A GENERAL HISTORY OF EUROPE

GENERAL EDITOR: DENYS HAY

A GENERAL HISTORY OF EUROPE

General Editor: Denys Hay

For many years the volumes of Denys Hay's distinguished *General History of Europe* have been standard recommendations for university students, sixth formers and general readers. They offer broad surveys of European history, in which the detailed discussion (on a regional or continent-wide basis) of social, economic, administrative and intellectual themes is woven into a clear framework of political events. They set out to combine scholarship with accessibility in texts which are both attractively written and intellectually vigorous. Now the entire sequence is under revision by its original authors – most of the volumes for the first time since they were published – and the books are being redesigned and reset. The revised *General History of Europe*, when complete, will contain twelve volumes, three of them wholly new.

★ *Available in the original edition*

◊ *New edition published in the revised format*

□ *New title in preparation*

EUROPE IN THE SIXTEENTH CENTURY

SECOND EDITION

H. G. KOENIGSBERGER,

GEORGE L. MOSSE

AND

G. Q. BOWLER

LONGMAN
LONDON AND NEW YORK

Longman Group UK Limited,
Longman House, Burnt Mill, Harlow,
Essex CM20 2JE, England
and Associated Companies throughout the world.

Published in the United States of America
by Longman Inc., New York

© Longman Group Ltd 1968
Second edition © Longman Group UK Limited 1989

First published 1968
Second edition 1989

British Library Cataloguing in Publication Data
Koenigsberger, H. G. (Helmut Georg), *1918–*
    Europe in the sixteenth century. – 2nd ed.
    – (A General history of Europe).
    1. Europe. Social life, 1517–1618
    I. Title   II. Mosse, George L. (George
    Lachmann)   III. Bowler, G. Q.   IV. Series
    940.2'32

ISBN 0-582-04615-7 CSD
ISBN 0-582-49390-0 PPR

Library of Congress Cataloging-in-Publication Data
Koenigsberger, H. G. (Helmut Georg)
    Europe in the sixteenth century / H. G. Koenigsberger, George L.
    Mosse, and G. Q. Bowler. – 2nd ed.
        p.   cm. – (A General history of Europe)
    Includes bibliographies and index.
    ISBN 0-582-04615-7
    ISBN 0-582- 49390-0 (pbk.)
    1. Europe – History – 1492–1648.   I. Mosse, George L. (George
    Lachmann), 1918–   II. Bowler, G. Q., 1948–   III. Title.
    IV. Title: Europe in the 16th century. V. Series.
    D220.K6 1989
    940.2'4 – dc19   88-13944
                                                            CIP

Set in Linotron 202 10/12pt Bembo

Produced by Longman Singapore Publishers (Pte) Ltd.
Printed in Singapore

CONTENTS

LIST OF GENEALOGICAL CHARTS

LIST OF MAPS

LIST OF FIGURES

PREFACE TO THE SECOND EDITION

A second edition of a textbook can vary between a simple updating of the bibliography and a completely rewritten text. A complete rewriting would have been necessary only if there had been a kind of Copernican revolution in the historiography and in our understanding of Europe in the sixteenth century. This has not happened. The outlines of the book, our views of the problems of the period, the relative importance we attached to different areas and topics – these have all, on the whole, stood up well to twenty years of reading. Nor has our basic outlook changed. We are still convinced that it is not possible to find single, underlying causes or inclusive models for the complexity of events in this century, even while we are quite willing to generalize about specific sets of events. All the same, we have rewritten more than half of the book and we have expanded it. Much detailed research has been done by historians. New areas of interest have appeared and, sometimes, new methods of research and analysis have been developed. We have added these to our text or expanded the treatment of some topics which we had been able to deal with only very briefly in the first edition. Many of them we have grouped together in a new chapter, 'Social Life'. It includes the new demography, the history of the family, of women and of attitudes towards children – all highly controversial topics – of witchcraft, of popular culture and its relation to elite culture – popular and court festivals here present a fascinating contrast – of the effects of warfare and of disease on the civilian population.

These and other new and expanded topics are not only interesting in themselves but they give us a better understanding of sixteenth-century European society and also of the classic historical topics of the Protestant and the Catholic Reformations and of the politics of the period. In the chapters on these topics and in those on cultural history we have included a great deal of the detailed work that has been done in the last twenty years. The chapter on literature has been completely rewritten and so have many sections of other chapters, notably in the history of ideas.

Inevitably, viewpoints, too, have shifted, both because of new research and because of the greater emphasis which historians now give to the history of attitudes, an approach which is certainly very valuable but not as original as some of its proponents claim, nor entirely absent from the first edition of this book.

The updated bibliographies have now been grouped together and the chronological tables have been considerably expanded, especially in the direction of social and cultural events.

It is true that every generation has to rewrite its history; but this does not mean that all historical knowledge becomes dated or that all historical judgements are completely relative. Knowledge and insight are cumulative, and we hope that this second edition is in fact a better and more useful, as well as a more up-to-date, history of the sixteenth century than the original.

TO DOROTHY, PAULA AND KAREN

1

INTRODUCTION

The sixteenth century seems an age of truly dramatic change. Traditional and established ways of men's thought about themselves and their universe were giving way to new and different concepts of heaven and earth. The quarrels of the Reformation about the proper standards of religious knowledge seemed to throw into the market place matters which had hitherto been accepted without much question. The first large-scale use of the printing press extended the circle of those who became involved in discussions which either challenged old traditions or attempted to find a new basis for the re-establishment of the vanished harmony of life.

The men of the Middle Ages had regarded the cosmos as a vast hierarchy stretching from God down to the smallest blade of grass. Angels, rulers, nobles and peasants all had their fixed place within this chain, determined forever by the law of God. The toad could never be a lion and the peasant could never become a lord. The root of all harmony, we are told as the century opens, is for every man to do his duty in the place on earth which God had reserved for him.[1] Such notions of an externally predetermined heavenly and earthly hierarchy were being undermined: the rise of capitalism meant greater social mobility, and the efforts to centralize political authority in the hands of the ruler attacked the ideal of hierarchy from another direction. Moreover, Protestantism destroyed the hierarchical chain linking God and man by confronting man directly with God, denying the need for intermediate hierarchies.

The old order was disintegrating, and it was in vain that William Shakespeare, at the end of the century, appealed to the stars in order

1

that the heavenly hierarchy might support the earthly division of 'degree and place'. The nobility could find solace in the reading of romances of chivalry, but the age of knighthood was past and illusion could not replace reality. The feudal order had dissolved and it was by no means settled what kind of new order would rise from its ashes. The classes which existed beneath the king and the nobility were warned in vain not to 'presume above their own degree' or to exceed their betters in dress, food or in any other manner.[2] The very fact that throughout the century such exhortations will never cease, shows us that many of the lower orders were in fact doing just that, and the need of the rulers for their support means that those who were supposed to guard 'degree and place' were in reality engaged in helping to destroy it. To the complaint that King Henry VIII of England was employing men of low degree in high office, Richard Morison raised the issue of careers open to talent. This did not prevent him from advocating a social hierarchy, and yet the door was opened to the dynamism of individual men.[3]

The European ideal of the Commonwealth represented a society cemented together by the rights and duties which all men owed towards each other. This concept implied social hierarchy but also social responsibility: political power existed for the protection of men's inherited rights, and personal property was a trust given for the benefit of the community, not individual gain. However, by the end of the sixteenth century the needs of the monarchies had substituted the concept of sovereignty, which concentrated political power in the hands of the ruler, for the older concept of a society of reciprocal rights and duties held together by the legal imperatives of immemorial custom. The 'divine right of kings' over their subjects substituted a moral check upon arbitrary power for the feudal safeguards of the rights due to each subject according to his place within the hierarchy. Throughout the century the monarchies, through administrative reforms, attempted to bolster the concentration of political power into their hands.

At the same time the growth of modern capitalism accelerated the concentration of economic power. The restraints which Christianity had traditionally put upon the taking of interest were weakened throughout the century. John Calvin was symptomatic in believing that money, far from being unproductive, could be allowed to reproduce itself like any other goods which men produce by their own labour. To be sure, interest could only be taken if this benefited the community, but 'if we wholly condemn usury', said Calvin, 'we impose tighter fetters on the conscience than God himself'. The novelty was not that interest was taken, for this had been done throughout the Middle Ages, but that now restraints upon this practice were consciously weakened. The ownership of property, even if still regarded as a trust for the community, increasingly became an instrument of exploitation.

Complaints against the rich multiply. They are blamed for the poverty of the many: driving the peasant from the land through enclosures, dismissing retainers and workers in order to increase their profits. The misuse of economic power for the purposes of gain and luxury was treated by the social critics of the age as a moral failing, part of the sinfulness of man which must be overcome, rather than as an aspect of the transition to a capitalist economy. Yet Christian morality seemed to adjust to the new economic facts rather than oppose them; the increasing laxity about rates of interest which could be taken, the failure to condemn enclosures as the work of Satan, and the luxury prevalent among some high Church men, all added up to give such an impression. At the same time the centralization of political power was justified by an appeal to Christianity and the realism of national and international politics was integrated within the framework of Christian morality.

To be sure, the age is filled with protests against the changes which were taking place. Not only did social critics call for the restoration of the foundations of Christian morality against the abuses of economic and political power, but rebellions were widespread throughout Europe. The nobility attempted to restrain monarchical power, and the bourgeoisie of the towns as well as other groups of the third estate, were ready to support changes in the political order which would increase their share in the making of policy. Such groups attempted to use national estates or parliaments in order to obtain an instrument through which they could transform their wishes into reality. The religious conflicts gave them a welcome opportunity to accomplish their ends. But in supporting whatever they regarded as the true religion against the king, men nevertheless accepted the new ideas of political power; they wanted to share in it, but very rarely (whatever they said to the contrary) return to the old order of things.

While the bourgeois sought change through the estates wherever this was thought possible, this did not keep them from joining with other social classes in the riots and rebellions which were the order

3

of the day. The sixteenth century was an age where violence was close to the surface of daily life, whether in public executions as popular festivals, or through the cruel treatment given to public and private enemies. Thus the dead bodies of criminals were dragged through the streets, dismembered and displayed, and corpses of those killed for religious or political reasons were given the same treatment. Riots might break out wherever a crowd assembled, most frequently at festivals and processions, but also at sermons in church which were not to some people's liking. Religious issues which dominated the age inspired most, if not all of the riots: even those whose cause was economic, like bread riots in time of famine,

BOVILLUS, *Liber de intellectu: The Orders of Nature and of Man*

Figure 1 Renaissance hierarchy in the orders of nature and of man – *Liber de intellectu*, etc., Paris, 1509, Bovillus (Charles de Bouelles). Just as the four orders of nature rise in stages, from passive rock, through vegetable, animal and man, so all of these capacities and states of mind are in man. Man exists, lives, feels and thinks. He perfects himself when he uses his intellectual capacity and keeps the others subordinate to it in the appropriate order. But man can descend as well as ascend; sensuality, especially the pleasures of the eye and of narcissism, is a seductive limitation. The lowest mentality is passive dumb and inert, like a stone. This text book is intended to teach the order. The pupil is encouraged to aspire to the highest intellectual state and not to behave like a beast. See p. 389.

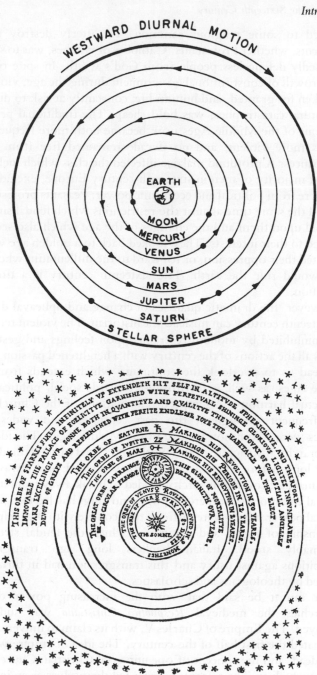

Figure.2 The Ptolemaic and Copernican universes.

appealed to some religious sanction. To utterly destroy one's opponents, whether Protestants, Catholics or witches, was to save a supposedly defenceless people from God's wrath. In spite of the slow growth of constitutional government during the age, violence was taken for granted, and human life, constantly at risk to disease and natural catastrophes, was held cheap. The traditional peasant rebellions of the Middle Ages now became both more frequent as well as more violent, and no decade remained free from such disturbances. A profound malaise infected the class which included the vast majority of men in sixteenth-century Europe, excluded as they were from political and economic power. Peasants protested at one and the same time against the restrictions which feudalism had imposed upon them and the changes of the age which also seemed opposed to their interests. They looked back to a golden age which pre-dated their oppression, or forward to the millennium when the poor would rule the earth. The sixteenth century is a time of revolution.

However, the dramatic qualities of change and upheaval during the sixteenth century can mislead the historian. The violent tenor of life, uninhibited by modern restraints upon feelings and gestures, invests all the actions of the century with a heightened passion. This may lead us to overlook the continuity which extends from the Middle Ages, as well as the impulse towards social, political and intellectual harmony. Attempted reformations of the Church had been frequent throughout the past centuries, and widespread heresies were a common feature of the Middle Ages. The ideal of the hierarchical structure of the world and society had clashed with reality long before the sixteenth century opened; and always the individual parts of that hierarchy tended to break away from it. The political ambitions of emperors, popes and kings had led to claims of political power which were difficult to reconcile with the reciprocal relationship of rights and duties for which the feudal structure presumably stood. Italian bankers long ago transgressed prohibitions against usury and this transgression had in turn been justified by theologians and scholastics.

Nor can it be said that with the increasing power of the monarchies the medieval *Respublica Christiana* was suddenly destroyed. The Empire of Charles V, with its claim to universalism, dominated the first half of the century. The idea of empire was far from dead, and the concept of one universal Christian Church was very much alive. The reformers regarded themselves as an integral part of the 'common corps of Christendom' which they did not intend to destroy, but rather to infuse with a new meaning. The national Churches, for all their desire for institutional independence, shared such sentiments.

Traditional attitudes and modes of thought only slowly gave way; there was no abrupt break with the past. If we read a work on the new astronomy like Johannes Kepler's *Astronomia Nova* (1609), its revolutionary nature is disguised by the emphasis upon the harmony which was said to exist between heaven and earth, the certainty which remained intact even though the stars were in movement. The effort to counter change through an emphasis upon harmony remains constant during the century and perhaps even increased in its last quarter, though it took many different forms. Some looked to the past and tried to recreate it in the present through attempting to restore the ideal of the feudal order. There were others who used the classical tradition, especially that of Plato, to arrive at an ideal of harmony which accounted for new ideas of infinity and movement within an ordered universe presided over by God. Many, especially on the popular level, longed for a return to a simple and uncomplicated society which had presumably existed in the golden age of the past; however, this longing was widespread in all ranks of society, as the popularity of pastoral romances can show us.

The continuity was as great as the change within all aspects of sixteenth-century culture. The violent tenor of life and its cruel publicity, which J. Huizinga has described so well for the fifteenth century,[4] continued throughout the sixteenth. The fear of the unknown, the scourges of famine and disease, the relatively short span of life on earth, sent men looking for safeguards against a world filled with catastrophes and unknown dangers. They found these in religious observance but also in the belief that God worked through nature in creating signs, wonders and portents. Astrology was especially important in attempting to read the awesome will of providence.

However awesome the spectacle which nature and the universe provided, many men were convinced, nevertheless, that men did possess the power to penetrate their mysteries. The widespread beliefs in astrology, magic and alchemy asserted the power of the human mind to unlock the secrets of God's universe. This assertion gave a new dignity to those who probed the workings of heaven and earth outside the framework of a theological tradition. Here, in spite of the attempted preservation of past harmony, was a change in attitudes which helped to prepare the way for the new scientific accomplishments of the age. However esoteric the learning produced by the majority of these men, when combined with the knowledge of mathematics, astronomy or geometry — with an emphasis upon the proper observation of phenomena — such learning did point the way to a fundamental change in the concept of that nature and heaven which surrounded man on earth.

Men's horizons were expanding in a wide spectrum of public and private life. Externally, Europe was breaking out of its be-leaguerment by Asian and African empires in which it had spent most of the thousand years of the Middle Ages. Now they turned the tables by the explorations and conquests of the Spaniards and Portuguese in Africa, Asia and America, and also by the Russians' reconquest of much of the vast territory lost in the thirteenth and fourteenth centuries to the Mongols and Tartars. Both the overseas and the continental expansions were to some degree at least all-European efforts, involving men, money and expertise from the whole of Europe and, at the same time, a rethinking, now with a new sense of urgency, of the old problem of the rights of Christians over pagans and unbelievers. In Europe itself the Reformation and the Catholic Reformation by stressing their different roads to the salvation of the individual, drew new social classes and also, very importantly, women into public life and into the political process on a hitherto unprecedented scale. It was not a process which pleased the ruling élites. On occasion, they tried to make use of it for their own purposes, especially during the French wars of religion; more usually, they did their best to minimize it, most typically, perhaps, in the Peace of Augsburg, with its principle of *cuius regio eius religio*, the principle that it was for the princes to determine the belief of their subjects. Yet the process of the widening participation in public life could not be, in the long run, fully reversed.

Just as the earth seemed to be expanding, so was the universe. By 1600 the limited Aristotelian–Ptolemaic cosmos, with the earth firmly fixed at its centre and comfortingly surrounded by God's celestial spheres, was giving way to a limitless universe in which the centrality of the earth and of man was no longer physical but merely theological. Here, too, sensibilities and attitudes changed only slowly. The churches fought a long rearguard action against Copernicanism. If the natural world, landscape, plants and animals were being observed more closely and accurately, they were also still regarded as having been created essentially for the sake of man. Leonardo's refusal to eat the meat of animals was held to be a pardonable eccentricity of genius — the concept of genius was itself relatively new. Giordano Bruno's suggestion of the existence of other worlds and other sentient beings was, even a hundred years later, regarded as unpardonable because it deliberately dethroned man from his central position in the universe.

Yet the nineteenth-century Swiss historian Jacob Burckhardt's characterization of the Renaissance as 'the discovery of the world and of man' has much truth to it. There was an intricate counterpoint to this discovery and the rediscovery of the ancients: greater awareness of the natural and the human world allowed men a better understanding of Greek and Roman civilization, so that this civilization, in turn, exerted a greater influence on European attitudes than it had been able to do in the middle ages. Herein, and not in greater admiration for the ancients, lies one of the main differences of the Renaissance from the succession of renaissances of earlier centuries.

It was also this counterpoint of contemporary experience and study of the ancient world which began to shake the religious and moral certainties of the early years of the sixteenth century. For these certainties were leading men to kill each other for their beliefs and ended by plunging large parts of Europe into civil wars — the very opposite of the order and harmony which the age prized so highly. The majority of men, it is true, remained convinced that harmony could only be maintained when the one and only and knowable truth was upheld and, if necessary, imposed by force. But, by the later part of the sixteenth century, there were those, like Michel de Montaigne, who revived the Hellenistic beliefs and attitudes of scepticism and began to doubt a belief in a certainty which resulted in the dreadful disasters they were witnessing all around them.

In spite of all efforts to resurrect the vanished harmonies of the past, the sixteenth-century impetus towards change could not be arrested. European civilization avoided the fate which, by the sixteenth century, had overcome many of the ancient civilizations of the orient and the near east: strangulation through the weight of a past which had become a rigid and formalized fear of change. The future was to belong to the European continent, and the older civilizations of the world were only to be awakened once more by contact with that civilization which had managed to forge ahead.[5]

The sixteenth century is a crucial age in the development of European supremacy: not because it managed to conquer the world by force, but because it laid the foundations for an attitude towards life which, in the end, proved favourable to those political, economic and social changes essential to the evolution of Europe into the modern age. Continuity and change exist side by side within any historical period, but within the age which this book analyses, the continuity did not obliterate the change. Instead, the new forces struggled from beneath the surface of things to their eventual victory.

NOTES AND REFERENCES

1 Edmund Dudley, *The Tree of Commonwealth*, ed. D. M. Brodie (Cambridge, 1948), p. 40 (written 1509–10).

2 Edmund Dudley, *The Tree of Commonwealth*, pp. 45–46.

3 Quoted in Arthur B. Ferguson, *The Articulate Citizen and the English Renaissance* (Durham, North Carolina, 1965), p. 381.

4 J. Huizinga, *The Waning of the Middle Ages* (London, 1924), ch. 1.

5 Thus the Arab awakening was fostered by European missionary enterprise. Georg Antonius, *The Arab Awakening* (New York, 1965), p. 35.

2

THE SOURCES

INCREASE OF SOURCE MATERIAL

There is a real change between medieval and modern European history in the nature of the sources available to the historian. The change was a slow one, and one can often find 'modern' sources in the Middle Ages; nevertheless, it is very evident. Broadly speaking, the medievalist has rarely enough source material for the study of even fairly large topics; the modernist usually has too much and is forced to make a selection, even in the study of fairly limited topics. Naturally, this does not mean that he always has enough of the type of sources which he would like to have in order to answer all the questions he is asking. The increase in the quantity of sources – an increase which continued strongly through the course of the sixteenth century – was due to a complex combination of causes which themselves throw considerable light on the course of European history of this period.

First, and most obviously, there was the invention of printing which vastly multiplied the number of books published and the size of editions. The possibility of reaching very much wider literate audiences than ever before was beginning to change the whole nature of political, religious, literary and scientific movements and controversies.

Second, far more was actually written than in any previous age. This is, admittedly, a somewhat deceptive phenomenon; for the question of the preservation and survival of written documents enters into it. More has survived from the year 1500 than from the year 1400, and more again from 1600, simply because there has been a shorter lapse of time and hence less opportunity for loss or destruction. The foundation, in the course of the sixteenth century, of safe depositories for government records, notably the deposition of Spanish government papers in the castle of Simancas, from 1543–45 onwards, greatly helped the survival of historical source material. But even such an extraordinarily rich collection of state papers as that of the archive of Simancas is far from complete for this period. Large quantities of official papers could still be lost, as happened for instance in the early seventeenth century when the papers of the Spanish-Sicilian government were lost at sea, *en route* between Palermo and Messina. More important still was the common attitude of this period which regarded official papers as the private property of the ministers and secretaries who wrote or received them. This accounts for much of the loss as well as for the dispersal of sources, as for instance the existence of the very large collection of Spanish papers in the British Library (cf. P. de Gayangos, *Catalogue of the Manuscripts in the Spanish Language in the British Museum*, 4 vols., London, 1875) or of French papers in the Public Library Saltykov-Chtchédrine, at Leningrad. Wars added to the dispersion of valuable source materials. For example, as a result of the defeat of the Elector Palatine in the Thirty Years War, the famous Heidelberg library (*Bibliotheca Palatina*) was brought to Rome where it now constitutes part of the Vatican Library.

In any case, the increasing scope and complexity of government in the sixteenth century enormously increased the paper work of government officials (see pp. 283, 287). The introduction of permanent embassies, in place of the occasional diplomatic missions of medieval times, produced an almost completely new type of source: the regular, weekly or even daily, diplomatic correspondence from all the major and some of the minor European capitals.[1] In some ways these are the easiest sources for the historian to handle, and many volumes of them have been published; but these represent only a small fraction of the manuscript material that survives in the major European archives.

PUBLISHED PAPERS: GOVERNMENT AND DIPLOMATIC

Some collections of sixteenth–century diplomatic and other government papers were published in the seventeenth and eighteenth centuries, notably the *Foedera*, by Thomas Rymer and Robert Sanderson, 20 vols. (London 1704–35), which is even now a most useful collection of the texts of international treaties. Or there are beautifully bound, and none too accurate, collections of miscellaneous state papers, apparently intended for a wealthy but politically amateur public. A good example of such works is the three volumes of the *Thesoro Politico* (Milan, 1601). But the systematic publication of such sources was undertaken in the nineteenth century and has continued in the twentieth, although usually on a less heroic scale. It is possible to mention only a few of the most important collections.

Ever since Ranke began to use them, in the 1820s, for his great works on the history of the sixteenth century,[2] the reports which the Venetian ambassadors read to their Senate, on the return from their missions, are still basic for all work on the political history of the sixteenth century. They are published by E. Albèri, *Relazioni degli ambasciatori veneti*, etc., 15 vols. (Florence, 1839–63). A well-chosen selection of these reports has been translated and edited by James C. Davis, *The Pursuit of Power: Venetian Ambassadors' Reports on Turkey, France and Spain in the Age of Philip II, 1560–1600*, (Harper Torch Books, New York, 1970). The regular correspondence of the Venetian ambassadors, in contrast to their reports, has been published for only some countries and for a few years of the sixteenth century. The bulk has still to be read in manuscript in the Archivio di Stato of Venice. They can be supplemented, however, by M. Sanuto, *I Diarii*, ed. G. Berchet and N. Barozzi, 58 vols. (Venice, 1879–1903), which cover much of the diplomatic information as it reached the Venetian Senate during the years 1496 to 1533.

Karl Brandi, the German biographer of Charles V, planned the publication of the emperor's complete correspondence. It was enormous and it is scattered over nearly all the major European archives. Brandi's plan was never executed, but the second volume of the biography, *Quellen und Erörterungen* (Munich, 1941), contains an all but complete list of all manuscript and printed sources for the reign of Charles V. The older published volumes, K. Lanz, *Korrespondenz Karls V*, 3 vols. (Leipzig, 1844–46), and the same editor's *Staatspapiere Karls V* (Stuttgart, 1845) are inadequate. There are various collections of documents about specific periods or incidents in the emperor's reign; but more important is the publication of his correspondence with his

Spanish family, M. Fernández Alvarez, *Corpus Documental de Carlos V*, 5 vols. (Salamanca, 1973), mainly from the archives of Simancas. From the Haus- Hof- und Staatsarchiv of Vienna H. Rabe, H. Stratenwerth and P. Marzahl are publishing registers of Charles V's correspondence, in the *Mitteilungen des Österreichischen Staatsarchivs*, (1976, in progress). Further documentation in G. Turba, *Venezianische Depeschen vom Kaiserhof*, 3 vols. (Vienna, 1889–96) and the *Nuntiaturberichte aus Deutschland*, published by the Deutsches Historisches Institut in Rome (ongoing).

Philip II has fared better than his father. A large number of the 112 volumes of the very miscellaneous and uneven *Colección de Documentos Inéditos para la Historia de España* (Madrid, 1842–95), are devoted, in whole or in part, to his reign. The two-volume catalogue of this collection, by J. Paz (Madrid, 1930–31), is indispensable. For Spanish relations with the Netherlands, the nineteenth-century Belgian archivist L. P. Gachard published *Correspondance de Marguerite d'Autriche, Duchesse de Parme, avec Philippe II*, 3 vols. (Brussels, 1867–1881), supplements by J. S. Theissen *et al.*, 3 vols. (Utrecht, 1925–42); and *Correspondance de Philippe II sur les affaires des Pays Bas*, 5 vols. (Brussels, 1848–79; lengthy summaries in French), with supplements for the period 1577–84 by J. Lefèvre, 4 vols. (Brussels, 1940–53). The Lepanto campaign is covered in *Correspondencia diplomatica entre España y la Santa Sede*, ed. L. Serrano, 4 vols. (Madrid, 1914). Most useful supplements to these collections are C. Weiss, *Papiers d'État du Cardinal de Granvelle*, 9 vols. (Paris, 1841–52), and C. Piot and E. Poullet, *Correspondance du Cardinal de Granvelle*, 12 vols. (Brussels, 1877–96).

For France we have, *inter alia*, A. J. C. Le Clay, *Négotiations diplomatiques entre la France et l'Autriche, 1491–1530*, 2 vols. (Paris, 1845); A. Desjardins, *Négotiations diplomatiques de la France avec la Toscane*, 6 vols. (Paris, 1859–86), A. Teulet, *Relations politiques de la France et de l'Espagne avec l'Écosse au XVIe siècle*, 5 vols. (Paris, 1862), and E. Charrière, *Négotiations de la France dans le Levant*, 4 vols. (Paris, 1848–1860). Mme A. Lublinskaja started editing two series of documents from Russian archives, *Documents pour servir à l'histoire des guerres d'Italie*, vol. I for 1547–48 (Moscow, Leningrad, 1963), and *Documents pour servir à l'histoire des guerres civiles en France*, vol. 1 for 1516–63 (Moscow, Leningrad, 1962). The correspondence of the rulers of France is not well represented in publications until we get to Catherine de Medici,

Lettres, 9 vols., ed. G. Baguenault de Puchesse (Paris, 1901), and the *Recueil des lettres missivies de Henri IV*, ed. Berger de Xivrey and J. Caudet, 9 vols. (Paris, 1843–76).

For the Netherlands, the most important collections are G. Groen van Prinsterer, *Archives de la Maison d'Orange-Nassau*, 8 vols. (Leiden, 1835–47) and Gachard, *Correspondence de Guillaume le Taciturne*, 6 vols. (Brussels, 1847–66).

In a class by themselves are the different series of the *Calendars of State Papers*, published for the Public Record Office, London. The documents are not published *in extenso* but in lengthy summaries in English, except for occasional passages which are quoted or translated verbatim. The most important series for the sixteenth century are *Letters and Papers, Foreign and Domestic, of the Reign of Henry VIII*, 21 vols. in 33 parts (London, 1862–1910), with addenda vol. I in three parts (1920); *Calendars of State Papers Spanish*, 13 vols. and 2 supplements, covering the period 1485 to 1558 (London, 1862–1954); *Calendar of State Papers Venetian*, 9 vols. for the period up to 1603 (London, 1864–98); and *Calendar of State Papers Foreign*, 23 vols. for the period 1547 to 1589 (London, 1863–1950).

PUBLISHED PAPERS: POLITICAL AND ADMINISTRATIVE

Published collections of source material for the internal political and administrative history of European states in the sixteenth century are rarely as extensive as those of diplomatic documents. They tend to be very varied and scattered, but their aggregate quantity is enormous. For the purposes of this chapter, it is best to select just one of the many topics in this field: parliaments and representative assemblies. These existed, in one form or another, in nearly every European country in the sixteenth century, and their relations with their princes were, whether this was clearly acknowledged or not, at the very centre of the problem of ultimate political power in the majority of European states. For the English Parliament the most important collections of sources are the *Journals of the House of Lords*, vols. I and II, for 1510–1614 (London, 1846); the *Journal of the House of Commons*, vol. I, for 1547–1628 (London, 1803); *The journals of all the parliaments during the reign of Queen Elizabeth*, by Sir S. D'Ewes (London, 1682–93);

T. E. Hartley, *Proceedings in the Parliaments of Elizabeth I, 1558–81* (Leicester, 1981); and A. Luders *et al.*, *Statutes of the Realm*, 2 vols. (London, 1810–28). For France there is the old publication of C. J. Mayer, *Les États généraux et autres assemblées nationales*, 18 vols. (Paris, 1788–89). For Castile the Real Academia de la Historia has published the *Cortes de los antiguos reinos de Léon y Castilla*, vols. IV–V (Madrid, 1882–1903). The University of Valencia has published *Cortes del Reinado de Fernando el Catolico* to *Felipe III*, 5 vols. (Valencia, 1972–73), photo-offsets of the contemporary publications of the acts of the cortes of the kingdom of Valencia. In Italy parliaments were important only in the peripheral areas, notably in Sicily for which we have A. Mongitore, *Parlamenti Generali del Regno di Sicilia*, 2 vols. (Palermo, 1749), and in Piedmont until 1560, after which date the dukes no longer summoned them – one of the very few deliberate moves, during the sixteenth century, to abolish a representative assembly completely, rather than, as for instance in Castile, simply to deprive it of its effective powers of resisting the demands of the crown (see pp. 112, 280). For the assemblies in Piedmont, we have A. Tallone, *Parlamento Sabaudo*, vols. VI and VII (Bologna, 1928–35).

The acts of the States General of the Netherlands have been published for the fifteenth century, but for the sixteenth publication begins only with L. P. Gachard, *Actes des États Généraux des Pays-Bas, 1576–85*, 2 vols. (Brussels, 1861–66), and is continued by N. Japikse, *Resolutiën der Staten Generaal van 1586 tot 1609* (The Hague, 1930). The publication of the acts of the Imperial Diet has, so far, reached the date of 1530: *Deutsche Reichstagsakten, Jüngere Reihe* vols. I–IV, VII (Gotha, 1893–1935), vol. VIII (Göttingen, 1970–71). At least another nine volumes are now in progress of publication, under the auspices of the Historische Kommission bei der Bayerischen Akademie der Wissenschaften and under the general editorship of D. Albrecht and A. Kohler.

The rather sporadic publication of the documents of the estates of the individual German states is listed in F. L. Carsten, *Princes and Parliaments in Germany* (Oxford, 1959). For Poland, a publication of the very rich sources of the estates of Royal Prussia (West Prussia), in German and Latin, is in progress, up to now 7 volumes: M. Biskup and I. Janosz-Biskupowa, eds., *Akta Stanów Prus Królewskich* (Societas Scientiarium Torunensis, Warsaw, 1954–86, in progress).

The International Commission for the History of Representative and Parliamentary Institutions is publishing a new series of
documents concerned with parliaments and representation. So far,
there is G. Griffiths, *The Parliaments of Southern and Western Europe
in the Sixteenth Century*, Studies presented to the International
Commission, etc. Ser. II, vol. I (Oxford, 1968).

THE CHANGING NATURE OF SOURCES

Closely connected with the increase in the quantity of sources
during the sixteenth century is a change in their nature. Not only
governments and all types of corporations, but also individuals,
wrote more, and in a much more personal way than they had ever
done before. This was due both to an increase in literacy, and to
safer and more settled conditions inside the European states,
which were accompanied by cheaper and more regular postal
services. Such private correspondence has proved a most valuable
source, especially for social and economic history, and for the
biographical part of the history of literature, art, music and
science. Burckhardt's thesis of 'the discovery of the individual'
during the Renaissance certainly receives some confirmation from
the change in the quality of our sources. Autobiographies and
memoirs, not unknown but still comparatively rare in the
fifteenth century, become common in the sixteenth, and more
especially in the second half. Outstanding, both for its literary and
psychological interest, and for the light it throws on social and
artistic life in Italy and France, is Benvenuto Cellini's *Autobiography*, trans. G. Bull, (Harmondsworth, 1956). Next to Cellini's
the most interesting autobiography is that of the Italian physician
and mathematician, Gerolamo Cardano (1501–76), *De propria vita*,
trans. as *Book of My Life* by J. Stoner (London, 1931). Important,
more as a symptom than for its contents, are the Memoirs of
Charles V which have survived in a Portuguese version and are
published by A. P. V. Morel-Fatio, *Historiographie de Charles-
Quint* (Paris, 1913).

A splendid collection of French memoirs is published by C. B.
Petitot, *Collection complète des mémoires rélatifs à l'histoire de France*.
Relevant for the sixteenth century are Ser. I, vols. XI–LII (Paris,
1819–1826), and Ser. 2, vols. I–XVI (Paris, 1820–22). For the

Netherlands there is the *Collection de mémoires rélatifs à l'histoire de Belgique, XVIe siècle*, 24 vols. (Brussels, 1858–66). For England there are no specific collections of memoirs except Richard Hakluyt's famous *The Principall Navigations, Voiages and Discoveries of the English Nation*, first published in London, 1589; modern edition by W. Raleigh (Glasgow, 1903–1905). But many individual memoirs and collections of letters have been published. The *Reports of the Historical Manuscripts Commission* list and calendar many of the MSS collections in private possession. Nothing quite like these reports exists in continental countries, and many important source collections in the hands of private families have remained sadly inaccessible to historians. There are, however, honourable exceptions, such as the archives of the Alva family. Of special interest for historians of the sixteenth century is the *Epistolario del III Duque de Alba, 1536–81*, giving extensive selections, edited by Jacob Fitzjames, Duque de Alba, 3 vols. (Madrid, 1952).

With this enormous increase in the volume and range of sources it is natural that the old-style chronicles, so important for the medievalist, should have become relatively unimportant for the modernist. In the sixteenth century itself their popularity greatly declined. They were indeed still written, but no longer by men of the intellectual calibre of a Matthew Paris or a Froissart. Their compeers in the sixteenth century would write histories, not chronicles. With exceptions, these histories are more important for the role they played in the intellectual life of European society than as sources for the modern historian. Some of the more important historians, notably the Florentines, are therefore discussed within the text of this book (for Machiavelli and Guicciardi see pp. 155, 101–2).

SOURCES FOR ECONOMIC HISTORY

Sources for economic history have mainly been published in the last seventy years. Outstanding as a selection of descriptive material is R. H. Tawney and E. Power, *Tudor Economic Documents*, 3 vols. (London, 1924). Statistical sources are available in the great series of publications on price and wages history. The most notable are: W. Beveridge, *Prices and Wages in England from the Twelfth to the Nineteenth Century*, vol. I, *Price Tables; mercantile era* (London, 1939); E. J. Hamilton, *American Treasure and the Price Revolution in Spain* (Cambridge, Mass., 1934). Some of Hamilton's statistical methods, as well as his interpretations, have been criticized (see p. 61n), and his tables must be used with caution; they are, however, still indispensable. N. W. Posthumus, *Inquiry into the History of Prices in Holland*, vol. I (Brill, 1946) unfortunately starts only with the year 1585. One of the best recent publications is C. Verlinden, J. Craeybeckx *et al.*, *Documents pour l'Histoire des prix et des salaires en Flandre et en Brabent, XVe-XVIe siècles* (Bruges, 1959). For France we have M. Boulant and J. Meuvret, Prix des Céréales extraits de la Mercuriale de Paris, 1520–1698, vol. I (Paris, 1960); and for Germany, M. J. Elsas, *Umriss einer Geschichte der Preise und Löhne in Deutschland*, 3 vols. (Leyden, 1936–49).

Statistical sources for the history of urban population are most easily accessible in R. Mols, *Introduction à la Démographie Historiques des Villes d'Europe*, 3 vols. (Louvain, 1954–56).

In a class by itself is Huguette and Pierre Chaunu, *Séville et l'Atlantique 1504–1650*, 8 vols. in two parts (Paris, 1955–59). This is the most detailed and thorough publication of commercial statistics for this period that has been attempted so far. The statistical analysis and historical interpretation of this material, by Pierre Chaunu (vol. VIII, in three parts), is brilliant but idiosyncratic.

Within the limits of this chapter it has been possible to list only a few of the most important publications of sources on a small number of the topics covered in this book. An extensive, though necessarily still selective, bibliography may be found in E. Hassinger, *Das Werden des neuzeitlichen Europas* (Braunschweig, 1959), pp. 399–486. Bibliographies for different countries are mentioned below, p. 20. We wish to provide, however, one example of a reasonably full discussion of sources and have, therefore, chosen one of the central topics of this book, the Reformation.

THE REFORMATION

The Reformation was the first major modern historical event to take full advantage of the invention of printing by moveable type in the mid-fifteenth century. With the sixteenth century we enter a period for which the historian finds a multitude of pamphlets and tracts at his disposal, a veritable flood after the dearth of earlier ages. Yet, in spite of this fact, there are still areas for Reformation history for which the historian has to depend entirely upon the archives rather than printed sources.

BIBLIOGRAPHICAL GUIDES

Bibliographical guides are of obvious importance in charting a course through the various reformations which took full advantage of the printing press, and which have maintained a high level of interest ever since. A valuable look at both source material and recent scholarship is *Reformation Europe: A Guide to Research*, edited by Steven Ozment (St Louis, 1982). Karl Schottenloher's excellent *Bibliographie zur deutschen Geschichte im Zeitalter der Glaubensspaltung* (1933–40; reiss. 1956–58) has been extended by a seventh volume edited by U. Thürauf (Stuttgart, 1966). Also useful for German events are the 10th edition of *Dahlmann-Waitz Quellenkunde der deutschen Geschichte*, ed. H. Hempel and H. Geuss (Stuttgart, 1965) and H. Grundmann, *Handbüch der deutschen Geschichte* (Stuttgart, 1970). For France H. Hauser, *Les Sources de l'histoire de France, XVIe siècle* (Paris, 1906–15) and P. Caron and H. Stein, *Repertoire bibliographique de l'histoire de France* (Paris, 1923–38) must be supplemented by the *Bibliographie annuelle de l'histoire de France* (Paris, 1953–). For England see Conyers Read, *Bibliography of British History, Tudor Period* (Oxford, 1959), Mortimer Levine, *Tudor England 1485–1603* (Oxford, 1968) and A. W. Pollard and G. R. Redgrave, *Short Title Catalogue of Books Printed in England, Scotland & Ireland and of English Books Printed Abroad* (London, 1926), as well its 1976 revision by Katherine Pantzer. E. J. Baskerville, *Chronological Bibliography of Propaganda and Polemic Published in England Between 1553 and 1558* (Philadelphia, 1979) is a guide to the pamphlet warfare of the Marian period while A. F. Alison and D. M. Rogers, *A Catalogue of Catholic Books in English Printed Abroad or Secretly in England* (Bognor Regis, 1956) is helpful for the Elizabethan Catholic press campaigns. For two journals listing primary sources and recent works see *Revue D'Histoire Ecclesiastique* and *Studies in Philology*.

POPULAR CULTURE AND HUMANISM

A serious problem which faces historians arises out of the paucity of materials concerning the popular culture which one must understand to appreciate the beginnings and evolution of the Reformation. The illiterate leave no written records and the most rewarding sources for their attitudes and opinions are often the writings of those who opposed their ideas or the trials of those accused of heresy. Much of the latter material is still archival but P. Fredericq, *Corpus documentorum Inquisitionis haereticae pravitatis Neerlandicae*, 4. vols. (Ghent, 1889–1900) provides a first-rate source for getting at the varieties of northern popular opinion. Georg Schreiber, 'Volk und Volkstum', *Jahrbuch für Volkskunde*, 3 vols. (Freiburg, 1936–38) brings together much material on Catholic piety. Wilhelm Peuckert, *Die Grosse Wende. Das apokalyptische Saeculum und Luther* (Hamburg, 1948) presents popular customs and superstitions before and during the Reformation. Those who seek sources for the study of popular belief in early modern England could not do better than examine the extensive notes and bibliography in Keith Thomas, *Religion and the Decline of Magic* (London, 1971). Once the Reformation started the availability of source material increases. Most useful for German pamphlets are the *Flugschriften aus den ersten Jahren der Reformation*, ed. O. Clemen, 4 vols (Leipzig, 1907–10). A project at the University of Tübingen seeks to make available on microfiche all German and Latin pamphlets produced in the Holy Roman Empire between 1501 and 1530; see H.-J. Kohler, ed., *Flugschriften des frühen 16. Jahrhunderts* (Zug, 1978–). For other microfiche collections see C. Augustijn, ed., *Dutch Pamphlets ca. 1486–1648* (Zug, 1979) and W. Balke *et al.*, eds., *Reformed Protestantism: Sources of the Sixteenth and Seventeenth Centuries on Microfiche* (Zug, 1979).

Humanists, of course, can be studied more easily than popular opinion because they wrote extensively and have been edited ever since. As an example of the material available, see Erasmus' complete works, the *Opera omnia*, ed. J. H. Wasznik *et al.*, (Amsterdam, 1969–) and the ambitious University of Toronto *Collected Works of Erasmus*. His correspondence can be found in the *Erasmi Epistolae*, ed. P. S. and H. M. Allen (Oxford, 1906–58). It has been translated in seven volumes as *The Correspondence of Eramus* by R. A. B. Mynors and D. F. S. Thomson

(Toronto, 1974) as part of the *Collected Works*. Yale University is producing new editions of the works of Thomas More and the major works of other humanists are also appearing in English translations.

THE WRITINGS OF PROTESTANT REFORMERS

Thanks to the indefatigable industry of nineteenth-century historians and editors, we possess several basic collections of the writings of Protestant reformers. The *Corpus Reformatorum* (Halle, 1834–) brings together in over a hundred volumes the important and even some of the less important works of most of the Protestant reformers throughout Europe. The collection, however, neglects the radicals. Martin Luther occupies much of the *Corpus Reformatorum* but is most reliably approached through the *Dr. Martin Luthers Werke* (Weimar, 1883–). *His Works*, eds., J. Pelikan, *et al.* in English occupy 57 volumes (Philadelphia, 1956–). For Martin Bucer there is the *Opera Omnia*, ed. R. Stupperich, (Gütersloh, 1960–) and the *Martini Buceri Opera Latina* (Paris, 1954–); see also *Martin Bucers, Deutsche Schriften*, ed. R. Stupperich (Paris/Gütersloh, 1960–), J. V. Pollet, *Martin Bucer: Etudes sur la Correspondance avec de nombreux textes inédits* (Paris, 1958–), J. Rott, ed., *Correspondance de Martin Bucer* (Leiden, 1979), and *Martin Bucer: études sur les relations de Bucer avec les Pays-Bas, l'Electorat de Cologne et l'Allemagne du Nord avec de nombreux textes inédits*, 2 vols. (Leiden, 1985). For Calvin there is *Ioannis Calvini Opera Quae Supersunt Omnia*, 59 vols., eds. Baum, Cunitz and Reuss, (Brunswick, 1865–80; reiss. 1964); the *Supplementa Calviniana* (Neukirche, 1936–) is steadily issuing sermons and critical notes. Calvin's letters have appeared in a variety of editions. Many are contained in the *Corpus Reformatorum* and in A.-L. Herminjard ed., *Correspondance des Réformateurs dans les pays de la langue française* (Geneva, 1866–97; reiss. Niewkoop, 1965). A collection not always reliably translated into English appeared in the nineteenth century, *Letters of John Calvin*, ed. J. Bonnet, trans., D. Constable and M. R. Gilchrist (Philadelphia, 1858). Calvin's Biblical commentaries are included in the 47 volumes of the Calvin Translation Society (Edinburgh, 1844–54; reiss. Grand Rapids, 1948–81). His masterpiece, *The Institutes of the Christian Religion* appeared in a two-volume edition by J. T. McNeill, tr.

F. L. Battles (Philadelphia, 1960). The *Calvin Theological Journal* publishes an annual bibliography on the Swiss reformer. The letters of Calvin's successor can be found in the *Correspondance de Theodore Bèze*, ed. H. Aubert (Geneva, 1960–). *Huldreich Zwinglis Sämtliche Werke*, ed. E. Egli *et al*, occupies 14 volumes in the Corpus Reformatorum and has recently been reissued (Zürich, 1982). Some of his works have been translated in W. J. Hinke, ed., *Zwingli on Providence and other essays* (Durham NC, 1922, reiss. 1983); see also S. M. Jackson, ed., *The Latin Works and the Correspondence of Huldreich Zwingli, together with selections from his German works* (New York, 1912; Philadelphia, 1922–29). Robert Stupperich has edited the works of Philip Melanchthon in the seven-volume *Melanchthons Werke* (Gütersloh, 1951–71). For his correspondence there is *Melanchtons Briefwechsel*, ed. H. Scheible, two vols., (Stuttgart, 1977). His central work is available in *Melanchton on Christian Doctrine, Loci communes 1555*, trans. and ed., C. L. Manschreck (Grand Rapids, 1965, repr. 1982). Other translated writings appear in *Melanchthon: Selected Writings*, eds. E. E. Flack and L. Satee (Minneapolis, 1962). Sources for the writings of other German reformers include the 6-volume *Osiander Gesamtausgabe*, ed. G. Muller and G. Seebass (Gütersloh, 1975–85) and *Dr. Johnannes Bugenhagens Briefwechsel*, ed. O. Vogt (Hildesheim, 1966).

There are still large gaps in the availability of primary sources for the study of the Reformation but a number of learned societies have made it their continuing task to publish editions of texts. For German Protestant history see the works of the 'Verein für Reformationsgeschichte'; for German Catholicism, the publications of the 'Goerres Gesellschaft' and for materials on the Swiss and Rhineland reformations, those of the 'Zwingli Verein' and the *Bibliothèque d'Humanisme et Renaissance*. The *Bulletin* of the 'Société de l'Histoire du Protestantisme Française' has issued documents on Huguenot history. Students of the English Reformation will find the 54 volumes of the 'Parker Society' invaluable, while the Camden series of the Royal Historical Society also reprints important texts. The *Library of Christian Classics* (S. C. M. Press, London; Westminster Press, Philadelphia) has translated a series of sixteenth-century tracts, some of them rather rare. Finally, no historian in search of source materials can neglect the many journals published by local historical societies, especially those in Germany and England.

THE RADICALS

Anabaptism in German-speaking lands is covered regionally in *Quellen zur Geschichte der Täufer* (Leipzig and Gütersloh, 1930–14); Dutch Anabaptist sources are covered in the *Bibliotheca Reformatoria Neerlandica* (The Hague, 1903–14) and in the more recent *Documenta Anabaptistica Neerlandica* (Leyden, 1975–   ). Swiss Anabaptist sources are contained in the multi-volume *Quellen zur Geschichte der Täufer in der Schweiz* (Zurich, 1973–   ) and a very valuable collection in English, *The Sources of Swiss Anabaptism: the Grebel letters and related documents*, ed. L. Harder (Scottdale, 1985). A compact selection is contained in W. Klaassen, ed., *Anabaptism in Outline: Selected Primary Sources* (Scottdale, 1981). For the German Peasant War see G. Franz, *Der deutsche Bauernkrieg*, 11th edn. (Darmstadt, 1977) and *Quellen zur Geschichte des Bauernkrieges* (Munich, 1963) and W.-H. Struck, *Der Bauernkrieg am Mittelrhein und in Hessen: Darstellungen und Quellen* (Wiesbaden, 1975). Sources in East German archives are discussed in H. Lotzke and R. Kluge, 'Quellen zur Geschichte des bauerlichen Klassenkampfes in Deutschland in Staatsarchiven der DDR', in G. Heitz, *et al.*, eds., *Der Bauer im Klassenkampf* (Berlin, 1975). Pamphlet literature of the war has been collected by A. Laube and H. W. Seiffert, *Flugschriften des Bauernkriegszeit* (Berlin, 1978). *Die älteste Chronik der Hutterischen Brüder* edited by A. J. F. Ziegelschmid (Ithaca, 1943) deals with the Hutterite experience while the Münster phenomenon is the subject of two volumes edited by Robert Stupperich, *Die Schriften Bernhard Rothmanns* (Münster, 1970) and *Schriften von Katholischer Seite gegen die Täufer* (Münster, 1980). For Thomas Münzer see H. Boemer and P. Kirn, eds., *Thomas Müntzers Briefwechsel; Politische Schriften*, ed. C. Hinrichs, and Günther Franz, ed., *Thomas Müntzer, Schriften und Briefe* (Gütersloh, 1968). Italian radical reformers, including Socinus, can be found in D. Cantimori and E. Feist, eds., *Per la storia degli eretici italiani del secolo XVI in Europa*, (Rome, 1937) and a collection of letters and documents in *Reform Thought in Sixteenth-Century Italy*, tr. E. G. Gleason (Ann Arbor, 1981). The beliefs of the founder of Mennonitism are set out in H. W. Meihuizen, ed., *Menno Simons. Dat Fundament des Christelycken Leers* (The Hugue, 1967). Some of Andreas Carlstadt's anti-Lutheran writings have been edited by E. Hertzsch, *Karlstadts Schriften aus den Jahren 1523–25* (Halle, 1956–57). Anabaptist source material has recently been issued on microfilm; see Irvin B. Horst, *The Radical Reformation Microfiche Project* (Zug, 1977).

THE CATHOLIC REFORMATION

The Catholic Reformation also possesses a monumental edition of the works of Catholic writers: *Corpus Catholicorum* (Münster, 1919–). The 'Goerres Gesellschaft' has published *Concilium Tridentinum, Diarorum, Actorum, Epistularum, Tractatuum novo collectio* (Freiburg, 1901–) in several volumes. This is not a complete collection and much still awaits publication. The *Monumenta Historica Societas Jesu* (Madrid, 1894–) is still indispensable for Catholic reform. For Germany see the *Acta Reformationis Catholicae Ecclesiam Germaniae*, ed., Georg Pfeilschifter (Regensburg, 1959–). There is much that is useful in the publications of the Catholic Record Society for material relative to the history of sixteenth-century English Catholicism, including the letters of Cardinal Allen and the Jesuit Robert Parsons. Most of the important orders of the Church have their own journals or historical series devoted to the history of their community.

CONTEMPORARY HISTORIES

The Reformation with its cry 'ad fontem' sparked a new interest in history, but usually the history of the early Church rather than that of contemporary events. However, there were contemporaries who chronicled the events in narratives which often bring out new data or lead to important insights. Sleidan's *Commentaries* concerning the state of religion and commonwealth during the reign of Emperor Charles V (first published 1555, English trans. 1560), are remarkably free from bias though they are the first important Protestant history of the age. More immediate and personal in approach is the *Geschichte der Reformation* by Friedrich Myconius, written in 1541–43 (published Leipzig, 1914, ed. O. Clemen). Though Myconius introduces himself as a man of learning and condemns the priests and monks who had a monopoly in the writing of history, his book is in reality the autobiography of a citizen of Gotha rather than a general chronicle of events. John Knox's *History of the Reformation in Scotland* (best edition by W. Croft-Dickinson, Edinburgh, 1950), written by the principal participant, is one of the most important sources for the Reformation in that country. The history of the French Reformation can be followed in the *Histoire de son temps* of Jacques Auguste de Thou and Theodore Beza's, *Life of John Calvin* and the *Historie Ecclésiastique des Eglises Reformées au Royaume de France*, ed. G. Baum and E. Cunitz (1883–9, reiss. Niewkoop, 1974). An antipapal account of Trent was offered by Paolo Sarpi in his *Istoria del Concilio Tridentino* (first published in 1619, new edition Bari, 1934). Sarpi was rebutted by the Jesuit Sforza Pallavicino, *Istoria del Concilio di Trento* (first published 1656–57) who, for the first time, was able to use material from the Vatican archives in the telling of the story. Among the most influential contemporary histories were John Foxe's *Acts and Monuments*, better known as his *Book of Martyrs* edited by G. Townshend and S. Cattley in 8 volumes (London, 1837–41) and Jean Crespin, *Histoire des Martyrs*, 3 vols., ed. D. Benoit (Toulouse, 1885–89). The English Catholic exile Nicholas Sanders published a scathing history of the English Protestant Church, *The Rise and Growth of the Anglican Schism*, trans. D. Lewis (London, 1877).

Clearly, in spite of the many publications of original sources, there is much that can only be read in the archives. But there are no central archives which can be said to contain most of the important unprinted materials. In England, for example, the Public Record Office must be supplemented by local archives. These can be county archives or those attached to cathedral churches; town archives may also yield important materials. The pattern is similar throughout Europe. Side by side with the national archives stand the regional or provincial archives and the municipal collections. The Vatican archives are of prime importance for the history of the Church, but even these, while containing (like all national archives) materials relevant to the central administration, must be used in connection with the episcopal archives of the regions in which the historian has a special interest. Lastly, there exists a greater continuity among the aristocratic families of Europe than is generally assumed. For this reason family archives can play a major role in historical research.

NOTES AND REFERENCES

1 Cf. the brilliant description of this development in G. Mattingly, *Renaissance Diplomacy* (Boston, 1955).

2 L. von Ranke, *Geschichte der romanischen und germanischen Volker 1494–1514 (1824); Fürsten und Völker von Südeuropa (1827); Die romischen Päpste (1834–36); Deutsche Geschichte im zeitalter der Reformation* (1839–47); *Französische Geschichte . . . im 16 u. 17 Jahrhundert* (1852–61); *Englische Geschichte . . . im 16 u. 17 Jahrhundert* (1859–68). Most of these works are available in English, although mostly in rather poor translations.

3

ECONOMIC LIFE

RURAL SOCIETY IN EUROPE IN 1500

In 1500 the vast majority of Europeans still lived in the country, in single homesteads, hamlets, villages or small country towns, just as they had done throughout most of the Middle Ages. With some exceptions, the peasants were no longer serfs but legally free, able to dispose of their property and, if they chose, to leave their native villages. Many were no longer engaged in subsistence farming but were raising cash crops — wool or flax, olive oil or wine — and many others spun wool, wove cloth or forged nails, part time or full time, not only for their own and their fellow-villagers' needs, but for sale in highly organized local or foreign markets. At the same time people's view of property was changing. In classical feudalism, from the ninth to the thirteenth centuries, property, especially property in land, was seen in a dual way. It gave rights to its owner, but it also imposed obligations on him: for a noble or free man, the obligation of fealty (loyalty) and military service to his feudal lord from whom he held his land; for a peasant or serf, the obligation of labour service, the payment of dues and also, sometimes, military service. With the disappearance of the obligation of military service and the loosening of the bonds of personal loyalty, in the later Middle Ages, property came to be regarded as an absolute right, with none but contractual obligations imposed on it. On the Continent the spread of Roman Law reinforced this attitude, but the same development occurred in England under the common law. It was a slow shift in conception and in attitudes, but it had far-reaching consequences. It gave landlords a legal claim, or at least a good conscience, for changing customary tenures or for incorporating common land in their own property. In political life the prince, no longer able to expect effective military support from his vassals *qua* vassals, had to claim wider powers and prerogatives over his subjects than he had previously needed. Especially important were his claims to a monopoly of military service from all his subjects and the right to impose taxes. Conversely, the prince's subjects were naturally anxious to limit these claims and, if possible, to control their exercise. Both theories of absolute princely power and of the subjects' right to consent to taxation were therefore developed at the same time. The political consequences of these changes in the general conception of property and of political theory will be discussed in chapters 11 and 13. By the seventeenth century, the view of property as an absolute right had become so firmly rooted in people's minds that they could hardly think of it in any other way and they came to base all their political philosophies on it.

In 1500 this change of attitude was not yet as obvious, at least at the village level. Over most of Europe the traditional village communities remained substantially intact. The nobility, the lords of the manors, the *seigneurs*, the *Grundherren*, continued to exercise many of their traditional rights over the local peasantry, over and above the rents due to them from the peasants for their land: special rents or fines, labour or personal services and, in some but not all countries, jurisdictional and police powers. Governments had rarely as yet challenged the nobles' local influence.

A situation so full of contrasts between tradition and change was not likely to prove stable, nor did contemporaries think that it would be. But just how unstable it was to prove, no one in 1500 could have foreseen, for no one could foresee the powerful new forces which were to act on the European economy in the course of the sixteenth century.

THE RISE IN PRICES

There is one economic phenomenon which affects everyone who does not live in a primitive natural economy, and that is inflation. When historians discovered this phenomenon in the sixteenth and early seventeenth centuries, they called it, with some exaggeration, the price revolution, and they contrasted it with the long period of static or declining prices of the later Middle Ages. To people living in the sixteenth century this revolution was not immediately obvious; prices, especially prices of foodstuffs, fluctuated within wide limits, both seasonally and with the quality of harvests. Over the century as a whole, the general upward trend was only 2 to 3 per cent per year; but, from about the middle of the century, the cumulative rise of prices was becoming evident, from Palermo to Stockholm and from London to Novgorod. At the beginning of the seventeenth century wholesale grain prices in England were, on average, some five times what they had been in the last quarter of the fifteenth century. In France they had risen more than seven times and in southern Spain even higher.

It seemed at first as if the inflation was due to the wickedness of individuals. Theologians and preachers thundered against monopolists and usurers. The German Diets blamed the Fuggers and the other great trading companies. The imperial knights thought it most unjust that the emperor would not countenance their time-honoured practice of kidnapping merchants and then cutting off the hands of these bloodsuckers if they failed to pay an appropriate ransom. In England the rackrenting landlord was a favourite target for attack.

> You landlords, you rent-raisers, I may say you step-lords (thundered
> Bishop Latimer, in a sermon he preached before the young king, Edward
> VI, in 1549), you have for your possessions yearly too much. For that here
> before went for twenty or forty pound by year (which is an honest
> portion to be had gratis in one lordship of another man's sweat and
> labour), now is let for fifty or an hundred pound by year. Of this 'too
> much' cometh this monstrous and portentous dearth made by man . . .
> that poor men, which live by their labour, cannot with the sweat of their
> face have a living, all kinds of victuals is so dear; . . . and I think verily
> that if it thus continue, we shall at length be constrained to pay for a pig a
> pound.[1]

The grain merchants were equally hated. Their houses and stores usually suffered the first attack during the many urban bread riots of the century. These popular beliefs had some foundation in fact. Monopolists did raise the prices of the commodities they controlled. Landlords did raise rents and, in consequence, the cost of agricultural production and prices. The grain merchants, having taken over the functions of the medieval markets with their concern for the interests of the consumer, were able by superior organization to supply large and growing cities with cereals shipped from the ends of Europe; but their trade was highly speculative and they exploited local shortages to the limit. Governments, fearing popular riots, legislated against such practices but, as so often in the sixteenth century, legislation and administrative practice were poles apart. Governments, depending on merchants for loans, had to close their eyes to many malpractices. Government agents were often corrupt and, even where there was no overt corruption, hard-pressed ministers sometimes found it difficult to resist the temptation of engaging in grain speculation on government account in order to relieve the frightening emptiness of overburdened treasuries.

But there were also more subtle explanations of the continuous inflation. The theologians of the university of Salamanca in the 1550s were the first to see a connection between Spanish imports of American gold and silver and rising prices.

In countries where there is a great scarcity of money (wrote Martin de Azpilcueta Navarro), all other saleable goods, and even the hands and labour of men, are given for less money than where it is abundant. Thus we see by experience that in France, where money is scarcer than in Spain, bread, wine, cloth and labour are worth much less (than at present in Spain). And even in Spain in times when money was scarcer, saleable goods and labour were given for very much less than after the discovery of the Indies which flooded the country with gold and silver. The reason for this is that money is worth more where and when it is scarce than where and when it is abundant.[2]

Azpilcueta and his colleagues had thus anticipated the famous quantity theory of money. Its almost universal acceptance as an explanation of the price revolution was due, however, to a pamphlet, *La Response de M. Jean Bodin aux paradoxes du Seigneur de Malestroit*, published in 1568. Malestroit, an official of the French royal mint, had argued that the rise in prices was apparent, rather than real, and was due to successive debasements of the coinage. Now it was perfectly true that many European governments had been debasing their coinages. This is not necessarily bad for a country's economy. In the later Middle Ages Europe had suffered from a serious gold and silver shortage. To provide enough currency to finance all economic transactions it was perfectly reasonable to try to break the link between money and precious metal. Pure paper money was not yet acceptable; but governments minted coins with a higher face value than the value of the coins' gold or silver content. This practice was becoming more and more acceptable, provided the discrepancy was not too great and provided also that the government accepted such coins at face value when it collected taxes.[3] With rapidly increasing taxation in the sixteenth century, this last condition, at least, was generally fulfilled. But only too often governments, in need of immediate cash, would greatly overdo the debasement. Between 1543 and 1546, for instance, the English government reduced the silver content of the shilling (testoon, 5p) from 100 to 40 grains. The mint paid £3 for every pound of silver and coined it into £7 4s. The difference, apart from the quite low expenses of minting, was pure profit. In the reign of Edward VI the silver content of the testoon was halved again.[4] Nevertheless, Bodin, famous among his contemporaries mainly as a lawyer and political theorist, had little difficulty in showing that prices in France had risen far more than they would have done if there had been no other cause than debasement. In England, after two successive, and eventually successful, attempts at recoinage, prices still continued to rise. In Spain and in some other countries, the coinage had not been tampered with at all when Bodin wrote, though in Spain this was to happen with a vengeance after 1597. Bodin, therefore, came to the same conclusion as the professors of Salamanca although, it seems, independently of them, viz. that the import of American gold and silver was responsible for rising prices in Europe.

AMERICAN TREASURE AND INFLATION

This view appeared to receive powerful support from the researches of modern economic historians. Many volumes of price histories, covering most European countries, have amply confirmed the phenomenon of rising prices in the sixteenth century (see above, pp. 18–19). Such figures as we have for the import of American treasure into Europe are far from satisfactory; but the trends they show are clear enough.[5] Quantities likely to affect drastically Spanish and European coinage were imported only from about the middle of the sixteenth century onwards and seem to have risen quite sharply until about 1600. It was mostly silver which was mined, with a new technical process using Spanish mercury, at Zacatecas and Guanajaco in Mexico, and at Potosi in Peru. Prices, however, had already started to rise in the first half of the sixteenth century and that, as some recent studies have suggested, in Spain at least at a faster average rate than during the second half of the century. Supporters of the quantity theory have explained this by the fact that, from about 1450, considerable quantities of silver were mined in central Europe. The mines of Joachimsthal, in Bohemia, were particularly famous and gave their name to that well-known silver coin, the thaler (which gave its name to the dollar).

Nevertheless, Bodin's theory of the price revolution, even in its most sophisticated modern form, has recently come under heavy and very damaging attack. For Spain there is too much evidence that much of the silver which came to Seville was very rapidly exported again: to pay for Spanish imports, to supply the pay and provisions of Spanish troops abroad, and to repay the loans which German and Genoese bankers made to the Spanish government. In consequence, Spain often suffered not from a surplus, but a shortage of gold and silver[6] and, at the beginning of the seventeenth century, she was even forced to adopt a billon currency, that is copper with only a small silver admixture. This coincidence of high prices and shortage of money would seem to indicate a credit, rather than a currency, inflation (see pp. 55 ff).[7] In Italy, the fluctuations, of silver imports did not coincide with the movement of prices.[7] But, most important of all, prices of different commodities did not rise as evenly as one would have expected in a purely monetary inflation. The really startling rises were, in fact, confined to agricultural products, notably grain and wool. Manufactured goods rose only about half as much. It would be unreasonable to suppose that American treasure had no inflationary effects whatever in Spain and western Europe. But it was clearly not the only and, perhaps, not even the most important cause of rising prices.

POPULATION GROWTH

The most commonly accepted alternative to Bodin's theory has recently come to be one based on the growth of population. The study of historical demography is beset with even more pitfalls than the study of prices. We have no censuses, and few reasonably reliable estimates, of the population of a whole European country before the eighteenth century. But there is an enormous mass of information about the population of individual towns, districts and even whole provinces. It has come down to us mostly in the form of censuses of households and land registers, usually compiled for purposes of taxation, of muster rolls for military service, and of parish registers.[8]

POPULATION IN TOWNS

In 1500 there were in Europe five giant cities of 100,000 inhabitants or more. Constantinople, most probably the largest of them all, was said to require eight ships laden with grain to feed its cosmopolitan population for just one day.[9] Naples, Venice and Milan had about 100,000 each, and Paris, the only transalpine city in this class, may have been even larger.[10] In the course of the sixteenth century Naples doubled its inhabitants and became the overcrowded, slummy and picturesque city admired by Goethe two hundred years later, and not so very different today. Venice rose to 168,000 in 1563, but the plague of 1575 reduced its numbers again. Milan reached 180,000 and Paris may have touched 200,000 at the turn of the century. By 1600 seven or eight more cities had reached or come near the 100,000 mark. Rome and Palermo more than doubled their inhabitants to reach about 110,000, with Messina, trebling its population, not far behind.[11] In Marseilles, officials estimated the city at between 80,000 and 100,000.[12] The new transaoceanic trade made Lisbon and Seville into boom cities which trebled their populations to 100,000 and 120,000 respectively. London rose to over 100,000 and Antwerp to over 90,000 in the 1560s; and while Antwerp declined again, its role as the greatest trading and banking centre of north-western Europe rapidly passed to Amsterdam which, in its turn, reached the 100,000 mark soon after 1600. For Moscow we have little more than guesses. Before the Tartars burned the city, in 1571, it was reputed to have over 40,000 houses or, presumably, as many as 200,000 inhabitants.[13]

The story of the smaller cities was similar. Few declined while the majority expanded — moderately by some 10,000 or 15,000, as did Florence, to a figure of 60,000–70,000, or Lübeck, with 40,000–50,000; rapidly, as did Vienna, Nuremberg, Augsburg, Strassburg, Hamburg and Danzig (Gdansk), which all started with about 20,000 inhabitants in 1500 and doubled their size in the course of the century; phenomenally, as did Madrid, an insignificant provincial town of a few thousand citizens which rose to the splendid position of capital of the greatest Christian empire. In 1600, most of its 60,000 new inhabitants were still housed in jerry-built squalor that contrasted sharply with the palatial towns houses of a few courtiers and grandees. Even so, sophisticated Italian visitors remarked, no doubt with patriotic exaggeration, that entering these palaces was like entering the stables.[14]

In 1500 there were in Europe, excluding Russia and Turkey, about 150 cities of 10,000 or more inhabitants, with an aggregate population of just under 3.5 million. By 1600 there were 220 such cities, with a total of nearly 6 million inhabitants. About half of this urban population in the sixteenth century lived in Italy and in the Iberian peninsula.[15] The old Mediterranean tradition of city-dwelling, going back to the Roman Empire and beyond, was still holding its ground. North of the Alps and the Pyrenees, only the relatively small area of the Netherlands had an equally dense urban population.

All these were big cities, by sixteenth-century standards. Below them were scores of medium-sized and hundreds of small towns which now were not only filling in the empty spaces which the plague of the mid-fourteenth century had left within their walls, but often found these walls too narrow and had to rebuild, or expand beyond, them.

This remarkable urban growth is an almost certain proof of an overall growth of population; for the mortality rate in towns was nearly always such that they could not maintain their population without immigration. Towards the end of the century, much excellent rebuilding took place in small towns and villages, much of which has survived, both in England and on the Continent. But in the bigger towns, especially those which were growing fast, housing and hygienic conditions got worse rather than better. The population growth originated in the countryside; its causes are still far from clear. It is possible that the virulence of the recurrent epidemics abated somewhat, although they could still be terrible killers, as Italy and other parts of Europe found in 1574–75. More effective central government and the end of baronial feuds and civil wars in most of western Europe may have given greater security on roads and rivers. This, in turn, allowed a much greater degree of regional specialization in agriculture with a consequent increase in output and the possibility of softening the worst calamities due to local harvest failures.

POPULATION PRESSURE ON LAND

Whatever the causes, all over western and southern Europe, growing numbers were competing for limited amounts of farm land. Except in Italy and in the Low Countries, there were still large areas of uncultivated land. But this was not always good farm land, nor easily accessible. It needed much capital to colonize and this was ofteñ either not available or not forthcoming. Where legal conditions allowed, as in parts of Italy, France and southern Germany, peasants would divide their holdings among their growing families. But there were limits to this process. Where peasants farmed their land on temporary leases, as was common though far from universal in England, their landlords could raise their rents, and there is plenty of evidence that they did so, quite apart from the sermons of bishop Latimer.[16] In either case, growing numbers of men were left without land or even without work on the land. Some of the young men would join the armies which were constantly being recruited. Others became vagrants or outlaws. They were a perennial and extremely intractable problem throughout the century, and in Italy and Spain the problem of banditry seems to have been at its worst in the last quarter of the century. Energetic governments had little difficulty in finding settlers for depopulated provinces or for overseas colonies. Franche Comté, after being devastated in the Habsburg—Valois wars, was largely resettled from Picardy and Savoy. The province of Granada whose Morisco population rebelled against Spain and was scattered over the whole of Castile (1570) was resettled from the north of the country. But most common of all was the continuous and unorganized migration of country people into the towns.

It has been estimated that the population of England grew from 2.5 million in 1500 to about 4.1 million in 1600, and that of the Empire from about 12 to 20 million. These particular estimates may be inaccurate but the trend, at least, is clear, and it seems to have been the same over most of Europe. In practice this meant a constantly increasing demand for bread and meat, for wool and flax, and for building materials and fuel. To meet this growing demand it was possible to improve some farming techniques, particularly by increased local specialization. Rice and maize cultivation spread in the Po valley. Viticulture tended to retreat from cold and rainy Normandy and to concentrate in the sunnier east and south of France. The market gardening of the Netherlands was imitated in the Ile de France and in Kent, where Paris and London provided expanding markets for fruit and the more sophisticated vegetables such as cauliflowers, carrots and peas. But other Netherlands inventions, such as the use of turnips and clover for animal fodder and a more scientific crop rotation than the traditional two or three field systems, were not introduced in other countries until the seventeenth century. All these improvements only touched the fringe of the problem. The great mass of European farmers could not read the new books on agriculture and, even if they did, they lacked the capital to make the recommended improvements. Thus throughout the century demand rose more rapidly than supply. Costs rose with rising rents, with the extension of cultivation to less fertile or less accessible land and, in the long run, with rising wages. The combined cost and demand inflation in European agriculture therefore can explain the main features of the price revolution and, especially, the discrepancy between the movements of agricultural and industrial prices.

WOOL PRICES AND SHEEP FARMING

The increasing demand due to a growing European population affected not only the price of foodstuffs but also the prices of other agricultural raw materials and not least of wool. This was especially important for England and Spain, for these were the only countries which produced wool for an international market. Until about the middle of the sixteenth century wool prices in both countries rose even more rapidly than grain prices. In England, arable land was turned into pasture already in the fifteenth century. Landlords enclosed common land and depopulated whole villages to make room for their flocks. Cardinal Wolsey even appointed a royal commission to inquire into enclosures. Turning arable land into pasture made the problem of food supplies even more severe. When, after 1550, a revaluation of the English coinage caused a sharp fall in the export of woollens, it became profitable again to enclose for arable, rather than for sheep farming.

In Spain the pattern was essentially similar. From the middle of the fifteenth century, a growing demand for the famous merino wool and rising prices made it profitable to breed huge flocks of sheep. In the arid interior of the Iberian peninsula, these flocks had to migrate, often over hundreds of miles, from summer grazing in the northern mountains to winter pastures in Estremadura and Andalucia. It was then, and it is still, a matter of controversy just how much damage to the sedentary farmers was done by the biannual passage of grazing and trampling sheep. Certainly the feud between the farmers and the armed shepherds of the *mesta*, the guild of sheep owners, was chronic and often violent. The *mesta* was allied with the rich wool exporters of Burgos and the Basque ports, and the crown supported them, in return for substantial loans. Indeed royal and *mesta* officials were often indistinguishable. Thence, the private interests of officials might determine royal policy; this happened frequently in the sixteenth century, and not only in Spain.[17] Just as in England, the result of this encroachment of sheep farming on arable land was a particularly sharp rise in grain prices. And, again as in England, there was a reversal of these trends in the second half of the century, when the demand for wool from the cloth industry of the Netherlands declined. The crown then gradually withdrew its support of the *mesta* while Spanish landowners began to enclose land for wheat growing.

In the long run population growth seems to have outrun food supplies. From the beginning of the seventeenth century, because of a rising death rate, population growth either slowed down or ceased. Even in the sixteenth century, those areas which were highly urbanized found it increasingly difficult to feed themselves. The Netherlands imported, on average, some 13 or 14 per cent of their grain requirements.[18] The great cities of Italy, especially Venice and Rome, depended on eastern Mediterranean or Apulian and Sicilian grain. For these latter supplies they had to compete with the constantly growing demand from Naples and Spain. In 1590–91 famine struck Italy, Spain and parts of France. From that date the whole of the western Mediterranean could no longer feed its population and had to rely on regular imports of grain. Venetian and Ragusan merchants had habitually shipped grain from Egypt and from the plains of Thessaly. But the enormous demands of Constantinople and of the Turkish fleet limited the quantities available for the west. There was only one area from which both the western Mediterranean and the North Sea areas could supply their deficiencies, and that was the Baltic.

The Danes levied tolls on all ships passing through the Sound, and from the Sound Toll Registers[19] we can observe the increasing number of Dutch and Hanseatic ships, laden with Prussian, Polish and Pomeranian rye, which sailed from Danzig and the smaller Baltic ports to London, Rouen and, above all, to Amsterdam. After 1590 they began to sail regularly through the Straits of Gibraltar. Leghorn (Livorno), the newly constructed free port of the grand duchy of Tuscany, became the distributing centre in Italy for northern grain, as well as for Dutch and English textiles and metal goods. The growth of Leghorn's trade was spectacular. In 1592–93 some 200 ships entered the port; in 1609–10 the number had risen to a little less than 2,500.[20] Soon Londoners and Amsterdamers were competing with the Italians for the carrying trade of the whole Mediterranean. With better crews and cheaper ships, with easier credit and lower freight rates, with Baltic grain, competitive cloths (Leyden says and Norfolk kerseys), the northerners enjoyed great technical advantages over their Italian rivals. They made this advantage overwhelming by adding 'the spirit of enterprise', as English and Dutch historians have called it. Italian historians, following contemporary opinion, have more prosaically seen it as a very efficient and quite unscrupulous combination of trading, privateering and systematic carrying of contraband by the fast-sailing and heavily gunned Dutch and English merchantmen. The Venetians who had successfully weathered the great crisis of Portuguese competition in the spice trade had no answer to Dutch and English competition in the Mediterranean and the Italian Ocean. From the 1590s, but not before, they and the other Italians began to lose their commercial pre-eminence in Europe.

MANUFACTURING AND BUILDING INDUSTRIES

While European agriculture was unable to expand its output as rapidly as the increasing demand from a growing population, this was not equally true of the manufacturing and building industries. Only a few industries, such as mining or iron smelting with the recently invented blast furnace, needed large outlays in fixed capital. More cloths could be woven, more nails could be forged and more houses could be built by just increasing the labour force. Since a growing population made labour easily available and relatively cheap, manufacturers were less concerned with labour-saving devices and the invention of new machinery than with the provision of capital to set labour working and with the discovery of new markets for its products.[21] To contemporaries, the greatest problems seemed to be chronic unemployment, with the consequent danger of social unrest, and the brakes which the guilds put on production and especially on the growth of large-scale industrial enterprise.

In Flanders and in the Rhineland, during the later Middle Ages, the guilds had had a heroic history of popular revolutions and political successes; but by the end of the fifteenth century they were in retreat almost everywhere before the powerful alliance of urban patriciates and territorial princes. In the most highly industrialized areas of Europe, in England, Flanders, south-western Germany and Italy, they had come to monopolize the organization of some of the most important industries, especially textiles. By regulating the price and quality of products, and by imposing limits on the number of apprentices and journeymen a master might employ, they blocked the capitalist entrepreneur who wished to employ large numbers of workers and lower, or just change, the traditional quality and price of a product, so as to reach a wider market. From the fifteenth century onwards the entrepreneurs reacted by moving out of the towns into the countryside, or into small, unincorporated country towns, where the rural population was only too willing to earn an extra income by spinning and weaving in their own homes. This was called the putting-out or domestic system, and it spread in England, especially in East Anglia, in Yorkshire and in the West Country. It also spread in Walloon Flanders, where a whole series of villages manufactured the famous says, the lighter and cheaper cloth that was to conquer the European and Levantine markets. Alternatively the entrepreneurs could take over the whole guild system and effectively employ the master craftsmen on piece rates. This method had been pioneered in medieval Florence and it now spread widely, particularly where guilds were only established in the sixteenth century.

For the guild system was spreading, at the very time when it was being attacked, evaded or taken over by the capitalist. In England, France and Spain, where the craft guilds had none of the revolutionary traditions of the Flemish guilds, they recommended themselves to conservative statesmen as a bulwark of the established social order against the social upheavals which so often seemed to follow the spread of capitalist industrial organization. The guilds could be easily controlled by the central government or its local officials, and in France guild offices were added to those which the government regularly sold. With this financial interest at stake it is not surprising to find the French crown issuing edicts, in 1581 and 1597, requiring all craftsmen to become members of a guild. Whether such official support for the system produced any advantages to the French silk or the English cloth worker, as against the exploitation he might otherwise have suffered under a capitalist putting-out system, is at least problematical. For the development of a country's industry, the guild system was almost wholly obstructive. England was saved from the most serious economic consequences of the system by the inability of her weak governments in the seventeenth century to uphold the guilds against the increasingly powerful interests on the other side.

WAGES AND PRICES

Custom and unemployment for a long time prevented wages catching up with rising prices. When they finally did — and that happened only in some areas — they rarely managed to keep up with further price rises. The discrepancy between the movement of money wages and food prices in the sixteenth century is startling. In southern England, for instance, the wages of building workers doubled in the course of the century, from 4*d* to 8*d* a day for labourers and from 6*d* to 1*s* for craftsmen. The prices of foodstuffs, however, rose to four or five times their original level. The relative movement of prices and builders' wages was very similar in Spain, France, Germany and Scandinavia[22]. Real wages, if reckoned by the amount of food a man could buy with his money wages, had been comparatively high in the fifteenth century. Nevertheless, a fall of some 60 per cent which the figures indicate would have been quite catastrophic and does not, in actual fact, seem to have happened. Retail prices did not rise as much as the wholesale prices from which historians have constructed their price indexes; for these are the prices they have found in their most conveniently usable sources. The cost of labour enters into the price of baked bread, for instance, and this did not rise as much as the price of grain. The prices of manufactures generally rose much less sharply than the prices of foodstuffs, though even they tended to outrun wages. All the same, there can be little doubt that the position of most European wage labourers tended to worsen during the sixteenth century and that this was due to the changed terms of trade between town and country, or, rather, between workshop and farm.[23] Laying the same number of bricks, or weaving the same length of cloth as formerly, the bricklayer or weaver would be able to buy less and less bread and meat as the century wore on.

He might not have realized this during the first two or three decades; for the long-term trends were masked by the usual violent seasonal and annual harvest fluctuations. The German peasant movements of the early sixteenth century and the great Peasants' War of 1524−25 did not spring from dissatisfaction with wages but had very different causes. (See pp. 171−3.) But, from about 1530, the disparity between prices and wages became too stark to be missed. From this period date the first significant wage increases and also, among contemporaries, a growing awareness of an undercurrent of discontent among the labouring population of western and central Europe. In 1534 it burst into open revolution when the Anabaptists set up their famous communistic and polygamous Kingdom of the Elect at Münster. (See pp. 173−4.) Contemporaries never forgot this shocking event, nor the explosive possibilities of the combination of unemployment or low wages with revolutionary religious propaganda. They were to see many more examples: from the popular movements in the German cities which forced patrician town councils into an unwilling acceptance of Lutheranism, to Kett's rebellion in Norfolk in 1549; from the image-breaking riots in the Netherlands, following the 'hunger winter' of 1565−66, to the popular dictatorship of the Holy League in Paris in 1589−90.

With real wages falling as they did, the wonder is that popular outbursts were not more frequent. What made the situation bearable for wage earners was that the great majority still lived in villages or small towns where they owned or rented a patch of land or garden − not enough to live on, but invaluable for supplementing an expensive diet of bought bread and meat. Characteristically, in the giant city of Antwerp where labourers could have no gardens, wage movements in the building industry were rather different from those in the smaller cathedral cities of England, France and Germany from which historians have constructed most sixteenth-century wage series. In Antwerp, too, the gap between prices and wages had become very large by the early 1530s; but from that time on, wages began to follow prices. By 1561 their relative level was again what it had been in 1500.[24] Almost immediately the estates of Brabant demanded the statutory reduction of wages.[25] The textile workers did not get an adequate rise until 1574. Belgian historians have suggested that this long delay may well help to explain the revolutionary role of the textile workers in the revolt of the Netherlands.[26]

Those who did well out of rising food prices and the increasingly favourable terms of trade for the countryside were, in the words of a contemporary, 'all such as have takings, or farms in their own maintenance, at the old rent; for where they pay after the old rate, they sell after the new; that is, they pay for their land good cheap, and sell all things growing thereof dear'[27] – provided always (and it was a most important proviso) that their holdings were sufficiently secure so that they could not be dispossessed by their powerful lords or neighbours. From about the middle of the sixteenth century, we find a new genre of painting and engraving by Flemish, Dutch and German artists, of whom Brueghel is the most famous: peasant feasts, peasant weddings and carnivals. The peasants are usually presented as loutish boors, with gross features, gorging themselves with food and drink. Since the peasants themselves are unlikely to have commissioned and bought such pictures (although they sometimes appeared in taverns), it has been argued that it was the bourgeoisie who provided the demand, as a gratifying and sophisticated, if essentially futile, comment on the changed terms of trade between town and country.[28] This may have been so, on occasion; but these paintings and engravings were often more ambivalent, giving a gratifyingly patriotic view of the natural vitality of the native peasantry, rather like the Tudor tradition of the sturdy English yeoman whose patriotic prowess had won the battles of the Hundred Years Wars. More simply, perhaps, the artists were depicting for a fascinated elite the well-known experience of fairs and festivals with their all-too-common drunkenness and brawling, not unlike the charivari of the French villages with their temporary reversals of social values.[29]

SOCIAL CONSEQUENCES OF RISING PRICES

Yet in spite of a great deal of local research and much controversy, we are still a long way from having a complete picture of the social consequences of the price revolution in rural Europe. There are, however, some conclusions we can state. In England, those small farmers with insecure land tenure often suffered from landlords who would dispossess them, either to farm the land themselves or to let it in larger blocks to tenants on short-term leases, which on expiry could be adjusted to rising prices. Over the course of the century a greater gap grew between the rich and the poor, especially between the prosperous yeoman with his security of tenure and the smaller farmers, many of whom were reduced to the class of common farm labourers. While the gentry and the yeomanry were able to thrive by taking advantage of the economies of scale, the number and economic position of the barely self-sufficient smallholders declined. The position of the higher aristocracy seems to have remained generally static.[30]

In England there was greater social mobility of both population and capital than in most other European countries. There was nothing new, in the sixteenth century, in men making money in trade and then investing it in land, so that they, or at least their children and grandchildren, should become gentlemen and even acquire titles of nobility. It was also an old story on the Continent. But in England, far more than on the Continent, some rural capital found its way back into trade, either by direct investment or by portions for younger sons. The sixteenth century with its expanding economy gave greater opportunities for this movement of persons and capital, but it did not alter the social structure of the country. Contemporary opinion generally deplored social mobility and was rarely even aware of the English phenomenon of the social mobility of capital, though the reverse, on the Continent, gave rise to much pessimistic comment by French and Spanish writers on economic matters and by the more perceptive of government officials. Cumulatively, and in the long run, this characteristic of English social and economic life was to give England a great advantage in her commercial and industrial development over that of her Continental rivals.

SOCIAL CONSEQUENCES OF RISING PRICES: THE CONTINENT

For the Continent we now have several excellent regional studies; but the overall effects of the price revolution on rural life are still a matter of controversy among historians.[31] In the northern Netherlands, especially in the province of Holland, the stimulus of nearby urban markets acted on a social structure in which lordship was traditionally weak and in which alternative employment for a surplus rural population was readily available in the nearby towns. Peasants could therefore avoid splitting their properties among their younger children and they could specialize in whatever type of farming was most suitable to the soil, the climate and their own skills. Thus they could give up growing grain for their own subsistence and concentrate on dairy farming and meat production. Their higher income, derived from more efficient farming, would then be reinvested directly in agricultural production, such as buying lifestock or improving farm buildings, and also in the infrastructure of the region, the roads, canals, dykes and polders (land reclaimed from the sea) which were to give Holland its characteristic modern appearance. Their purchases of grain (for their own consumption) and of manufacturers from the city markets further stimulated Dutch trade and industrial production. It was a slow process, reaching its climax only in the seventeenth century; but it provided the solid economic basis for the 'golden age' of the Dutch Republic, the comfortable bourgeois lifestyle of a large section of its population, its pre-eminence in painting, music and science, and its role as a great power in European politics.

Further south, in the noble-dominated province of Hainault, for which we possess quite good figures for income from land, it looks as if the owners of medium-large properties benefited by rising agricultural prices and did relatively better than the owners of small properties.[32] The situation may well have been similar in the other Walloon provinces of the Netherlands where the nearby industrial cities of Flanders provided excellent markets. But even for the neighbouring French provinces the position is much more doubtful.

In France and Italy, many of the lower nobility do not seem to have been able to make their rents keep pace with rising prices. The eagerness with which the lower nobility of France joined first the royal and then the different confessional standards in the foreign and civil wars of the sixteenth century may well be an indication of an economic malaise of large sections of this numerous class. Even so, it is uncertain how far such a malaise applied mainly to younger sons. In the course of the sixteenth century the nobility of many parts of Europe, and especially in northern Italy, came to adopt legal devices to keep the bulk of the family estates in the hands of one heir. The appearance of quite large numbers of impecunious noblemen — and on the Continent, unlike England, all sons inherited noble status — was therefore not necessarily a sign of the economic decline of the nobility. The law courts of the continental monarchies were constantly encroaching on the nobles' rights of jurisdiction and of raising taxes and dues from their vassals and tenants. The nobles reacted by entrenching themselves ever more rigidly behind their privileges. They developed the doctrine of *dérogeance*, and in 1560 they persuaded the French crown to make it law: any nobleman who engaged in trade, especially in retail trade, or in any handicraft, lost his noble privileges.[33] By the end of the sixteenth century this principle was generally accepted, if not always legalized, in much of northern Italy as well as France.

The principle of *dérogeance* meant that rural capital would rarely be invested in trade or industry, except in some big trading companies and indirectly, through taxation by the government — a function which governments did not perform at all systematically until the second half of the seventeenth century. The immobilization of capital in land applied *a fortiori* when a former bourgeois had bought land and acquired a title; for he would generally be doubly anxious to conform to the rules of his new status.

However, in western and southern Europe the nobility as an order, and especially the higher nobility, managed to weather the economic storms of the price revolution with considerable success. They had many different ways of doing this. The Roman nobility depopulated the Roman Campagna by turning arable into grazing land, in order to exploit the expanding Roman market for meat and cheese.[34] In Spain the government decreed maximum prices for grain, the *tasa*; but in practice this was a method of keeping down the price paid to the peasant producers while the nobility marketed the peasants' grain well above the *tasa* prices.[35] But more important than such tricks was population pressure on land, which generally made it possible for landowners to raise rents or entry fines at least as fast as prices.[36] While the peasants were legally free in most parts of western and southern Europe, they were often still subject to heavy feudal dues and seignorial monopolies, such as those for milling, brewing or oil and wine pressing.

In large parts of France the peasants met increasing population pressure by subdividing their holdings among their children. The lords, unable by law and custom to dispossess their peasants and to group holdings together in larger and more efficient units, as English landowners were beginning to do, encouraged the process of subdivision, for it gave them more rents and entry fines. The peasants, with their fragmented holdings, had to maintain their traditional inefficient subsistence farming. There was therefore little chance of a Dutch-type rural prosperity providing a growing market for urban manufactures. In southern France and in other Mediterranean areas this rural blight was made even worse by the development of sharecropping (French: *métayage*, Italian: *mezzadria*) by which lord and tenant shared the harvest in a fixed proportion. It was a practice which gave the landowners easy returns with minimal effort on their part and, in a period of rising prices, allowed them to take advantage of favourable market conditions; but it gave no encouragement to investment in agricultural production by either lord or tenant, nor to the adoption of more efficient methods of farming.

It was said that in Portugal the peasants on the big estates were little better off than negro slaves. In Castile a strong monarchy managed to protect the peasants from the worst excesses of arbitrary increases in feudal dues and from the even greater arbitrariness of seigneurial jurisdiction; but it did nothing to save them from economic exploitation. In Aragon and Catalonia, this same monarchy had no powers whatever to protect the peasantry from exploitation by a nobility which prided itself on administering its estates as independently as if they were kingdoms. In Naples and Sicily its rights, and hence its economic opportunities, were almost as extensive.[37] From time to time a vigorous Spanish viceroy attempted to limit the nobles' right to tax their vassals. The nobles fought such measures as being tantamount to confiscation of property, and a legalistically-minded king in Madrid failed to back his viceroys, for fear of antagonizing the nobility over a question in which his own jurisdiction was not directly involved. Not until the seventeenth century did the kings of Spain grant, or sell, powers of jurisdiction to the south Italian nobility, as of right; but many of them had exercised it already in the sixteenth century. In Sicily this included the *ex abrupto* procedure by which a criminal could be tortured before the indictment was read to him. The nobles petitioned against its use in the royal courts, but found it convenient in their own seignorial courts.

The high nobility — the peers and princes of the blood of France, the grandees of Spain, the princes of the old Italian families, the peers of England and the Knights of the Golden Fleece of the Netherlands – rarely had to rely on purely economic methods to recoup or enhance their family fortunes. They were the first and most substantial beneficiaries of royal patronage; for no European monarchy could do entirely without the support and the services of the high nobility in the highest military and administrative posts, and this service had to be rewarded with a generosity that befitted the status of both the giver and the recipient. Contemporaries liked to compile lists of incomes of the leading families of different countries. The figures are hardly very accurate, but both individual family incomes and the aggregates for the high nobility rise regularly with each successive list, and this trend was undoubtedly correctly observed.

In western Germany the nobility found it more difficult to cope with the price revolution. On the other hand, the feudal obligations of the peasants, and even serfdom, had remained much more important, although serfdom was far from universal; on the other hand, surviving customary law could not be abrogated unilaterally, and the peasants therefore enjoyed a certain degree of protection. The nobility found it difficult to raise rents, except in Bavaria and Austria where serfdom was more common and where the dukes and archdukes supported the claims of the lords to raise entry fines. If the non-princely lords and the knights found themselves hamstrung, this was not the case with the scores of small princes, prince-bishops and prince-abbots in south-western Germany and in the German-speaking Alpine regions. They could introduce autocratic Roman law in place of local custom; they could arrogate to their own courts village and seigneurial jurisdiction; above all, they could impose new taxes. For more than a generation before the Reformation such policies had produced chronic peasant unrest until, in 1524–25, south-western and central Germany and the Alpine lands exploded in the great Peasants' War. (See pp. 171–2). The defeat of the peasants benefited the princes rather than the lesser lords. The former could continue to impose taxes (subject, however, in many principalities, to some quite effective brakes applied by representative assemblies), while the nobility found it no easier to raise their rents now than before the Peasants' War. Since in most German states burghers from the towns were not permitted to acquire noble estates, there was little of that inflow of commercial capital into agriculture that was so characteristic of England, France and Italy. For more than two centuries rural life in western and southern Germany stagnated. The country nobility, unable to maintain their rental income, had almost no choice but to enter *en masse* the service of the princes.

RURAL SOCIETY EAST OF THE ELBE

Quite different, however, was the history of rural society north and east of the river Elbe. In Holstein and Denmark the nobility found the growing cities of north-western Germany and the Netherlands excellent markets for their grain and dairy produce. Like the Spanish nobility, they interposed themselves between the peasant producers and the market and found it profitable to sell directly to foreign, rather than Danish, merchants. Where possible, they extended their own demesnes at the expense of the peasants, working them, at least partly, with servile labour.[38]

In north-eastern Germany and Poland, the landed nobility did even better. The declining population of the later Middle Ages and peasant migration to the towns and to newer lands further east, had left the nobles with large demesnes on their hands. The price revolution and the growing western and southern European market for rye, timber, furs and other forest products now presented them with a golden opportunity, provided they could find cheap labour for extensive demesne farming. This they did by tying the peasants to their holdings and exacting labour services from them and their families. The 'new serfdom' grew slowly in the course of the later sixteenth and the seventeenth centuries; but it was imposed by draconian laws and enforced by the lords' seigneurial and police powers. The electors of Brandenburg, the dukes of Mecklenburg, Pomerania and Prussia, and the kings of Poland were too feeble to protect the peasants. As large landowners, moreover, their own interests coincided with those of the nobility on whom they were dependent for money grants in the assemblies of estates. Thus the *Junkers* built up their *Gutsherrschaft* (in contrast to the medieval *Grundherrschaft*, the manorial system), that combination of capitalist and feudal estate management, more similar to the Spanish *encomiendas* in America than to a contemporary English or French estate. On the extensive river and lake system of central eastern Europe they shipped their grain to Danzig (Gdansk) and the other Baltic ports where, like the Danish nobles, they preferred to do business directly with the Dutch and English merchants from whom they could often obtain credits. In the second half of the sixteenth century Poland trebled or even quadrupled her exports of rye and, in the first two decades of the seventeenth century, doubled them again.[39]

Thus the urbanization and industrial advance of western Europe in the sixteenth century was directly linked with the triumph of a new commercial 'feudalism' east of the Elbe and the depression of a once relatively free peasantry into serfdom and the decline of the east German and Polish towns (see p. 112) – just as it was linked with the slave trade and the plantations worked by slave labour in the New World. On the other hand, developments in Bohemia and Hungary were essentially similar, and this without exports of grain to western Europe. The markets here were the armies and fortress garrisons of the Turkish wars and, later, the Thirty Years' War. In much of central eastern Europe an economically and politically triumphant nobility identified the interests of the state with its own. They did this either by the virtual destruction of royal power, as happened in the aristocratic republic of Poland, although not irretrievably until the seventeenth century, or by allying with the prince, as in Brandenburg-Prussia: the later absolutism of the Hohenzollerns notoriously did not extend to the estates of the *Junkers*. In the west, by contrast, the structure of society and the structure of governments was, and remained, much more complex, richer and more flexible. Towns and countryside, merchants and farmers, nobles and bourgeois, princes and subjects struggled with and balanced each other in varying unstable combinations, until the political and industrial revolutions of the late eighteenth and nineteenth centuries transformed both the societies and their governments, and forced on serf-owning eastern Europe and slave-owning America the painful necessity of adapting themselves to the political and economic demands of industrial capitalism.

INTERNATIONAL TRADE

There is one further element in the complex phenomenon of the price revolution which has, so far, only been hinted at: the increase in trade and in the velocity of the circulation of money. We know comparatively little about the local and retail trade of thousands of villages, small towns and weekly markets, all over Europe. Historians have rather concentrated on regional and international trade and banking, partly because the sources for such studies are more easily accessible, but also because international trade has been seen as the pacemaker of economic development.

In 1500 the geography of European international trade was still essentially what it had been for the previous two or three hundred years: northern Italy and Flanders, the most highly urbanized and industrialized areas of Europe, were the two hubs of an economic axis. Both areas manufactured high quality woollen cloth for the European market. Italy further specialized in silks and other rich fabrics, while Flanders also produced linens, lace and tapestries. Both areas had advanced shipbuilding and metal industries. Venice had established a virtual monopoly of the Levant trade in oriental spices and other luxury goods from the east which Venetian and German merchants distributed over Europe. Contact between Italy and Flanders was both overland and by sea, and there were lateral lines of connection at all points of the Italy-Flanders axis, south-westwards, towards France and Spain, and east and north to Germany and the Baltic. The axis extended north-west to England which, while it no longer supplied the raw wool that had made the fortunes of Ghent and Florentine clothiers, was still exporting semi-finished cloths for the finishing industries of Flanders and Brabant. Spain had taken the place of England as the principal international supplier of high-quality raw wool.

There were, of course, many more commodities in international trade than textiles and spices. Timber, grain and furs from Norway and the Baltic were exchanged for French and Portuguese salt and wines. Fish, cheese, butter, wines and beer, metals and arms of every kind, were commodities commonly shipped over long distances. An English customs list of 1582 even has the intriguing entry 'Wolves living; the woulf Xs'.[40] Not least in importance was the slave trade; for domestic slavery had never died out in southern Europe. During the sixteenth century, the recruitment of galley slaves for Mediterranean warships of all nationalities became a specially brutal type of slave trade in convicts. Characteristically, it was only the Erasmian humanists who attacked this practice. The Spanish crown was content to forbid its sea captains to throw galley slaves overboard at the end of a campaign.

Goods sent overland were more often packed on mules and horses than loaded in wagons; for roads were bad. Where possible, people preferred to transport goods and to travel by ship at sea, or by barge on rivers. It was cheaper and more comfortable, often quicker and sometimes, but not always, safer than travel by road. From Venice to Brussels one reckoned to take ten days, to Paris, twelve, to London twenty-four, and to Constantinople something over a month. It could be less − the shortest recorded journey from Venice to Paris was seven days, and to Constantinople fifteen − but it could also, and often did, take very much longer.[41] The Italians led the world in commercial, banking and insurance techniques, in double entry bookkeeping, and in all the most sophisticated credit transactions by which merchants financed their business, speculated on exchange rates and avoided clerical censures in the earning of interest on loan capital, even though the Catholic Church was tightening up its prohibitions of usury.

EFFECTS OF OVERSEAS DISCOVERIES

The first big change in the geographical pattern of European trade came as the result of the Portuguese exploration and circumnavigation of the coasts of Africa, and of the Spanish discovery of America. Before this, European merchants rarely got beyond the Mediterranean ports, where they had bought West African slaves and gold, Indian pepper and ivories and Chinese silks from Arab merchants. Now, for the first time, they established direct contact with the producers of these commodities. In the New World, they opened completely new markets for European goods, paid for in solid gold and silver which, in its turn, helped to expand European trade with the east. The blow to Venice was immediate and sharp. The loss of the spice monopoly, lamented the Venetian Girolamo Priuli as early as 1501, was like the loss of milk to an infant.[42] But by the middle of the century the Venetians had fought their way back to the position of leading suppliers for the European market, and for the rest of the century they held the Portuguese in an uneasy balance. Together with their Arab suppliers, they had the advantage of long-established expertise and of the shorter Red Sea and Persian Gulf routes. Connoisseurs held that spices deteriorated during the long voyage round the Cape. The Portuguese, involved in interminable naval wars with the Arabs in the Indian Ocean, found their overheads rising. In the end, victory turned on the hard facts of naval and commercial efficiency. In the seventeenth century, the Dutch and the English proved themselves superior in both these qualities to Arabs, Portuguese and Venetians alike.

The possibilities of trade with the New World were not appreciated so quickly. At first, the Spaniards simply sent back looted gold. Unlike the Portuguese in Africa and Asia, who were content to set up trading posts protected by forts, the Spaniards in the West Indies and on the American mainland conquered and settled huge areas of land. The settlers had to be supplied with every type of commodity, from foodstuffs and horses to clothes and arms and, quite soon, with labour, in the form of negro slaves. Thanks to the monumental work of Pierre and Huguette Chaunu, we now possess excellent statistical information about the Spanish Atlantic trade.[43] From the early years of the century to about 1550 the number of ships and their loads which sailed annually between Seville and the New World expanded steadily to about 200 ships and an aggregate of nearly 30,000 tons (1 ton = 2.8 m³), for the outward and inward journeys together. Then, for about twelve years, there was a recession. The early phase of looting the New World was over and the volume of trade fell to little more than 20,000 tons per annum. The colonies had to organize a ranching economy and develop the new methods of extracting and refining silver. From the early 1560s, the transatlantic trade began to expand again until, in 1600, there were again more than 200 ships sailing both east and west, and the tonnage had risen to about 50,000.[44] This was the high water mark, although there were still a few exceptionally good individual years to come, and it roughly coincided with the high water mark of silver imports into Spain; for the colonies had few other goods with which to pay for their imports. The Spanish government channelled this trade through Seville and reserved it to inhabitants of the kingdom of Castile; the other subjects of the kings of Spain were excluded, at least in theory, because, it was argued, the Castilians had organized, manned and financed the expeditions for the discovery of the Indies. Thus, the crown could control the trade and claim its share, the quint, or 20 per cent of all silver shipped and, though this was not the original intention, it enabled the crown, from time to time, to confiscate the private silver of the merchants. The officials of the crown also liked this arrangement, for they could cooperate with merchants and ships' captains to smuggle unregistered silver into Spain. The quantities of silver smuggled have been variously estimated as from rather less to rather more than 10 per cent of the official quantities; but there is, in the nature of the problem, no means of knowing more exactly.

Castilian industry was quite unable to supply more than a small proportion of the goods exported to the colonies. The bulk came from the rest of Europe, especially from the Netherlands and northern Italy. Soon, Netherlanders, Germans and Genoese took over most of the trade with the colonies, though mostly under the cover of names of Castilian firms. The greater proportion of American silver, therefore, simply passed through Spain to pay for the goods shipped to the colonists or, in so far as it was crown silver, to pay for the Spanish armies in Italy and the Netherlands.

ANTWERP

From the beginning of the sixteenth century, the rhythm of the Portuguese East Indian and the Spanish Atlantic trade affected, directly or indirectly, the economic fortunes of the rest of Europe. The connecting link was the market of Antwerp. At the very beginning of the century, the commercial alliance of the Portuguese and South German merchants started Antwerp on its meteoric rise. In return for their spices, the Portuguese needed from the Germans copper and metal goods, cloth and, above all, silver from the central European mines. The Germans promptly expanded copper mining operations in Hungary and began to finance the Portuguese voyages to the Indies. Just as important was the commercial alliance of the German and English merchants, though it was an indirect one. The English Company of Merchant Adventurers had established its staple at Antwerp (from time to time, for tactical reasons, it moved the staple to the smaller towns of Middleburg or Bergen-op-Zoom) and was exporting the famous English white cloths which were dressed and finished by the Antwerp finishing industry before being distributed by the Germans to markets in central Europe. English exports rose from about 50,000 cloths in 1500, to an average of 100,000 in the 1540s.

This expansion and concentration of the international commerce in spices, metals and textiles carried with it its own impetus and attraction. Baltic grain came to Antwerp (more and more *via* the grain market of Amsterdam), both for consumption in the Netherlands and for re-export to Portugal and Spain. Sugar from the Canaries, Italian silks and alum (from the papal mines at Tolfa), French and Rhenish wines, cheese from Gouda, beer from Haarlem and fish from Zealand, and countless other commodities converged on Antwerp, to be transhipped to other parts of Europe or to Africa, Asia and America. Much of it, however, was used in the industries of Antwerp itself: in the cloth finishing and dyeing industries, in armaments and other metal work, in furniture and tapestry workshops, in glass, paper and instrument making (both scientific and musical) and, not least, in book publishing. The publishing and printing firm of Plantin possessed twenty-two presses and employed up to 160 workmen. It was one of the biggest industrial enterprises, outside the mining, building and shipbuilding industries.

Comparatively little coined money entered into the transactions of the Antwerp market. The merchants preferred the more convenient and safer method of giving and taking credit. Inevitably, the richer merchants acted as bankers; and since banking and finance were no more risky and much less exacting than shipping goods in a world full of both natural disasters and human predators,★ more and more merchants came to prefer this type of investment. Thus, the Antwerp bourse became the most important centre of finance in Europe, followed, at a considerable distance, by Lyons, the rival finance centre sponsored by the French monarchy.

While speculation in pepper futures or foreign exchanges could produce handsome profits for those with skill and luck, the really big fortunes were made almost invariably in conjunction with government finance. Jacob Fugger, who succeeded to the control of the family capital of 200,000 florins in 1511, left the firm with assets worth 2 million when he died in 1525. The phenomenal annual average of over 50 per cent profit was achieved by obtaining monopoly contracts for silver and copper mining in the Tyrol, Hungary and elsewhere in central Europe, in return for loans made to the emperors Maximilian I and Charles V. Fugger boasted that he had lent Charles V half a million florins for his election campaign in 1519 and that without this money he might never have been elected.

★*Bassanio*: Hath all his ventures failed? What, not one hit?
From Tripolis, from Mexico, and England,
From Lisbon, Barbary and India?
And not one vessel 'scape the dreadful touch
Of merchant-marrying rocks?
Salerio: Not one, my lord.

Shakespeare, *The Merchant of Venice*, III, 2.

This was true enough. It was equally true that the Fugger mining monopolies and the elaborate marketing organization which made the monopolies commercially effective would not have survived for a week against the attacks of the Fugger's many and bitter enemies — both potential rivals and the German estates — had they not had the backing of the imperial government. The symbiosis of governments and private bankers led to a colossal expansion of credit operations in Antwerp. The rate of interest on government loans steadily dropped, from an average of about 20 per cent at the beginning of the century, to 10 per cent in the 1540s. Although the Netherlands, the Spanish, the Portuguese and the English governments were now borrowing unprecedented sums, running into millions of florins, there appeared to be no shortage of funds: small merchants, hopeful of getting a cut from the rich pickings of government finance and monopolies through the apparent safety of the great banking firms, were willing to chance their money in the loans these firms made to the government.

This great expansion of commercial and government credit operations, together with the steep increase in taxation in most countries, must be regarded as an additional cause of the price revolution, especially as, owing to dehoarding, this expansion of credit is likely to have been accompanied both by an increase in liquidity and in the velocity of circulation.

About the middle of the sixteenth century Antwerp reached its apogee. For the first time in history there existed both a European and a world market; the economies of different parts of Europe had become interdependent and were linked through the Antwerp market, not only with each other but also with the economies of large parts of the rest of the world. Perhaps no other city has ever again played such a dominant role as did Antwerp in the second quarter of the sixteenth century.

It did not last. In 1549 the Portuguese withdrew their spice monopoly from Antwerp. They could get the silver they exported to the Indies more easily and more cheaply from the Spanish silver fleets. The Germans and other distributors of spices transferred their factors to Lisbon and to Venice. But that did not save the German silver mines whose production costs now proved too high to compete with American silver. In 1550 the English governments' devaluation of silver enabled the Merchant Adventurers to export the record total of 130,000 cloths to Antwerp. This caused a temporary glut which coincided with the attempted revaluation of sterling in the following year and a consequent sharp rise in the price of cloth. For more than a decade the trade did not recover and in the rest of the sixteenth century it never reached the record figures of 1550 again. At the same time, as we have seen, Spanish-American trade experienced its first prolonged slump, and this may well have reduced the volume of Spanish imports from the rest of Europe. In 1552 the war between France and the emperor broke out again and immediately proved to be more expensive than earlier conflicts of the century. In 1555 and 1556 the harvest failed in western Europe. Grain prices rose to three or four times their normal level, and grain imported from the Baltic, to prevent the poor from dying of hunger, had to be paid for in silver coin. Interest payments for Netherlands government loans rose from 425,000 livres (Artois) in 1555 to 1,350,000 livres in 1556. The Spanish government, with its own debt standing at about 25 million ducats, was in no position to help. Early in 1557 the war with France which had died down after Charles V's failure to take Metz, flared up again, and with it came an embargo on trade with France and greatly increased French privateering.[45] In June 1557 the Spanish government forcibly transformed all its debts into state bonds (*juros*) at 5 per cent. The Netherlands government had no choice but to follow suit and it dragged the Netherlands municipalities with it into bankruptcy. Soon the French government declared a similar moratorium on its debts. In 1560 the Spanish government once more reduced payments on its debts and so did the Portuguese government. These bankruptcies, especially those of 1560, caused the first big wave of international bank crashes. Bankers who had lent to governments suddenly could not meet their own obligations, and many financiers, especially in Antwerp and in South Germany, were in serious trouble. Smaller investors, who usually suffer most in bank crashes, were in this case probably mainly hit in the bond market when the Netherlands government had difficulties in paying the regular interest on bonds (*rentes*).

Antwerp never fully recovered from these blows, though the city remained immensely rich and its commercial activities sound. The most famous and glowing description of this city, by the Florentine Lodovico Guicciardini, was not written until 1565. A commercial war between England and the Netherlands had then caused further damage, and the very next year Antwerp became one of the centres of the image-breaking riots – those riots which precipitated the revolt of the Netherlands, the sack of Antwerp by the Spanish troops in 1576, and the closure of the Scheldt by the Dutch, in 1585. Antwerp survived all these disasters, though with a much reduced population, and its role as the fulcrum of European trade was at an end. For the rest of the sixteenth century, the merchants of north-western Europe took over the functions of Antwerp by going much further afield than they used to. The Merchant Adventurers, belying their name, only wandered from one small North Sea port to another, until they finally settled their cloth staple in Stade, on the Elbe below Hamburg (1587). But more adventurous English merchants founded companies to trade with Russia, with the Baltic, with the Levant, with Morocco and, finally, with the East Indies. More important still, Hollanders and Hansards now provided the link between northern and southern Europe. Even the Eighty Years War between the Dutch and the Spaniards[46] did not stop this traffic; for Spain and Portugal needed grain, copper and manufactured goods for themselves and their colonies, while the Dutch and their customers needed Indian pepper, Spanish wool and American silver.

BANKERS AND GOVERNMENTS

The bankers, too, were undismayed by the fall of Antwerp. The dazzling prizes of mining monopolies, tax farms and colonial concessions which the Spanish government could offer, attracted not only the Fugger, the Welser and other south German firms but also the Genoese into ever greater investments in Spanish government loans. In 1528 Andrea Doria took the city republic of Genoa from the French into the imperialist camp. The way had already been prepared by previous Genoese investments in Spain. Now, the Doria, the Grimaldi, the Spinola, the Pallavicino and other Genoese families were able to make profits comparable to the south Germans and, in their turn, attracted investments from all over Italy. The German and Italian merchant-bankers were not the typical exponents of rising capitalism, still less of a rising middle class or bourgeoisie. Jacob Fugger called himself 'merchant by the grace of God', but he bought many noble estates and accepted titles of nobility. As imperial counts, the Fugger found that, with their type of money, bourgeois origins were no bar to rapid entry into the highest aristocratic society of Europe. The Genoese bankers belonged, in any case, to one of the oldest and proudest patrician aristocracies of Europe, although they were not averse to acquiring new ducal and princely titles in the kingdom of Naples whose trade and tax-farming they all but monopolized. The financiers, whatever their social origins, were essentially the creatures of the great monarchies who needed them but always could, and did, break them when reason of state demanded it. It was rare for a merchant to accumulate more than a modest capital without government contracts and monopolies, and for purely commercial operations vast capital accumulations were not necessary, as the merchants of Venice and Amsterdam demonstrated. In the early sixteenth century it was still possible even for the financiers to work on a truly international level, making contracts with different governments. Gaspar Ducci, the Italian financier of Antwerp, was the greatest virtuoso of those who worked with both the imperial and, at least indirectly, with the French governments and who gambled on, and manipulated, the exchanges of both the Antwerp and the Lyons bourses. In 1550 Ducci ran into political trouble. From that time, the financiers had to bind themselves to one or other of the great monarchies as, indeed, the Fugger had done from the beginning. The Genoese and most of the south Germans attached themselves to Spain; the remaining German firms and most of the Florentines and Lucchese worked with the French crown. Twice more before the end of the century, in 1575 and 1596, the Spanish government defaulted on its debts, spreading financial disaster far beyond the circle of its creditors. Had they not made excellent profits since coming to Spain? was Philip II's cold reply to the Genoese when they remonstrated against the bankruptcy of 1596. Financial needs, not the financiers, determined the policies of sixteenth-century governments. By 1600 most of the south German firms were bankrupt and, in the seventeenth century, the Fugger and the Genoese were ruined, or driven out of business, by the inability of the Spanish government to repay its enormous debts.

WAS THERE A WORLD ECONOMY IN THE SIXTEENTH CENTURY?

By the end of the sixteenth century Europe was importing gold and silver and very small quantities of exotic products, such as tobacco, tomatoes and pineapples, from the American colonies. In return it exported European and African manpower (the latter as slaves) and a wide range of manufactured goods. From Asia Europe imported spices and luxury textiles and exported mainly silver. The American silver mines and, later, in the seventeenth and eighteenth centuries, the American sugar and cotton plantations geared their production mainly to a West-European market. Similarly, the Polish and Prussian *Junker* estates of cenral-eastern European geared their agricultural production mainly to a West-European market. Western Europe also imported timber and furs from that region. In return it exported manufactures, salt and, as in the Asian trade, silver. In both cases, much of this silver had come from America. It is on the basis of these connections that some historians have claimed that here we have the beginnings of the modern world economic system. Western Europe, with its growing capitalist mode of production and its free agricultural labour, is held to have exploited the American colonies and central-eastern Europe, with their underdeveloped manufactures and their agricultures based on slavery, peonage and serf-labour. The more rapid advance of western Europe to about 1750 is then held to have been dependent on this exploitation.

The economic links between these areas undoubtedly existed. Slaves, peons and serfs were certainly exploited by the masters and lords for whom they were made to work. Some individuals and a few cities, such as Lisbon, Seville, Antwerp and, more indirectly, Genoa made spectacular fortunes out of overseas trade. But these links and fortunes did not add up to a system which regulated the economy of Europe or which can explain its development. American treasure was only one and, as we have seen, not the most important cause of the rise in prices in the sixteenth century. This rise contributed nothing to the development of technology in Europe and it is doubtful whether it contributed much to capital formation. Overseas trade represented only a fraction of total European trade. Even for Antwerp, the greatest international trading centre of the sixteenth century, English cloth was more important than Asian spices. Antwerp's trade with Germany, Italy, France and Spain was more valuable than its trade with the Baltic. By far the greater part of the gross economic product of Europe was still agricultural, and the greater part of this agricultural product was consumed locally. The Dutch peasants, with their advanced farming techniques, sold a much larger proportion of their produce to the

Netherlands cities than the Polish and Prussian *Gutsherren* could spare for shipment to Amsterdam from their large but inefficient serf-labour estates. While the economy created by the European colonists in Latin America was, to a considerable extent, dependent on the West-European market, the *Gutsherrschaft* which developed in central-eastern Europe was created by local landowners and was only partially dependent on the West-European market. The colonial and the Baltic trade of the early modern period undoubtedly benefited the West; but it did not determine or even greatly influence European economic development. In short, the sixteenth century saw, at most, the modest beginnings of a world economy; but this world economy was still a long way from determining, or even greatly influencing, European economic development.

NOTES AND REFERENCES

1   H. Latimer, *Sermons*, ed. G. E. Corrie (Cambridge, 1844), pp. 98 ff.

2   From *Commentario resolutorio de usuras*, 1556, quoted in M. Grice-Hutchinson, *The School of Salamanca* (Oxford, 1952), p. 95.

3   H. A. Miskimin, *The Economy of Later Renaissance Europe 1460–1600* (Cambridge, 1977), pp. 158–60.

4   R. de Roover, *Gresham on Foreign Exchange* (Cambridge, Mass., 1949), pp. 50 ff.

5   E. J. Hamilton's well-known figures for Spanish silver imports from America (*American Treasure*, pp. 34 ff) have been criticized in detail R. Carande, *Carlos V y sus banqueros*, vol. 1 (Madrid, 1943–49), pp. 145 ff. Moreover, he sometimes confuses averages and aggregates, and his quinquennial figures cannot be used statistically.

6   e.g. quotations by R. Carande, *Carlos V*, vol. 1, p. 156.

7   C. Cipolla, 'La prétendue révolution des prix', in *Annales Economies, Sociétés, Civilisations*, vol. X, 1955.

8   The use of parish registers in the new demography will be discussed in chapter IV.

9   Braudel, *The Mediterranean and the Mediterranean World in the Age of Philip II*. Trans. S. Reynolds (Collins, London, vol. 1, 1972) p. 350.

10 Figures, or even orders of magnitude, for non-European cities in the sixteenth century hardly exist. Cairo and Aleppo may well have been larger than any European city except perhaps Constantinople Tenochtitlan (Mexico) before the Spanish conquest may have been much larger and the same may have been true for some Indian and Chinese cities.

11 R. Mols, *Introduction à la Démographie Historique des Villes d'Europe* (Louvain, 1954–56), vol. 11, pp. 505 ff. The figures for Palermo and Messina seem rather high. Cf H. Koenigsberger, *The Government of Sicily under Philip of Spain* (London, 1951), p. 74, n. 2.

12 Braudel, *The Mediterranean*, pp. 345 and 356. Some modern authorities think the figure is far too high.

13 Dr. G. Fletcher, *Of the Russe Common wealth*, in Hakluyt Society, *Russia at the Close of the Sixteenth Century* (London, 1856), p. 17

14 Braudel, *The Mediterranean*, p. 635.

15 J. de Vries, *European Urbanization 1500–1800* (London, 1984), pp. 28–31, 269–78.

16 E. Kerridge, 'The Movement of rent 1540–1640', *Economic History Review*, second ser., vol. VI, no. 1.

17 F. Braudel, *The Mediterranean*, pp. 38 ff. J. van Klaveren, *Europäische Wirtschaftsgeschichte Spaniens im 16. und 17. Jahrhundert* (Stuttgart, 1960), pp. 211 ff. Cf. also this author's suggestive but controversial thesis in 'Die historische Erscheinung der Korruption, und Fiskalismu s – Merkantilismus – Korruption', in *Vierteljahrschrift für Sozial- und Wirtschaftsgeschichte*, 1957–60.

18 C. Verlinden, J. Craeybeckx, E. Scholliers, 'Mouvement des prix et des salaires en Belgique au XVI siècle', in *Annales*, vol. X, 1955, p. 179.

19 For an appraisal of this difficult and not always reliable source of commercial statistics cf. A. E. Christensen, *Dutch Trade to the Baltic about 1600* (Copenhagen, The Hague, 1941), ch. 1.

20 F. Braudel and R, Romano, *Navires et marchandises à l'entrée du port de Livourne (1547–1611)* (Paris, 1951), p. 22.

21 F. J. Fisher, 'The sixteenth and seventeenth centuries', *Economics*, 1957.

22 E. H. Phelps Brown and Sheila V. Hopkins, 'Seven centuries of building wages', *Economica*, 1955; 'Seven centuries of the prices of consumables', *ibid*, 1957; 'Builders' wage-rates, prices and population', *ibid.*, 1959. These articles have comprehensive bibliographies

23 *Ibid.*, 1959, p. 298.

24　H. Van der Wee, *The Growth of the Antwerp Market and the European Economy*, vol. 11 (The Hague, 1963), pp. 192 ff.

25　C. Verlinden and J. Craeybeckx, *Prijzen- en Lonenpolitiek in de Nederlanden in 1561 en 1588–1589* (Brussels, 1962), pp. 35 ff.

26　C. Verlinden *et al.*, 'Mouvements des prix etc'., *Annales*, 1955, p. 194. This is one of the very few cases where we have any wage figures for textile workers.

27　*A Discourse of the Common Weal of this Realm of England, 1549*; (now attributed to Sir Thomas Smith). R. J. Tawney and E. Power, *Tudor Economic Documents*, vol. III (London, 1924), p. 306

28　B. H. Slicher van Bath, *The Agrarian History of Western Europe*, trans. O. Ordish (London, 1963), p. 194.

29　M. D. Carrell, 'Peasant festivities and political identity in the sixteenth century', *Art History*, vol. 10, no. 3, 1987.

30　Joyce Youings, *Sixteenth-century England* (Harmondsworth, 1984), pp. 304 ff.

31　See T. H. Aston and C. H. E. Pilpin, eds., *The Brenner Debate: Agrarian Class Structure and Economic Development in Pre-Industrial Europe* (Cambridge, 1986).

32　H. G. Koenigsberger, 'Property and the price revolution (Hainault 1474–1573)', *Econ. Hist. Rev.*, second ser., vol. IX 1965.

33　F. B. Grasby, 'Social status and commercial enterprise under Louis XIV', *Econ. Hist. Rev.*, second ser., vol. XIII, 1960, p. 24.

34　J. Delumeau, *Vie économique et sociale de Rome dans la seconde moitié du XVI siècle*, vol. II (Paris, 1959), pp. 566 ff.

35　J. van Klaveren, *Wirtschaftsgesichichte Spaniens*, pp. 207 ff.

36　Braudel, *The Mediterranean* II, pp. 709 ff.

37　W. G. Coniglio, *Il Viceregna di Napoli del sec. XVII* (Rome, 1955), p. 63

38　Malowist, 'Baltic countries', *Econ. Hist. Rev.*, 1959, p. 180; A. Nielsen, *Dänische Wirtschaftsgeschichte* (Jena, 1933), pp. 145 ff.

39　F. L. Carsten, *The Origins of Prussia* (Oxford, 1954), ch. 11; Malowist, 'Baltic countries', *Econ. Hist. Rev.*, 1959.

40　T. S. Willan, ed., *A Tudor Book of Rates* (Manchester, 1962), p. 65

41　Braudel, *The Mediterranean*, p. 362, quotes a fascinating table with normal, average, maxima and minima, and the frequency relations between minimal and normal travelling times. Cf. D.

Hay, *Europe in the Fourteenth and Fifteenth Centuries* Second Edition (London, 1966), pp. 391–92.

42   Quoted Braudel, *The Mediterranean*, p. 543.

43   P. and H. Chaunu, *Séville et l'Atlantique, 1504–1650*, 8 vols. (Paris, 1955–59).

44   *Ibid.*, vol. VI, I, pp. 324 ff.

45   H. Van der Wee, *The Growth of the Antwerp Market and the European Economy*, 3 vols., (The Hague, 1963) vol. II, pp. 214 ff.

46   1568–1648. This is the name by which the wars which followed the revolt of the Netherlands are known in Holland.

4

SOCIAL LIFE

PARISH REGISTERS AND DEMOGRAPHY

In the last twenty years historical demography has been
transformed by the study of parish registers. Registers of births,
baptisms, marriages, deaths or burials first appeared in the later
Middle Ages but became common only in the course of the
sixteenth century. As with so many statistical sources, we find them
first in Italy. In Switzerland they appeared, at least in some parishes,
with the introduction of the Reformation. In England the
government decreed the universal keeping of parish registers in
1538, following the Act of Supremacy and the establishment of royal
control over the Church and its organization (see below, p. 291). But
it did not need the Reformation to introduce the practice of keeping
parish registers, and some provinces of Catholic France, such as
Anjou, are particularly well endowed with them. Nevertheless, it
was only in the seventeenth and eighteenth centuries that registers
came to be kept in the majority of European parishes. Inevitably,
many have since been lost or destroyed by warfare, fire, the
tranformation of parishes or simply by neglect.

The statistical basis for the new method of population study in
the sixteenth century is therefore patchy. The method itself, of
collecting and correlating hundreds or even thousands of entries for
even one parish over a period of time, is highly laborious.
Nevertheless, it has been possible to draw some very interesting
conclusions by 'reconstituting' average families and tracing
movements of people into and out of parishes. The average age of
marriage for girls in Elizabethan England was about twenty-two,
with a median (the point at which there are as many instances above

as below) at over twenty-four. This latter figure was influenced by the large number of widows who remarried; for, with high death rates, many people found themselves widows or widowers at relatively young ages and they tended to marry again. The wicked stepfather or stepmother of the fairytales had their basis in quite common experience, even if the wickedness was often not so much a matter of evil inclination as of family jealousies over the actual or prospective inheritance of property. For men, the average and median figures for first marriage were about twenty-four and above twenty-six years of age. Shakespeare's Juliet, told by her mother that marriage and even motherhood at fourteen was common among the ladies of Verona,★ would in fact have had a most unusual experience in most of western Europe, except among royalty. By contrast, in Spain and in eastern Europe women married earlier and in Muslim countries earlier still.

The reasons for late marriage in western Europe were practical. In most, although not in all, areas the extended family, with all generations and with uncles, aunts and cousins all living together, had long since given way to the conjugal or nuclear family of husband, wife and unmarried children only. A prospective young couple therefore had to wait for some property or an opportunity to make a living, before getting married and setting up their own household. Many girls would save up for their dowry by spinning or by going into service in another household. The result of late marriage and of the low rate of illegitimacy (another conclusion drawn from the parish registers which runs counter to much literary tradition) was relatively small families. On average, women did not bear more than five or six children. There is some difference of opinion among demographers over the rates of infant and child mortality. They were certainly appallingly high, and the survival rate of children into adulthood was only 2.5 to 3 children per family on average.[1] Such an average, however, was sufficient to produce a steady growth of population, although such growth might well be interrupted by sharp temporary rises in mortality. The conclusion of steady growth, at least for the sixteenth century, is also supported by such overall figures as we have.[2]

★*Lady Capulet*: Well, think of marriage now; younger than you
                Here in Verona, ladies of esteem,
                Are already made mothers.

Shakespeare, *Romeo and Juliet*, I.3. Cf. P. Laslett, *The World We have Lost – Further Explored* (London, 1983), p. 80 ff.

THE FAMILY

The social life of sixteenth century men and women was to a large extent centred upon their community: the village, the guild or the congregation. This was a public sphere which affected their private lives at every turn, and yet it was the family which focused their emotional life, was their primary economic unit and the principal school for all that was worth knowing. Family structures varied widely throughout Europe. For example, while primogeniture was the rule in many peasant families, and others divided the land between brothers, in parts of southern France brothers shared the same roof and farmed their land jointly in order to improve their economic situation. There were peasant families in Austria where the aged father could secure his future through a retirement agreement with his son, and English families who abandoned their elderly kin to the charity of the parish.

The predominant family unit was not the extended and multi-generational family, but the nuclear family of parents and children. The average sixteenth–century English family contained about five members, and in north-western Europe fewer than 6 per cent of all families held more than two generations. Nevertheless, households throughout Europe were crowded, filled with servants and visiting relatives. For example, the families of city guildsmen housed a multitude of apprentices as family members. If crowding was the rule in rural and urban establishments, noble and royal households with their retainers and courtiers constantly about could not make up in space for the press of people.

MARRIAGE

The Church emphasized that no one should marry without consent, but in practice severe constraints were imposed when it came to choosing a mate; the disposition of land and family alliances were too important to be left to the discretion of the young. The lower orders, especially servants and labourers who had to leave home to seek employment, had relatively more freedom of choice, though this was limited by social expectations. European society disapproved of marriages where there was a disparity of age, status, religion or wealth. At festival time bands of town or village youths used to pillory those who had broken the norms imposed upon marriage: old husbands with young wives, husbands who had let themselves be deceived by their wives, and husbands who beat their wives in May, a month thought special for women. Those who had married outside the locality were apt to receive rough treatment as well, having deprived local youth of a possible choice. Such men and women were mocked by what the English called 'rough music', the Italians, 'mattina'[3] and the French 'charivari': banging of pans, rough language and often public humiliation and beating as well. This was social control from below, without the aid of secular or ecclesiastical authority, popular culture in the service of established norms of sexual behaviour.

Late marriages were common, and men usually waited until their mid to late twenties in order to marry after taking their inheritance at the death of the father. The long delay between physical maturity and marriage meant that a great strain was put upon the sexual continence of young people, especially as sexual contact outside marriage was officially banned. Prostitutes abounded in Europe, and the rate of extramarital pregnancies could be quite high. These unwanted children were often abandoned and many European cities erected hospices for their care. Erasmus's renowed *Colloquies* (1522), used as a schoolbook to teach morality, contained a discourse between a young boy and a prostitute in order to warn youths against such women. It was taken for granted that children knew about them: they were not concealed in an age where sexuality was only beginning to be associated with shame and embarrassment. Prostitutes often acted like a city corporation and sometimes defended themselves publicly against competition and stood up for their rights.[4] If young men were warned against premarital sex, they were offered other outlets for their high spirits during festivals such as the carnival where they sometimes acted out plays or were permitted to openly mock society, and through noisy masked demonstrations (the charivari) take the punishment of social transgression into their own hands.

CHILDBIRTH

Once married, the husband and wife were expected to be faithful and sexually available to one another. The Catholic Church instructed its confessors to inquire into sexual behaviour with the intention of discouraging the use of contraception, as well as intercourse during the twenty forbidden weeks of the year. Protestants did not have a confessional, but their attitude towards sexual behaviour was the same. Nevertheless, despite official disapproval, contraception was widely practised; spermicidal preparations and those supposed to facilitate abortion were in evidence, but only marginally, as were professional abortionists mostly frequented by prostitutes. The most common measures to restrict or postpone childbirth were, aside from late marriages, coitus interruptus and breast feeding. The latter was often continued well into the child's second year and beyond, though wet nurses were frequently hired by the nobility and by those women whose employment required freedom from breast feeding. Infanticide was the resort of the truly desperate, particularly women who had been seduced and abandoned. The too-frequent incidence of child suffocation by 'over-laying' clearly included many deliberate deaths, and led to demands that sleeping in the same bed as an infant be made illegal.

Childbirth was dangerous in the sixteenth century and could easily claim the life of mother and child; it has been calculated that for every thousand births, twenty-five mothers died. This was a high figure, considering that, for example, in England women bore an average of six children; infant mortality was even higher. Childbirth was under the control of midwives, and the risks involved were reflected in their vulnerability to accusations of witchcraft. But the high rate of death at childbirth probably had little effect on family relationships: parents were not indifferent to children because their lives might be short, or husbands callous about the death of their wives. To be sure, remarriage was usually rapid as single parent families were all but unknown, and excessive mourning was discouraged in Protestant regions. Death was a constant companion to Europeans of all ages in a century when men and women faced disease and natural catastrophes without much protection.

SEXUAL ATTITUDES

The sixteenth century saw important transformations in attitudes towards human sexuality, not so much in the family or in the relationship between men and women, but as associating the human body and its sexual functions with shame and embarrassment. Both the Catholic and the Protestant Reformation sought to forbid frank discussion or representation of human sexuality as tempting men and women to indecency, and indecency was equated with impiety. For example, when Michelangelo was commissioned to paint the ceiling of the Sistine chapel in 1536, Pope Paul III at first supported his design which called for nude figures which hid nothing from view. But these figures soon became controversial and Paul III changed his mind, siding with those who accused Michelangelo of indecency. Between 1559 and 1566 that nudity in the Sistine Chapel thought most offensive was covered by draperies. The Council of Trent condemned nudity in religious art which left the sexual organs exposed to view. To be sure, so it was said, Christ was crucified in the nude — such had been the medieval tradition — but he himself would wish to be decently veiled.[5] Ordinances in Protestant regions made much the same point: such exposure, indeed all nudity, encouraged the sins of the flesh. This attempt to tighten morality was reflected in the attacks against popular culture as well. Here sexual licence was one of many sins which popular culture seemed to condone, especially at festival time. Protestants attempted to abolish such occasions for sin, Catholics wanted them purified. The Catholic and the Protestant reformations wanted to enforce virtue: a moral order which seemed necessary for the purification of a corrupt faith.

But it took nearly another century to assure the victory of respectability. As yet, for example, Erasmus in his *Colloquies* talked openly to young boys about their sexuality, without mincing his words. At the very start of the seventeenth century the future king Louis XIII of France, just seven years old, preached a sermon on 'men who sleep with women' and though it would later be considered indecent to even think about such a subject at the king's age, what he actually preached reflected the new morality in the ascendant: decency and chastity were his themes. At the same time that morals were being more tightly controlled, refinement in manners was slowly spreading from the court to other classes: the use of an implement like the knife or fork instead of the hand while eating, no longer blowing one's nose into one's hand, or spitting on all occasions. Modern manners were slowly being forged together with the ideal of respectability, and good manners in turn would become an indispensable part of the moral universe which the reformations had set in motion. But during the sixteenth century itself use of the term respectability still applied to legitimate or upper-class birth rather than to manners and morals.

FAMILY HIERARCHY

The attempt to regulate and control private and public morals corresponded to the belief in order and hierarchy, to the quest for an orderly world. The family was regarded as a little monarchy presided over by the father. 'Marriages are the seminaries of states', so reads a preamble to a French ordinance strengthening the paternal power within the family.[6] The father's role was to protect and provide for his family, serving as an example of piety and virtue. He might discipline his family with corporal punishment as a means to educate his children or to punish the servants. Together with his wife he was to ensure that the children and the household staff were raised in the true religion and were imbued with the proper morality. The servants and the children were dependents in the literal sense of the term, though excessive maltreatment of servants could be appealed to law courts such as the English Quarter Sessions. The wife tended the children, supervised the servants and cared for her husband in good or bad health. She was not to chastise her husband, but advise him with deference lest the neighbours think her a scold and submit her and her husband to communal derision, and perhaps even to a charivari at festival time.

Children were subject to their parents' command until they left to take up employment or married. Urban children were often sent to serve in other households, but rural children were employed from an early age as farm labour. The concept of childhood as a carefree and innocent age developed among the privileged class only late in the century. Children were not segregated from the adult world, they dressed like adults, were addressed like adults – as we saw in Erasmus's *Colloquies*, while ten- and twelve-year-olds joined in carnivals or political riots. Yet adolescence was recognized as a distinct stage of human development where youth needed outlets for its exuberant spirit. These were provided, as we have mentioned, by carnivals and other festivals.

Should the marriage be unhappy or unfruitful, there were very few ways out. Divorce was impossible in Catholic countries and Protestant England, but with great difficulty annulments could be obtained by citing one of the numerous impediments to the original marriage. Divorce was possible in Switzerland and Protestant Germany for a number of reasons, of which adultery was the most common, allowing the injured party to remarry. Among other grounds for divorce in Switzerland for example, impotence or sexually incapacitating illness were accepted as were deliberate desertion, grave incompatibility or threats against life. However, in most of Europe the only realistic way out of a marriage was desertion, usually by the husband. Towards the end of the century, one married woman in twelve in Norwich had been abandoned by her husband. Pauperhood was the almost inevitable result.

THE ROLE OF WOMEN

John Calvin's statement about the qualities he would like to see in his future wife was typical for the sixteenth century: she must be chaste, if not too nice or fastidious, economical, patient, and interested in his health. The dominance of men over women was anchored in theology, law and medicine. After all, Eve had been responsible for Adam's fall from Paradise, giving rise to speculation about women's weakness of will and inability to reason. She seemed a creature of emotion and as such needed a steady hand. More proof of women's inferiority could be found in Mosaic law and in St Paul's injunction that women should be silent and submissive. There were counter examples in theology as well. Sarah had rebelled against Abraham and Delilah destroyed Samson, but these were taken as isolated cases over against a dominant mode of thought. Aristotle's judgement that women were incomplete creatures 'botched men' as it were, still carried weight: the notion that the sexual organs of women were merely male sexual organs in reverse position. Such ideas reduced women to frail shadows of men, and here medicine played at least as important a role as theology.

Sixteenth-century medicine emphasized that women's dominant humours were cold and moist, resulting, to be sure, in superior imagination and retentive memory, but leaving them vulnerable to passions, deceit and infidelity. The uterus, because it, unlike male sexual organs lacked ventilation, was thought to induce hysterical ailments such as lovesickness, listlessness and depression. Women's cranial construction did not allow humours to escape from the skull, causing perturbation of the brain and irrationality.[7] Roman Law added its voice, claiming that women were of diminished mental capacity and should receive lesser penalties for crimes they committed. Sixteenth-century men and women believed in the importance of warm and cold, moist and dry humours and cranial construction as determining mental and physical health. The perceived inferiority of women was part and parcel of a generally accepted system of medicine and theology, making their stereotype all the more effective. Physical appearance and bodily structure also played a role in the diagnosis of illness or health: witches, for example, expressed their perverse attitudes through their old and ugly appearance, and if they were beautiful, it was a beauty which transcended the norm. Woman was stereotyped in the sixteenth century as she had been in previous centuries, and this stereotype was regarded as truth, even though the functions women actually performed in society flagrantly contradicted notions of their weakness and instability.[8]

Though there are indications that their economic status declined over the course of the sixteenth century, women still played an important role in the economy of Europe. They were found in almost every profession from construction worker to farm labourer, to goldsmith and physician. They were even allowed to enter some of the guilds. Women whose husbands were engaged in trade and commerce usually were active in their husband's business at a time when the private household and the commercial establishment were usually under one roof. However, upper-class women could not find employment deemed suitable to their status and usually, if unmarried, had to enter a convent, their only refuge.

The great number of women rulers, from Catherine de Medici to Queen Elizabeth challenged the dominant view of women during the sixteenth century; they were required to possess virtues which were contrary to those usually ascribed to women. Some, like the Italian Torquato Tasso in his *Discourse about Feminine Virtue* (1582) argued that the first duty of a princess was to her royal status, that here she was a man by virtue of her birth, and therefore masculine standards of morality applied. However, usually the assertion sufficed that women rulers were the exception, and that women in general were not suited to command. Yet within the reality of the sixteenth century the fact that women did occupy positions of command was not as contradictory as it might seem at first glance. In spite of the stereotype of women, they did rule, not only nations, but as prioresses or abbesses as well, and in the family they commanded servants and children. But then this was a society where everyone was both a governor and a governed: women in the family, their husbands in the social and political hierarchy and even the ruler under God.

Was there a change in the perception of women during the sixteenth century? Some like Baldassare Castiglione in his *Courtier* (1528), writing about society at court, held that men and women had an identical capacity for virtue, but at the same time upheld the social conventions which made women subject to men in the family and in a court of law. More basic changes seemed in the making when some scholars disassociated humours and mental faculties, and began to stress the role of the will and reason in controlling bodily passions. The heightened worship of the Virgin Mary after the Council of Trent associated women with spirituality but also served to emphasize their primary duty to motherhood and the upbringing of children. The sixteenth century did not on the whole lead to a basic change in the perception of women; this was as yet, far in the future. Only in court society did women attain a somewhat greater equality.

The status and the task of various members of the family were thought fixed and taken as a given. But the cycle of work and family life was interrupted during the year by various public festivals which were the principal occasions for amusement and relaxation. But amusement is much too simple a term to describe the social significance of public festivals in the sixteenth century.

PUBLIC FESTIVALS

The highly structured and hierarchical society of the sixteenth century needed a safety valve, a place where men and women could escape its dictates for a limited time. Yet, people also felt a need to strengthen the communal sprit which existed apart from hierarchies of birth and privilege. Popular festivals fulfilled such contradictory longings, they provided a safety valve and a renewed sense of belonging. Through their regular rhythm they gave additional coherence to the calendar year. The most important public festival of the year was the Carnival, the time when the population passed from its normal regime to Lent, a time of penitence symbolized by abstinence from meat or flesh. Carnival occurred from three to six days ending in Shrove Tuesday or Mardi Gras. It was supposed to bring sin to light, in order that it might be got rid of in time for Lent. Thus Carnival was a season when men and women as sinful creatures could indulge themselves bodily as well as in their fantasy life. Gluttony was the order of the day, eating meat and drinking. The figure of the Carnival himself was visually represented as a fat man, hung with sausages or other meats, while Lent was shown as a thin old woman. But Carnivals were more than merely occasions to eat, drink and make merry; above all, they allowed men and women to act out their individual and collective fantasies.

People dressed up, wore masks and acted out the roles they had chosen as clerics, devils or fools. There was much cross-dressing as men dressed as women and women as men, and servants dressed like their masters. This was a world turned upside-down, reversing the social and natural order. Thus, for example, a horse was made to walk backward with the rider facing its tail. The meaning of such spontaneous reversal of roles is not clear, perhaps it was simply exuberance at authorized unruliness, turning fantasy into reality. But this was not just playfulness, for it often led to criticism of the existing order through songs and plays. Rulers had reason to look with suspicion at this world turned upside down, the more so, as such criticism was part of a general climate of violence and hostility at festival time, which went beyond symbolic expression. As one historian of the Carnival has written, this was a time 'when the collective expression of envy, anger and enmity is legitimate.'[9]

Competitions provided one outlet for these feelings, in the mock battles and foot races which occurred in all carnivals. Thus at the Roman Carnival the aged, youth and children had to race each other, while the Jews were forced to run in the nude to the jeers of the crowd. Carnivals often went beyond such competitions to collective riots; for example, in 1517 the carnival at Berne turned into a peasant revolt. Other public festivals took on a similar appearance to the Carnival, and in London in 1517 the festival of May Day ended with a riot against foreigners. The carnival atmosphere also encouraged charivaris, the public humiliation of those who had broken social norms. Finally, sexual fantasies played a large part in carnivals, where people were masked and free of the ordinary social restraints. Phallic symbols, poems and songs with their double meaning were obligatory, prostitutes essential. Sex, food and violence were major themes at all carnivals.[10] This then was a time when forbidden behaviour and modes of expression were authorized.

Festivals were part of the public sphere which affected private life at every turn, through the town or village community, the guild or the Church. Public festivals like a mirror image, can tell us much about the restraints of society as opposed to the often brutal or playful expressions of individual passion and fantasy.

EDUCATION

Education was part of social life, supposed to instil Christian morality as well as to teach literacy and knowledge. There was much opposition to education in the sixteenth century, and many nobles, gentlemen and peasants did not see learning relevant to their style of life. Poor families feared the loss of income involved in schooling a child who could help earn a living; the ruling classes feared the effect learning might have upon their volatile subjects, while many clergy worried lest literacy lead to heresy. Almost everybody feared that educating girls might take them away from their domestic duties.

Yet despite these and other obstacles, education made considerable headway in the sixteenth century. For example, the demands of the new national bureaucracies meant that being accomplished in equestrian and martial arts was no longer sufficient recommendation for service to the state. Increasingly in the sixteenth century the acquisition of a new type of education became important to social and professional élites. This education was that of Renaissance humanist pedagogy, which had developed in Italy and been introduced into northern Europe by the schools of the Brethren of the Common Life. Its essentials, as expounded by humanists such as Erasmus, were fluency in the Latin language and the study of classical literature, taught with the aim of fostering eloquence, critical skills and moral responsibility. Its champions included both Protestants and Catholics. Luther, in pleading with Germans to support this sort of education, demanded, 'where are the preachers, jurists and physicians to come from, if grammar and other rhetorical arts are not taught? For such teaching is the spring from which they all must flow.'[11]

They were to come from the Latin secondary school which attracted many children of the middle classes. After an elementary training in literacy, taken from primary schools or private tutors, students progressed through a series of grades from the rudiments of Latin to reading Cicero's prose, the drama of Terence, and the poetry of Virgil and Ovid, on to original composition of Latin verse and oratory. In many schools Greek was studied in the upper forms but mathematics and the physical sciences seldom found a place in the curriculum. In crowded classrooms, students were arrayed on benches (often in order of academic standing, which was considered a spur to diligent study) from 7.00 a.m. until the noon meal and then from 1.00 to 4.00 p.m., with only one afternoon and Sunday free. Discipline was maintained by masters and senior students with liberal use of praise and shame, frequent examinations and competitions and, ultimately, corporal punishment. Though most educational writers urged moderation in beating students, thrashings seem to have been a frequent part of school life.[12] Such discipline was used to reinforce social values as well. Students were taught to revere their parents and all figures of authority, suppress their sexuality and place the needs of society above their own. Whether humanist education was actually superior at instilling morality, as its proponents claimed, is doubtful but it gradually became the cultural norm for the upper classes throughout Europe and the key to professional careers.

Those seeking a career in medicine, law or the Church proceeded to university where they would continue their education in the liberal arts before taking an advanced degree in their chosen profession. The sixteenth century saw the founding of many new universities, though sometimes the student bodies were very small. Increasing numbers of clergy were educated at universities and the numbers of gentry attending increased as well. Though the sons of the middle class used university for professional training, the gentry attended more often for a social finishing than to take a degree. The increasing presence of such young men added to disciplinary problems.[13] The young gentleman might also sample legal education (very useful to the landowning class), or choose to take the Grand Tour of Europe, accompanied by a tutor and armed with numerous guide books.

But education, the transmission of a society's skills, knowledge and values, cannot be equated in the sixteenth century with a single model; instead, there was a different approach appropriate to each social order. The education of an aristocratic heir had other aims than that of an apprentice brewer or a peasant girl and, as a consequence, the young people of Europe were subject to a variety of instructional methods. For most, a humanist education was of no practical benefit; far more useful was an initial grounding in literacy followed by job training. Elementary education in the vernacular was available in a number of forms. It could be offered by an unlicensed private schoolmaster or by a municipal orphanage, by song schools attached to chantries, or in primary grades attached to a grammar school. Letters could be learned at a mother's knee or from the parish priest. In the countryside, education accommodated itself to the agricultural economy with school hours and terms flexible enough to allow children to work at planting and harvest times but many children attended only long enough to acquire reading (but not necessarily writing which was often taught later); and many did not acquire even that. Though a few bright boys might be sent on to a Latin school if they had impressed someone as a future cleric or civil servant, most children, after this early schooling, were either set to work in service or agriculture or taught a trade.

In the cities the most common method of commercial education was apprenticeship, an arrangement whereby, in return for a premium, a master agreed to train a youth in his trade for a specified number of years. The contract between parent and master also set out clothing required, probationary period and duties involved. In England, after the 1563 Statute of Artificers, urban apprentices trained until age 24, usually for a period of seven years and most often living in the master's house and being closely regulated by him. On the Continent conditions were different – the length of apprenticeship was variable and could be as short as a year for glaziers or two years for brewers.

EDUCATION AND THE REFORMATION

The Reformation and the religious struggles which followed had contradictory effects on the course of education in the sixteenth century. The destruction of church property, the disruption of monastic orders and the diversion of funds once spent on education meant considerable dislocation in countries undergoing religious reform, setbacks which sometimes took years to repair. In addition, the disappearance of careers in the priesthood and obscurantist tendencies in some forms of Protestantism discouraged many parents from investing in their children's education, much to the despair of Reformers. However, there was a great deal in Protestantism that advanced learning. Literacy was encouraged so as to promote Bible reading and many reformers insisted on schemes of compulsory education for both boys and girls. Luther and Melanchthon helped develop Protestant Germany's school system. Calvin insisted that the Genevans erect an academy, while in Scotland John Knox wanted widespread public education. In Strassburg, Johannes Sturm's Gymnasium became a model for secondary schools throughout Europe. Like most Protestant educators, Sturm adopted humanist pedagogy but always with a generous measure of religious content. Though fathers were encouraged to participate in the educational process by catechizing their children, and repeating sermons to servants and offspring, one effect of the Reformation was to strengthen the position of the public school and the professional teacher at the expense of the family.

The Catholic Reformation sought to remedy deficiencies in existing Catholic education – clerical training was improved, the importance of parish education was emphasized and new orders such as the Ursulines and the Jesuits took particular interest in schooling. The Jesuits were not concerned with mass education and specialized in the secondary and university humanist pedagogy which won them wide fame. Aside from theological training, Jesuit schools differed little from Protestant academies in curriculum. There was perhaps less emphasis on corporal punishment and more stress laid on emulation and competition among the boys, rewarded by praise, prizes and privileges such as membership in élite youth groups. As with Protestant schooling, Jesuit education could have a corrosive effect on traditional family values. Children from Protestant backgrounds were actively encouraged to repudiate their fathers' influence and become Catholics. Moreover, the Jesuit emphasis on Marian theology stressed the maternal influence which threatened to reverse the family hierarchy.[14]

A point on which some educators and religious reformers agreed was the necessity for more education for girls. Humanist scholars such as Luis Vives, Roger Ascham and Thomas More produced a generation of learned women in England, including Queens Mary and Elizabeth, while in France many upper-class women presided over literary salons. Luther too wanted girls to benefit from education but in ways that would enable them to serve the Christian family as household managers and transmitters of the true religion to their children. Chastity was always viewed as a prime asset in young women and care was taken not to teach boys and girls together after primary education. Neither reformers nor humanists (except for those tutoring princesses) conceived of female education as leading to careers outside the home. Thomas More, for example, told his daughter that, despite her humanist education, she should not aspire to more than pleasing her father and husband. For most girls, literacy and education in domestic arts such as sewing was considered sufficient.

LITERACY

Though educational opportunities seem to have proliferated during the sixteenth century, what effect did this have on the literacy of Europeans? This is an important question for, although much culture remained oral or visual, illiteracy would have cut off the majority of the population from each other and from political communication. One method of answering it is to determine the percentage of those able to sign their own names on documents such as wills, court records or petitions. If this is used as the standard it becomes evident that rates of literacy varied widely, depending on occupation and the need to read and write. Among the gentry (who had estates to administer and who were often involved in lawsuits) and in occupations such as the clergy, the apothecary business or printing trade, literacy was extremely high; urban artisan rates varied between 50 to 75 per cent, depending on their craft; while for gardeners, the construction trade or day labourers, rates were low, perhaps no more than 10 to 15 per cent. The lowest rates for male workers seem to have been among agricultural labourers. Far fewer women than men were literate, especially in the rural areas; only 2 per cent of women could sign church court documents in the diocese of Durham during the seventy years after 1651. Certainly no more than 30 per cent of Europeans could have been literate throughout the sixteenth century.

COURT SOCIETY

At the top of European society the courts constituted a world of their own. Princes had had courts from time immemorial; but during the Renaissance the courts developed a lifestyle which, at one and the same time, set them apart from the rest of society and made them models, to be imitated as money and opportunity allowed. Courts came to be seen as microcosms of the society of the rich and the powerful. The codes of late-medieval chivalry merged with the artistic, literary and musical tastes of the Italian and the French-Burgundian urban élites to create a distinctive way of life. At the beginning of the century Count Baldassare Castiglione painted a portrait of the ideal courtier as a man who excelled in courage, piety, good manners and artistic and literary taste and who was matched by the highly educated court lady to whom the male courtier's behaviour must always be acceptable and pleasing. Castiglione's famous dialogue, *The Courtier*, found many imitators in the course of the sixteenth century. Books of manners were particularly popular and evidently very necessary since they taught such practical matters as table manners — the use of the fork, for instance, was only just beginning to be common — how to blow one's nose discreetly and when and when not to spit. The words courtesy and courteous in all Romance and Germanic languages indicate the civilizing influence of courts on the manners of European society.

For Castiglione the courtier was the quintessential Renaissance individual, the man who had developed his personal faculties to the full. In practice, however, court life also stressed two other and, in a sense, anti-individualist aspects of social behaviour: rank and ceremony. The two were closely connected. Rank was the affirmation of the God-given structure of society, indeed of the universe. Ceremony confirmed rank and made it inviolable. It allowed the prince to be presented as a superhuman being, standing apart from and above all ordinary men. This could be done in different styles. The king of Spain, and especially Philip II, lived withdrawn from his subjects and was rarely seen even by the greatest among them. The king of France, by contrast, lived out his life in public view, or at least in view of his courtiers. Even his bedroom was the scene of a public *levée*, when the king rose ceremonially from his rest. Every courtier also had his or her definite rank, from the grand-chamberlain or the queen's ladies-in-waiting to the gardeners, stable boys and kitchen maids, all defended by ceremony but also attacked by envy and intrigue. To the rest of the country and especially to ambitious individuals, court society seemed immensely attractive for its glitter, its opportunities for employment and for both receiving and dispensing patronage, and for its close association and intermingling with the centres of political power. At the same time, court society was notorious for its artificiality, its increasing remoteness from the lives of ordinary citizens and for the fierce and uncharitable rivalries of the courtiers at all levels of rank. There were in early modern Europe always those who detested court life, although for third parties it was not always easy to know whether this detestation was the result of philosophical or religious conviction or, more mundanely, of a failure to enter the charmed circle.

COURT FESTIVALS

Such ambiguities were particularly evident in the contemporary public reactions to court festivals and also in their appreciation by modern historians. Court festivals were organized both as entertainment for the courtiers and as propagandistic affirmations of the greatness of the prince and of his court. These festivals had almost nothing in common, except perhaps the love of food and drink, with public festivals like the carnival which we have discussed. During the Renaissance they developed a style which derived, in varying proportions, from ceremonial church festivals and religious processions, from late-medieval tournaments and from what was known of the triumphs of the generals and emperors of ancient Rome. There would be enormous and gluttonous banquets, with cooks vying for culinary pre-eminence, knightly jousts, literary and musical competitions and elaborately staged theatrical presentations, often with a spendid water festival. (The 'floats' of modern popular processions are a reminder of these water festivals.) Often the prince and his family took part in these presentations. The festivals projected a complex set of imagery, usually derived from classical history or mythology and celebrating cosmic harmony, of which the state and especially the court were the earthly images. The prince, often in the guise of a Greek god, would put strife and hatred to flight and bestow the blessings of peace on his country. The festivals often had a popular as well as courtly audience, but in the course of the sixteenth century they became more and more exclusive.

In 1520 the biggest, longest and most magnificent festival was staged for the meeting of Francis I and Henry VIII, the famous Field of the Cloth of Gold. King Francis's tent was 'as high as the tallest tower' and his party had almost another 400 tents, surrounding that of the king. King Henry's appearance was no less splendid. The two kings spent most of their time watching or taking part in the competitions and displays. They left serious diplomacy mostly to their ministers, and there was not much of that. Contemporary moralists, such as John Fisher, bishop of Rochester and, later, a Catholic martyr and saint, pointed to the enormous waste of money, the dust and the dirt mixed with the courtly splendour – there was, of course, no modern sanitation – and contrasted the tawdriness of earthly luxuries and the fickleness of princes with the untarnished glories of heaven and the immutability of God. It was a valid point, but too easy to make. The upbringing of the European aristocracy was essentially military; the relations of princes were those of competitive power politics. The destructive nature of this ethos had always been clear to the more perceptive. Out of this perception there had developed attempts to tame and civilize this society and its propensity towards violence, without giving up its traditional ideals of what constituted manly behaviour. Tournaments and court festivals were at least partly designed for this purpose, and they had the further advantage over war of creating an important and meaningful role for women as judges in the jousts and competitions. Francis and Henry wanted and needed to impress each other and the rest of the world. They could do this either by war or, in a much more civilized and eventually cheaper way, by a highly formalized and symbolical display.

In the second half of the sixteenth century the greatest of the impresarios of court festivals saw the matter in just this way. For Catherine de Medici these occasions were a deliberate tactic of proclaiming the splendour and apparent resources of the virtually bankrupt French monarchy and of its pursuit of peace and religious harmony in a country torn by religious civil wars. It was the tragedy of Europe and the pathos of the Field of the Cloth of Gold and of Catherine's festivals that they, like all other imaginative attempts to find alternatives to war, could not counterbalance the passions of military ambitions, envy and religious hatreds. Francis I and Henry VIII quickly broke their vows of eternal amity. Catherine, although she did not plan it that way, climaxed her grandest peace festival, celebrated in honour of the marriage of her daughter with the Huguenot Henry of Navarre, with the massacre of her Huguenot guests. But it was the impassioned moralists and preachers of the word of God, as much as the princes and barons, who were responsible for the massacres and wars of the century.

WAR AND SOCIETY

To Shakespeare's Jaques the soldier's life was one of the seven ages of man:

> Full of strange oaths and bearded like the pard,
> Jealous in honour, sudden and quick in quarrel,
> Seeking the bubble reputation
> Even in the cannon's mouth . . .*

War was an inescapable part of sixteenth-century life: but only a small proportion of young men became soldiers. In Shakespeare's England, from 1585 to 1603, only 1.3 per thousand of the population were recruited annually for foreign service — perhaps five per 1,000 of all adult males. In Castile, a much more highly militarized country, the annual recruitment figure was only one per 1,000 of the total population. Armies were small, both because they were expensive and because it was difficult to get men to serve. Soldiers' pay was lower than that of unskilled labourers and, during the inflation of the sixteenth century, tended to deteriorate further. While in theory men owed service to their princes and while sometimes they were pressed into service, most armies relied on voluntary recruitment. Even then, desertion rates were often up to a third of total numbers. But men would join when there was no work or no prospect of making a reasonable living at home. Some at least served for love of adventure and some for the sake of honour, but most joined in the hope of booty and plunder. There were just enough examples to make this plausible, such as the sack of Rome, in 1527, and that of Antwerp, in 1576. Where there was long-term rural overpopulation,

*Shakespeare, *As You Like It*, II.7.

as in South Germany and in the Swiss Alpine valleys, traditions of military service grew up and were passed from generation to generation of young men, with soldiers sometimes organizing themselves in brotherhoods, rather like civilian craft guilds.

But for most men the hope of riches turned out to be vain.

> We be soldiers three
> Pardonnez-moi, je vous en prie,
> Lately come off from the Low Country,
> With never a penny of money.

The period was rich in soldiers' songs, though not always written by soldiers, and with the braggadocio one would expect they also produced much cynicism. The great fortunes were made by those who financed wars and supplied the armies or, sometimes, by mercenary leaders who looked on war as a business. They were the men who as colonels recruited the regiments of German *lanzknechts* and Swiss halberdiers. In effect, they gave credit to the governments who employed them and they therefore needed funds of their own or, more usually, access to the credit network which operated among the Central-European nobility. They also needed a sufficient reputation as military leaders to attract the captains of companies who, in their turn, provided them with credit. It was obviously useful to be a great lord, or even better, a minor German or Italian prince. But, at least in the first half of the century, even a commoner could, exceptionally, succeed. The outstanding career was that of Sebastian Schertlin von Burtenbach (1495–1577), the son of a forester, who counted among his many employers the emperor, the Schmalkaldic League and the king of France. With a long life, a great deal of sheer luck and with his eye always fixed on the main chance, he ended up as a nobleman and the owner of property reputed as worth a million thalers. In his old age Schertlin wrote his memoirs in which he lovingly detailed all his financial gains, including very substantial ones even in the disastrous campaign of the Schmalkaldic league whose forces he commanded against the emperor.

It was of course well known that the captains and colonels and the suppliers of arms and provisions defrauded both the soldiers and the governments who employed them. The problem was how to prevent it. In Spain there was a lively debate, during the later years of Philip II's reign, about the relative merits of military administration by the king's own officials or by contracts to private entrepreneurs. The theoretical arguments of these debates centered on the authority of the king and his control of patronage and appointments. Actual decisions were usually taken for practical reasons: the notorious sixteenth-century difficulty of recruiting enough reasonably honest and efficient civil servants and, more important still, the government's need to rely on the credit which the private military entrepreneurs could provide. By the early years of the seventeenth century the commander of the Spanish armies in the Netherlands was the aristocratic Genoese banker, Ambrogio Spinola, who had started his military career by raising the considerable force of 9,000 men on his own account.

While relatively few soldiers fought and fewer still were killed in battle, rather than by hardship and disease, far more civilians were involved in war. Most directly and most dreadfully this happened to women and children in towns taken after a long siege or, perhaps even worse, during a siege. For garrisons would drive out 'useless mouths' and the besiegers would drive them back, so that most of them would die from hunger and exposure under the walls of their own town. Even Admiral Coligny, the later Huguenot leader with the reputation for incorruptible uprightness, did this to the women and children of St Quentin when he was defending the town against Philip II, in 1557. Neither friend nor foe regarded such action as dishonourable. But when Coligny was, probably wrongly, accused of complicity in the assassination of the duke of Guise, his fate was sealed, even though it took the Guise family many years to get the opportunity for 'revenge'.

The indirect results of war affected whole populations. Armies spread diseases which killed civilians by the thousands. In 1590, when Henry IV besieged Paris, some 13,000 Parisians died of starvation. On top of increased taxes, people were forced to house and feed soldiers and to provide digging, trenching and carting services. The soldiers could blackmail villages and towns into money payments on pain of being burnt down (*brandschatting*). At times, as in Provence during Francis I's Italian wars and in Ireland during the Elizabethan's wars retreating armies would carry out a scorched earth policy of their own territories. But worst of all were the bands of unpaid soldiers who 'ate up the poor country folk', as people said. An English writer called soldiers 'the very scum, thieves and rogues of England', and thought the country well rid of them if they died abroad. The sentiment was echoed by many, all over Europe. Often enough peasants took their revenge on small groups of stragglers, and in France towards the end of the civil wars, whole provinces rose in rebellion against the hated soldiery, regardless of whether they were Protestants or Catholics. But already at the beginning of the century Erasmus had summed it all up in the lapidary words: 'War is a fine thing to those who know it not.'

DISEASES, PLAGUES AND HOSPITALS

It was not only the soldiers who spread diseases. Outbreaks of bubonic plague recurred regularly in Europe, although at gradually lengthening intervals, ever since the Black Death in the middle of the fourteenth century. It could still wipe out whole families, as virtually happened to that of Benvenuto Cellini who lost all but one sister, in 1528; or it could devastate a large city, as happened to Lisbon in 1580, when 35,000 people died. There was a particularly virulent outbreak in Italy in 1575−78 and an even worse one in the whole Mediterranean world in 1596−1600, when 600,000 died in Castile alone. Besides bubonic plague there was the whole gamut of epidemics which continued into our own century. An especially deadly strain of influenza struck western Europe in the 1550s.

For most people such calamities still represented visitations inflicted by God on a sinful world or the malign influence of a certain conjunction of the stars and planets. The two explanations were not necessarily regarded as contradictory. The rich would temporarily move out of the cities where, it was generally recognised, mortality was always at its highest. For most people there was no such escape. The medical profession, ascribing epidemics mainly to noxious airs, had no answer beyond the perfectly reasonable advice to people to eat moderately, drink only fresh water and, if possible, live in salubrious air, away from swamps. At least one Italian physician, who in true Renaissance style was also a physicist and a poet, the Venetian Girolamo Fracastoro (c. 1478–1553) developed a theory of contagion which comes remarkably near the modern germ theory of disease. Fracastoro thought that disease was caused by rapidly multiplying minute bodies transmitted directly from person to person, through infected clothing or through the air. But, in the absence of microscopes (invented only in the last decade of the sixteenth century) and of a

87

theory of immunization, Fracastoro's and other physicians' insights or inspired guesses had little practical effect.

Since the Black Death, the major Italian and some northern cities had appointed permanent health officials (*provveditori di sanita*) who supervised hospitals, apothecaries, sewage systems (where these existed), refuse disposal and burial grounds. When plague broke out they imposed quarantine regulations and tried to organize the burning of the clothes of people who had died from the infection. In the 1575 plague the authorities of Palermo ordered the killing of all dogs, but characteristically exempted the hunting dogs and the lap dogs of the lords and ladies of the aristocracy. Many people, and especially the grave diggers who also had the best opportunities, were so poor that they would steal the clothes from the plague victims, even though the penalties were ferocious: hanging or, at best, service in the galleys for men and in hospitals for women.

Many hospitals were founded in the sixteenth century, mainly from charitable bequests, and were run either as private charities or as public services by the municipal authorities. In both Catholic and Protestant countries there was a lively debate throughout the century about the practical advantages and the theological justification of public versus private welfare administration. But hospitals were refuges for the destitute and the helpless, not medical centres for anyone who could possibly afford a physician or even a quack. Some of the religious orders and many members of the Protestant churches did devoted work in the hospitals. But it was hard and dangerous work, and there were never enough of them. Hence the impressment of criminals as hospital workers — another reason why no one would willingly go there if he could possibly avoid it.

ATTITUDES TOWARDS DEATH

Death was omnipresent and witnessing it was everyone's experience. The dying could not be, nor would they want to be, isolated from the rest of the household. Preachers and moralists pointed to death to counter human vanity. All over Europe, from the fourteenth to the sixteenth century, church and cemetery walls were decorated with Dances of Death: Death, no longer represented as he had been in the earlier Middle Ages as an avenging angel of

God, but as a mummified, decayed body or as a skeleton. He was either leading a procession of pope and emperor, through the orders of society, to peasant and beggar; or each member of the social procession was led a dance by his own death figure. Woodcuts (a Chinese invention which became popular in Europe around 1400) came to be a favourite method of propagating the picture of the Dance of Death and its chilling message. This message certainly contained an aspect of social irony, for Death was evidently no respecter of rank; but it brought no special comfort to the poor for they, too, were subject to Death's power.

Nor was the Dance of Death by itself a symbol of Christian hope or redemption. Such a role was performed rather by the very popular books of the *ars moriendi*, the Art of Dying. They were written in analogy to the humanist books of instruction on manners and morals and also in analogy to the business ledgers with their credit and debit accounts. Only that in the *ars moriendi* it is the whole life which is accounted. At the moment of death the dying person was thought to witness a dramatic struggle between supernatural forces around his bed: angels and devils were fighting for his soul. The crucified Christ and the Virgin were always thought to be present and God was seen less as a judge than as the arbiter in the struggle between the forces of good and evil. The books stressed the importance of resisting the temptations of the devil, for those who gave in to him at this time of greatest human despair would have to spend endless years in Purgatory.

NOTES AND REFERENCES

1   This is nearly 50 per cent. See M. W. Flinn, *The European Demographic System 1500–1800* (Brighton, 1981), pp. 14–18. Laslett, *The World we have lost*, cit., p. 112, suggests a 25 per cent mortality rate of children before 10.

2   R. Mols, *Introduction à la démographie historique des villes d'Europe*, 3 vols. (Louvain, 1954–56).

3   Christiane Klapisch-Zuber, *Women, Family and Ritual in Renaissance Italy*, (Chicago, 1985), p. 263.

4   Merry Wiesner, *Working Women in Renaissance Germany* (New Brunswick, N.J., 1986), p. 100.

5   Jean-Claude Bologne, *Histoire de la Pudeur* (Paris, 1986), p. 281.

6   Natalie Zemon Davis, 'Women on Top', in *Society and Culture in Early Modern France*, (Stanford, 1975), p. 128.

7   Ian Maclean, *The Renaissance Notion of Women* (Cambridge, 1980), p. 41.

8   Merry Wiesner, *Working Women in Renaissance Germany* (New Brunswick, 1986), p. 195.

9   Julio Caro Baroja, quoted in John Bossy, *Christianity in the West, 1400–1700* (Oxford, 1985), p. 43.

10   Peter Burke, *Popular Culture in Early Modern Europe* (London, 1978), p. 186.

11   Martin Luther, 'A sermon on keeping children in school' (1530), in *Luther's Works* vol. 46 (Philadelphia, 1967), p. 252.

12   Gerald Strauss, *Luther's House of Learning: Indoctrination of the Young in the German Reformation* (London, 1978), p. 179.

13   Rosemary O'Day, *Education and Society, 1500–1800* (London, 1982), p. 90.

14   R. P. Hsia *Society and Religion in Münster, 1535–1618* (New Haven, 1984), pp. 65–66.

5

TOWNS AND CITIES

THE SOCIAL AND POLITICAL STRUCTURE OF TOWNS

The cities of the Middle Ages had been founded, or refounded from Roman survivals, with varying degrees of emphasis, as centres of trade, military refuges, seats of ecclesiastical administration or even as prestige symbols. So that the cities could properly fulfil these functions in an agrarian and feudal world, their inhabitants had had to develop a separate body of law and a concept of citizenship which differed from the various lord-and-vassal relationships of the time. The high town walls with their massive towers, the church and cathedral spires, and especially the imposing town halls on the market squares, represented at once the means of carrying on and protecting the life of the Christian commune and the visual symbols of its autonomy and separateness. Hamburg and Bremen reinforced this symbolism by erecting a giant statue of the legendary Roland in front of their town halls. Florence set up a whole series of symbols of liberty in front of its Palazzo Vecchio, of which Donatello's Marzocco, the lion of Florence, and his Judith, the tyrant slayer, are the most famous.

By the end of the fifteenth century, the towns were almost everywhere governed by an oligarchy, a patriciate of rich merchants and property owners. The composition of these oligarchies varied considerably. In England there were hardly any patrician dynasties: after one or two generations of urban success, patrician families and their property tended to be reabsorbed, by intermarriage and land purchase, into the upper strata of rural society. This is one, though not the only, reason for the relatively small size and restricted autonomy of English provincial towns. As a further consequence, the smaller English boroughs were frequently dominated by one or several great county families, who, from the fifteenth century on, tended more and more to represent the boroughs in parliament. In Hamburg members of the knightly class were not allowed to reside in the city. In Lübeck, by contrast, the patriciate were generally landowners. In Frankfurt a small ring of families monopolized the town council. Most Italian cities had tamed the country nobility of their regions by forcing them to live for at least part of the year in the city; but the cost of urbanizing the feudal nobility was high: it introduced their family feuds into the cities where they became mixed up in the social and faction fights of town politics. Only Venice escaped these feuds; but the Venetian patriciate became the most exclusive ruling class in Europe, looking down even on the oldest nobility of the Venetian mainland who could trace their families back to the Lombards of the seventh century. From 1381 until 1646, the Venetian patriciate admitted no newcomers to its ranks[1] – a unique degree of exclusiveness among the European aristocracies of the time. In the rest of Europe the variations were equally great, from the hidalgo-dominated cities of Castile to the complex of business and aristocratic groups ruling the Netherlands cities, with the banking and mercantile plutocracy of Antwerp as another extreme.

In the Mediterranean cities there were considerable numbers of domestic slaves: Circassians, Levantines, Berbers and Negroes. Apart from these, however, the inhabitants of the cities were legally free. In the fourteenth and fifteenth centuries the guilds had won some notable victories against the patricians. In many Flemish, Rhineland and Italian towns they had forced their way into the town councils. But by 1500 the patricians were everywhere reasserting their authority and the guilds were on the defensive. In most European towns, the majority of the citizens had very few active political rights.

They were also very poor. In Coventry, in 1524, nearly 50 per cent of the inhabitants could not pay the minimum rate of four pence of the lay subsidy. On the other hand, 2 per cent of the taxable population owned 45 per cent of the taxable wealth. The figures for other English towns were similar, and the price revolution of the sixteenth century caused the disproportion to increase.[2] Wherever we have figures for property distribution, for the small towns of Hainault for instance, or for Turin in northern Italy, we find a similar picture.[3] Nor were conditions better in the large cities. Their tenements within the city walls, and their suburbs without, were notorious: 'Dark dens for adulterers, thieves, murderers and every mischief worker', as Henry Chettle, a London dramatist, called them in 1592.[4] The slums of sixteenth-century towns were as dark, damp, evil-smelling and unhealthy as the more famous slums of the industrial revolution. Sanitation was primitive, and only towards the end of the century did some municipalities in Italy and the Netherlands begin to organize the regular cleaning of streets and the removal of refuse. Nevertheless the cities, especially the larger ones, could offer many attractions to their inhabitants and even to those of their poor who had no reason to hide from the authorities. Taverns, theatres and spectacles of all sorts, preachers in the cathedrals and large churches whose thundering sermons could rouse men in a way the poor, semi-literate village priests never attempted, the companionship and, sometimes, the help in sickness and distress which the guilds provided for its members and their families – all these drew men from the countryside into the towns. But perhaps most important was the lure of opportunity. The popularity of the many stories of poor young men who set out to make their fortunes is an indication of a very real longing. Since giants, hidden treasures and princesses immured in high towers were woefully uncommon, outside fairy stories, there remained four main ways in which a young man without connections might better himself: in the church, in the army, in overseas exploration and colonization, and in the city. In all four he would need more than uncommon luck and ability to succeed; but life in a city presented the easiest and most comfortable way of trying.

The vast majority, of course, did not succeed. With half the population of nearly every European city living on the poverty line, city politics tended to be explosive. When, in the course of the sixteenth century, the traditional, and almost respectable, bread riots of the urban poor came to be tinged with religious fanaticism, the results could be very nasty, as Antwerp, Paris and other cities were to find (see pp. 307–9, 314).

As a general rule, the degree of independence or autonomy of cities varied inversely with the strength of the monarchies. The Holy Roman Empire, that is a broad belt from central Italy to the

North Sea and the western Baltic, where the central authority was particularly weak, contained the areas of greatest urbanization and the cities with the greatest degree of independence. In Brabant 35 per cent of the population lived in towns, 45 per cent in Flanders and over 50 per cent in Holland.[5] Some parts of northern Italy may have been as highly urbanized. Elsewhere, the percentage of towns people was much lower, and many inhabitants of the smaller towns still lived by agriculture.

Again, as a general rule, the commercially most active towns in this part of Europe had the greatest degree of political independence. Venice, Florence, Genoa and the other Italian city republics were independent states. Lübeck, Nuremberg, Augsburg and the other free imperial cities of Germany recognized the authority of the emperor, but otherwise were as independent as the electors of Saxony or the dukes of Bavaria. The great Flemish cities, Bruges, Ghent and Ypres, had never become independent city states but enjoyed autonomous administrations and exercised considerable jurisdictional and police powers over their surrounding countrysides. Antwerp and Amsterdam, which developed commercially later, under a more powerful central government, never gained any control over theirs. By contrast, the political fragmentation of southern Germany had allowed some quite small cities to become free imperial cities.

THE CONTADO

Like ancient Athens and Rome, the late-medieval city states of Italy had extended their territory over considerable areas, the *contado*, and in the process had reduced other cities to political dependence. Venice had done this in the fifteenth century, mainly to defend itself against the aggressive policy of the Visconti dukes of Milan. Most of the others, especially Florence and Genoa, were themselves the aggressors, possibly because of the noble element in their city governments. The defeated cities were rarely willing subjects. Guicciardini, the Florentine statesman and historian, observed that it was an axiom of politics that a republic 'grants no share of its grandeur to any but the citizens of the chief city, while oppressing all others'.[6] In Guicciardini's own youth, the recently restored Florentine republic waged a long and ruinous war against Pisa which had rebelled against Florentine rule (1494–1509).

Even if they did not conquer other cities, the city states needed their *contado* to assure their food supply, although for a city as populous as Venice even its large *contado* was insufficient for this purpose. Equally important, at least for cities with textile industries, was the control of rural manufacturing. Ghent and Bruges tried to prevent the weaving of woollens in their surrounding countrysides, and from time to time the city weavers would march out to smash peasant looms. The Florentine clothiers had preferred to control and integrate the rural with the urban industry, although by 1500 Florentine cloth production had sadly declined from its early fourteenth-century peak. The citizens of Basle prevented the immigration of propertyless workers into their city and forced them to live and work in the surrounding villages, in complete economic and political dependence on the city. Basle thus exploited its *contado* as ruthlessly as Ghent or Florence, and its policy had the added advantage of preserving the city from internal social struggles until the nineteenth century.[7]

In Germany, the *contado* of the free imperial cities remained much smaller than in Italy and never included other cities. The reason was, perhaps, the smaller size of the German cities and the relatively greater power of both the emperor in Germany and of the surrounding territorial princes or, simply, that most of the cities were not interested in, nor had a tradition of, territorial expansion. Only the Swiss towns, although neither as rich nor as populous as the great Italian and German cities, managed to dominate an extensive *contado*. Moreover, their confederation with the free peasant communities of the forest cantons, Schwyz, Uri, Unterwalden and Glarus, celebrated breeding grounds of infantrymen, gave the Helvetic League a military potential out of all proportion to the economic importance of its cities. The Swiss cities were ruled by small patriciates, like most other European cities, and even the forest cantons were far from democratic; but the Helvetic League was by far the most successful anti-monarchial institution in Europe. Its regiments of highly trained and savage pikemen from the overpopulated mountain villages had crushed Charles the Bold in 1476 and 1477, and had repulsed Maximilian I in 1499. Francis I defeated them at Marignano, in 1515, and put an end to Swiss expansionism in the Lombard plain; but, before the wars of the French Revolution, none of the great powers was willing to attack again the heartland of the Confederation. The only other really successful antimonarchical experiment of the sixteenth century, the United Provinces of the Netherlands, looked for a model to the Swiss Confederation, rather than to the German or Italian city states, and hardly at all to republican theory.

REPUBLICANISM

Since the rediscovery of Aristotle's *Politics*, in the twelfth century, the educated elites of the European cities had become familiar with the concept and language of republicanism. In this language republics stood for liberty, both from outside domination and from the domination of one of their own citizens. It was not usually thought that the concept could apply to anything much larger than a city and its surrounding countryside. Many sixteenth century cities affixed a variation of the famous Roman SPQR (Senatus Populusque Romanus – the senate and the people of Rome) to their town halls, such as SPQA on the new town hall of Antwerp. It was a sort of republican parallel to the *dei gratia* (by the will of God) which emperors, kings and princes claimed as a justification for their position, and which is still inscribed, with the reigning king's or queen's image, on British coins. Since city republics could not claim such a divine justification for their existence they made up for this lack by inventing a long ancestry of freedom. The Florentines insisted on an Etruscan and Roman-republican foundation. The cities of the Netherlands claimed the freedom-loving Batavians as their ancestors. When the citizens of the small North-German town of Emden chased out their duke (of Eastern Friesland) in 1595, they justified their rebellion by citing the liberty of the ancient Frisian inhabitants of their region. French cities could not usually pretend to republican foundation; but some of them could at least find themselves a Roman emperor as founder, preferably a famous Christian one such as Constantine or Theodosius, thus making the city's ancestry more venerable than that of the French monarchy which dated only to the fifth century A.D.

Yet, in spite of the classical education of all the European ruling elites, the republics found themselves in a hostile political and intellectual climate. To most Europeans monarchy appeared as the natural, God-given form of government; for Heaven itself was represented as a kingdom with Christ as its king. In almost universally mouthed metaphors, the king was likened to the head and his subjects to the members of the body politic; or, alternatively, he was the father and his subjects were his children. Both feudal and Roman law reinforced the duty of loyalty and obedience to the person of the prince. In return, princes were expected to distribute patronage and encourage and reward the quest for personal glory of their subjects. And while such glory would usually be military, in the Renaissance courts of Europe it was also coming to be literary and artistic.

All this produced a gut-feeling in favour of royalty. The republics could set against it only the much more abstract duty of loyalty to the state or the *patria*, the native country; and this *patria* was a city or, at most, a region, such as a Swiss canton, but not a large country, such as Italy or Germany or France. All republics stressed the need to practise republican or civic virtues: soberness and frugality, the acceptance of equal burdens in taxation and in the defence of the *patria*, and the enforcement of equal justice, although not necessarily of equal social status or equal political rights. Military success and honours were to be earned for the glory of the republic and not for the reputation of the individual. The public benefits of these virtues were often presented visually in paintings and decorations of town halls. Such, for instance, were the frescoes in the *palazzo pubblico*, the town hall, of Siena where these benefits were dramatically contrasted with the disasters flowing from tyranny. Such also were the many Venetian paintings in which the Venetian Caterina Cornaro, widow of the last independent king of Cyprus, was represented as spontaneously and virtuously making over her kingdom to the Republic of St Mark, i.e. Venice. In fact, the Venetians had gained control of much of the economy and administration of the island in the course of the fifteenth century and, in 1488, they bullied and bribed the helpless queen into this surrender of sovereignty to the republic.

If the republican virtues appeared austere, yet liberty, the rule of law and self-government were highly prized by many, and even by those who acknowledged the ultimate sovereignty of the king of England or France or of the Holy Roman Emperor. With the dissolution of feudalism and manorialism, in western and central Europe in the later Middle Ages, many peasant communities and small towns had achieved previously undreamt-of degrees of self-government. In large areas of Alpine and South-German lands this came to include the control of local jurisdiction and tax collection. The Swiss had gone all the way to full republicanism by abolishing princely and noble powers completely. In the non-urban forest cantons they had also gone a long way towards democracy, for there even the peasants had full political rights. In the sixteenth century the inhabitants of the Grisons and of the Valais deprived their rulers, the prince-bishops of Chur and Sion, of all their political authority and concluded alliances with the Swiss Confederation.

These were extreme cases; but in the first quarter of the sixteenth century there was a distinct possibility that many South-German cities might 'turn Swiss', i.e. effectively renounce the authority of the Emperor and join the Swiss Confederation. Basle actually did this; but most cities eventually decided against this course, not least because their ruling families feared that in the Confederation they might have to share power with the 'common man'. The peasants' war of 1524–25 spread precisely in those areas, from the Alps to Thuringia, where a considerable degree of self-goverment by the better-off peasantry had developed in the latter Middle Ages. There was much sympathy for the peasants in many towns. Nevertheless, the rebellion frightened the urban patriciates, and the defeat of the peasants also meant the defeat of those who wanted to 'turn Swiss'. (See below, pp. 171 ff.)

Outside Italy republicanism was generally more a matter of attitude than of the acceptance of a fully-argued republican theory. Even during the revolt of the Netherlands (see below, pp. 311 ff), the most spectacular success of republicanism in the century, very few people thought of the United Provinces as a republic until at least a generation after the Act of Abjuration, the Dutch declaration of independence from their ruler, Philip II of Spain, in 1581. Self-governing cities relied on specific privileges, on their charters and liberties, rather than on classical political theory. There was, moreover, the constant temptation for the rulers of the town halls to regard themselves as princely rulers and to look on their non-privileged fellow citizens as subjects. By the seventeenth century this had become the common practice in the free imperial cities of the Holy Roman Empire and even in some of the Swiss cities, such as Berne. The great families of the Venetian aristocracy, having closed their ranks against newcomers already in the fourteenth century, vied with each other in the princely splendour of their life styles in their *palazzi* on the Grand Canal. In the early seventeenth century a Venetian ambassador claimed precedence over a Dutch ambassador because the Republic of St Mark ruled over three kingdoms, Cyprus, Candia (Crete) and Negroponte (Euboea), while the highest titles included in the United Provinces of the Netherlands were only dukedoms. Only with such snobbery, it seems, could republicanism survive in an essentially royalist Europe. Political privileges, the rule of law and the rights and liberties of subjects could be safeguarded in monarchies by representative institutions (see below, pp. 280 ff). Only when this method did not work any more, which happened in most Continental countries by the eighteenth century, was republicanism resurrected, but now no longer as a regime for a city but on a nation-wide scale and with a degree of democracy which had been unacceptable outside the Swiss forest cantons in the sixteenth century.

VULNERABILITY OF CITY STATES: FLORENCE

By that time, the last quarter of the sixteenth century, it had become clear that the city states were vulnerable both to overthrow from the inside and to attack from outside powers or their own princes. The political instability of the Italian city states had shown itself as early as the fourteenth century. Family feuds and faction fights within the ruling oligarchies, and the bitter class struggles between patricians and *popolani*, presented military leaders with easy opportunities to set themselves up as despots. By the end of the fifteenth century many of the despots had found it convenient to dispense with the popular support on which their rule had at first rested. The Sforza in Milan, the Gonzaga in Mantua, the Este in Ferrara, the Montefeltre in Urbino had acquired the titles of dukes or marquises. Their courts, not as yet stifled, as they were later to be, by Spanish etiquette and Counter-Reformation piety and puritanism, became brilliant centres of Renaissance art and learning.

But it is in Florence that we find the fiercest struggles between republican freedom and princely authority, the most complex interaction between internal party strife and external pressures, and, as we would expect in this epicentre of Renaissance civilization, the most brilliant intellectual reaction to these struggles. In 1494, under the shadow of the French army, the popular party and the republicans overthrew the rule of the house of Medici which had made the tactical mistake of opposing Charles VIII's march to Naples. From that moment, the republicans and *popolani* were bound to rely on the French for support, and the Medici on the support of the enemies of France. The internal politics of Florence therefore became indissolubly linked with the politics and campaigns of the great powers for the control of the peninsula.

After a brief interlude, during which Florence foreshadowed Geneva in accepting the moral domination of a preacher, the Dominican friar Girolamo Savonarola, who introduced some more democratic elements into the constitution, the republic returned to traditional oligarchical government (1498). For a decade and a half Florence manœuvred uneasily between the great powers and at the same time fought against the rebellious city of Pisa in a war that was financially ruinous and ideologically unjustifiable. In 1512 the Medici marched into Florence with a papal and Spanish army and re-established their domination as it had been in the days of Lorenzo the Magnificent. It was under the impact of these events that Machiavelli wrote his famous treatise, *The Prince* (see p. 155).

The Medici were supreme, but not yet all-powerful; nor did they attempt to stifle political discussion. In treatises, political dialogues and histories, the Florentine intellectuals analysed the problems of the city republic. Many of them met privately in the Oricellari Gardens to discuss politics and literature. The climate of opinion was still distinctly republican. Machiavelli became a member of this group in 1515. We now know that it was probably only at this time that he began to compose his greatest political work, the *Discourses on the Ten Books of Livy*, and not, as used to be thought, both before and after the writing of *The Prince*.[8] It is, therefore, no longer necessary to try to harmonize the two works. For the Machiavelli of the *Discourses* is a republican who looks to the Roman Republic, rather than, as in *The Prince*, to the Roman Empire as a model. He has become aware of the psychological difficulties of advocating the type of political conduct he extolled in the earlier work; for 'very rarely will there be found a good man ready to use bad methods . . . nor yet a bad who, having become a prince . . . will use well that authority he had acquired by bad means'.[9] When in 1519–20 Leo X and Cardinal Medici (later Clement VII) asked the leading political thinkers of Florence for advice on the best constitution for the city, Machiavelli argued that in countries where there was great social inequality and a strong nobility, as in Naples, the Papal States, or Milan, only a monarchy could give stable government. But in the cities of Tuscany, where there were no such strong social divisions, a free republic was best. His practical advice was for a regime which would leave the Medici with supreme power in their lifetime, but which, after their deaths, would automatically make Florence into a republic again.[10]

THE END OF THE FLORENTINE REPUBLIC, GUICCIARDINI

The actual course of events was more dramatic. In 1527 the unpaid and mutinous imperial army captured Rome and made Clement VII a prisoner in his castle of St Angelo. The Florentines seized this opportunity to overthrow Medici rule once again. The last Florentine republic, however, was doomed as soon as the Medici pope made his peace with the emperor. In October 1529 papal and imperial troops began their march on Florence. This time, the republic's defence was more determined than in 1512. Michelangelo himself superintended the building of the fortifications. But inside the city the faction fights reached a new pitch of intensity. The patricians (*ottimati*) were divided between Medicians, moderates and republicans; the *popolani* pursued them all with a common hatred. After months of resistance against overwhelming military odds, the city had once more to open its gates to the Medici (August 1530). It is not surprising that the majority of the *ottimati* welcomed them. It seemed that only with Medici support could they now protect their social and economic position against the hatred of the *popolani*.

Francesco Guicciardini, the statesman and historian, and the other leaders of the Florentine aristocracy joined enthusiastically in the Medici policy of revenge against the republicans and *popolani*. They thought they could control the Medici; in fact, they became the prisoners of the more powerful partner of the alliance.

101

The development of Guicciardini's ideas was symptomatic, both for the attitude of the Florentine aristocracy and for the contemporary retreat from the republican ideal. Guicciardini had never shared his friend Machiavelli's belief in the possible *virtù* of the ordinary citizen. His ideal was rather a mixed monarchical and aristocratic constitution; but this seemed less and less attainable. 'The stability and security of the state does not consist in (constructing) models', he wrote in 1532.[11] The humanists had seen the state 'as a work of art' (Burckhardt's phrase), and this idea still dominated Machiavelli's political thought: man, as a political animal, could control his own destiny, and good constitutions and laws could make good citizens. This fundamental optimism, however much tempered, in Machiavelli's case, by scepticism, now gave way to an equally fundamental and pervading pessimism. The state was to be preserved no longer by the civic virtues of its citizens, but by the power of a ruler who would defend the personal security and private property of the individual. Guicciardini stands at the beginning of the long tradition of antirationalist, empirical conservatism. It was not a big step, although not an inevitable one, and certainly not one taken by Guicciardini himself, from this position to the justification of monarchy as divinely established for the good of the body politic – a doctrine which was to become the commonplace of political thought at the princely courts of the later sixteenth century.

In his last years, from 1535, Guicciardini wrote his famous *History of Italy* (effectively 1494–1534). Remorselessly unromantic, realistic to the point of cynicism about men's motives, overloaded with detail yet fast moving, Guicciardini's *History* has set the pattern for the historiography of the period, right up to our own time: for here we find the idealization of the Florence and Italy of Lorenzo the Magnificent, and the year 1494, the year of the French invasion of Naples, as the beginning of all the disasters which befell Italy and from which, unlike the older Machiavelli, Guicciardini could hope for respite, but no longer for deliverance.

Alessandro de' Medici and, after his assassination and a last, unsuccessful, republican revolt in 1537, his successor, Cosimo, did not abolish the political institutions of the city state; he simply bypassed them by building up an alternative administration, staffed by his own nominees. Some *ottimati* were, on occasion, still appointed to important offices of state; but these were personal appointments. The class as such was excluded from office. Gradually they withdrew from the city. They invested their money no longer in commerce and banking but in their country estates, and they looked for advancement to the hispanicized court of Cosimo, now duke of Florence and, from 1569, grand-duke of Tuscany. The urban patriciate, the former upholders of republican liberties, were being transformed into a landed nobility of the kind which Machiavelli had rightly seen as the mainstay of monarchy. Characteristically, the duke achieved what the republic had never even attempted: the equalization of the Florentines and their former subjects in the *contado*. All were now equally the duke's subjects.

For about two decades after the fall of the last Florentine republic, the Florentine historians of the older generation continued the passionate discussion of the reasons for the failure of the republic and its free institutions. Most of them were agreed that the relentless social and party strife within the republic had made the victory of the Medici inevitable. Cosimo allowed this open, and often hostile, discussion. But Guicciardini and Varchi, Nerli, Segni and Pitti had no successors. The ever more rigid and hispanicized court life of the increasingly absolutist Medici dukes and grand-dukes provided none of the inspiration and challenge for acute political thinking which the free republic had done. In place of the clash of parties and principles there were court intrigues, and in place of the defence of a free republic against foreign despotisms there were the manœuvrings of a Spanish satellite pretending to a spurious independence. In the second half of the sixteenth century historical and political writing in Florence, centred no longer on the free and informal Oricellari Gardens but on a stuffy ducal academy, deteriorated to the dull encomium of the Christian virtues of the now absolute Medici dukes.[12]

VENICE

It is possible that the Florentine historians took too gloomy a view of the internal instability of their republic, and that the Medici only won because two successive Medici popes, Leo X and

Clement VII, were able to marshal overwhelming outside forces against the republic. In the case of Venice, there can be no doubt that her decline as a great power was due almost entirely to outside attacks. At the turn of the century Venice was at the height of her power. Philippe de Comines, the soldier, statesman and historian who had served both the dukes of Burgundy and the kings of France, thought Venice 'the most triumphant city I have ever seen . . . [and] the most wisely governed'.[13] In 1495, when Comines visited the city as French ambassador, the Venetians were just organizing the league which was to chase the French from Italy.

Venice was the most powerful of the Italian states; but neither the Venetians nor the other Italians had as yet adjusted their thinking to the vastly increased scale of military power which followed the invasion of Italy, first by the French, and then by the Spaniards, the Swiss and the Germans. In 1508 the Venetians still defeated the emperor Maximilian singlehanded; even to Machiavelli it seemed that they were aiming at the domination of the whole peninsula, just as the Romans had done. It was only with the hindsight, born of a whole generation of Italian disasters, that Guicciardini in 1535, when he wrote his *History of Italy*, appreciated fully the dreadful blow which the Italians themselves had struck at their liberty when they joined the League of Cambrai against Venice.

This league, an alliance of nearly all European powers with ambitions in Italy, was inspired by Pope Julius II. We know this old Genoese, with the long white beard and imperious nose, from the famous portrait by Raphael. His contemporaries were impressed by the force of his personality and called him an *uomo terribile*. He was the patron of Raphael and of Michelangelo, from whom he commissioned the ceiling of the Sistine Chapel, and a monumental tomb of whose projected forty figures only the Moses and the captive slaves (now in the Paris Louvre) were finished. Like Machiavelli, and indeed many of the Venetians, Julius dreamt of an Italy freed from the foreign barbarians. Yet, in his politics, as in his relations with Michelangelo, obstinacy and peevishness flawed his great conceptions. For the sake of reconquering for the Papal States a few towns in the Romagna, he was willing to bargain Venetian territory to the French, the Spaniards, the Swiss, the Hungarians, and the emperor, as well as promising the smaller Italian princes a share of the booty.

The French, first in the field, shattered the Venetian army at Agnadello (14 May 1509). The patriciates of the cities of the Veneto made common cause with the allies whose armies were now closing in on the lagoons. Soon news reached the Rialto that on 3 February the Portuguese in India had won a decisive victory over the Egyptians, the allies and trading partners of Venice. Italy, as a contemporary put it, had ceased to be 'the inner court in the house of the world'.[14] But Venice refused to surrender. The common people of the subject towns preferred the just and efficient rule of Venice to the tyranny of their own patricians and the insolence of the foreign armies of occupation. City after city raised again the standard of St Mark. Foreseeably, the League of Cambrai broke apart. Julius II, belatedly thinking again of the liberation of Italy, was bought off by the surrender of the Romagna towns. 'If Venice did not exist, it would have to be invented', he remarked,[15] anticipating the formulation of Voltaire's *bon mot* about God. Thus Venice survived the crisis, with most of her possessions intact,[16] but her role as a great power was at an end.

Old attitudes, however, die hard. In 1529 the Venetian ambassador to Charles V, Niccolo de Ponte, reported him as saying that he did not want to become a *monarca*, that is, ruler of a *monarchia universale*, a world empire, as some had slanderously said, but that he knew others who did. He certainly had the French, or just possibly the Turks, in mind. De Ponte, however, wrote in his report: 'He meant the Venetians.'[17] The illusion did not last. In 1546 Navagero, another Venetian ambassador to Charles V, advised his doge that there were only three great powers left, the Turks, the French and the emperor. 'Peace, most Serene Prince,' he cried, 'Peace! But if it must be war, let it be far from home.'[18]

It was a good characterization of what was to be Venetian policy for the rest of the century. The republic had lost its position as a great power but had preserved its liberty as a city state. More and more, both in Italy and across the Alps, Venice came to be recognized as the prototype (though a curiously unimitated one) of the state in which liberty was maintained by an almost ideal constitution. In the commonplaces of political thinking – those unoriginal and repetitive clichés that often tell us more about the attitudes and motivations of practical politicians than the disquisitions of the great thinkers – the mixed constitution of Venice, monarchical (doge), aristocratic (senate) and democratic (great council), became synonymous with liberty.

LÜBECK

The only other city state which, in 1500, could rank as a great power was Lübeck. Though past her apogee, and inclined to commercial and political conservatism, Lübeck was still the leader of the Hanseatic League, the staple market for much of the Baltic and north German trade, and the carrier of grain, timber and furs to western Europe. Intellectually and artistically, she was also a sort of staple market for Netherlands and French culture which she translated into her own low German language (the *lingua franca* of much of northern Europe) and spread over the Baltic littoral. But just as the economic position of Venice came to be threatened by the Portuguese circumnavigation of Africa, so Lübeck's economic position came to be threatened by the Dutch circumnavigation of Jutland. As early as 1497, the year for which we have the first Sound Toll Registers, the lead of Dutch shipping over the Hansards was clear.[19] But, to contemporaries, the commercial rivalry between the Dutch and Lübeck seemed as yet far from decided. It involved Lübeck in Danish politics, for Denmark controlled the all-important passage through the Sound, and here the intervention of the powerful Lübeck fleet could still be decisive. It sailed to Stockholm, in 1522, and decided the issue between Gustavus Vasa and the Danish king, Christian II, against the latter. In the following year it helped the duke of Holstein to drive Christian II from Denmark itself. The two new kings by the grace of Lübeck, Gustavus I of Sweden and Frederick I of Denmark, had to renew and extend all the old commercial privileges of Lübeck and the Hanseatic League.

It was not to be expected that Sweden, Denmark or the Dutch would permanently accept this situation and in the long run they were likely to win, as they had the greater resources. The dramatic collapse of Lübeck, like that of Venice, was, however, largely of her own making. The government of the city state was traditionally controlled by a tight ring of some ninety families. But the financial strain of the Danish war of 1522–23, coupled with the spread of Lutheran teaching, gave the burghers their first real chance against the patricians. Once the patrician council had been forced to make concessions, in 1529, the swing to the 'left' rapidly gathered momentum. By the spring of 1531 the popular and Protestant revolution was complete. The new regime, under the leadership of a Hamburg immigrant into Lübeck, Jürgen Wullenwever, badly needed a foreign policy success to maintain itself against the unforgiving hostility of the patricians. In 1533, Lübeck intervened once again in a Danish succession struggle in order to safeguard Hanseatic privileges against Dutch competition. But while in 1522–23 she had helped to break up the Union of Kalmar, the personal union of the crowns of the three Scandinavian kingdoms, she now tried to break up the kingdom of Denmark itself and set up Copenhagen and Malmö as independent city states. Lübeck herself was to acquire the fortresses of Elsinore (Helsingør) and Helsingborg, controlling the Sound, and the big Baltic islands of Bornholm and Gotland.

Here was a city state imperialism which matched that of Venice. It was, moreover, linked with social and religious revolution, for the burghers and peasants of Denmark rose against the hated nobles and prelates. In the summer of 1534 they controlled most of the country and the flagship of Lübeck levied the Sound tolls. In Rostock, Wismar and Stralsund, Wullenwever's agents helped to engineer the overthrow of the patrician councils. But the fear of social revolution, and Wullenwever's arrogant and inept diplomacy, brought Lübeck's neighbours together in an alliance as formidable as the League of Cambrai. Frederick I's son, Christian III, reconquered Denmark, in alliance with Danish and north German nobles and princes. The Lübeck squadrons were captured or surrendered to the combined Danish, Norwegian, Swedish and Prussian fleets – through the treachery of Lübeck's aristocratic commanders, it was said. In August 1535 Wullenwever resigned from his burgomastership. He was later captured and, apparently illegally, condemned to death (1537). Only the common people mourned him:

The Lübeckers will, to their very last breath,
Lament Master Wullenwever's death.*

'Die von Lübeck werden in allen Tagen
Den Tod Herrn Jürgen Wullenwevers beklagen'

Quoted in O. Kaemmel, *Illustrierte Geschichte der Neueren Zeit*, vol. 1 (Leipzig, 1882), p. 266.

The restored patrician regime of Lübeck cut its losses and concluded a not unfavourable peace with Denmark (Peace of Hamburg, 14 February 1536), leaving Copenhagen and Malmö to their fate: surrender to Christian III. Just like Venice, Lübeck survived her defeat commercially; but her role of a great power was at an end.

THE SOUTH GERMAN CITIES

Like Lübeck and the Italian city states, the south German cities, at the beginning of the sixteenth century, were under pressure from their princely neighbours. The princes wanted the towns to bear the cost of imperial government and defence while denying them the right to vote in the imperial Diets. The Diet of Nuremberg, 1522–23, proposed both the virtual destruction of the great trading and banking companies and an imperial customs duty which would fall chiefly on the merchants. The cities sent a joint delegation to the emperor in Spain and persuaded him to reverse the Diet's policy which the imperial government of his brother Ferdinand had, at first, accepted. For some years the emperor and the cities found it convenient to cooperate. At the Diet of Speyer, in 1526, a coalition of Catholic and evangelical cities persuaded Charles V to proclaim a religious truce. It seemed as if the cities had become a major political force in Germany. But the emperor's willingness to compromise on the religious issue, which was one of the principal reasons for his entente with the cities – the others were common economic interests and a common hostility towards the pretensions of the princes – was a purely tactical move, determined not by his position in Germany, but by his relations with France, the Papacy and the Turks. At the second Diet of Speyer, 1529, he returned to a severely anti-evangelical position. Some evangelical cities joined the evangelical princes in their famous protest; the coalition of Catholic and evangelical cities broke up, and the entente with the emperor dissolved.

Of the Protestant cities, only Nuremberg consistently maintained its pro-imperial policy. With their relatively large *contado*, constantly threatened by jealous neighbours, with their European-wide trade connections, and with the city's traditions as seat of the imperial government and frequent meeting place of the Diets, the Nuremberg patricians refused to join the Schmalkaldic League, Nuremberg managed to maintain both her independence and her Protestant religion; but she lost her political initiative and influence. So, equally, did the cities which joined the Schmalkaldic League; for Saxony and Hesse were its leaders and involved all its members in a common defeat, 1546–47 (see p. 239).

Only Strassburg, the leader of the south-west German cities, maintained an effective Protestant and independent policy of European significance throughout the reign of Charles V. Compared with Nuremberg, it was the very limitations of Strassburg's trading interests, in the upper Rhine valley, and her comparative remoteness from the centre of Habsburg power that enabled the city to pursue its anti-imperial policy. But, in the long run, Strassburg's resources were too limited to sustain the role of a great power. The defeat of the Schmalkaldic League drove her back onto the imperial side, and when she protested against some of the provisions of the Diet of Augsburg in 1555, no one took any more notice.

Thus the political importance which the south German cities seemed to enjoy in the early years of the Reformation was a spurious importance that depended on the vacillations of imperial policy. When these vacillations ceased, or even simply changed direction, the cities sank quietly and undramatically back into their customary political insignificance.

THE CITIES IN THE NETHERLANDS AND IN FRANCE

Outside the central European city belt, the towns had never been fully independent, but had often achieved considerable administrative autonomy. From the fifteenth century, the princes began to attack this autonomy. By 1500 the dukes of Burgundy had already greatly reduced the liberties of the Netherlands cities. Justice and police powers were in the hands of ducal officials and the central government exercised considerable influence over the appointment of the town councillors. In the sixteenth century the Habsburg rulers of the Netherlands used the pretext of every rebellion, or even bread riot, to eliminate the last vestiges of medieval popular rule, the participation of the guilds in the government of their cities. One aspect of the revolt of the Netherlands against Philip II was an attempt by the towns to reverse this trend and regain some of their former liberties (see p. 317).

In France the monarchy pursued an urban policy similar, at least in principle, to that of the Habsburgs in the Netherlands. 'The general government and administration of the kingdom . . . and also of our good towns and cities . . . belongs to us alone', Louis XI had declared as early as 1463.[20] In 1555 the supervision of city finances and, in 1567, all civil jurisdiction was placed in the hands of royal officials. But many cities obtained exemption from such interference and, even where the king's officials were received, they tended to become simply one more privileged and independent group inside the town, recruited locally and with local interests, manœuvring for power against the city corporation, the cathedral chapter, the parlement or any other body with autonomous rights.[21]

During the Wars of Religion the towns suffered heavily. 'The present war is waged only against the burghers of the towns and the people of God . . .' declared a famous political pamphlet of 1594,[22] 'the nobles and soldiers are having a good war and the burghers are paying for everything'. At the same time, the citizens of the towns became the political pacemakers of the civil wars. It was they who made the effective revolutions and perpetrated the worst massacres. But the Huguenot citizens of La Rochelle or Montauban, and the Catholic citizens of Paris or Toulouse, were not thinking in terms of city state politics but were acting as members of nationwide political-religious parties. Nevertheless, while the monarchy was weak, the cities undoubtedly regained much of their medieval autonomy. Only in the seventeenth century, with the development of the system of intendants, did royal control over the towns become an administrative and political reality.

CASTILE AND THE REVOLT OF THE COMUNEROS

It was in Castile that the struggle between monarchy and towns occurred in its starkest political form in the sixteenth century; for here there were no religious issues involved. Traditionally, the

Castilian towns had been allies of the monarchy in its fight against the overmighty magnates – the exact opposite of the position normally obtaining in the Netherlands, where the dukes were usually allied with the great nobles against the overmighty cities. At the beginning of the sixteenth century the crown-town alliance in Castile began to break down. The towns resented the crown's insistence that their deputies to the cortes, the Castilian parliament, should have full powers; for this meant that they were more likely to accept the crown's tax proposals than if they were bound by definite instructions from the constituents. Even more, the towns disliked the corregidors, the royal officials who supervised their administration. During the eighteen months' regency of Cardinal Jiménes de Cisneros, between the death of Ferdinand the Catholic (January 1516) and the arrival of the new king, Charles of Burgundy (later, Charles V), the position of the crown deteriorated sharply. Grandees and towns manœuvred against each other, but combined to thwart the orders of the government. Charles, with his Burgundian court, neither reassured nor managed to impose himself on the Castilians. His election as emperor caused increased fears that he would neglect the country and leave it a prey to grasping foreigners.

The break came over a royal demand for money to finance Charles's journey to Germany. At the cortes of Coruña and Santiago in April 1520 the government had to bribe a large number of deputies to obtain even a bare majority of the votes of the eighteen towns traditionally represented at such assemblies. As Charles set sail, leaving the Netherlander Adrian of Utrecht (later Pope Hadrian VI) as governor, the towns, led by Toledo and Valladolid, repudiated their deputies, formed a league and set up a revolutionary government (junta).[23]

The royalists accused the comuneros of wishing to set up independent communes (Spanish: *comunidades*) on the Italian model; and in many of the towns the citizens did come together, deliberately and by oath to form a commune, to appoint their own officials and to govern themselves. But they went much further. The cities, they claimed, did not seek their private interests, as the nobles did; together they *were* the kingdom. It was a formulation that was even bolder than the official (though not private) claims of the Third Estate during the French Revolution in 1789, for these did not deny, as the comunero claim at least implicitly did, the existence of the orders of the clergy and nobility. It contrasted sharply with the orthodox sixteenth-century view, expounded by the government spokesman, bishop Mota, at the cortes of Coruña, that the estates were members of the king's person. To give effect to their claims, the junta demanded for the cortes the right to assemble on their own initiative and discuss all matters relating to the benefit of the crown and kingdom.[24]

Characteristically, the revolutionary implications of comunero claims were only fully appreciated when, in the winter of 1520–21, in the towns themselves power shifted more and more to popular and radical elements. The great nobles had at first remained neutral; for they, too, had been offended at the king's Burgundian councillors and their much-exaggerated plunder. Now they began to take alarm at a movement that was threatening to turn into a genuine social revolution and spread disaffection to their estates. In the towns most of the urban nobility deserted to the royalists. The nobles raised an army and routed the comunero forces at Villalar, 23 April 1521.

The defeat of the comunero movement broke the will and ability of the towns to resist the crown. Inevitably, the same was true of the cortes. On all important issues, especially taxation, the crown could now always get its way. Only in the kingdom of the crown of Aragon, Aragon itself, Catalonia and Valencia, did the Spanish towns maintain their autonomy unimpaired. This was still to become a major issue in the seventeenth century.

THE TOWNS IN EASTERN EUROPE

East of the central European city belt, in Brandenburg, Prussia and Poland, the monarchies had won their struggles against the autonomy of their towns as early as the fifteenth century by an alliance with the nobility; for both parties were agricultural producers who wanted to break the towns' control of their export trade. Only the largest cities, notably Danzig (Gdansk) and Königsberg, were still able to resist. But Berlin and most of the smaller towns lost the right to elect their town councils. Even where this did not happen, as in the Polish capital of Cracow, the role of the cities in the assemblies of estates became more and more insignificant. In Russia the towns, with the exception of the city state of Novgorod, had never developed as autonomous communes and were therefore in no position to resist the growing autocracy of the tsars. Even Novgorod had fallen to Ivan III, in 1475–78. Ivan IV abolished the last vestiges of its independence, in 1570, on the pretext of a pro-Lithuanian conspiracy in the city. His armies, which entered Novgorod without encountering any resistance, are said to have massacred some 15,000 of its inhabitants and transported thousands to Moscow and other places.

THE SOCIAL COMPOSITION OF TOWN COUNCILS

The sixteenth century saw the defeat of the independent city state, in both Italy and Germany, and the loss of administrative independence and autonomy of most towns in the great monarchies from Spain to Poland. In England, with the exception of London, the towns were small and never enjoyed a political independence equal to that of the great continental cities; there was nothing for the crown to attack. The social consequences of this defeat of the towns were everywhere similar: a strengthening of the patrician and conservative elements in the towns. The property-owning oligarchies were becoming, even more than they had been earlier, a kind of urban aristocracy. Public offices in the towns came to be monopolized by lawyers, sons of merchants, perhaps, but no longer merchants themselves. In France, in particular, they swelled the ranks of the same *noblesse de robe*, the 'pen of inkhorn gentlemen', as contemporaries called them, who filled the higher positions in the king's courts and who intermarried with the *noblesse dépée*, the older nobility, and this despite the anguished protests of the more conservative members of that order. They promoted the development of that strongly graded and intensely status-conscious class of the privileged which was to dominate the social and political life of France until the Revolution.

There was a very similar trend in the still independent cities of Germany and even in the only city which actually became an independent city state in the course of the sixteenth century, Geneva. While the community of citizens as a whole was regarded as the owner of the city's liberties, the citizens took an oath of fealty to the council. In practice the relationship between council and citizen body was therefore very similar to that between a prince and his subjects. It led to periodic conflicts

113

between them, especially over taxation, and tended to throw up the fundamental question of who had the ultimate right of decision. The answer to this question in Germany, even in the seventeenth and eighteenth centuries, was often a surprising one: the emperor.[25]

FOUR TYPES OF SUCCESSFUL CITIES

It was the cities trying to defend their medieval independence or autonomy which suffered defeat or decline in the sixteenth century. Other cities, pursuing different policies and fulfilling different political and economic functions, were remarkably successful. There were four types of these: first, the city which profited by new developments in international trade; second, the city which linked its economy deliberately with that of a great country (and this did not have to be the country in which it was situated); third, the capital of a monarchy; fourth, the city, or group of cities, which dominated a country larger than that of the usual medieval city state.

These types, especially the first three, were not mutually exclusive. To the fourth belonged the Swiss Confederation which we have discussed above (see p. 95) and the United Provinces of the Netherlands which are discussed in a different chapter (see pp. 311, 318). Antwerp was the archetype of the first two groups, exemplifying in its dazzling rise and dramatic fall both the opportunities and the dangers of trying to hold the centre of the stage of sixteenth-century economic life (see pp. 54ff). The career of Seville was scarcely less spectacular, but its decline, in the seventeenth century, much less precipitate. Antwerp and Seville were doing much too well within the framework of the Spanish empire to have any very strong hankering after political autonomy. Augsburg and Genoa, on the other hand, were old and proud city states. They belonged to our second group, of cities which deliberately linked their economy with that of a great country in which they were not situated. Socially, and even more, psychologically, their entrepreneurial class was very different from the tradition-bound patricians of Venice and Lübeck, anxiously trying to defend a crumbling commerical monopoly. The aristocratic merchants and bankers of Augsburg and Genoa turned resolutely towards new and expanding economic fields. In the process, Augsburg became as effectively a Habsburg city as Antwerp. Its one attempt at independent political action, when the popular Protestant party disastrously led the city onto the losing side of the Schmalkaldic War, only emphasized Augsburg's dependence on the Fugger and their imperial connection. In Genoa, the Doria family successfully maintained their, and the Spanish faction's, domination of the city. From the gaily painted façades of the splendid palaces, built for them by Galeazzo Alessi (1512–72), and in their refined faces and proud bearing which we know from Van Dyck's portraits of the 1620s, we can still catch a glimpse of this elegant and ruthless aristocracy who bargained an outlived dream of civic independence for fat commercial and banking profits and for Spanish and Neapolitan titles.

Scarcely less spectacular was the rise of Lisbon and of London, the one as centre and staple for the gold of Africa and the spices of Asia, the other as the export centre for some 80 per cent of English foreign trade. London and Lisbon fitted into both the first and the third of our groups, for they were, of course, capitals as well as trading centres. In the long run, this position was, even commercially, more useful to them than their medieval charters. Cities, however, could grow as capitals without being trading centres at all.

It doth infinitely avail to the magnifying and making cities great and populous the residency of the prince therein according to the greatness of whose empire she doth increase (wrote an acute Italian observer, Giovanni Botero, in 1588) for where the prince is resident, there also the parliaments are held, and the supreme place of justice is there kept. All matters of importance have recourse to that place, all princes and all persons of account, ambassadors of princes and of commonwealths, and all agents of cities that are subject make their repair thither; all such as aspire and thirst after offices and honours rush thither amain with emulation and disdain for others. Thither are the revenues brought that pertain unto the state, and there are they disposed of again.[26]

PARIS

Botero may well have had Paris in mind. Its only important institution making for 'greatness' that he did not mention was its

famous university with its even more famous theological faculty, the Sorbonne. Paris had never acquired a charter granting its citizens political liberty or their own jurisdiction. It had voluntarily taken the royal *fleur de lys* into its coat of arms. The Provost of the Merchants, the head of the corporation, was not a merchant at all, but a royal official. He and the aldermen (*échevins*) enjoyed noble status and, in consequence, were forbidden to exercise a trade. The rest of the corporation was a narrow oligarchy of property owners, easily controlled by the king – unless Paris was in a state of revolution.[27] Yet Paris was never a mere residence of its monarchs in the way that Florence came to be under the grand-dukes of Tuscany, or innumerable small *Residenzstädte* in Germany. In fact, the Valois kings often preferred to reside outside its oppressive and sometimes menacing urban atmosphere. But, from at least the fourteenth century, Paris played its role of capital, consciously and deliberately, in a way that no other European city, after imperial Rome and medieval Byzantium, had ever done. It was not only that the lawyers of the Parlement of Paris, and the jurists in their legal treatises, spread the customs of Paris over the whole of France; it was rather that Paris set the tone for the political life of the whole country. It was Paris which started the massacre of the Huguenots; it was Paris which organized the Holy League against Henry III and drove him from the city; and it was for the sake of Paris that Henry IV had to abjure his Protestant faith.

ROME

For Paris the sixteenth century was simply one, though a very important, century in its long rise. For Rome it was the century which transformed a relatively small medieval town of barely 20,000 inhabitants into a city of over 100,000, and the capital, not just of the Papal States, but of Catholic Christendom. It changed the name of the *campo vaccino*, the cow field, back to Forum Romanum, as an archaeological site and a tourist attraction. In 1526, just before Rome was sacked by the imperial armies, it had already 236 hotels and inns; at the end of the century, there were at least 360, plus innumerable furnished houses and rooms to let. Thus it was that during the jubilee year of 1600, Rome could

117

accommodate over half a million pilgrims. Everything was geared to this: there was one wineshop for every 174 inhabitants; there were hundreds of tailors, goldsmiths, manufacturers of *objets d'art* and religious souvenirs and, inevitably, street vendors. Yet all attempts to introduce a textile manufacturing industry into the city failed. Rome lived on the contributions of Catholic Europe, on the income of ecclesiastical offices and church lands, spent by their owners in the Eternal City; but, above all, it lived on its visitors: a city of beggars and prostitutes, of devoted clergy, pious pilgrims and indifferent tourists, of nobles and princes of the church, displaying their wealth and ruining their fortunes by sumptuous buildings and princely dowries to their daughters and nieces. Two things were necessary for success in Rome said St Carlo Borromeo, to love God and to own a carriage.[28]

IMPORTANCE OF AN URBAN NOBILITY

As towns lost their character of medieval communes, and as jurisdictional distinctions between town and country began to break down, the nobility began to play an ever-increasing role in city life. In Italy this was not a new phenomenon. Botero saw its implications. Noblemen living in cities would erect splendid town houses and spend large sums on their families and their retinues, and on entertainment, from which 'sundry arts of all sorts and kinds must needs increase to excellency'.[29] Botero contrasted the urban habits of living of the Italian nobility with the rural habits of the French and English aristocracy. Yet it was the Italians of the Renaissance who had also rediscovered the Roman practice of gracious country living in villas. In the third quarter of the sixteenth century, Andrea Palladio created a new, superbly elegant, classical style of country house architecture in the Veneto where the Venetian noblemen could live privately on their estates: publicly, the great senatorial families continued to reside in their magnificent Gothic and Renaissance *palazzi* on the Canal Grande. A century later, the English aristocracy began to imitate the Palladian style in their own country houses, but, characteristically, gave up the intimacy of Palladio's houses for the sake of size and magnificence.

Yet even in England and France the pull of the court, and the growing centralization of political and cultural life, attracted the aristocracy into the capitals. By 1600 London, Paris, Madrid and smaller capitals, such as Brussels, Munich and Vienna, could boast of fine, aristocratic town houses even if, in size, they rarely compared with the great *chateaux* on the Loire, the larger Elizabethan country houses or the baroque palaces of Rome. Gradually, the aristocratic taste for urban life began to spread. By the eighteenth century, the tone of Paris and London, even of Dublin and Edinburgh, was very aristocratic indeed.

FORTIFICATIONS AND TOWN PLANNING

It was inevitable that the political, economic and social transformations of the cities should be accompanied by transformations in their appearance. The round towers, linked by high curtain walls, so characteristic of medieval towns and castles, had to give way to low, thick earthworks, to withstand the greatly increased fire power of sixteenth-century artillery. Star-shaped bastions provided flanking fire against the attacker and became a characteristic feature of fortified cities until the beginning of the twentieth century. All this, however, was enormously expensive, and by 1600 not all fortress towns had been refortified in this way.

Even slower, because even more expensive, were the effects of a changing attitude towards town planning. Medieval towns, though often highly functional in their construction, were not strictly planned. Streets were often just passages between houses, and the central market square was simply a space left unbuilt. Even the famous grid pattern of the *bastides*, the new towns of the thirteenth century, was little more than a convenient surveyor's method of allotting individual building plots – just as it was to be in the towns of the American midwest. During the Renaissance the idea developed of combining functionalism with beauty by deliberate and rigorous planning. Leon Battista Alberti sketched an ideal city plan, closely modelled on one by Vitruvius. Leonardo devoted a few pages of his notebooks to the problem, with suggestive sketches of a city on three levels: the top one 'exclusively for the use of gentlemen. The carts and burdens for the use and convenience of the inhabitants have to go by the low ones,' the lowest level being canals.[30]

Palladio attached similar importance to the separation of pedestrians from wheeled traffic and hoped to achieve it by the extensive use of arcades, a method which, in fact, came to be widely adopted. Palladio wanted wide and beautiful avenues, leading from the city gates straight to the main square and subsidiary squares.[31] The most popular town plan, in the sixteenth century, was the radiocentric plan, in which all principal avenues radiated from a central square to the city gates. Such a plan satisfied both military and aesthetic requirements better than the grid pattern which was, however, still used in the middle of the century for the building of the new capital of Malta, Valetta. In 1593 the Venetians used a radiocentric plan by Scamozzi to build the small fortress town of Palma Nova, near Udine, where it can still be seen, almost unchanged. Other Italians and their pupils built the

Figure 4 Palma Nova, 1598.

small radio centric fortress towns of Vitry and Hesdin, in northern France, of Coeworden, in the Netherlands, and of Zamość, in southern Poland.

More important, however, than the building of small new towns was the systematic replanning of old cities. This could only be done partially and, in the sixteenth century, was confined mainly to Italian towns. The finest examples are in Venice and Rome. Jacopo Sansovino gave the Piazza San Marco and Piazzetta, in Venice, the famous shape and appearance which we now know. Equally well known is the Capitol (Campidoglio) in Rome with its open, sloping and irregular square and the dramatically placed antique equestrian statue of Marcus Aurelius. It was reconstructed, from 1564 onwards, from plans by Michelangelo. About this time, the popes, and especially Sixtus V (1585–90), began a systematic attack on the medieval jumble of Roman housing. Some of the great avenues planned and constructed during the last quarter of the sixteenth century, especially those radiating from the northern entrance to Rome, the present Piazza del Popolo, still dominate the modern topography of Rome.

The greatest period of pre-industrial town planning, from the seventeenth to the early nineteenth century, was still to come; but both its aims and problems were being outlined in the sixteenth. It was becoming clear that town planning was possible only where there was a strong political authority willing, if the need arose, to override private property rights. This existed both in Rome and in Venice, but it did not exist in London. Even where it did exist, people had to learn to use it. In 1517 Francis I founded Le Havre, simply as a harbour on the estuary of the Seine. But it soon became clear that a harbour could not function without a town, and the early history of this unwanted and unplanned town was a sorry one of land speculation, legal chicanery and feuds between officials and local magnates. Only in 1541 the crown accepted a plan for a proper town and set up the necessary authorities. It was not completed until the seventeenth century.[32]

The functional and aesthetic aims of the town planners were also becoming clear. Insofar as they were not military, they were closely connected with each other. The city was meant to impress, firstly by its layout, in which its different parts and subordinate centres were to be connected by straight avenues, very much like the formal Italian gardens which were just beginning to be imitated beyond the Alps. Secondly, the city was meant to

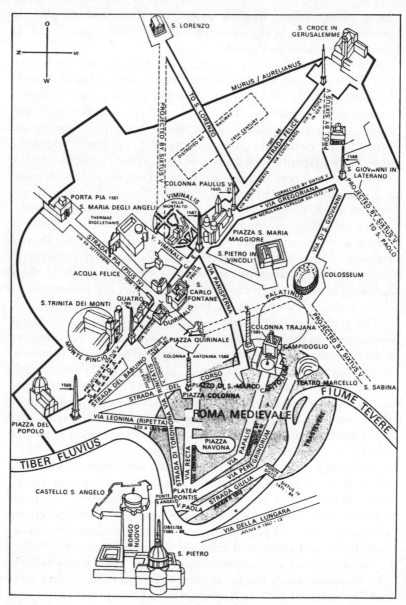

Figure 5 Rome: planning under Sixtus V.

impress by the magnificent façades of its churches and palaces, and by elaborate public fountains. Thirdly, and perhaps most important, it was meant to impress by monumental perspectives. The architects and town planners had learned this from the Renaissance and mannerist painters whose idealized architectural compositions they now began to translate from canvas into stone. To heighten the dramatic effect of perspective Sixtus V set up obelisks in front of St Peter's and in the Piazza del Popolo. Where the Renaissance statue had been related to a building – Verrocchio's Colleone in Venice, for example, or even much later Cellini's Perseus in Florence – the mannerist and the baroque statue was moved into the centre of a square, related no longer to a building but to a view. The possibilities of this new fashion for the glorification of the subject of such monuments were not lost on kings and princes. The baroque towns, as they began to be planned in the sixteenth century in Italy and developed over much of Europe in the seventeenth and eighteenth, became part of the deliberately dramatic and theatrical appeal of absolutist monarchy. Just as the new Baroque style of church decoration developed a deliberate popular appeal by making the interior of the church, and especially the high altar, into the kind of stage where mass was celebrated almost as a theatrical performance for an audience-like congregation, so the Baroque city became a huge theatrical setting for the display of the court, the princes of the church, the nobility and other rich and powerful persons. It was the visual aspect of the political and social change from the city state, with its free citizens, to the capital of the absolute monarch, with its court and its subject inhabitants.

· However, in spite of the growing importance and splendour of the cities, the peasantry still provided the modes of popular thought and aspirations for the vast majority of the European population. The Lutheran Reformation, as one of the most important events of the century, was set in a region devoid of large or important towns. Moreover, Martin Luther's own background was essentially non-urban (contrasting with that of Calvin). The peasants themselves were to play an important part, not only within Luther's closeness to popular piety, but also as a social and economic group in determining the course of his Reformation.

Nevertheless, many German cities and towns did adopt the reformed religion. To be sure, social resentments and economic tensions played their part: Lutheranism could be used as a cause in factional struggles and in the quest for municipal independence. However, in a city like Nuremberg, so important in the Reformation, such considerations seemed to have played a minor part in the adoption of Lutheranism.[33] A truer motive lay in the question asked by Lazarus Spengler, an important citizen: 'The fundamental question is: "Shall we be Christians or not?" ' The struggle for the Reformation was indeed over Christ and His Gospel . . . not politics or taxes or Luther himself'.[34] Despite the advances and growing complexity of urbanism and society in general, the appeal of the Reformation was directed towards man's fears and doubts, towards clarifying his existential situation. As such it proved to have a dynamic of its own, which, in turn, reacted upon the historical reality of the century.

NOTES AND REFERENCES

1   J. C. Davis, *The Decline of the Venetian Nobility as a Ruling Class* (Baltimore, 1962), p. 18 and *passim*.

2   W. G. Hoskins, *Provincial England* (London, 1963), pp. 83 ff.

3   Koenigsberger, 'Property and the price revolution', and 'The Parliament of Piedmont during the Renaissance', in *Estates and Revolutions* (Ithaca and London, 1971), pp. 144–65: 42–47.

4   Quoted in V. Pearl, *London and the Outbreak of the Puritan Revolution* (Oxford, 1961), p. 38.

5   P. Mols, 'Die Bevölkerungsgeschichte Belgiens im Lichte der heutigen Forschung', *Vierteljahrschrift für Sozial- und Wirtschaftsgeschichte*, vol. XLVI (1959), p. 509.

6   Quoted in M. V. Clarke, *The Medieval City State* (London, 1926), p. 165.

7   H. Mauersberg, *Wirtschafts- und Sozialgeschichte zentraleuropäischer Städte in neuerer Zeit* (Göttingen, 1960), p. 119.

8   H. Baron, 'Machiavelli: the Republican Citizen and the Author of "The Prince"', *English Historical Review*, vo. LXXVI, no. 299, 1961.

9   Machiavelli, *Discourses*, bk 1, ch. 18. Quoted *ibid.*, p. 232.

10   'Discorso delle cose florentine dopo la morte di Lorenzo', also quoted *ibid.*, p. 235.

11   Quoted in R. von Albertini, *Das florentinische Staatshewusstsein im Ubergang von der Republik zum Prinzipat* (Berne, 1955), p. 232.

12   The foregoing discussion follows Albertini, *Das florentinische Staatshewusstsein*, pp. 282 ff. The Florentine writers of the first half of the sixteenth century are still very readable. There are several English translation of Machiavelli and Guicciardini.

13   P. de Comines, *Les Memoirs*, ed. G. Calmette, vol. III (Paris, 1925), p. 110. Also quoted in F. Chabod, 'Venezia nella Politica Italiana de Europea del Cinquecento', in *La Civilta Veneziana del Rinascimento* (Venice, 1958), p. 29.

14   Quoted in L. von Ranke, *History of the Latin and Teutonic Nations*, transl. G. R. Dennis (London, 1909), p. 297.

15   F. Gregorovius, *History of the City of Rome in the Middle Ages*, trans. A. Hamilton, vol. VIII, pt. 1 (London, 1902), p. 63, n. 1.

16   For the economic recovery of Venice, see p. 52.

17   E. Albèri, *Relazioni degli Ambasciatori Veneti*, ser. LL, vol. III, p. 178.

18   *Ibid*, ser. I, vol. I. pp. 339 ff.

19   R. Häpke, 'Der Untergang der hansischen Vormachtstellung in der Ostsee', in *Hansische Geschichtsblätter*, vol. XVIII (1912), pp. 95 ff.

20   Quoted in C. Petit-Dutaillis, *Les Communes françaises* (Paris, 1947), p. 238, n.a.

21   Cf. 'The Monarchies', pp. 286 ff.

22   *Dialogue d'entre le Maheustre et le Manant* (Paris, 1594), p. 33.

23   H. G. Koenigsberger, 'The Powers of Deputies in Sixteenth-Century Assemblies'. *Estates and Revolutions*, pp. 183–9.

24   For a discussion of the political thought of the comunero movement, cf. J. A. Maravall, *Las Comunidades de Castilla* (Madrid, 1963).

25   O. Brunner, 'Souveränitätsproblem . . . in den deutschen Reichstädten . . .'. *Vierteljahrschrift für Sozial- und Wirtschaftsgeschichte*, vol. 1. (Nov, 1963).

26   G. Botero, *Of the Greatness of Cities*, trans. Robert Peterson, 1606; ed. P. G. and D. P. Waley (London, 1950), bk II, ch. II.

27   R. Mousnier, *Paris, Fonctions d'une capitale*. Colloques, Cahiers de Civilisation (Sèvres, 1963), pp. 66–71 and *passim*.

28   For the last paragraph cf. J. Delumeau, *Vie économique et sociale et Rome dans la seconde moitié du XVIe siècle*, 2 vols. (Paris, 1957–59).

29 G. Botero, *Of the Greatness of Cities*, bk. V, ch. 10.

30 Leonardo da Vinci, *The Literary Works*, vol. II, 2nd edn, ed. and trans. by J. P. Richter (London, 1939), pp. 21 ff.

31 A. Palladio, *I Quattro Libri dell'Architettura* (Venice, 1570), lib. 3, cap. L.

32 P. Lavedan, *Histoire de l'Urbanisme. Renaissance et temps modernes* (Paris, 1941), pp. 93 ff.

33 Gerald Strauss, *Nuremberg in the Sixteenth Century* (New York, 1966), p. 169.

34 *Ibid.*, p. 173.

6

CHRISTIANITY, POPULAR CULTURE AND HUMANISM

The Reformation was the central fact which dominated the first half of the sixteenth century. Martin Luther wrought his deed against a background of political tension and social change, but even more relevantly against the canvas of men's lives themselves. The kind of life which men lived at the turn of the sixteenth century, and the questions which they asked about it, are essential to an understanding of the Reformation, and beyond this to the sixteenth century as a whole. Concrete fears and very real dilemmas determined the structure of men's thought, although in the sixteenth century the meaning of life and the final answers about what life holds in store for men were cast within a Christian context, and it is the tone of Christian life at the turn of the century which provides the indispensable background to the rise of Protestantism and the end of the *Respublica Christiana* of the Middle Ages.

THE TENOR OF LIFE

The life which men lived varied greatly according to the social position in which they found themselves. Not only did this hold for the material comforts but also for the cast of mind with which they approached the problems of their times. Class differences were enormous and generally recognized as such. The princes and nobles were one class which decisively influenced events, but the members of the world of learning, the intellectuals, formed another separate class at a time when their number was relatively small. The urban

127

classes were rising in importance and becoming selfconscious. The vast majority of the population consisted of peasants, far removed from the other classes which were rapidly becoming more sophisticated in their attitudes towards life. But separate though these classes were, and indeed thought themselves to be, they still shared an attitude towards life, not just Christian, but linked also by irrationalism and fear. The gap between the peasant and the educated was much less in the realm of thought than in the realities of power and style of life. For example, the intellectuals, the humanists, can no longer be regarded as the first modern rationalists, since it is now recognized that they shared many of the irrational presuppositions and prejudices of their less learned, indeed ignorant, fellow men. All these diverse classes were linked in a Christian piety which, however diverse, embraced the religious excitement and the heightened search for answers to life's problems which dominated the period between the fifteenth and the sixteenth centuries.

RELIGIOUS SENSIBILITIES

Historians have been struck by this singular ferment within Christianity, the heightened religious sensibilities, the almost obsessive preoccupation with death, salvation, and the future of man. There were good reasons why this should have occurred. Times were bad, beyond anything which men could recall. Several factors built up a momentum which took on catastrophic proportions. The last decades of the fifteenth century were years of price fluctuation caused by bad harvests; the year 1500 saw a total crop failure in all of Germany. The peasants reacted with violence. In Alsace they founded a conspiratorial organization to overthrow the existing order (*the Bundschuh*) but everywhere in the Empire looting and pillaging took on such proportions that by 1501 a paid police force became a necessity for the first time.

Rising prices and bad harvests were accompanied by the ravages of war. The wars of rival factions in Switzerland (1499) affected not only this region but also Swabia and the Tyrol. Whole villages were depopulated and the bonds of the old and settled order were utterly destroyed. For all this, these scourges which descended upon man were less important than the inroads made by epidemics. The plague, and a new disease, syphilis, seemed to herald a coming change in the order of things, that great catastrophe which precedes the 'total reformation' of man and society about which medieval prophecy had spoken so eloquently.

Few epidemics have been more upsetting to the life of western man than the plague. It was an epidemic which struck with deadly force, and would subside only to return again. Thus it seemed to be a wilful and arbitrary chastisement: it was deemed impossible to know when it would strike and what could be done to make it vanish. The fourteenth century had seen at least four major outbreaks of the Black Death and now, at the end of the fifteenth century, the plague struck once more. Between 1499 and 1502 the populations of many regions of Europe were decimated, and it has been estimated that in the Rhineland and Swabia half the population died.

But death seemed to have not one but two scythes. Syphilis flared up in a sudden, intense, and epidemic manner in the last years of the fifteenth century. Contemporaries thought it to be 'new', were appalled by its ravages upon the human form and by the painful death which most often terminated the disease. Great efforts were made to combat it. For example, towards the end of the fifteenth century, the city of Frankfurt provided not only free medical treatment, but also tax exemption for the duration of the cure. However, at the beginning of the new century it was regarded as a catastrophe for which the only explanation could be the wrath of God. From 1500 on it became usual for preachers to call for penance and special pilgrimages in order to stem the inroads of syphilis. All efforts were in vain, for syphilis had come to join the plague in order to demonstrate further the dangers and brutality of life to the peoples of Europe.

Such is the background to the heightened religious sensibility at the turn of the century which gripped all the diverse classes of the population. Men believed that there must be some sense to this chaos and they found it by turning to various sources of inspiration in order to overcome the unpalatable present. The approach of the learned, the humanists, was obviously different from that of the vast majority of the population. But they were also affected by the search for solutions which influenced popular forms of thought and expression. No new modes of expression were 'invented', but instead medieval traditions were used and given a heightened application.

POPULAR PIETY AND PROPHECY

'Popular piety' is the phrase best suited to describe those forms and modes of expression which were shared by a majority of the population at a time when men's consciousness of themselves and their world moved within a Christian, if not always orthodox context. Popular piety represents the hopes and aspirations of the multitude whose religious awareness tends to be immediate and naive. The practices of popular piety functioned as dynamic social myths, reaffirming community and kinship ties, reconciling man to God and seeking to secure divine aid for the problems of human existence.

Popular piety looked to the Church as a reservoir of magical assistance available to men and women in their every-day lives. Its blessings in the form of holy water, exorcisms and charms, could ward off fire, disease or sudden death. The ringing of consecrated church bells might prevent storms, while formal priestly curses protected crops from the ravages of insects and weeds. Holy water was generally thought effective against animal disease, and peasants crossed over from Protestant to Catholic regions in order to obtain this medicine. The saints of the Church could always be petitioned in the case of need: St Margaret availed for labour pains and St Job was sought by those suffering from the pox.[1] The local saint was of special importance, and whole villages or towns considered themselves under his protection, turning to him first in times of crisis such as the plague, famine or civil discord. The rituals and processions which popular piety prescribed for the veneration of saints reinforced communal ties and enhanced local pride. Local or professional loyalties were channelled into many religious confraternities as well, in which laymen could participate. Based on the guild or the neighbourhood, these groups, which employed their own salaried clergy and often had their own chapel, functioned as devotional associations and as means to ensure prayers and masses for deceased members. But they also functioned as service clubs, sponsoring religious drama and local festivals and took an important part in carnivals, the most popular festivals of the year which preceded the fasting season of Lent.

The sacraments of the Church provided an essential focus for popular piety. Baptism, first communion and weddings were not only religious ceremonies but also rites of passage marked with banqueting, dancing and singing, often in a carnivalesque atmosphere. Events in the Church calendar such as St John's eve or the Feast of the Assumption could prompt bonfires in which the Christian message had to compete with folk ritual and custom. Indeed, any special occasion in the Christian year was used to celebrate festivals. This mixture of the sacred with the profane was a marked feature of pre-reformation popular piety which saw nothing untoward in using the Church or its ceremonies for purposes that were not exclusively religious.

The revival within popular piety of ideas of prophecy and hope were of greatest importance, and fuelled the medieval search for the millenium.

While the present could only be viewed with pessimism, there might be hope for the future: the age of darkness would give way to the age of light. Pessimism led to a belief that the end of the world was in sight, that the world was running towards the abyss. Martin Luther himself lived in the expectation of such an end. But this view of the end of the world did not stand in naked isolation; it was systematized and elaborated. The thought of the medieval mystic Joachim of Fiore (d. 1201) proved decisive here, as it had been in previous centuries. Joachim believed that history ascended through three successive ages culminating in the 'age of the spirit' which would be the golden age enduring until the Last Judgment. But every new age was ushered in by a period of incubation which saw great disturbances in the existing order of things. Such a view coincided with the interpretations of the books of the Apocalypse in the Bible: here also it was thought that bloody wars and chaotic conditions would be necessary to unseal the book with the seven seals. Obviously such thought fitted the pessimism of the times, yet gave hope that this was a prelude to better things.

Astrology went hand in hand with the Joachimite prophecies. Typical of this was the most popular book of prophecy in central Europe: Lichtenberger's *Prognostications*. Written in 1488, it went through one edition after another; Luther read it and discussed it in his 'Table Talk', and so did most men from the learned to the ignorant. For Lichtenberger the stars are demonic powers; the world of the skies is connected with the world of man; the upper influences the lower in the hierarchy of world and heaven. The conjunction of planets has an immediate effect upon men. Saturn being traditionally a planet much feared by astrologers, the conjunction of Saturn and Jupiter was held responsible for the appearance of syphilis on earth; the bad planet had eclipsed Jupiter, the good one, and won his omnious victory. Lichtenberger set up a series of horoscopes which, for several short decades, prophesied wars, rebellions and plagues. But he ended by forecasting a golden age, a 'new Reich', and universal peace. The present age was, therefore, an age of continual transition, providing an uninterrupted series of catastrophes.

THE JEWS

The conjunction of stars was unfavourable, but there were those who symbolized on earth the evils which the heavens portended. The Jews, the witches, and the corrupt Church were (for such prophecy) an unholy trinity which must be replaced by a Christianity restored. For Lichtenberger the triumph of Saturn meant that the Jews would rise for a time to dominant positions in the Empire. The Jews were the anti-Christians, and the many legends of their desecration of the host are always combined with the miracles which even the host so desecrated still performs. The years between 1450 and 1510 saw an almost floodlike increase in the accusations of ritual murder: the Jews were accused of slaughtering a Christian child in order to drink its blood. It was such an accusation which served as the ostensible reason for the expulsion of the Jews from Spain (1492). There can be little doubt that this increase of the 'blood accusation' was connected with the atmosphere of pessimism and catastrophe we have described. It was one more sign of the times which were 'out of joint'. Even the arch-humanist Conrad Celtis repeated such accusations against the Jews.

The belief in the Jew as Antichrist was combined with the equally deeply held belief that his conversion was a necessity in order that the Joachimite 'age of the spirit' might begin. The depth of their evil contrasted with the anticipated glory of their conversion. The book of the Apocalypse provided the evidence. The harvest must be reaped before the book of the seven seals would reveal its mystery. Luther shared this belief fully. If his was the true reformation of Christianity, the harbinger of the new age, then the Jews would be converted. They refused, and he now advocated eradicating them from the surface of Europe, burning their synagogues and forbidding their religion. The guilt they represented must now be exterminated in radical fashion, and Luther believed that those like Thomas Münzer who distorted the true faith were in fact building on Jewish doctrine.

The Jews themselves were in particular need of encouragement as the sixteenth century opened, having passed through a painful period of persecution such as their expulsion from Spain (1492). They found new hope in Martin Luther as they saw their persecutor, the Catholic Church, discomfitted, and, more important, because many Jewish sages believed that this reformation of Christianity was a first step in Christianity's return to Judaism, deemed essential before the Messiah could come.[2] Both Luther and the Jews were disappointed in the role which they had assigned to each other's conversion as heralding the golden age. But for the Jews the consequences of this disappointment were grim, as mainstream Protestant persecution often proved more unyielding than that of the Catholic Church. They were caught between the two reformations, forced in the sixteenth century to attend Christian 'services of conversion', and this in both Protestant regions like Hesse and in Catholic regions including the City of Rome. However, in the end, Jews tended to side with the Catholic and Imperial cause, and this in spite of the fact that it was precisely the Catholic reformation which attempted to bring about the complete isolation of the Jews.

The first ghetto was established in Venice in 1516 on an island which had been the site of a foundry: the name 'ghetto' derives from the Italian, to pour or to cast. Here the Jews were confined to a walled-up quarter which they were only to leave on certain hours of the day. Jews had been admitted to Venice as useful money-lenders only in 1509, and this against the strenuous opposition of the Church, and it was under clerical pressure that the ghetto was established. Pope Paul IV (Carafa), the most intransigent pope of the Catholic reformation, introduced the ghetto into the papal states and in addition forbade Jews to hire Christian servants or to own real estate.[3] He justified this action in his Bull, *Cum nimis absurdum* (1555), claiming that the Jews were condemned to eternal slavery because of their guilt. Some Italian states like Florence and Padua followed the Pope's example, while a few cities in Central Europe created their own ghettos. The very word 'ghetto' eventually became diluted, often applied to dense areas of Jewish settlement, like those in nineteenth century Russia, even though Jews had freedom of movement and lived among Christians. The true meaning of 'ghetto' designated a separate system of government under which Jews were forced to live as a result of Christian fervour demanding as complete a separation as possible.

Yet in reality this separation was never anything like complete, Jews and Christians interacted even as ghettos were being established and the pressure for conversion increased. They dealt with each other not just in trade and commerce but on an intellectual level as well. Jewish scholars were in demand as teachers of Hebrew and of the mysteries of the Cabala. The Christian humanists were interested in penetrating secrets about the universe which the medieval Church seemed to have hidden from view, but they also sought to study the Cabala for what it might tell them about the coming of Christ. This Christianization of the Cabala distressed Jewish scholars, but still they introduced Christians to its symbols and to the Hebrew language. Perhaps here was one of the first times when Jewish learning was of direct influence upon Christian scholarship. Thus, for example, the famous Jewish scholar Leon of Modena entered into a dialogue with Christian humanists from out of the ghetto of Venice where he lived. Such lively intellectual exchange did not touch official hostility or the increasing efforts to control and isolate the Jews during the sixteenth century.

The image of the Jews as Antichrist and as evil usurer remained much more effective than that of the Jewish scholar, especially in times of bad harvests and rising prices. Jews continued to be viewed as an evil, part of humanity's burden of guilt, which had to be made evident through their treatment. This image of the Jew was encouraged by great preachers in an age fond of preaching. Thus Fra Bernardino da Feltre incited the population to violence against the Jews (using above all, the ritual murder accusation) throughout Italy and on the borders of Germany as well. At the same time he established loan banks (Monte di Pietà) in order to eliminate what he called 'jewish usury'.

Here the trend in popular culture diverged from the thoughts of those who constituted the learned classes of Europe. Many humanists deplored this finding of guilt. Melanchthon, Luther's good right arm, a humanist, rescued Jews from accusation of ritual murder. The emperor Charles V, who had received a humanist education, gave to the Jews the most liberal privileges then in existence (1554): accusations about ritual murder must wait upon his own personal judgement, and no Jew should be physically attacked and deprived arbitrarily of his belongings. This privilege forms a startling contrast to Luther's attitude, and indeed to that of popular culture. The search for those guilty in the present, and the expectation of the golden age, combined to see in the Jews the Antichrist who according to prophecy would come to the fore in a time of troubles.

The Jews were the victims of the general drive to Christianize Europe, to bring any form of belief or behaviour not sanctioned by the established Church under control. The Jews were caught in this drive regardless whether the official Church was Catholic or Protestant, but the primary target was popular piety, itself hostile to Jews. This piety consisted of folk beliefs and customs which, though of Christian inspiration, threatened to bypass the Church and its dogma. The mass persecution of witches in the sixteenth century was in part an attempt to come to grips with popular piety in order to Christianize peasant society.

WITCHES AND NECROMANCERS

Witches were joined to Jews as demonstrating the preponderance of evil which flowed from the 'house of Antichrist'. The belief in witchcraft had its roots in popular culture, white magic was said to be good and black magic was considered evil. Magic was taken seriously as a practical undertaking, a way of making sense of the universe. People were afraid for good reason, given the mortality rate, frequent famine and recurrent outbreaks of the plague. They distrusted all natural and human forces and instead turned to the supernatural for protection, to the Saints, to wizards, and to the use of magic potions, all of which not even the Reformation could stamp out in its territories. The witch was the malignant opposite of the Saints and those helpful wizards who could find lost property, capture thieves and cure disease. Why the witch craze should have spread through Europe precisely in the years from roughly 1500 to 1680 is still not satisfactorily explained. To the daily fears of men and women was added the feeling that they were living in a final period of time, just before the end of the world and the Last Judgement. More concretely, the drive by Catholics and Protestants to christianize rural society played an important part in unleashing the witch craze, and once the persecution began the accused under torture implicated others until many thousands were involved. Moreover, the judicial bureaucracy now took beliefs in witchcraft for granted and acted accordingly. They did not, as did the common people, view witchcraft in terms of the harm done by witches, but saw in it the result of a pact with the devil which challenged all secular and ecclesiastical authority.[4]

Thus the accusation of heresy added to that of black magic around the year 1500 was crucial to the extent and effectiveness of the accusations which followed. The witch had become a tool of the devil as in the *Malleus maleficarum* (The Witches Hammer) compiled between 1487 and 1488 by the Dominicans Heinrich Institorus and Jacob Sprenger. The book codified the belief in witches for the sixteenth and seventeenth centuries, a handbook used at witch trials. They were now said to be slaves of the devil and his sexual lovers besides. The orgies which were said to take place at their meetings with the devil, the so-called witches sabbath, saw gluttony, riotous dancing and the practice of so-called perverted sex with the devil and among themselves. The witch stood society on its head, the counter-type to all that was considered normal and acceptable. The devil literally branded the witch as his creature, and finding the 'devil's mark', an insensible spot or scar, was a regular feature of witchcraft trials. Here the belief of the educated in the reality of the devil reinforced popular fears, but never entirely: in England, for example, the accusation of devil worship was never important, instead witchcraft trials were mainly based upon popular fears of black magic.

The vast majority of witches were women, though a great many men were also tried. Women were the most vulnerable members of the community, considered sexually more voracious than men, emotionally unstable and needing the firm guiding hand of a husband. Their position was dangerously exposed if they practised a profession like midwifery, or were poor and dependent widows or beggar women, village scolds or gossips. Giving birth in the sixteenth century entailed high risk for mother and child, surrounded by magical incantations and blessings. The midwife was always under suspicion if something went wrong, and from the mid-fifteenth century on, some authorities made midwives swear on oath never to murder a new born child or to disguise the mother's maternity. Poor beggar women or widows were usually dependent upon the community, and if they had been refused charity were thought to lay a curse upon households and livestock.

These women, including the scold and the gossip, stood out from those women who conformed to the passive role assigned to them and therefore were ready targets for witchcraft persecutions.

Demographic factors played their role in this attack upon women as witches. The sixteenth century saw a sizable increase in single women from 5 per cent of the population to even 15 or 20 per cent in some regions of Europe. Late marriages also increased the pool of single and dependent women. These stood outside the established family hierarchies, no doubt giving additional currency to the widely held notion that women were disorderly and rebellious unless taken in hand by men. The mass persecution of women as witches addressed deep-seated fears of society that the hierarchical order, symbolized by the patriarchal family, might be in danger: such women without men might turn the world upside down. Moreover, the fact that the mortality of men in the periodic outbreaks of the plague was much greater than that of women, not only meant that women were open to accusations of causing plague, but must have led to a still greater awareness of the potential threat of women to male society and therefore to the established order of things. The Protestant Reformation did not affect the witch craze which, for example, was encouraged by Jesuits and Huguenots alike.

The end to the witchcraft craze in immediate terms came because it had run itself dry. The anarchy caused by the trials, the potential menace to so many innocent people, produced a kind of revulsion tinged by fear. Witch hunters became uncertain of how to find still more witches for their judicial machine, and though they themselves still believed in the existence of witches, became increasingly disenchanted with their task.[5] But the end of the belief in witchcraft came with the slow rise of scepticism and rationalism among the intellectual elite who refused to entertain any more witchcraft persecutions by the beginning of the eighteenth century, though a changing image of women also cut much ground from under the accusations of witchcraft. The opposition which was finally to triumph was already foreshadowed in the sixteenth century, during the height of the witchcraft craze. The Reformers believed in the devil and in witches, but their contention that it was impossible to live a chaste life served to lessen the sexual frustrations so obvious in the invention of the witches' sabbath, and their advocacy of the partnership of marriage as central to the christian life, eventually served to increase the status of women, though this would not be obvious for another century and a half.

More important, a book like Reginald Scott's *Discoverie of Witchcraft* (1584) anticipated learned opinion in the next century, when it denied the possibility that witches could have made a pact with the devil or used the supra-natural for their own purposes. They were cunning women who probably used poison to accomplish their end. He was not concerned with the contention whether they were witches or not, but solely with the claim that they performed miraculous works. Similar isolated and sceptical voices, searching for a reasonable answer to witchcraft can be found on the continent of Europe. But it was not until the seventeenth century that doubt became a respectable philosophy and that even most theologians gave up the belief in the corporeal existence of the devil. The belief in witches continued as a part of popular piety, increasingly divorced from educated opinion. But in the sixteenth century the common search for explanations of evil times did not stop with Jews and witches, some saw the unreformed Church itself as responsible for the evils which the times portended.

THE CHURCH ACCUSED

In the course of his prophecies Lichtenberger had lamented the decline of the Church: 'like a tree without fruit, the head of the Church will leave this world'. The present state of the Church seemed to symbolize the times as much, or indeed even more, than Jews and witches. Here everyone was immediately involved; if there was to be salvation, the instrument of salvation was contaminated. It was the 'blind leading the blind', as a north German poem has it. For the more sophisticated, the clergy were a constant target for ridicule, for the simple, an open scandal. The often characterized 'abuses' of the Church must be seen within this context.

The popular play *Of the Rise and Fall of Antichrist*, one of the oldest German popular dramas, was often performed in the sixteenth century. Antichrist triumphs over the kings and emperors, but especially over a Church which had already received him in its heart for a long time. This is proved by the vanity of the clergy: 'God does not love worldly priests.' Though in the end God destroys Antichrist in the play, it was a much more difficult matter to destroy an Antichrist who, as part of existing reality, owned nearly a third of the German lands.

The objection was not merely to the wealth of the Church, to its administrative and political preoccupations, but to the fact that all of these endangered the Church's mission. It was intimately involved in existing society and politics and therefore was a part of the corruption and decline of the period. The Church should give an example of the 'age of the spirit' to come, but how could it do this when it served as a prop of the age that was in being? It sold ecclesiastical offices (simony) just as any territorial ruler, a fee was levied for the grant of bishoprics, and claims for taxes like 'Peter's Pence' in England completed a popular picture of greed rather than piety. Satires like Sebastian Brant's *Ship of Fools* (1494) pictured all clerics as greedy and worldly, part and parcel of the worst side of the existing order. Such attitudes were not new; indeed, Joachim of Fiore and some Franciscans had held them during the Middle Ages. Now such thought again had relevance. It became a part of the call towards a 'total reformation' which would not only take in the Church but go beyond this to change the whole of the present in order to prepare for a brighter future.

A 'TOTAL REFORMATION'

Typical for this desire is the *Reformatio Sigismundi* (1439), a document which appeared at the end of the Hussite wars in Bohemia, and which appealed for a change in the hierarchial feudal order. The appeal found an echo, for its popularity lasted well into the sixteenth century.[6] It did call upon the Emperor Sigismund to put an end to senseless war but, below the emperor, the whole structure of society was to undergo revolutionary change. Clerics must become mere state officials, monasteries and convents be stripped of their worldly possessions — indeed the priesthood as a special class was to be eliminated. In addition, other powerful interest groups must be abolished: the big trading companies which drove up prices and the guilds which perpetuated the power of one man over another. Finally, serfdom must vanish from the land. Under the mantle of demanding a 'total reformation' as the way out of present dilemmas, this was a revolutionary document. It advocated not only a return to complete poverty by the Church, but also an equalitarian social order where serfdom was abolished and wages and prices fixed to serve the interests of the poor. What is most important for our period is the despair in the Church's ability to reform itself. Instead, the *Reformatio* looked to a reformed emperor to restore a decayed Church.

Joachim of Fiore had already called upon a secular king to chastise the corrupt and worldly Church. Such ideas never died out in the Middle Ages, regardless of the actual course of the struggle between pope and emperor. For Joachim such a king was part of the Antichrist who would eventually be destroyed but who first had the task of putting an end to the corrupt Church. The dream of the 'emperor saviour' transformed him into the prophet who would indeed end the present order, who was needed to usher in the golden age. Catastrophic times lend themselves to dreams of an earthly Messiah who would come to the rescue, and we find this in all European countries as the sixteenth century opens. A concrete fact came to the support of the dream, for the emperor had tried to reform the Church at the councils of Constance and Basle. Moreover, an elementary kind of nationalism is involved; the decline of the Church, of Christianity, meant the decline of the nation as it did of the whole world. Within the Empire it was a 'future Emperor Frederick' who was to put down Jews and clerics, make the poor rich, and reform the papacy. He was to be the emperor of the golden age, who, now asleep in the Thuringian mountains, would rise again. The *Reformatio Sigismundi* at times spoke of a peasant emperor, and so did the chronicles which come to us from Bohemia.

The ideal of the peasant emperor as saviour was typical of that trend in popular culture which wanted to liquidate present society by going back to the original man, to come as close to the biblical paradise as possible. Adam was believed to have been the first peasant (thus those who held these ideas were called the Adamites) and this image implied a social and economic equality now denied to most men. Radicals like the Lollards in England and some of the Hussites occasionally adopted such ideas. But even the learned Carlstadt, Luther's colleague, bought a farm after becoming a radical reformer and became for a short time a peasant, the Wittenberg professor behind the plough. Here messianic longings and romanticism were mixed with a real social urge towards an equalitarian society.

Side by side with the 'emperor saviour' an older Joachimite idea also persisted: that of the *pastor angelicus*, the pope who would arise in order to usher in the age of the spirit which a strong king had helped to prepare. But the idea of empire seemed stronger than the *pastor angelicus*. In France, Charlemagne replaced the German

Frederick as the centre of these longings. The Spanish kings regarded themselves as messiah–emperors in this tradition; Spain had undertaken the final conversion of Jews, Muslims and gentiles foreshadowing the rapid approach of the end of the world. Here another factor enters: the founding of the Spanish world empire. The Spanish discovery of the new world was linked to the millenarian and apocalyptic vision of converting all the races of the world. This seemed to be the Spanish mission, and therefore the Spaniards were the chosen people, their king the 'emperor saviour'. Columbus himself firmly believed in this mission. The gold of the Indies was to be used to rebuild the temple of Jerusalem; the discovery of America was a crusade, the last crusade, for it heralded the end of the world. By 1501 Columbus proclaimed himself the Joachimite messiah who had helped usher in the 'age of the spirit', and indeed the discovery of America had brought the world to the threshold of the Last Judgment, the fulfilment of human history.[7]

SAVONAROLA

Not only were these ideas current in the north of Europe and in Spain, but Italy provides the most direct example of a 'prophet reborn', of a people believing themselves to be chosen to reform the world and to liquidate the present age. The Dominican friar Girolamo Savonarola (1452–98) started, like many others, by calling the citizens of Florence to do penance in order to absolve the guilt of humanity for the catastrophes of the times. But he became much more than such a prophet during his domination of the city of Florence (1494–98), which began when King Charles VIII of France successfully invaded Italy. For him Charles VIII was God's avenging instrument, the Antichrist so necessary to punish evil and to make possible a new age. God had decided to cleanse his Church with great punishment and to institute reform. These are the same ideas which we have seen expressed in the north of Europe. For Savonarola the *pastor angelicus* of the Joachimite tradition, the reforming pope, would after all these tribulations restore the Church to its purity and thus save mankind.

But such medieval tradition was combined with civic, Florentine, pride. Charles VIII had bypassed Florence, and this was now taken to mean that the city was selected as the divine instrument of reform. From this Savonarola derived his idea of choosing Christ as king of Florence, making the city directly subject to His law. Florence was the nucleus of the coming millennial world. Its leadership would be primarily spiritual, but in actual fact Savonarola was deeply involved in governing the city. His attempted reforms (such as establishing pawnshops for the poor) show once again the social implications of this millenarian thought as well as a practical approach to the city's problems. Much has been made of his opposition to Renaissance art and philosophy, but modern scholarship has pointed out that he shared with the Italian humanists their ideal of civic liberty and opposition to despotism, and that his friends included many able men from humanist circles. The priory of San Marco, of which he became prior in 1491, had always served the intellectual interests of the city, and under Savonarola it continued to do so. The link between the humanist tradition and his prophecy was the civic pride they both shared.

Yet for all this Savonarola belongs to the tradition of popular culture we have discussed, and it was this which enabled him to appeal to a larger section of the populace than the Florentine humanists. The state of the Church is once more typified by the fact that it was not theological opposition but an administrative quarrel which led to his excommunication. He fought for the independence of the Tuscan Dominican houses from the Lombard congregation against the wishes of the pope. Once excommunicated, he was delivered to the instability of popular support in Florence. When this turned against him (1498) he fell from power and was burned at the stake. Here also monkish rivalry was the immediate cause. A representative of the Franciscans challenged Savonarola to a 'judgment of God' which one of his followers rashly accepted. The trial by fire was organized, but in the end washed out by rain; and for this the crowd blamed Savonarola. A medieval trial by fire stood at the end of his career, but it is not possible to write him off as a purely medieval phenomenon in a Renaissance world. Savonarola was a part of that heightened religious sensibility which was immediate to the sixteenth century. The distinction between medieval and modern is meaningless here. Men were waiting to escape a world of corruption and catastrophe. The millenarian rule in Florence had failed, just as thirty-six years later the second experiment in millenarian rule, in Münster, failed once more. The answer to the religious tensions, which reflected the tensions of life, was to come from a different direction.

THE QUEST FOR RELIGIOUS SAFEGUARDS

No emperor saviour appeared, and no *pastor angelicus*. Instead, popular piety became ever more introspective, preoccupied with its fears. The result was a heightened search for religious safeguards, a clinging to them in a frightening world which might end soon. The fear of purgatory, the stage which souls had to pass through after death, was especially widespread. Here the veneration of relics of saints and the granting of indulgences entered the picture. The castle church at Wittenberg contained 17,443 relics which could help a person reduce his stay in purgatory by as much as 2 million years. No wonder that such an atmosphere meant abuse in the issuing of indulgences. Originally an indulgence was a relaxing of the punishment (penance) imposed by the Church for transgression against some religious commandment. At first such indulgences were conferred by the popes upon those who risked their lives fighting against the infidel. Gradually, however, such active service for the common good of Christendom was extended to include financial gifts for worthy spiritual causes, even if the donor did not actively participate in them. The financing of cathedrals, monasteries, and hospitals was at times designated by the papacy as warranting an indulgence. Thus good works could lead to a remission of punishment. But by now such a remission had come to mean the relaxing of punishment not just by the Church itself, but by God, and a right to expect God's mercy. Could not the pope, as custodian of that surplus of good deeds accumulated by Christ and augmented by the saints through the ages, grant remission of divine punishment?

Indulgences became all-important in a period obsessed with the fear of death, believing in the end of the world and the coming of the Last Judgment. They came to imply that good works by themselves could merit divine mercy and, as indulgences were often sold for cash, this seemed to commercialize the grace of God himself. Luther came to regard indulgences in this light, as typifying not only what was wrong with the Church, but also the faults of a popular piety which concentrated on religious safeguards. Small wonder that the reformers denied the existence of purgatory and changed the concept of good works. What had happened was an abuse of Church doctrine, another evidence of its involvement in the world. For the territorial rulers got a part of the proceeds from indulgences collected on their territory, and indulgences were, at times, proclaimed to help princes faithful to the Church out of monetary difficulties or to benefit, indirectly, papal coffers. Such was the case with the indulgence of 1514–17 which led to Luther's protest. Albrecht of Hohenzollern, already twice a bishop, was appointed to the important archbishopric of Mainz. Because of this singular instance of pluralism the pope required him to pay an extra assessment apart from the regular annates. The indulgence was proclaimed in order to help Albrecht make the payment.

Popular piety, encouraging the search for religious safeguards, led to such abuses of traditional Church doctrine, for no saviour 'prophet' had appeared. Instead, Luther had his reformation, not the 'total reformation' of society for which all of this popular culture longed, but an attempted renaissance of Christianity.

The background of popular piety is important, perhaps even decisive, for Luther's own path towards reform, in spite of attempts by modern historians to transform him into a humanist. His parents were peasants who had become small-scale entrepreneurs, owning a mine in Thuringia, demonstrating that a certain social mobility was not unknown in the age. Luther's emphasis upon himself as *rusticus* is therefore not quite true. But the dangerous profession of mining no doubt reinforced the atmosphere of popular piety in which he was brought up. Throughout his life Luther believed that the end of the world was approaching, in the prophecies of the Apocalypse (as we saw when discussing the Jews) and in devils and demons as well as witches. For him also two worlds were in collision: the present world, shot through by evil, ruled by Antichrist (the pope), and the world which could be redeemed through a renaissance of Christianity. He wrote a preface to a new edition of Lichtenberger, criticizing above all the astrology which could lead to a determinism excluding the hand of God from the world, but accepting much else in this book of popular culture. Luther shared the fears and terrors of his contemporaries, indeed their basic view of the world. But in him this was tempered by the learning he acquired, which brought him into the company of humanists. He made a sharp distinction between revelation and reason, faith and knowledge. In the compartment of faith we shall find many reminders of this popular piety in which the man, who proudly called himself a peasant to the end of his life, had grown up.

The humanists themselves, learned though they were, shared with the ignorant the concerns and traditions of the age. For humanism, as scholars have recently shown, was not an abrupt break with the medieval tradition of learning. Here also medieval inheritances were continued and applied to meet new conditions and challenges.

SIXTEENTH-CENTURY HUMANISM

The term 'humanism' is a nineteenth-century reading of the attitude reflected by men who, as a part of the Italian Renaissance, seemed to centre their thought upon the dignity of man and his privileged position in the world. But as P. O. Kristeller has shown, in reality the early humanists did not have one single coherent philosophy or attitude towards life. What gave them a semblance of unity was their enthusiasm for the rediscovery of the Latin and Greek classics and the application of the diverse values they found in them to literature and morals.[8] However different their individual conclusions, they emphasized elegance of writing and speech as well as a morality which stressed the uniqueness of man, his feeling and his potential.

This humanism first grew up in Italy, closely associated with the urban society of the peninsula. The movement, if such it can be called, typifies a gradual shift in the attitudes of lay society, the growth of its literacy, wealth, and political power. Italy was first here, but this same shift penetrated Europe as a whole, coming earlier to some regions than to others: in England, as A. G. Dickens has shown, it can be observed fully a century and a half after it reached its climax in Italy.[9] Wherever this shift took place, it was influenced by humanist considerations, though in diverse ways. Indeed we can envisage it as a dialectic: on the one hand a realism about man and the world which was new as against the medieval context; on the other hand, a sharing of religious concerns which were closely related to medieval life and thought. Humanists, like all men of their age, were affected by the heightened religious tensions which reflected man's existential dilemma in those troubled and rapidly changing times. In common with all the men and movements we have discussed they attempted to propose solutions which would lead to peace of mind.

Concern for religion is markedly evident in that humanism which developed into the sixteenth century. One consequence of the rediscovery of the ancients had been a renewed interest in Plato, though it must be emphasized that this did not, at first, mean direct opposition to the Aristotelian tradition which derived from the Middle Ages. What appealed especially were the Platonic doctrines of the eternal presence of universal forms in the mind of God, the ability of human reason to grasp these, and the emphasis upon the immortality of the human soul. It is the proposition of the immortality of the soul which raised the most important controversy among the Italian humanists towards the end of the fifteenth century. We are once more plunged into a basically religious concern, even though it is discussed on a more sophisticated level.

By contrast, Aristotle was also rediscovered, shorn of his medieval connection with Christian thought and treated like other ancient philosophers. This meant a distinction between reason and faith which Platonism seemed to deny, and some humanists believed in addition that Aristotle denied the immortality of the soul. As Aristotle continued to be taught in the universities, but with such changed emphases, his influence took two directions. The divorce of faith and philosophy led towards a greater irrationalism of faith as against reason, the latter being regarded as applicable only to earthly pursuits. For all his damning of Aristotle, Luther's division between faith and the world has striking similarities with this interpretation of the ancient philosopher. But Aristotelianism could also fuse with the concept of the mortality of the soul, lead to a kind of atheism which became increasingly popular in some Italian universities towards the end of the sixteenth century. Once again, this represents, on a more sophisticated level, the ancient popular heresy of 'soul sleeping': that there is no immortality of the soul until the resurrection. Calvin had to write his first tract against such a heresy, but it continued for the next two centuries as a wide variety of heresy trials in England and the Continent can testify.

While Aristotle did not vanish before the impetus of Platonism, Plato was of more immediate importance for the first part of the sixteenth century. For his ideas could be combined with religious feeling, as indeed Aristotle's had been in the Middle Ages. Marsilio Ficino (1433–1499) tried to do just this. Man's highest good is the enjoyment of God, but as man can rise only imperfectly to this vision, his ends must be achieved in the life after death. Man is, however, given a central part to play in this universe (here is humanism); he is the link between the material and the spiritual, the microcosm of the universe which is composed of both of these. Such syncretism had increasingly irrational elements built into it.

This is demonstrated by Ficino's ideal of love as desire for beauty, a love which can rise by stages to the love of God Himself and of His infinite beauty (see p. 389). Moreover, Ficino believed that in the last resort the universe was shrouded in 'secret'; he writes about the 'world soul' and puts this into the sun. Here is a 'final secret' which can only be mystically penetrated.

Small wonder that Ficino made a great impression not only in Italy but also in the north, where the preoccupation with 'secrets' which would unlock the universe, or which (like the Jews) prevented it from being unlocked, was more intense. The search for means to penetrate the universe occupied these Neoplatonists, the more so as they believed that man could accomplish this end. 'Platonic mysticism' led Giovanni Pico, count of Mirandola (1463–94), to rediscover in the Hebrew Cabala an esoteric symbolism of value to Christian scholars, a part of the necessary 'unity of truth'. But together with such an irrational approach to cosmology he also believed in the freedom of man to determine his own fate. This Platonism, then, had two sides: the mysticism which diffused the universe and which has to be unlocked, and the power and freedom of man himself.

How this differs from Aristotelianism can be illustrated through the ideas of Pietro Pomponazzi (1462–1524). For him also the soul can rise to grasp universal truths, and thus participate in a relative immortality. But the soul cannot function independently of the body. Pomponazzi meets with the Neoplatonists in proclaiming the centrality and the dignity of man, but the mysticism is absent and man tends to become autonomous: virtue and vice are their own rewards. As humanism spread to the north, it was Platonism which became influential, rather than the Aristotelianism of Pomponazzi. Here the shifting attitudes towards the centrality of man in the universe could be combined with a religious mystique close to popular culture.

Plato became the 'divine Moses', the discoverer of many dark secrets, hidden during the Middle Ages. It is typical in this regard that many of the most famous humanists believed in astrology, while a man of immense learning like Johannes Reuchlin took up Hebrew in order to fathom the mysteries of the Cabala.

A view of the humanists as the ancestors of modern rationalism can no longer be upheld without serious qualification. They were men of their own times and, especially in the north, their learning and sophistication mixed with Platonic mysticism and the traditions of popular and medieval piety. For example Melanchthon, the humanist reformer, believed in astrology, signs and dreams. The sun, moon and stars are the oracles of God's fate, and such a concentration upon astrology did not prevent him from combining the most meticulous scholarship of the time with belief in the primacy of scripture. Yet the basic dialectic between such views, and that new realism about man and the world which Pomponazzi reflects, was to remain a theme in the sixteenth century. After all, Luther and Machiavelli were contemporaries. We cannot expect the shift of attitudes on the part of the more literate, selfconscious laity to be immediate or total. Hence condemnation of Machiavelli throughout most of the century merges with increasing realism.

THE 'DEVOTIO MODERNA'

Northern humanism was influenced by the humanism of the South, especially by its Neoplatonic elements. But it was equally, if not more, indebted to a Christian impetus which had its origins in the Netherlands. There, in the fourteenth century, a mystical spirit had resulted in laymen asserting themselves to produce a 'Christian renaissance'. Gerard Groote (1340–84) had founded an order of laymen, the Brethren of the Common Life, which influenced Thomas à Kempis (1380–1471) and was joined by such figures as Wessel Gansfort (1419–89). Luther was to see in Gansfort's ideas similarities to his own, and indeed this whole 'modern devotion' (as it came to be called) had a pietistic emphasis similar to that of the Reformation. Both movements were largely laymen's revolts against a Church absorbed in temporal rather than spiritual concerns. The *devotio moderna* taught that the essence of Christianity is a spiritual communion with God through Christ. Such a communion would transform the lives of men; the example of Christ experienced in immediate, personal, terms could then be carried into practical daily living. Christian life was more important than Christian doctrine, and the inspiration for this life was set forth clearly in the gospels and the Acts of the Apostles. Scripture reading and an inner spirituality were essential.

This movement was usually orthodox; it did not break with the Church or deny its role in the world, but it challenged the scholastic method of arriving at religious truth. Such a challenge was basic to all humanism, but here it was inspired not by the examples of classical arguments alone but instead by an undogmatic concept of Christianity. Members of the *devotio moderna* founded schools, and thus spread its influence. It is from their schools that some of the principal humanists such as Erasmus graduated. Here was a shift of emphasis, from a Christianity approached through scholastic argument, the posing of questions 'from outside', to a more immediate Christian experience bolstered not through the analysis of secondary sources, but through the reading of scripture. In the age as we have attempted to describe it, the question of how one could lead a good life in an evil world was answered by such men not through concern with the outward signs of God's hand in the world, but through actual, personal living.

Erasmus called for such a 'Christian renaissance', but the ideas of this Dutch movement were not the only ones involved. For as humanists these men believed passionately that the literature of Christian, and not just pagan, antiquity could restore the 'philosophy of Christ'. It is in this manner that the true sources of a living piety could be revitalized. To be sure, the mystical ingredient of the *devotia moderna* could easily fuse with Platonic mysticism. A humanist like Johannes Reuchlin was concerned both with the esoteric Cabala and with scripture. Whatever the influences upon them, northern humanists believed in going back to the original sources of Christian inspiration. These sources, stripped of scholastic logic, would enable man to 'come to Christ' and thus to live a moral life on earth. In reaction against scholastic argument the purity and simplicity of the gospel were their ideal for living and for learning.

DESIDERIUS ERASMUS

In December of 1500 a Dutch clergyman wrote a letter seeking support and promising that his patron would win more glory through his writings than through other theologians. 'They merely deliver humdrum sermons,' he announced, 'I am writing books that may last forever . . . my books will be read all over the world; in the Latin west and in the Greek east and by every nation.'[10] This prediction, in fact, proved correct and Desiderius Erasmus (1466–1536) became a highly influential writer and the acknowledged leader of early sixteenth-century humanism.

To his contemporaries Erasmus seemed to exemplify the Christian humanist effort to make religion meaningful within the life of all men on earth. The attempt to live a Christian life seemed to have been perverted through an excessive emphasis upon religious observance or swamped by millenial urges. Practical piety was very much a part of the humanism which Erasmus advocated — a piety which was a matter of the human spirit and not of formal observances. The philosophy of Christ must no longer be taught in an 'involved fashion' but through reading scripture. Yet this primacy of scripture did not lead towards an understanding of the word of God through 'illumination' or through faith alone. Instead, scripture was to be taken out of the hands of the theologians and placed in the hands of the philologists and men of letters who would purify it by going back to the ancient sources and, by cleansing it of the accretions of scholasticism, make it understandable once again. Clearly, the humanist asserted a monopoly over the source of divine inspiration against the scholastic disciplines which held scripture in their custody during the Middle Ages. The effect of such an approach was equally obvious: humanist learning must accompany piety.

For Erasmus, religion tended to become intellectualized. Learning and piety were fused. The pious Christian must have a clear conscience, and make his peace with God; a clear conscience meant a mind open to the pleasures of learning, study and the writing of good literature. Learning was essential to an understanding of theology, humanist not scholastic learning. But piety had to accompany this and provide the goal. In the last resort, faith would lead beyond learning itself to a transcendent unity with God. But the result of this was envisaged in pragmatic terms, leading to an ethical, Christian life on earth. All humanists, whether north or south, shared the concern with a revived morality and sought to have this realized in daily life.

Erasmus's works exemplify such attitudes: his edition of the New Testament, his editorial work upon the Church fathers, and his works of exhortation to piety such as his *Handbook of a Christian Soldier* (1503). Yet Erasmus's popularity was not only that of a reformer, but increasingly that of a critic of contemporary society. His most popular works were the *Praise of Folly* (over six hundred editions since its publication) and the *Colloquies* (over three hundred editions). In both these works Erasmus views folly as the dominating principle of a fallen world, and he criticizes the Church at precisely that point where it had become involved with this world. Thus his own criticism touches the fundamental problem already raised by the criticism of the Church in popular piety — it had lost its true mission and had become integrated into corrupt and evil society which constituted the existing present. In the *Praise of Folly* (1509) the monks, clergy, and priests are an integral part of the whole procession of corruption which takes in scholars, kings and nobles. Unlike some other humanists, Erasmus despised war and military glory, saying that princes would have to answer to God for each drop of blood spilled. To Erasmus, violent behaviour was a product of human culture and thus might, in time, be eradicated.[11]

The way out did not lie in the emotionally heightened sensibilities of popular piety. Indeed Erasmus castigates these as leading to undue emphasis upon religious safeguards, like the 'worship' of saints and the excessive obsession with pilgrimages. Instead, like all humanists, Erasmus put his faith in education. Man can be helped to be good for he has free will, though this free will must be aided by divine grace. Erasmus was in this respect in the medieval catholic tradition; his belief as expressed in his book *De Libero Arbitrio* (1524) tries to maintain a sometimes confusing balance between justification by faith and the necessity for man's will to perform ethical acts.

But how could man's will be directed? Through the combination of learning and piety which we have discussed. Thus a humanist education joined to piety would make it easier for the human will to use its freedom correctly. Consequently, humanists, like Erasmus's close friend John Colet, founded schools and academies. For Erasmus this way to perfection meant the creation of a society where a prince, educated in humanist fashion, would rule justly and where, in imitation of Christ, there would be peace instead of war. The ideal society which a humanist like Erasmus wanted to create remained a Utopia, but the ideal of a ruling elite imbued with humanist culture became a near reality. In a society where kings and nobles set the tone, the libraries of even the minor nobility begin after the mid-century to show an impressive range of interests. The ancients, the Italian and northern humanists are represented, side by side with works of an older Christian devotion. There is some justice in Franz Palacky's remark that the strength of the Bohemian nobility around 1500 was due to the fact that it produced more than its share of men of intellect and culture[12] and this at the identical time they were depressing their peasantry into serfdom.

The impact of such a complex personality, who poured out an endless and sometimes contradictory stream of words, is difficult to assess. He founded no sect; indeed he was orthodox, believing in the functions of the priesthood and the sacraments, in a Church Catholic but reformed according to the criterion of Christian living. His influence exalted learning as a vital part of religion, intellectualized faith, and thereby made for a more tolerant attitude of mind. Such greater tolerance was implicit also in the ideal of the perfectibility of man through education. Erasmus was fond of contrasting learning with force, and in an age of violence this tended to connect Christianity with pacifism as well as with a refusal lightly to persecute those who differed in opinion. How typical that Erasmus, in defending the freedom of the human will against Martin Luther, praised that man *qui non facile definit*, who does not easily form categorical judgments. Erasmus here provided a definition of the intellectual which was to outlast the sixteenth century.

Erasmus's humanism exerted a profound influence upon many men in his own time and during the next centuries. His disciples constantly searched for a middle way between the categorical judgments made by Protestants and Catholics alike, which led to a hardening of men's minds towards each other. Calvin and Luther were fond of using the word 'fortress' to describe the security which true religion gave to the believer, while Erasmians tried to pull down the walls between men and attempted to keep open the dialogue between them.[13] They stressed the love of God for men rather than God's stern judgment upon men's actions. Catholic reformers like Reginald Pole and Contarini, Castellio in Geneva and the Italian radicals as well, are the heirs of this attitude. Erasmus's tolerant definition of Christianity also explains his enormous and almost immediate popularity in Spain, in part attributable to the *conversos*. These people, whose immediate ancestors had been converted from Judaism to avoid expulsion from Spain, had a real interest in furthering a philosophy of tolerance, a Christianity which had little regard for outward ceremony.[14] Nor is it surprising that the court of Charles V was Erasmian in outlook. Erasmus's ideas found fertile soil in the Netherlands, the home of the 'modern devotion' and the land of Charles's birth. Moreover, the universalism of Erasmian ideas could reinforce the imperial ideas of the emperor (see p. 236).

Erasmus's attacks upon the Church further deepened the distinction between Christian living and Christian doctrine. In these ways he affected the moderates in both the Catholic and the Protestant camps. Especially the learned chancellors and advisers of rulers tended towards Erasmianism in an age of unleashed religious passions which seemed to ignore learning, the weighing of evidence, and the secular interests of the state.

THOMAS MORE

Erasmus and the northern humanists considered themselves the teachers of Europe, believing intellectual freedom to be vital if the standards of justice were to prevail in a corrupt world. Thomas More, the friend of Erasmus, was imbued with such an aim and sought to exemplify it in his *Utopia* (1516). He shared with Erasmus, and with popular piety, the sense of the corruption of present society; but, unlike both of these, he was imbued with a greater sense of realism. He was specific about the abuses which characterize this corruption and did not use Erasmus's method of satire and allegory. Much more than Erasmus, the Englishman was convinced of the sinfulness of man, and his own optimism, at least in the *Utopia*, was singularly subdued. The root of the evil present was the cardinal sin of Christianity, that of pride. To tame it the *Utopia* became a state which rigorously disciplined men through its police and an ascetic mode of life. The essence of the good society, however, was the abolition of the money economy and private property.[15]

More abolished these not merely because they led to the sins of pride, greed and envy, but because their abolition made possible the concentration upon the common, not the private, good. More conceived the state and the rulers as part of an integrated community of men. The just, Christian life was not merely a personal matter but part of the making of a proper community. The *Utopia* was for him only a beginning, because it lay in a part of the world where the light of Christianity had not yet penetrated. But if such a community could be based on natural reason, how much further could a community based on Christianity itself advance; if the present contrasts so vividly with this Utopia, how much further removed was it from the commonwealth which was not merely just but also Christian? More returned to the sense of community held by Florentine humanists a century earlier, but he did so from a northern Christian, humanist standpoint. Here humanism typifies a preoccupation with the idea of community which we shall meet again in the Protestant Reformation. More himself, however, hated Protestantism as a perversion of the true pillar of Christianity, the Church.

THE HUMANISTS AND THE CHURCH

The humanists shared with popular piety the sense of the evil of the present, and the need to change this towards a golden age. They attempted to cut through the ever-present dilemmas by advocating a reform of man's life on earth which would also lead to a reform of the Church. The Church itself was more tolerant towards popular piety. It did nothing to stem the tide of prophecy or the ever greater reliance upon religious safeguards. But it did try to strike at humanist criticism, if with divided counsel. The most famous episode is that in which the Dominican friars of Cologne persecuted Johannes Reuchlin for heresy. He gave them an opening through his interest in Hebrew at a moment in which one of the many drives against the Jews and their 'perfidious' religious books was taking place.

The humanists in the north had no special fondness for Jews, but a man like Reuchlin did regard Hebrew and Hebrew literature as part of the learning necessary to penetrate to the sources of Christianity, even if he was influenced by the Neoplatonic 'mysticism' of the Cabala. The Dominicans took the opportunity to accuse Reuchlin of heresy while the other humanists rallied to his defence. In the *Letters of the Obscure Men* (1515−17) they produced a satire upon the Dominicans (and the clergy in general) which has the same point to make as the *Praise of Folly*. The struggle itself ended inconclusively (Reuchlin died while it was taking place) and it can only be regarded as foreshadowing the Reformation in a most general way. What the humanists obviously shared with the reformers was the anticlericalism which they did so much to promote. This sprang out of a common criticism of present society and of the Church's integration within it. But such criticism was also shared by the whole tradition of popular piety. Another connection, however, was implied in the answer given by both humanists and reformers: back to the sources of the faith, and here popular piety was ambivalent and overlaid with superstitions of its own from which even humanists like Reuchlin were not free.

Scholasticism, whose method had been decried by the humanists, still had an important contribution to make both to humanism itself and to Luther's own development. A philosophy which had emerged out of a lively scholastic controversy added its influence to the diverse modes of thought we have considered. The medieval nominalism of men like William of Occam put forward an hypothesis that ideas apart from reality have no existence, are mere names (*nomina*), and transferred this to theology. This involved a sharp cleavage between reason, applicable to existing reality through experience, and revelation; between knowledge and faith. Nominalism influenced humanists and reformers in two major ways. Occam implied the absolutism of a God who could never be understood by humans. Man was saved and damned by His inscrutable will alone. For Martin Luther this meant a heightened uncertainty about man's salvation; belief in a God who seemed removed from man by an impassable chasm. But Luther's own division between the world and faith owes something to this thought, and Calvin's concept of God owes much to nominalism. For humanists like Melanchthon such ideas pointed the way back to faith from Church dogma and from the power of the contemporary Church. What mattered, in the last resort, was God's will and the revelation of Christ as seen in the Bible. Moreover, such nominalism could lead to a more pragmatic attitude towards living one's life on this earth, combined with a purely inward faith and piety.

If nominalism contributed its part to the new religious impetus of the age, so did the very antithesis of such ideas and fears about man and his place in the world. The emphasis upon learning, the good Christian life on earth, faced another kind of pragmatism which derived from the Italian Renaissance and which, for better or worse, came to be associated with Niccolo Machiavelli (1469–1527). His ideas are a part of the dialectic which we have already mentioned: the heightened religious sensibilities on the one hand, and the shift towards secularism on the other. Both vitally influenced the thought of men in the sixteenth century.

NICCOLO MACHIAVELLI

Northern humanists and reformers equated Machiavelli's writings with atheism, and further saw in the Florentine politician a menace to the good society which could exist only upon an explicitly

Christian base. Christian living, which they all prized so highly, must pervade every aspect of life: politics as well as private attitudes. But this is just what Machiavelli seemed to deny. Politics, as he contemplated it after having finished his own active life in Florence (but not given up his ambitions), has its own laws of existence.[16] These laws are not properly speaking Christian, though presumably Machiavelli had no objection to men who lived a Christian life — provided they left politics alone. Political action depended upon three forces, characterized by three words Machiavelli uses constantly: *virtu, necessita,* and *fortuna.*

Virtu was not a Christian term: it denoted the strength and vigour which were necessary in order to construct a politically successful society. *Fortuna* is the element of chance, of capriciousness in human affairs which must be harnessed to political life. Basically, it represents the element of change which means a struggle to control unpredictable events, and here *virtu* is necessary. Necessity creates opportunities for man, which he must exploit, once more through the use of *virtu.* Political life consists of constant struggle against *fortuna* which, however, can be controlled through taking advantage of all opportunities, and for this strength and vigour are needed. Machiavelli's regard for the man of *virtu* is very high: such a man accepts his fate but attempts to control it.

The difference between Machiavelli's ideas, up to this point, and a Christian view of life is clear; the opportunities to be exploited are connected to *fortuna* and necessity rather than to God's providence. *Virtu* means strength and force, meeting the continued struggle of political life on its own terms, rather than countering evil with good. Political life made its own rules of behaviour and, since Machiavelli felt the active political life was the most meaningful life on earth, this seemed to produce a programme which left out any immediate relationship to the Christian faith. The ideal society was not one of justice like More's *Utopia,* but a republic in which all citizens were united by *virtu,* generating the strength and power of will which could cope with ever-present change and thus survive. A citizen army was more important than any transcendent moral system. It is this which struck his Christian critics with special force. And well it might, if we remember that to a large extent the nobility still set the tone and that a concept of 'virtue' also stood at the centre of its life and thought. But this was a 'virtue' composed of Christian ideals of faith, hope and love, to which were joined justice, wisdom, bravery and moderation as of special relevance to life in this world.

Such 'noble virtues' could bear no relationship to Machiavelli's councils. The prince, to succeed, must exploit the 'necessities' of the weaknesses of his enemies wherever possible, and by any and all means at hand. Machiavelli's view of man was pessimistic; he believed that in his own time *virtu* was not to be found. A prince could, if he possessed it, help to restore Italian politics to a greatness which Machiavelli saw in the past. As a humanist of the Italian Renaissance, he looked to Rome, for here a society had survived the changes of history (*fortuna*) for the longest time.

His aim was not to lead men back to Christ, but to lead them back to the *virtu* which he saw in the Republic of Rome. This meant that men had to overcome their weaknesses, jealousies and personal concerns. For him, as for More, the community was central; and he also advocated the equalization of private property in order to change the focus of man's ambitions. But that community was a political one, geared to constant change, inspired by strength of will and the opportunity to see those necessities which could be exploited — those weaknesses of the enemy which could be bent to the community's own advantage. The Bible, for Machiavelli, was merely a story book, and the actions of Moses were to be judged on the same political level as the actions of any Roman politician. What then is new here? Not the realization of the necessity of political action which might not be in tune with the accepted, eternal mortality. What is new is the exaltation of this into a way of life essential to the construction of the golden age. The political community itself is conceived of as man's highest end. Machiavelli was not a great systematizer; his books were no literary exercises like More's *Utopia*, but a part of his attempted comeback into Florentine politics. Yet to most readers it did seem as if he had constructed a system opposed to everything they held dear, to the whole atmosphere of both popular culture and that humanism which went into the making of sixteenth-century thought.

THE 'MIRRORS FOR PRINCES'

Machiavelli examined the present by referring to the Roman past, however much he changed his examples to make them fit his own preconceptions. The contrast between him and the continuing Christian tradition stands out if we contrast his view to that typical of so many 'Mirrors for Princes' which were current throughout the century.[17] The popular English *Mirror for Magistrates* (seven editions between 1559 and 1587) was not much different from Erasmus's 'Mirror' or a host of others. Princes must obey Christian morality, and subjects their princes, or both would be punished by God. The *Mirror* told, for example, 'How King Richard the second was for evil government deposed from his seat', or how the traitor Jack Cade was punished for his rebellion. Punishment follows an evil deed 'as rain drops doe the thunder'.[18] The whole humanist exhortation to morality, the belief in the perfectibility of man, is brought to bear upon the problem of government. The contrast with Machiavelli could hardly be greater.

The sixteenth century was still a Christian century, though the ambiguous relationship of many of its leading figures to Machiavelli's ideas points to the future. The shift to a lay society and more secular attitudes of thought accompanied the Christian renaissance both in Catholicism and in Protestantism. Popular piety remained the religion of peasant life and with its rites and customs presented a challenge to the more educated reformers.

NOTES AND REFERENCES

1   Keith Thomas, *Religion and the Decline of Magic* (London, 1971), pp. 30–31.

2   Hayim Hillel Ben-Sason, 'The Reformation in Contemporary Jewish Eyes', *Proceedings of the Israel Academy of Sciences and Humanities*, vol. 4 (1969–70), p. 288.

3   B. Ravid, 'The Venetian Ghetto in Historical Perspective', in *The Autobiography of a Seventeenth-Century Rabbi: Leon Modena's Life of Judah*, ed. M. R. Cohen (Princeton, 1988).

4   Robert Muchembled, William Frijhoff and Marie-Sylvie Dupont-Bouchat, *Prophètes et Sorciers dans le Pays-Bas* (Paris, 1978), p. 11.

5   H. C. Erik Midelfort, *Witch Hunting in Southwestern Germany, 1562–1648* (Stanford, 1972).

6   Four editions of the work appeared between 1520 and 1522, on the eve of the Peasants' War, Manfred Straude, 'Die Reformatio Sigsmundi', *Die Frühbürgerliche Revolution in Deutschland* (Berlin, 1961), pp. 108–15.

7   John Leddy Phelan, *The Millennial Kingdom of the Franciscans in the New World* (Berkeley, 1956), pp. 19 ff.

8   Paul Oskar Kristeller, *Renaissance Thought* (New York, 1955), p. 10.

9   A. G. Dickens, *The English Reformation* (London, 1964), pp. 9 ff.

10 Cited in Richard L. De Molen, *Essays on the Works of Erasmus* (New Haven, 1976), p. 1.

11 James D. Tracy, *The Politics of Erasmus: A Pacifist Intellectual and His Political Milieu* (Toronto, 1978).

12 Franz Palacky, *Geschichte von Böhmen*, vol. V, I. Abteilung (Prague, 1865), p. 397; Otto Brunner, *Adeliges Landleben und Europaeischer Geist* (Salzburg, 1949), pp. 158 ff.

13 Friedrich Heer, *Die Dritte Kraft* (Frankfurt, 1960), p. 256.

14 J. H. Elliott, *Imperial Spain 1469–1716* (London, 1963), p. 151.

15 J. H. Hexter, *More's Utopia* (Princeton, 1952), *passim.*

16 Felix Gilbert, *Machiavelli and Guicciardini* (Princeton, 1965), pp. 177, 178.

17 Cf. Quentin Skinner, *The Foundations of Modern Political Thought*, vol. 1, (London, 1978), p. 128 ff., where he deals with the differences between *The Prince* and mirror-for-princes literature.

18 *The Mirror for Magistrates*, ed. L. B. Campbell (Cambridge, 1938), pp. 111, 112, 171.

7

THE REFORMATION

For some time it had been evident that the chances for the continued unity of Western Christianity were small. Though the Church of Rome still emphasized universalist claims it was becoming increasingly obvious that it had outlived the functions that had made it uniquely valuable in earlier centuries. Then, as the only international organization, it had provided an impoverished and backward Europe with a sophisticated administrative structure and with it educated personnel, drawn from many countries but all speaking the international language of Latin. However, as Europe had grown more prosperous and regional cultures had become able to supply their own requirements, the need for this sort of an international organization had diminished. Heresies and reform movements of all kinds challenged the Church. The fifteenth-century conciliar movement might have allowed the Church to accommodate itself to the growing centrifugal forces in Christendom while still preserving an overall unity but the defeat of conciliarism and the obsession of the papacy with Italian politics left the Church unable to adapt to new and difficult circumstances.

These challenges came from the printing press and the national monarchies. The invention of printing in the mid-fifteenth century had led to an increased availability of the Scriptures to European laymen who were now able to read and interpret the Bible themselves. Without the monopoly of scriptural interpretation the claim of the Church to act as the indispensable intermediary between God and man was critically undermined in a way that would have been impossible before the great technological change wrought by Gutenberg. At the same time this was happening, national governments in Europe were taking over areas of jurisdiction which had once been reserved for the international

Church. By 1500 the papacy had been forced to abandon much of its control over church administration and personnel to the great monarchs who could now not only fill the important ecclesiastical benefices but also regulate the publication of papal briefs inside their kingdoms. The extent to which these Catholic princes were willing to threaten Church unity can be seen in two incidents early in the sixteenth century. In 1508 Ferdinand of Aragon threatened to withdraw all of his kingdoms from obedience to the papacy if the pope insisted on sending a bull of excommunication into the kingdom of Naples. In a furious letter to his Viceroy in Naples Ferdinand pointed out that by sending such a bull the pope would increase his influence throughout Europe and demanded that the papal messenger be arrested, forced to declare he had never delivered the papal brief and then hanged for his impertinence. Three years later Louis XII of France called an anti-papal Council at Pisa in an attempt to challenge the pope with a revival of the doctrine of conciliarism; this ill-fated council issued a decree of suspension against Pope Julius II. With such erosion of support for Rome it was clear the unity of the Church could no longer be taken for granted.[1]

Yet the irrevocable break in Church unity, when it finally came, was to be only part of a much larger process, the Reformation, which would bring profound changes in religious sensibilities, changes which would affect the social, intellectual, artistic, economic and political life of much of the world for centuries to come. These changes cannot be thought of without Martin Luther, the man whose moral and physical courage challenged the established way of things and provided an example for other would-be reformers to imitate.

MARTIN LUTHER

Though Luther's religiosity eventually stressed the simplicity of an active faith, Luther was not a simple man. He was formed by nearly all the contemporary cultural and religious patterns. Hans Luther, his father, had left the land to become a small-scale entrepreneur, the owner of a mine in Thuringia. A man of ambition, he wanted Martin to rise still further in the social scale through the study of law, and he was bitterly disappointed when his son became a monk. For all this mobility, Martin Luther was born into a world where the peasant cast of mind was dominant, and it never left him completely. He believed in evil spirits, in their struggle against the good – even a few days before his death Luther saw the devil sitting outside his window. For Luther, especially in his youth, this meant viewing the universe as filled with secret dangers, a realm of constant fear where one lived beneath the 'cloud of unknowing'.

It is not surprising that he made his vow to enter a monastery when he was frightened by a bolt of lightning. But the Augustinian Order which he joined was devoted to teaching and learning; Luther was destined to achieve the kind of education which his father had lacked. At Erfurt he was taught a doctrine of the universe which was connected with the philosophy of William of Occam – nominalism, with its view of the chasm between God and men, reason and revelation, fitted in with Luther's fear of the unknown. He was deeply affected in two ways by this theology: firstly, in making a distinction between reason and revelation, the order of the world and the sphere of faith. This enabled him to give due weight to reason in secular learning on one hand, and, on the other to combine this with a passionate belief in a mysterious universe peopled by angels and devils. Modern scholarship has made much of the fact that Luther was a part of the humanist movement as he took up his professorship at the University of Wittenberg (1508). He did advocate more education, the learning of languages and the knowledge of history. His method was that of the humanists, and like them he condemned the scholastics. But the realm of faith was something else again; for Luther it was given by the grace of God alone and man's learning, his free will, had nothing to do with it – though they would make man better, motivated by love, and thus indirectly reflect upon the culture which he advocated.

For Luther sought to close the gap between God and man, and this was the second effect which Occamism had; it heightened the fear of the unknown in the young Luther, and he sought to come to terms with it. Such is the basis of his struggles in the monastery and beyond: he toyed with mysticism to get close to God. But it would not work for him. He sought refuge in the minute observance of religious practices, to grasp at every safeguard which existed to protect man against a hidden and predatory God. Luther knew whereof he spoke when he condemned the preoccupation with works, for he had experienced this in his own person.

JUSTIFICATION BY FAITH

Luther's solution to the dilemma of how man could face his God came from a scholar's insight, for he obtained it when studying and lecturing upon St Paul's epistles at the University of Wittenberg. There was, after all, a bridge between God and man, and this was faith alone (*sola fide*). Faith is a free gift from God, whom man must trust; 'trust' and 'faith' took the place of 'fear' and 'works'. This faith freely given by God was made possible by the sacrifice of Christ who had died for all men. For Luther, Christ became the symbol of hope, not the Christ bowed down by his passion and suffering who had, in popular piety, been the symbol of an evil and despairing world. The centrality of such faith corresponded to the centrality of scripture where God had revealed his plan for salvation. *Evangelium est promissio:* it is not merely 'law' or a part of the divine tradition; instead, it contains the hope of mankind God's promise to man.

This view of scripture was to be one of the driving forces of the Reformation. For Luther believed that the text was clear to the understanding of those who approached it with trust in God and the faith which springs from such a trust. Therefore, not only must the Bible be accessible to all in their own language, but it must also be constantly spread abroad through the spoken word. That is why, in an age of mass illiteracy, preaching was so important to Luther, indeed to the whole Reformation. This preaching must, of course, be based solely upon the scripture. We shall return to the problems which this raised, for the peasants were to read the book of hope differently from the princes and from Luther himself.

When Luther encountered the indulgence of 1517, he saw blatant substitution of works for faith. He called for a debate in the usual manner by posting his objections publicly at the Castle Church which contained, ironically enough, the greatest collection of relics in north Germany. For Luther, penance was the humility of faith, and had nothing to do with atonement through works or payment of money. No debate took place then, but within the next two years Luther had to confront the learned and orthodox Johannes Eck in the customary disputations of contested theological points. The most crucial of these debates took place in Leipzig (1519) and here Luther was pushed into questioning the divine appointment of the papacy and, worse, into admitting a sympathy with some of the ideas of both Wycliffe and Hus. Luther did not completely follow Hus's accentuated predestinarianism, nor Wycliffe in his sacramental heresies, but their stress upon the equality of all believers, their criticism of Church practices, provided a common bond. In reality Luther shared with them, and now expressed, criticisms which were common to much of medieval thought.

Criticism does not constitute a doctrine. Luther never really became a systematic theologian; the great compendium of evangelical thought stems not from his pen, but from that of his fellow professor and close friend, Melanchthon. In his three tracts of 1520 Luther came as near as he ever did to drawing out the consequences of his original 'tower experience'. *The Babylonish Captivity of the Church* faces the theological consequences of his criticism. The supremacy of faith dictated the abolition of priests as a separate caste endowed with special mystical functions: all Christians were priests. Faith and trust, the knowledge of scripture, were attainable by all men. Ordination as a sacrament was abolished, reducing the Catholic Mass to a celebration of communion or the Lord's Supper. No longer was the priest alone endowed with the power to perform the miracle of the bread and wine; no longer, therefore, was the Church the sole custodian of the body of Christ. Moreover, only two sacraments were left standing: the Baptism and the Lord's Supper. Religious service became a communal action in which the entire priesthood of believers participated. The symbol of this participation was the hymn, and Luther published the first evangelical hymnbook in 1524. Luther's change in the service of the Mass was combined with a change in the Thomist view of transubstantiation. In his view, the bread and the wine were not transformed into the actuality of Christ's blood and flesh, nevertheless, because of Christ's universal presence, God was in some manner corporeally present as well. The gate was opened to the sacramental controversies which were to plague the Reformation, as they had troubled the Church throughout earlier centuries. This was a matter not to be taken lightly, for whether Protestant or Catholic, the worship of God through Christ was the central core of religious faith.

THE CHURCH

The basic doctrinal pillar of the Church structure had been swept away. But this change was not so apparent. The confessional remained intact, and indeed much of the service followed the old rites, if now in the German language. Throughout the first part of the century we find priests who impartially served both Evangelical and Catholic congregations. The break was not so abrupt to contemporaries as it seems to us today, and in this very fact lay a factor essential to Luther's success. Men are reluctant to change liturgy which outwardly expresses their faith, and though criticism of the Church was widespread, as we have seen, abrupt change might have led to defection – not abrupt change in the clerical establishments (anticlericalism had struck root) but change in liturgy. This was avoided; indeed Luther himself was far from clear about the exact form services should take. His central idea of the supremacy of faith made him reluctant to dictate any set way of celebrating Mass, for the external order of the Church was to him of secondary importance.

But order there had to be, and from the structure of the Church which he had pulled down, Luther turned to the secular authorities – what else was left? This was, once more, not a new step, for throughout the late Middle Ages, in the quarrels between emperor and pope, the partisans of the emperor had held that he must regulate a corrupt Church and, indeed, control it. Wycliffe had seen reform coming from above and not from below. The Lutheran Reformation stood in this tradition. The popular longing for the 'emperor saviour' also aided such a point of view. Luther's *Appeal to the Christian Nobility of the German Nation* (1520) called upon the German ruling classes to repulse the pretensions of the Roman Church, to strip it of worldly power and wealth which disguised true faith. Thus he began to endow rulers with the duty to reform the Church and to supervise such a reformed Church – for were they not a part of the priesthood of all believers, and that part singled out as the 'powers that be, for they are of God'?

But what, then, was the exact relationship between the external order and the liberty of inward faith? The third tract of 1520, *Concerning the Liberty of a Christian Man*, was supposed to give the answer. Christian liberty was not outward social or political freedom, but inward liberty which springs from a faith freely found. Luther attempted to make a clearcut division between inward and outward liberty, based upon the unquestioned primacy of man as a spiritual being. Such an attitude also affected the meaning of good works, the importance of which Luther by no means denied. But good works themselves are 'externals' and therefore 'good works

165

do not make man good, but a good man does good works'. It was not that Luther was indifferent to the downtrodden or opposed to good works, but for him, for whom inner freedom and certainty were the only concerns, worldly rebellion and stress upon good works were signs of insufficient attention to the real business of life, which lay in the attainment of faith.

As Luther had to face these problems growing out of his religious experience, he was also forced to confront the problem of how much free will man has in his own actions. Erasmus through his emphasis upon the human will stung Luther to reply in the *Bondage of the Will* (1525). Submission to God's commandments, the opposition to 'works', led Luther in this tract to emphasize predestination. But the harshness of such a doctrine was mitigated by an equal stress upon the saving grace of Christ's revelation. Earlier in his life Luther had emphasized the element of predestination, but now he did his best to take the sting out of this doctrine. It is precisely the incontestable will of a hidden God which makes Christ so necessary to man. Scripture has given us the hope of salvation, if we only trust and love — and do not inquire into the final will of God which man can never understand. Luther's idea of predestination is without the harshness which Calvin was to give to this doctrine. With Luther there is no fear of God's will, a fear of which Calvinists could never rid themselves and which made for a heightened tension in their life, a tension which Luther wanted to avoid for he had himself experienced so much of it.

FRIENDS AND FOLLOWERS

Not Luther but Philip Melanchthon (1497–1560) wrote the first systematic statement of Protestant theology, the *Loci Communes* (1521), which went through many editions. Melanchthon was both a systematizer of the new faith and pressed by Luther into service as the diplomatic representative of his cause. He followed Luther all the way, but with some typical deviations due to his own humanist outlook. Thus he came to believe that man has the power to accept or reject God's gift of salvation. Here he was closer to Erasmus than to Luther who had attacked the Prince of Humanists for his advocacy of free will. Moreover, Melanchthon systematized the distinction between the essentials and non-essentials of faith, putting religious ceremonial into the non-essential category because it was not static but could change. After Luther's death this led to a bitter controversy within Lutheranism. On one side were the followers of Matthias Flacius Illyricus (1520—75), who thought that liturgy reflects doctrine and who, at a time when Lutheranism was hard pressed by the emperor, held that outward forms of religion did matter. These 'Protestant scholastics' were opposed by Melanchthon and his followers, beginning a struggle among Lutherans which was to last most of the century.

Luther had made his spiritual discovery at the university, and it was in front of the assembled students and professors that he burned the papal bull which excommunicated him (1520). At Wittenberg he found his first disciples, and from the university the first missionaries went out to convert other regions. The disciples whom they attracted into the faith were not necessarily united upon the consequences which they drew from Lutheranism. The emphasis upon scripture opened the door to diversity of thought, and more influential than the tracts was Luther's own translation of scripture (completed translation published 1534) which made accessible the divine basis by which all interpretations of faith must be tested. However, we can divide these followers into four categories which will accompany the Reformation throughout its history. For all their diversity, whether prince, humanist, radical or mere adventurer, all Luther's followers shared his faith in the basic importance of scripture, whatever conditions they drew from it.

Ulrich von Hutten (1488—1523) typifies the type of adventurer who was also a humanist and a patriot. He was learned in history, wrote Latin, but put these skills largely in the service of anti- papal propaganda. Hutten called upon the emperor to reform Church and papacy, to keep Germany from being dominated by Rome. For Hutten the issue was simple: restore what he believed to have been the past independence of the Empire and all would be well. This meant also a restoration of the knightly class to which Hutten belonged, and which was losing its status in a world of growing cities and gunpowder. Though Hutten felt the decline of his class, modern scholarship has contested the notion that the knights were in full retreat before the modern forces of the age. Some knights did manage to adapt themselves and change functions. Thus Hutten's relative profited from the new type of warfare and became the commander of the powerful Swabian League. For all that, the piratical attack upon the city of Trier (1522) which Hutten organized, together with other imperial knights, was an assertion by the traditional knights against their traditional enemy. This was an ecclesiastical principality, and thus the pope would be indirectly attacked in the name of Luther's reformation. The attack failed. German princes came to the aid of the city in crushing the last attempt of the knights to compete with the princes in the game of political power. Worse, this attack had been made in the name of spreading the Lutheran reformation. The liberty of faith had been transformed into an activism bound up with political ambitions and social concerns. Luther repudiated Hutten, and the knight who had exalted the Empire found himself dying in exile. But the adventure of the knights was not the only attempt to link Luther's definition of freedom to a change in the existing society, nor was it the most important portent for the future.

THE RADICALS

In that same year (1522) Luther's fellow professor Carlstadt took the lead in instigating a reformation at Wittenberg, for Luther was far away at the Wartburg, sheltering from the wrath of the emperor. The Catholic Mass was abolished, as were all images in churches. Such radical action led to an enthusiasm for reform which expressed itself in riots, the smashing of all that was thought to be connected with the traditional Church. Moreover, to add to the ferment, some men arrived from the neighbouring textile centre of Zwickau preaching a radicalism which had been no part of Luther's thought or intention. Carlstadt (1480–1541) himself was drawn into the vortex of this 'radical reformation'. These radicals attempted to capitalize on Lutheranism rather than being, properly speaking followers of the reformer. They also based themselves on scripture, though this was not the infallible test of faith: it merely confirmed the faith of those who already possessed it. Direct revelation, visions, and belief in the immediacy of the millennium characterized such thought. It is closely linked to an unchanging urge in popular piety, rather than to the Lutheran Reformation. The present was viewed as the age of Antichrist and it must be overcome through those elected by God for the purpose: then the millennium would be ushered in. Those so elected are given direct revelation, are 'filled with the spirit', are constantly in touch with God himself. Radicals believed in a 'continuous revelation' made by God to his special children because of their important task; therefore, no earthly powers or agreements could bind them. We find such ideas not only among the radicals of the Reformation, but wherever such radicalism surfaced as, for example, in Hussite Bohemia in the fifteenth century and in the English revolution of the seventeenth where it caused Cromwell much the same concern it had already caused Luther.

The radicals envisaged themselves as not only standing outside the establishment but also in direct opposition to the present order. They had been given a special mandate to destroy it, for with its false idols and injustices that order was the work of Antichrist. Radicalism was the religion of the poor, of those who stood outside the establishment of the powerful, the priests and the learned. While at first these 'Anabaptist' movements attracted people of all classes (though the majority of the membership was poor) by the end of the sixteenth century, after so many persecutions, almost only the poor remained.[2]

Such people were influenced by the millenarianism of popular piety and its heightened religious sensibilities, while a humanist like Melanchthon had adopted astrology, a belief in signs and portents, without including such millenarian hopes. Thomas Münzer (1489—1525) became for a while the leader and the theoretician of this radicalism. From being a follower of Luther, Münzer moved away to preach the eternal covenant of the elect with God, the bestowal upon them of the Holy Spirit, after a period of doubt, unbelief and suffering. The poor, spiritually impoverished, would provide the group of elect whose mission was to bring about a 'total reformation'. In a sermon delivered in 1524, Münzer attempted to persuade the Saxon dukes that they were the predestined instruments to lead the elect against the rest of the world.

Theology and social longings were mixed: the restoration of primitive and true Christianity after the battle was won, would also mean a good life for those to whom it was now denied. Here the Reformation had become a revolutionary doctrine far removed from Luther's concept of liberty. Luther returned from the Wartburg to put an end to the disturbances which Carlstadt and the men of Zwickau had caused. But this complex of ideas erupted in action twice more during Luther's lifetime. The peasant wars infused their concrete demands with this revolutionary ethos, and a decade later the Münster experiment brought it to its zenith.

THE PEASANTS

The peasants were aroused by popular religious feeling and their religious enthusiasm encompassed their social and economic ambitions. The natural catastrophes of the age, famine and disease, struck hard at the countryside, and in regions like Thuringia the small independent peasant was hard pressed. The problem was how he could maintain himself in face of the legal and economic pressure from the great landlords to take over his land and repress him into serfdom which was becoming the rule in eastern but not in western Europe. Thus the strong and self-assertive Bohemian nobility depressed the peasantry of the country into virtual dependence during the first decades of the century. In the south-east of Europe the crushing of peasant rebellions led to the same consequences. These uprisings, of which the one of 1514 was the most serious, were directed both at the encroachments of the Turks and the attempts of the lords to impose hereditary subjection upon the peasants. When the rebellions failed, stringent feudal obligations were imposed in Hungary, Transylvania and Slovakia — and the peasant was 'forever' bound to the land over which the lord assumed complete jurisdiction. However, the peasant uprisings which fill the century were not always directed against the slipping status of the peasantry. At times they were due to the breakdown of the lord's ability to protect the peasants, his *quid pro quo* for their services and obedience to his jurisdiction. In eastern Austria when the lords retreated into their castles in face of the Turkish onslaught, the peasants united first against the invader and then against the lords who had abandoned them. Similarly, the repeated peasant uprisings in lower Austria from 1596 to 1597 were due to the need to call upon the peasants to fight the Turks after the Hungarians had been beaten. Politics entered in: the serious peasant rebellion in Latvia (1577) was actively encouraged by the Russian nobles in order to depose the German lords of that region. It was begun by the failure of these lords in war, and the consequent prohibitions against the peasants carrying arms was not to end the constant unrest.

The peasant wars in Germany did not affect these regions, but they were no isolated incident. The German peasants were also crushed in the end, yet they were not depressed into virtual serfdom. However, the same noble ambitions were at work in Germany as in the rest of Europe, even if they were to fail in the west. There were great advantages to be gained in making the peasant, father to sons, completely subject to the lord's will. The small number of days which he worked the lord's land under latterday feudal custom (usually twelve a year) could be transformed into regular and unpaid labour on the estate. The 'common land' so essential to the peasants' economic survival could be taken from him (as happened in the English enclosures) and his rights to hunt in the woods discontinued. This meant that the judicial functions which the village community shared with the lord must be eroded, and the lord assume sole jurisdiction over his estates and the people who lived upon them.

The inroads made by Roman law in the Empire were used by the nobility to this end, stressing the maxim that 'whatever the Prince commands has the force of law'. The nobility resisted this maxim when it was used by kings against their power, but they were content to make full use of it within their own jurisdictions. But this use of Roman law, indeed such noble ambitions, would have been illusory if the lords had not already exercised vast rights over the peasantry upon their estates. These they now sought to extend, not only through law, the abolition of fixed manorial dues, but also through taxation. Here nobles annexed rights which belonged to another and rival authority. As the century opens they had in large measure usurped the tithe from the Church, and this was a burden from which the peasantry in central Europe suffered extensively. Moreover, a fairly rapid growth of the population worsened the proportion of land available to the individual peasant and raised the call for a fairer use of the common lands. But the nobles wanted to take over common lands altogether, abolish the autonomy which remained to the villages, and increase the burdens of serfdom. Their goal was to create a uniform group of subjects.

THE PEASANTS' WAR

The peasants in their German revolt were well aware of these threats to their existence, and their aims were designed to counter them. This was true though the Peasants' War differed in complexion within the diverse regions of Germany. In the more northerly territories the declining status of the peasant was the main source of anxiety. But in south-west Germany the aims of the peasants were slightly different. Here they not only wanted to maintain their customary rights, but indeed to extend them as over against the landlords and state power. Their revolt was primarily directed against the state, rather than against the local feudal lord. This situation foreshadowed the peasant rebellions which were to plague the next century — when the local lords encouraged rebellions against the encroachment of the state and its tax collectors upon both landlords and peasants alike.

The Peasants' War was not a coordinated rebellion but took place in several regions of central Europe: Switzerland, Swabia and Thuringia being the most important. The demands known as the Twelve Articles (1525) provided the glue which held at least some of the rebellion together. Two of the demands were basic to the entire programme: the call to replace customary law by godly law, inspired by the protestant reformation, and emphasis upon the autonomy of the community as represented by the peasant village. The primacy of godly law meant that the principles of equality inherent in the gospel must replace ancient and discriminatory custom.[3] Serfdom as well as all feudal restraints must be abolished and, just as important, the common lands should no longer be enclosed for the use of the privileged. The tithe, also, was contrary to God's commandments. Moreover, pastors should be elected and dismissed by the village community itself, and the village must control its own jurisdiction. The equality inherent in the law of God was to benefit the community as a whole, for the village was the focal point of the peasants' identity. But the primacy of the law of God had a liberating effect which transcended the peasant community and attracted some cities and even minor nobility to the peasant cause. The Twelve Articles became a fully fledged revolutionary doctrine through the preachers who had joined in the war and whose sermons radicalised the cause.

Thomas Münzer called the peasants the 'elect', having their divine duty, an assured victory, and as the Peasants' War started he painted social equality as a part of the new society they would bring about. The leaders of the peasants were, for the most part, not peasants at all; they were preachers like Münzer (though his actual association with the revolt was short), minor nobles like Florian Geyer, and even men of a middle-class background. They toyed with the idea of a peasant parliament to reform the Empire, even with a 'parliament of saints' such as Cromwell put into unsuccessful practice in his 'Barebone's Parliament' over a century later.

Linked to the longings of popular piety these ideas were to have a long life in all of Europe, both in religious and social terms. From this point of view the 'radical Reformation' must stand side by side with the other Reformations which retained their link to, and the support of, the 'powers that be'. The peasants were crushed (1525) and Münzer executed, but the peasants did not relapse into apathy; they were from now on a force to be reckoned with in German politics. Their demands were discussed at an Imperial Diet the next year, and though no action was taken, individual towns and regions went far towards resolving some of the peasant's grievances. Moreover, this was the beginning rather than the end of radical revolt. The next eruption at Münster (1534—35) shows this well. It began harmlessly enough, with a not unusual dispute between the city and its bishop who was its secular lord and indeed not even ordained. To strengthen their hand the guilds invited preachers who were inclined towards the cause of the Reformation. The same thing happened in Geneva, where a dispute between city and bishop was also the beginning of reform. But in Münster the reformed cause soon slid out of the control of the guilds, and indeed out of the hands of the settled and respectable elements of the community.

THE MÜNSTER EXPERIMENT

Preaching extended the Reformation, as preaching was the lever by which the reformed Christianity was introduced into all of Europe. It is not difficult to see how in a largely illiterate society listening to preaching was a major outlet for men's frustrations and desires — we know how men and women waited all night to hear a popular preacher in the morning. Bernard Rothmann was such a preacher in Münster. He managed to get Anabaptist refugees admitted to the city, and they in turn provided more preachers to spread the faith. With them the unemployed and discontented began to immigrate from the neighbouring Netherlands. By 1534 the 'takeover' was complete and a Dutch immigrant, Jan Matthys, by his control of the town council, prepared the way for the dictatorship of his fellow countryman, John of Leyden. Where earlier a sympathetic town council had proclaimed liberty of conscience, and had given the Anabaptists legal recognition, by 1534 most of its members had fled and the 'holy community' had come into being.

The Münster theocracy guided the social revolution in the town.

The distinction between 'mine' and 'thine' was to vanish in favour of trust in God; the existing order must be exterminated and with it its symbol, private property, unknown in the primitive and true Church. Money was not used in the town, only in its dealing with the outside world, and communal ownership over all commodities (including food and housing) was established. This was a community of the elect and 'no Christian or Saint can satisfy God if he does not live in such a community'. John of Leyden established polygamy, using the Old Testament patriarchs as his example.

All phases of life were regulated, including a strict division of labour. But such regulation led to increasing terror. John proclaimed himself 'king' and presided at executions in the market place. The 'good society' coincided with the needs of a city under siege, and Münster held out longer and more successfully than any other city under similar conditions. But the end came, and massacre succeeded the victory of the princes leagued against the town. Defeat did not destroy the dream of the new Jerusalem which had, for a moment, existed: a dream whose menace the princes and the established reformers were quick to see.

ANABAPTISTS AND SPIRITUALISTS

Anabaptist belief created a community of the Godly to whose discipline men and women submitted voluntarily and which was enforced by admonition and the ban. Adult baptism for believers signified entry into this exclusive community from whose religious practices, such as the Lord's Supper, non-believers were excluded. The community was democratic: honesty was to be the rule and no oaths were to be sworn, while the pastor was supported and disciplined by the congregation. Such a tight-knit community united by faith, dedicated to separation from the ungodly, was well suited to function as a centre for the seizure of power. Indeed, Anabaptist Münster was the centre of a widely spread conspiracy to seize cities in the Netherlands and western Germany.

During the siege of Münster Anabaptist leaders in that city hoped that other Anabaptists would relieve them, and in response thousands of Dutch Anabaptists marched towards Münster only to be intercepted and crushed. Even after the fall of Münster, Anabaptist violence died only a slow and lingering death,[4] though the overwhelming majority of Anabaptists turned quietist under persecution, holding that pacifism and love were the Christians' proper response to violence and evil. God was now said to judge between the 'believers' and their enemies – when the time is ripe. Anabaptism withdrew into its own self-contained communities, adopting a waiting posture. To be sure, with the passage of time such a retreat from the world led towards a strict biblicism which triumphed over the millenarian impetus. Even before the failure of the Münster experiment such a self-contained Anabaptist community had already been founded by Conrad Grebel of Zürich (1525). The 'Swiss brethren' continued to exist throughout the sixteenth century. Another important centre of Anabaptism was Moravia, where Jakob Hutter had made communism a part of his community, though in a more restrained way than had been the case at Münster. It is difficult to make a typology of this radicalism or to confine it to one region, for it is found everywhere. Its spiritualism, belief in continuous revelation, and the ideal of prophecy, lent themselves to the most diverse kind of interpretation.

Some figures stand out, however: Kaspar Schwenkfeld with his deification of man, Sebastian Franck whose mysticism was related to stoic ideals, and the spiritualism of Valentin Weigel. To Luther it seemed as if he had unleashed a tempest and had attacked one creature of Antichrist only to raise up a horde of others. To be sure, his Reformation had stimulated radicalism, and many of the 'prophets' had passed through Lutheranism on their way to a new Jerusalem; but Luther clung increasingly to another group of followers: those in power. Luther has been blamed for forging a close tie between throne and altar, but it must be remembered that without it his Reformation could not have survived. Moreover, he himself sincerely believed that no one could truly regulate a faith freely found, which formed the essence of his 'Christendom restored'.

LUTHER AND WORLDLY AUTHORITY

Luther gave rulers power to regulate the externals of the Church, but for all this, his view of secular authority was essentially negative during the first part of his reformation. Laws existed to restrain men, tempted by Satan, and the task of rulers was to keep the peace and protect one man from another. This meant an inequality of persons, a necessary secular hierarchy under which man must live. Without such inequality 'a kingdom cannot stand' and the result of its fall would be chaos in which the devil could do his work unhindered; the true Christian community is aided by such a secular order, surrounded as it is by enemies on all sides. However, in 1531 Luther grew somewhat bolder, and in his *Warning to His Dear German People* wrote that he would not oppose violent resistance in order to defend Protestantism. But this new permissiveness did not basically change Luther's view of the secular order. Princes who defended Protestantism had to receive continued support against all other authority, but it was quite another matter to support subjects against their rulers. Luther lacked Calvin's doctrine of the intermediate magistrates, interposed between rulers and people, who can call for resistance against an ungodly ruler. Perhaps Luther's greater willingness to entertain some resistance theory at this point was part of the older Luther's fears that his enemies were constantly increasing: the radicals, the Turks, the Jews and the pope. Luther's essentially patriarchal and hierarchical concept of society explains his opposition to the peasants, his advocacy in the main of passive resistance only — even if the magistrate commands evil actions. Not only would God punish evil in his own good time, but to upset the established order would make the work of Christians all the more difficult in the end. These are the underlying factors in his own mind of why he turned to and supported 'the powers that be'.

Frederick the Wise of Saxony held the key to Luther's success, for without his support the professor could have been delivered into the hands of emperor or pope. Frederick had been the pope's candidate in the election to the office of emperor which went to Charles V. He had a financial stake in the relics at the Castle Church, and he was hardly of a radical turn of mind. Frederick moved to the support of Luther on the basis of his political opposition to the emperor and his alarm that the greatest ornament of his cherished university might be driven away from Wittenberg. Had he not founded that university to outshine his rival in ducal Saxony? Frederick, by temperament a moderate, believed for a long time that the religious quarrel could be settled by compromise.

Luther's key supporter at court was the humanist chancellor Georg Spalatin. Undoubtedly this man influenced the elector in Luther's favour, until Frederick himself became convinced of the inherent rightness of Luther's cause. Winning the support of the ruling powers was greatly facilitated by the humanists who acted as their chancellors and diplomats. Such men, even if not outright supporters (like Spalatin), were apt to be Erasmians, working for moderation and compromise in matters religious.

Luther obtained support not only from Frederick or Philip of Hesse, but also from other princes for whom political ambition for greater power and independence also entailed a religious commitment, in an age where religion was always at hand. The Lutheran Reformation proved especially successful in German towns and cities. There the medieval Church with its system of pilgrimages, indulgences, penance and special offerings seemed to strangle individual initiative in meriting heaven on the part of ever more self-confident townsmen. Lutheran doctrine seemed to liberate men from the relative impersonality of a universally prescribed system of religious duties. Good works could now be performed from a sense of grateful joy rather then out of fear. The individual freedom which Luther's ideas brought to people in towns was joined to a long standing, if vague, sense of German pride as well as anticlericalism directed at Rome and its agents. The urban Catholic clergy was often perceived as standoffish, unwilling to share the responsibilities of city life. Evangelical missionaries and printers, speaking directly to the middle and lower orders, rapidly found an enthusiastic audience in German cities. In Strassburg, for example, it was the parishioners, led by the gardeners' guild, who heedless of the illegality of their action installed Martin Bucer as their preacher. It was such pressure from below which persuaded city councils and ruling oligarchies, anxious to preserve civic unity, to declare openly for the Reformation. This process of preaching, popular pressure and magisterial acceptance was sometimes slow as, for example, in the triumph of Calvin at Geneva, but its success in Germany can be measured by the fact that, of the 65 Imperial Cities, 50 eventually saw Protestantism accepted or tolerated.[5]

In immediate terms, princely support for the Reformation encouraged resistance against the emperor. When at the Diet of Speyer (1529) the emperor rushed through a resolution confirming the edict of Worms against Luther and forbidding all ecclesiastical innovations, the evangelical princes made a strongly worded protest, and though the emperor ignored this, it was clear that Luther had attracted powerful and vocal support. At the next Diet, in Augsburg (1530), Charles asked Johannes Eck to make a catalogue of all heresies which were plaguing his empire. To this the

Protestants responded once more, this time with the Augsburg Confession. Melanchthon wrote this Confession, and at a difficult moment. Charles for once had his hands free to deal with the empire, and the Protestant princes themselves were divided on how to approach the emperor at so dangerous a juncture.

Was the Augsburg Confession a compromise? Luther, though temporarily alarmed that it might be, in the end accepted it joyfully. The document is couched in a moderate tone and seeks to conciliate, but all the tenets of Luther are firmly stated and carefully explained. It was to remain the classic statement of the Lutheran faith. In the Augsburg Confession we can see clearly the dilemma which was to lead to the close union of throne and altar. It is stated that outward uniformity of religious service is not necessary, but further on the remark is made that such service must proceed in good order. Who was to preserve this order? The dilemma was solved when the secular authorities began making binding orders for church services, whether it was the duke of Prussia (1525) or, in the same year, the city of Stralsund. The magistrate came to stand not only *in loco parentis* but also *in loco Dei*, he came to unite the two swords in his person. The time was past when reformers like Zwingli advised that the Protestant communities themselves might elect and dismiss their pastors. This had been a demand of the 'Twelve Articles of the peasants', and the defeat of the peasants also spelled the end of a Protestantism which sought its roots in community control. The cultural attitudes which sprang from the union of Church and state were to affect Germany into the twentieth century. Secular authority, such as the state, has to be obeyed for the sake of order; this is an 'external' matter not to be questioned. The true liberty resides within man, an idealistic definition which does not extend into the public realm. Luther's growing conservatism, as evidenced in his immensely popular *Table Talk* (jotted down by his guests and published after Luther's death), supported such attitudes. But it must be added that the original alliance between throne and altar was ambivalent, that in some German states like Württemberg it did not support the prince but strengthened the estates.

CULTURE AND COMMUNITY

Luther's Reformation had other far-reaching consequences in the secular realm. He was vitally interested in education, now open to new experimentation as it passed out of the hands of the Church into that of the secular magistrate. Education must have faith as its object, but Luther's division between the world of faith and the human world where reason could be used led him to advocate universal compulsory education, not merely religious but also practical. Languages were important in discovering the meaning of scripture; the study of nature was advocated as well. The knowledge of the external world should include the skills used within it, even mundane subjects like book-keeping. In this way Luther contributed to a reorientation of education which corresponded to the more practical interests of the bourgeoisie in the cities. Another issue which Luther had to confront was that of the poor. Charity given out at the monastery door had come to an end in Protestant regions. Luther's answer in the *Leisniger Kassenordnung* (1523) was that the community would have to take over their support. The parish received social duties in addition to religious ones. All reformers faced this problem, and all solved it in the same manner. Similarly the sick and insane were now viewed as a communal responsibility, and former monasteries were converted for their care.

The regulations which Luther laid down for the Saxon town of Leisnig never became reality, but they show in excellent fashion his emphasis upon the total community of believers. The whole parish was to meet in order to elect ten 'guardians', half of them to come from among the parishioners themselves and half divided roughly between city councillors and the peasants of the surrounding countryside. As a matter of fact this was a more direct and, from our vantage point today, a more democratic representation than that which Calvin was to set up for his church later. These 'guardians' looked after the communal treasury, the care of the poor and sick – but they had other economic duties as well. The 'guardians' were to buy up wheat when it was cheap and store it in order to sell, loan or give it to members of the community in times of high prices.[6]

Luther's individualism was an inward one; for the priesthood of believers as a whole he strengthened the sense of community, for rulers their feeling of social responsibility. Faith through love of God also meant loving your neighbour and this in turn led to an emphasis upon the Christian as part of a social community. Luther believed in social hierarchy, but he also stressed social justice within the community and thus called for a restoration of the medieval 'just price'. Luther's ideal of the community, his ideal of parish organization, must be put side by side with his strengthening of the authority of the magistrates.

This community was the 'fortress' within which the true believers found shelter and comfort. Luther's increasing intolerance excluded the possibility of a dialogue between his followers and those who differed in religious opinion. He was fighting error not men, and whenever he saw in an enemy a disposition to embrace the truth, the polemic was dropped.[7] Luther's unyielding fight against error is not surprising in a man who was not only certain of the truth he had discovered, but also took considerable risks in proclaiming it. From the very beginning of his career as a reformer there was no intrinsic reason why he would not be burnt as a heretic in the usual way, and he was fully aware of the danger he courted. Such is the setting of his fierce and polemical demands. By 1530 he called for the extermination of adversaries such as the Anabaptists, just as he had demanded the extirpation of the rebellious peasants at an earlier time. Those who disagreed were children of the devil, and as the world seemed to be peopled by devils, no quarter could be given. Luther encouraged the persecution of witches and called for the burning of Jewish synagogues: the refusal of the Jews to convert, now that the true Christianity had been revealed, could only mean that they were the devil's creatures. Moreover, according to the *Book of the Apocalypse*, the conversion of the infidels was a necessary precondition to the second coming of Christ, and by their refusal to convert the Jews were impeding the coming of the millennium. The concept of the community of believers went hand in hand with an ever greater exclusiveness. As Luther told the papal legate in 1535, 'the Holy Ghost has given us certainty and we need no general council of the Church. But [the rest of] Christianity needs one in order to convince them of the errors which they have practised for so long a time.'[8]

The nineteenth-century contention that the Protestant Reformation furthered individualism can no longer be upheld. Calvin allowed usury only for the good of the community, the Anabaptists stressed a perfect community – and the Reformation as a whole gave new social tasks to the community of believers. The problem of individualism seems beside the point. Instead Luther inaugurated a new stage in the evolution of secular society. Not only did secular activity receive a direct religious sanction, but it was on the road to social legislation of which the Elizabethan Poor Law at the end of the sixteenth century can stand as a not untypical example.

Meanwhile the Reformation had spread to western Europe and into eastern Europe as well. This was accomplished by men who, with the example of Luther's struggles before them, managed to avoid millenarianism or prophetic radicalism. Like Luther they launched movements which were to influence the destiny of men and nations far into the future.

NOTES AND REFERENCES

1   H. G. Koenigsberger, 'The Unity of the Church and the Reformation', in *Politicians and Virtuosi* (London, 1986), pp. 169–178.

2   Claus-Peter Clasen, *Anabaptism: A Social History, 1525–1618* (Ithaca, N.Y., 1972), p. 330.

3   Peter Blickle, 'Biblicism versus Feudalism', in Robert Scribner and Gerhard Benecke, eds., *The German Peasant War of 1525 – New Viewpoints* (London, 1979), p. 142.

4   James M. Stayer, *Anabaptists and the Sword* (Lawrence, 1972), p. 284 ff.

5   A. G. Dickens, *The German Nation and Martin Luther* (London, 1974), p. 180.

6   Aemilius Ludwig Richter, *Die Evangelischen Kirchenordnungen des Sechzehnten Jahrhundert* (Leipzig, 1871), pp. 10–15.

7   This point is made by Roland H. Bainton, *Studies on the Reformation* (Boston, 1966), p. 91.

8   Quoted in Friedrich Heer, *Die Dritte Kraft* (Frankfurt, 1960), p. 202.

8

A CONTINUED REFORMATION

THE 'MAGISTERIAL' REFORMATION

Within the many reformations which followed Luther's we can distinguish two main types: the radical reformers and those who carried through their task supported by the secular authorities. The radicals, Anabaptists for the most part, also made a bid for secular power, but after their failure at Münster was followed by equal failure at Strassburg, such radicals either withdrew into a rejection of the world or split into a myriad of sects, each with its own leadership. However, this radicalism did not vanish. In the England of Oliver Cromwell it made one more bid for secular power – and failed again. With its own doctrine of 'election' for those infused with the 'holy spirit', it came to provide a revolutionary dynamic for the lower classes of the population, keeping up the role it had played during the peasant wars.

Luther had considered these radical ideas a menace to faith and order, and so did the other reformers who worked hand in glove with secular authorities. They have been called the 'magisterial reformers', because of their reliance upon the magistrates, and it is to them that the immediate future within the sixteenth century belonged. Here also the centrifugal tendencies of the Reformation were at work, and of the many reformations of this type we can select for discussion only the most portentous. Huldreych Zwingli, Martin Bucer and John Calvin possessed an influence which went well beyond their immediate small territories and affected all of western Europe and some of eastern Europe as well.

HULDREYCH ZWINGLI

Luther was an important example to all these men, but both Zwingli and Calvin arrived at their break with Rome independently. Zwingli did not become familiar with Luther's work until after he was called to be minister at Zürich, and humanist influences were more important in forming his attitude towards traditional theology than Lutheranism. As a pastor in the town of Glarus, and at the monastery of Einsiedeln, he had always been in touch with the work of the Christian humanists. Brief study at Basle combined with the reading of the works of Erasmus gave Zwingli a different Christian education from that which Luther had received. The sale of an indulgence pushed Zwingli upon the threshold of his reformation in 1519; for Luther also the selling of an indulgence had been instrumental in crystallizing his opposition to Rome. The actual reformation in Zürich began in 1520 and was complete five years later. The powerful council of the city of 5,400 inhabitants was favourably inclined to Zwingli from the beginning, but it desired, if possible, to proceed legally without provoking imperial authorities or the bishop of Constance within whose diocese Zürich was located.

METHODS OF REFORM

The change in Zürich was accelerated by the use of methods which were general to the Reformation as a whole. Preaching was essential, and the reformer was usually attached to a leading church; Zwingli, for example, was a minister at the Münster of Zürich, Bucer at Strassburg Cathedral. Such men were superb preachers in an age which set great store by preaching. The attempt of the reformers to cut through Catholic dogma made for simple and direct preaching which the people could understand and by which they could easily be swayed. Zwingli filled his sermons with Swiss patriotism and references to contemporary events.

When Zwingli faced representatives of the bishop for disputation (1523) this became a demonstration in favour of the most popular preacher at the cathedral. The city council, pushed on by the popular pressures the reformer himself had created, gave his reforms the support they required. Marriages of priests were increasingly condoned and 'images' removed from churches. Finally, in 1525, the abolition of the Mass completed the reformation which Zwingli desired. Zwingli's changes in religious service were more radical than those which Luther had produced. Zwingli's humanism and his intense concern for the corporate character of the Church asserted themselves. The Lord's Supper was not merely a memorial service but was indeed filled with Christ's 'real presence'. However, this presence was not within the bread and wine, nor even affected by the individual believer, but was instead diffused among the whole corporate body of believers worshipping together. Such a stress upon the corporate nature of the Church worked to equalize clergy and laymen within it, but it also played its part in the ecclesiastical discipline which Zwingli instituted. The Church was a unity, forming a 'holy community' within which secular tasks and religious worship were closely linked. Where Luther had separated the kingdom of God, *communio sanctorum*, from the secular order, Zwingli tied the two together, and Bucer in Strassburg was to follow his example. Calvin, as we shall see, took a middle position between Luther and Zwingli on this important question.

The social effects of the Zürich reformation were immediate and profound. Monasteries were abolished and monastic charity became a communal concern. This happened wherever the Reformation established itself, and it took much the same course in all Protestant Europe. Monastic wealth was used to support the poor and the monasteries themselves became poor houses or, at times, hospitals for the insane. Each parish was forced to pay tithe, both for the support of the poor and for the maintenance of the pastor. In Zürich these new responsibilities were established by the city council during the year 1525, when the jurisdiction hitherto exercised by the bishop was transferred to the civic body. Through these changes the civil administration greatly extended its jurisdiction and power.

Zwingli, however, did not wish to grant to secular authority the power to oppress which he had found objectionable on the part of the Church. He became the first reformer to advocate violent resistance to an ungodly tyrant: not only must the people depose a ruler who demanded wicked actions, but any individual commissioned by God was justified in assassinating such a tyrant. The considerable secular and ecclesiastical powers granted to rulers was reserved only for those who governed according to the reformed religion.

MORAL DISCIPLINE

The new law court concerned with marriage disputes, hitherto part of the bishop's jurisdiction, developed in a significant way, for it became the watchdog over the general manners and morals of the city. Through spies it discovered and punished lovers who stood in doorways or behind barns, women who received male visitors, and even innkeepers who failed to report on the moral behaviour of their guests. When church attendance was made compulsory in 1529, those who did not attend regularly were also punished by this court which had become in fact a board to enforce moral discipline, composed of the clergy, the magistrates and two elders of the Church.

Moral discipline was supervised jointly by Church and State: Zwingli everywhere minimized the distinction between ministers and laymen. The community must include both Church and State in order to become a 'holy community'. Zürich provided one possible example for the Geneva of Calvin and of the 'rule of saints' in revolutionary England. But why did Zwingli emphasize such a disciplined community? Zwingli had come under humanist influence, and it is not without interest that it is precisely the humanist reformer who insists upon such rigid moral discipline. For Luther, justification by faith had meant that man's life remained one of penance, that faith was God's free gift, which does not essentially change man's character or free him from the imputation of sin. But for Zwingli, justification by faith freed man from the *necessity* of sinning, and enabled him freely to fulfil God's will.

Zwingli supposed a predisposition in man towards virtue, a goodness which originated in God but nevertheless existed in human creatures. He emphasized man's will – the damned were those who, having heard the word of God, refused to follow it. Man must show that he has realized his potential through obeying the word of God as revealed in the Bible. Discipline was to help man by educating him to a holy life but this must be combined with that thorough knowledge of scripture which is central to all of Zwingli's thought.

Not only was the religious service simplified to consist of Bible reading, a sermon and the distribution of bread and wine, but daily Bible readings supplemented such services. These *lectiones publicae* trained laymen in biblical analysis and interpretation, for they could take part freely in these exercises. Zwingli called these daily exercises 'prophesyings', and as such they were taken up by other Protestant sects, especially the English Puritans who used them to harry the Anglican Church of Elizabeth.

This democratic element within his reformation seemed to put Zwingli into dangerous proximity to the Anabaptists. Zwingli saved himself from such association by stressing the necessity of human justice as well as divine justice: the power of the magistrate over all citizens was combined with that of the clergy. Nevertheless, Zwinglianism was constantly accused of Anabaptist leanings, and it cannot be denied that, especially in Strassburg, the two movements had some sympathy for one another.

Such accusations of radicalism were furthered by Zwingli's interpretation of the two sacraments which to him, as to Luther, retained their validity: baptism and communion. For the humanist reformer these were sanctifications, but only as signs of belonging to the corporate church. It was on this doctrine that the effort of union between the two reformations foundered – for Luther's individualistic, inner-directed faith such an interpretation could have little meaning. A 'board of moral discipline' would have made no sense to the German who emphasized 'trust' in God rather than outward discipline.

Zwingli's importance for the Reformation lies not merely in the changes which he made in Zürich. He gave the whole movement a new and important direction. The humanist emphasis upon man's potential meant that a holy community could exist on earth, strengthened by moral discipline and the excommunication of those who refused to see the truth of scripture. The fusion of Church and state which Zürich represented was not followed by most other reformers. Here the way in which this reformation had come about as well as Zwingli's own political involvement must be taken into consideration. His doctrine of resistance to authority as a way to safe-guard the true religion had a future before it. He was a patriot and kept up a constant agitation against the Swiss custom of forming mercenary armies for foreign employers. Zwingli spoke from experience about this problem as he had accompanied one such army to Italy as a chaplain and been present when the French bloodied the Swiss at Marignano.

THE ESTABLISHMENT OF THE 'REFORMED' FAITH

It seemed only logical for Zwingli to take the lead in the political and military events which occurred once Zürich had accepted the Reformation. He attempted but failed to win over the other Swiss cantons; they resented his bid as a move towards greater centralization within the Swiss confederation. The powerful cantons which had originally formed the nucleus of that Confederation (Urkantone), Luzern, Uri, Zug, Schwyz and Unterwalden, remained militantly Catholic. Here a fear of centralization was mixed with resentment against Zwingli's opposition to the recruiting of mercenary soldiers, their greatest export. Austria supported these cantons, for it had no desire to see a more centralized Swiss state menacing its flank at a time when Swiss soldiers were considered the best in Europe. A showdown within the Confederation was not slow in coming, and the first victory belonged to Zürich (1529). This induced the powerful cantons of Berne and Basle, though themselves embracing Protestantism (1528), to join in opposition to Zürich's growing power. At the second and decisive trial of strength that city was defeated. At the battle of Kappel (1531) Zwingli, who fought as a volunteer, was killed and his body quartered and burnt.

Defeat did not end the Reformation in Zürich or its influence. Heinrich Bullinger, Zwingli's successor, was a man no less remarkable than the reformer himself, though his talents took a different direction. Bullinger had the makings of a mediator, and he was consulted in all the great quarrels among the different branches of the Reformation. When English Protestants fled during the reign of Queen Mary they made use of his services, not only as host but as mediator in their own quarrels. During the reign of Elizabeth he was consulted by both the Puritans and the queen, though he finally sided with the English government in the controversy over the use of the vestment or cope during religious service. His reputation was pre-eminent, though Calvin's was to eclipse it. Bullinger himself brought the Zürich Reformation into close contact with that of Geneva, preparing the way for the common front of the two Reformations with the acceptance by both of the *Consensus Tigurinus* (1549). All Zwinglian churches in Switzerland joined this agreement in points of theology.

MARTIN BUCER

By the time of the battle of Kappel, the influence of Zwingli had spread beyond Switzerland, up the Rhine valley, and had found support in one of the chief cities of that valley – Strassburg. The Reformation in Strassburg had been accomplished by Capito (1525) together with the chief magistrate, Johannes Sturm. However, the Strassburg Reformation took a direction which increasingly alarmed the other leaders of the 'magisterial reformation'. Strassburg had become a place of refuge for persecuted Protestants from France and the Netherlands who had brought with them Anabaptist ideas. Capito himself was close to Zwinglianism, but that faith had enough similarities to this despised radicalism for Capito to have acquired Anabaptist sympathies. Was Strassburg to go the same way which Münster followed nearly a decade later? It was Martin Bucer who made his name by successfully fighting the Anabaptists and Zwinglians in Strassburg, until he had become the city's leading reformer (1527). Bucer's lasting importance was due not only to his victory in Strassburg, but also to the development of his own political ideas during this struggle. For when the young Calvin came to Strassburg he not only was a close friend of Bucer, but was also influenced by Bucer's ideas in his own thought about the Church and society.

In opposition to Anabaptist beliefs, Martin Bucer stressed predestination; no human could believe himself saved merely by the certainty which he possessed of his own faith. Therefore the Church cannot merely embrace the 'company of saints' as the Anabaptists believed, but must embrace all men. This Church was a divine institution to which God had given a task, and no sect had the right to separate itself from it. Like Zwingli, Bucer stressed ecclesiastical discipline and the use of excommunication. Such a view of the Church meant the expulsion of radicals and the establishment of a magisterial reformation in Strassburg.

Bucer's formulation of the relationship of Church and state was more important for the future than his views of Church organization (similar as they were to Zwingli's). He made the Church an independent power standing beside the State. Unlike Zwingli's organization, the board to enforce moral discipline must in Bucer's view consist wholly of clerics, and only the Church should wield the weapon of excommunication. Bucer was not able to realize this ideal fully in Strassburg, as, later on, Calvin was never to realize it fully in Geneva. Excommunication was too powerful a weapon to be left solely in the hands of the Church: expulsion from the society of Christians meant, in effect, expulsion from the city as well. Bucer did manage to put his ideal of Church–state relations into effect in Hesse; and that State came to exemplify the ideal of the Calvinist Church in this respect.

Bucer's political theories were first set down in his *Commentary on St Matthew* (1530) and they were to influence Calvin's own political thought.[1] In his book Bucer emphasized that the Church must be independent of the State in order to fulfil its divine mission in the world. But of still greater importance was his opposition to the centralization of power in the hands of one supreme ruler or magistrate. Bucer did not depart from the view that a Christian has to regard existing laws and rulers as willed by God. But for the citizen of Strassburg not only the emperor, but also the authorities in self-governing cities were directly instituted by God as magistrates. The same held for all the German princely states. Strassburg was a city within the Empire and for Bucer the demand of religion to preserve the order established by God implied the conservation of political variety within the Empire itself.

Such a political theory conferred a special responsibility upon the inferior authorities: God, Bucer wrote, did not want the rule of absolutism on earth – Saul was given to the people of Israel only in God's wrath. Hence if the emperor attacks the Church, then the inferior magistrates must act to preserve it against the highest secular authority. Calvin in his *Institutes* adopted this mode of political thought. For Calvin, not city councils and princes but parliaments and estates were the 'inferior' magistrates, and he gave them a status which legitimized opposition to any absolute ruler hostile to the 'true church'.

Bucer's stress upon the role of the inferior magistrate, and his emphasis upon the independent role of the Church in the State, were his principal contributions to the Reformation. To be sure, he also attempted to mediate between the different reformations. But these attempts were failures, and led only to the Wittenberg Concord (1536) by which the Strassburg reformer yielded to most Lutheran theological demands. When Sturm humbled the city before Charles V's interim (1548) (see p. 219) Bucer fled to England and in his *De Regno Christi* (1551) tried to influence Edward VI to accept his plans for the organization of the English Church. But London was to be no Strassburg. Bucer the theoretician was vastly more influential than Bucer the active reformer. Though Calvin received his ideas from many other sources, Bucer was crucial as the first magisterial reformer decisively to separate the functions of Church and State and to put forward a political theory which, in Calvin's hands, was to make the Reformation an instrument of political as well as theological change.

JOHN CALVIN

John Calvin's background has a certain similarity with that of Martin Luther. Calvin's father was also a self-made man who had risen to importance as a lawyer in his native Noyon. However, the elder Calvin sprang from artisan, not peasant stock, and the mother of the reformer came from a bourgeois family. Calvin was not raised against a background of popular piety but, largely, in a humanist and urban environment. Like Luther, Calvin started upon an ecclesiastical career; as a matter of choice, rather than through the shock induced by a bolt of lightning. He spent five years at Montaigu College, a part of the Sorbonne. There he was taught the theology of Occam and the fear of heresy. There is no evidence that Calvin suffered any of the mental torment which had plagued Luther when confronted with the same theology and a similar discipline.

Calvin left theological studies, not because he was troubled, but because his father wished him to study law. Through this study, at Orléans and at Bourges, Calvin came in contact with the French Renaissance and French humanism. These were to leave a profound mark upon his mind, especially through the study of law. The Roman law as he was taught it by the French masters formed a vital part of his political thought. The maxim that the ruler is the sole legislator (*Princeps legibus solutus est*) recurs in his writings after he had become a famed reformer, though for him the ruler was always bound by the laws which he had made. Throughout Calvin's mature thought there runs an emphasis upon law and legal terminology: God is the judge and His authority does not only mean the exercise of supreme power but has a legal corollary as well. God's will is the best and most rational rule of law.

To his legal training was added a preoccupation with the ancients, the mark of all humanists. This is reflected not only in Calvin's emphasis on style but also in the quality of his thought. The ideal of the organic state, where all members are interrelated, has origins in the medieval analogy of the state and human body. But for Calvin it was Seneca who confirmed this interrelatedness. However, his edition of Seneca's *De Clementia* (1532) represented a typical humanist exercise rather than a work fundamental to his development. Perhaps he was already questioning some humanist presuppositions at that time, for one year later he was definitely identified as a reformer. That year (1533) the rector of the Sorbonne, Nicolas Cop, delivered an official address which was filled with Erasmian sentiments. He called for the substitution of love for force in persecution of heretics and stressed justification by faith. Calvin probably had no hand in writing this speech, though it was believed at the time that he had, and the storm which the incident aroused forced him into hiding. There he wrote a tract against the soul-sleeping heresies in popular piety (see p. 146), showing that he was now definitely on the road towards evangelical commitment. But this development did not put Calvin in an isolated position, as Luther had been in his struggle. For French humanism in one important aspect tended towards ecclesiastical reformation.

FRENCH HUMANISM AND ECCLESIASTICAL REFORM

Two such humanist groups were especially active, and Calvin had contacts with both of them. Francis I's sister, Margaret of Navarre

(1492–1549), had made her court into a centre of both Renaissance literary modes and humanist learning. Rabelais resided at her court and pursued his satirical world. But increasingly Margaret turned towards a spiritual attitude: she had the Psalms translated into French and herself wrote a book many of whose stories castigated the existing Church and called for a true spiritual revival within the human heart (*Heptameron*). Margaret became something of a mystic, combining this with an emphasis upon salvation by faith. Calvin, like Luther before him, eventually repudiated such mysticism: no such mediating attitude was needed between God and man.

Another similar group of humanists existed at the court of Guillaume Briçonnet, the bishop of Meaux. There Lefèvre d'Étaples in his biblical commentaries had reached a position close to 'salvation by faith' and predictably filled with a mild kind of mysticism. Lefèvre's faith was nourished by the study of the Bible and by that Neoplatonism which was so important to many humanists. The Platonic tradition seemed to lead both Lefèvre and Margaret of Navarre close to pantheism. Denounced by the Sorbonne as heretical, the circle of Meaux fled to Margaret's court until the speech by their friend Nicolas Cop threw down the gauntlet to the ecclesiastical establishment.

The key figure in the controversy which now erupted was Margaret's brother, King Francis I. By 1533 it seemed that Margaret was pushing her brother in a reformist direction. Sermons calling for reform were openly preached at court. But Francis discovered that reforming sentiment, once left free play, was difficult to control. When posters (placards) attacking the Mass appeared at Paris street corners (1534), the king called for an abrupt halt. Why should he wish to see a fundamental change in a Church he already controlled? (see p. 277). Francis was a true Renaissance monarch, not interested in religion except as it touched upon politics. The king had no intention of letting religious radicalism become a menace to public order – reformation could easily escape royal control and lead to an attack upon constituted authorities. The year of the affair of the posters against the Mass was, after all, also the year when the Anabaptists were transforming the city of Münster into their new Jerusalem.

The placards against the Mass seemed indeed to menace public order. The people of Paris rose in righteous indignation against the 'foreigners' who were said to have perpetrated the outrage. Francis, the religiously indifferent monarch, executed an about-face. Those suspected of heresy were sacrificed to popular indignation. Rich and poor, the prosperous textile manufacturer and the poor printer of Margaret of Navarre's *The Mirror of a Sinful Soul* were burnt alive. Francis led a procession to the cathedral of Notre Dame in order to ask God's forgiveness for his earlier tolerance. The king held fast to the course of action he had chosen. Towards the end of his life (1545) he unleashed a 'crusade' against the Waldensians in southern France brutally destroying their villages. From 1533 onwards France was bent upon discontinuing a religious latitudinarianism which had made that country into a centre of Christian humanism. The orthodox at the Sorbonne had gained their victory, however temporary.

Calvin, Cop and Lefèvre fled France. After brief stays at Basle and Ferrara, Calvin secretly returned once more to Paris, intending to proceed from there to Strassburg at Bucer's request. However, the wars between Francis I and Charles V had closed the border between France and the Empire, forcing Calvin to travel *via* Geneva. There he found William Farel attempting to reform the city. The shortage of learned men who could help in such a reformation was great, and Farel asked Calvin to become a reader and commentator on Holy Scripture in Geneva. Strassburg would have to wait.

CALVIN AS REFORMER

After his flight from France Calvin emerged as a full-fledged reformer, and the first edition of the *Institutes of the Christian Religion* was published in Basle (1536). Revised continuously until the final edition of 1559, this book summarized the religious mission of John Calvin. He was accused of being a 'Lutheran', and with Luther he shared the belief in salvation by faith alone, and also the doctrine of the direct confrontation of God and man through belief in the mission of Christ. But Calvin's precise legal mind led to certain shifts of emphasis which had far-reaching consequences. The absolute power of God faced the irremediable sinfulness of man within the 'theatre of the world'. The basic theme of all the editions of the *Institutes* is that man belongs to

God, that it is man's duty to sacrifice himself to God and through such sacrifice to seek union with Him. The sense of the awesome power of the 'hidden God' and of the sinfulness of all men made Calvin reject the optimism of the humanists about the possibilities inherent in man's free will (as Luther had already rejected this before him), as well as the mild mysticism of many of his fellow French humanists.

Man's function in the 'theatre of this world' was obedience to both God's commands as laid down in the moral imperatives of the Old Testament, and to the commands of Christ, without whom nothing can be known about God's justice. It is through the mediation of Christ that God has called some men to be saved (the 'elect'), just as others are forever damned. The doctrine of election can be found in Luther as well, but here it is spelled out in detail and emphasized against the background of God's unchanging justice.

Calvin did not mean predestination to lead men and women into passivity and utter despair, nor did he want God's power to annihilate the individual. Men and women are still responsible for their own acts, and if they should receive God's call, they had the freedom to respond through the way in which they led their lives. God himself sees to it that individual life has meaning. Calvin always moved precariously between God's absolute power, his awesome grandeur, and God's goodnees; one makes people humble and responsible for their actions, while the other keeps them from despair.[2] Calvin himself in revising his *Institutes* increasingly tended to dwell upon God's power in predestination, and later Calvinists often removed any ambivalence in that concept through treating men and women as passive objects of God's will. Always, however, the elect are an aristocracy, not of society, but of God's grace, for they are also tainted by sin like the rest of humanity. But the elect set an example of obedience through their struggle against sin. Small wonder that the aristocracy of grace tended to become a social aristocracy as well, in spite of Calvin's rejection of such a definition of election.

Calvinism became a disciplined way of life because of the tension between human nature and God's wishes and, still more important, because of the positive attitude towards the world within which man has to act. For Calvin life on earth was hard and full of unrest – and we must not retreat from reality for God has created this for us. The emphasis upon unrest exemplifies the dynamic which runs throughout Calvin's world view. Man must always act through work; he must always struggle to build a better society and strive to safeguard the Church which Christ has created. Satan must be defeated both in the world and within each human being. The inward battle is joined to the outward struggle.

Man's conscience was his direct link to God. 'The conscience of man . . . is man's judgment of himself according to the judgment of God of him.'[3] Thus a clear conscience was the only sign of election, an 'inner certitude' that God's battles were being fought. Calvin's God commanded the consciences of man, and like an absolute ruler he abolished all authorities intermediate between Himself and His creatures. Medieval and Renaissance thought had believed the cosmos to be a vast hierarchy stretching from God through angels and saints to popes, kings and bishops. The heavenly and the earthly hierarchies complemented each other in a great chain of being. Luther had already demolished the heavenly hierarchy while clinging to the hierarchy on earth, and Calvin himself stressed the necessity of intermediate authorities in wordly government, while denying them a function in the ordering of heaven or indeed of the Church.

Both Calvin and Luther denied that the levelling of the cosmos also meant the destruction of the social and political hierarchies within a commonwealth. Yet as Calvinism became ever more revolutionary such an idea could strike root. The place of men or angels in the great chain of being had been conceived of as static: none of its parts could hope to climb nearer to the divine source. Within Calvinism, however, it was not simple being that mattered but instead man's behaviour induced by a clear conscience. Should those who fulfilled this criterion not move to the top, regardless of any other considerations in State or Church? Through drawing out the implications of the doctrine of conscience, and the destruction of the great chain of being, a Calvinist revolutionary elite, like the Puritans, defined its place in the governance of the world.

A clear conscience did not mean certainty; there was a constantly present inner struggle against the 'old Adam' as well as the outward struggle to transform the world according to God's plan. Calvinists lived in a state of permanent war. These tensions both outside and within man would only be truly resolved at the Last Judgment, but in his discussion of them

Calvin rejected extremes. There must be no stoic resignation to God's providence. For the God who rules all through his providence also puts challenges in the way of man which make it possible for him to fight this battle with himself and within existing reality. No doubt Farel's request that the reformer should stay in Geneva was such a challenge applied to Calvin himself. The necessity to exploit all opportunities which God creates for human action was to further both the dynamic of Calvinism and its political flexibility. An argument is provided which will be used by John Winthrop in New England to justify war against the Indians, and by a member of Parliament in order to urge Queen Elizabeth to cut off the head of Mary, Queen of Scots. For if she did not do so, the queen would be guilty of refusing the means 'now miraculously offered by God unto her'.

However, Calvin believed that there must be moderation in all things. Restlessness does not mean chaos or confusion. God's law is, after all, the most rational rule of law. Calvin expressed this wish for order in terms of the harmony which must prevail in society as it does in a clear conscience.

Moderation and harmony were bolstered, if men did their duty in their 'calling'. God has 'called' man to a profession in this life and to do one's duty in this station is therefore part of a religious obligation. This further encouraged application to work, but it did not necessarily prevent social mobility. For both Luther and Calvin man was put by God into his 'calling', but for both (while man should not lightly leave his profession) all 'callings' should be open to the common people. Calvin thought of such *vocatio* as aligning man with his duty to God in all aspects of his life, as an integral part of the harmony of man and his universe. Here the Reformation made a contribution to the advance of European civilization which cannot be overlooked: new status was given to the professions, indeed to all work, for to perform it was part of a religious duty. If we add to this Calvin's emphasis upon action, the opposition to a withdrawal from reality, a pattern of life emerges which did transform European attitudes whatever its actual economic consequences may have been. For Calvin economic success was not yet a part of this picture, election was a matter of clear conscience only – but given the emphasis upon acting to transform this world it was only a step to regard wordly success as a reward for doing one's duty – and the very ability to obey God and to take advantage of the opportunities He puts in man's way as a sign of election.

In the world no distinction can be made between elect and reprobate for no one possesses the kind of perfection which would automatically set him apart. Calvin, in common with all the 'magisterial' reformers, rejected the elitism of the Anabaptists. Membership in the community of believers is essential, for it is only through this true Church that life and society are possible. Otherwise man and all he creates are so corrupt that life would (in Thomas Hobbes's later phase) be 'nasty, brutish and short'. The reign of Christ through his Church makes possible the restoration not only of the Church itself but of the whole *corpus* of society.

The Church is therefore a communion of all Christians; this aspect was stressed by both Luther and Calvin. For both reformers Church officers should be elected by the community, but Luther never consistently enforced this and the 'emergency' control many rulers assumed over his Church became permanent. Calvin, however, did lay down firm principles for such elections, combining his love for order with the concept that power should flow upwards from below. Briefly, as put down in the 1543 edition of the *Institutes*, the pastors take the lead, examining candidates and proposing those whom they have selected. The community acclaims those proposed. The principle of inequality of function is important, not only for the sake of order, but also because the community includes the elect and those who are not – thus in a truly 'free election' the hypocrites would make themselves felt. By 1561 the Geneva ordinance still further reduced popular participation through providing merely for the 'silent approval of the people'. It is difficult to see the origins of modern parliamentary democracy in this form of election, the more so as the reformer followed a practice which had already been used in elections during the Roman Republic.

CALVIN'S POLITICAL THOUGHT

The Church had its own function to perform, and though it gave life and direction to society, this must be independent of the State.

Magistrates were members of the Church with 'special dignity' and Calvin hoped that they would be among the 'elect'. But within the Church they were to act as private persons, and from 1560 onwards the Geneva Syndics were no longer allowed to bring their staff of office to the consistory of the local church. They must support the Church, but not interfere with its functions. What then of a ruler who opposes the Church? Calvin supported the absolutism of Justinian's law, and was neutral as to the form which secular government could take – with a preference for aristocracy. This preference comes into play when the ruler persecutes the Church and when a legitimate prince is transformed into a tyrant. It was a commonplace of medieval thought that ungodly tyrants might be deposed, and Calvin followed this course. But who was to do the deposing?

Calvin, like Bucer before him, came to stress the responsibilities of 'inferior magistrates', those authorities 'appointed for the protection of the people and the moderation of the power of kings'. As an example of such authorities Calvin pointed to assemblies of the three estates, just as Bucer had spoken of the city governments of the Empire.

These ideas fitted in both with the reality of the situation, and with Calvin's aristocratic bent. The Reformation had been supported by city magistrates against the emperor, and the nobility who dominated the assemblies of estates often proved friendly to Calvinism. Moreover, Geneva provided another example; there the council had pushed through reforms against the legitimate overlord, the bishop, and the house of Savoy. These intermediate authorities were called upon to resist and overthrow the tyrant: the people did not participate. In Calvin's mind such authorities were not 'representative' of the people but were rather guardians of their rights. A judicial, but hardly a democratic, approach governed his attitude towards resistance to authority.

CALVIN'S GENEVA

Joining William Farel in Geneva, Calvin found a city whose long history had been shaped by the struggle to maintain its privileges. The right to elect magistrates (syndics) and representative councils was jealously guarded. But Geneva was surrounded by powerful and dangerous neighbours: the duke of Savoy to the south and the Swiss canton of Berne to the north-east. The immediate menace to independence came from the duke of Savoy who attempted to obtain control through the appointment of the bishop of Geneva. Geneva allied herself both with the Catholic canton of Fribourg as well as with Berne against the duke. The alliance was successful. First the bishop fled Geneva (1533) and then the allied army defeated Savoy (1535).

The war had been waged for the sake of political freedom, but religious issues could not be ignored. The failure of the bishop of Geneva and the duke of Savoy had been a blow to Catholic prestige within the city, and Protestant Berne now pressed for reform. It was that powerful canton which sent William Farel to Geneva. Political considerations helped Farel's work; Catholic Fribourg broke with Geneva and allied herself with Savoy, and in these circumstances Berne was the city's best hope for maintaining its independence.

Berne was Zwinglian, Church and state were fused, and the civil authorities also exercised ecclesiastical power. Such a model was attractive to the councils and syndics of Geneva, but it was unacceptable to Calvin himself. The creation of an independent church organization met great resistance from the Geneva oligarchy, and for the next twenty years Calvin had to battle for the 'true Church' he desired. The actual control of the city was in the hands of the long-established families: out of a population of 13,000 some 1,500 had the vote. Two councils existed, the Big Council of 200 and the Little Council of twenty-five members – both were elected, but it was the Little Council which held most of the strings of power and whose members bore the patrician title 'Seigneur'. The syndics were usually chosen from a list drawn up by the Little Council. In the last resort, the issues within the city were decided by the powerful oligarchy which held most of the important offices.

No sooner had Calvin arrived in the city (1536) than he and Farel submitted articles of faith which were accepted by the Councils. However, a year later Calvin submitted a new Confession of Faith (1537) to which all Genevans were supposed to swear public allegiance. Moreover, it bound the citizens to Church discipline. All his life Calvin regarded such confessions of faith as essential to maintaining order among the reformed communities. Luther had shied away from such formalism but Calvin believed in systematization, and as the Reformation grew older his viewpoint won out. Quite rightly the Councils saw in the Confession of 1537 an attack upon their authority, while others were afraid of a new ecclesiastical despotism – and Catholic sentiment undoubtedly still existed within the city. The Reformers had gone too far and too fast, and they were asked to leave the city (1538).

Calvin now went to Strassburg, but not for long. Geneva asked him to return two years later (1540). The reason was, once more, political: the anti-Calvinist councils had made a treaty with Berne which seemed to threaten the sovereignty of Geneva. They were discredited and Calvin's friends returned to power. His Protestantism, differing from the Zwinglianism of Berne, would mean a greater independence from the powerful ally to the east. Now Calvin pushed through his order for the Church: the *Ordonnances ecclésiastiques* (1541) served as a model wherever Calvinism took root. The central organism of the Church was the consistory composed of ministers and a dozen members of the council co-opted by the clergy. The 'Venerable Company of Pastors' included all the ministers of the city and county of Geneva. They prepared legislation for the consistory and proposed the new ministers to be elected to office. Laymen were represented on this council by twelve elders, elected by the congregations and then proposed for membership by the councils.

The triumph of Calvin in Geneva came at the end of a painfully slow process of conversion, one which was not confined to Geneva but can be traced to many other cities where the Reformation attempted to establish itself. First one or more charismatic Protestant ministers began a period of preaching, followed by disputation and agitation, and finally the new religious forms were legalized and institutionalized. Although reforming edicts can be dated precisely, the whole process of implementation could take as long as one generation. For example, Geneva officially adopted the reformed religion in 1534 but it took another generation to fully establish Calvin's control of the city.

Such control did not necessarily mean that Geneva or any centre of Protestantism constituted a community of godly Christians, not to mention a kingdom of true believers. Years of Lutheran indoctrination did not automatically re-Christianize the ordinary German, and even English areas thought heavily Puritan may

have contained only a relatively small flock of believers. Elizabethan ministers complained frequently of their unruly congregations which during sermons jostled each other, spat, talked and
even on occasion discharged firearms. We shall never know what
percentage of those who lived under some form of Protestantism
were true believers, yet there is some reason to think that a great
number of people hardly believed at all, a fact hinted at in the
frequent ignoring of the Sabbath, some deathbed confessions and
the lack of the conventional religious preambles in wills coming
from localities reputedly firm in their faith.

Ecclesiastical discipline was essential not only to encourage
believers but to restrain the cynical or indifferent as well as those
hostile to any established religion. Popular piety was difficult to
penetrate as well, not only for the Protestant reformers but for
all established religion. The drive to Christianize popular piety
was part of the reason for the century's witch craze. Calvin with
his belief in the sinfulness of all men and women paid close attention to ecclesiastical discipline in order to come as close as possible
to instituting an ideal Christian community as he saw it.

ECCLESIASTICAL DISCIPLINE

The consistory was the most important and controversial body
of the Church. It exercised ecclesiastical jurisdiction, and thus
symbolized the autonomy of the Church which Calvin desired.
But this autonomy was not complete until 1555; only then did
the Church get the right to pronounce excommunication, which
meant not only religious damnation but social and economic ruin
as well. Moreover, the consistory not only judged heresies, and
acted as a marriage court, but was charged with maintaining
church discipline. Two members of the consistory, accompanied
by the local minister, made regular rounds of each parish in order
that 'their eyes might be on the people'. This supervision was not
regarded as punitive, but was considered to be an aid to the
constant struggle every Christian had to wage against his own
baser nature. Calvin's stress on order and on the community was
also involved. The 'theatre of God' was a communal affair, and
scandal could not be tolerated. Still, the soberness of this new
Jerusalem has been overstressed.

Calvin was not opposed to art and music as such, only when they represented spiritual elements which could not be grasped by man's reason. His attitude towards music was ambivalent. It may have frightened him, approaching the 'vanity' which he detested. When Calvin praises music he does so because Plato had seen in it a harmony which should pervade all the world (see p. 407). Once more the classical influence upon his thought becomes apparent. He encouraged the representation of historical subjects in the visual arts. Such art, however, should only show those things which could be grasped by the eye rather than by the spirit. Some reforms had to be abandoned: the closing of local taverns, for example, which met intense popular resistance. The emphasis was constantly, relentlessly, on moderation and frugality. Predestination was the best pillar upon which to rest one's quest for salvation, but it was not a pillow to rest on. Ecclesiastical discipline was meant to encourage the pursuit of holiness.

But it also served as a warning to civil authority: several times members of powerful families had to humble themselves for blaspheming or for attacking the doctrine of predestination. The most famous case when heresy was confronted was, however, that of the Spaniard Michael Servetus (1553). Here the civil and ecclesiastical authorities acted in harmony. Servetus did indeed throw down the gauntlet to the beliefs Calvin held dear: he represented the radical Reformation in Italy, where humanism was combined with mystical religious ideas leading to pantheism. Such thought was, typically enough, fused with the possibility of man's rising to God through Christ by way of love, a love which was superior to belief. From this point of view the Spaniard criticized the Trinity; Christ was not of the same nature with God the father, but instead God infused his nature into Christ and thus exemplified the possibilities inherent in all men.

These ideas had found fertile soil in Italy, and especially in Venice, but for Calvin they typified the worst aspects of a humanism turned towards religious concerns. Servetus, passing through Geneva, attempted to debate with Calvin, for he believed in free debate with all the fervour of his religious enthusiasm. But Calvin, instead of engaging in a debate which would have proved a veritable sensation, had him imprisoned. Servetus was tried and then, despite Calvin's request that he be beheaded, burnt at the stake. The Swiss churches gave this action their unanimous approval and even the moderate Melanchthon expressed his gratitude. Servetus's radicalism was a menace to the whole 'magisterial' reformation, rightly associated in their minds with that Anabaptism against which they had fought so fiercely. For Calvin the very foundations of faith were denied and the community of Christians, which he stressed so much, disrupted.

Satan had no place in the new Jerusalem. Ecclesiastical discipline kept order, and by 1555 the Church had gained its independent status standing beside the secular authorities. The edifice was crowned by the founding of an educational system which ran from the primary and secondary schools up to the Academy (1559). Here, once more, Calvin's talent for building a coherent system comes to the fore.

CALVIN'S SOCIAL THOUGHT

Such an urge for harmony also governed the reformer's social thought. Calvin supported commercial activity as a sign of the interrelatedness of all human endeavour, and money was not looked upon as merely a necessary evil, but as an instrument of God for the support and sustenance of society. The use of money must not be governed by the lust for profit or wealth. Man must discipline himself to see in this God-given instrument a mere necessity, to be used according to the laws of justice and equity, and always with the good of the whole community in mind. Calvin instituted price control in Geneva for those goods considered as necessities of life: wine, bread and meat. Such control was a part of ecclesiastical discipline. But what about the taking of interest? It is important to understand Calvin's attitude towards this problem, for the relationship between Calvinism and capitalism has preoccupied many historians in the twentieth century.

Calvin's view of commerce and money produced a novel effect here also; interest is allowed if it is for the good of the community as a whole.[4] The reformers here broke with the medieval scholastics who had rationalized usury. Luther condemned all taking of interest, for he held that money was unproductive and should not multiply of itself without work. But Calvin now distinguished between a productive loan and usury: to lend in order to increase capital, to make production possible, was not a sin – in that way money was just as productive as any other merchandise. Moreover, with his usual realism, Calvin refused to be involved in fixing once and for all allowable rates of interest; circumstances must be taken into consideration (and they were made by God).

It should be clear that in a vague way Calvin did make a breakthrough towards capitalism. But he did this *not* by emphasizing individualism or free enterprise. Instead Calvin linked economic activity to the needs of the community as a whole, connecting the duty man owes to God with his membership in the holy community; indeed with all human endeavour. It was upon such interrelationships that Geneva was based, and it is little wonder that, in spite of all its imperfections, the small city came to represent for Calvinists the godly society in working order.

THE IMPACT OF CALVINISM

The impact of Geneva was great. Calvin always regarded his mission as a universal one. From Geneva pastors were sent out to other congregations in the west. They usually first took a position in French-speaking Switzerland (especially in Lausanne) and then moved to congregations in France. Every community where Calvinism took hold formed a company of pastors (sometimes called *classes*) which were responsible to the civil government for providing clergy. These pastors considered themselves an elite, and their rigorous training in the Genevan educational system was designed to mould them into such an aristocracy. In their congregations they took the lead in proselytizing and resisting outside pressures. John Knox of Scotland was only one of such pastors; within a few years some 161 had infiltrated France. But Geneva itself was affected in becoming the centre of such a large endeavour. Refugees entered the city and became citizens, further bolstering Calvin's political support.

By the time of Calvin's death (1564) not only was Geneva firmly under his control but Calvinist churches existed in France, Scotland, the Netherlands and eastern Europe – and it even looked as if England might yet become a Calvinist power. Zwinglianism had established a common front with Calvinism in Switzerland itself (see p. 188). But Calvin had not succeeded in making a *rapprochement* with Lutheranism, and for the same reason that Zwingli had failed in this attempt. At Marburg (1529) Luther had refused to compromise on the presence of Christ's body and blood in the sacrament of communion. After Luther's death his successors refused to meet Calvin's definition that in taking communion Christ is not bodily but spiritually united with the believer. This formulation was however accepted in the *Confessio Helvetica* (1566) and the breach between the Lutheran and 'reformed' (Zwinglian and Calvinist) Churches was made complete. The 'magisterial reformation' was split between these main branches (the English; was soon to be added see p. 289), while the radicals continued to exhibit renewed vigour.

Theodor Béza (1519–1605), Calvin's successor at Geneva, had to deal with the rapidly shifting religious and political scene of the last decades of the century. Personally tolerant, he was pushed increasingly to sharpen several of Calvin's ideas. Continued attacks upon the idea of predestination meant increasing concentration on this part of Calvinist orthodoxy, and Béza combined such an emphasis with a stress upon the elite of preachers. A growing authoritarianism within the faith contrasts with his writings upon the doctrine of resistance to secular authorities – for Calvinism was hard pressed on all sides. But for all that, the appeal of Calvin's faith and its dynamic continued unabated.

The attraction of Calvinism cannot be confined to one nation or to one class of the population. To be sure, the urban middle classes 'on the make' found much that was attractive in the faith, but so did the lesser nobility in France and the great nobles in Scotland. Many joined for reasons of salvation, for Calvin, like Luther before him, gave a feeling of certainty in a restless world. Given the various strains of popular culture of the century, this appeal must not be minimized, and it cut sharply across class lines. Moreover, many adhered for political reasons: the doctrine of the right of resistance to authority, as formulated by Calvin, had a great future before it. Calvin, who loved order and harmony and maintained discipline in Geneva, founded a fighting faith which did not fear established authority and trembled only before the Lord.

NOTES AND REFERENCES

1 Hans Baron, "Calvinist Republicanism and Its Historical Roots", *Church History*, 1939, pp. 30–42.

2 Eric Fuchs, *La Morale selon Calvin* (Paris, 1986), p. 36 ff.

3 William Ames, *Conscience with the Power and the Cases Thereof, etc.* (n.p. 1639), bk 1, p. 1

4 André Biéler, *La Pensée économique et sociale de Calvin* (Geneva, 1959), p. 457.

9

THE CATHOLIC REFORMATION

Ironically, it was the shock of the Protestant Reformation which provided the Catholic Church with new opportunities for survival as a universal church in at least part of Europe. The Reformation convinced those who still wanted to preserve the old Church that it was necessary to have a thorough reform of its pastoral and educational work, and of its administrative structure and personnel. Controversial dogmas had to be clearly defined. Above all, the Reformation convinced many powerful rulers that it was safer to protect the old Church, which was in any case largely under their control, than to unleash the unknown, but evidently powerful social, political and moral forces which seemed to support the various Reformation movements. This success was not won easily or over a short period of time. Though in the 1530s and 1540s it appeared as if Europe might become Protestant, a century later the picture was reversed – Catholicism had ended its decline and was showing a vigour and dynamic that compared favourably with a now rigid Protestantism.

THE NEED FOR REFORM

What had the Church done or left undone in the early sixteenth century to have fallen on to such hard times? The lack of priests was undoubtedly an important factor; from Germany, Italy and England we hear that while in the past there was an abundance of monks and priests, now there are none to be found. Moreover, this lack was combined with the increasing remoteness of bishops from their flocks. This was a complaint which had been made for centuries. Many bishops no longer resided in their dioceses, and some of them held several large dioceses widely separated one from another. Moreover, the bishop had become primarily an administrative officer with more political than religious responsibilities. He acted as chancellor to princes, or within the Empire, and if his see was of sufficient importance, was himself a prince. Absentee bishops were important as administrators in the papal court in Rome.

Religious indecisiveness went hand in hand with such political involvement. The English bishops, with few exceptions, docilely followed the lead of Henry VIII in his break with Rome, while those of the Empire refused to enforce the Bull against Luther because they feared strengthening the emperor's power more than they feared heresy. The people were thus left largely to their own devices, and no resistance was shown to the excesses of popular piety which had alarmed Luther and were to alarm the Catholic reformers. To these factors we must add the inroads of Erasmian humanism with its tolerant attitudes, which produced indecision when it came to confronting heresy and schism.

The orders of mendicant friars had stepped in where the regular clergy failed, emphasizing direct contact with the people, and preaching in a highly emotional vein. It was in such a role that many of the Protestant reformers must have appeared to the people they sought to influence. Indeed, the failure of the Church to establish a viable contact with the people gave the reformers their chance, and they used it to the full. The mendicant orders produced problems of their own, created by their support of popular piety and, above all, by the fact that they were freed from the jurisdiction of the local bishop. No one seemed to be able to exercise any effective control over their activities.

In this situation some efforts at reform had been made long before the advent of Protestantism: the *devotio moderna* was such an attempt in north-west Europe (see pp. 148). Though laymen took the lead, they were joined by priests and monks, foreshadowing the kind of organization which was to provide one approach to reform from within the church; the 'brotherhood' which, joining priests and laymen together, devoted itself to piety and to a sanctification of individuals' lives through a mystical kind of faith. Such brotherhoods were also founded in Italy, starting with the 'Oratory of S. Girolamo' in Vicenza (1494) and climaxing with the founding of the 'Oratory of Divine Love' in Rome (1517). This brotherhood in Rome included in its membership many important dignitaries of the Church. It practised prayer, frequent confession, communion, and charity in the visitation of hospitals. Here was a nucleus of men devoted to reform, to the 'imitation of Christ' as the title of the most famous book of the 'modern devotion' had summarized its aims.

The Oratories based themselves upon an alliance with those religious orders which had preserved the strictness of their original charters, as well as upon the new religious orders founded out of the felt need for reform. For example, the *Oratoria* at Vicenza had sprung up under the influence of the Observant Franciscans who still practised a certain amount of poverty and lived relatively austere lives given over to religious devotions. The Carthusians also managed to carry on their solitary life of contemplation. Small wonder that these were the religious orders in England which most effectively resisted the actions of Henry VIII. Gian Pietro Carafa, a member of the Rome Oratory, was instrumental in founding the Theatine Order (1524) whose task was to remedy the deficiencies of the regular clergy by concentrating upon preaching and the cure of souls. Among the other new religious orders (such as the Barnabites and Ursulines) the Capuchins were of special importance. These, with the Conventuals and the Observants, in practice constituted a third Franciscan Order. Their constitution (1529) stressed total poverty — preaching was to be one of the most important tasks combined with ministering to the people in times of catastrophes, pestilence and famine. The foundation of the Capuchins was an attempt to make the Church relevant once more to the common people surrounded as they were by dangers and natural catastrophes. Little wonder that preaching was stressed, for this was, after all, the best way to reach down among the people who thirsted for it. Bernardino Ochino, the superior of the Capuchins, was one of the most famous preachers of his time. But the dangers inherent in such a reforming order were soon to be manifest.

The emphasis on humility, charity, and on preaching could not but contrast with the as yet unreformed state of the Church. Such considerations must have weighed with Ochino himself in his development towards religious individualism and a spiritualistic piety. He was converted to Protestantism, and in 1542 he fled Italy to settle in Calvin's Geneva. This was a severe blow to the Church and to reform. But the order survived (to become a principal rival of the Jesuits) and so did the movement. However, another kind of religious foundation was to take the lead: the disciplined Jesuit order whose task was to work from the top down rather than to start reform from below with the people themselves.

THE JESUIT ORDER

Ignatius Loyola (1491–1556) was a Spaniard, and indeed most of the early Jesuit leadership came from that nation. This fact is significant, for Spain was on the road to that orthodoxy which was to make it a pillar of the Catholic Reformation. To be sure, there had been an initial advance of heresy in Spain as in all of Europe, but the Spanish Inquisition was working hard to crush such sparks and Loyola was interrogated in his youth and forbidden to preach for three years. The religious orders had remained powerful and, in many cases, had recovered much of the strictness of their original principles. Moreover, in Spain both the medieval knightly tradition as well as a religious mystical fervour was still alive. The crusade against the Moors had aided the union of race and religion which seemed to give Spain its selfconsciousness.

The *conversos* constituted a minority which was tainted by suspicion of both political and religious subversion, thus keeping alive an orthodox religious impetus. Loyola was influenced by the religious fervour of his native Spain, but he was also touched by the mystical and Erasmian influences which orthodoxy condemned and which the *conversos* furthered (see p. 226). His conviction that he could find God whenever he wanted Him led to the belief that man experiences God through all his senses. Here is the basis of the sensualism which affected the Jesuit's use of art and architecture as part of the needed religious reform, while leading their critics to accuse them of a mysticism which threatened to leave the path of orthodoxy. Moreover, Loyola never joined those who wanted to 'purify' the Church from the *conversos*: the unity of faith and purity of blood which the Spanish Inquisition attempted to enforce was not the unity he desired. Indeed the early Jesuit order contained many *conversos*, and Diego Lainez, who was to succeed Loyola as the second general of the Jesuits, was the child of Jewish parents. Only towards the end of the century did the Jesuits exclude everyone of Jewish ancestry from their community.

Loyola's youth was that of an adventuresome and undisciplined scion of the Basque nobility. Eventually he entered the service of the emperor. Wounded in battle, he read lives of saints and Christ (a common form of medieval literature) in his convalescence. He was left crippled and his mind turned to fighting the infidel rather than France. After all, the notion of leading a crusade was a part of the Spanish experience. But he failed in this aim. His little band of followers was turned back by Venice which wanted money for the passage to the Holy Land, and this Loyola did not possess.

He now went to study theology at the Sorbonne, and here conceived the idea of fighting heretics in Europe as well as the infidel in Palestine. In 1534 Ignatius and a small group of friends swore an oath to serve the pope in the Holy Land or, indeed, wherever he would send them to do battle. The constitution of the new order assured its success, for it was based upon military principles of organization and a militant piety. The individual was to give strict obedience to the whole of the order, ruled by a 'general' elected for life. Conditions for admission were strict, at the very least a novitiate of two years' duration being required. Next to the general were the 'provincials' who governed a region and then the 'rectors' of the individual houses.

But the organization would not, by itself, have been effective, and it was accompanied by a piety expressed through the 'spiritual exercises' which each member of the order had to hold for roughly thirty days. These exercises are best described as a disciplined mysticism building on a Spanish tradition as well as that of the 'modern devotion'. By weekly stages the mind was trained through contemplation to lift itself towards a complete union with Christ and thus to complete obedience to His commands. After the contemplation of sin and hell, there follows a survey of Christ's passion and martyrdom. Those taking the exercises must imagine themselves actually present at the events of Christ's life, '. . . taste the loaves and fishes with which Jesus feeds the multitude'. Ignatius Loyola here clearly expresses the sensualism which the Jesuits used as part of their means to lead men back to the Church; religious experience involves all of men's five senses and they must all be set to work. This includes the imagination and it was used by the 'Exercises' to train and discipline the human will. Selfish thought and the temptations of the flesh must vanish for the sake of obedience, just as private judgment must be set aside in favour of that of the Order. The similarity to Calvinism is striking here: both stressed physical and spiritual discipline.

However, this spiritual discipline was not supposed to abrogate the freedom of the will in which Jesuits believed. Instead, the 'spiritual exercises' were supposed to educate that will freely to follow Christ's commands. Gasparo Contarini, the Erasmian moderate, took the exercises, and they strengthened his resolve to mediate between Catholicism and Protestantism. The Jesuits also stressed understanding in their approach to the conversion of heretics: the discipline which was kept within the order must not be taken to mean an emphasis upon force and terror in order to compel men to orthodoxy. Flexibility of approach and methods characterized Jesuit activity and gave scope to the talents of those who joined the order.

The greatest strength of the Jesuit order may well have been in the calibre of men it was able to attract. With unbounded energy such Jesuits plunged themselves into a wide variety of tasks. Peter Canisius, in Germany, illustrates this well. He acted as teacher, preacher, confessor, diplomat, university rector and wrote theological tracts besides. He was not an isolated case. The primary weight of Jesuit activity fell into two spheres, working with rulers and inaugurating educational reform. As confessors and diplomats to the powerful they could exercise great influence. The Jesuits substituted detailed confessions of sins, and detailed advice to the confessed, for the shorter procedures which had been followed previously. The foundations of schools and universities was equally important. The aim was to train an elite of young men who would be dedicated to the faith, and to restore the prestige of theological studies.

Jesuit success in primary and secondary education was considerable. This was due in no small measure to the discipline which they kept among the children, and which parents liked. Moreover they integrated all aspects of education: games had been frowned upon, but the Fathers realized that youthful instincts could not be suppressed and that therefore it was better to harness them. Dancing was taught to give boys the right deportment. Play-acting, both scared and profane, found its way into the school in order to stimulate spoken Latin. The aim of education was not a sterile moralizing but instead to give purpose and direction to basic human passions — in harmony with the Catholic doctrine of free will. Upon such a basis the Jesuits were to achieve their greatest educational triumph in the next century. For the excellence of their schools provided one of the most important factors in the Catholic reconquest of Poland.

But universities also were involved. All over Europe discipline among students had fallen into decline, and here too the Jesuit colleges tightened the reins. The competition of Jesuit colleges forced the University of Paris to reform itself in the first years of the seventeenth century by instituting new principles of order and discipline. The centre of the whole Jesuit educational system was the *Collegium Romanum* in Rome (1551).

This was missionary work, and under this heading all the aspects of Jesuit activity must be viewed. Such work was not only carried on in Europe, but Francis Xavier achieved startling success in India (Goa) as well as in Japan. Indeed, by the end of the century not only was the Catholic Church surging back in Europe, but a whole new Christian era seemed to have dawned in the Far East. This however was not to be — by the next century most of the far eastern churches were destroyed through persecution. Torture and persecution also awaited Jesuits in Protestant Europe. It is typical of Jesuit thoroughness that they sought to prepare their novices for such eventualities, and the way they went about this shows their desire to integrate all endeavour towards the main goal to be reached, to make use of all legitimate methods. Thus art was used in this work of preparation. The novices' refectory was painted with the most gruesome scenes of torture in order to accustom the future Fathers to the fate which might await them (the paintings can still be seen on the walls of the Church of St Stefano Rotondo in Rome). The Jesuits used art as they used the mystical tradition in order to further the victory and domination of the Church. This they also had in common with Calvinism: an emphasis upon the interrelationship of all human endeavour and therefore the integration of all parts of human activity.

However, unlike Calvinists, the Jesuits stood upon the doctrine of human free will and of the constant possibility of man's redemption by God's grace if only he would help 'pull the barge ashore'. The 'spiritual exercises' trained the will of the elite, but ordinary man needed help, both on behalf of his will and his senses — he had to be 'guided' towards the truth. Here the Jesuits made good use of the Catholic emphasis upon the visual aspects of piety which had always appealed to the longing for colour and form inherent in popular piety. Catholicism, as the Jesuits understood it, depended largely upon sermons, spectacles, gestures and symbols, while Protestantism centred upon sermons, scripture reading and the singing of hymns. The emphasis upon the visual on the part of a reconstructed Church had great popular appeal, while the intensely verbal aspects of Protestantism projected a seriousness and sobriety which this Catholicism seemed to lack. In their desire to symbolize the majesty and triumph of Catholicism the Jesuits built their own model church, the 'Gesù' in Rome (1568–75). The Renaissance style was developed into a highly theatrical setting where the altar resembled a stage and preaching was emphasized as part of the drama, as the pulpit was placed in the centre of the Church. Catholic churches throughout much of the world were to follow the Gesù's architectural example: the way was prepared for the baroque style of the next century, though other factors also went into its making.

The Order was attacked by Protestants for its use of persuasion, and for making religion easy to get into. But in reality the so-called 'casuistry' used by father confessors was simply a method to guide men in given situations without the harshness of predestination. Adjustment to the realities they faced was important to Jesuits; both in their fight against heresy which had to be waged on a political, tactical level (for they were a small elite and no mass army) and in their casuistry as well. How much they went beyond the morally permissible depends upon a study of individual cases, but cannot be charged against the Order as a whole.

POPES AND REFORM

The Jesuits served the papacy directly, and Paul III gave them official recognition (1540). The papacy was bound to play the key role in reform, in spite of all the initiatives taken by brotherhoods, religious orders and individuals. A small and short beginning was made when Charles V's tutor, Hadrian VI (1522–23), became pope and brought with him the humanist impulses of the Netherlands. But his immediate successors reverted to the pattern of the Renaissance papacy with the support of the curia — that is, those ecclesiastics who served in Rome and who feared any reform as a diminution of their powers. Leo X and Clement VII, as Julius II before them, were preoccupied with securing and extending their territories by balancing the interests of France against those of the

Empire. Leo X, in office at the beginning of the Reformation, attempted to stem the tide of heresy in Germany through concessions to loyal rulers and through mediation. Clement VII was to continue along these lines, but with even less success. His foreign policy opposed him to Charles V, the very emperor who had to be relied upon to fight heresy in the north. Charles, in turn, used Lutheran mercenaries in his campaigns against the papal states. The sack of Rome (1527) by his army provides a landmark in the relationship of papacy to reform only in that no later pope returned to the Renaissance pattern of life – and in that, by delivering Clement into the emperor's hands, the loss of England was accelerated.

But the sack itself stunned Europe. It seemed to many a punishment which had descended upon the worldly papacy. Looting and murder were the order of the day, aged cardinals were dragged through the streets amidst abuse in which Spanish troops and Lutheran mercenaries joined. This was an army which had mutinied because it had not been paid: the sack of Rome was not intended by Charles, though once it had taken place he took advantage of the control it gave him over the weak Clement.

For all that, little happened in the way of reform until, after Clement's death, Paul III (1534–49) ascended the throne of St Peter's. The Farnese pope created a reform commission (1537) on which the men connected with the Oratory of the Divine Love predominated. Three members of the commission merit special attention. Contarini (never a member of the Oratory) was a Christian humanist, a leader in the sentiment which called for a reconciliation with the Protestants. Cardinal Reginald Pole had left England, and remained in exile, in fear of his life, for having openly opposed Henry VIII. He was devoted to the cause of reform and in many ways his own piety drew him towards sympathy with some aspects of Protestantism. Thus he advised one pious lady to believe in salvation by faith, but to act as if works were important also. His groping, hesitant nature did not fit him for statesmanship – a fact which became obvious when he attempted to guide the much more energetic and decisive Mary Tudor (see p. 295). G. P. Carafa was, perhaps, the most interesting of the group: deeply pious, ascetic, he was later to become the most intransigent of popes.

This group not only drew up plans for reform, but tried to come into conversation with the Protestant reformers. In this they succeeded, but the Colloquy of Regensburg (1541) proved a bitter disappointment.

This colloquy was certainly the most spectacular effort to overcome the schism. Luther sent Melanchthon and even Calvin was present. In the background, Charles V did his best to encourage unity. The beginning was hopeful: quick agreement was reached upon a formula concerning justification by faith and upon the role of Christ as mediator between God and the world. But transubstantiation proved an insurmountable obstacle to more general unity, as it had proved an obstacle to the unity of Luther and Zwingli twelve years earlier. Discussions on the powers of the papacy and the veneration of saints were inconclusive.

In the end both Luther and the pope rejected even the agreed formula on justification by faith, while Contarini remarked that he was unwilling to make a hypocritical agreement with the Protestants, and that this was the only kind of agreement which seemed possible. A similar meeting the next year, also at Regensburg, demonstrated to all concerned the hopelessness of such attempts at an agreed solution.

At the same time the general plans for reform were sabotaged by the curia. This was mainly caused by the condemnation of non-resident bishops, for many of the curia officials held such bishoprics *in commendam*. They had no wish to leave the central administration of the Church for administration in the provinces. This was a problem destined to provide a continuing obstacle to the course of Catholic reform.

The failure of the men of the Oratory deflected Paul on to a different course. Reconciliation with Protestants had failed, while heresy was making advances even in Italy itself. The pope now based himself increasingly upon the Spanish methods of orthodoxy. The Jesuit Order had been recognized, and in 1542 the papal Inquisition was reorganized in Rome. Every bishop traditionally possessed the right of inquisition into heresy. From the thirteenth century this had been supplemented by a papal Inquisition (mainly staffed by Dominicans and others in Italy and southern Europe). Now the pope established a congregation or central office in Rome. In spite of this change of policy to meet the challenge, the failure of reconciliation with the Protestants had put Pope Paul into a difficult position — for pressure now mounted for the calling of a general council of all Christendom which might succeed where the papacy had failed: both in healing the split within the universal church and in putting through the necessary reforms.

THE COUNCIL OF TRENT

The pope had some reason to dread such a council. The memories of the Councils of Constance and Basle were still fresh, councils which had asserted their own superiority over the papacy. The Protestants had appealed for such a general council, but with some hesitation. At the famous Leipzig disputation with Johannes Eck, Luther held that even a general council of Christendom could err – for had the Council of Constance not put Hus to death? Charles V was the major figure pressing for a council; it would help him reunite his empire and, if the Protestants should refuse to participate, strengthen his hand in dealing with them. Pope Paul had, at first, resisted this pressure as best he could. However, the failure of the Reform Commission and of the Colloquy of Regensburg made such resistance more difficult, while the increasing Protestant infiltration into Italy alarmed the pope. On 22 May 1542 a council was called to the city of Trent. However, the actual work of the council began only after the peace between the emperor and the King of France in 1544 gave both pope and emperor a free hand to proceed.

The papal bull summoning the council had listed as its task both the defining of dogma and church reform. The definition of dogma was a pressing matter, indecision on points of theology had harmed the cause of the Church. For example, priests and bishops had negotiated with Luther long after he had been excommunicated. Erasmianism was partly to blame, but the medieval liturgy of the Church had permitted many variations and even papal directives dealing with ceremonial and liturgy never had the quality of outright 'commands'. It is important to realize that the Council of Trent no longer 'suggested and approved' as the medieval popes had done in such matters, but, instead, 'stated and declared' – while from that time on the papacy was no longer afraid to 'make laws' concerning the liturgy.[1]

The Council of Trent laid down guidelines for dogma and pointed towards a greater centralization within the church. The pope was only an indirect beneficiary of such centralization inasmuch as the Council was careful to respect his prerogatives. The bishops as the 'intermediate authority' in the church emerged greatly strengthened, with much wider authority over the clergy as well as in the ordering of their services. In a wider sense the Council of Trent was a part of the new spirit of uniformity which coincided with the rise of a new centralized political order in the West. Not only Catholics, but Protestants, through their 'Confessions of Faith', by the end of the century, enforced a religious uniformity which contrasts markedly with Luther's earlier permissiveness and the latitude of much medieval theology.

Reform was equally important, and became part of an overall plan jointly supported by pope and emperor to end the schism. First the Lutheran Schmalkaldic League was to be defeated, then Protestants must be forced to attend the Council while at that precise time church reform would make reunion possible. The Schmalkaldic League was defeated, the Protestants did appear at one session, but the theological definitions already agreed upon made it impossible for them to remain. The timetable broke down at the very start of the Council. The first session (1545—47) took place before, not after, the League was defeated, and it proved to be one of the most fruitful sessions not for reform but for theological definitions.

The Council found against the primary Protestant contentions: the apostolic tradition of the Church must be accepted with the same 'holy reverence' as scripture. The authentic text of scripture was held to be the Vulgate (as against Protestant Bible translations). The Protestant emphasis upon original sin was rejected in favour of stress upon baptism which transforms original sin into a 'pull towards evil' which can be resisted. The Council reaffirmed Catholic doctrines on human free will: man's will plays a part in justification by faith through God's grace. Moreover such Divine Grace heals man. Finally, the efficacy of the traditional sacraments was affirmed.

Theological definitions proved easier to achieve than reform. This first session did forbid pluralism in the holding of bishoprics, but it bogged down in the problem of non- resident bishops, an issue that was to haunt all the sessions of the Council of Trent. Charles V had pressed for reform rather than theological definition, always having in mind the importance of healing the schism. He was distressed when the Council moved briefly to Bologna, closer to the pope, the plague having broken out in Trent. The pope took advantage of the situation to sabotage the emperor's German policy, a vital part of which was Charles V's attempts to involve the Protestants in the Council's proceedings. The emperor, finally victorious over the Schmalkaldic League, now took reform into his own hands when he promulgated the 'Interim' for the empire (1548) (See p. 239 for the political situation.) His greater tolerance meant concessions to the Protestants, such as communion in two kinds and approval of marriage for priests.

But now Pope Paul's successor, Julius III (1550–54), recalled the Council to Trent, and the Protestants, beaten in war, made an appearance. This second session (1551–52) proved successful only in reaffirming the 'real presence' of Christ in the sacrament and in stressing the importance of oral confession. The Protestants on their appearance immediately made demands which proved totally unacceptable, claiming that the bishops must be freed from their loyalty to the pope and that all the theological matters already agreed upon be taken up once more. The resulting stalemate led to the suspension of this session. It hardly looked as if the Council would meet again. For Carafa succeeded Julius as Pope Paul IV (1555–59) and he was suspicious of councils, indeed of any reform that might touch upon the might of the papacy. He had been a member of the Oratory, witnessed the failure of its efforts, and believed that now only change carried through with an iron hand from the centre of the church would have success.

Pope Paul exemplified this effort in his own ascetic life, in his hatred of all that smacked of heresy. It was this pope who accused his former friend, Reginald Pole, of heresy at the very moment when Pole was helping Queen Mary Tudor lead England back into the Catholic Church. Indeed the 'new' Carafa is part of a type which came to pervade much of the Catholic Reformation. Such men were its second generation, in a manner of speaking, as Calvin was a second-generation protestant reformer. Fighting for the true Church meant a rigid outlook combined with dynamic action directed against every suspicion of heresy. Deep attachment to a beleaguered faith resulted in a personally ascetic life, filled to the brink with the consciousness of a crusade undertaken to defeat Satan. Both Mary Tudor and Phillip II, Carafa's younger contemporaries, were reformers of such a breed.

Paul IV as pope was also a temporal ruler, and the conflict between his religious fervour and his ambitions as an Italian prince led to irreconcilable actions. He pursued a policy of nepotism hardly in tune with reform. Moreover, he became embroiled in a losing war with Philip II. Nor was the cause of reform really advanced during his pontificate. A man of such a dogmatic cast of mind, so little given to compromise, found it impossible to deal effectively with the great administrative apparatus of the church.

Pius IV (1559–64) recalled the Council once more. He was under the influence of his nephew, Carlo Borromeo, who as archbishop of Milan came to exemplify, by the care he devoted to his diocese, the prototype of the truly reformed bishop. However, a new and more important threat had appeared upon the horizon. Up to this point it was Charles V, involved with the Lutherans, who had provided the urgency behind the calling of a Council. Now it was to be the king of France facing the Calvinist threat. Francis I had died, his successor had been killed in a tournament and France was faltering under what proved to be a series of royal minorities. Moreover, in 1559 the first general synod of the Calvinist churches of France had met in Paris. The next year the king of France called for the meeting of the national council of the French Church under his own auspices in order to end the religious strife which threatened civil war. Such an open threat to his power goaded Pius IV into action: the third and final session of the Council (1562–63) met at Trent in the same year as the long and bloody civil war broke out between Huguenots and Catholics. Perhaps the reconvening of the Council might also solve an additional problem; England, barely regained, might be lost once more. However, the new queen, Elizabeth, refused entry into the country to the delegate bringing the invitation to attend the Council.

For the first time a sizeable French delegation attended, led by the Cardinal of Lorraine. Calvinism now proved to be the major threat in western Europe. At the same time, in spite of the emperor's active support of the Council, the German delegation was small. Princes and bishops were fearful of upsetting the religious balance obtained at the peace of Augsburg. Spanish bishops, dedicated to reform, attended in larger numbers and with the enthusiastic backing of King Phillip II. Among the slightly more than 200 prelates present at the height of the Council, the Italians had a majority.

Theological matters were, once more, quickly disposed of. The Mass and the traditional role of the priests in the Mass were confirmed. At the same time the abuses of the Mass (such as the proliferation of masses said for special occasions) were castigated. The Council also affirmed the true veneration of saints as against the superstitions of popular piety.

The great crisis of this session erupted, once more, over the reform of bishops. The French desired a greater share of ecclesiastical authority for bishops, and this the curia, supported by many Italian bishops, resisted. Papal power did become involved, for the reform party wanted to establish as a canon of faith that bishops held their office *iure divino*, a fact which would have made the pope's control over them problematical. The first papal legates were not able to resolve this impasse and it was the arrival of Giovanni Morone as presiding legate, possessing the pope's full confidence, which made possible the successful conclusions of the Council.

The issue of how the bishops should hold their office was side-stepped and provisions for ending non-residency were not written into the decrees of the Council but merely suggested to the pope. Instead Morone concentrated upon the 'cure of souls' as the chief task of bishops. Pluralism was forbidden, regular visitations of the diocese were demanded and, above all, provision was made for the education of the clergy. Nothing specific had hitherto been laid down for their theological education. Clergy could, of course, if they desired, embark upon long and arduous study at a university. Cardinal Pole had pioneered in attaching a school for priests to each cathedral in England. The Council now decreed that every diocese must have a seminary. Though attendance was not yet made compulsory for the clergy, this constituted a most meaningful reform against the background of constant complaints about uneducated priests who could hardly read the services. General rules were also formulated for religious Orders, focused upon the stricter observance of their aims.

The pope affirmed the actions of the Council (1564). A special commission was formed to implement the decrees, while another, at the Council's request, revised and reissued the list of books dangerous to the spiritual health of the layman (*Index librorum prohibitorum*). The first such *Index* had been commissioned by Pope Paul IV, following many earlier attempts by universities like the Sorbonne or Louvain. The effort at theological definition may have been more important than the attempted reforms. Both were arrived at through compromise with the various national ecclesiastical interests present at Trent. Such an important matter as the relationship between pope and bishops was not mentioned in the decrees, and the abuses of popular piety were easier to condemn than to check. The Council of Trent provided guideposts, but did not immediately cause the greater effectiveness and centralization of the Church in subsequent years. A new Catechism (1566), Breviary

(1568) and Missal (1570) were issued only later by the pope, this time with an effort to enforce them upon all the faithful.

For all that, the Council had provided increasing certainty upon the most important points of theology. The Church was engaged in an increasingly bloody battle with the Protestants and such certainty gave a clarity to this battle which eventually would lead to greater religious dedication and therefore to reform. In this manner the Council of Trent laid the foundations for the great spiritual and and political revival of Catholicism of the next century.

POPULAR PIETY

Yet, the Catholic Reformation challenged not only Protestantism but many aspects of popular piety as well. The Church, in answer to Protestant criticisms, had a new view of the relationship of the sacred and the profane which was soon to clash with many popular practices. The old rituals containing local customs or pagan elements were now suppressed in favour of more rigorously orthodox rites. Processions which had overtones of fertility rites, or raucous gatherings of young people, were replaced by sober parades in which the clergy played a prominent role. At times student disputations or theatre performances were substituted for processions which encouraged indecency. Popular customs surrounding funerals were attacked as superstitious, and the attempt was made to substitute the veneration of new Counter Reformation saints such as Ignatius Loyola and Francis Xavier for traditional, but perhaps apocryphal, saints. The old lay confraternities were frowned upon: some had degenerated into mere dinner clubs while others were too independent for the new centralizing tendencies of the Council of Trent. New, more pious confraternities were established, firmly under the control of the clergy. A sense of separation was urged on the reformed Catholic clergy; distinctive dress and hairstyle was mandated and priests were forbidden to stand as godfathers to parish children, a practice which had once reinforced their community ties. Religious ceremonies which had also served as family and communal festivals were subject to new regulations designed to emphasize their sacred nature. Clergy in Strassburg, for example, decreed that marriage was to be celebrated 'without tumult, mockery, taunts, scuffles, jokes, and foul and immoderate speech which is customary at betrothals and weddings'.[2] Dances and fairs were forbidden on church grounds and graveyards were ordered fenced off to remind the populace that they were sacred ground.

The goal was to make the reformed parish the centre of Catholic worship. The enforcement of this and other measures, which often clashed with traditional popular piety, was made easier by two important results of the Council of Trent, the introduction of parish registers and changes in confession and penance. Every birth, baptism, marriage, communion or death in the parish was to be noted, a practice which heightened the clergy's powers of social control. This was especially so when coupled with the abolition of the old custom of public confession and penance and the introduction of the private confessional. Such challenges to popular piety sometimes ran into the sort of resistance met by Luther's reforms. This was often the case among laymen in rural areas who found their traditional role in parish institutions such as confraternities, charities, and hospitals diminished, while clerical influence increased. The Catholic Reformation did find supporters though, particularly among women who were able to play a wider part than ever before in religious life. Their enthusiam for the Catholic Reformation is shown by the generosity of their bequests to the Church throughout this period.

But for all this new emphasis on theological clarity, austerity and self-discipline, the Catholic Reformation maintained the Church's tradition of religious spectacle and visual display. The visual orientation of the Catholic Church, the theatrical representation of its majesty and power, was furthered by the Jesuits as part of their effort at conversion. Popular piety was attacked, but not defeated. Indeed, within the stricter system of clerical control, popular piety retained a place, and many folk customs were integrated into the ritual of the Church. The Saints kept their efficacy and so did various magical cures such as the use of holy water or amulets, even if the so-called black magic of witchcraft was sought out and persecuted.

The Lutheran Church itself kept many pre-reformation practices and traditions, especially in regions where Lutheranism was not seriously challenged — such as central and eastern Germany. Processions and pilgrimages were continued and, at times, even monasteries (now Lutheran) remained intact. There existed an interrelationship between the traditions and practices of the two faiths on the popular level, and this local conservatism slowed down not only the establishment of a true reformed Church, but the Catholic Reformation as well. Thus the 'ancient custom' of priests living in concubinage was difficult to break, and from Catholic Westphalia we hear of priest dynasties who held ecclesiastical livings generation after generation. Even in a region comparatively untouched by the struggles of the Reformation, like the inner Catholic cantons of Switzerland, a visitation of 1600 found over half of the priests living in a married state.

Piety and attachment to the Catholic Church increased towards the end of the sixteenth century, but old 'abuses' embedded in local customs also remained — especially in Germany. But Germany became a backwater within the Catholic Reformation which got its impetus from Spain, where the firm foundations of religious enthusiasm had not been eroded, and from France, where the religious wars gave a new impetus to Catholic piety. Though the Catholic Church sought to bring a new discipline to its believers, its approach to man's life on earth remained different from and less sober than that of the Protestant reformers. Not that Luther, or even Calvin, lacked a joyful spirit, but their sense of original sin and their stress upon predestination shifted the emphasis of a life of duty and work. Calvin, especially, heightened the tensions of life which both popular piety and Luther had wanted to overcome. The Catholic Reformation with its belief in free will distinguished between a mortal sin and one for which absolution through penance could be obtained. For man would err, and the effort must be directed towards training his will to choose the good, to collaborate in the obtaining of God's grace. The liturgy of the Church would help to guide fallible man, for he needs an infallible authority, the divine Church, to govern his life. This was quite different from Calvin's view of man who 'naked but for his conscience' does battle in the 'theatre of the world'.

Two different cultural patterns, growing out of two different views of man and his capabilities, confronted each other. The difference between and north and south of Europe, between, for example, England and Italy, are not so much due to different climates but to the fact that one region became Protestant and the other was caught up in the Catholic Reformation. Concentration on economic factors has obscured this difference. Capitalist economics made rapid strides in parts of Italy as well as in the north; the people of the south do not necessarily work less than those of the north. But their attitude towards this work, towards their profession, indeed towards all of life, is of a different and lighter texture. Not all sin is equally mortal; to be healed through grace does not mean accentuating the inner and outward tensions of life. The Church provides an infallible guide and in capturing rather than eliminating the urge towards colour and form, so evident in all of popular piety, it did provide a marked contrast to the Protestant way of life.

The sixteenth-century reformations were not merely political events, they did not merely break the always-challenged unity of Christendom, but also led towards a division within Europe around the vital problem of man's attitudes towards life. At its extreme one need only compare the *Roma Triumphans* – the reconstruction of Rome begun in the last decade of the sixteenth century (which still dominates present-day Rome) with the Puritan meeting house. In between there existed many diverse shadings within both the Catholic and Protestant ways of life.

The appeal of the Catholic Reformation was as general as that of Protestantism; we find people of all classes in its ranks. But it tended to appeal most to two segments of the population, though never exclusively so. The peasant had, at one point, risen on behalf of his rights and the new faith. But by mid-century the fusion of religion and popular piety proved attractive enough to bring him back to Catholicism in large numbers. In most regions outside parts of Germany he had never left it at all. The Jesuits were correct in concentrating on ruling élites. Many of these saw in Catholicism a guarantee of order, for its religious approach worked well for those who actually held power in their hands. Hierarchy was deeply ingrained in the thought of the Catholic Reformation. It is typical that an examination of the 'Miracle Books' of local patron saints has demonstrated that miracles were exclusively performed upon those of high birth.[3] But this factor must not be over-emphasized. Catholicism also developed a radical doctrine of resistance to authority in its battles against Protestant rulers, and Calvin, after all, also held an aristocratic view of the social hierarchy.

RELIGION AND THE STATE

With all the successes which the Catholic Reformation was to book against the Protestants, there were danger signs on the horizon

225

which came from a different direction. The nation state entered a crucial phase of its development in the religious wars which broke out even as the Council of Trent was ending its deliberations. National monarchs, such as Henry IV of France, refused to receive the decrees of the Council into their states for fear of increasing the independence of their clergy. Powerful Venice, which had to resist the encroachment of the Papal States, coined the motto: 'first Venetians, then Christians' (1609). Fra Paolo Sarpi from the city wrote an extremely hostile account of the Council of Trent itself and sympathized with the Gallicanism of France.

The growth of the concept of national churches in the second half of the century threatened the success of Catholic reform and, together with the established Protestantisms, put limits upon its expansion. Behind such national churches lurked the spectre of toleration practised for political or economic reasons by the rulers — a course of action which might prove the Reformation battles to establish one sole 'truth' to have been fought in vain.

There was, however, another and opposite danger to Catholic reform: an excessive and, in the long run, culturally, socially and even religiously stifling imposition of orthodoxy. This happened in Spain. The Spanish Inquisition had been established by Ferdinand and Isabella, partly in response to popular anti-semitism, to deal with the suspect Christian orthodoxy of the *conversos*, the converted Jews. The Inquisition fulfilled this task with great efficiency and committed literally thousands to the flames. At the same time, Ferdinand had also seen the Inquisition, which was a royal as well as an ecclesiastical court and whose personnel were appointed by the king, as an instrument to increase royal control over the Spanish Church and to isolate it from papal influence. From about 1530 the Spanish Inquisition virtually gave up the hunt for judaizing *conversos*, probably because there were hardly any left, and concentrated on the Moriscos and on unorthodox 'old Christians', especially the followers of Erasmus. When these latter had been eliminated, by about 1560, the Spanish Inquisition took on the task of supervising the implementation of the doctrines and practices of Tridentine Catholicism at the local level. Death sentences and burnings at the stake now became relatively rare, although other penalties imposed by the Inquisition remained ferocious. Correct beliefs and strict sexual morality were enforced on both clergy and laity by the supervision of the whole population through a network of local inquisitions, helped by the ubiquitous lay familiars —

anything from thuggish bodyguards for the inquisitors to aristocratic patrons — and by the encouragement of popular denunciations of actual or supposed deviations from orthodoxy. Because women were strictly excluded from religious discourse, the Spanish Inquisition assigned both the utterances of some mystically inclined nuns and the spells or sorceries mumbled by witch-women to the realm of unimportant female vapourings. They were dealt with relatively leniently or the women were simply declared insane and locked up.

As religious conflicts sharpened in the latter part of the sixteenth century, a stricter enforcement of correct religious beliefs and an increased supervision of popular morality and of all forms of verbal and literary expression was practised in both Catholic and Protestant countries (see pp. 201 ff, 383). The differences lay less in the aims of the different confessions than in their ability to enforce orthodoxy. It was here that the Spanish Inquisition was most effective. Its dramatically staged *autos da fe* (acts of faith) and the secrecy and irreversibility of its proceedings inspired in the popular mind a mixture of devotion and terror. The terror was further heightened by the ability of the Inquisition to strike at even the most exalted personages. Such a one was Archbishop Carranza of Toledo who was kept in an Inquisition prison for seven years before the papacy managed, after great efforts, to have him and his case transferred to Rome. Of course, the case was complex. Carranza was resented as a social upstart, he had offended some of the established great ecclesiastical families and he had laid himself open to charges of heresy by writing on theology. These charges were later proved to be unjustified or of the most trivial kind; but Philip II was prepared to defend the Spanish Inquisition in order to uphold its reputation, even if it condemned an innocent man. At least once, in 1591, he used the Inquisition for overtly political purposes to override the laws of the kingdom of Aragon. His action provoked an armed rebellion which could only be mastered by a regular military campaign. The sixteenth-century intermingling of religion and politics could not have been demonstrated more clearly.

The reformers had not meant to break up the unity of western Christendom: they achieved this result in spite of their intentions. Within the Europe of their time the national state had not yet replaced the concept of empire; either in theory or in the reality of political life. The empire of Charles V provided the setting for the

Reformation, and other empires existed at the fringes of Europe. To be sure, the Reformation affected the evolution of the European monarchies; it was involved, despite itself, in the tensions between these monarchies and the empires of the sixteenth century.

NOTES AND REFERENCES

1   See David Hecht and George L. Mosse, 'Liturgical uniformity and absolutism in the sixteenth century', *Anglican Theological Review*, XXIX (July, 1947), pp. 158–66.

2   Cited in Philip T. Hoffman, *Church and Community in the Diocese of Lyon, 1500–1789*, (New Haven, 1984), p. 84.

3   Georg Schreiber, *Deutsche Mirakelbücher* (Dusseldorf, 1938), p. 68.

10

EMPIRES

THREE EMPIRES WITH UNIVERSALIST CLAIMS IN THE FIRST HALF OF THE SIXTEENTH CENTURY

The sixteenth century is traditionally regarded as the age of the break-up of the medieval unity of Christian Europe and of the rise of the new monarchies. Yet, in the first half of the century, there appeared in Europe no less than three empires with universalist claims; and these claims were better founded in political reality than those of any political structure in Europe during the previous 500 years or more: that is in the area these empires controlled, in the influence they wielded beyond their borders and in the hold they won over men's minds. These three empires were the empire of Charles V, the Ottoman Empire of Selim I and Suleiman the Magnificent, and the Muscovite Empire of Ivan IV, the Terrible. The first and the last of these grounded their claims ultimately on their succession to the Roman Empire; and even the second, the Ottoman Empire, did so to a certain extent. Furthermore, two European nations, the Spaniards and the Portuguese, conquered empires on the basis of a somewhat different universalist claim, a claim based on a papal grant to them of 'all islands or mainlands whatever, found or to be found . . . in sailing towards the west and south . . .' (*Dudum siqiudem*, the last of four successive and ever more comprehensive papal bulls, 1493). This claim, being Christian and Europe-centred, was therefore closely related to the universalist claims of two of the three European empires, and, of course, especially to that of Charles V. Thus Hernán Cortés, the conqueror of Mexico, wrote to Charles in 1524 about his plans on the coasts of the Pacific Ocean which, he

229

said, would make the emperor ruler over more kingdoms and dominions than were known hitherto and 'that if I do this, there would be nothing more left for Your Excellency to do in order to become ruler of the world'.

THE EMPIRE OF CHARLES V IN EUROPE

Charles V came perhaps nearer to this ideal than any of his rivals — much nearer than his great contemporary, the Emperor Babur, whose conquest of northern India was based on no other claims than self-aggrandizement and descent from Timur and Genghis Khan. In Europe, Charles V owed his position to heredity, without any conquest at all. Ferdinand and Isabella had united the houses of Aragon and Castile; Maximilian and Mary those of Austria and Burgundy. Between 1516 and 1519 the succession of all four houses devolved on Charles of Habsburg, eldest son of Philip of Burgundy and Joanna (the Mad) of Castile.

Austria and parts of southern Germany, the Netherlands, Franche-Comté and Spain, together with Spain's Mediterranean dominions, Naples, Sicily, Sardinia and the Balearics, and her rapidly expanding overseas empire in the New World — these diverse and scattered countries now all acknowledged the same ruler. In 1519 Charles defeated Francis I of France in the election for the imperial title. While the general German distrust of France had gravely handicapped Francis, the election of Charles was not so much a manifestation of German nationalism — Charles was hardly more German than his rival — as the result of the superior military and financial position of the Habsburgs in Germany. Charles's agents paid out to the electors and other German princes and their ministers more than half of 850,000 florins, which was the total cost of the election campaign (and of which more than 500,000 florins was loaned by the house of Fugger). Only a month before the election, the army of the Swabian League, an alliance of south German princes and cities of which Charles was the head, drove the duke of Württemberg, the leader of the French faction, from his country. Francis could rival neither the bribes nor the blackmail.

The union of the crowns of different countries in one person was neither new nor very remarkable in the early sixteenth century. Thomas More made some apposite and very biting remarks about it in his *Utopia*. But to the lord of Chièvres and the other great Burgundian lords who managed the young Charles's government of the Netherlands for him, it seemed perfectly natural that they should help to make good their prince's claim to the crowns of Spain in 1516. They had helped his father, Philip, in the same way some ten years earlier. Nevertheless, the accumulation of crowns and lordships in Charles's hands was unprecedented. 'God has set you on the path towards world monarchy', said the grand-chancellor, Gattinara, in 1519. Charles, it seems, agreed with him. Dynastic alliances and inheritance, not wars and conquests from Christians, had made this empire; and dynastic alliances remained the emperor's favourite policy for strengthening his power in Christian Europe. For thus, he was convinced, he was fulfilling God's purpose.

The precise nature of God's purpose Charles learnt from many sources, but above all from Gattinara. This Piedmontese lawyer and humanist, a great admirer of Erasmus, saw the imperial title and authority just as Dante had seen it, as 'ordained by God himself . . . and approved by the birth, life and death of our Redeemer Christ'. The emperor was to be not so much the direct ruler as the moral and political leader of Christendom, and he was to lead against the enemies of Christ, the Muslim Turks and, later, the Lutherans and other heretics. The crusading ideal inherent in this concept fitted well with the Spanish tradition of the *reconquista* within the Iberian peninsula, and with Isabella the Catholic and Cardinal Jiménez's policy of conquest in North Africa during the first decade of the sixteenth century. It was in this vein that Charles's spokesman at the cortes of Coruña, in 1520, interpreted his new title of emperor and proposed a kind of imperial programme: the defence of Christendom against the infidel.

Yet, at least in 1520, the majority of Spaniards were unimpressed. To be king of Castile was as good as, or better than, being emperor of Germany, they argued, and at the first taste of the financial obligations which the new empire imposed on them the Castilian towns rose in rebellion (see pp. 110 ff.). The nobles defeated the towns. But the real victor was the monarchy and, indirectly, Charles V's imperial idea: no longer could the Castilian towns resist heavy taxation for the benefit of their king's imperial policy. The nobles still could and did resist such taxation. Effectively, they managed to contract out of the financial obligations of the state and the empire. In return, however, they gave the emperor their personal support, in both army and administration and, perhaps unwittingly, they helped to transform Charles V's universal empire into Philip II's Spanish empire.

CHARLES V, LUTHER AND THE PAPACY

Two urgent problems faced Charles V when he arrived at Aix-la-Chapelle for his coronation (October 1520) and at Worms for his first Imperial Diet (January–May 1521). The first problem, Luther's heresy, seemed as yet a comparatively minor one. Charles composed his own reply to Luther's famous declaration at the Diet. He was descended from most Christian ancestors, he said, German and Spanish, Austrian and Burgundian, and he would follow their example in holding fast to and defending the Catholic faith. 'Therefore', he concluded, 'I am determined to set my kingdoms and dominions, my friends, my body, my blood, my life, my soul upon it.'

It was a declaration of intent no less absolute than Luther's. It derived directly from Charles's view of his imperial dignity as transcendental. As the Lutheran and other heresies continued to spread, the direct result, it seemed, of the generally acknowledged shortcomings of the Catholic Church, the emperor saw the reform of the Church as a part of the duties God had imposed on him. But this was a position no pope could accept. Already in 1521 the papal legate, Aleander, protested against the Edict of Worms condemning Luther; for what business had the emperor and the Diet to judge in a religious matter which the pope had already settled in his bull of excommunication against Luther? At subsequent Diets, notably at Augsburg (1530) and at Regensburg (1541), the emperor's theologians actually tried to negotiate on matters of doctrine with Lutheran theologians, and for twenty-five years the emperor was pressing the pope to summon a general council, or worse still, threatening to do so himself (see pp. 214 ff.). It is doubtful whether the emperor ever fully understood how intolerable this was to Clement VII and Paul III, although he did understand their hostility to the imperial domination of both northern and southern Italy. The threat of heresy and the Turks kept pope and emperor together in uneasy alliance. But the popes continued to intrigue with France against Charles and, on one disastrous occasion in 1527, Clement VII actually engaged in open war with the emperor (see pp. 215, 234–5).

HABSBURG SUCCESSION IN HUNGARY AND BOHEMIA

The second problem, or rather set of problems, facing the emperor in 1521 was political. It seemed at this time the much more urgent one. Firstly, a government had to be organized for Germany. Charles appointed to this his brother Ferdinand, and made over to him the direct control of the Habsburg lands in Germany and Austria. Ferdinand married Anne of Hungary and his younger sister, Mary, married Anne's brother, King Louis II of Hungary and Bohemia. Five years later Louis II perished in the battle of Moháacs (29 August 1526) when a huge Turkish army shattered the brave but disorganized and squabbling Hungarian forces. Buda and Pest and the greater part of lowland Hungary fell to the Turks. Since Louis and Mary had had no children, Ferdinand now inherited the crowns of both Hungary and Bohemia. Once again it seemed that, through dynastic alliances and inheritance, God had raised the house of Habsburg, even in the teeth of a Christian disaster. But the inheritance raised new and formidable problems. Not only was Ferdinand now directly threatened by the Ottoman Turks – in 1529 they reached Vienna but failed to take it, and in 1532 they raided deep into Styria – but he had to make good his claims against John Zápolyai, prince (*voivode*) of Transylvania, who was proclaimed king of Hungary by a strong party of Magyar nobility and who was, logically, supported by the sultan.[1]

THE HABSBURG–VALOIS RIVALRY

In 1521, however, it was the French problem which overshadowed all others. Chièvres, the French-speaking nobleman from Hainault, had seen the secret of his master's success in maintaining peace with France. Thus he had confirmed French rule over Milan, which Francis I had won by his victory over the Sforza duke and his Swiss army at the battle of Marignano (13–14 September 1515); and in return France had not interfered with the Spanish succession. But the very success of Chièvres's policy made continued peace with France impossible. Charles had now succeeded to the political traditions and obligations of the Spanish kingdoms in North Africa and in Italy. The first brought the emperor into collision with the

Turks and involved him in a struggle not only for the control of the North African coast but for the whole of the central Mediterranean. The second involved Charles in the rival Aragonese and Angevin claims to the kingdom of Naples and, inevitably, in a struggle with France for the political control over Italy; and control over Italy, as Gattinara, the Italian humanist steeped in Roman history, now argued, meant the dominant position in Europe and the world.

The court of Francis I thought in very similar terms, although in France the concept of empire was an even more ambiguous one than at the court of Charles V. Both Francis I and Henry VIII of England thought their respective kingdoms to be empires, by which they meant that they did not recognize any secular superior. Nevertheless, both kings appeared as candidates in the imperial election of 1519. Francis I took this candidature quite seriously, even though later he flippantly compared the election and the beginnings of his personal rivalry with Charles V to the pursuit of the same lady by two knights. In terms of power politics, the lady in question was not just the imperial crown but the dominant position in Europe, and in the end, the *monarchie* or *monarchia*. This was the contemporary term for a world empire.[2]

Chièvres's death in 1521 removed the last obstacle to the now inevitable war. Gattinara wanted to elimate France once and for all as a serious rival to his master. The French were to be pushed out of Italy. An imperial attack on France was to synchronize with an English invasion and a rebellion by the Connétable, Charles de Bourbon, the greatest magnate in France, who had private scores to settle with King Francis. The emperor was to reward him with the hand of his sister, Eleanor, and a kingdom carved out of southern France.

This was pure power politics, whatever the emperor's and his grand chancellor's ultimate Christian intentions. Neither the French nor the rest of Europe ever forgot it, especially when these policies lacked the only condition which would have made them acceptable – success. The French fought back tenaciously. The imperial and English invasions of France turned into costly failures. Bourbon's vassals and tenants preferred loyalty to the person of the king and the advantages of royal service to loyalty to their immediate feudal seigneur: Bourbon had to flee, alone, to the emperor's court. In 1524 Clement VII concluded an alliance with France. The emperor reacted by suspending pressure on the German Lutherans, an action which the pope, in his turn, found unforgivable. But the scales turned again. On 24 February 1525 the imperial armies crushed the French at Pavia. King Francis himself was among the prisoners.

The humanist imperialists at the emperor's court were jubilant. He would now establish his *monarchia*, reform the Church, heal its schisms and finally lead a united Christendom against the Turks. Once more Gattinara proposed the dismemberment of France. To his dismay, Lannoy, viceroy of Naples and the victor of Pavia, brought the captive king to Madrid. This Walloon seigneur wanted conciliation with France, in the spirit of Chièvres and the Burgundian traditions of chivalry. The Peace of Madrid (14 January 1526) was a compromise between these two policies. Francis married Charles's sister, Eleanor, and gave up all French claims in Italy and to the duchy of Burgundy.

The treaty achieved neither conciliation nor a serious reduction of French power. Back on French soil, Francis repudiated it on the grounds that it had been signed under duress and that the fundamental laws of the kingdom would not allow the alienation of any French territory. The war started again. On 6 May 1527 the unpaid imperial armies stormed and plundered Rome and made Clement VII a prisoner in his own castle of St Angelo.

DIFFERENT CONCEPTIONS OF EMPIRE

There were many, especially at the imperial court and in Germany, who thought that Charles should immediately exploit this spectacular, though unplanned, triumph over the pope in order to force him to summon a council and reform the Church — just as some of the great medieval emperors had done. But Charles found his victory embarrassing and allowed the opportunity to pass. Once again, the confusions and contradictory pretensions associated with Charles V's imperial title prevented the pursuit of a consistent imperial policy. It may be well here to recapitulate the more important of these imperial pretensions, remembering that they often overlapped, were partly contradictory and were almost never kept clearly apart in the minds of Charles V's contempories or, as far as one can see, in the emperor's own mind.

There was, first, Gattinara's idea of a hegemony or imperial leadership of Europe against the infidel, with no actual domination of other powers. This was Charles's official policy. Then there was the idea of the Imperium, interpreted by the humanists of Charles's court as involving a kind of resurrection of the original Roman Empire, with Rome as the emperor's capital city. Many of the emperor's actions, however, followed rather from the traditional claims of the medieval Holy Roman emperors to reform the Church and strengthen the *Reichsregiment*, the imperial government of Germany. In this context, Empire meant the Holy Roman Empire, that is the kingdom of Germany plus parts of northern Italy.[3] Lastly, there was the quite novel and, to many contemporaries, rather sinister idea of a world empire. Charles V himself denied such pretensions, but many of his supporters made the claims for him. To his opponents the spectre of the *monarchia* always appeared as a very threat to their security and independence.

But the war against France went well for the emperor, especially after he managed to draw Andrea Doria, the admiral of the Genoese fleet and virtual dictator of the city state, into his service. From then onwards the emperor enjoyed complete naval superiority in the western Mediterranean, and this, even more perhaps than the tactical superiority of Spanish over any other infantry at the time, assured for Spain the ultimate victory in Italy. In the Peace of Cambrai (summer 1529) Francis I once more renounced his claims in Italy while Charles gave up his to the duchy of Burgundy, that is to French territory.

Gattinara, with his career now nearing its end — he died in the following year — had thus achieved a substantial part of his imperial programme. France was defeated, at least for the time being, and Charles dominated Italy without having had to acquire any further Italian territory. In Bologna the pope crowned him as emperor. He would now proceed to Germany, to bring the Lutherans back into the Church, and then finally turn his full powers against the Turks. But the grand chancellor had been less successful in the internal organization of the empire. It was not for want of seeing the need. He had plans for a treasurer-general to coordinate the finances of all the emperor's dominions; he proposed a common imperial currency; the emperor was to be the legislator for the whole world. But the interests and traditions of the separate dominions were too strong and Charles himself saw his empire in terms of allegiance to his person rather than as an independent political structure held together by imperial institutions. The only practical outcome of Gattinara's vision was the *Carolina*, the German criminal code, to which the emperor gave little more than his name (1532).

The grand chancellor's own authority and that of the old Burgundian Council of State had extended over all of Charles V's dominions. With its Netherlands, Spanish and Italian members it was a truly international body. Important decisions, however, tended to be taken more and more by a small cabinet of close advisers whom the emperor chose to consult on particular issues. The Council of State therefore failed to develop into a body truly representative of the different parts of the empire. Only in Spain did Gattinara manage to continue the traditions of Ferdinand and Isabella by giving the Castilian Council of State and War competence over the whole of Spain and the Council of Aragon over the Spanish dominions in Italy. This institutional advance in Spain, and the greater administrative efficiency that was its consequence, played its part, together with finance, in gradually making Spain the centre of Charles V's empire.

After 1530 Charles V did not appoint a new grand chancellor. His paper work was done by a Spanish secretariat with competence over Spain and Italy, and a French-Burgundian secretariat with competence north of the Alps. The emperor himself remained the only link between his dominions, keeping in touch by weekly, or even daily, correspondence with his viceroys and governors. Where possible he appointed members of his family to these key positions: his wife, son or daughter in Spain, his brother in Germany, his aunt or sister in the Netherlands. There were no other members of the family, and the viceroys of the Italian dominions had therefore to be found from among Spanish grandees, Burgundian seigneurs or the oldest and most aristocratic Italian families. All important decisions and appointments, together with the control over local patronage, the emperor kept for himself. Thus he maintained personal control over his empire, but at the cost of constant journeying from dominion to dominion, of great administrative inefficiency and of many lost opportunities.

For the Burgundian seigneurs, for Spanish grandees and Italian princes there were rich opportunities for making their reputations and enhancing their fortunes as generals, governors and viceroys in the emperor's service. Hundreds of the lower nobility flocked to his standards for a quick chance of advancement, glory and plunder. For humanists and lawyers the empire was not only a fulfilment of classical dreams but provided dazzling careers in the imperial councils. But what was there for the great mass of the emperor's subjects, except the hope for peace within Christendom? This was the one part of the emperor's universalist claims which ordinary people fully understood. Yet it was precisely this peace which Charles V could not give them; for the very existence of his empire made the other European states his mortal enemies, fearful for their own independence.

CONTINUING WAR WITH FRANCE AND THE TURKS

The Diet of Augsburg (1530) failed to produce the theological compromise which was to have healed the schism in the Church. With the Turks threatening, both in Hungary and in the Mediterranean, Charles had to shelve the religious problem once again. In 1535 he was finally ready for his great counterstroke: he himself commanded the ships and soldiers which recaptured Tunis from the Turks. It was his greatest triumph, the justification of his empire and of his own position as the leader of Christendom. But it was only an interlude. The death of the last Sforza duke of Milan gave Francis I another opportunity to reassert the old French claims to Milan. To Charles it appeared an irresponsible breach of the Peace of Cambrai. Before the horrified pope and the assembled court and ambassadors he proposed to settle his differences with King Francis by single combat, as a judgment of God. His own ministers immediately disavowed this proposal of their quixotic master to their French colleagues.

Twice again, in 1536 and 1544, the emperor's armies invaded France. Francis countered by concluding a formal alliance with the Turks and justified it with the need to save the liberty of the European states from the tyranny of the emperor's *monarchia*. Charles and Ferdinand, in their turn, treated with England and with the Turks' northern and eastern enemies, the Poles, the Muscovites and the Persians. At the moment when the religious unity of Europe was breaking apart, not only the whole of Europe but large parts of Asia and North Africa were being drawn ever closer into the orbit of the rivalries of the great European powers.

In the Peace of Crépy (19 September 1544) Francis I agreed to support Charles against his recent allies, the Turks. He also agreed to support the emperor against the Protestants if they should refuse to accept the decisions of the council that was to meet at Trent (see

p. 217). In return Charles promised to marry a Habsburg princess
to the king's second son and bestow either Milan or the Netherlands on the couple. It was a remarkable arrangement: after four
successful wars against France Charles was willing to concede
nearly all French territorial claims and to contemplate the cession
of his own original Burgundian inheritance, all for the sake of
achieving effective leadership of a Catholic and united Christendom. Soon afterwards, however, the French prince died, much
to the relief of the hard-headed politicians at the imperial court.
They persuaded Charles not to renew the offer for another of
Francis's sons. The Franco–imperial alliance collapsed. But Francis
I, prematurely old and tired, did not try to renew the war.

THE PROBLEMS OF GERMANY AND THE
IMPERIAL SUCCESSION

At last the emperor had time to concentrate on Germany. From the
emperor's point of view, the German problem was particularly
intractable because of the alliance of the Reformation movement
with the ambitions of a number of princes and great cities. For more
than twenty years he had tried to solve the religious question as part
of a general reform of the Church without attempting to deal with
the political and constitutional problem of imperial power in
Germany. This policy had failed. Protestantism continued to spread
and the Schmalkaldic League of Protestant princes and cities was
intriguing with France. Charles now reversed his policy. To deprive
the Lutherans of their political backing, which apparently made
them unwilling to accept a reasonable compromise, he struck at the
Schmalkaldic League, ostensibly to punish its leaders, the elector of
Saxony and the landgrave of Hesse, for rebellion. At Mühlberg his
general, the duke of Alva, with German and Spanish troops, won a
complete victory over the elector (24 April 1547). The landgrave
and the rest of the League submitted.

It was the high point of Charles's reign. Titian painted him as a
victorious knight on horseback – a great contrast to the even
better-known portrait of the same year (1548) of a contemplative,
somewhat sceptical-looking Charles sitting in his armchair. But the
emperor's victory alerted all his old enemies. The pope had already
withdrawn his troops from the imperial army before the battle of

Mühlberg. When he transferred the Council from Trent to Bologna he sabotaged the emperor's policy of imposing a religious compromise on the German Protestants. Even after his great victory Charles was not strong enough to do it alone, and the Catholic princes of Germany were as unwilling as the Protestants to reform the constitution of the Empire in order to increase the effective power of the emperor (see p. 271). In the rest of Europe, from London to Constantinople, the French were working hard to mobilize opinion against Charles. The war against the Schmalkaldic League had thus failed to resolve either the religious or the political problems of Germany and Europe.

This failure precipitated a crisis over the imperial succession. In 1530—1, when his own son, Philip, was only four years old, Charles had persuaded the electors to elect his brother, Ferdinand, as king of the Romans, that is as prospective heir to the imperial title. But now Philip was a grown man. He would, in any case, inherit Spain and the Netherlands. More than ever Charles was convinced that only with the support of these countries could imperial power become effective in Germany and Europe. Ferdinand, however, refused to resign his title to Philip. In an acrimonious family debate they finally reached a compromise by which Ferdinand remained Charles's successor to the imperial title but would himself be succeeded by Philip, with his son, Maximilian, succeeding Philip in his turn.

This was the deathblow to Charles V's universalist aims. They depended on his own position and title, and he had not been able to bequeath them to his son. Moreover, the rift in Habsburg family solidarity was to have serious consequences. When, in 1552, Maurice of Saxony and other German princes, in alliance with the new French king, Henry II, attacked Charles and forced him to flee for his life, Ferdinand's attitude remained at least equivocal. The renewed Franco-imperial war was a purely power- political war, even though Charles still clung to his old arguments about defending the unity of Christendom and the French still talked about defending the liberty of the Christian states. Both sides used the familiar arguments about the escalation of potential disasters: if we lose a certain, admittedly unimportant, position we may then lose an important fortress, followed by the loss of a province and, then, of the whole state of empire. Both sides were determined to negotiate from strength or, as contemporaries put it, only after they had won some substantial military success. Both sides made play with the moral turpitude of the enemy who had first to show some public sign of repentance before he could be trusted: the French because they had allied themselves with the Turks and the heretics; the imperialists because they had wantonly planned to destroy the French monarchy and state. Between the two parties stood the new pope, Julius III, who spoke of peace between Christians but who played the traditional power game because he was convinced that the papacy could be genuinely independent only if its political position in Italy was assured.

Thus the war dragged on and men, viewing the rigid and unimaginative policies of the great powers, spoke with increasing despair of a *Christianitas afflicta*.[4] Only Ferdinand was ready for a compromise in Germany; for he knew that eventually he would have to live with the German princes without the Spanish and Netherlands resources on which his brother, the emperor, was always able to rely. In the face of the sullen hostility and, sometimes, active interference of Charles, Ferdinand piloted a religious and political compromise through the Diet of Augsburg, in 1555. The main provisions of the Peace of Augsburg were later summarized as the principle of *cuius regio eius religio* – the right of the princes (and of the magistrates of the free imperial cities) to impose their own confession on their subjects. This applied only to Catholics and Lutherans. The Calvinists were left out of the peace and many problems were simply shelved, notably the relations between the princes and the Imperial Crown for whom the *cuius regio eius religio* principle meant a heavy defeat, a formal abdication of authority to the princes over a field which Charles V had always considered to lie peculiarly within the emperor's prerogative. The bitter fruits of these failures were still to be tasted in the following century; for the next fifty years, however, the Diet of Augsburg gave Germany peace – not a mean achievement after nearly a decade of intermittent civil and religious wars.

CHARLES V'S ABDICATION

It is not clear how far Charles V was convinced that his imperial programme had failed. His last great success, the marriage of his son Philip to Mary of England, seemed a triumph in the best Habsburg dynastic imperial tradition. He could not know that, like the English queen, it would turn out to be barren. Yet the emperor's failures were very evident. The Church had not been reformed in such a way as to heal the schism, nor had the Protestants been finally crushed by force of arms. France and the Turks were as threatening as ever. Julius III's successor Paul IV (Gian Pietro Carafa) was working for an open breach with Spain. On 25 October 1555 Charles V abdicated his sovereignty over the Netherlands to his son Philip. In the following months he did the same with his other titles.

No one had any doubt that his successor Philip II was a Spaniard and nothing but a Spaniard. The German electors would have nothing to do with him and cheerfully ignored the Habsburg family agreement by electing Ferdinand's son, Maximilian, king of the Romans. Already in the later part of Charles V's reign his empire had become more and more Spanish. The military superiority of Spanish troops, the greater willingness of Castile, as against the Netherlands, to pay for the cost of empire, the rapidly increasing flow of American treasure into Seville — all this inevitably shifted the empire's centre of gravity. Spaniards and Hispano-Italians displaced the Netherlanders in the emperor's councils, monopolized all high positions south of the Alps and even began to appear in the Netherlands and Germany. In Spain itself, Erasmianism, the great spiritual force behind the emperor's vision of Church reform and reconciliation with the Protestants was dying. Its last surviving exponents were imprisoned or in flight before the triumphant Inquisition. Even in his lifetime Charles V's universalist Christian empire, with its Burgundian core and Erasmian inspiration was changing into Philip II's Spanish empire, with its Castilian core and its inspiration derived from the Catholic revival of the Counter-Reformation.

THE OTTOMAN EMPIRE

The claims to universal empire by the Turks and, more specifically, by their ruling house of Osman, had their foundation in the will of God, just as much as those of Charles V; but they were also based on the concept of the justice of conquest. God had imposed on Muslims the duty to propagate Islam by force of arms, and the Koran adjured believers 'not [to] think that those who were slain in the cause of Allah are dead. They are alive and well provided for by

Allah; . . .'[5] This duty of holy war with the promise of martyrdom attached to it was not held to apply to all individual Muslims in all circumstances. But the Ottoman Turks had risen as warriors on the Anatolian marches of the decaying Byzantine Empire and had, traditionally, seen their primary (though not their only) duty in conquering the Christian provinces of this empire. The conquest of Constantinople by Mohammed II (the Conqueror) in 1453 gave a further dimension to the Ottoman concept of empire. One of the oldest and greatest ambitions of Islam had now been achieved. The sultans found a decaying and depopulated city and made it again into a flourishing centre of an expanding empire, a capital with a multi-racial and multi-religious population whose numbers and trade rapidly surpassed those of all other cities in the Christian and Muslim world. The hoped-for conquest of the world by Islam did not imply the forced conversion of all non-believers. In contrast to the Christians, the Turks were remarkably tolerant. Jews and Christians had to pay special taxes from which Muslims were exempt; but they were allowed to practise their own religions unhindered. There was still a patriarch of the Greek Church in Constantinople and, later in the sixteenth century, the English and Spanish ambassadors in Constantinople enjoyed greater freedom in practising their own version of the Christian religion than they enjoyed, respectively, in Madrid and London. To the sultan's Christian subjects who called him *Basileus*, the title of the Byzantine emperors, and even to many western Christians, it seemed that the East Roman Empire was reborn. And if such ideas probably meant little to the majority of Muslims, the sultans themselves were certainly aware of their Greek heritage, though they looked back as much to Alexander the Great as to the East Roman emperors.

Nevertheless, while Ottoman power was confined to Anatolia and the Balkan Peninsula, the sultan's claims to world empire were hardly impressive, as Scanderbeg, the undefeated Albanian leader, had tauntingly pointed out to Mohammed the Conqueror.[6] This was still the position in 1500. But during the first decade of the sixteenth century Shah Ismail Safawi, the ruler of Persia, broke the old tradition of toleration between the Sunni majority and the Shiite minority in the Muslim world and imposed Shiism on his subjects by force. When his followers spread their activities to Anatolia, a clash between the two major Muslim powers became inevitable. It took the form both of a religious war between Sunni orthodoxy and Shiite heresy and of a struggle for political supremacy in the Islamic world. In 1514 Sultan Selim I, seeing himself as a new Alexander (whose history he knew from Persian sources), marched to the conquest of Persia. He entered Tabriz but finally failed to defeat Shah Ismail and conquer his country. In the following years, perhaps because Selim still saw himself as following in the footsteps of the great Alexander or, perhaps, to prevent a Persian-Shiite counteroffensive towards the south-west, the Turks conquered Syria and Egypt from the feeble and inoffensive Mamluk sultans (1516–17). Soon afterwards the corsair kingdom of Algiers acknowledged the suzerainty of Constantinople. In 1534 Suleiman I conquered Bagdad.

LIMITS OF THE OTTOMAN EMPIRE

The Turks did not manage to unite the whole of Islam. In India the Sunni Moghul empire of Babur and Akbar remained sublimely indifferent to Constantinople. Shiite Persia proved to be unconquerable. The frontier in Asia remained very much what it had been at the time of the Roman Empire, except that the Turks held on to Mesopotamia, which the Romans had succeeded in doing for only a short period. But the sultan's authority was now acknowledged (although not always effective) from the Don and the Danube to the Gulf of Aden, and from the Tigris and the Gulf of Persia to the Sahara and the Atlas Mountains. Suleiman I, whom the Christians called 'the Magnificent', ruled over the holy cities of Mecca and Medina, and over the seats of the former caliphs of Bagdad, Damascus and Cairo. There was now substance to his title of *Padishah-i Islam*, the emperor of Islam, 'the king of kings, the greatest emperor of Constantinople, the lord of Egypt, Asia and Europe . . . the master of the universal sea'.[7] According at any rate to a Christian tradition, Khair ad-Din Barbarossa, the corsair king of Algiers, tried to persuade Suleiman the Magnificent to attack Tunis (1534), specifically as a move towards the conquest of Rome which Suleiman's great-grandfather, Mohammed the Conqueror, was supposed to have planned in order to reunite the Eastern and Western Roman Empires.[8]

If Suleiman harboured such an ambition, he failed. But he captured Belgrade in 1521, Rhodes in 1522, Budapest in 1526 and Tripoli in 1551. By 1560, the imperial ambassador at Constantinople, the Flemish humanist Ghislin de Busbecq, wrote pessimistically: 'On their side are the resources of a mighty empire . . . experience and practice in fighting . . . habituation to victory, endurance of toil, unity, order, discipline, frugality and watchfulness. On our side is public poverty, private luxury . . . broken spirit, lack of endurance and training. . . . Can we doubt what the result will be?'[9]

Busbecq was certainly correct in thinking that the social, political and military institutions of the Ottoman Turks had all been developed with a view to conquest. Their rulers, having started simply as leaders of a band of free Turkish warriors, had, through the influence of Persian theologians, come to regard their authority as virtually absolute. Nevertheless, even as sultans they had to observe the Holy Law of Islam which was divine and immutable. Muslims in general, and the Turks in particular, were notoriously conservative in their interpretation of this law. The sultans' real power therefore depended not so much on a political–religious theory of absolutism as on the effectiveness with which they could make their will obeyed. This was done by building up an army and a civil administration from the sultan's personal slaves.

THE 'DEVSHIRME'

These slaves were recruited not only from outside the ranks of the old-established Turkish families but from outside the Muslim population altogether, from Christians. Prisoners of war, slaves bought from dealers, or even volunteers, that is Christian renegades, could serve; but the most important method of recruiting slaves was the system known as *devshirme*. This was a regular levy of boys from Christian families, mostly in the Balkans. The boys had to become Muslims and received an education that was as methodical and rigorous, in its own way, as that of the novitiates of the Jesuit Order. They were carefully selected according to aptitudes. The majority received a military training and joined either the regiments of the household cavalry, the Sipahis of the Porte, or the even more famous infantry, the Janissaries with their long cloaks and feathered turbans, and with their scimitars and arquebuses – the most highly disciplined fighting force in the world. They were forbidden to marry, so that no cares for wife and family should interfere with their loyalty to the sultan and their singlemindedness as warriors of the faith. A minority of boys were trained for the sultan's service, either in his household or in his administration.

The system aroused mixed feelings in Christian observers. They marvelled at the Ottoman contempt for considerations of birth and lineage which were so central to the structure and ethos of European society; for could not a peasant boy from Serbia, a shepherd from Albania or a fisherman from Calabria rise to the dignity of a *beglerbeg* (governor of a province), of an admiral of the fleet, even of a grand vizier who effectively ruled the whole empire, amassing enormous wealth and aspiring to the hand of the sultan's own sister or daughter? Yet they all remained the sultan's slaves and were even proud of it; their property was his to dispose of, their children had few privileges. Westerners with a classical education, like Busbecq, could even imagine that the Turkish system of slavery resembled that of ancient Rome and that slavery was the cause of the greatness of both the Roman and the Turkish empires.[10]

The Janissaries and Sipahis of the Porte were only the nucleus of the Turkish army, no more than 12,000–15,000 each. The bulk of the regular army was formed from the holders of the *timars*, military fiefs, who had either themselves to serve as cavalry or provide a number of horsemen according to the size of the fief. There were also client armies of princes who acknowledged the suzerainty of the sultan and, always, vast hordes of irregulars. On the Aegean islands the system worked similarly, with holders of the *timars* serving in the Ottoman fleet. These fiefs were not hereditary in the holder's family, as they were in classical western feudalism, but only in the class of *timar* holders as a whole. They were redistributed after the holder's death. At the accession of a new sultan there was a wholesale redistribution, in theory at least, according to military services rendered by individuals in the *timar*-holding class. In consequence, this class had a vested interest in constantly pushing the frontiers of the empire outwards in order to provide more land and *timars* for distribution.

WEAKNESSES OF THE TURKISH SYSTEM

From about the middle of the sixteenth century a number of fundamental weaknesses began to become apparent in the Ottoman system, weaknesses which brought to a halt the further expansion of the empire. The central pillar of the whole system was the sultanate. It was protected from succession troubles by the notorious, but effective, custom of strangling the new sultan's brothers on his accession. The institution of the harem served to free the sultan from family attachments as effectively as celibacy freed his Janissaries or the priesthood of the Roman Catholic Church. It was therefore an ominous sign for the future when Suleiman the Magnificent raised the ambitious young Roxolana above all his other wives, had his gifted and popular son of an older wife murdered and fixed the succession on Roxolana's worthless offspring, Selim II. From Selim II descended the long and only rarely broken succession of cretinous or paranoiac sultans of the two following centuries.

The personal deficiencies of the sultans following Suleiman the Magnificent could be, and often were, made good, at least partially, by energetic and devoted grand viziers. But a slave system, even when started in an ideal form, is unlikely to continue in this way. 'Bribes to officials are an incurable disease. Oh God, save us from bribes!' wrote a retired grand vizier, Luṭfi Pasha, already in the 1540s.[11] Yet Luṭfi's successor, Rustem Pasha, a creature of Roxolana's, systematically introduced the sale of offices to the highest bidder; and, since office holders had no security against an even higher bidder, they usually made the most of their opportunities while they had the chance. Turkish corruption and oppression became proverbial. Where the Turkish horse sets foot, it was said, there no grass will grow again.[12] In earlier days the Christian peasants of the Balkans had often welcomed the Turks as liberators from the oppression of their own nobility. Yet, in the second half of the sixteenth century all the Venetian ambassadors at Constantinople speak of the depopulation of the empire's European provinces and of the misery of the survivors.

The empire had reached its limits. At 800 or 1,000 miles range from its base, and in repeatedly plundered country, the mighty Ottoman army could be held up for vital weeks by the determined resistance of a small fortress. This happened to Suleiman before Sziget, in western Hungary, during his last campaign, in 1566. It was the same in Persia and in the central Mediterranean. In 1565 a huge combined operation just failed to take Malta from the Knights of St John – the real turning point in the naval war against the Christians.

With the change from moving to fixed frontiers, the social-military institutions that had been designed for conquest began to deteriorate. The *timars* came to be distributed, no longer for prowess in battle, but to serve the ambitions and greed of provincial governors who gave the *timars* to their friends and clients and, frequently, to men who could not fulfil the military obligations attached to them. Already during the reign of Suleiman, the Janissaries obtained the right to marry. On the occasion of Selim II's accession — always a weak moment for the sultan — they forced him to allow their sons to join the corps. When the Persian wars at the end of the century swallowed up the best Ottoman armies, the ranks of the Janissaries were opened to born Muslims. The elite troop of the Ottoman army had shed all its traditions except one: its rigid conservatism in the arms and tactics it was willing to use. Worse was to come. Like the Praetorian Guards of the Roman Empire, the Janissaries began to interfere in politics. Under Murad III (1574—95) they demanded and obtained the heads of ministers who had made themselves unpopular with them. In 1622 they murdered Osman II — the first of a melancholy series of murdered sultans. The slaves had become the masters.

The Venetian ambassadors who, among many other observers, described this decline in the second half of the sixteenth century, were under no illusions about the still formidable might of the *Signor Turco*. Yet even his ambitions had become paltry. At the moment when the Moriscos were engaging the whole might of the Spanish empire in their last great revolt in southern Spain (1568—70) and were anxiously calling on the sultan for help, Selim II preferred to attack the inoffensive Venetian Republic in Cyprus, near his own bases. The Turks managed to conquer Cyprus but brought on themselves the revenge of the combined Spanish, Venetian and Papal fleets. The crushing naval defeat of Lepanto (7 October 1571) had few immediate consequences. The Christian alliance soon broke up and the lost fleet could be rebuilt; but the blow to Muslim morale was tremendous. The legend of Ottoman invincibility at sea was shattered, once and for all. Worse still, it had become clear that the sultan had failed as the leader of Islam against the unbelievers. Cut off by the Shiite schism from its Persian and central Asian religious and cultural roots (roots from which the long since exhausted and, to the Turks, alien Arabic-Egyptian tradition was no substitute)[13] the Ottoman Islamic empire, with its universalist claims, was becoming a limited Turkish empire — no more than one of several great military powers in Europe and Asia.

MOSCOW, THE THIRD ROME

It cannot be said that Europe took the universalist claims of the grand princes of Muscovy in the sixteenth century as seriously as those of the Habsburgs and the Ottoman sultans. Those who were near enough to the Muscovites to be directly involved with them — the Turks, the Emperor, the Poles — rejected them outright. Those who, like the English, were far enough away to be concerned only with trading relations, were quite willing to humour the grand prince by calling him an emperor;[14] but it signified nothing. Yet, to the Muscovites themselves their universalist claims were clear and irrefutable.

They were developed, in the first place, by the Russian church, from the last quarter of the fifteenth century onwards, and they received their most famous formulation in the letters of the monk Philotheos of Pskov, during the reign of Vassily III (1503–33). The first Rome had fallen because of the Apollinarian heresy, Philotheos argued.[15] The second Rome — East Rome, Byzantium — had betrayed the true Christian faith by its union with the Church of the pope of Rome,[16] and its fall to the Turks was the divine punishment for this betrayal. This left the Russian Orthodox Church as the only true and direct heir, with its centre in the blessed city of Moscow, the city where the holy Virgin Mary had died. The tsar was the only true ruler over all Christians; for, according to the books of the prophets, 'two Romes have fallen, but the third [Moscow] stands, and there will not be a fourth'.[17] Moscow, therefore, like Rome and Byzantium before, was the *Civitas Dei*, the City of God; but, unlike its predecessors, it placed itself at the end of an irrevocable historical development.[18] Gradually, an elaborate supporting mythology was built up. It was claimed that the house of Rurik was descended from a brother of the Emperor Augustus; that the Byzantine emperor Constantine Monomach had given his own crown jewels to the grand prince Vladimir Monomach of Kiev in the twelfth century; even that Moscow, like Rome, was built on seven hills.

THE TSARS

The rulers of Muscovy themselves were rather more cautious in their claims than their enthusiastic clerical protagonists.

Nevertheless, they developed their own political claims in the same direction. Ivan III, whose second wife was the niece of the last Byzantine emperor, began to use the double- headed imperial eagle in his seal. From about 1480 he used the title of tsar, at first only in relations with his weaker neighbours, the German Order in Livonia and the Hanseatic cities. Vasily III rejected an offer of the title of king from the emperor Maximilian and insisted on the imperial title which, however, Maximilian did not concede. The claim to this title had undoubtedly a religious significance. Ivan III justified his campaign against Novgorod, in 1471, as a means of preventing its Orthodox Christian inhabitants from losing their faith under a Roman Catholic ruler, the king of Poland. Ivan IV, the Terrible, claimed that he conquered Kazan to protect its Christians from outrages by the Muslim Tartars and he instructed his agents abroad that they were to point to the immediate foundation of Christian churches in his newly conquered provinces. The sacramental character of the ruler's position had a long tradition in Russia. A large number of Russian princes had been saints, either because they fought for Christianity or because they bore their deaths as Christ bore His cross. In popular belief these two categories seem to have included every single one, even Ivan the Terrible; for were they not all mediators between God and their people? In contemporary iconography they were portrayed with little individuality but with the emphasis on their attributes of power and with a close resemblance to the traditional manner of representing the Apostles and the fathers of the Church.[19] This was the traditional iconography of the Byzantine emperors. The theory of the succession to Byzantium, the *translatio imperii*, emphasized this tradition and gave it a universal significance.

As a matter of practical politics, however, the rulers of Muscovy, whether they called themselves grand princes or tsars, were in no position even to dream of universal empire in the manner of a Charles V or a Suleiman the Magnificent. A Russian attack on Constantinople, for instance, though regarded as ultimately desirable and, from time to time, even encouraged by western powers and the pope, never seriously entered the realm of practical possibilities during the sixteenth century. The Orthodox Christians in the Ottoman empire had to be left to their fate. They probably preferred it that way. Even a serious attack on the sultan's vassals, the Crimean Tartars, was held to be too risky. This left the possibility of expansion towards the west and towards the south-east. There were theoretical justifications for both; for the tsar, the ruler of all the Russians, claimed the right of succession to the princes of Kiev and other medieval Russian rulers. Lithuania had annexed the communities of Little, Black, White and Red Russia, that is all the western areas of Russian-speaking peoples, while the Great Russians were fighting for their lives against the Tartars.

IVAN IV'S CONQUESTS

Ivan IV's campaigns against the enfeebled successor states of the Golden Horde were brilliantly successful. Kazan fell in 1552; Astrakhan in 1556. The whole of the enormous Volga basin was now in Russian hands and, with it, not only the trade routes to Central Asia (soon to be exploited, among others, by merchants of the English Russia Company) but also the way for Russian expansion through Siberia and, eventually, to the Pacific Ocean. The Russians who for centuries had been oppressed by the Tartars became their heirs and recreated the northern steppes part of Genghis Khan's Eurasian empire of the thirteenth century. But this development still lay in the future.

Expansion on the western frontier proved much more difficult. Its southern part, the Ukrainian steppe, stretching from the Don to the middle Dnieper and the Carpathians, was the domain of the Cossacks, an ethnically mixed group of frontiersmen, fighting as free warriors on horseback and alternating primitive farming, cattle rearing and fishing with raids on settled communities. They were the arch-enemies of both Russian boyars and Polish noblemen whose peasants or serfs they had frequently been and whose estates they now happily plundered. Rather than attempt to subjugate such unpromising territory it was clearly better for the tsars to follow the Polish example and take some of the Cossack bands into their pay, as brave even if unreliable auxiliaries.

Almost equally unpromising, in the face of the formidable Polish cavalry armies, was a move directly westward for the possible conquest of Smolensk and White Russia. This left the north-west. Here the weakness of the German Order in Livonia seemed to give a chance of a Russian advance to the Baltic with all the enormous strategic and economic advantages this would bring. Ivan IV justified his attack on Livonia with the argument that the Germans and Lithuanians were not Christians, by which he meant Orthodox Christians.[20] Between 1558 and 1582 the Russians fought in Livonia with varying success, sometimes in alliance with, more often against most of the other Baltic powers, Poland-Lithuania, Sweden, Denmark and the Hanseatic League. In the end, and at enormous cost in manpower and devastated provinces, they failed completely against the superior military organization and naval power of the Baltic states (Peace of Yam Zapolsky, 1582).

While the tsars could not yet successfully challenge the western powers they could make themselves supreme in Russia itself. Over the whole vast area north of the Oka and the Volga they had extended their rule as over a private estate. No regional and provincial autonomies, nor any corporate cities had been able to develop. Where the tsars found autonomous corporations already in existence, as in the city of Novgorod, they smashed them. Thus the struggle against royal absolutism, which in western Europe so often took the form of a defence of regional and corporate autonomies, lacked in Russia one of its strongest bastions. The Church was, of course, a corporation and, in a crucial Church council in 1503, it successfully defended its property against Ivan III's plans for secularization. In all other matters, however, including the choice of the metropolitan, the right to convoke councils and even in jurisdiction over heresy, the Church acknowledged the authority of the tsar and, following Byzantine tradition, preached his absolute power.

THE DEFEAT OF THE BOYARS

This left the boyars as the only counterweight to the tsars. They were the great landowners, many of them descended from minor Russian princes or even, like the Shuisky, from the house of Rurik itself. Against them, the grand princes of Moscow had built up the *dvoriane*, the service nobility or gentry who performed military services with their retainers according to the size of their estates. Like the holders of the *timars* in the Ottoman empire, they clamoured for wars of conquest to obtain more land. But perhaps even more important, in a country as sparsely populated as Russia, was the landowners' need for peasants for their estates. Inevitably, landowners competed for peasants, and here the rich boyars had great advantages over the service gentry. Equally inevitably, these latter looked to the tsar for help against the economic competition of the boyars.

Here were sufficient reasons for a struggle between the monarchy and the boyars. But Ivan IV also had personal reasons for hating them. During his long minority (1533–47) several of his relatives and the boyars had fought each other for power and misruled the country. Like Louis XIV of France a hundred years later, Ivan could never forget the indignities he had suffered as a child at the hands of overmighty subjects. Obedience to the tsar must become absolute; for, as Ivan wrote to Prince Kurbsky, a boyar who had defected to the Poles, all divine writings teach that children must not resist the father, nor the servant the master, 'except in the cause of faith', nor 'only the good [prince] . . . but also the froward . . . and if you are just and pious, why do you not permit yourself to accept suffering from me, your froward master, and [so] accept the crown of life?'[21]

Having thus, to his own satisfaction, and in accordance with the traditional teachings of the Russian church, established the irrelevance of his own character to the office of tsar, Ivan gave his subjects ample opportunity to win their crowns of life. In 1565 he set up an organization, called the *oprichnina*, in which first 1,000, later up to 6,000 of his most loyal followers were given land confiscated from boyars and other landowners. Some of the boyars were given compensation in frontier areas, to the south and east, but much of their old influence was now broken. The *coup* was staged with exemplary brutality. There were mass executions and thousands were evicted from their homes in the middle of winter. It is not for nothing that Ivan IV has come to be known as Ivan the Terrible. Within the area of the *oprichnina*, about half the territory of the state, the tsar was left with absolute power. In the rest of the country, the *zemshchina*, the old boyar duma (assembly) continued to function. Ivan even summoned a new type of assembly, the *zemsky sobor*, which had some of the characteristics of the representative assemblies of the rest of Europe, although its members were mainly men in government service.

SOCIAL AND POLITICAL RESULTS OF IVAN IV'S REIGN

The results of Ivan's *coup d'etat* were far-reaching. It greatly accelerated the disintegration of the remaining free peasant communes, for the new owners of the confiscated estates needed tenants. Since conditions were harsh, great numbers of peasants simply fled, either east to the lower Volga where the state needed colonists, or south to the Cossacks. But in central Russia, around Moscow, and even more in areas suffering from the Livonian war, population declined disastrously. This forced the tsars to support the landowners in imposing serfdom on the Russian peasant, and it was this support which, in turn, assured the loyalty of the service nobility to the tsars and their unquestioning acceptance of tsarist absolutism.

These were the long-term effects of Ivan IV's policies. They did not solve the immediate problems of the Russian empire. As in the Ottoman empire, too much depended on the personality of the ruler, and Ivan's tyrannies and cruelties left his successors with an appallingly difficult task. His autocracy had been still largely personal. The *oprichnina*, although it vastly increased his authority, was not a centralized administrative apparatus which could govern the country. A Tartar raid on Moscow in 1571 showed only too clearly how far the Livonian war and the action against the boyars had weakened the military strength of the country. When Ivan died in 1584 the country was 'full of grudge and mortall hatred', as the English ambassador, Dr Giles Fletcher, wrote four years later.[22] Ivan himself had entertained fears for his position. For years he pressed Elizabeth I most insistently, and finally obtained from her the promise of refuge in England should he need it. He had himself killed his eldest son. A younger son, Fedor, was weak minded and the third a child of two. To all Russia's troubles was now added the problem of disputed successions.

For a time Boris Godunov, the maternal uncle of the weakminded Tsar Fedor, governed successfully, rather like an Ottoman grand vizier. But by 1600, when Fedor had died, the country was rapidly sliding into civil war between warring palace and boyar factions, while Poles and Cossacks intervened to try and control the fate of Muscovy. The Cossacks were then at the height of their power, not least because of the influx into their ranks of peasants who had fled from Ivan the Terrible's Russia.

RUSSIAN IMPERIALISM

Yet the Russian state survived, and with it Russian imperialism; for imperialism was what the universalism inherent in the idea of the Third Rome had become. Many western travellers in Russia in the sixteenth century remarked on the extremes of Russian xenophobia. It was part of the Russian Church's belief in its unique orthodoxy and it meant that the idea of the universal church had become nationalized, so to speak. Ideally, the Russian church would have liked to cut the country off from all contact with the schismatic west. But the tsars brought a steady stream of Italian architects, German engineers and soldiers and English merchants into the country. Sigismund II of Poland saw the implications of this policy, and he was afraid. 'We know and feel of a surety,' he wrote to Elizabeth I, by way of protest against English trade with Russia, 'the Muscovite, enemy to all liberty under the heavens, daily to grow mightier . . . while not only wares but also weapons heretofore unknown to him, and artificers and arts be brought unto him: by means whereof he maketh himself strong to vanquish all other . . . Therefore we that know best, and border upon him, do admonish other Christian princes in time, that they do not betray their dignity, liberty and life of them and their subjects to a most barbarous and cruell enemy . . .'[23]

THE PORTUGUESE OVERSEAS EMPIRE AND ITS JUSTIFICATION

When Vasco da Gama sailed to India in 1498 he was acting within the tradition of Portuguese maritime exploration, then already three-quarters of a century old.[24] Its motivation lay both in the chivalric and crusading tradition of fighting the Moors and of converting the heathens, and also in the quest for gold, slaves and profitable trade. Later, in the third quarter of the sixteenth century, Camões, himself a voyager to the Indies, sang of Vasco da Gama's exploits:

> Armes, and the Men above the vulgar File,
> Who from the Western Lusitanian shore
> Past ev'n beyond the Trapobanian Isle,
> Through Seas which never Ship has sayld before;
> . . .
> Likewise the Kings of glorious memory,
> Who sow'd and propagated where they past

The Faith of the New Empire . . .

. . .

My Song shall spread where ever there are Men . . .★

Vasco da Gama's men themselves put it more prosaically: 'We have come to look for Christians and spices', they said as they disembarked in Calicut.[25] Some Tunisian merchants, on the same occasion, put it even more succinctly when they said to the Portuguese: 'What the devil has brought you here?' To the Muslims in general, and to the Arab traders in particular, the Portuguese discovery of the sea route to India was an unmitigated disaster, even if, in the long run, it may have strengthened, rather than weakened, the hold of Islam on the shores of the Indian Ocean.[26]

If the Portuguese needed any further justification for empire, successive fifteenth-century popes had provided it by a series of grants, and especially by the bulls of 1493 (see p. 229). These papal bulls were a kind of Donation of Constantine[27] in reverse. Since Portugal and Spain were their exclusive beneficiary, they were naturally not accepted by the rest of Europe. 'I should be very happy to see the clause in Adam's will which excluded me from my share when the world was being divided', said Francis I.[28]

There is little evidence that, during the sixteenth century at least, the Portuguese ever seriously questioned the pope's right to grant them an empire, or their own to conquer it. In 1501 Manuel I assumed the title of Lord of the Conquest, Navigation and Commerce of Ethiopia, India, Arabia and Persia. This was a considerable exaggeration. The Portuguese rarely held more than coastal fortresses and trading stations; but they did attempt to establish a monopoly of the eastern spice trade and they justified this not only on commercial grounds but also as a weapon against the greatest enemies of Christ, the Muslims. Constant warfare against the Muslims and the attempt to spread the gospel went hand in hand with commerce. This combination of aims often led to sickening cruelties, perpetrated especially on East African Muslims, and to a revulsion against Christian hypocrisy by many highly civilized Asians. Yet there were also many Portuguese, especially Dominicans and Jesuits, who attempted to mitigate the worst evils

★Luis de Camões, *The Lusiads*, trans. Sir Richard Fanshawe (1665), ed. G. Bullough (London, 1963), Canto I, Stanzas I, 2. See also p. 365.

of conquest, colonization and greed. Their greatest success was probably in Brazil where the Jesuits in particular worked hard for the domestication and conversion of the American Indians, the education of both white and coloured children, and the reformation of the morals and manners of the colonists 'which', as a modern historian has remarked, 'like those of most European pioneers in the tropics were apt to be based on the theory that there were no Ten Commandments south of the equator'.[29]

RACE RELATIONS IN THE PORTUGUESE EMPIRE

The Portuguese crown, again under the influence of the theologians, insisted that all Christians, regardless of colour, were to be treated as equals, and in 1562 and 1572 it translated these beliefs into laws. The colonists, however, and even the colonial clergy, largely disregarded these laws. The Italian Jesuit, Alessandro Valignano, for instance, argued that Indians should not be admitted into his order, 'both because all these dusky races are very stupid and vicious . . . and likewise because the Portuguese treat them with the greatest contempt'. This attitude did not apply to the Chinese and Japanese, nor were Indian and African Christians prevented from becoming secular clergy. For all their race prejudices, the Portuguese often intermarried with native women. In Brazil and, to a lesser extent, in those parts of the East Indies which they held, they gradually developed an interracial, though still white-dominated society.

THE SPANISH OVERSEAS EMPIRE AND ITS JUSTIFICATION

The motives which led the Spaniards to conquer their overseas empire were, perhaps, an even more complex compound of greed and Christian ideals than were those of the Portuguese. Pizarro, the conqueror of Peru, did not even pretend that he was bringing Christianity to the Peruvian Indians. 'I have come to take away from them their gold', he declared.[30] He was followed by many with similar aims but without his bravura. The colonial society they created was devastatingly characterized by Cervantes:

The refuge and haven of all the poor devils of Spain, the sanctuary of the bankrupt, the safeguard of murderers, the way out for gamblers, the promised land for ladies of easy virtue, a lure and disillusionment for the many and a personal remedy for the few.*

Cervantes, the author of the most famous anti-heroic novel, naturally stressed a very different type of motivation from Camões, the author of the most famous heroic poem in modern literature. Hernán Cortés, with his quest for personal glory, as much as for wealth and power, with his ability to pick up humanist tags and his visions of himself as the instrument through which Charles V should conquer his universal empire, was perhaps a more complex character than even the heroes of the *Lusiads*. Most of the early Spanish *conquistadores* would probably have agreed with Bernal Diaz, soldier in, and chronicler of, Cortés's expedition: 'We came here to serve God and also to get rich.'[31]

The qualities which enabled a few hundred Spaniards to conquer vast empires in Central and South America were their complete conviction of the justice of their cause and their consequent heroic determination and almost unbelievable daring, their superior weapons and knowledge of the art of war and, perhaps more important still, their flexibility of mind, compared with the mental inflexibility of their brave, but tradition-bound, opponents. It was this flexibility which enabled the Spaniards to deal successfully with situations which no European had ever encountered before.[32] Perhaps it was this same flexibility of mind which also led some Spaniards to think about the problems of colonial conquest and empire, and of the relations of human beings of different races and religions in an entirely new manner. The Portuguese won their colonial empire in a struggle mainly with the Muslims. Perhaps this was the reason why they never completely freed themselves from traditional crusading ways of thinking. God's standard bearer, they called their country — the same phrase which Charles V had used for himself when he sallied forth to the conquest of Tunis. But, in America at least, then Spaniards met only relatively primitive and pagan peoples. The problem which they faced was therefore

---

*Miguel de Cervantes, *El Celoso Extremeño*, opening; quoted and translated in Boxer, *Race Relations*, p. 86.

twofold: firstly, what right did Christians have to make war on, conquer and take away the land of, pagan peoples? and secondly, how best were these pagan peoples to be converted? — for that they must be converted everybody was agreed.

The most common answer to the first question was, of course, the papal grant. Both Charles V and Philip II usually thought it sufficient justification. Many Spaniards, however, both in the New World and in Spain, did not think so or felt the need for further elaboration. They invented mythologies designed to prove that the Aztecs had originally been brought to America by an ancestor of Charles V, or that the New World was identical with the Isles of the Hesperides, called after a mythical King Hespero who reigned in Spain in the seventh century B.C. Alternatively, as we have already seen, the universalist conception of Charles V's empire was taken to apply specifically to the new discoveries.[32] Very different from such fantasies were the arguments put forward by Francisco de Vitoria and the Salamanca school of theologians. They denied the pope's claim to temporal power over the world and his right to dispose of it to the kings of Spain and Portugal. Nor did they consider that any rights could flow from the fact of discovery. A canoe-load of Indians, arriving at the mouth of the Guadalquivir, might otherwise claim the discovery and possession of Spain, said Vitoria. Paganism was not, in itself, a justification for war because, in natural law, pagans had property rights just as much as Christians. Only unnatural practices, such as cannibalism or human sacrifice, Vitoria conceded, would justify a war of conquest for the protection of the innocent.

THE TREATMENT OF THE AMERICAN INDIANS: BARTOLOMÉ DE LAS CASAS

These discussions were not limited to the lecture rooms of the universities. As early as 1511 Antonio de Montesinos, a Dominican friar, preached a sermon to the Spanish colonists of Hispaniola accusing them of cruelty towards the natives. It was the first shot in a long struggle which the Dominicans waged with the colonists over the treatment of the American Indians. It was not that all Spanish colonists were deliberately cruel; but they had come to make money and they wanted cheap labour. The disruption of the social structure of the Indian communities, the breaking up of families, forced labour and, worst of all though unintentional, the devastating effects of European diseases, produced catastrophic results. In the West Indian islands the native population disappeared altogether. For Central Mexico some recent authorities suggest a decline from about 25 million, at the time of the conquest in 1519, to little more than 1 million, at the end of the century.[33] From the seventeenth century onwards there was a slow increase again. The rate of decline, following the conquest, varied in different areas of Central and South America and it was usually worst in the coastal areas. Later, and right into the nineteenth century, the European settlements on the North American continent were to prove similarly catastrophic for the native population. The main difference was that the Dutch, French and English colonists for the most part did not have nearly such a bad conscience about it as the Spaniards.

Both sides, the colonists and the Dominicans, appealed to the crown, and successive kings of Spain were willing to listen to their arguments and to frame policy and legislation accordingly. The most effective spokesman of the Dominicans was Bartolomé de las Casas. Throughout his long life he fought with extraordinary energy and skill to establish his view that the Indians were not inferior to the Europeans. With government support he sponsored social experiments, designed to show that the Indians could live like Spaniards and that it was possible to propagate the gospel peacefully among them. It is easy to see now why the attempts to impose, in such a short period of time, Spanish institutions and Christian values on peoples of a completely different culture should, at best, have met with only very partial success. There was nothing obvious about this in the sixteenth century, for no one had had any experience of such a problem. The colonists, finding their own observations of the apparent inferiority of the natives happily coinciding with their economic interest in slave or forced labour, did their best, first to sabotage Las Casas's experiments and then to disregard and sabotage the New Laws of 1542 by which the crown attempted to erect safeguards for the Indians. Nor did the colonists lack intellectual spokesmen in Spain. In 1547 the humanist lawyer Sepúlveda, a friend of Cortés, wrote a treatise based on the Aristotelian argument of the natural inferiority of some races who should be enslaved for their own good and, in the case of the American Indians, for the purpose of making them Christians. Las Casas successfully prevented the publication of Sepúlveda's treatise, and in 1549 the Council of the Indies refused to sanction further conquests in America until the theologians and jurists had decided whether or not they were morally justified.

In the two formal debates which followed, in 1550 and 1551, Las Casas claimed not only the spiritual equality of the American Indians to the Europeans — this had already been conceded in a papal pronouncement of 1537 — but also their equality in nature. 'All peoples of the world are men . . . all have understanding and volition . . . all take satisfaction in goodness and feel pleasure with happy and delicious things, all regret and abhor evil.'[34] At the very end of his life, but apparently not before, Las Casas drew the logical, but psychologically most difficult, conclusion from his arguments. In his last will he included the Negroes as complete equals with the whites and Indians. This will was not published until a quarter of a century after his death in 1566.[35]

Las Casas won the debate and his views remained orthodoxy for the Spanish government. Their practical effects were more problematical. Yet there can be no doubt that government legislation, however imperfectly enforced, together with the efforts of Las Casas and his fellow clergy in the Spanish colonies, at least mitigated many of the worst cruelties of empire. It is one of the ironies of history that Las Casas's deliberate indictment of the Spanish *conquistadores* and colonists should have become one of the sources of the 'black legend' against Spain, used as anti-Spanish propaganda by nations whose colonial record was to be no whit better than that of the Spaniards and who hardly even began to discuss the moral problems of empire until the eighteenth century.

THE NEW WORLD IN THE OLD

For a thousand years Christian Europe had been on the defensive, a fortress defending itself against assaults from pagans and Muslims from Asia and Africa. The Christians' one great series of sorties, the crusades, had been a costly failure. Even in the sixteenth century Christian Europe still remained on the defensive against the Ottoman Turks and suffered terrible losses in the Balkans and the eastern Mediterranean. The Portuguese and Spanish and, later, the French, English and Dutch discoveries and conquests marked a decisive turning point. The Europeans did not burst upon a world peacefully minding its own business. Almost everywhere the strong were seeking to dominate the weak, from the Muslims in India and Southeast Asia to the Aztecs in Central and the Incas in South America. Where the Europeans could not impose direct political rule they still imposed their trade and, gradually, their value system.[36] They did this, moreover, without being united and, in consequence, they transferred their own rivalries also to the rest of the world.

There were many who recognized the historical importance of these events. López de Gómara, in the dedication of his *History of the Indies* to Charles V (1552) wrote: 'The greatest event since the creation of the world (excluding the incarnation of him who created it) is the discovery of the Indies.'[37] Charles V took as his emblem the Pillars of Hercules (i.e. the Straits of Gibraltar) with the device *plus ultra* ('always further'), pointing symbolically to the New World under his imperial sway. Humanists and poets did not tire of pointing to the providential coincidence of the discoveries with the emergence of the 'New Charlemagne'. Yet, to most Europeans not directly involved in the overseas conquests or trade the New World remained a marginal experience. In the sixteenth century four times as many books were published about the Turks and Asia than about America.[38] Gold and silver, of course, had their effect (see pp. 29, 32–3), but that was what the Europeans had been looking and hoping for. Spices from the East Indies were also expected. But the new products, tobacco, potatoes and tomatoes, made only the rarest appearances before the end of the sixteenth century, and tea and coffee not until the seventeenth. Dürer, seeing the Aztec treasures Cortés had sent to Charles V, in Brussels in 1520, was one of the few to see them as more than titillating exotica:

All these days of my life I have seen nothing that rejoiced my heart so much as these things, for I saw amongst them wonderful works of art and I marvelled at the subtle *ingenia* of men in foreign lands.[39]

NOTES AND REFERENCES

1   Ferdinand claimed the crowns of Bohemia and Hungary by inheritance. The Bohemians and Hungarians held that their crowns were elective. The Bohemian Diet elected Ferdinand in

1527. The Hungarians remained divided on the issue for a long time.

2   M. François, 'L'Idée d'empire en France à l'époque de Charles Quint', *Charles Quint et son temps*. Colloques Internationaux du Centre de la Recherche Scientifique (Paris, 1959), pp. 23–35.

3   Empire with a capital E is here used to signify the Holy Roman Empire; with a small e the Habsburg monarchy of Charles V. The distinction, however, was not always clear to Charles V's contemporaries.

4   See the brilliant book with this title by H. Lutz (Göttingen, 1964).

5   *The Koran*, trans, N. J. Dawood (Harmondsworth, 1956), p. 409.

6   Quoted in R. Knolles, *The Generall Historie of the Turkes* (London, 1603), p. 391.

7   B. Lewis, *Istanbul and the Civilisation of the Ottoman Empire* (Norman, Oklahoma, 1963), p. 45. Knolles, *Historie of the Turkes*, p. 571.

8   Knolles, *Historie of the Turkes*, p. 638.

9   G. de Busbecq, *The Turkish Letters*, trans. E. S. Forster (Oxford, 1927), letter III, p. 112.

10 Busbecq, *The Turkish Letters*, p. 101 ff.

11 R. Tschudi, 'Das Asafnâme des Luṭfi Pascha', *Türkische Bibliothek*, ed. G. Jacob (Berlin, 1912), vol. XII, p. 13

12 Quoted among others by Marcantonio Barbaro, 'Relazione dell' Impero Ottomano, 1573', in E. Albèri, *Relazioni degli Ambasciatori Veneti*, ser III. vol 1. (Florence, 1840), p. 309.

13 Cf. the very revealing *Journal d'un Bourgeois de Caire. Chronique d'Ibn Iyâs*, trans G. Wiet (Paris, 1960), vol. II, *passim*.

14 Cf. Shakespeare, *Winter's Tale*, Act III, sc. 2 '*Hermione*: The Emperor of Russia was my Father'. One might speculate on the sort of letter which Ivan the Terrible, for instance, might have written to Leontes. It is unlikely that he would have accepted Hermione's plea to look on her trial 'with eyes of pity, not revenge'. On 24 October 1570 he actually did write to Elizabeth I: '. . . wee had thought that you had been ruler over your lands . . . but now wee perceive that there be other men that doe rule, and not men but bowers [i.e. peasants] and merchaunts . . . and you flowe in your maydenlie estate like a maide'. G. Tolstoy, *The First Forty Years of Intercourse between England and Russia 1553–1593* (St Petersburg, 1875), p. 114.

15 This was pure fantasy. The papacy had not been guilty of this heresy nor was it the cause of the schism between the eastern and western churches in 1054.

16 The union of the eastern and western churches, at the Council of Florence 1439, by which the Bystantine emperors hoped to get western help against the Turks. The Russian Orthodox Church had rejected this union from the beginning.

17 Quoted in H. Schaeder, *Moskau das dritte Rom*, 2nd edn. (Darmstadt, 1957), pp. 75 ff.

18 G. Stoekl, 'Russland und Europa vor Peter dem Grossen', *Historische Zeitschrift*, vol. 184 (1957), p. 545.

19 M. Cherniavsky, *Tsar and People. Studies in Russian Myths* (New Haven and London, 1961), *passim*.

20 J. L. I. Fennell, *The Correspondence between Prince A. M. Kurbsky and Tsar Ivan IV of Russia* (Cambridge, 1955), p. 17.

21 Letter of 5 July 1564, *ibid.*, p. 21.

22 Quoted in Fennel, 'Russia, 1462–1583', *New Cambridge Modern History*, vol. II, p. 561.

23 Tolstoy, *England and Russia*, pp. 30 ff.

24 Since this volume is a history of Europe, and not a history of the world, or of European expansion outside Europe, we do not propose to relate the history of the Portuguese and Spanish overseas conquests in the sixteenth century, nor to discuss the effects – mostly disastrous – of these conquests on non-European peoples and civilizations. We shall discuss only the attitude of the Portuguese and Spaniards towards their overseas empires. Their economic effects on Europe have been treated in chapter 3. There are excellent and easily accessible works on the conquests; e.g. the relevant chapters in the *New Cambridge Modern History*, or J. H. Parry, *The Age of Reconnaissance* (London, 1963), which has a bibliography of works in English.

25 H. Cidade, *A literatura Portuguèsa e a Expansao Utramarina* (Coimbra, 1963), vol. I, p. 19.

26 C. R. Boxer, *Four Centuries of Portuguese Expansion 1415–1825* (Johannesburg, 1961), pp. 14, 35 ff.

27 Unlike the western churches, the Russian church, in the sixteenth century, still accepted the genuineness of the Donations of Constantine and, in 1551, incorporated them into Russian Canon Law, as a counter to the tsars' attempts to secularize church lands. W. K. Medlin, *Moscow and East Rome* (Geneva, 1952), pp. 112 ff.

28 Quoted in L. Hanke, *The Spanish Struggle for Justice in the Conquest of America* (Philadelphia, 1949), p. 148.

29 C. R. Boxer, *Race Relations in the Portuguese Empire 1415–1825* (Oxford, 1963), p. 87.

30 Hanke, *The Spanish Struggle for Justice*, p. 7.

31 Quoted in Hanke, *The Spanish Struggle for Justice*, p. 7.

32 This is very evident from Bernal Diaz's account, *The Conquest of Mexico*, trans. I. A. Leonard (New York, 1965), *passim*.

33 S. F. Cook and W. Borah, *The Indian Population of Central Mexico 1531–1610* (Berkeley, 1960) and *The Aboriginal Population of Central Mexico on the Eve of the Spanish Conquest* (Berkeley, 1963).

34 Quoted in Hanke, *The Spanish Struggle for Justice*, p. 125.

35 We owe this point to Professor C. R. Boxer.

36 Now, in the second half of the twentieth century, direct political domination has largely been liquidated. How far this is also true of European/American economic and intellectual domination is still very problematical.

37 Quoted in J. H. Elliott, *The Old World and the New* (Cambridge, 1970), p. 70.

38 *Ibid.*, p. 12.

39 Quoted in J. B. Ross and M. M. McLaughlin, *The Portable Renaissance Reader* (New York, 1958), pp. 231–32.

11

THE MONARCHIES

NATIONALISM IN THE SIXTEENTH CENTURY

The contrast between the empires and the other monarchies of the sixteenth century was not one between medieval universalism and modern nationalism. The universalist ideas of the period, although based on medieval, and even ancient, traditions, were the product of the problems and opportunities of the later fifteenth and the early sixteenth centuries. Much the same was true of the nationalist ideas and emotions of the period. They had their medieval roots in the xenophobia of peasant societies which had emerged from the tribalism of the age of the barbarian invasions but which clung tenaciously to their own languages and dialects – Germanic, Slavonic, Celtic, Romance, or pre-Indo-European, like Basque – and which might yet, like the Northumbrians and the Border Scots, reserve their greatest hatred for the men of the next valley who spoke, if not exactly the same, a mutually comprehensible language, observed similar customs, prayed to the same saints and indulged in the same murderous pastime of mutual cattle raiding. The pre-medieval, ancient traditions of nationalism were essentially literary – emotions for those who had received a classical education or were under the influence of someone who had. By 1500 this included an already sizable part of the European court, aristocratic and official society and of the richer townsmen.

To outsiders, the identity of a Frenchman, a Spaniard, even a German, seemed clear enough. But to these men themselves such definitions often meant little compared with the 'nations' to which they gave their first loyalties: Normandy or Provence, Aragon or Castile, Bavaria or Saxony. The Lübeckers and the other Hansards regarded themselves as Germans, in contrast to Danes, Swedes or Poles. Yet, at least until the patrician (but not the lower) classes adopted the High German language with the Reformation, the cultural affinities of Lübeck were never with the High German south, with Nuremberg or Augsburg, but always with the Netherlands and, by way of the Netherlands, with Paris and London. In this, the north German cities were at one with their Scandinavian political and economic rivals. Together they developed a Baltic culture whose commercial *lingua franca* was Low German but whose inspiration was western European. This same inspiration was still strong in Poland; but the Poles, and even more their southern and south-western neighbours, the Hungarians, Austrians and Bavarians, looked as much to Italy and the Mediterranean as to the Netherlands and the North Sea. Indeed, through the activities of the Socinians, even Protestantism had an Italian flavour in Poland (see p. 347).

Language could and did become a unifying force, but this happened mainly on the literary level and it usually represented the victory of a particular dialect, that is, of the language of a particular, small area, over the rest. This might be accomplished by royal command, as happened in France where the king ordered all official acts and pronouncements to be written in the *langue d'oil* (Ordinance of Villers–Cotterets, 1539). More usually, however, it was the result of the literary prestige enjoyed by one dialect: Tuscan in Italy, or the High German of central Germany which experienced a kind of linguistic apotheosis in Luther's translation of the Bible.

But even in Italy, where literary nationalism was older and more pervasive than in any other country, it did not become a political driving force. The rulers of the separate Italian states, both republican and princely, deplored the domination of the Spaniards and the French, and formed leagues with the express purpose of ridding Italy of the 'barbarians'. But, when it came to the point, they were always more anxious to win advantages over each other than cooperate effectively against the common enemy. Nor is this surprising. For most men a large country, a nation in the literary sense, was too vague an entity to command loyalty, compared with traditional and more familiar institutions: the community of the town, of the county or province, above all, the person of the ruler. Rulers of small states and local authorities were themselves not at all anxious to encourage loyalties to outside bodies or ideas. Where some sense of the wider community of the whole country had developed, as had happened in England, this had been the result of an exceptionally strong monarchy which had early imposed an effective authority over all rivals.

The Reformation contributed only indirectly, at first, to an awakening sense of nationality centring upon the wider community. The opposition against Rome or against Protestantism led to a deepened feeling of national unity in some parts of Europe. Thus Ulrich von Hutten appealed to a national spirit against the 'alien' oppression of Rome, while the Spanish stress upon the unity of faith and purity of blood was meant to counter the threat of heresy. Above all, the presence of a political and ideological enemy indirectly strengthened the hands of the national monarchs. When Henry VIII of England annexed the spiritual jurisdiction to the crown (1533) England was called an 'empire'. This claim was justified by the supposed fact that an imperial crown had descended upon English kings in a direct succession from Emperor Constantine.[1] Elizabeth furthered similar views, and as the enemy became ever more menacing some Englishmen began to call their island 'a new Israel, His chosen and peculiar people'.[2] But the full effect of such thought, which was, in the end, to lead men to make a distinction between the nation and the monarch, was not properly felt until the Puritanism of the next century.

Kings and their propagandists could and did identify their interests with those of the nation and, in the face of an actual enemy, such a fusion could have a powerful appeal. But even the defence of the *patria* was often interpreted in a purely provincial sense. The militias which sixteenth-century kings raised for the defence of their kingdoms regularly refused to fight outside their own provinces. It was this parochialism, as much as the military incompetence of most militias, which forced princes to rely on professional mercenaries for an effective campaign.

LOYALTIES, MOTIVES AND AIMS IN EUROPEAN POLITICS

Sixteenth-century loyalties were rich, varied and rarely exclusive. Perhaps the best illustration is provided by the Netherlands. The dukes of Burgundy (a junior line of the French ruling house of Valois) and their successors, the German Habsburgs, had acquired the seventeen provinces by marriage, inheritance and conquest.

Geographically compact, but linguistically, economically and socially highly diverse, the provinces did not even have a collective name until, around the middle of the sixteenth century, the cumbersome and unimaginative *les pays de pardeca* gave way to *les pays bas*, the Low Countries. The provinces had their separate political and legal institutions and laws; they insisted that only their own natives should hold office and that official acts should be in their own particular language. Their economic policy was often deliberately directed against the interests of the other provinces and they could even fight separate wars, as Holland did in the Baltic during the 1520s and 1530s. Yet, as early as the fifteenth century, there had appeared an undeniable feeling for a Netherlands community, or nationality, distinct from the feeling of loyalty to the common ruler. In 1477 the provinces rebelled against the centralizing absolutism of their last duke, Charles the Bold; but they maintained their union and at least some of the central institutions which the dukes had created: the States General and the supreme court at Malines. In the sixteenth century they were to argue for the validity in all provinces of the great charter of Brabant, the *Joyeuse Entrée*.

Since in general, however, loyalty to their prince was for most men a stronger emotion than loyalty to the abstract concept of the nation, it seemed perfectly natural that princes should wish to extend their dominions outside the confines of their own nation. The so-called national monarchies — a modern and not a sixteenth-century term — were all composite states, including more than one nationality. English monarchs ruled over Celtic Ireland and incorporated Wales into the realm of the English crown, and none of them, not even Elizabeth I, gave up territorial ambitions on the Continent; the royal title included the phrase 'King of France'. The kings of France ruled similarly over Celtic Brittany and had ambitions in Italy. So had the kings of Spain who had incorporated the Basques and Moriscos into the kingdom of Castile and hoped to do the same with French Navarre, but made no attempt to do this with their Aragonese, Catalan and Valencian subjects. The political driving force of sixteenth-century politics was nearly always dynastic; territorial claims usually had a basis in public law (most frequently but not always the laws of inheritance), and were felt to have an objective validity, irrespective of the nationality of the inhabitants of the territory in question.

Commercial or other economic reasons played their part, though it is easy to exaggerate this. England wanted Calais for its wool staple, although even by 1500 English exports of raw wool were comparatively unimportant, compared with the export of cloth to Antwerp, and it is difficult to believe that Elizabeth's strenuous efforts to get Calais back, after its loss in 1558, were motivated by concern over English trade. The Hollanders, Lübeckers, Danes and Swedes fought wars for the control of the trade through the Sound; but for the Danes and Swedes this represented a financial rather than a trading interest. Ivan IV coveted Narva and Livonia, among other reasons because they offered a commercial outlet to the Baltic; but, as his famous letter to Elizabeth made clear, he was the last man to have his policies determined for him by merchants and their interests (see p. 263n). Even Venice, the commercial republic *par excellence*, had few genuine economic reasons for its disastrous policy of territorial aggression on the Italian mainland (see p. 104). The kings of France fought campaign after costly campaign in Italy to make good their dynastic claims to Naples and Milan; in the later stages of the wars perhaps also to counter Spanish dominance in Italy and Europe. The alternative of pushing towards a Rhine frontier, in pursuance of a supposedly 'French national interest', was not even considered; for in the climate of sixteenth-century opinion it would have been very difficult to justify.

The only French advance in this direction was the annexation of Metz, Toul and Verdun, in 1552; but this was done in agreement with a section of the princes of the Empire and with the invitation of a strong French party in these cities. Officially, moreover, Henry II acted only as imperial vicar in the cities although without the consent of the emperor. By contrast, the French were particularly resentful of Gattinara's plans for dismembering France (see p. 234) for which there was no dynastic nor other legal justification. But Gattinara was an Italian, and the Italians had developed the idea of pure power politics much further than the rest of Europe and they had also invented the concept of the balance of power.

DYNASTIC POLICIES AND THE NOBILITY

Support for an aggressive dynastic policy came mainly from the nobility and from the lawyers and professional administrators of the royal councils. Perhaps the majority of the European high nobility had received a military education, either privately or attached, as boys or young men, to the suite of some famous general. Membership of the older orders of chivalry – the Order of the Garter in England, of the Golden Fleece in the Netherlands, of St Michael in France, of Santiago, Calatrava and Alcántara in Spain – carried with it great social prestige and sometimes, as with the Golden Fleece, valuable political privileges. War meant military commands, glory and plunder; conquests meant chances of acquiring confiscated estates and governorships of fortresses, provinces and even whole countries. Nearly everywhere in Europe, the high nobility found these prospects more attractive than the now outmoded cause of local independence. The great monarchies could even attract foreign noblemen into their service. The Gonzaga and the Colonna preferred careers in the service of the Spanish monarchy to the doubtful fame and poor rewards they could expect in the provincial politics of the small Italian states. The Guises, close relatives of the dukes of Lorraine, acquired vast estates in France by serving Francis I and Henry II, and managed to marry their sister to James V of Scotland and their niece, Mary Stuart, to the Dauphin, later Francis II of France. Duke Francis of Guise and his brother Charles, the Cardinal of Lorraine, prided themselves on their voluntary allegiance to the kings of France; but they were completely gallicized and were the principal protagonists of an aggressive French policy, both in Italy and in Metz, Toul and Verdun.

The Hungarian and Polish nobility succeeded in turning their countries into aristocratic republics; yet even they were often surprisingly willing to follow their kings in the latters' dynastic wars. The attractions of warfare in eastern Europe were very similar to those in western Europe. Only the Germans were different. Long before the year 1500, their high nobility had become virtually independent princes, concerned only with their own principalities or at most, and that usually very half-heartedly, with the defence of the Empire against the Turks. The emperor's dynastic policies – the successful marriage alliances of the house of Austria – were for the German princes a cause for alarm, rather than an opportunity for their own advancement. But while the greatness of the kingdom of Germany, or the Empire, held no promise for the German princes, their own dynastic policies were very similar to those of other European monarchs. They managed to attract the lower nobility to their courts in much the same way as the great western monarchies,

271

especially after they had smashed the last attempt of a section of the German imperial knights to compete independently with them in the general game of conquests and plunder (1523) (see p. 168).

THE UNIONS OF CROWNS

The primacy of dynastic aims in the foreign policies of sixteenth-century monarchies explains the continued popularity of the medieval tradition of personal unions – the union of the crowns of two or more countries in one hand. The empire of Charles V was, in origin, a whole complex of such personal unions and, as we have seen, to most of his contemporaries it was never more than this. The ruler who acquired another crown usually agreed that all constituent countries of the union should maintain their own laws and institutions and that their offices and benefices be reserved to their natives. Such arrangements were relatively easy to maintain where the union had been voluntary or by inheritance, as for instance between the crowns of Aragon and Castile or between Poland and Lithuania. But where a king had to make good his dynastic claim by war, whether against an outside rival or a native pretender, it was almost inevitable that the newly acquired country should fall under the domination of the ruler's original countrymen. This happened to Naples and Milan, both under Spanish and French rule, and to that part of Hungary which was under Habsburg rule. The Spaniards themselves maintained that it had happened to them when Charles V came with his Burgundian court to claim the hereditary succession to the Spanish kingdoms. But even in purely voluntary unions, outside pressures and the ambitions of courtiers and officials could have the same effect. In either case the result was likely to be civil war. Thus it happened in Castile in 1520–21, and in Hungary after 1526 (see p. 233).

In Castile and in Hungary, as in Naples and Milan, the Habsburgs eventually won and the unions were preserved. In Scandinavia the originally voluntary union of the three kingdoms of Denmark, Norway and Sweden (Union of Kalmar, 1397) broke up. The Norwegians were reasonably content with the union; the Swedes, however, despite their closely related language and not very dissimilar cultural traditions, had even in the fifteenth century re-established an effective independence from the kings in

Copenhagen and were governed by a regency of the Swedish family of the Stures. After 1515 the regent Sten Sture the Younger quarrelled violently with Archbishop Trolle of Uppsala. In 1520 Christian II intervened in favour of Trolle and the pro-Danish nobles in Sweden, many of whom owned estates in both kingdoms. Sture was defeated and killed, and Christian had himself proclaimed hereditary king of Sweden. He celebrated the event by the execution of more than eighty of his leading opponents. Voluntary union had been succeeded by rule of the Danish king and his partisans.

GUSTAVUS VASA

The young Gustavus Vasa, who now took up the struggle against Christian II, could count on Swedish dislike of the Danes and especially on the revulsion inspired by the 'blood-bath of Stockholm'. He had the support of the survivors of the Sture party; he skilfully used the economic discontent of the peasants and miners of Dalarna to recruit an army among them; and he harnessed the normal anticlericalism of the age, recently fanned by Lutheran preaching, against Archbishop Trolle and the Swedish hierarchy. Nevertheless one may doubt whether this national uprising (if it can be called that) would have managed to overthrow King Christian and Trolle's party without outside help. But Gustavus had the support of Lübeck (see p. 106) and, indirectly, that of the Danish opposition to Christian II who forced the king to flee from Copenhagen (1523). Christian had made himself unpopular with the Danish nobility and higher clergy by favouring the towns and peasants. Their resentment overflowed when the king fell more and more under the influence of the low-class mother of his young Dutch mistress. In the same year, 1523, Gustavus Vasa was elected king of Sweden by the Diet (*Riksdag*) of Strangnäs. At the end of his long reign, in 1560, the position of the independent Swedish monarchy was finally secure. Gustavus, one of the most astute and ruthless politicians of the age, secularized and confiscated large amounts of church property and effectively made Sweden a Lutheran country. He broke the economic stranglehold of the Lübeckers over Sweden. He put down further rebellions of the peasants of Dalarna (this time directed not against the Danes but

273

against the 'national' king) and he smashed both the Trolle and the Sture parties. After that the succession of his sons was assured.

The Union of Kalmar was dead, and the kings of Sweden now had the opportunity to start their own aggression on the eastern shores of the Baltic. They accepted an invitation from the city of Reval to protect it from the Russians and went on to annex the whole of Esthonia (1560–1581). In 1587 King Sigismund, the grandson of Gustavus Vasa and a convert to Catholicism, had himself elected king of Poland. Even by sixteenth-century standards this was one of the most unlikely and arbitrary unions of crowns, and it did not last. Once more there was civil war and foreign intervention in Sweden. Once more a Swedish 'national' party, led by Sigismund's uncle, Duke Charles of Södermanland, exploited the enmities of noble factions and the strong Lutheran feeling against the Catholic Sigismund and his Jesuit friends. By 1600 the duke had won and was crowned as Charles IX in 1607. The union with Poland was effectively dissolved; but, since Sigismund and his sons did not renounce their claims to the Swedish crown, the light-hearted ambitions of the Vasas were to leave a half-century of futile and destructive wars between Sweden and Poland.

POLAND–LITHUANIA

Poland's previous experience of union had been happier. In 1385, Jagiello, grand prince of Lithuania, had succeeded by marriage to the throne of Poland. Although this throne was nominally elective, it was effectively hereditary within the ruling family, and the Jagiellos reigned over both countries until the family died out in 1572. Three years before, in the Union of Lublin, the two states merged their diets and also those of German-speaking 'royal Prussia' (West Prussia) and of Lithuania's Ruthenian dominions in White Russia and the Ukraine. It was a remarkable achievement; for this vast union, stretching from the Baltic to the Dniester, was multilingual and multireligious, tolerating not only Jews and almost all types of Protestantism in the officially Catholic Poland (see p. 346), but also comprising in Lithuania and Ruthenia a majority of Orthodox Christians. The reasons for this success were the danger to Lithuania from the constant raids of the Crimea Tartars and from Muscovite imperialism. Against both, Lithuania needed Polish help. The Lithuanian nobility had become largely Polonized during the long period of the purely personal union of the crowns. The Union of Lublin now extended to them also the enormous political, legal and economic privileges enjoyed by the Polish nobility. Sigismund II Augustus, the last Jagiello king, had himself helped to negotiate the Union of Lublin; but it represented a major defeat of the monarchy by the Polish and Lithuanian nobility, for the crown now became as weak in Lithuania as it was in Poland. In 1596 the union was taken yet one step further by a religious agreement between the Catholic Church and the majority of the Greek Orthodox hierarchy of Lithuania (Union of Brześć).

The choice of kings following the extinction of the house of Jagiello in 1572 showed the extent of the victory of the nobility – the freedom of the Polish Republic, as it was optimistically called; for the peasants and townsmen were carefully excluded from it. It is difficult not to regard the election of Henry of Anjou, fresh from organizing the massacre of St Bartholomew (see p. 308),[2] as an altogether fatuous piece of political manœuvring by men who were trying to be too clever. Henry was allowed powers that were little more than nominal. He was kept a virtual prisoner and, predictably, he escaped back to France as soon as he heard of his own succession there, as Henry III, in 1574. The next election was more sensible. Stephen Báthory, prince of Transylvania, was a forceful personality and an experienced soldier. In three brilliant campaigns, 1579–1581, he captured Polock and Livonia from the Russians and set back Moscow's hopes for an outlet to the Baltic for more than a century. Báthory seems to have had plans to conquer Moscow itself and create for himself an immense Christian empire in eastern Europe, with the ultimate aim of driving the Turks from Constantinople. But he died in 1586 and even before his death it had become clear that the Poles would not support the almost limitless personal ambitions of their king.

Once more the Polish and Lithuanian nobility would not consider a native king. The election of Sigismund Vasa, they hoped, would assure them of Swedish cooperation against Muscovy, without saddling them with a king who, like Báthory, would want to exercise royal power. Because of the Swedish civil war the first hope was to be disastrously disappointed; because of Sigismund's incompetence the second hope was to be equally disastrously fulfilled.

THE MONARCHIES OF WESTERN EUROPE

It was in western Europe that conditions were particularly favourable for the development of strong monarchies in the sixteenth century. They had ceased to be elective and had become hereditary centuries before. By 1500 the monarchies of England, France, the Netherlands and Spain had all emerged victorious from long periods of civil wars with overmighty subjects. It now seemed reasonable to assume that in future the kings and their partisans would always win such struggles, that indeed such struggles would be very rare, for their subjects were most anxious to escape from renewed civil war. The French nobility showed this unequivocally when they refused to support the Connétable Bourbon against the king (see p. 234). Moreover, the authority of the king was often preferable to that of the local magnate. As the Spanish chronicler and royal councillor, Hernando Pulgar, said, perhaps a little too pointedly: men 'wanted to leave lordship and place themselves under the freedom of the king'.[3] Yet neither assumption, that men would not rebel or that, if they did, the king would always win, was to prove correct. New and powerful motives for rebellion arose in the course of the sixteenth century which, when they mingled with the traditional ones, were to cause more formidable revolutions and more destructive civil wars than any which the later Middle Ages had known.

Up to about the middle of the sixteenth century, the monarchies were able to consolidate the victory they had won. Theoretically there was nothing very new in the powers they claimed. 'Absolute royal power' and 'supreme jurisdiction' over the kingdom, terms which we find used with great emphasis for instance in the will of Isabella the Catholic, had a long and respectable history, although their interpretation was very much a matter for debate. The problems facing the monarchies were practical problems, and the attempts to solve them were also essentially practical. They were of three kinds: firstly, the need to free the state from interference of outside authorities; secondly, the need to make the monarchy militarily more powerful than any of its internal rivals and as safe as possible from external ones; and thirdly, the need to build up an effective administration.

RELATIONS BETWEEN CHURCH AND STATE

The first problem was essentially the problem of the relations between Church and state or, more specifically, between the monarchies and the papacy. Ferdinand and Isabella, by supporting the pope's political aims in Italy, obtained from him the right to submit to him nominations for all bishoprics and many other ecclesiastical offices in their kingdoms. The clergy therefore had to look to the crown, rather than to the papacy, for advancement. In Sicily, Naples and Milan the Spanish kings could also prevent the publication of any papal bull (right of *exequatur*), and when Julius II disregarded this, Ferdinand threatened to break off relations with the papacy — some twenty years before Henry VIII of England actually did it. In Sicily the control of the crown over the Church was even more extensive; for the king claimed (although the pope never acknowledged) the position of permanent apostolic legate for himself (the *monarchia sicula*). He could not claim such powers in Spain itself. But in the Spanish Inquisition he had an ecclesiastical court whose members were appointed by the crown and whose jurisdiction was superior to any other ecclesiastical court in Spain and, for practical purposes, independent of Rome itself. 'There is no pope in Spain', said a president of the Royal Council, and there was only a little exaggeration in the boast.

The French made no such boast, nor did they have a French Inquisition, like the Spanish. But in 1516 Francis I obtained a Concordat from Leo X which gave the effective right of appointment to the 600 most important ecclesiastical positions in France. The king's *droit de vérification* was as effective a censorship on papal bulls as the Spanish king's *exequatur* in Italy. In the second half of the century, the efforts of the popes to regain lost positions caused much friction with the French and Spanish monarchies and many problems of divided loyalties for their clergy. But the popes could not seriously challenge effective royal control over the Spanish and Gallican churches. These monarchies had thus won a double victory: virtual freedom from outside interference and an enormous increase of power within the state. Patronage over the Church assured the monarchies not only the loyalty of the clergy, with its enormous spiritual and educational influence, but also helped to assure the loyalty of the nobility who now had to look to the crown to provide ecclesiastical careers for their younger sons. From a practical point of view the position of kings had not changed much. For centuries strong princes had appointed bishops and taxed the clergy in all parts of Europe. But the sixteenth-century popes were prepared at last to recognize the *de facto* limitation of their powers as *de jure* and thus sealed the victory of the monarchies.

THE PROBLEMS OF FINANCE

The second problem, that of the military power of the monarchies, depended, in the last analysis, on money. Only with ready cash could the kings hire the professional infantry which had proved itself decisively superior to the old feudal cavalry; and only with ready cash could they buy the cannon and muskets which their generals now deemed necessary, build and equip warships and reconstruct the fortifications of cities and fortresses to withstand the fire of contemporary artillery. This cash might be obtained on credit, but it still had to be obtained. For if the soldiers were not paid they would 'eat up the country people', as their plundering and marauding was called or, worse still, go over to the enemy. Not surprisingly, finance became the central practical concern of European governments. There is hardly a letter between a king and his ministers or generals which does not, among other matters, discuss money. Money, men kept repeating to each other (as if they did not know already) was the sinews of war. Warfare was incomparably more expensive than any other government activity, not excluding the rapidly expanding diplomatic services and the sumptuous royal building programmes.

By 1500 the normal resources of the west European monarchies – domain lands and regalia, such as certain customs duties, mineral or mining rights and crown monopolies – were no longer sufficient to meet the steadily increasing cost of warfare, and this even though the monarchies had repossessed themselves of much alienated crown land and added to it by generous confiscations from their defeated opponents. The Spanish monarchy had managed especially well by taking over control of the three orders of knighthood, Santiago, Calatrava and Alcántara, with their vast estates and patronage. The price revolution which was only just beginning was always increasing costs, but not always income from crown lands. It became necessary to tap new sources of revenue. This could be done by the renewed sale of crown property or (as in England and other Protestant countries) the confiscation and resale of former Church lands, by insisting on the fiscal side of otherwise decayed feudal relationships, by loans and by new taxation. All these methods were used and came to be highly elaborated in the first half of the century.

THE SALE OF OFFICES; LOANS

In France, Spain and Italy the sale of crown property came more and more to include the sale of government offices. In France, where the practice was pushed to its furthest extent, offices were often created specifically for the purpose of being sold. They reverted to the crown on the death of the holder, but it became a frequent practice to buy the succession for one's heir. Such offices were sold in practically the whole range of the royal administration, from the local toll collectorships and the market police to the councillorships of the *parlements* of Paris and Bordeaux. In Spain and Italy the monarchies sold offices in much the same way. Rome was particularly notorious for this practice, despite the stigma of simony which attached to the sale of ecclesiastical offices. Even the efforts of the saintly and puritanical Pius V only touched the worst abuses of the practice. To abolish it would have meant either buying back all offices, which no monarchy could begin to afford, or expropriating the office holders, which would have been both unthinkable in the contemporary view of private property and politically suicidal.

Sale of offices was certainly not unknown in the rest of Europe, even though the Germans, in particular, prided themselves on their public morality, which they compared happily with French corruption. But it seems to have been mostly lack of opportunity in the still comparatively undeveloped civil service systems of the German principalities which accounted for the comparative rarity of the sale of offices in the sixteenth century. In the seventeenth the practice spread quite rapidly. In England Henry VII and, much later, James I sold offices. During most of the sixteenth century, however, and especially during Elizabeth's reign, it was not the crown but the office holders themselves who sold offices. The principle, the view of an office as private property or a freehold, as it was called in England, was the same as on the Continent. The difference was that, quite characteristically, in England the buying and selling of offices had, to a large extent, become a matter for private enterprise. This enterprise was largely controlled by the court nobility and was part of the latter's system of patronage and bribery on which much of its power depended. The crown, as the actual employer, obtained from this system few financial but considerable political benefits.

While not all kings sold offices, they all took up loans. There was nothing new about this except the scale and the sophistication of the credit operations (see p. 55). The ability to raise large sums of money gave the monarchies a further enormous advantage over even the greatest of their subjects. By contrast, one might speculate how much the absence of an advanced credit organization helped the magnates of Poland in their successful efforts to keep the Polish monarchy weak. From about 1520 an additional and quite new method of raising loans was introduced in western Europe; the sale of life annuities funded on earmarked government revenues or guaranteed by the revenues of provinces or cities. Here were the beginnings of a system of national debts. The issuing of annuities spread rapidly in France, the Netherlands, Spain and Italy, and it was not long before annuities came to be freely bought and sold in the great financial centres of western and southern Europe.

TAXATION: SPAIN

In the end, however, the monarchies had to meet their rising expenditure by increased taxation. In 1500 the ancient doctrine was still firmly established, practically all over Europe, that princes needed their subjects' consent to new taxation and that such consent was normally given through a representative assembly. The fundamental opposition of interests between rulers and subjects tended to crystallize during the meetings of these assemblies. Prelates, nobles, towns and provinces set their traditional privileges and autonomies against the king's centralizing policy. His demands for money and his subjects' unwillingness to pay were the key to this relationship. Ultimately it was a question of power. The incompatibility of the claims of the two sides had finally to be resolved by the victory of one or the other; but until this happened – as it happened sooner or later in every country – the balance of power between the two sides tended to be unstable. At the same time, both sides were usually anxious to carry on the practical business of government; the struggle was more often latent than acute. The States General of the Netherlands, a congress of delegates from the assemblies of the separate provinces, was willing to grant huge sums for Charles V's wars against France. It was a matter of pride or, at least, a good propaganda point, that the Netherlands lived in greater freedom than the subjects of the king of France. On his side, Charles V never attempted a frontal attack on the estates. But his government in the Netherlands was acutely aware of how its increasing demands for money made the balance of power between crown and estates ever more precarious and their willingness to cooperate with the government more and more doubtful.[4] The final confrontation was to come in the next reign.

In Spain it had come already at the beginning of Charles V's reign, although neither side had planned, or even foreseen it. It was characteristic of the nature of the problem that the *comunero* movement should have arisen out of the rejection of a royal demand for money and become, almost immediately, a struggle for ultimate political power in Castile (see pp. 110 ff.). It was also characteristic that the nobles won the civil war for the monarchy but that the monarchy emerged as the stronger partner of this alliance. It could maintain a standing army with the money which the towns in the Castilian cortes now voted although they did so reluctantly and not always as much as the crown demanded. Once, in 1538, the nobles themselves refused a royal tax demand. Charles V gave way but, from then on, ceased to summon the nobility to the cortes. The monarchy thus allowed the Castilian nobility to contract out of all financial obligations towards the state while still reserving for this class most of the benefits of the empire. In return, the nobility tacitly conceded complete political victory to the monarchy.

The immediate result was a shift in the burden of taxation. Much more heavily than before it came to fall on the *pecheros*, the classes which were not exempt like the nobles and *hidalgos* (gentlemen). This proved to be a serious burden on the economically most active classes of the country. It largely accounts for the phenomenon which greatly perplexed contemporaries, viz., that Castile, in spite of all the American treasure she received, was experiencing an increasingly serious shortage of funds for investment in trade and industrial production. The political victory of the monarchy in Castile helped to create, or at least perpetuate, the conditions of Spain's economic weakness, a weakness which became an ever more serious handicap in her struggle with her economically more progressive European rivals.

TAXATION: FRANCE

It was the ability of the kings of France to levy the *taille*, a direct tax on persons and property, as well as the *gabelle* on salt and certain customs duties, without the consent of an assembly of estates that impressed contemporaries with the extraordinary powers of the French monarchy. When to this ability was added the 'unity and obedience of the kingdom', wonderingly observed by the Venetian ambassadors, together with the king's powers of legislation, it seemed that here was truly the *rex legibus solutus*, the king above the law. This was the position which the Roman lawyers in government service all over Europe claimed for their princes. It was generally acknowledged that France had fundamental laws which no king could alter: the Salic law of male succession and the king's inability to alienate his own powers and lands. But these fundamental laws were held to strengthen, rather than weaken, royal power and the coherence of the state. It was fashionable to contrast, with varying degrees of approval or disapproval, the absolutism of the kings of France with the constitutional limitations imposed on other European princes by their subjects. Sir John Fortescue's *De laudibus legum Angliae*, first published in the reign of Henry VIII but written in the fifteenth century, set the tone for a long tradition of English disapproval of French absolutism. The emperor Maximilian I's attitude was more ambiguous when he remarked that he himself was a king of kings because no man did his bidding, the king of Spain was a king of men because his subjects reacted as men, sometimes obeying and sometimes disobeying his commands, and the king of France was a king of beasts because his subjects always obeyed all his commands. Francis I would gleefully repeat Maximilian's joke to impress foreign ambassadors.[5]

The *taille* was specifically imposed for defence expenditure and, in consequence, the nobles and clergy claimed to be exempt from it.

(The clergy granted the king voluntary *aides* in their local or national assemblies.) Effectively, all higher officials and professional men and most rich and influential persons managed to claim exemption. Villages, districts and whole cities, like Rouen, bought themselves off. It seems as if in France, unlike Castile, at least some sections of the economically most active classes managed to escape from the heaviest forms of taxation. For the rest of the population of France the *taille* was a very heavy, and probably increasing, burden, even though during the reigns of Francis I and Henry II it does not seem to have risen much more than prices.[6] In 1542, for instance, the Venetian ambassador reported peasants fleeing from the land, without even knowing where to, in order to escape from the *taille*,[7] and this was not an isolated incident.

ADMINISTRATION

The third great problem for the monarchies was that of building up an administrative organization that could translate their political victory into effective government. To contemporaries this meant that the king must be able to make his will obeyed and also that he must be able to provide equitable justice for his subjects, in accordance with their rank and privileges. A problem neither new nor as obsessive as finance, this proved to be just as difficult to handle, for it involved, once again, but this time on a hundred different levels, the question of political power within the state.

The king's greatest vassals had traditionally claimed the right to give him advice and, therefore, to be members of the royal council. Strong kings had always been able to select their councillors from among their magnates; but the political victories of the monarchies in the latter part of the fifteenth century made them, for the first time, complete masters in their own councils. At the same time, the single royal council was divided into several councils with different functions. This was not entirely new; but earlier divisions had remained fairly rudimentary and even those of the sixteenth century were not as rigid as the names of the new councils might suggest. Both their membership and their functions still tended to overlap in varying degrees. In almost every case, however, the old officials of the royal household, with their splendid names of seneschal, steward, chamberlain, etc. were reduced to mainly ceremonial functions. The kings of Spain led the way with the most elaborate new conciliar organization, both for different governmental functions — Councils of State (nominally for matters of high policy), of Finance, of Military Orders, of War, of the Inquisition, of the Mesta — and for their different dominions — Councils of Castile (which effectively performed many of the functions that the Council of State performed nominally), of the Indies, of Aragon (with competence for all the realms of Aragon) and, later, of Italy. All these councils acted both as government departments and as courts of law.

In France the functional divisions of the royal council into different sections, or new councils, took place more gradually. Judicial work was reserved to the *Grand Conseil*, at the very end of the fifteenth century. Francis I and his successors came to rely for all important political decisions on a small inner council, sometimes called the *Conseil des Affaires*, while the larger council tended to divide finance from the rest of its work. In England, during the reign of King Henry VIII, Thomas Cromwell also organized an inner ring of councillors into a government board: the Privy Council. This coordinated the work of bureaucratic departments of state and was meant to oversee the reorganized finances of the king. Such was the foundation of efficient Tudor government though, in the last resort, its working always depended upon the ruler himself.[8]

The council possessed not only administrative functions but also judicial powers. The judgments of the council in Star Chamber, without the traditional jury trial, produced much controversy during the century. The chancellor's court was even more important, for it drew to itself most equity cases. But all these courts used common law and the principles of equity. Roman law was used only in Admiralty and in Church Courts. But for all the exercise of the council's jurisdiction as an arm of the monarchy, Roman law never defeated the common law in England as it did on much of the Continent. The common law soon found a champion in parliament against the increasing power of the monarchy.

The Tudors also used their council to pacify and then to rule those parts of the country which had a tradition of disorder and rebellion. Under the supervision of the Privy Council, the Council of the North was established after the Pilgrimage of Grace had raised rebellion against King Henry VIII (1536) (see p. 294). The Council in the Marches of Wales, founded in the fifteenth century, had authority over the regions bordering that rebellious province. Conciliar government was the instrument through which the

Tudors exercised their rule, and Thomas Cromwell's reorganization strengthened its powers as an effective instrument if the monarch chose to use it to its full advantage.

Parallel with the new system of royal councils developed that of the royal secretaries. They provided the link between the councils and the king who could not attend all their sessions in person. The political and administrative power of the secretaries increased rapidly in the course of the century. Having constant access to the king they knew his mind better than most of the councillors, and since the king came to rely on their advice, they often came to dominate royal patronage. Most of them became very rich.

THE PERSONNEL OF GOVERNMENT

Now that the kings had the power to do so, it was obvious that they would prefer to choose as secretaries and councillors men who owed their careers entirely to royal favour. Again, this was not a new policy, but in the sixteenth century the kings came to practise it much more systematically than before. Anyone not a member of, nor closely linked to, one of the great aristocratic families was considered eligible. In practice, recruitment was mostly from the lower nobility and from the sons of professional men and well-to-do bourgeoisie. They had to have a law degree or a professional administrative or financial training in government service itself. Understandably, the older nobility was intensely jealous of them and, not always without reason, despised their careerism and narrow-mindedness. They were men, said Juan de Vega, one of Charles V's viceroys of Sicily, who knew nothing of chivalry and honour and who treated the viceroys of Sicily and Naples as if they were the mayors of Salamanca or Avila.[9] Nevertheless, the professional servants of the monarchies were not representatives of the bourgeoisie as a class, invading the king's councils to further its economic and social interests as against the economic and social interests of the nobility. On the contrary: the king's servants usually tried very hard to rise into the ranks of the higher nobility, and the top men often managed to marry their children, especially their daughters, into titled families. These latter, for all their vociferous dislike of upstarts, were not averse to alliances with men who had the king's ear and a finger in the patronage pie.

The quest for the cardinal's hat by the king's principal ministers (in the case of those of them who were bishops) was perhaps the most effective gambit for these men to rise to the social level of the high nobility. Jiménez, d'Amboise and Wolsey, in the early sixteenth century, Granvelle and Espinosa in the second half, and Richelieu and Mazarin in the seventeenth century were, with the possible exception of Jiménez, all purely 'political' cardinals, and all of them of gentry or bourgeois origin. Laymen found it a little more difficult to raise their social status quite as rapidly as the most successful 'clerks'; but it could certainly be done, as was demonstrated, for instance, by Thomas Cromwell when Henry VIII made him Earl of Essex. None of this was altogether new in the sixteenth century; but it became much more common than it had been in the Middle Ages. Moreover, since the complete assimilation of social upstarts into the high nobility often took several generations, there appeared a new type of administrative nobility, the *noblesse de robe*, in contrast to the *noblesse d'épée*, who tended to monopolize the highest judicial and administrative posts. This happened not only in the *parlements*, the supreme courts of France, but also in the secretaryships. The Villeroys in France, the Pérez in Spain, the Perrenots de Granvelle in the Netherlands and elsewhere in imperial and Spanish service, the Cecils and Bacons in England, all followed from father to son.

The professional lawyers and administrators who were making such successful careers in the royal councils and courts naturally wanted to increase their own power and importance. Save in England, where common law prevailed, the precepts of Roman law and the demands of equity and Christian justice could happily all be adduced to justify the extension of the jurisdiction and competence of the royal courts at the expense of the seignorial courts of the nobility. Together with the royal attacks on the autonomy of the towns, this policy consituted the most systematic movement towards royal absolutism and centralized government of the century.

SALARIES, PROFITS, PATRONAGE AND CORRUPTION

Nevertheless, the practical difficulties of running an effective centralized government were still enormous. In the first place, there were the ambiguities in the contemporary conception of public office. Philip II was very clear about it in his secret instructions to his viceroys of Naples:

Your principal object and intention must be to work for the community which is your charge . . . to watch that it may sleep . . . and to take heed that you are not accepting this office . . . for any benefit of your own, but only for the peace and quiet and good of the community.[10]

But it was one of these viceroys of Naples who used to say that one ought not to wish to hold this office because of the pain of leaving it.

Even when offices were not bought and sold — and the highest administrative offices (councillors, governors of provinces, commanders of armies or fortresses, etc.) never were — they were often given as reward for political services or in expectation of further political support. The men who filled them would naturally make the most of their opportunities, financial and social, which the possession of such offices offered them. The morality of such action was generally accepted. The career of Montaigne, son of a merchant and parvenu landowner, is typical and was regarded as strictly honourable in its progression, through the purchase of various provincial offices and estates, to a noble name and to the dignity of a gentleman of the king's chamber. Men would expect fees for the performance of an office, where letters had to be written or documents issued. There was, therefore, a built-in tendency for paper work in government offices to increase. Parkinson's Law was valid even in the sixteenth century and was recognized to be operating, although naturally not with this name. The real income of office holders varied tremendously, but it was usually greatly in excess of official salaries.[11] In Italy and Spain there were even theoretical justifications for this pattern, based on the idea of a just salary (in analogy to the medieval idea of the just price) and of the decline of the real value of fixed money wages in a period of rising prices. Corruption was regarded as depending on the amount charged and on the intentions of both the giver and the recipient. But to those who required the services of the office holder the situation was both simpler and more sinister: it required bribery. For the great majority of the population of western Europe, the victory of the centralizing and paternalistic monarchies meant at least a partial escape from the often arbitrary and tyrannical, but also traditional and personal, authority of the local magnate. But it also meant the spread of a new corrupt and very expensive officialdom. It is not surprising that, for instance in France towards the end of the century, local landowners and their peasants began to combine against the hated royal officials.

Not all officials were corrupt, at least by sixteenth-century standards, and some had as high a conception of the duties of their office as Philip II expected them to have. But there was simply not a sufficient number of reasonably honest and efficient civil servants available for all the tasks for which they were required. If the monarchies wanted to translate their orders into administrative action, they still had to rely on the cooperation of the traditional local authorities. The collection of the *taille*, that symbol of absolutism, needed the cooperation – the forced cooperation, it is true – of the small town and village communities to determine exactly how much each individual had to pay. Above all, the monarchies still needed the nobility. The governor of a province or a fortress, the commander of an army or a fleet had to be a great lord. He had to have the habit of command and the expectation of being obeyed. Philip II's choice of the inexperienced duke of Medina Sidonia to command the Armada was motivated by a clear and inescapable social logic. A man of lower degree, a simple gentleman like Martínez de Recalde, would simply not have commanded sufficient authority to make himself obeyed, for all that he was perhaps the most experienced and efficient naval commander in Spanish service at the time. Although the great noblemen had lost their hereditary right to sit in the royal council and to treat the king as the first among equals, they were still perfectly willing to serve the crown. They would expect to be paid the salary attached to the office they held; but, equally, they might be willing to advance money to their prince or guarantee a government loan with their private property. They would expect recognition of their services later, and this might take the form not only of money payment but of some public honour or privilege. It was a slight on a man's honour and self-esteem to be expected to serve his prince without such public rewards. It undermined his standing with, and usefulness to, his own friends and clients who had attached themselves to him in hopes of advancement and profit. For the rewards granted by the prince also took the form of benefits to third parties at the request of their patrons. When Charles V failed to reward the marquis of Pescara who had won the battle of Pavia for him (1525), the Milanese chancellor, Girolamo Morone, was led to believe, quite logically but, as it happened, erroneously, that Pescara might be induced to change sides.

The control of patronage was therefore regarded by all sixteenth-century rulers as the key to effective government, and the desks of their secretaries were always piled high with requests for titles, honours, ecclesiatical benefices, pensions and, above all, for public offices. Royal patronage tended to centralize political life, but it also preserved powerful loyalties in society which were neither national nor monarchical. These were the loyalties depending on the horizontal links of family alliances and the vertical links between patrons and clients. When joined to the loyalties generated by popular religious movements, they could still challenge the authority of sixteenth-century monarchies as dangerously as the leagues of overmighty subjects could challenge the monarchies of the fifteenth.

STATE AND CHURCH IN ENGLAND

The evolution of the monarchies in the sixteenth century cannot be separated from the all-pervasive influence of the Reformation. Historians used to believe that the Lutheran reformation in particular meant an increase in the ruler's powers over his subjects. But it is doubtful if the rulers of all principalities actually gained much power through the Reformation. To be sure, the Reformation was usually introduced without consultation with the Estates, but these nevertheless came to play a vital part in the establishment of the new order. This was the case, for example, in Denmark where the diet furthered the Lutherans, and in Sweden where the Diet of Westerås concentrated the spiritual power in the hands of Gustavus Vasa, expelling the chief leader of the Catholic party (1527). The collaboration between king and parliament in fuelling the English Reformation did not constitute an isolated example.

When the political situation demanded it the tensions between Church and State, as well as the latent anticlericalism of educated lay classes, could be used to bring parliaments into line with the ruler's demands for religious reform. At its beginning the English Reformation was a political act, for the Church itself was neither particularly weak nor always unpopular. Lutheran ideas had penetrated the island, but their reception was only half-hearted at best. Moreover, a native tradition of heresy persisted ever since the Middle Ages. The Lollards were anticlerical and opposed to the Catholic Mass long before the Reformation. Lollardy was reinforced when William Tyndale's translation of the New Testament reached England (1526). Just as important, influential sections of the gentry and merchant classes were being alienated by the Church's aggressive defence of its coercive jurisdiction. While some doctrinal opposition to the Church existed, the growing anti-clericalism of many elements of the population was of greater importance.

Christian humanism played its part in England through influencing the educated classes in the direction of Church reform. Yet at first humanism in England as on the continent wanted to reform the Church from within. Thomas More, the friend of Erasmus, attempted to regenerate the Church from inside its medieval tradition. This tradition, which included the universalism of the papacy, was, for him, a part of the law of God. More had taken the lead in persecuting those English heretics who seemed to endanger the divinely commanded fabric of the Church, long before he himself was executed as a traitor against the king (1535). But More represents an isolated example of resistance to royal authority in high places. English bishops, like their counterparts abroad, were royal and ecclesiastical administrators. With the exception of John Fisher, bishop of Rochester, they soon abandoned all resistance to the king's wishes.

WOLSEY AND CROMWELL

The rule over the Church and State by Cardinal Wolsey (1515–29) crystallized the latent anti-clericalism of powerful and envious sections of English society. However, if the crisis over the king's divorce had not arisen, it is difficult to envisage any forces powerful enough to have driven England to break with the papacy at this particular time. Dynasties were fragile in the sixteenth century, and no English king had lost as many children as Henry VIII. To be sure, Catherine of Aragon had given a daughter to the dynasty, but female rule was thought to be insecure and dangerous. Moreover, the queen was an active Spanish agent, whose influence had already involved England in a useless war with France. Royal divorce was not unknown, and Henry could bring forward a strong theological justification: Catherine had been married to his brother. But the hands of Pope Clement VII were tied. Charles V was his master at this critical moment of Henry's divorce proceedings (see p. 215) and the emperor had no desire nor reason to sacrifice his aunt, and thereby offend the pride of his touchy Spanish subjects.

Wolsey fell from power when he failed to obtain the divorce, and Henry was now constrained to follow a course of action which inevitably led England into a reformation which the king himself at first scarcely desired. Pressure was brought upon Rome through curtailing the power of the English clergy, and through gradually transferring the rights of the papacy over the Church into the hands of the monarch. Taking Parliament into partnership, the king obtained a series of statutes (1531–34) which abrogated the tie between Rome and the English Church, establishing Henry as its 'Supreme Head'. The king gained a great advantage from this mode of proceeding: the anti-clericalism of lawyers, merchants and gentry led parliament to press ahead, while the king could always call a halt, provided the pope granted his wish. But Parliament gained an equally great advantage. Instead of meeting intermittently, as it had done before, the Reformation Parliament sat for seven years. The House of Commons evolved a set of procedures, and even began to keep a journal. Moreover, Parliament's composition changed: the removal of 29 abbots from the House of Lords shifted its balance away from the Lords Spiritual, while the House of Commons expanded rapidly from 296 seats to 398 by 1558. The laicization of Parliament made it increasingly an arena for ambitious laymen.

There can be no doubt that through its part in the Reformation, Parliament was strengthened to such an extent that no future ruler could do without it: not only because the financial needs of the monarchy had to be met, but also because the religious change had been accomplished by statute law, and to change it would therefore require once more collaboration between the monarch and his parliament.

The confrontation between ruler and parliament was a general phenomenon in the sixteenth century. As we saw earlier, in most nations the ruler won. But in England the partnership between crown and Parliament continued uneasily, and the tensions between them mounted as the century advanced. The final confrontation was postponed until the next century, and the way in which the Reformation was accomplished in England provides one of the chief reasons both for the increased rivalry between ruler and parliament and for the delay in the ultimate confrontation between them.

Henry VIII chose Thomas Cromwell to carry through the actions which king and parliament had taken. Cromwell exemplifies the new type of dedicated civil servant upon whom the monarchies were coming to depend. He mobilized support for the king's battle with Rome, recruiting important humanists as propagandists for the king's cause. These attributed vast powers to the monarch while arguing for non-resistance to authority. But even they never made the King *legibus solutus*: he was always subject to divine and natural law, sharing some of his powers with parliament. However, Cromwell strengthened the crown in a more concrete manner as well, trying to take advantage of the situation, not only to reorganize the government, but also to better the finances. The dissolution of the monasteries gave him his chance, and he attempted to use the new-found wealth in order to establish a permanent endownment for the crown. However, contrary to his wishes, the monastic lands were soon alienated through sales to men who were inclined to Protestantism and to others whose allegiance belonged to the old order. Religious preference made little difference in this scramble for wealth or land speculation. Small wonder that Queen Mary was not able to restore English monasticism, or that her parliament insisted upon safeguarding the new owners of monastic lands.

Cromwell's sudden fall from power and his execution were partly occasioned by his foreign policy. He tried to push the king into an alliance with the German Lutherans as a safeguard against the threat to England's security arising from Spain and France. But a price had to be paid for gaining such allies: the marriage to Anne of Cleves was undertaken by Henry with ill grace, but to follow Lutheran teachings was something he would not undertake at all. Cromwell had placed the king in an awkward position while seeming to foist upon England a faith against which Henry himself had written a book many years earlier. Equally important in his downfall were disgruntled nobles and clergy, conservatives held back from power. This court faction dangled the vivacious Catherine Howard as bait and fed the love-struck and suggestible king stories of Cromwell's treason and supposed Anabaptist heresy.[12] The execution of Cromwell (1540) illustrated not only the fierceness of the struggle for power at court, but also that political motives underlying the English Reformation could not sidetrack the religious issues which the king's actions had inevitably raised.

THE HENRICIAN SETTLEMENT

Henry VIII liked to be his own theologian and, especially in his old age, was prepared to consider, but not really act on, theological novelties such as the abolition of the Mass. His reformation of the Church was conservative rather than radical, assuring much continuity, for men and women were not prepared to accept sudden changes in their manner of worship and in its traditional meaning. The Six Articles (1539) which were supposed to settle Church dogma, stressed belief in transubstantiation, auricular confessions, clerical celibacy and private masses. All pressure upon the king for doctrinal reformation proved in vain. Thomas Cranmer was Henry's archbishop of Canterbury, the chief agent of the king in the control of the Church. Cranmer had finally divorced the king from Catherine (the first of several divorces and remarriages he was to carry through for his sovereign). The archbishop was of Protestant leanings, but during Henry's reign his only success in this direction was the establishment of the English Bible as a feature of national life. This was of some importance: it went far towards assuring victory over papal authority and the cult of saints.[13]

But once the old framework of authority had been destroyed, religious opinion never became stabilized. When Henry died, important elements at court supported Protestantism, including the Queen, the Archbishop of Canterbury, the heir's uncles and reform-minded courtiers such as Sir Anthony Denny,[14] as well as a limited circle of gentry, merchants, clergy and intellectuals. The vast majority of Englishmen adopted a waiting posture, as yet uncommitted to any course of religious reform.

EDWARD VI AND THE CHURCH

The short reign of Edward VI (1547–53) witnessed a sharp turn away from Henry's settlement of the Church. It is still puzzling why Henry VIII had his young son tutored by several committed Protestants or appointed such men to the council which was to exercise the regency. Perhaps he wanted to obtain a balance of forces, either envisaging his son's minority or in order to contain the factions at court. At any rate, Edward Seymour, earl of Hertford (later made duke of Somerset) seized power in the council and established an unprecedented toleration in religious matters. A convinced Protestant, he began far-reaching religious reforms. The new Prayer Book (1549) was a study in ambiguities, but these were weighted in favour of Protestantism. When John Dudley, earl of Warwick (later duke of Northumberland), replaced Somerset (1549), a statute allowing clerical marriage was pushed through parliament. The second Prayer Book of Edward VI's reign (1550) while keeping much of the ambiguous wording of the first, eliminated the word 'mass', abolished all vestments except the surplice, and forbade the adoration of the eucharist. England seemed to have entered the mainstream of the Reformation, and foreign Protestants such as Bucer, fleeing from Charles V's Interim (see p. 219), were welcomed in the island.

Thomas Cranmer was instrumental in this reform. Historians have held that he moved increasingly towards Zwingli's doctrinal position. It seems more likely that he himself arrived at a Protestantism which diverged from Continental models: the sacrament was an 'outward' ceremony of remembrance, but inwardly it did become the body of Christ, Cranmer was an enigmatic personality. He survived Henry's reign and under Mary converted to Catholicism before he finally decided to die a martyr's death (1556). The explanation for his seeming cowardice may well lie in Cranmer's desire to preserve national unity through a consensus of belief whose enforcement depended upon the ruler. The monarch was, after all, the divinely appointed governor of the Church.

The whole course of the English Reformation was accompanied by rebellions which took advantage of the dislocation of hitherto firmly established ecclesiastical institutions. The north and the south-west of England were especially prone to such uprisings. The conservative north was a border region, kept in military training by the Scots and dominated by a feudal nobility. The Pilgrimage of Grace (1536) in Henry's reign, and the rising of northern earls (1569) under Queen Elizabeth demanded a return to the traditional order of things. The Western Rising (1549) also demanded a return to Catholic practices, while economic grievances, mainly directed against the gentry, played only a minor part in the revolt. The Western rising was the biggest of these rebellions, all of which were inspired by a religious cause while at the same time expressing dissatisfaction with the new monarchy, its centralizing tendencies and its bureaucracy, which excluded the old nobility from power. The new monarchy was associated with the new religion and by calling for the restoration of the old religion these rebels also supported the old order of things.

Robert Kett's 1549 revolt in Norfolk was the only true peasant revolt among all the Tudor uprisings. The rebel demands, in some ways, resembled the Twelve Articles (1525) which had contained the demands of the peasants in the earlier German Peasants Wars.[15] Kett's revolt was part of the general peasant unrest in Europe which seized the opportunity of the unsettled religious situation in order to press their demands for peasant autonomy and to call for redress of economic grievances. This revolt had a decidedly Protestant and anti-clerical flavour, but it was mainly directed against the Norfolk gentry. Thomas Wyatt's rebellion in Mary's reign (1554) masked its Protestant learnings under protests against the queen's proposed marriage to a Spanish prince and the dangers that foreign influence posed for England.[16] During her reign, her opponents would eventually come to openly pair Protestantism with national pride, a link which would become even stronger with the passage of time.

Kett's rebellion brought about the fall of Somerset. However, court intrigue had already brought Northumberland to the fore as Somerset's rival for power. England's turn towards Protestantism was accompanied by the most sordid court politics, and by a financial crisis which was not solved through the further expropriation of Church property. Mary's accession to the throne (1553) was greeted with joy, and Northumberland's effort to substitute the Protestant Lady Jane Grey was doomed to failure. The golden dawn of her accession convinced the daughter of Catherine of Aragon that a Catholic restoration could be accomplished smoothly and with some ease. When this proved to be far from the case, the disappointed queen retreated into personal bitterness and the merciless persecution of Protestant heretics.

THE CATHOLIC RESTORATION

Mary encountered strong parliamentary resistance on the road to reunion. Parliament not only refused to restore Church lands but also restricted the power of papal bulls in England, while depriving Philip II, Mary's husband, of any real say in English affairs. This, even though all Reformation statutes were soon repealed. But more was needed to root Catholicism in England. The queen's chief adviser was Cardinal Reginald Pole, and this in itself proved a handicap. Pole was a Christian humanist who in the past had tried to reconcile Catholicism and Protestantism. While Pole's lack of sympathy with the course of the Catholic Reformation led his former friend Pope Paul IV to accuse him of heresy, this had an even more serious consequence. Pole refused Ignatius of Loyola's offer to train young Englishmen in Jesuit colleges. Such dedicated missionaries were badly needed in England, but their education had to wait until Cardinal Allen founded his colleges during the reign of Elizabeth. Mary regarded England as a Catholic nation which had been perverted, rather than as a missionary province. She was mistaken; not only did a Protestant underground remain in existence,[17] but most of her subjects had learned to take a waiting posture in the midst of rapid religious change which seemed to breed only confusion.

For all that, Mary did revive Catholicism in England.[18] Monasticism was given new life, seminaries were established, and some monastic land was returned to the Church. But above all, she managed to restore the morale of Catholicism to the point that when Elizabeth succeeded her sister many clergy and students went into exile in order to preserve the faith and to prepare for its possible return to England. There was nothing inevitable about the triumph of Protestantism, and in England Catholicism would continue to contest the Protestant ascendancy for another century and a half.

However, Mary also contributed indirectly to the strength of English Protestantism. She was not, on the whole, successful in reconverting her subjects. Moreover, many of the best intellects among the Protestant clergy and laity were driven to the Continent where they came in contact with Calvinist influence. Above all, the increasing persecution of heretics produced a popular sympathy with Protestantism which led many to abandon their waiting posture. The fires at Smithfield consumed not only the mighty, but also simple workers and peasants. About 282 people were burnt at the stake. To be sure, some may have been radicals, Anabaptists who had been persecuted even under Edward VI, but the vast majority were simply opposed to Catholicism. John Foxe's *Book of Martyrs*

(1563) made sure that Mary's victims were not forgotten and became, after the Bible, the most popular book of piety, edifying generations of Englishmen.

Equally important for the future growth of Protestantism was Mary's marriage to Philip II of Spain. The half-Spanish queen seemed to bind England to the most menacing power on the Continent, and the arrogant behaviour of Philip's retinue in England added fuel to the fear and dislike of Spain. Catholicism and foreign tyranny became linked in the minds of many Englishmen, a handicap (reinforced by the Armada) which it took Catholicism two centuries to overcome.

The English Reformation began as an act of state or, more correctly, as an act of blackmail against the pope in order to assure the security of the Tudor monarchy. However, change in the structure of the Church could not be divorced from those religious currents which flowed so strongly throughout the century – though Henry VIII attempted to contain them. Other national Churches also had their beginnings in acts designed to fulfil political ambitions, but they were soon settled on a Lutheran or Zwinglian base. Not so England, which, in a relatively short span of time, ran through a variety of religious doctrines each one enforced by law. Slowly a state Church was emerging which was to find a solution within a latitudinarian framework to the support which these diverse, partly divergent doctrines, had received. Though we can see this foreshadowed by the ambiguities in the Prayer Books of King Edward VI, it was Queen Elizabeth who finally settled her Church upon such a foundation.

The monarchy had gained new power through the Reformation, but so had Parliament, and the competition between these two centres of authority prevented any claim towards monarchical absolutism in England. The composition of Parliament reflected the transformation of a feudal and ecclesiastical society to one dominated by an educated laity which was gaining ever greater self-confidence. Such laity could now be found in all of Europe, and their existence represented a potentially dangerous challenge to the monarchy, one which could not be met solely through administrative or financial reform. The loyalties generated by popular religious movements continued unabated, drawing within their orbit not only the grievances of the lower classes but also the threat to monarchical power represented by the estates and the older competition for power among the nobility. The second half of the sixteenth century saw many a monarchy engaged in the fight for survival.

NOTES AND REFERENCES

1   A. G. Dickens, *The English Reformation* (London, 1964), p. 117.

2   John Lyly, *Euphues and His England* (1580), quoted in Hans Kohn, *The Idea of Nationalism* (New York, 1944), p. 160.

3   Quoted in J. A. Maravall, 'The origins of the modern state', *Journal of World History* vol. VI, no. 4, 1961, p. 798.

4   H. G. Koenigsberger, 'The States General of the Netherlands before the Revolt', in *Estates and Revolutions* (Ithaca, 1971), pp. 125–43.

5   M. Dandolo, 'Relazione di Francia, 1541', in Albèri, *Relazioni*, ser. 1, vol. IV, p. 32.

6   Figures for the *taille* in R. Doucet, *Les Institutions de la France au XVIe Siècle* (Paris 1948), vol. 11, pp. 556 ff.; and G. Zeller, *Les Institutions de la France au XVI Siècle* (Paris, 1948) pp. 258 ff. For wheat prices of. M. Boulant and J. Meuvret, *Prix des Céréales extraits de la Mercuriale de Paris* (1520–1698) (Paris, 1960), vol. I, p. 243.

7   Dandolo, 'Relazione', in Albèri *Relazioni*, ser. 1, vol. IV, 4, p. 39.

8   G. R. Elton, *The Tudor Revolution in Government* (Cambridge, 1953), ch. VII.

9   *Papiers d'état du Cardinal de Granville*, ed. C. Weiss (Paris, 1844), vol. V, pp. 144 ff.

10   British Library Add. MS. 28 701, fo. 86.

11   For Milan in the late sixteenth century we have comtemporary lists of official and unofficial incomes, showing variations ranging from 30 per cent in the case of the grand chancellor, to 800 per cent in that of the office porters. This pattern may well have been typical for much of Italy and western Europe. Cf. F. Chabod, 'Stipendi nominali e busta paga effectiva dei funzionari dell' administrazione milanese alla fine del cinquecento', in *Miscellanea in Onore di Roberto Cessi* (Rome, 1958), vol. II, pp. 187–363.

12   J. J. Scarisbrick, *Henry VIII* (Berkeley, 1968), p. 378.

13   A. G. Dickens, *The English Reformation*, pp. 137, 189.

14 Maria Dowling, 'The Gospel and the Court. Reformation under Henry VIII', in Peter Lake and Maria Dowling, eds., *Protestantism and the National Church in Sixteenth-Century England* (London, 1987), p. 71.

15 Barrett L. Beer, *Rebellion and Riot, Popular Disorder in England During the Reign of Edward VI* (Kent OH, 1982), p. 108.

16 'The *Vitae Mariae Angliae Reginae* of Robert Wingfield of Brantham', ed. Diarmid MacCulloch, in *Camden Miscellany*, 4 ser., vol. 29 (London, 1984), pp. 274, 279.

17 J. W. Martin, 'The Protestant Underground Congregations of Mary's Reign', *Journal of Ecclesiastical History*, 1984, pp. 519–38.

18 D. M. Loades, *The Reign of Mary Tudor* (London, 1979), p. 465.

12

WESTERN EUROPE IN THE AGE OF PHILIP II

THE PEACE OF CATEAU-CAMBRÉSIS

The almost interminable wars between the Habsburgs and the French monarchy were settled by the Peace of Cateau-Cambrésis (1–3 April 1559). *Christianitas afflicta* was to be finally healed by peace and a common front of the great Catholic powers against the further spread of heresy. In traditional style the peace was sealed by dynastic marriages: of Philip II with Henry II's daughter, Elizabeth, and of Emmanuel Philibert of Piedmont-Savoy with Henry's sister, Margaret. But the rest of the terms made it clear that the treaty of Cateau-Cambrésis was a power-political arrangement between France and Spain. The French withdrew from Piedmont, some two-thirds of which they had held since 1536, except for garrisons in Saluzzo and five other cities. Spain was left supreme in Italy, with Sicily, Sardinia, Naples, Milan and five coastal fortresses in Tuscany under her direct control. The Neapolitan Pope Paul IV who, in his almost insane hatred of the Spaniards, had provoked the last round of the Habsburg-Valois wars (1556), had suffered humiliating defeat. Emmanuel Philibert, despite his French marriage, owed his return to Savoy to Spanish arms and so, earlier, did the Medici dukes of Florence who were allowed to keep their recent conquest of Siena – another Italian city republic which had fallen to outside attack (1555). The Doria family had bound Genoa by financial and political bonds indissolubly to Spain. Of all the Italian states, only Venice remained truly independent. But France kept Calais, which the duke of Guise had conquered from the English in 1558, at a time when Philip II was husband of Mary Tudor and joint king of England. France also kept Metz, Toul and Verdun. To obtain peace Philip II had thus unsentimentally liquidated the last remnants of his father's imperial plans and obligations. His own subjects in the Netherlands were not slow to draw the conclusion that they had been made to fight France so that Spain should win Italy.

Without his father's imperial title and without his transcendental vision of a universal Christian empire, Philip II was left with only one justification for his Spanish empire, beyond the purely personal allegiance of his multi-national subjects: the defence of the Catholic Church. 'You may assure His Holiness', Philip wrote to his ambassador in Rome in 1566, 'that rather than suffer the least damage to religion and the service of God, I would lose all my states and a hundred lives, if I had them; for I do not propose nor desire to be the ruler of heretics.'[1] Yet Philip had no intention of losing any of his states, whether in Spain or Italy, in Franche-Comté, the Netherlands, America or East Asia. Not only were they rightly his, by inheritance or Christian conquest, but their possession was necessary for the defence of the Church. For Philip, therefore, championship of the Church and Spanish reason of state tended to be the same thing. For everyone else, both allies and opponents, and not least the popes, the two often looked flatly contradictory. Philip was caught in the dilemma of all those who champion a universal cause from the base of a limited territorial power with its own limited but imperative interests. For this reason the Peace of Cateau-Cambrésis could be no more than a truce. Kings and their advisers thought in terms of power, and the basic problem of power between the two greatest Christian monarchies, the Spanish and the French, had not been resolved. France still had her footholds in Italy and could count on potential allies if ever Spain should suffer a reverse. The old border quarrels with the Netherlands were shelved, not settled. Both powers had their allies and clients among the German princes and the leaders of the Swiss Cantons. English policy was unpredictable, except that Elizabeth would want to regain Calais at the first suitable opportunity. Worse still, neither the English nor the Scottish regimes seemed stable. Both France and Spain might seize a chance to intervene and upset the balance of power in western Europe.

All this was clearly recognized; but it proved just as impossible to act consistently according to the dictates of pure reason of state as it was to ignore practical advantage for the sake of pursuing a universal cause. Neither princes nor their ministers were fully immune from the religious emotions which dominated their subjects; not even Elizabeth, who would not 'open windows into men's souls'; much less Philip II who felt himself directly responsible for his subjects' souls. The national rivalries of the great powers therefore became entangled in the religious struggles within the different states and in the international patterns of religious loyalties.

THE SPREAD OF CALVINISM

Up to the middle of the sixteenth century the Reformation had generally been successful only where it had been supported by the public authorities. The relative ease with which the German peasants' movements and the Anabaptists of Münster and Holland were defeated, demonstrated conclusively that there was no chance of success for a creed that appealed only to the lower classes. The rise of international Calvinism changed all this. Here was a creed that could become as effectively revolutionary as that of the Anabaptists and which yet remained socially respectable, appealing to great seigneurs and rich bankers as much as to unemployed artisans. In an age when most men thought of economic and political problems in religious and moral terms, social discontent proved a fertile soil for revolutionary religious propaganda. Rising prices and taxes, lagging wages and periodic unemployment, burnt harvests and lost livestock brought misery to townsmen and country people. After two generations of royal wars, thousands of young men, both nobles and commoners, had no training but for warfare. Peace left them unemployed, unemployable and bored. Many were converted. Many more flocked happily to the standards of the leaders of religious movements, often without caring too much whether it was on the Catholic or the Calvinist side. The governments of all states in western Europe were therefore confronted with actual or potential military movements within their frontiers and, since these movements had international connections, with the threat of foreign intervention. Even Spain had its 'fifth column' in the Moriscos, the potential allies, as the Spaniards saw it, of their most powerful enemy, the Turk.

Here was the greatest crisis that the monarchies of western Europe had yet to face: revolutionary movements with organizations that came to match those of the monarchies and with patterns of loyalty which, at times, were not only more powerful than those the monarchies could call on, but which stretched across national boundaries. The crisis might still have been overcome by firm and experienced leadership. The monarchies still held many trump cards. 'You know, sir, how difficult it is to persuade a multitude to revolt from established authority', wrote two Scottish opposition leaders who had experience of the matter.[2] But firm and experienced leadership was precisely what disappeared at this moment. In 1559 government in France and the Netherlands passed into the hands of children or women. In England, Scotland and Portugal this had happened already a few years earlier.

THE PROBLEMS OF MINORITY AND FEMALE SUCCESSIONS

The systematization of central administration (see pp. 283 ff.) had made it possible to carry on the ordinary business of government even under rather incompetent kings, like Henry II of France. Personal loyalty to the sovereign and the knowledge that ultimate decisions depended on him, an adult male, kept the ambitions and rivalries of princes and magnates, like the Guises and the Montmorencys, within constitutional bounds. But a child or a woman, especially if she was only a regent and not herself a reigning sovereign, could command no such loyalty and obedience. Under such rulers the manœuvrings of court factions not only turned into deadly struggles for power and survival but also became entangled with the religious passions of the moment.

This chain of events was not entirely fortuitous. What we know of the high mortality rate of infants and children, the prevalence of syphilis, the frequency of childlessness and the relatively low life expectancy even of adults during this period, suggests that ruling families could expect to die out, or suffer a minority or female succession, on average every second generation.[3] This probability was a fundamental and inescapable weakness of the institution of European monarchy, and it goes a long way towards explaining the slowness with which effective absolutism was established in most countries.[4] Kings, moreover, often took appalling personal risks, even before assassination became the greatest professional hazard of rulers, as it was soon to be after 1559. Already in 1551 the Venetian ambassador commented on the dangers of Henry II's hunting habits.[5] At the tournament held to celebrate the Peace of Cateau-Cambrésis the king characteristically showed off his jousting prowess to the point of exhaustion when an unlucky lance penetrated his eye. He died a few days later (10 July 1559), leaving a boy of fifteen, Francis II, to succeed him.

THE HUGUENOTS: CONDÉ AND COLIGNY

Almost immediately the crisis in France became unmanageable. Calvinism was spreading at an astonishing speed. It was a situation similar to that of Germany during the imperial election of 1519 and the early, hesitant years of Charles V which had allowed many of the princes and imperial cities to ignore the papal and imperial condemnations of Luther's teaching. By 1562 the Huguenots claimed to have 2,000 churches all over France. They were organized in tiers of synods, up to provincial and even national level. Their spiritual direction was in the hands of preachers, trained and sent from Geneva. The conventicles practised a rigid discipline, as befitted the Lord's 'elect'. After 1559 the nobility began to join in large numbers with their retainers and clients. Calvin was deliberately aiming at converting them, and many of the preachers sent from Geneva came originally from French noble families. Very rapidly the nobility came to dominate the conventicles and superimposed upon an ecclesiastical organization a political and military one. It was necessary; for Francis I and Henry II had issued stringent edicts against heretics, and the conventicles had to be defended against the attacks of the Catholics. When Condé and Coligny joined the movement it acquired not only the support of the vast network of the Bourbon (Condé) and Châtillon (Coligny) connections but, more important still, a determined political direction. Coligny, the nephew of the

Connétable Montmorency, had grown up in the king's service. A strict royalist, he never wanted to impose any political or constitutional limitations on the monarchy but only to secure freedom of worship for the reformed churches and perhaps, if that were possible, the religious conversion of the whole of France. Condé's aims were more ambiguous. A younger brother of King Anthony of Navarre, he claimed, as a Bourbon and a prince of the blood, the constitutional right of participating in the government during the minority of the king. Condé's religious convictions have remained suspect, not least because Calvin himself distrusted him. These two essentially conservative men thus found themselves in control of a potentially revolutionary party with a religious, political and military organization the like of which had never been seen before.

At first, they used it simply to put pressure on the government. Francis II's government was dominated by his wife, Mary Stuart, as well as her uncles, Duke Francis of Guise and his brother Charles, Cardinal of Lorraine (see p. 271). As royal favourites and provincial governors, the Guises had built up a vast network of clientage among the lower nobility of eastern and northern France. Inevitably their ascendancy was resented by the other great families, the Bourbons and the Montmorencys. The disastrous state of the royal finances, the legacy of Francis I's and Henry II's wars, left them little room for manœuvre. With debts standing at some 40 million livres and with the traditional forms of taxation already pushed beyond the limits of the country's endurance, there was no alternative but to summon the States General. It presented Condé and the Huguenots with a most useful weapon and propaganda platform for their attack on the government, a weapon, moreover, of which Calvin himself approved (see p. 198). In the provinces royal authority was dwindling almost daily while religious and partisan passions were rising. In March 1560 the government gave up its attempts to enforce religious unity and issued a series of edicts granting liberty of conscience but prohibiting armed assemblies. It soon proved to be just as difficult to impose toleration as it had been to impose religious unity; for on both sides there were too many who thought this a betrayal of the true religion. When Francis II died, in December 1560, the queen mother, Catherine de Medici, seized the control of the government of the new king, Charles IX, who was only ten years old.

CATHERINE DE MEDICI: THE FRENCH CIVIL WARS

Descended from a Florentine family of popes, on her father's side, and from the highest French nobility on her mother's, Catherine was neither a bourgeoise nor, strictly, a foreigner in France, as her opponents liked to claim. With neither religious convictions nor, it seems, any real understanding of religious passions, Catherine's one aim was to preserve the French monarchy of France intact for her sons. To do this she must gain time which might allow a settlement of the religious differences or would at least let tempers cool and prevent one or other of the factions from controlling the monarchy in its own interests or, worst of all, give Philip II of Spain a chance to do so. Quite logically, therefore, Catherine continued the policy of limited toleration.

None of the parties was satisfied. Even the chancellor, Michel de l'Hôpital, who opposed force in matters of conscience, declared: 'The division of languages does not divide kingdoms, but that of religion and law does and makes two kingdoms out of one. Hence the old proverb: one faith, one law, one king.' Since Catherine had neither the power nor the will to impose such unity she could do little more than play the parties and personalities against each other. She has been accused of making mistakes in this game. It was, however, inevitable that the situation should escape from her control. Three times, from 1562 to 1568, the country slid into civil war. The Huguenots, outnumbered and at times outgeneralled, lost battles but remained on the offensive. They had some help from England and from the Palatinate, just as the Catholic party had some help from Spain. But the main Huguenot strength lay in Coligny's leadership and in superior organization. Where they dominated whole provinces or cities, as they did in the south, they took over all functions of government. Where they did not, they infiltrated public offices until there was a Huguenot hierarchy of officials intermingled with the royal administration. 'Thus they could, in one day, at one definite hour, and with all secrecy start a rising in every part of the kingdom', wrote a Venetian ambassador, with only slight exaggeration.

The third civil war (1568–70) left the Huguenots more powerful than ever. They preserved the right to exercise their religion (a right which they rarely allowed to Catholics in those regions which they dominated) and were granted the further right to garrison four towns in southern France (Edict of Pacification of St Germain, 8 August 1570). Once more Catherine tried to solve all the kingdom's problems on a personal level. Her daughter Margaret was to marry the young Huguenot leader Henry of Navarre, the son of Anthony de Bourbon. Coligny came to court, in June 1572, and joined the king's council. For several months before the king himself had been in touch with both Louis of Nassau and Elizabeth of England. There was talk of a virtual partition of the Netherlands between France, England and the house of Orange-Nassau. Coligny was, rightly, sceptical. Elizabeth, while willing to play Charles along and to give some help to the Sea Beggars, was determined not to break completely with Spain or to see the French permanently established in Flanders. But when a small contingent of Huguenots marched into the Netherlands and was promptly annihilated by the duke of Alva's army (17 July 1572), Coligny swung round to the need for full-scale French intervention. Perhaps he hoped that he could unite France in a war against the Spaniards. If so, he was vastly over-optimistic about the ability of an exhausted France to face the duke of Alva's formidable *tercios*, the famous Spanish infantry regiments. This prospect terrified the queen mother, and the military experts in the king's council agreed with her. But Coligny persisted. His followers talked of changing the king's council to make it amenable to their plans. What the Huguenots had never even hoped for in three civil wars, they seemed now on the verge of achieving peaceably: the capture of the king's government.

THE MASSACRE OF ST BARTHOLOMEW

Everything seemed to hinge on Coligny. Catherine therefore determined to have him murdered. But the plot misfired; Coligny was only wounded. The Huguenots breathed vengeance; the king promised an investigation. Catherine was desperate, but she managed to persuade the unstable young king that the Huguenots were now planning a *coup*. 'Then kill them all', he is reported to have shouted. This does not seem to have been Catherine's intention. She seems to have wanted to do away with some dozen

Huguenot leaders. But once more and, one may think, again inevitably, events escaped from her control. On the sultry summer's night of 24 August 1572, St Bartholomew's Day, Catherine's son, the duke of Anjou (later Henry III), the Guises, the municipal authorities of Paris and, above all, the Paris mob transformed the selective killings into a general massacre of the Huguenots (and anyone else they disliked) in Paris and in the provinces. This time Coligny did not escape.

It was the worst of the century's religious massacres and in the following two months it was repeated in a dozen French cities. But it was not the first. Both Catholics and Huguenots had for more than ten years indulged in violence. The Huguenots usually attacked the objects of Catholic worship, crucifixes, statues and pictures of saints, stained glass and even the host of the eucharist. All these they held to be the abominations of the pagan and devilish 'Romish' worship, but sometimes their anger also led to the murder of priests or monks. The Catholics tended to attack persons, the perpetrators of such horrors against their venerable beliefs. If the regular religious and secular authorities failed to act, or were thought to fail to act against those who spread the poison of heresy then the people themselves undertook to purge the Christian community, often assigning the bodies of the murdered Huguenots to the symbolically cleansing elements of fire or water. The involvement of 'the common man' in the religious controversies of the age was reaping a harvest unforeseen by either the Protestant or the Catholic reformers.

The civil wars started again. Huguenot organization held firm, was indeed further perfected, but was now confined to a broad arc from Dauphiné through Languedoc and Béarn to Guienne. For the first time the Huguenots were completely on the defensive. But their opponents were more disunited than ever. The massacre of St Bartholomew had a cathartic effect on many Frenchmen; if the quest for religious uniformity led to such horrors, it would be better to sacrifice it for the sake of political unity. This was the belief of the Politiques, a mixed group of Erasmian nobles and businessmen, lawyers, royal officials and all those Catholics who, for various reasons, hated the Guises (see p. 305). This latter group included the Montmorency family and Catherine's youngest son, the duke of Alençon. They were even willing, at times, to support the Huguenots.

Thus the civil wars continued intermittently and with shifting alliances. War had now become part of the structure and habits of French society. The great princely houses, the Bourbons, the Guises, the Montmorencys, knew that war increased their hold over the central government or at least over the provinces they governed. The lower nobility, impoverished by inflation and the devastation of their estates, sought to recoup their fortunes by military service with one or other of the parties. With marauding armies leaving trails of desolation over hundreds of miles, young men came to prefer the life of the plunderer to that of the plundered. The accession of the duke of Anjou, as Henry III, in 1574, made little difference. Much more intelligent than his father or brothers, he yet lacked his mother's persistence and capacity for hard work. Despised by the military nobility of France for his supposed homosexuality and his growing distaste for war, he was not the man to impose himself on the warring factions.

Nevertheless, after 1580, Catherine's ceaseless and exhausting negotiations with party leaders all over France produced some sort of equilibrium. The energies of all parties were diverted into the expedition of the duke of Anjou (formerly Alençon) to the Netherlands (see p. 318). It was characteristic of the dilemma in which Philip II found himself that this situation drove him to negotiate with Henry of Navarre in order to keep alive the civil wars in France and stop French intervention in the Netherlands. Navarre was too canny to fall into this trap; but Philip was soon to have a better opportunity to paralyse France once more.

PHILIP II IN SPAIN: THE MORISCO PROBLEM

After 1559 Spain was the only country of western Europe with an adult male ruler. It was also the country most impervious to all the different Reformation movements. Yet, even here, the mixture of social and religious problems that was so typical of the age could become explosive. This was, at least partly, the king's own fault. Intelligent, conscientious and hard-working, Philip II was a man who found it difficult to make decisions. Yet he was determined that all decisions should be his and he distrusted, or came to distrust, nearly all of his servants who wielded independent power. 'His smile and his dagger are very close to each other', said even his official biographer, Cabrera de Córdova. His unreliability poisoned the politics of his court and turned political and personal rivalries (which he encouraged) into just as deadly struggles for power and survival as they were at the courts of the boy-kings of France.

Philip's system of government was directly responsible for the outbreak of the revolt of the Moriscos of Granada in 1568. Protestantism was never a major problem in Spain, perhaps because heterodoxy had a Jewish or Moorish taint for a people who had come to equate orthodoxy with racial purity. The 'New Christians', the Moriscos, had been forcibly converted in name, but had been assimilated neither in language nor in customs and religious practices; for there was neither the money nor the trained personnel to carry out mass education. The Moriscos remained second-class subjects, exploited, hated and feared by the 'Old Christians' and plagued by bandits of their own race who, when the occasion arose, would make common cause with Moorish sea-raiders from North Africa. As the Turks were launching their great Mediterranean offensives in the 1560s it seemed to the Spaniards that they were harbouring a mortal enemy in their own country.

Two courses seemed possible, and both had their advocates: either to keep the loyalty of the great majority of the Moriscos by closing an eye to their Moorish customs and to continue the very slow process of assimilation by precept; or to repress all Moorish customs and Christianize the Moriscos if necessary by force. But the Spanish system of government made it impossible to pursue any consistent policy at all. All the public authorities in southern Spain were manœuvring for power against each other or quarrelling over land, precedence and authority over the Moriscos: the captain-general, responsible for defence and internal security, which meant the Moriscos and the bandits, was at loggerheads with the Inquisition, both of them with the *audiencia*, the supreme court of southern Spain, and with the municipal council of Granada which, in its turn, was quarrelling with the archbishop who was not on speaking terms with his own cathedral chapter. The government in Madrid sent a special commissioner to settle the disputes over property, and he managed to quarrel with everyone. The weakest group, the Moriscos, suffered most from these quarrels. All parties appealed to Madrid where their disputes became entangled with the factional fights in the king's councils. Philip was slow to interfere.

The quarrels were, after all, not directed against his own authority, even though they virtually paralysed the administration of southern Spain. When he was finally, and characteristically, persuaded to support a policy of rigorous action against the Moriscos and entrust this, not to the experienced captain-general, but to the inexperienced *audiencia*, he turned paralysis into chaos. The Moriscos, feeling completely betrayed, rose in rebellion (Christmas 1568). It took the quarrelling Spanish generals over two years to win a war marked by appalling cruelties on both sides. The defeated Moriscos were driven from their homes and resettled, in small groups, in Castile. It was one more attempt to achieve assimilation and it, too, was to fail.

THE CRISIS IN THE NETHERLANDS

In the Netherlands the crisis would probably have matured even without Philip's mistakes; its ingredients were similar to those of the crisis in France. When Philip left the Netherlands in 1559 he followed his father's custom of appointing as governor-general a member of his family, his half-sister Margaret, duchess of Parma, who was a native of the Netherlands. This was a perfectly proper move and so was Philip's next one, which also followed his father's custom and which was to associate the native high nobility with the government. He appointed them to governorships of the separate provinces and three of the most distinguished seigneurs also to Margaret's Council of State: William of Nassau, prince of Orange, of a German family and the greatest landowner in the Netherlands, the successful general Count Egmont and his friend, Count Hoorne. But whether, as seems likely, Philip did not fully trust them, or whether he simply wanted to keep personal control over the Netherlands government, he secretly commanded his inexperienced sister to consult in all important matters merely with a *consulta* of only three men, two of whom were nonentities. The third, who really mattered, was Cardinal Granvelle, a Franche-Comtois career civil servant whose father had already served Charles V as chancellor.

The result was the opposite of what Philip had intended. Instead of a broadly based government, strongly led and closely linked with Madrid by the able and completely loyal Granvelle, the king had created divisions which rapidly paralysed the Netherlands government and fatally weakened his own authority. Balked from participation in the central control of the Habsburg empire and, now, despite appearances to the contrary, effectively excluded from the running of their own government, the Netherlands seigneurs set themselves to exploit their provincial governorships by arrogating to themselves powers belonging to the government, by interfering in the elections of the town councils and by systematically placing their friends and relatives in key positions in local goverment. In the absence of the king, Granvelle retaliated by using government patronage to build up his own, personal, following in the provinces.

This was bad enough; but the king's reorganization of the Netherlands Church, in 1561, entangled the struggle between the nobles and Granvelle with a much more complex problem and awakened forces and passions which neither side could fully control. To reform an admittedly corrupt Church and to intensify the fight against heresy, Philip obtained from the pope bulls creating fourteen new bishoprics. Granvelle became archbishop of Malines and the new primate of the Netherlands with all the control this gave him over an enormously increased ecclesiastical patronage, much of it taken from the high nobility. Orange saw it both as a dangerous strengthening of royal authority and as an extension of the religious persecution which to him, as to many of the aristocratic and patrician compatriots of Erasmus, was utterly hateful. He and his friends now concentrated their fire on Granvelle, and in this they were skilfully supported by the propaganda of the Protestants which suggested (wrongly) that the new bishoprics were meant as a first step towards the introduction of the dreaded Spanish Inquisition. There existed in any case a highly unpopular papal Inquisition, introduced into the Netherlands by Charles V.

The government was in a weak position. The servicing of the enormous debts left by the late wars was swallowing up most of current revenue. Appeals to the provincial estates gave the opposition a platform for attacking Granvelle and the *placards*, the laws which decreed death for all heretics. Some of the high nobility, notably the duke of Aerschot, of the great Walloon house of Croy, supported Granvelle because they personally disliked Orange and Egmont. Just as in France, the parties tended to crystallize around the family rivalries of the great noble houses.

The king was in no position to intervene, as long as he did not go to the Netherlands himself. Philip held that his father had wasted far too much time, energy and money by his constant travels. He failed to see that these travels had enabled Charles V to remain in personal touch with his subjects, that his personal dispensation of patronage for the loyal and punishment for the rebellious were necessary to keep together an empire which depended not on a common feeling of unity, nor even on institutions, but on the person of the ruler.

But even more important in Philip's view was that Spain desperately needed both his presence and all its financial resources at a time when it was defending itself in the Mediterranean against the most determined Turkish offensive yet. With his son, Don Carlos, showing increasing signs of madness, there was no one to whom Philip could entrust a regency in Spain during his own absence. He therefore tried to placate the opposition by dismissing Granvelle (1564). He had, however, no intention of altering the policy of suppressing heresy nor of giving up his own close control of policy in the Netherlands. He was as determined as ever not to give in to the opposition demand of summoning the States General to solve the religious problem.

Nevertheless, Granvelle's departure weakened the Netherlands government still further. Just as in Germany after 1517 and in France after 1559, it was the weakness of central authority and the conflicting, or apparently conflicting signals of royal intentions which paralysed consistent action, against the reformers. Protestant preaching, both by native Netherlanders and by foreigners coming in from France, Germany and England, was spreading steadily. As yet, the Protestants were not as highly organized as the Huguenots were in France and, again unlike France, they were not led by members of the high nobility, although some of them undoubtedly sympathized with the reformers. Orange, Egmont and Hoorne now returned to an equivocal membership of the regent's Council of State. But by 1565 the Calvinists talked of armed resistance to the *placards* and of seizing towns, in Huguenot fashion. Harvest failure in the autumn of 1565 and war in the Baltic pushed prices to famine level in the winter of 1565–66. Unemployment and hunger were sharpening an already explosive situation. In the early summer, food prices came down, but people remained afraid. A slight rise, at the beginning of August, seems to have been the signal for the outbreak of mob violence.

The Catholics blamed the preachers; but it has never been conclusively proved that the outbreaks were organized. In Antwerp, Ghent and other great cities there was an orgy of church-sacking and image breaking that lasted up to two weeks. The government in Brussels was helpless.

Then the inevitable reaction set in. Noblemen who had only recently presented Margaret with a petition to abolish the Inquisition hastened to assure her of their support. Egmont and most of the high nobility took a new oath of loyalty which Margaret imposed on her council. Philip, for once, sent money and the regent could now raise troops. The armed bands of the Calvinists were dispersed; their leaders were killed or fled. Orange joined them in Germany. He had tried to pursue a moderate policy, supporting the demands of the opposition, but preventing an armed attack by the Calvinists on Antwerp. It earned him bitter denunciation from both sides.

ALVA IN THE NETHERLANDS

It was a commonplace of sixteenth-century statecraft that rebellions should be crushed in their infancy. The Scottish and French governments had failed to do this, and the disasters which had followed this failure were only too apparent. Philip therefore decided to send the duke of Alva, his best general and the advocate of a policy of ruthless suppression of all opposition, to the Netherlands, at the head of a large force of Spanish and Italian troops (1567).

The situation was now very different from that of France. The Netherlands had suddenly acquired a government able and willing to use all necessary means, constitutional or not, to suppress heresy, sedition and, indeed, every type of opposition. Alva arrested, and later executed, Egmont and Hoorne, their privileges as knights of the Golden Fleece notwithstanding. He had always regarded these two, with Orange, as the originators of all the troubles in the Netherlands. He set up a new court which tried and condemned 12,000 persons for having taken part in the previous year's rebellions. So terrified were the Netherlanders that not a single town rose to support the prince of Orange when he invaded the Netherlands from Germany in 1568. But a policy of terror rarely wins friends. As in France after the massacre of St Bartholomew, many good Catholics, like the duke of Aerschot, now began to look for national unity, rather than religious uniformity imposed by Alva's methods. They had friends in Madrid, and Alva knew that he could not count on Philip's indefinite support. With time running out he must, above all, make his government financially secure. A 10 per cent tax on all sales, like the Spanish *alcabalá*, plus a tax on property would certainly do this. Yet Alva, for all that his government was now as absolute as any in the sixteenth century, did not have the machinery to raise such taxes, even after he had modified them to meet the most violent objections. He still needed the cooperation of the local authorities, and to obtain this he summoned the States General, promising an already sceptical Philip that it would be as tame as the cortes of Castile. It was not; and before Alva could bully it into submission, the political situation had become completely transformed, and the 'Tenth Penny', as the tax came to be called, was never levied.

THE REVOLT OF HOLLAND AND ZEELAND: WILLIAM OF ORANGE

In April 1572 the Sea Beggars, Netherlands privateers licensed by the prince of Orange, captured the little port of Brill in Holland. By the summer of 1572 most towns of Zeeland and Holland had fallen to them. A highly organized and skilfully led military and naval force, they could always count on the support of a minority in the town councils and of sections of the artisan classes. The majority of the patrician councils of the Dutch towns were Catholics and loyal to the king, but detested Alva and his regime of terror. They usually agreed to let the Sea Beggars into the towns. Once inside these latter usually broke the agreements, purged the councils of royalists, handed over churches to Calvinist preachers and terrorized the mass of the Catholic burghers into compliance. In July 1572 the estates of Holland met at Dordrecht and invited the prince of Orange to return as governor, nominally still in the name of the king. Orange did his best to stop the terror but he continued to make use of the Beggar movement and organization.

The breach between Philip and William was now complete.

The king saw himself responsible to God for the salvation of his subjects and obliged to safeguard them from heresy. The means he should use to attain to this divinely appointed end were a matter of tactics; they might have to include the most ruthless political despotism, although for Philip such despositism was never an end in itself. William, on the other hand, detested all religious persecution. His political career started in the defence of his aristocratic rights, mostly against the estates of Holland who wanted to tax his property in the province, then progressed to the defence of the rights of his order, and finally came to be identified with the defence of the rights and liberties of his whole country and of the individual conscience against political absolutism and religious persecution. Unlike Coligny, he ceased to be a royalist. He owed his position to the estates and came to lead and manage them with unequalled virtuosity.

Alva had been unable to concentrate on Holland and Zeeland because he had to meet Louis of Nassau's invasion from France. The massacre of St Bartholomew relieved him from his greatest anxiety on his southern flank, a full-scale French attack; but it was then already too late to recapture Holland and Zeeland against the naval superiority of the Hollanders. In 1573 Philip recalled him. Alva's successor, Don Luis de Requesens, stopped the terror but failed both to win back the Netherlands' good opinion of the king or to reconquer rebellious towns protected by broad rivers and flooded marshes. Since the Tenth Penny was never collected, the cost of the war now fell almost exclusively on Spain. In 1575 the Spanish government went bankrupt again. With the collapse of its finances, its military power in the Netherlands collapsed as well. When Requesens died in March 1576 his unpaid troops mutinied. At this point events in the Netherlands completely escaped from the king's control. For almost a year he was neither financially nor, apparently, psychologically capable of even trying to regain it.

THE PACIFICATION OF GHENT

In Brussels, Aerschot and his Politique friends in the Council of State seized the initiative. The estates of Brabant levied troops to protect the country from the mutinous and marauding Spaniards.

They summoned a States General of all the provinces and, on 8 November 1576, they concluded the Pacification of Ghent with Holland and Zeeland. The civil war, it seemed, was at an end. A few days before, however, the Spaniards had put Antwerp to a gruesome sack. But for the moment at least the Spaniards had lost all political power and the king was willing to make every concession demanded of him, except for the maintenance of the Catholic religion and the preservation of his own ultimate authority. He sent his young half-brother, Don John of Austria, the hero of Lepanto and Tunis, as the new governor-general, to preside over the great reconciliation.

But no one could any longer reconcile the divergent interests of the parties or control the fears and passions which revolution and repression had generated. Holland and Zeeland refused to accept Don John's compromise with the States General by which the Spanish troops were to be withdrawn but the Catholic religion restored in all the provinces. Don John, by profession a soldier and by temper an autocrat, found his relations with the States General increasingly frustrating, especially when it had become clear to him that they would not support his plans to liberate and marry Mary Queen of Scots. In 1577 he reverted to a more congenial role and restarted the war by seizing Namur.

Almost immediately it became a civil war again. In Holland and Zeeland the Sea Beggars had made use of the mob; but the patricians remained in control of the town councils and, in consequence, of the assembly of estates. Some patrician families were displaced by others; but there was no social revolution. Even in religion the Calvinist councils were content to exert a steady but peaceful pressure for a very gradual conversion of the majority of the population. But in the much larger cities of Flanders and Brabant the artisans and their guilds had a long tradition of revolutionary action in defence of popular rights. They had as yet gained nothing by the Pacification of Ghent. Now they carried the anti-Spanish revolution a stage further. In Antwerp, Brussels, Ghent and other cities they set up popular war councils, usually dominated by extreme Calvinists. They dismissed the regular magistrates and terrorized the Catholic burghers. In Ghent, a popular Calvinist dictatorship, based on rigid organization and demagogic preaching, held the city in a reign of terror and spread the popular Calvinist revolution through the length and breadth of Flanders.

THE UNIONS OF ARRAS AND UTRECHT

To the Catholic Walloon nobility this seemed a worse tyranny than that of the duke of Alva. The old Croy-Nassau rivalry set them at cross purposes with Orange. In January 1579 the Walloon provinces joined in the Union of Arras and concluded a treaty with the king in which he conceded all their old provincial and aristocratic privileges in return for their renewed allegiance and, of course, the re-establishment of the Catholic religion. The northern provinces formed their own union, of Utrecht, at the same time. This was a Calvinist alliance in which power was effectively shared between the estates and the house of Nassau. In an Act of Abjuration (1581) they renounced their allegiance to Philip II.

Don John had died – luckily for him, for he was already in disgrace at court. The new governor-general was Philip's nephew Alexander Farnese, Margaret of Parma's son. Coldly and methodically, without massacres and with little victimization, he set about the task of reconquering the provinces. Town after town surrendered. Desperately Orange cast about for help. He induced a reluctant States General to swear allegiance to Henry III's brother, the duke of Anjou (formerly Alençon). They needed his troops but were unwilling to give him political authority. Once more the lines of political and religious allegiance were crossed. More and more the Netherlands were becoming the focal point for all the political and religious struggles of western Europe – the only place where, as yet, France and England were beginning to challenge the hegemony of Spain.

SPAIN TAKES THE OFFENSIVE: PORTUGAL

For the first twenty-five years of his reign, Philip II had remained on the defensive, reacting to circumstances, rather than taking the initiative. Such a role suited him temperamentally; his epithet, the Prudent King, was well deserved. But this role was also forced on him by his political and financial situation. He was fighting the greatest military and naval power in Europe, the Turks, and even after Don John of Austria's brilliant tactical victory of Lepanto (7 October 1571), the Spaniards could only just hold the central Mediterranean against renewed Turkish attacks (see p. 248).

In 1580, however, Philip signed a truce with the Sultan. Both empires were turning their attention outwards, away from the Mediterranean where neither could break the stalemate. In the same year Philip conquered Portugal. It was his first genuine initiative, and it was a brilliant success.

In 1578 the young King Sebastian of Portugal led a crusade into Morocco. In the battle of Alcazar-el-Kebir he was slain and his army annihilated. King Sebastian had no children. His successor, the last legitimate member of the house of Avis, the elderly Cardinal Henry, was not expected to live long. Once again, the failure of a royal line produced a major political crisis. Philip II had good hereditary claims to the Portuguese crown: but it was immediately clear that neither the majority of the Portuguese nor the European powers were willing to accept a Spanish succession. An illegitimate member of the old ruling house, Antonio, prior of Crato, tried to organize the resistance to Spain. Elizabeth I of England and Catherine de Medici encouraged him. When the cardinal-king died in 1580 Philip sent the duke of Alva with an army into Portugal. The majority of the Portuguese ruling classes had been won over by bribes and promises. English and French help for Antonio, predictably, did not materialize. Lisbon and Oporto fell after a few weeks to the last of the old duke's typically brilliant and atrocity-stained campaigns. It left bitter memories which the pretender, Antonio, continued to exploit. But for the time being the Portuguese ruling classes were well enough satisfied. Philip left them in possession of all their privileges and of the administration of their colonial empire.

The moving spirit and organizer of the annexation of Portugal had been Cardinal Granvelle now, for the first time, in Madrid as the king's principal adviser. The cardinal and Philip's Spanish advisers continued to press for a determined retaliation against French and English interference in Philip's concerns. Their pirates, euphemistically called privateers, were disrupting Spain's legitimate trade with her colonies; their soldiers were supporting the rebels of Portugal and the Netherlands. Gradually, Philip was persuaded.

HENRY III AND THE LEAGUE

Once again, the crisis broke with a death in a ruling house. In the spring of 1584 the duke of Anjou died. Henry III had no sons, and the Bourbon Henry of Navarre therefore became the next legitimate heir to the French crown. The prospect of a Huguenot king immediately upset the precarious equilibrium in France which Catherine de Medici had achieved after so much trouble. In Paris a number of priests, professional men and other bourgeois organized a Catholic party among the artisans, shopkeepers and public officials of the capital. In other cities similar organizations sprang up, often with Parisian inspiration and usually in close communication with Paris. In the countryside there had been local organizations of Catholic noblemen, in some places already from the beginning of the civil wars. In 1576 these had coalesced into a Catholic League covering most of France; but when Henry III had tried to make himself head of this League, it had dissolved itself. Now, in 1584, it reappeared, but with Henry duke of Guise as its head, and with the support of the whole enormous Guise connection. When Guise took up contact with the Paris League, he found himself, like Condé and Coligny on the Protestant side, at the head of a highly organized and potentially revolutionary party. In town after town the League replaced royalist commanders and officials by their own men. On 31 December 1584 Guise concluded a formal treaty with Spain. Philip had thus achieved what his father had always vainly striven for: a Franco-Spanish alliance in the Catholic interest, and with Spain as senior partner. As yet, he had got it with only one party in France; but it looked as if the League might prove to be the strongest one. In the summer of 1585 civil war broke out again in France. France was therefore out of action, and Philip could concentrate on his other enemies.

ENGLISH INTERVENTION IN THE NETHERLANDS

Only England could now help the Netherlands, and the Union of Utrecht needed help urgently. On 10 July 1584 Orange fell to the bullets of a fanatical assassin whose family were duly given the reward which Philip II had promised for such a deed. William's legend, which started from the moment of his death, helped to keep alive the will to resist and, eventually, to develop a new national identity of the provinces forming the Union of Utrecht. But the immediate prospects looked black. That summer and during the following spring Farnese captured most of the big cities of Brabant and Flanders. Antwerp surrendered in August 1585. Elizabeth now made up her mind and concluded a regular alliance with the Union of Utrecht. The earl of Leicester was to have a seat in the Dutch council and to take an English army of 5,000 to the Netherlands.

It was a hard decision. For twenty-five years the queen and her chief adviser, Lord Burghley, had manœuvred between the great powers, France and Spain. Traditionally, and by virtue of her geographical position, France represented the greater danger to England. The marriage alliance of the Guises with the Scottish royal family (see p. 271) was a deadly threat, especially to the English queen whose legitimacy was questioned by many Catholics. Mary, on the other hand, had a legitimate claim to the English throne. The Protestant revolution in Scotland (judiciously supported by Elizabeth) and Mary Stuart's political ineptitude removed the direct threat from Scotland. But Mary remained a menace, even after her flight to, and imprisonment in, England (1568), especially after Pius V excommunicated Elizabeth. Moreover, not only France but Spain too might intervene in Mary's favour. To be sure, neither of the great powers was at all anxious to see the other dominate England; but this was a very unreliable safeguard. The queen's own life was constantly threatened by plots. If any of them were to succeed, so her anxious subjects feared, their country could hardly escape civil war and foreign domination.

Elizabeth was therefore as anxious as Philip II to see the civil wars continue in France – and as anxious as Catherine de Medici to see them continue in the Netherlands. Her positive aims were more modest: the return of Calais from France and plunder from the Spanish colonial empire. These aims did not make her relations with France and Spain any easier; nevertheless it was in the interests of all three powers to avoid a complete breach. Even while the States General of the Union of Utrecht (now generally known as the United Provinces) proclaimed Leicester governor-general (contrary to Elizabeth's declared wishes) she continued to negotiate with Philip. She hoped that her military intervention would force him to grant a reasonable settlement both to herself and to the United Provinces. But the Dutch had ceased to believe in the possibility of such a settlement. They looked on the Anglo-Spanish negotiations as a downright betrayal. More than Leicester's personal incompetence and his mishandling of a very difficult situation, these divergent aims turned his mission into a fiasco. Elizabeth's reputation on the Continent never fully recovered.[6] For fear of Spain, the common enemy, England and the United Provinces remained in uneasy and distrustful alliance. But the Dutch patricians had learnt their lesson. No longer would they look for a foreign sovereign but they would claim sovereignty for their own estates.

THE 'ENTERPRISE OF ENGLAND'

In the spring of 1585 Philip made up his mind to strike at England. If he succeeded, the remainder of the rebellious provinces of the Netherlands would be easily reconquered, Spanish preponderance in western Europe would be unchallenged, and the Catholic religion would be restored at the very centres of heresy. Neither the king nor any of his advisers were under any illusions about the enormous difficulty of the 'Enterprise of England', least of all of the superiority of English naval gunnery or the tactics which the English fleet was likely to pursue; but all of them thought the enterprise was feasible and would work. For three years Philip doggedly pushed ahead his preparations, despite the inevitable administrative muddles, the enormous cost, the death of his supreme commander and Drake's destructive raid on Cadiz in 1587. In Philip's favour were the vastly increased imports of American silver, the fine naval traditions of his Spanish and Portuguese subjects and, not least, his and their conviction of the justice of his cause. France was kept out of action by Philip's alliance with the League. In May 1588 Henry III was driven from Paris by a rising in favour of Guise. This 'Day of the Barricades' was organized by the Paris League and seems to have been engineered by the Spanish ambassador in Paris to coincide, as far as possible, with the sailing of the Armada. Farnese, now duke of Parma, was to be in readiness with an army of 30,000 which he was to take across to England in barges, once the Armada had gained control over the Straits of Dover.

Parma, offended that he would have to share the command of

the expedition with the admiral of the Armada, veered between optimism and pessimism. Not until early in 1588 did he appreciate that the Dutch fleet would sink his barges and that the Armada, without a deep-water harbour on the Netherlands coast, would never be able to protect him, even if it had defeated the English fleet. But if Parma believed that the 'Enterprise of England' was doomed from the start, he never actually said so.

On 30 July 1588 the Spanish Armada entered the English Channel. For a whole week it fought a running gunnery battle with the English fleet. It was the biggest sea battle fought up till then and the first of a long series, stretching into the Second World War, fought entirely by artillery.[7] Neither side managed to do very much damage to the other. The decision came when the Armada, without the shelter of a deepwater port, had first to face English fire ships and then a close-range gunnery attack that, for lack of ammunition, it could no longer answer. This was the end of the Armada as an effective fighting force, although it suffered its greatest losses on the reefs of the Scottish and Irish coasts. In the end about half of the 145 ships which had left Spain managed to reach Spanish ports again – in the circumstances a fine achievement for the Spanish admiral, the duke of Medina Sidonia. To his contemporaries Medina Sidonia became the scapegoat of the disaster; only recent scholarship has restored his reputation as a brave and far from incompetent leader. Philip II never blamed him. He did not lack a certain magnanimity and he always showed a sincere humility before God's inscrutable purpose.

England was now ranged irrevocably alongside Spain's enemies. Both sides made plans for renewed attack. The English ones, in 1589 on Portugal and in 1596 on Cadiz, were spectacular but strategically ineffective. Several Spanish attacks were wrecked by storms. In 1601 the Spaniards landed in Ireland. But this was no longer an invasion attempt by a great armada. When their Irish allies had been defeated, the small Spanish force at Kinsale had to surrender.

More and more Philip's efforts came to be concentrated on France. Here, it seemed to him, he might yet retrieve the disaster of the 'Enterprise of England'. This disaster had given Henry III renewed courage. But the French king was still thinking of politics as he had done in 1572, at the time of the ascendancy of Coligny. On 23 December 1588 he had Guise assassinated and, a day later, despatched the duke's brother, the Cardinal of Guise.

THE PROBLEM OF A HUGUENOT SUCCESSION TO THE FRENCH THRONE

There was an immediate feeling of revulsion against the king. The Sorbonne declared his subjects to be absolved from their oath of allegiance to him. The League recognized Guise's brother, the duke of Mayenne, as lieutenant-governor of the realm. Soon the king's authority was reduced to his fortresses in the Loire valley. Rather than abdicate the authority of the monarchy to an openly revolutionary party, he now allied himself with the Huguenot leader, Henry of Navarre. But assassination for religious reasons had been justified too often (see pp. 333 ff). Europe was now swarming with would-be tyrant killers. On 1 August 1589, Henry III himself suffered the fate of Coligny and Guise. Dying, he recognized Navarre as his successor if he agreed to become a Catholic.

At first, Navarre's chances did not look good. Few Catholic royalists would, as yet, support him. Twice Parma intervened with his veteran army from the Netherlands and relieved the king's sieges of Paris (1590) and Rouen (1592). Elizabeth gave help, but she could not match the scale of Philip's intervention. After the death of Pope Sixtus V, in 1590, Philip's ambassador in Rome engineered the election of three successive pro-Spanish popes. The majority of the college of cardinals were dependent, in one form or another, on Spanish patronage; but never before had the Spanish monarchy used this power so ruthlessly. For the first and last time, the political and military alliances in western Europe coincided completely with religious affiliations. In France it looked as if the Catholics were the winning side.

But the aims of the different partners of the Catholic alliances were too divergent. Mayenne found it impossible to reconcile the aristocratic and the popular wings of the League – just as Orange had found it impossible in the parallel situation of the Protestant revolution in Flanders and Brabant ten years before. In Paris the League was dominated by the bourgeoisie and organized under a Committee of Sixteen (for the sixteen quarters of the city). The Reformation, among its many other effects, had, for the first time in European history, brought forward intellectuals as an important political force, rather than just as inspirers of others, propagandists and rationalizers. They were prominent in the Huguenot towns. In the Paris League they displayed that characteristic mixture of rationalism and fanaticism with which we have since become familiar in revolutionary movements. They were openly hostile to the nobility and the Parisian patricians, while their special hatred was reserved for the conservative parlement of Paris whose president and two councillors they arrested and executed for alleged treason (November 1591). Mayenne reacted half-heartedly by arresting several of the members of the Committee of Sixteen but refusing to destroy their organization completely. This action lost him the support of the popular wing of the League without placating the outraged nobility and the parlement.

The duke was aiming for the crown for himself; but his paymaster, Philip II, was trying to place his daughter, Isabella Clara Eugenia, on the throne of France. The dukes of Savoy and Lorraine had ambitions in the same direction but contented themselves with claiming kingdoms in Provence and Champagne respectively. In 1592 the college of cardinals finally grew tired of being bullied by the Spanish ambassador and, in the most dramatic conclave of the century, rejected his candidate by one vote. Instead they elected a young cardinal who was not directly dependent on Spain. Clement VIII still supported the League; but he had room for manœuvre and was prepared to listen to Henry IV's envoys. No longer was the pope willing to be 'the king of Spain's chaplain'.

HENRY IV AND THE END OF THE CIVIL WARS IN FRANCE

The crisis came with the States General of 1593. Mayenne had reluctantly summoned them because Philip wished them to set aside the Salic Law in favour of his daughter. Henry IV chose this moment to announce his return to the Catholic Church. He alone, it seemed, could prevent the breaking up of France and its complete domination by Spain. Now that he was no longer a heretic, 'France threw herself into his arms', as a prominent member of the League said. The League collapsed. On 22 March 1594 Henry entered Paris. As was his habit, he took no revenge but only banished for a short time a small number of preachers and leaders of the League. One after another, its aristocratic leaders made their peace with the king – always on generous terms, for thus Henry hoped to end the civil war. When he declared war on Spain in 1595 he had a practically united France behind him. As leader of the Huguenots he could no more have achieved this than Coligny when he tried it twenty-three years before. As king of France and a Catholic who was willing to tolerate the Huguenots, he now could.

To achieve effective toleration was not easy. Henry himself had no doubts about its necessity. But the old hatreds and suspicions on both sides were not easily stilled. The Edict of Nantes (April/May 1598) was a compromise in the tradition of compromises by which Catherine de Medici had so often tried to restore peace. The Huguenots were allowed freedom to worship where they had worshipped before, except in Paris, and they were granted some hundred places of security – small towns, which they garrisoned at royal expense. It was the state within the state which even non-fanatical Catholics, like the chancellor l'Hôpital, had always sought to prevent. But for the time being no one was willing to start the civil war again on this account.

THE REVOLUTIONARY PARTIES OF THE SIXTEENTH CENTURY

Henry IV, like Condé and Coligny, and also like Guise, Mayenne and Orange, had been the leader of a revolutionary party. No more than these other leaders had he created his party. His aim, as that of many aristocratic rebels before him, had been to capture the existing machinery of government without overturning the existing social order or the political structure of his country. Yet he, like the other leaders, had been carried far along the paths of political and social revolution by his party. These parties were effectively revolutionary by virtue of their combination of religious beliefs, ambitions and fears with political and social discontents. It was religion which kept together in one organization nobles and merchants, princes and artisans. It was not, however, so much the dogmas of a particular religion which made it revolutionary but the fact that its adherents felt themselves threatened by, or wanted to capture, a hostile state. Preachers and propagandists had no more difficulty in giving a revolutionary twist to the most respectable and time-honoured dogmas of the Catholic Church than to the ambiguities and equivocations of

Calvin's theology of political power. The Catholic bourgeois of Paris were as effectively revolutionary as the Protestant artisans of Ghent. Yet the revolutionary parties were all inherently unstable and success always broke them up; for the nobility would never be reconciled to a popular dictatorship, Protestant or Catholic. Both William of Orange and Henry IV understood this perfectly and both tried to take religion out of politics, once they had achieved their own, mainly political, purposes. For William this was bound to mean co-operation with the patrician States General. Once the revolutionary organization of the Sea Beggars had served its purpose and could be dismantled, William could have no other possible backing. For Henry it meant the reconstruction of royal absolutism. This fitted in with his distinctly autocratic temperament; but it also followed logically from the anti-absolutist position of both the religious extremist parties in France, the Huguenots and the League. Against them, Henry represented the Politique view, and this had come to be identified with royal absolutism; for only a strong monarchy could guarantee both the religious peace and the integrity of the state.

Those who lost out were, in every case, the politically radical preachers or priests and the lower classes. Neither in the United Provinces nor in France were the Calvinist preachers allowed to set up a rigid theocracy on the Geneva (or, later, New England) model; nor were the League preachers allowed to maintain their Catholic popular dictatorship. Revolutionary action in France changed into a melancholy succession of peasant revolts, directed against rents, tithes and *taille*, regardless of religion or political party. In the United Provinces, Calvinist preachers and popular leaders maintained some sort of alliance and were, from time to time, made use of by the house of Nassau in its struggles with the patrician oligarchy of the Estates. The crisis of European society was not resolved; but at the end of the sixteenth century the traditional ruling classes were still as firmly in power as they were at the beginning.

SPAIN AT WAR WITH ENGLAND, FRANCE AND THE UNITED PROVINCES

Henry IV's declaration of war on Spain broke the religious alignment of western European power politics. In international relations, as in the internal affairs of France, the Franco-Spanish war was a victory for the Politique idea of the primacy of reason of state over that of religion. The European state system was beginning to solidify. The United Provinces, no longer in search of a foreign sovereign, were accepted as equal partners in an alliance by the king of France and, with characteristic reluctance, by the queen of England. Spain was no longer engaged in putting down a rebellion and intervening in a civil war, but in open warfare against the major powers of western Europe.

This war she could no longer win. In 1596 Philip II's government went bankrupt for the third time. Even the obedient cortes of Castille were now openly questioning the wisdom of continuing the war. Parma's diversions into France had killed the last chance of defeating the Dutch. Parma died in 1592, like his uncle, Don John of Austria, only just in time to avoid his public disgrace. The young Maurice of Nassau, William's son, methodically reconquered all the offensive positions on the southern and eastern flank of the United Provinces that Parma had built up with so much skill in the previous years. Except for occasional sorties by one side or the other, the front now remained relatively stable, along the line of the great rivers. The unrepentant Protestants from the southern provinces had long since fled to Holland and there helped to found its spectacular economic success. The south, aristocratic and Catholic, had maintained its privileges and much of its political autonomy. Modern Belgium was beginning to emerge, with its own feeling of unity, different and separate from that of the United Provinces.

The anti-Spanish alliance was as unstable as the Catholic alliance had been. Here, too, the interests of its partners were too divergent. On 2 May 1598 France and Spain concluded the Peace of Vervins, on substantially the same terms as the Treaty of Cateau-Cambrésis. A few months later Philip II was dead (13 September 1598). The great plans of his last fifteen years had been checked. But he had fulfilled his original intention of preserving his dominions and defending the Catholic faith wherever he could. The northern Netherlands were lost, but not yet, he hoped, irrevocably. He had fought off the Turkish threat; he had acquired the crown of Portugal with its great empire, and, by his intervention in France, he had perhaps even saved that country from being ruled by a heretic king; for while this was not the intention of Philip's intervention, would Henry IV have otherwise been obliged to return to the Catholic Church? These were great achievements. Yet to attain them he had sacrificed the treasures of the Indies and the blood and property of his Castilian subjects. Philip II left Spain with its imperial tradition confirmed but with an economy unable to bear the strains which this tradition had come to involve. There were Spaniards who could see this clearly enough. No one, as yet, could foresee the full extent of the decline of the seventeeth century.

The political and revolutionary struggles of the age of Philip II were closely linked to the forces which the Reformation had unleashed. Within the context of the changing political scene in the second half of the sixteenth century we can see a change in men's attitudes towards authority, the nation state and toleration. The religious thought which evolved from the Reformations had become an integral part of man's attitudes towards life as a whole, fusing in this manner with the necessities of his political environment and his social as well as his economic aspirations.

NOTES AND REFERENCES

1   *Correspondance de Philippé II sur les affaires des Pays-Bas*, ed. P. L. Gachard (Brussels, 1848), vol. pp. 446 ff.

2   Earl of Argyll and Lord James Stuart to the English agent in Scotland, 6 August 1559. *Calendar of Scottish Papers*, vol. 1. p. 240.

3   S. Peller, 'Births and deaths among Europe's ruling families since 1500', in *Population in History*, ed. E. V. Glass and D. E. C. Eversley (London, 1965). We wish to thank Professor C. W. J. Granger, of the University of Nottingham, for working out this probability from the available data. We still lack a thorough statistical analysis of the ruling families of Europe during this period. It would be well worth having; but we doubt whether the result would be very far out from the present calculation.

4   After the death of Louis XI, in 1483, France had only one succession of an adult son following directly on his father (Henry II following Francis I, 1547) before the end of the monarchy. There were six minorities; Charles VIII, Francis II (effectively, if not legally), Charles IX, Louis XIII, Louis XIV and Louis XV. By contrast, the effective establishment of absolutism in Prussia depended in no small degree on the fact that the Hohenzollern were spared minorities during two crucial centuries. Few ruling

families were as lucky; certainly not the Tudors. Henry VIII, with six wives and living to the age of fifty-six, left only one sickly male heir and two females to succeed him.

5 Lorenzo Contarini, 'Relazione di Francia', in Albèri *Relazioni degli ambasciatori veneti* (Florence, 1839), ser. 1, vol. IV, p. 60.

6 This is so even in modern Continental historigraphy. Arguments based on the exigencies of reason of state, or even national security and perhaps survival, have an unfortunate habit of appearing to outsiders like special pleading. *Mutatis mutandis*, this applies of course to the historiography of Philip II, Henry IV and William of Orange as much as to that of Elizabeth I.

7 This point is made by G. Mattingly, *The Defeat of the Spanish Armada* (London, 1959). For the important problems of gunnery, see M. A. Lewis, *The Armada Guns* (London, 1961) and C. Martin and G. Parker, *The Spanish Armada* (London, 1988).

13

POLITICAL THEORY AND RELIGIOUS STRIFE

THE SPREAD OF THE REFORMATION

By mid-century the Reformations were solidly established. The year 1555 saw Lutheranism recognized in the Empire at the Peace of Augsburg and Calvin's final and decisive victory in Geneva. It was also the year in which King Sigismund II Augustus of Poland granted freedom of worship to all Protestants, including the radicals. The Catholic Reformation had embarked on its course: the second session of the Council of Trent at which the Lutherans had made a brief appearance was over, and in 1555 Paul IV ascended the papal throne, typifying the radicalization of Catholicism in its opposition against the Protestants. Poland, in the east, seemed definitely lost, but England that same year was returning to the Catholic fold.

The second half of the sixteenth century opened against the background of a fluid situation; only Spain was firmly settled in her religion and the Empire had gained a breathing space at the Peace of Augsburg which was to last for the rest of the century. The clashes and disputes which tore the other nations apart had a twofold aspect: not only did Protestant fight against Catholic, but one form of Protestantism was pitted against another. Europe paid the price for the failure of attempts at reconciliation among Protestants as well as among Protestants and Catholics. Many nations, like England, had to fight a war on two fronts: against the 'Antichrist' of Rome and against those who spread 'satanic' opinions from within the anti–Catholic fold.

These battles became an integral part of the national rivalries of the great powers, both within the different states and in the international patterns of religious loyalties. The evolution of political and religious thought was largely determined by the international and civil wars which dominated the last decades of the sixteenth century.

THEORIES OF RESISTANCE IN ENGLAND

Protestantism had never lacked self confidence, nor had it shunned conflict and even war in order to establish itself. However, it was in the second half of the sixteenth century, when the battle between Protestantism and Catholicism was equally joined, that it began to construct elaborate theories of resistance to authority. English Protestantism took the lead here; it had tasted power, and when Catholic Mary I succeeded her brother Edward VI, had lost it again. At that time many of her Protestant subjects fled to exile on the continent and conducted a vigorous campaign in print against her and her religious policies. A common theme in these tracts was the question of obedience to a persecuting monarch. Some advised flight or martyrdom rather than obeying an ungodly command; others proclaimed that a proper response to tyranny was violent rebellion. Though these advocates of resistance were clearly inspired by the writings of the Reformers themselves, most of whom had approved resistance under certain conditions, the English exiles were far more radical than their mentors. Where European Protestants would sanction rebellion only when the true religion was imperilled, many English writers urged their countrymen to rise up for a number of economic and political reasons. For example, some tried to appeal to the country's widespread hostility to the Spaniards who had arrived since the Queen's marriage to Philip of Spain by enumerating Spanish extortion and atrocities in other countries, while others urged rebellion because the queen was not only a tyrant but was also a usurper, without a legitimate title to the throne.

The most articulate of those who urged violence for secular reasons was John Ponet, the exiled Bishop of Winchester, who in *A Short Treatise of Politic Power* (1556) maintained that the basis of any ruler's power was a contract with his people; that they would obey him as long as he maintained justice and ruled without tyranny. Should he break this contract through religious persecution or by depriving his subjects of their goods or murdering them, the people might justifiably rebel and replace him with a leader more to their liking. In most cases, this resistance ought to be carried out by representatives of the sovereign people, such as parliament or officers of the state, but Ponet had little faith in his own country's political class who had proven too weak and greedy to withstand the Queen. For this reason, he directed his readers' attention to the long and honourable history of assassination, and sanctioned tyrannicide by anyone who felt called by God to eliminate an evil ruler whom the nation had tolerated for too long.

Such ideas were taken up by other Englishmen who tried to put them in practice in a wide variety of conspiracies and even through an invasion of Yorkshire by a band of patriots and mercenaries. In 1557, however, England was at war with France and many who had exiled themselves for primarily non-religious reasons came home to fight for their country. One consequence of this was a shift in the propaganda directed against Queen Mary; secular reasons for rebellion were no longer advanced and the leadership in this campaign against Mary passed into the hands of exiles living in Calvin's Geneva. This colony of Englishmen and Scotsmen had always considered themselves more rigorous in religion and less open to compromise than other exiles, and their resistance theories reflect this boldness. Had Englishmen, for example, followed the advice of Christopher Goodman, *How Superior Powers Ought to be Obeyed* (1558), the result would have been revolutionary. Goodman believed that England was bound by the convenant that Moses and the Israelites had made with God, in which they had promised to be His people and obey him. As prescribed in the Book of Deuteronomy, a ruler could only be a native-born male of the true religion, qualifications Queen Mary failed to meet. Because they had ignored Scripture and followed human rules, Englishmen were cursed with a murderous queen, who meant to yield the country to foreign idolaters. Faced with such a tyrant violent resistance was legitimate. Though this should first be undertaken by inferior magistrates, resistance was the responsibility of the people themselves should their leaders fail to act.

This attack on female rule was not a new theme and had been discussed in exile tracts before Goodman's, but it was to receive its most famous and comprehensive treatment in a work by John Knox, *The First Blast of the Trumpet Against the Monstrous Regiment of Women* (1558). Using an array of Greek philosophers, Church fathers and observations from nature to bolster his scriptural arguments, Knox claimed that women were a weak and unstable sex whose rule often led to idolatry, a sin which Protestants equated with the Catholic Mass. As God had forbidden women to rule, any queen was therefore a usurper and could be deposed. Though he believed the inferior magistrates should lead the opposition, Knox made it clear that the common people had a role to play in this process as well. Like Goodman, he believed sixteenth-century Christians were bound by the Israelites' covenant with God, a covenant which obliged even the commons to destroy idolatry and take a hand in ridding themselves of their tyrannous rulers.

The very year that saw the appearance of these controversial writings also saw the death of Queen Mary and the succession of her Protestant sister Elizabeth. The Marian exiles headed home to help rebuild the English Church but their opinions on women's rule had made Knox and Goodman so unpopular with the English government that they went to Scotland instead. Though Knox and Goodman were for a time unwelcome, most of the exile ideas about resistance remained current under Elizabeth, not because they were directed against her but because they were useful in countering the claims of Mary Queen of Scots[1] and in defending the actions of European Protestants in their civil wars.

THEORIES OF RESISTANCE IN FRANCE

Civil war broke out in France in 1562 but it was not until after the massacre of St Bartholomew in 1572 that French Protestant writers openly advocated violent resistance to the monarchy. Until then they had shared Calvin's own distaste for conspiracy and had focused their propaganda on the threat to the crown and nation from the Catholic Guise faction. The massacre of August 1572 forced Huguenot writers to confront the French monarchy as tyrants and to advocate, in different ways, the idea of popular sovereignty and resistance by the people or their representatives.

The most restrained and learned of these Protestant writings on resistance was *Francogallia* by the lawyer Francis Hotman, which appeared in 1573.[2] Hotman wished his conclusions to have the widest possible readership and so grounded his arguments, not on Protestant polemic or the Bible, but in over a thousand years of constitutional history. By showing that the original constitution of the French people was a mixed one, giving very limited powers to the king, and by demonstrating that this principle had continued throughout succeeding centuries. Hotman hoped to undermine the power of the persecuting monarchy. French kings, he said, were originally nothing more than magistrates elected for life with the real power residing in the assembly of the people. This assembly, not the king, had the power to make laws, decide on war or peace and confer honours. Moreover, the assembly had the power to depose kings for useless or tyrannous rule and to appoint a successor. Hotman maintained that the ancient constitution was still in effect. Huguenot strength lay among nobles and in the provinces and any theory which inflated the importance of the Estates-General where they could make their influence felt would be to the benefit of the Protestant party.

Theodore Beza, Calvin's successor at Geneva, believed that there was an implicit contract between a ruler and the people, with their obedience conditional on the prince's good government. Should he prove to be a tyrant, they might call on either inferior magistrates or the Estates to resist him. In *The Right of Magistrates over their Subjects* (1574), Beza discounted the rights of the commons to defend themselves but did suggest that an individual assassin might act against a usurper or against a legitimate ruler turned oppressor if inspired by God. There were other more radical advocates of resistance. The anonymous *Political Discourses* (1578) allowed the people themselves to exterminate a tyrant and scorned those who would restrict tyrannicide to only those with a special calling from God. (In fact, assassination became somewhat of an epidemic among both Protestant and Catholic extremists, claiming the lives of three leaders of the Guise faction, two kings of France and William of Orange, on whose head Philip II had placed a bounty.)

THE COVENANT

Many, perhaps most, resistance theories appealed to the biblical covenant between God and people against the exercise of arbitrary power.

Calvin had written about the covenant which God had made with man and which He had fulfilled for the elect through Christ's redemptory role. Now it was up to man to keep his side of the bargain through obedience. Such ideas had been extended by the

1580s, largely through the work of Heidelberg theologians, to incorporate the whole range of life on earth. This was done through the 'Covenant of works' which did not just apply to the 'elect' but to all men. It had been made between God and Adam who represented all mankind. This Covenant fastened religious and secular obligations upon man, whether elect or not. The state contract theory by which the government has its roots in the people contracting together was incorporated within it.

The *Vindiciae Contra Tyrannos* (1579), the most famous Huguenot tract, posits a double contract: between the king and people jointly on the one hand, and God on the other, and a second contract between the people and the king. The first contract bound the community to the true Church, the second contract (being also a part of God's order) could be used to put down a tyrannical monarch. For the people had given their power to the monarch only conditionally (the essence of any contractual theory of government) – that he rule well and justly and keep the faith. As long as the king fulfils his functions he must be obeyed, for his power is from God. But if he does not, he can be deposed; however, the people themselves take no part in this action. Once more power is delegated, and the 'inferior magistrates' must take action. They were, as Calvin had held, the guardians of the rights of the people – in the terms of the *Vindiciae* they were the guardians of the covenants.

This use of covenants stripped the king of that personal, inherited, magic with which he had been endowed as part of a cosmic hierarchy encompassing both heaven and earth. Protestantism destroyed that hierarchy. It was now no longer the personal status of the king which mattered, but how well he fulfilled his office and practised his 'vocation'. The ruler was put upon the same level with all Christians, to be judged by how well religious duties were fulfilled, and these included all 'vocations', however humble. This is what both Hotman and the author of the *Vindiciae* meant when they held that magistracy is ordained by God for the benefit of men.

CATHOLIC RESISTANCE THEORY

The propagandists of the Catholic League argued first that no heretic could rule and some even used arguments similar to Knox and Goodman in insisting that the Book of Deuteronomy be followed in determining a king. Eventually, however, the League grew more radical and turned on Henry III who had murdered the Guise leadership. This necessitated arguments for resistance that would sanction violence against even a Catholic ruler.[3] Convinced that the great majority of Frenchmen were loyal to their cause, and that inferior magistrates were not needed, members of the League produced works emphasizing popular sovereignty and the right of the people to depose a tyrant. When Henry III was assassinated in 1589, and Henry of Navarre succeeded him as King Henry IV, some League writers, treated the assassin as a religious and patriotic martyr. The best of the League works was *The Just Authority of a Christian Commonwealth* (1590), which may have been written by an English exile, William Reynolds. The work advocated an end to inherited kingship and called for the popular election of rulers after candidates had been ruled fit for office by the Church. Should the ruler prove to be a tyrant by seizing his subjects' goods, breaking laws or attacking religion, the people may declare him subject to tyrannicide.

Both Huguenots and French Catholic theorists were able to see their ideas on resistance put into practice but another group of dissident writers was not. These were the English Catholic exiles who called on their countrymen to rise up against the heretic Elizabeth.[4] The most important of these Catholic works was Robert Person's *A Conference about the Next Succession* (1595), which agreed with earlier tracts in supporting popular sovereignty, that the people themselves may cast off an evil ruler. Person's book became a sourcebook for many seventeenth-century discussions of resistance, quoted and reissued by both Catholics and Protestants.

Jesuits throughout Europe were the most active theorists about the right to resist an ungodly ruler as the sixteenth century came to a close. Some like the Spaniard Juan de Mariana emphasized the necessity of tyrannicide, even by private persons, and saw one of his books burned by the public executioner in front of the Cathedral of Notre Dame in Paris. But the influential Jesuit theorist, Robert Bellarmine (1542–1621), took a more legalistic position in face of the newly strengthened national monarchies. A tyrant could be deposed, to be sure, but only for actually endangering the people's souls, and solely by the pope before whom all men are equal according to divine law. Bellarmine sought to make a sharp distinction between the secular and the spiritual – only the latter can transform a ruler into a tyrant. His theory of the 'indirect power of the papacy' attempted to base the secular aspects of government upon the people who delegate them to the king, while the religious aspects come directly from God and of these the pope is custodian.

Though Bellarmine's ideas remained current, in the long run such a distinction was difficult to maintain. Monarchs like Henry IV intended to rule their own Church. The future lay with the national monarchies who wanted to protect and define their powers as over against resistance theories which seemed responsible for religious strife. Such attempts at strengthening the king's power by providing the appropriate theory took a great leap forward in the religious wars: they expressed in theory what Catherine de Medici and Henry IV wanted to accomplish in practice, while fitting the ambitions of other hard-pressed national monarchs such as Queen Elizabeth of England.

SOVEREIGNTY AND THE DIVINE RIGHT OF KINGS

Jean Bodin became their most famous theoretician, and his *République* (1576) a work of great influence. Within the chaos of civil war he made an assertion which was new: that there *must* be an authority in the state which is supreme, and that this authority must unite the making, enforcing, and judging of law, in its own hands. Bodin believed that no state could exist without this kind of sovereignty. Something new and revolutionary was thus formulated out of the French experience: the modern doctrine of political authority. Medieval political thought, and that of Bodin's Huguenot and Jesuit contemporaries, had stressed the 'shared' authority of the ruler; with the estates, under the law — sovereignty here was mixed. Bodin went back to the Justinian tradition of Roman law and held that sovereignty could never be mixed but must have a clearly defined centre of authority. To be sure, he still included some medieval limitations in his theory; the sovereign must not break contracts or take property without consent. But these held only in normal times, and in an emergency the ruler's authority was absolute.

This was a clear response to doctrines of resistance, to attacks upon the national monarchies. The French kings made good use of this doctrine, in order to circumvent the Estates and traditional magistrates; indeed it became part of the constitutional theory of the old regime.[5] Yet for Bodin himself such a theory was still hedged around with abstract conceptions of ultimate justice. No one doubted that the ruler was, in the last resort, responsible to God. But such a responsibility could not take the place of medieval constitutionalism or of the covenants which the *Vindiciae* advocated. Indeed this responsibility could be used to exalt the national monarch even further.

The growth of Bodin's idea of sovereignty goes hand in hand with the growth of the concept of the 'divine right of kings'. The dangers which this theory was designed to counter become clear when we consider its content. Kings were established upon their thrones by the direct command of God. They had a divine right to their office and authority, and this right was hereditary. Thus not only the pope but the ruler was directly commissioned by God, not merely delegated by the people as Bellarmine and the Huguenot writers had supposed. Moreover, neither the pope nor inferior magistrates could interrupt the royal succession which also rested upon a command of God.

Rulers whose right to succession was disputed could make excellent use of this theory. Moreover, the 'divine right of kings' gave them a means of controlling their own Church against both Catholic and Protestant pretensions. This was first used with some effect by the Royalist party, supporting King Henry IV against the League which seemed willing to permit papal domination over purely French affairs. The king affirmed his leadership over the Gallican Church; did he not also represent God on earth? A ruler like Henry IV, once in power, did not claim competence in spiritual matters, but he did desire to control his Church aided by the national and local assemblies of French clergy.

However, control over the Church was just one of the claims to authority which the 'divine right' monarch could fasten upon his realm. Because he was instituted directly by God, the ruler lent life to the laws, justice, and those general rules by which society was governed. The monarch was constantly guided by God himself, and consequently he must combine in his own person the functions of law maker, judge and magistrate. The idea of sovereignty was bolstered by this theory, and the medieval limitations which forbade the ruler to take property or to break contracts, except in emergencies, could be ignored.

Even in England divine right theory proved useful in small doses. In order to counter Catholic resistance theory and attempts by fanatics on the life of Elizabeth, Protestant writers cloaked the Queen in divine trappings. They referred to her 'sacred person', called her 'The Greatest' and claimed the birds of the air would report whispered treasons to her. Though one of her court claimed that the monarchy possessed 'power full and perpetual' over every subject,[6] Elizabeth did not attempt to practise absolutism. Instead the 'Homily on Obedience' which she commanded to be read from every pulpit justified her superiority only as part of the 'excellent and perfect order' which God had ordained in the world. Degree and rank were part of this order and the queen merely held the highest rank in the commonwealth, placed there by God Himself. She always remembered that, in some matters, she had a parliament and a political class to take into account, nor was she willing to solve the religious question with the divine right theory. Instead, she attempted to persuade her dissidents to be content with the latitudinarian state Church.

Divine right theory did find an enthusiastic defender in Elizabeth's successor. James VI of Scotland published his *True Law of Free Monarchies* in 1598, five years before he journeyed south to take up his English throne. Here was the theory in its fully developed form where kings were said to exercise 'a manner or resemblance of divine power upon earth' where they might deal with their subjects at their pleasure as a father might dispose of the inheritance of his children.[7] In Scotland James, like the French kings, had embraced the theory to bolster the monarchy in a country torn by the reality of civil strife; in England the theory was to prove a disaster in the struggles of the seventeenth century.

By the end of the century the 'divine right of kings' had become a popular theory among the monarchs who were attempting to build strong national states. Small wonder that, after Henry IV's assassination, one writer talked about the king's call to heaven in order to be crowned by God as the prince of all virtues,[8] or that, in the next century, Charles I of England had Rubens paint his father's apotheosis. Monarchs all over Europe bestowed their patronage upon writers and poets who praised their divinity. When patronage was the only way many writers could make a living, this drive for recognition of royal divinity was accompanied by a shrewd use of propaganda. But in an age where heaven and hell were still live concepts, the idea of responsibility, of being a father to one's people, did temper such absolutism with a sense of moral obligation.

CHRISTIANITY AND POLITICAL ACTION

The attempt to take into account the growth of the nation state, and the enhanced claims of the national monarchies, was always combined with a sustained effort to keep the traditional Christian framework of morality intact. Machiavelli's contention that the demands of politics must be placed above all others continued to be sharply rejected. Nevertheless, in the age of the religious wars, theorists saw themselves confronted with a political reality which pressed with increased weight against the Christian ideal of what constituted good and evil actions. In consequence, the older view, shared by Erasmus and the English *Mirror for Magistrates*, (see p. 157), that a virtuous prince was bound to triumph just as an evil ruler was bound to fall, gave way to more realistic theories about the relationship of Christianity to political action.

The 'divine right of kings' was useful here as well, for guided by God all royal actions (even if they had the appearance of evil) must be informed by Christian virtue. But for Catholics and Protestants who did not believe in the divine right theory, the problem was not so easily solved. Giovanni Botero in his *Reason of State* (1589) gave the Catholic answer to this problem. He accepted Bodin's definition of sovereignty and based himself upon the identity of interest between the Church and the king. In order to arrive at such an identity he made one all-important assumption: without the support of true religion no political action can succeed. But once this support has been obtained, Machiavellian means could be used freely in order to attain political success. The consent of true religion was given through the father confessor of the monarch. Here a device for linking Church and monarchy was readily at hand, one which the Jesuits (to whom Botero belonged) had long used for an identical purpose. Botero did suppose that the father confessor would bring religious conscience into play when advising the king on political action, but as he explicitly countenances force and cunning, the means and the ends become separated — reminiscent of Machiavelli rather than of Erasmus or traditional Christian political thought.

As long as the political aims of the Church and the king coincided, the ruler was freed from following a traditionally virtuous path of political action. The Protestants, though they could not use the device of a father confessor, followed a similar course. They based themselves upon scriptural precedent, such as Joshua's stratagems

341

against his enemies, which had direct divine sanction. Moreover, the imperative need to use any opening which God puts before men, in order to build His City on earth, was used to justify Machiavellian political action for the sake of the goal in view. The commands of God's providence must be accepted, even if this means the use of supposedly evil actions and political stratagems.[9] William Perkin's *Discourse of Conscience* (1596) follows this casuistry and stresses the importance of man's intentions, which must be to do God's work, and which are more important than the 'outward means' used to fulfil them.

William Perkins, the English Puritan, and Giovanni Botero, the Italian Jesuit, attempted in similar ways to reformulate religious ideals in the light of a changing political reality; and they were not alone in this quest. Unlike Machiavelli, such writers did not place the demands of politics above all other considerations, but rather attempted to integrate the necessities of ruthless politics into the Christian framework of life. However, the result of their efforts was to give religious sanction to what had, in the past, been considered most un-Christian behaviour.

The Catholic–Protestant conflict had, in the last resort, furthered the growth of the nation state, though it had also laid the groundwork for theories which were to prove revolutionary in the next century. The reformers had made desperate efforts not to destroy the traditional forms of government, but in the spread of the Reformation these forms were now challenged. The uncertainty introduced here was paralleled by the uncertainty introduced as to the standards of religious truth. The magisterial reformers' attempts at fixing religious orthodoxy had been no more successful than their efforts at maintaining political conformity. Radicalism continued to flourish, even if it often remained underground.

EVOLUTION OF RADICALISM

Catholics and Protestants joined in persecuting the radicals; but within their diaspora — which extended over the length and breadth of Europe — they did begin to crystallize into a multitude of clearly defined groups. To their enemies they were all known as 'Anabaptists', but in reality their ideas were quite different from group to group, and even from man to man. What they had in common was the idea of the regeneration of man through the Holy Spirit, and that man so regenerated was indeed free from the sins of the flesh, at liberty to live according to the will of God. Such a life meant one lived within the 'holy community' of equals who shared and shared alike; for all were 'new' men. The ban was to be used in order to maintain a pure community within an evil world. Along such lines the Mennonites developed in Holland and the Hutterites in Moravia.

A great deal of the spiritualism of the age was integrated with the radicals' view of man and God. Men like Kaspar Schwenckfeld and Sebastian Franck influenced all the radicals. Such Germans were religious enthusiasts with an undisciplined, burning, passion to experience the outer limits towards which faith could be driven. They held that man participated directly in the divine nature of Christ, that man's nature and the divine were compatible. The radicals were prone to believe in man's gradual rise towards divinity and viewed the deification of man as the ultimate goal of God. That is why they came to deny the Trinity. Neither Christ nor the Holy Spirit could exist independently of the elect. They must enter the body of those men who are especially chosen, in order to enable such elect to share with them in the nature of God. This mysticism made radicals the sole possessors of God — Christ's heavenly flesh had fused with theirs.

Such ideas continued the millennial dynamic of popular piety. Often one man would think himself a 'prophet' who had received direct divine inspiration and seek either to found a community of his own or to redeem all mankind, especially those now excluded from the benefits of society. We find such 'peasant preachers' among the weavers in Silesia, an economically depressed area, and they were to come to the fore in the English Revolution of the next century. Indeed this radicalism fuses with a deep stream of popular aspirations which expressed itself through a heightened mysticism, a millennialism continuing unabated from the Middle Ages to the non-industrial regions of nineteenth-century Europe.

But a further aspect of such ideas is even more important for the sixteenth century: their taming into viable organizational forms. This meant shedding much of the millennial fervour. Jacob Hutter (d. 1536) and his successors managed to found lasting Hutterite communities in Moravia because they stressed leadership and discipline. Theirs was a 'holy community' (or rather a series of them) in which all goods were shared but over which a bishop presided. Similarly, Menno Simons (1492–1559), the founder of an influential strain of Anabaptism, believed the Church was a voluntary association of believers, open to any man who could attain to 'active sainthood'. No one was irrevocably damned. His community was plagued by the same problem which haunted the Hutterites; a centrifugal tendency which made all sorts of splits inevitable.

THE LOGIC OF PETER RAMUS

The emphasis upon the direct outpouring of the 'holy spirit' gave an individualistic cast to all radical sects. Even the Bible was no restraining factor; for when they read it the Holy Spirit was apt to be at work, making for individualistic interpretations. Calvin had wanted to avoid such individualism by laying guidelines and keeping discipline. Calvinists added to this a certain formal logic to be used when 'dissecting scripture' – advocated by Peter Ramus (1515–72), a victim of the Massacre of St Bartholomew. The basic principle of Ramean logic was the contention, derived from Plato, that the universe is a copy of the ordered hierarchy of ideas existing in the mind of God. Ramus's logic '. . . is really a way to divide and subdivide matters'. This prevents obscurity and confusion. Ramus desired clarity and order, he held that ideas could be arranged symmetrically: individual ideas are formulated first and then put together into general axioms; ideas, in turn, are of two sorts – those which are established upon our own experience and those which are based upon an authority like the Bible. Moreover, ideas must be paired with their counterparts: the sun with the moon, man with woman, cause with effect. Ramean logic was a way of laying out ideas in a systematic form; once this had been done the meaning of the ideas was thought to be self-evident.

Ramean logic did seem liberating to those who had grown up in scholastic argument. The division and distribution of concepts according to a simple order of things seemed to correspond to the rationality of the universe in which all Calvinists believed. They structured their writings and sermons according to this logic, and in England the Puritans took it over with great zeal. Ramus's logic was a coherent system and as such it served to set boundaries to any individualistic interpretations of scripture, and closed the door to that mysticism and millenarianism which always seemed to threaten the faith. To all such efforts to stifle the religious imagination the radicals were opposed and in consequence their own ideas of organization and discipline clashed with their concepts of the deification of man and each man's separate mystical contact with God.

ITALIAN HERETICS

Radical ideas appeared all over Europe. But in Italy they had found a specially fertile soil, and here they led to a further development of some importance. Among the Italian radicals the exaltation of man in the humanist tradition fused with the spiritualization of religion. The synod of Italian Anabaptists meeting in Venice in 1550 declared Christ to be a mere man, though filled with the grace of God, and went on to emphasize the justification of the elect. Moreover, the existence of hell or of the devil was denied. Spiritualistic religion and rationalism existed in close proximity among the Italian Anabaptists, as indeed among the whole of the Italian Reformation. Ever since Juan Valdès and his circle in Naples during the first half of the century, Erasmian ideas had stood side by side with a spiritualization of faith.

Venice, with its antipapalism, had seen the meeting of an Anabaptist synod. But immediately thereafter the Inquisition began to drive the Italian heretics from their native land. The radicals, at first, found a haven in the Grisons, a part of Switzerland. As early as 1526 the diet of Ilanz had decreed toleration between Catholics and Protestants, and the Alpine valleys became hotbeds of sectarianism. These groups were not tolerant, whether in Switzerland, Holland or elsewhere; the synod of Venice had expressly reaffirmed the ban as the instrument to exclude those who were not elect and therefore did not 'belong'.

But among the Italians the execution of Servetus led to reflections about toleration and the sceptical, inquiring, spirit which some had brought from the south did the rest. Sebastian Castellio insisted that the Reformation can gain victory only if it fights with the weapons of the spirit, not the sword. This argument leads him, in his famed *De Haereticis* (1554), to reduce Christianity to a moral attitude, a virtue which would triumph over vice. All the dogma which was needed was belief in Christ as the redeemer. Thus the necessary belief was reduced to a minimum. At the same time Laelius

Socinius (1525—62) bombarded men like Calvin and Bullinger with questions about every part of dogma. He believed that intellectual clarity was essential for religious belief. But doctrines like the Trinity did not lend themselves to such an analysis. The heir to this attitude was Faustus Socinius (1539—1604), the nephew of Laelius. His work could no longer be done in Switzerland. The Grisons had discontinued their toleration of Anabaptists at the same moment that a new nation had opened its doors to them.

Poland's toleration was not due to general principles, but to its backward political organization. The Polish kings had been unable to develop their royal authority and were elected by the diet which the nobles controlled. Moreover, during the weak reign of Sigismund II Augustus (1548—72) the nobles had gained control of legislative and executive functions. Each noble was therefore a king in his domain and could determine its religion. All that was needed to establish a faith was the support of one or more members of the large noble class. Small wonder that all forms of Protestantism spread into Poland. When, after Sigismund's death, the diet passed the Compact of Warsaw (1573) affirming religious liberty, it was at the same time affirming the autonomy of the Polish nobility.

Conditions in neighbouring Transylvania, formerly part of Hungary, but since 1526 under Turkish suzerainty with a virtually independent ruler, were also favourable to the radicals: its prince was not able to force unanimity of religious opinion upon the German settlers and the Magyars who lived there. Morever, Transylvania contained a sizable population of Rumanians who were Greek Orthodox Christians. Indeed within this territory religious differences were closely tied to other diverse nationalities who made it their home. Catholic Hungarians, Protestant Germans and Orthodox Rumanians equated the safeguarding of their religious differences with the preservation of their own national consciousness. Moreover, each of these nations lived within well-defined territorial boundaries. In these circumstances, the national assembly of the region took the only possible way out; in 1554 it proclaimed religious freedom to adherents of all faiths. For all this, one modern historian has questioned whether Transylvania can rightly be regarded as a seedbed of modern freedom. The granting of religious tolerance did not mitigate the harsh executive authority of the ruler over other aspects of life.[10] During the sixteenth century, religious freedom did not inevitably lead to political freedom as well.

THE SOCINIANS

It was in Poland and Transylvania that Faustus Socinius spread his beliefs and organized his Church. His was not a modern rationalism, for he held that man's reason and his power of will were limited by revelation. It was necessary to follow the example of Christ in order to release man's strength and his virtue. Christ, however, was not a God but a man miraculously born as an example of the perfection to which all men could attain. Socinius stripped Christianity of all dogma except revelation; instead it was man's moral posture which counted. The object of man's striving must be to live a Christian life and such a Christian life was contrasted with sterile dogma. The First (1580) and Second (1605) Catechism issued from the city of Rakow, the centre of Socinianism, disclaimed the binding force of the Confessions of Faith of other Protestants.

The followers of Faustus Socinius were first known as 'anti-Trinitarians' and, finally, as 'Unitarians' because they stressed the 'oneness' of Christ's human nature. Scepticism towards belief and dogma did lurk underneath Unitarianism, and this was to have an important future in the next century. For it was to find friends wherever men opposed religious orthodoxy and Calvinist predestination. Thus in the seventeenth century Unitarians were to join hands with the Dutch Arminians.

To the rest of Christendom this was a dreadful heresy, an atheism which denied Christ's divinity and substituted a pragmatic moral criterion of behaviour for Christian dogma. The number of Unitarians was small, but what they stood for loomed large: had the religious divisions, the inability of orthodoxies to maintain themselves, led to a rejection of the possibility of finding dogmatic religious certainty? Early in the seventeenth century many men were to make a distinction between leading a Christian life and Christian dogma.

GIORDANO BRUNO

In the sixteenth century most radicalism was as yet filled with religious certainty. But the strong mystical component of this radicalism could also dissolve itself into a pantheism which, in its turn, would deny the relevance of Christian dogma. If everything was of God and God was everything then Christ could not but be irrelevant, then the reality of nature, and man surrounded by nature, was all that mattered – filled with God even unto each leaf of a tree. Giordano Bruno (1548–1600) extended these ideas beyond the limits of nature to include an infinite universe, composed of innumerable worlds. This cosmos reflects the infinite divinity of God of which man and nature are an integral part. Nature links man to this image of the divine nature which is innate in every man. If man can make nature yield up her secrets, he will become an 'adept', knowledgeable about the infinite extension of reality which constitutes the true revelation of God. Bruno believed that man must expand himself to an infinite extent, so that he may receive the vision of God's miracle: an infinite universe populated by innumerable worlds, all animated by God. This pantheistic religion transforms faith into a 'secret science', a magic which builds upon the mystery religion of the Christian agnostics, the Cabala and the Hermetic school of mystical religious thought supposedly derived from Egypt.

Bruno accepts the Copernican revolution in astronomy, but he also represents a continuation of mystical ideas, a fascination with magic which had occupied some of the humanists before him.[11] He did not make Christianity a meaningful part of his thought; it can play no role in such pantheism. Small wonder that he found himself a wanderer, expelled from one academic position after another. His execution by the Inquisition in Rome (1600) could not stop the dangerous onslaught of such pantheism, which, like the moralism of the Socinians, dissolved religious orthodoxy. It did away with the difference between nature and revelation (all is the relevation of God) and opposed any use of force to uphold a purely outward conformity.

ORTHODOXY AND TOLERANCE

The rejection of such conformity by most of the radicals led to more tolerant attitudes, and these were given impetus through the fossilization of religious orthodoxy. The scholastic argumentations of Lutheran or Calvinist ministers, turning around details in Confessions of Faith, seemed to recreate the very religious situation against which the Reformation itself had come into being. Indeed, Confessions of Faith became the rule in Protestantism during the second half of the sixteenth century. The French Church produced the *Confessio Gallicana* (1559); its example was followed: the

Confessio Belgica (1559) became the enforced Calvinist creed in the Netherlands by 1618, and the *Confessio Scotiana* (1560) codified John Knox's reformation. The *Heidelberg Catechism* (1563), originally promulgated by the Count Palatine, proved to be the most widely adopted definition of Calvinist orthodoxy. Luther had never desired to make his rule of faith into a rule of law, but the *Book of Concordance* (1580) became binding on two-thirds of German Protestantism. The Confession of Faith included Luther's Catechisms, the Confessions of Augsburg and the articles of the Schmalkaldic League — even the printers' mistakes in these documents became sanctified and binding. This development within Protestantism was a natural consequence of the fear of radicalism and the need for order in the magisterial reformation. The radicals took a different view of such enforced orthodoxy.

Radicals, whether anti-Trinitarians, Christian mystics or pantheists, considered themselves as holding open a door which the established Protestant churches seemed to have closed. Many remained 'seekers' who believed that God would give them a continued, ever fresh, revelation involving them in an open-ended mysticism. But as these radicals formed groups, they in turn began to close the door to unbelievers through the use of the ban. Persecution made for an enforced coherence. Instead, radicals contributed most effectively to the growth of toleration through the variety of opinions they managed to sustain. Moreover, they rejected many fixed and traditional dogmas, thus broadening the scope of the admissible, and, last but not least, exalted man as an individual human being on a basis of social and economic equality.

Still more powerful agencies working for tolerance were political circumstances and economic necessity. The economic factor enters meaningfully only in the next century when impoverished rulers were to encourage complete religious tolerance in order to attract wealth to their cities.

Poland provided a model for toleration in the second half of the sixteenth century, and here political circumstances were decisive. They benefited not only all types of Christians but also the Jews, who came to enjoy a freedom in Poland (and Transylvania) not equalled elsewhere. Jews were not tied to money-lending or petty trade, as in the rest of Europe, but worked in all professions and manufacture; as peasants and craftsmen. Yet, these favourable conditions did not produce a cultural flowering comparable with that which had occurred in Islamic Spain. Instead, the most productive Jewish cultural centre was once again in an Islamic region, which had a longer history of tolerance. The chief codification of Jewish law and ritual, *The Prepared Table (Shulhan Aruch,* 1567) by Joseph Karo, was prepared in Safed, a hill town in Palestine. The new impulse of Cabalic mysticism came from Safed as well, reflecting the shock over the fate of Spanish Jewry.[12]

Polish Jewry could show no comparable accomplishment. This cultural ferment in Safed was the last movement to affect all of Judaism. From now on for Jews and Christians alike national surroundings were to be of ever greater decisiveness. The golden age in Poland ended for the Jews at the same time as for the Protestants: with the Catholic reconquest which was begun in the reign of Sigismund III (1587–1622) but not completed until the middle of the next century.

But Poland was an exceptional case; the future of religious tolerance lay not with the feudal, backward nations but with the newly strengthened national monarchies. Political necessity forced them to travel this road. It is no coincidence that Jean Bodin, the formulator of the modern doctrine of sovereignty, believed that it was impossible for mere men to judge between the different religions. The conversion to God of a purified soul was a personal matter, and men should not be dictated to about their faith. Political allegiance was what mattered in this world. The growing consciousness that there was a difference between political loyalty and religious opinion is crucial both for the development of the modern state and for the idea of toleration. Hand in hand with the new theory of sovereignty, this consciousness countered the traditional argument that religious heresy could not be separated from political treason. The age of the religious wars saw merely the first hesitant steps in this direction. Such steps were taken not only through the political necessity of tolerating two different faiths within one nation (as in France), but also by making the national Church so broad that it could contain within it a divergence of religious opinion. The traditional framework was kept: religious conformity was vital to political loyalty, but this conformity was made as latitudinarian as possible — sometimes approaching closely to the radicals' ideal of a minimum of necessary belief.

Such a broad Church had been in the mind of Charles V struggling to preserve his empire, and it was certainly an ideal of Henry IV of France as it had been that of Catherine de Medici. But Queen Elizabeth of England came closest to realizing it in practice.

THE ELIZABETHAN CHURCH

Elizabeth at her accession had no choice but to be a committed Protestant. The Catholics considered her a bastard and in Mary Queen of Scots presented a rival candidate for the throne. Queen Elizabeth was determined from the start to restore Protestantism based upon the Royal Supremacy and the Prayer Book of 1552.[13] She faced opposition from Marian bishops and conservative peers, but outmanœuvred her opponents by having some of them arrested and keeping others from attending parliament. The religious settlement which emerged, based on new Acts of Supremacy and Uniformity, tried to appeal to a wide spectrum of religious opinion. Elizabeth styled herself not 'Head' but 'Governor' of the Church and approved an ambiguous use of words on the question of the real presence in the sacrament.

Threats to this settlement came from both outside and within England. Astute diplomatic action kept Philip of Spain neutralized — he had no wish to see Mary Queen of Scots and her powerful French connections take the English throne and was, for a time, encouraged by Elizabeth's talk of a Habsburg marriage partner. Elizabeth had to replace Catholic bishops and clergy but for the first ten years of the reign English Catholics were not actively persecuted in the way Mary I had treated her Protestant subjects; many behaved as 'Church-papists', publicly attending the Protestant service but holding Catholic observances in private. Anti-Catholic penal laws became increasingly harsh, however, as the Catholic Reformation moved against England. Missionary priests, many of them Jesuits, smuggled themselves into the country to stiffen the opposition of English Catholics. Catholic propaganda challenged Elizabeth's right to rule, and there were the plots to assassinate the queen and replace her with Mary. Most Catholics were probably unwilling to associate themselves with violent resistance and remained politically loyal to Elizabeth throughout her reign.

THE PURITANS

The most concerted attacks on the settlement, however, came not from an increasingly isolated Catholic minority, but from those Protestant enthusiasts known as 'Puritans'. The names 'Puritan' and

'Precisian' had been first applied in an insulting way in the 1560s to those who wished to carry out a more complete reformation of the English Church. They were distinguished by the intensity of their feelings on a number of issues: Puritans regarded the Church of Rome as the embodiment of Antichrist with whom true Christians must always be at war; they believed preaching and Bible study more important than church ritual and they were fervently committed to an evangelism which would convert England and result in the imposition of a godly discipline on the populace.[14] The overwhelming majority of Puritans remained committed to membership in the Church of England, however imperfect an instrument it might be. Nor was the form of Church government the issue, but the decisiveness of its doctrine.

Clarity had been all-important to Calvin, and so it was for the Puritans. This was true not only in understanding the Bible whose study was their prime concern, but in preaching as well. In attempting to bring the reformation to England once more, they placed an emphasis upon preaching which had been a common factor in the spreading of the reformation as a whole. They also wanted to arouse the people through plain and simple preaching, through the logical construction of their sermons. Puritans opposed the licensing of preachers by the Church, and the Anglican Church came to see in Puritan preaching one of the greatest dangers to its stability.

Puritans looked at the universe as a single and organized plan in the mind of God and, like their continental models, gave instructions on how man must fulfil this plan. A disciplined piety was the result; Tudor Puritans kept diaries to see how their battle with sin was progressing. They were eager to detect if they were of the elect, and this eagerness led to a self-awareness which stressed the manner of their performance on earth. Puritans knew with great certainty in what such a performance must consist: God's plan was known, and books as well as sermons served to describe the proper disposition of a godly mind.

Many of the leaders of early Elizabethan Puritanism had spent the years of the Marian persecution in exile on the continent where they had seen other Protestant Church practices they hoped to imitate in England. While Elizabeth could accept much of Calvin's theology, the queen was not in favour of abolishing the traditional ceremonial which the Puritans found objectionable or of going down the road of Church reform. Against the opposition of the government, Puritans failed to win changes in convocation or in Parliament. Press campaigns to back Puritan demands, notably the 1572 *Admonition to Parliament* and the 1588–89 'Marprelate tracts', aroused controversy but were failures. There were further defeats for Puritanism outside of parliament. Elizabeth, despite the objections of Archbishop Grindal, ordered the public preaching assemblies, known as 'prophesyings' suppressed. The attempts, led by Thomas Cartwright and John Field, to form a national presbyterian system inside the Church of England succeeded only locally and for a short time before Whitgift, Grindal's successor, dispersed the movement. By the 1590s Puritanism, as a political movement, had been rendered impotent. Its usefulness as a counter-weight to the Catholic menace had ended with the execution of Mary Queen of Scots in 1587, and the defeat in the following year of the Spanish Armada. Its patrons at court were dead and its clerical leaders were in difficulty, edging towards separatism or emigration. Government and Church leaders portrayed the movement as the product of radical sectarians eager to overthrow the established political and ecclesiastical order.

But Puritans should not be seen only as critics. The religious settlement of 1559 by no means completed the English Reformation but, rather, marked the beginning of a long process of planting Protestantism into the national consciousness, an undertaking in which Puritanism was often in the forefront.[15] The Elizabethan regime had first to create a reliable body of Protestant clergy. This was a lengthy task and in the beginning the government had to rely on returned exiles and others of a Puritan bent whose Protestant loyalties were unquestionable. They purged the episcopacy of Catholics and tried, as far as possible, to root them out of positions in the universities, churches and judicial system. But it was not enough to remove Catholic supporters or decree the elimination of Catholic imagery and ceremonial. The Protestant message had to be presented to the people, especially to the political elites, and this required preaching and publishing.

Their most effective publication was the *Geneva Bible* which they printed in 1560 and whose glosses, printed in the margins, had Calvin's approval. This was to be the most popular Bible of Elizabethan times.

Puritans, whose enthusiasm for preaching was unquenchable, were given positions in parish churches and in cathedrals; they found university posts where they could raise up new generations of Protestant enthusiasts. Puritans were particularly useful in the remoter parts of England where Catholicism was strong and rewards for Protestant ministers few. Their value in such sensitive areas was acknowledged by Church and government for as Archbishop Grindal observed, 'where preaching wanteth, obedience faileth'. Puritans had an elevated sense of the importance of the 'godly magistrate' in furthering the Reformation and succeeded in making alliances with civic officials and in winning patrons among the nobility and gentry. In this way Protestantism took a firm hold in many towns and counties as magistrates and magnates provided lectureships or benefices for Puritan preaching, even in the face of government disapproval.

Just as popular piety and popular culture had been affected by the moral rigour of the continental reformations, so in England they were influenced by the Puritan aspect of the Elizabethan reformation. Puritans demanded a new moral discipline, not only of themselves, but of the whole community as well. They were opposed to many folk customs as well as amusements, such as May-poles, morris dancing, ballad singing and plays. They wanted a clear line to separate the sacred from the profane, calling for an end to Sabbath breaking, elaborate funerals, and the use of churchyards as places for public gatherings and festivities. As in other sixteenth-century reformations, they wanted to stamp out semi-magic rituals, such as the purification of women after childbirth. In these aims they were supported by many officials who believed that this reformation of morals reinforced their own responsibilities in keeping the people in order and subjection. Puritanism offered a popular religion based on sermon attendance, Bible study, anti-Catholicism, intense moral self-scrutiny and domestic piety. Fathers were to evangelize their wives, children and servants, conduct family prayers, catechize their dependents and enforce the holiness of the Sabbath. It is this household religion which survived, and indeed thrived, in England when political Puritanism had been eclipsed.

PARLIAMENT

Parliament was often the arena for Puritan attempts to win further reform in the Elizabethan church. Some historians have seen in this conflict a struggle between the crown and an opposition in the House of Commons under the direction of radical Puritans and their allies.[16] In this view, which tends to treat the House of Lords, really the more efficient chamber, as of no great importance, the Commons is seen to grow slowly in significance and independence becoming the forum for all issues of national consequence. A more recent school of thought has denied the existence of such a leadership and has challenged long-held assumptions about the importance of Parliament and, particularly, the House of Commons.[17] Parliament, it is said, was an 'occasional instrument' called infrequently by the crown to provide needed tax revenue or particular legislation, not for purposes of political debate. The clashes which earlier historians described as opposition were in fact manipulated by the Privy Council to pressure the queen.

It is true that Parliament made no real legal or institutional gains during the reign of Elizabeth. Freedom from arrest had been granted to members in the reign of Henry VIII but the queen did not believe that the principle applied against the crown and had several members of Parliament imprisoned. Free speech was limited by Elizabeth's express command only to matters she wanted discussed, while Chancery, and not the Commons, decided disputed elections. Members were interested in attending parliaments for a number of reasons, including angling for a position in government service. The seventeenth-century struggles between king and parliament must not be read back into Elizabeth's reign, yet we must not underestimate the importance of politics in Elizabethan parliaments. In addition to the debates on the often divisive matter of religious reform, Elizabethan parliaments saw many other clashes over national issues, including social welfare, the succession to the throne, anti-Catholic measures, national security, freedom of speech, and abuses of the queen's prerogative in purveyance and monopolies. No matter why the crown called parliaments, in every sitting members were anxious to debate issues of national importance, with or without the support of members of the Privy Council. Prompted by love of true religion, patriotism or their consciences, they could speak out boldly against queen or council without feeling themselves disloyal or alienated.

Elizabeth's handling of parliaments and politics was usually deft but when she died in 1603 she, nonetheless, left her successor the problems which she had postponed rather than solved. Faction-fighting at court had got out of hand; the economy was fragile; the political class was increasingly recalcitrant and both Puritans and Catholics pressed for religious change. King James was to dash the hopes of both Puritans and Catholics, maintaining the broadly based English national Church which combined old concepts of allegiance with new ideas of minimum belief, or at least with a certain officially sanctioned approach to the freedom of conscience. Small wonder that Richard Hooker emphasized rationalism in his defence of the Church against the Puritans. Man's reason was the highest court of appeal amid the bewildering theological controversies of the age. This reason is limited by God but it also springs from the divine, it governs everything which is not specifically laid down in scripture. This includes ecclesiastical policy and human government. Both, as they exist in England, are best suited to the prevailing circumstances, for they assure a universal harmony which is essential, according to Christianity and reason. Political obligation provides the foundation for such an order and Church policy was only one part of civil society. Reason, law and political allegiance are more important than controversy over doctrine; in spite of the piety which pervades his *Laws of Ecclesiastical Polity* (*c.* 1594–97) Hooker points to a time when the 'vanity of dogmatizing' will be rejected. Such opinions lie in the future, yet the national Church represents a vital development towards this point of view, and beyond it towards scepticism and religious indifference.

PROTESTANT OPPOSITION TO THE EMPEROR

Religious indifference was encouraged by religious strife. Inside the border of the Empire opposition to the crown combined with moves for religious reform in lower Austria and Bohemia. While Lutheranism had made substantial inroads in Austria, in Bohemia the largest group of the Hussites (Utraquists) had united with Catholicism in 1525. Yet even here there remained a group of 'radicals' devoted to the Reformation. Faced with this situation the emperor had temporized, and in 1568 Maximilian II granted a limited toleration to the Lutheran nobility in Austria in return for taxes with which to fight the Turk.

But from 1576 onwards under the rule of his sons, the Counter-Reformation received earnest support and could book initial successes. Such pressure led to a radicalization of the Protestant nobility which now turned to Calvin's doctrine of resistance to authority. They attempted to use the estates which they dominated in Austria, Moravia and Hungary, as a weapon against the emperor, just as in England the Puritans had tried to use parliament as a forum to pressure the queen. However, not England but the Netherlands inspired the assembled estates (1608) to demand freedom of religion and to mutter about the advantages possessed by 'free Republics'. It was too late to reimpose Catholicism for this would now entail the destruction of the power of the estates. However, in the next century, the emperor was to ignore all such dangers in the name of the true faith, as Philip of Spain had done before him. The Empire was drifting towards the Thirty Years War (1618).

The similarity of the problems faced by the national states in Europe during the second half of the sixteenth century are obvious. The spread of the Reformation had taken under its wings those groups which opposed the national monarchies for religious, social, economic and political reasons. These, whether in France, Scotland, or Austria, found a power base in the nobility or in the estates and, at times, in both of them. Small wonder that ideas of sovereignty and the 'divine right of kings' seemed to come to the rescue of rulers, though such ideas of absolute rule could be transferred to estates and parliaments as well. But all these strains worked to weaken the fabric of the faith itself, to turn it away from the single-minded enthusiasm of belief which had inspired the reformers, Protestant or Catholic.

THE RISE OF SCEPTICISM

The result was not only an emphasis upon political unity rather than religious commitment. The sixteenth century made a contribution of its own towards the rise of scepticism and religious indifference. For outside all the controversies within Christianity, it witnessed a revival of the form of Greek scepticism called pyrrhonism. Michel de Montaigne (1533–92), the most impressive representative of this attitude, came from a family divided by religious conflict; his father was a Catholic, his mother was half Jewish and Protestant. For Montaigne, doubt and the suspension of all judgement are the finest of human achievements., We cannot know the truth about ourselves or other things, the only course human reason can take is to assert that some judgements seem to be more reasonable than others. We can, in fact, never tell if our ideas correspond to real objects and thus there can never be any kind of certainty.

Montaigne has a place for religion in his thinking: it is blind faith because man's reason and even his senses can only produce doubt and suspended judgement. Such fideism is found among some radical Protestants as a thoroughgoing anti-intellectualism, but Montaigne reasons out his argument and that in itself was new. In common with the revival of scepticism he leans upon the *Outline of Pyrrhonism* of Sextus Empiricus (second century A.D.) and the men who followed this thought were called the 'new Pyrrhonists'.

NEOSTOICISM

One of the other foundations of Montaigne's thought was stoicism. The late sixteenth century saw a revival of interest in the literature of the Roman Empire, particularly that of Tacitus and Seneca. From a study of these texts European writers, in the midst of civil war and religious strife, developed a philosophy that stressed the individual's self-discipline and resistance to the world's troubles. Men were to act, not under the influence of their emotions but according to right reason, with a strength of mind that was not swayed by either good fortune or disaster. Shakespeare expressed such thoughts through Hamlet:

Blest are those
Whose blood and judgement are so well commingled,
That they are not a pipe for fortune's finger
To sound what stop she please. Give me that Man
That is not passion's slave . . .

The chief figure in Neostoicism was the Belgian professor Justus Lipsius (1547–1606), author of a series of very influential books, notably *Constancy* (1584) and *Six Books of Politics* (1589). Neostoicism was not just a guide to personal behaviour. The ideas of Lipsius also influenced political and military affairs throughout Western Europe for over a century.[18] Roman practices in military, governmental and financial affairs became models as Lipsius stressed the values of a standing army, centralized civil service and a disciplined populace, ideas that helped shape the absolutism of European states. He also allowed the ruler to practice deceit if necessary for the good of the state. The scope of his career demonstrates the universal appeal of his work; educated by Jesuits, he taught at Lutheran, Calvinist and Catholic universities, and his ideas found favour in monarchies and republics.

So influential was stoicism that attempts were made to tie the philosophy closer to Christianity. Guillaume du Vair in his *Holy Philosophy* (1600) was, like all stoics, concerned with erecting a defence against the human passions. Such a defence depended upon the strength of will within every individual, for the will can regulate all actions through reason. Man's reason must follow nature – and if we stop here stoicism does give justification to the libertinism of the turn of the century: use your free will to follow where your own human nature leads you, and all will be well.

But du Vair attempted to fasten his ideas on to Christianity. For du Vair, God is the regulator of nature, we cannot follow nature unless we are pious. God has given the law to man and this includes free will in order to overcome the passions. In spite of this 'Christian Stoicism' such movements of thought reinforced the concept of man's natural virtue which gained currency from another direction as well: those Protestants who made a distinction between Christian life and Christian dogma also tended to judge man by his own proven virtue rather than through his belief. Ideas usually associated with the eighteenth century have their beginnings in the disgust with doctrinal controversies and the religious conflict of the sixteenth. This concentration upon curbing the passions, upon living the virtuous life, rather than bothering about theology, is the consequence of the violent struggles which the Reformation had unleashed. The increasing latitudinarianism of the state Churches also belongs here, as does the assimilation of Machiavellism into political thought. The reformers themselves, Luther or Calvin and the others, were willing to jeopardize their work upon points of theology and their followers agreed. But by the end of the century in many instances this was no longer the case – the consequence not only of battle fatigue but also of a growing Protestant orthodoxy and its hair-splitting custodians.

However, the religious enthusiasm which had fathered the Reformation also continued to exist within the dynamic of the radicals, the Puritans and even in some measure among the orthodox. Not only radical Protestants but the Catholic Reformation took up the ideal of 'faith alone' in order to attack Calvinist theorizing about God, and to assert that God can only be known through faith.

Catholicism was entering upon its great age of religious revival as the sixteenth century closed. European civilization grew in complexity, and that was its strength. If one result of the spread of the Reformation was a tendency toward religious indifference, another made towards a decisive religious commitment. The inscription 'one faith, one king, one law' over the door of the Sorbonne might be outmoded by the events; the coexistence of two faiths in one political organism had not proved destructive, and yet the rulers continued to be challenged by those who put their particular religious truth above all human authority. But at the same time the 'divine right of kings' gave new status to rulers, the idea of sovereignty strengthened the nation state, centring the making and execution of laws in the hands of the sovereign. All these contradictory results of the age of religious strife went on into the next century, which was to be not only an age of absolutism but also an age of revolutions.

NOTES AND REFERENCES

1   Gerald Bowler, "An Axe or an Acte"; the Parliament of 1572 and Resistance Theory in Early Elizabethan England', *Canadian Journal of History*, 1984, pp. 349–59.

2   Much of the book was written before the Massacre. The standard English translation is in R. E. Giesey and J. H. M. Salmon, eds., *Francogallia by François Hotman* (Cambridge, 1972).

3   Frederick Baumgartner, *Radical Reactionaries: the political thought of the French Catholic League* (Geneva, 1975) gives summaries of many of these works.

4   Peter Holmes, *Resistance and Compromise: the Political Thought of Elizabethan Catholics* (Cambridge, 1982), pp. 147–65.

5   Julian Franklin, *Jean Bodin and the Rise of Absolutist Theory* (Cambridge, 1973).

6   Charles Merbury, *A Brief Discourse of Royall Monarchie* (London, 1581), p. 41.

7   *The Political Works of James I*, introduction by Charles Howard McIlwain (Cambridge, Mass. 1918), xxxix.

8   Roland Mousnier, *L'Assassinat d'Henri IV* (Paris, 1964), p. 187.

9   See George L. Mosse, *The Holy Pretence* (Oxford, 1957).

10 See the works of the Hungarian historian Gyula Szefku, written during the 1920s.

11 Frances A. Yates, *Giordano Bruno and the Hermetic Tradition* (Chicago, 1964), p. 246. For Bruno see also p. 430.

12 Gershom G. Scholem, *Major Trends in Jewish Mysticism* (New York, 1946), pp. 286, 305.

13 This account of the Settlement is drawn from Norman Jones, *Faith by Statute: Parliament and the Settlement of Religion* (London, 1982).

14 William Hunt, *The Puritan Moment* (Cambridge, Mass, 1983), x.

15 Patrick Collinson, *The Religion of Protestants* (Oxford, 1982), 1; Penry Williams, *The Tudor Regime* (London, 1980), p. 258.

16 J. E. Neale, *Elizabeth I and her Parliaments*, 2 vols (London, 1953–57).

17 M. A. R. Greaves, 'Thomas Norton the Parliament Man: An Elizabethan M.P., 1559–1581', *Historical Journal*, 1980, pp. 17–35; G. R. Elton, *Parliament in England 1559–81* (Cambridge, 1986).

18 Gerhard Oestreich, *Neostoicism and the early modern state*, H. G. Koenigsberger and Brigitta Oestreich, eds (Cambridge, 1982), p. 8.

14

SIXTEENTH-CENTURY LITERATURE

Literature can serve a number of functions. It can, in forms ranging from the courtly masque to the jests of the village storyteller, entertain. It can educate, passing on a culture's skills, attitudes and moral values, and it can attempt to persuade, to urge men and women to action or meditation. It can, depending on its presentation, heighten social tensions or purge and soothe them. In the sixteenth century literature served all these purposes in very important ways. Literature could not, of course, have remained free of the period's turmoils in church, society and state; indeed, the literary world saw much upheaval itself. This was a century when old literary forms and conventions were challenged by new preoccupations and themes; popular cultures clashed with elite cultures. This was also a time when languages themselves arose, stagnated or declined. Central to an understanding of all these changes is an appreciation of the influence of the printing press.

THE PRINTING PRESS AND LITERATURE

Before the invention of the printing press in the Rhine Valley in the mid-fifteenth century every book was handwritten. By 1500, however, mass-production of literature had resulted in as many as 7.5 million books circulating in Italy alone. The technology spread rapidly; in the early sixteenth century 40 French urban centres had printing shops while in 181 German towns 1,058 different printing establishments operated. These shops were capitalist endeavours, with constant challenges posed by capital investment, labour problems, rigorous competition and international trading connections; but they were also more than that. Printing houses were important centres of the literary arts. Here, in an inter-disciplinary setting, technicians, writers, translators, illustrators, editors and scholars mixed in a new kind of forum with the printer acting as a press agent, impresario, business man and operator of a refugee shelter for wandering or exiled literati.[1] Printing was always an occupation fraught with perils. Shops that invested too heavily in editions that proved unpopular or theologically suspect could find themselves bankrupt; those who ran afoul of censorship authorities could have their presses smashed. Patronage was often as important for printers as writers. Governments played a part in keeping the industry healthy by granting profitable monopolies to print law-books, school-books or Bibles. This was to compensate printers for refraining from printing unauthorized works and also served to give governments a material hold on printers who feared to lose their livelihoods.

The development of printing brought important changes to European literature. Its economies of scale meant that more people than ever before could now afford to buy books, that they could buy more of them and that there were now more titles available to choose from. This expansion of the market allowed printers to reach not just the clergy, scholars and members of social elites who had been the primary buyers of manuscript books but also to appeal to a wider readership with different sorts of taste – popular literature took on a new importance. Moreover, not only could writers reach new classes of readers but new classes of writers now appeared: artisans wrote of their trade-craft, discontented groups distributed manifestos, female authors became more commonplace and elements of popular culture such as carnival songs or charivari verses now entered into print. Printing allowed a new sort of relationship between writer and reader as authors called for responses to their work in the form of criticism, corrections or new material that might be reflected in later editions. Dissemination of books became more rapid and more widespread, enhancing the international dimension of European literature. New sorts of literary forms were now possible. The poetic collection with a unified theme sprang into prominence as did the emblem book – an integration of verse and picture impossible before printing.[2] That the nature of reading itself changed from a public, oral activity to a silent, private one can be seen in a change in the size of books, from a folio size suitable for lecterns to smaller books which could be held in one's hand. Printing also helped determine which languages would become national, literary languages and which would become isolated, regional dialects. Where a linguistic form such as Tuscan in Italy or Castilian in Spain found writers and printers to champion it, it might become a standard literary language; where it did not, like Scottish Gaelic, it might decline to local, oral usage only. This could be a slow process. Though books were printed in Cornish, Breton and Provençal early in the sixteenth century, less and less literature emerged in these languages as time went by and as writers abandoned them for English or French.

Much of sixteenth-century literary culture was oral: popular religious drama, jests, riddles, folk tales and ballads were preserved by the arts of memory and passed on by word of mouth. The advent of printing had an impact on this literature. It gave permanence in print to traditional material, taking much of this regional, oral literature and disseminating it throughout Europe so that Parisians could sing songs of the countryside and Englishmen could laugh at German comic tales. Printing also strengthened oral culture in other ways. Books could be shared by reading aloud, giving the illiterate other topics to talk about and new ways of viewing human experience. There was even a strong oral element to more refined genres; the Italian *commedia dell'arte* staged improvised drama without a script and the popularity of the dialogue as a literary form shows an 'oral residue' in prose. In the sixteenth century at least, it seems that the effect of printing on oral culture was not a destructive one.[3]

POETRY IN THE SIXTEENTH CENTURY

Few doubted in the sixteenth century that the most elevated of all literary forms was poetry. Sir Philip Sidney (1554–86) claimed in his *Defence of Poesie* that it was the best vehicle for imparting moral values, 'the right description of wisdom, valour and justice'; superior to philosophy and history for giving insights into the nature of man; and unmatched for creating 'with the force of a divine breath' visions of a better world: 'Nature never set forth the earth in so rich tapestry as divers poets have done; neither with pleasant rivers, fruitful trees, sweet-smelling flowers, nor whatsoever else may make the too-much-loved earth more lovely. Her world is brazen, the poets only deliver a golden.'[4] Neoplatonism encouraged poets to think of themselves as creators with god-like powers and most poetical theorists assigned the highest rank of poetic creation to the epic.

THE EPIC

Throughout the century poets took Virgil as the model for the composition of their epics. His *Aeneid* had told the story of the Trojan Aeneas whose troubled journeys eventually led him to Italy where his descendants would establish the city of Rome. Sixteenth-century epics too would deal with quests: to defeat the infidel, reach the Indies or worship at the court of the Faerie Queen.[5] The century's first great attempt at this form was *Orlando Furioso* (1516; final version 1532) by Ludovico Ariosto (1474—1533) who wrote at the Este court in Ferrara. The poem deals with the struggle between the knights of Charlemagne and the invading Saracens, weaving into its complicated plot stories of madness, love and the heroical origins of the Este family. *Orlando* inspired other poets to outdo Ariosto in creating epic hymns of national or dynastic pride. Luis de Camões (1524—80) took as his subject the great deeds of the Portuguese, particularly the explorer Vasco da Gama, in his 1572 *The Lusiads*. Less successful artistically was the attempt by Pierre de Ronsard (1524—85) in *La Franciade* (1572) to do the same for the French. *Jerusalem Liberated* (1581) by Torquato Tasso (1544—95) dealt with the conquest of the Holy City by the knights of the First Crusade, including, because Tasso also resided at the Ferrara court, yet another imaginary ancestor of the Este clan. In many ways the poem is an expression of the new earnestness of the Catholic Reformation and Tasso would eventually rewrite parts of it to strengthen its religious content. Tasso was also careful to use elevated language appropriate to his work's high moral tone. The Englishman Edmund Spenser (1552—99) in his unfinished masterpiece *The Faerie Queene* (1589—96) used Arthurian legend to present a complicated allegorical tale full of references to the court of Elizabeth I. These marvellously constructed Virgilian epics attempted to offer the reader a comprehensive interpretation of history and human experience but because of their obsession with knighthood they were, at the same time, out of touch with the realities of the sixteenth century.

THE PASTORAL

Nowhere was the tension between reality and illusion greater than in the pastoral poems, romances and plays which linked an ancient tradition to the Renaissance belief in Aristotle's aesthetics: the poet must represent the universal as well as the particular. The pastoral setting was thought to typify the universal which was common to all men, the genuine life and thought of the golden age. The pastoral, said Sidney, 'sometimes under the pretty tales of wolves and sheep, can include the whole considerations of wrong-doing and justice'. The close link between man and nature in pastoral literature provides stability in the midst of change; man himself (the shepherd or shepherdess) becomes an abstract entity whose task it is to provide a foundation for all that men have in common. The simplicity and genuine emotions of those who were thought to exemplify Arcadia suffuse the plot, while the action centres upon the pure love which man and woman have for each other.

The *Arcadia* (1504) of Jacopo Sannazaro (1458–1530) was a mixture of poetry and prose, telling the story of the unhappy love of Sincero who consoled himself by sharing in the life of shepherds. It proved to be enormously influential and its theme was often imitated. Jorge de Montemayor (1519–61) placed Arcadia in Spain in his intermingling of prose and poetry, the 1559 *Diana*, a pastoral continued by the 1564 *Diana enamorada* of Gaspar Gil Polo (1519–85). The form reached England where Edmund Spenser's *Shephearde's Calendar* was published in 1579 and George Peele's verse play *The Araygnement of Paris* was played before Queen Elizabeth in 1584. Sir Philip Sidney's *Arcadia* (1590–93) combined chivalric romance and elements of the pastoral, with kings living in the wilderness and princes disguising themselves as shepherds. There is certainly an element of neo-stoicism in the pastorals and they were to have a continuing popularity, offering a vision of man living the simple life within nature, demonstrating the harmony which infused all men before their corruption by modernity.

LYRIC POETRY

Because of the flowering of Renaissance poetry later in the century many have tended to overlook the rich native traditions of poetical expression that were found in many countries when the century began. In Spain the courtly love-song flourished and the old folk ballads continued to inspire poets. The enormous collection of traditional and contemporary verse in the 1511 *Cancionero general* of Hernando del Castillo reveals how closely Spanish poetry was linked to music. This was also the case in Germany where the 'Volkslieder', songs about love, heroes in battle or religious devotion, were a fundamental part of early sixteenth century poetry. The Meistersingers were urban guilds of poets, highly organized, with strict rules governing their creativity and progress. The most famous of these poets, and one who went outside their conventions, was Hans Sachs (1492–1576), a shoemaker of Nuremberg. Extremely prodigious in his output (he may have produced nearly 1,700 poems and 200 plays), Sachs became the leading poet of German Protestantism and saluted Luther's activities in the 1523 'Wittenberg Nightingale'. Luther's great hymns are part of the popular medieval strain. Urban guilds also featured in the poetry of the Netherlands – the 'Rederijkerskamers', or chambers of rhetoric, produced rather undistinguished poets interested in literary theory and bound by complex rules of composition. English poetry of the early sixteenth century has often been criticized for its drabness or clumsiness and poets who felt themselves children of the Renaissance sought to distance themselves from their literary forerunners. Sidney called them 'base men with servile wits' who by 'their own disgracefulness disgrace the most graceful poesy'. This is unmerited harshness. While poets like Stephen Hawes (1474–1511), author of the allegorical *The Passetyme of Pleasure* (1509) and Robert Crowley (1518–88), the indefatigable Protestant versifier and pamphleteer, are by no means poets of the first rank, their work is vigorous and often very interesting; the metric versions of the Psalms by Thomas Sternhold and John Hopkins, first published in 1549, were extremely popular with English Protestants for centuries.

Many areas, particularly at the periphery of Europe, were able to continue their folk and medieval poetic traditions undisturbed by the Renaissance throughout the sixteenth century. In Russia, for example, which the printing press did not penetrate until the 1560s, poetry still concerned itself with epic renditions of battles and acts of national heroism against the Tartars and the Poles. In other countries, however, native poetry suffered an eclipse. Italian poetry, under the influence of Petrarch, had developed new poetic conventions that were to prove appealing to foreign poets as well. In Spain, through the efforts of Juan Boscán (1487—1542) and Garcilaso de la Vega (1501—1536), Italian poetic effects and themes were introduced. Older metric forms were abandoned and writers took up the sonnet, blank verse and the ottava rima; the pastoral and themes from classical mythology now entered Spanish poetry. This movement was not unopposed and the innovations of Boscán and Garcilaso aroused resistance from poets who continued to champion their medieval inheritance. At the court of Henry VIII, two poets in particular tried to demonstrate the virtues of Italianate poetry to Englishmen. Sir Thomas Wyatt (1503—42) and Henry Howard, Earl of Surrey (1517—47) attempted to popularize the sonnet but it was not until the reign of Elizabeth that Renaissance poetry achieved dominance, as we can see in Sidney and Spenser. In France, Pierre de Ronsard, Joachim du Bellay (1522–60) and the Pléiade poets absorbed both Petrarchan and older classic styles to produce a new school they thought could rival both the Italians and the ancients. French poets were among the leading exponents of emblem books which tried by artful arranging of graphics and text to produce a neoplatonic unity of image and poetry in illustration of the Idea. In Maurice Scève's *La Délie* (1544) fifty emblems are placed at regular intervals, tied by motto to the text of the poems following. The court of James VI patronized a new wave of Scottish poetry, influenced by French models but which aimed at a distinctive national school. King James himself wrote poetry, including an epic celebration of the battle of Lepanto.[6]

The cultivated artificiality and self-conscious grand style of much of this work led to poetry becoming stilted and strangled in its own conceits, though real feeling occasionally managed to break free of conventions as in the poetry of the great Michelangelo Buonarroti (1475—1564). Michelangelo's devout but unconventional Catholicism led him to seek direct communion with Christ and many of his poems may be seen as prayers meant only for the eyes of God.[7] His anguished sublimation of earthly passions filled his poetry with a genuineness that many contemporary writers were unable to approach. In the end, however, the problems of imitating past styles and adhering rigidly to theoretical conventions threatened to overwhelm the poetic imagination. At the end of the century the Italian poet Giambattista Marini (1569–1625) exemplified this trend and gave the name 'Marinism' to a whole school of poetry. Marini's poems are filled with ingenuity and brilliance, word plays and rhetorical devices but the hyperbole and ornamentation ultimately weary the reader. His style would lead to the Baroque but his poetry is only one expression of the sixteenth century's infatuation with classic imitation and a clinging to things past, a trend which can also be seen in much drama and love of such prose as the chivalric romances.

PROSE FICTION IN THE SIXTEENTH CENTURY

Prose fiction did not have as high a reputation in the sixteenth century as poetry, particularly if it were written in the vernacular. Much of it was held in low esteem because it appealed to the vulgar masses and did not take a sufficiently didactic tone. Its subject matter often failed to impress contemporary critics as well. Speaking of the chivalric romance, Malory's *Le Morte D'Arthur*, the humanist Roger Ascham said that its pleasures consisted of two main attractions: 'open manslaughter and bold bawdry'. Even authors of romances were hesitant to bill their works as such, preferring to call them 'histories' or 'mirrors'. Nonetheless, such works were extremely popular throughout the century. The chivalric *Amadis of Gaul* by the Spaniard Garcia de Montalvo, first published in 1508, created a hunger among European readers for sequels or imitations of its tales of heroic derring-do, feats of arms and rescues of fair maidens. Not only was *Amadis* translated into many languages but Amadis himself became the father of a dynasty of knights errant whose sons, grandsons and nephews became the heroes of countless new tales and who continued the family tradition of slaying giants and overcoming evil spells.[8] Despite the disfavour of literary critics, this fiction found readers among all classes, from the nobility who identified with the aristocratic heroes to the common sort of reader who relished the passion and violence. Romances always sought to evoke a sense of awe and wonder;

every literary effect was practised to excess. They fashioned imaginary worlds where passionate sex and violence powerfully gripped their readership.[9] Eventually, however, romances fell out of favour with the well-to-do and became the proverbial reading of servants, children and old women.

DON QUIXOTE

Miguel de Cervantes (1547–1616) wrote his novel *Don Quixote* (1605) in opposition to the illusions which formed the essence of chivalric romances. In fact Cervantes has two of his characters fuel a bonfire with books of romances, though *Amadis* was one of only two volumes spared from the flames. The knight Don Quixote, driven mad by reading romances, lives in a world of chivalric illusions, not understanding himself or the real world about him. Whenever, with the best of intentions, he wants to do good he merely succeeds in making the situation worse. Don Quixote lives in a world where every transitory experience becomes a major event, and where reality is of little account; windmills become giants, inns become castles and village girls become noble ladies. Yet for all that, the knight's view of himself and his surroundings allows him to cope successfully with reality as seen in his own terms. People do help and are polite, in spite of his crazed state of mind. By contrast, the primitive common sense of his squire Sancho Panza cannot readily cope with the unsolved and unsolvable problems of reality.

Cervantes professed to view his masterpiece as nothing more than an 'amusement' but there is, in addition to the obvious theme of parodying the romances to which his fellow-Spaniards were addicted, a deeper intention shown in *Don Quixote*. The knight's world-view, however disjointed it may appear to the outside world, is harmonious and forms a coherent unity. The sickness of Don Quixote contrasts markedly with the confusion and fatalism of his times; his sickness may be needed to heal the even more serious sickness infecting Spain. The harmony of the individual personality must be restored in an age for which the knightly ethos can no longer serve as example. Cervantes's attack on illusions springing from a dead past goes hand in hand with the rejection of a confused and atomized present.

THE PICARESQUE NOVEL

A different diagnosis of contemporary society is rendered in the picaresque novel, a genre dealing with the adventures of poor but clever rascals, which appeared first with the publication of the anonymous *Lazarillo de Tormes* in 1554. Lazarillo is portrayed as a man of no attachments who must live by his wits and who goes through a variety of employments in which he tries to better himself by trickery. Forced, as a young child, to be the servant of an evil blind man, he escapes and steals his master's money. Serving, in turn, a priest, a nobleman, a seller of papal bulls and a notary, Lazarillo recounts with a keen satirical tone the shortcomings of these representatives of Spanish society. These novels, the best of which was the 1599 *Guzmán de Alfarache* by Mateo Alemán, reflect a society whose values are distegrating, where a rogue can hope to prosper by adopting the hypocrisy of his social superiors. The author of *Lazarillo de Tormes* and Alemán are thought to have been 'conversos' which may account for the image of the anti-hero, on the fringe of society. In later examples of the picaresque, however, there is much of the Catholic Reformation's zeal for repentance and conversion of the degenerate heart. The picaro, thinking himself to be the freest man on earth, was in reality at the mercy of fleeting circumstances. The longing for harmony, so much a part of the age, shines through here.

SHORT FICTION

The fourteenth-century Italian Giovanni Boccaccio had popularized with his *Decameron* the genre of short witty tales, full of ribaldry and amorous intrigue. Two centuries later he had many successors, such as Marguerite of Navarre and the authors of Italian 'novellae'. Marguerite's *Heptameron* (1558) follows the convention of a disparate group of people brought together by disaster (in Boccaccio by the plague, in Marguerite on account of a flood) who pass the time by recounting stories to each other. The work is interesting for a number of reasons: its strong female characters, its insights into contemporary views on love and marriage and the uncompromising nature of its anti-clericalism.[10] The predominant theme of the *Heptameron* was love, but Marguerite's handling of the topic is more refined and moralistic than Boccaccio. Like Marguerite, Bonaventure des Periers (1510–44) found the short story an attractive genre and, like her, used it for anti-clerical satire, though of a gentler sort. His *Joyeux Devis* (1558) are lighter and less concerned with moral elevation. More lurid and sensational were the Italian short stories, the 'novellae'. Matteo Bandello (1485–1562) was the leading author of this sort of tale, many of which offered the reader versions of contemporary events, embellished with scenes of cruelty and licence. Giovan Francesco Straparola's *Pleasant Nights* (published in two parts in 1550 and 1553) was a collection of seventy-four tales and introduced such folk stories as 'Puss in Boots' and 'Beauty and the Beast'. The extremely wide readership for this short fiction shows the growing importance of middle-class taste to European literature.

RABELAIS

The sixteenth century was an age of huge appetites. It was nothing unusual when Melanchthon, on a visit to Nuremberg, was offered a meal of eight courses, all either meat, fowl or fish. At such a dinner, unpalatable to modern stomachs, each guest consumed a third of a litre of wine with each course. Drunkenness went hand in hand with gluttony, and nearly every government passed laws against such behaviour. The giant heroes of the novels of Francois Rabelais (1494–1553) enter fully into this life; indeed, Gargantua's first words on being born are 'Drink, drink, drink!'. In Rabelais' *Pantagruel* (1532), *Gargantua* (1534) and the later books, the coarseness that was so much a part of contemporary life, especially in the peasant excesses of Carnival, plays a large part.[11] Better than any other writer of this time, Rabelais describes the zesty life of the market-place, the oaths of the common man and the popular humour of the streets. But it would be a mistake to see Rabelais only in these terms – his books are also satires on the learned and powerful, on churchmen, scholars and soldiers. They comment on the role of women, the demands of education and the need for ecclesiastical reform. Rabelais was a committed Christian, an admirer of Erasmus whose longing for a purer Church cleansed of medieval abuses is evident in his writings. The contribution of Rabelais to French prose is also considerable. In championing a vigorous vernacular, in injecting movement and a sense of the natural, he opened the language to new possibilities.[12]

DRAMA

It is not surprising in an age when most men and women could not read that the literary form which reached most people was an oral one. Drama, in the form of pageants, pantomimes and civic or church processions, had been used for hundreds of years to impress religious and social values on an illiterate audience; indeed, early in the sixteenth century this aim was still a major factor in European theatre. Throughout the course of the century drama would undergo important changes but the didactic element would remain strong.

This can be seen in the lingering popularity of those medieval genres, the morality and mystery plays. Moralities, an allegorical form which personified virtues and vices, instructed viewers all over western Europe: Scottish nobles watched at court, Cornish audiences crowded open-air amphitheatres, while the most famous of all moralities, *Everyman*, originated in a Dutch rhetorical competition. In Iberia, where religious drama was highly valued, the most distinguished writer of moralities in the sixteenth century was the Portuguese poet Gil Vicente who from 1516 to 1519 produced his trilogy, *The Ship of Hell, The Ship of Purgatory* and *The Ship of Heaven*. In England, urban guilds shared responsibility for these plays, providing both finances and actors for the production. Similar to the morality was the mystery play. Though less allegorical than the morality, it, too, had didactic purpose, depicting the lives of saints or Biblical scenes, and often relied on civic groups for its production. In Paris, for example, passion confraternities held a virtual monopoly. In the French countryside mystery plays were staged annually or to meet a special need such as propitiating heaven over a plague or bad harvest and their presentation could stretch over a considerable period of time. In 1547 in Valenciennes a mystery took twenty-five days to enact while in Bourges a play on the lives of the Apostles lasted a full forty days. Despite considerable imagination in stage settings, both the morality and mystery plays went into decline in the sixteenth century. They tended to lose their simple, direct appeal by increasing intrusions of comic scenes or pompous

373

language and they began to appear to educated audiences as quaint relics of an earlier, unsophisticated age. The talented writers who might once have been attracted to these forms turned to other means of dramatic expression as pressures of the Reformation and Counter Reformation served to extinguish their performance. This does not mean the religious element abandoned the theatre, only that it would find different channels. All sides in the religious struggles would find drama an effective weapon. Even persecuted sects wrote plays presenting their views; English Anabaptists wrote the drama *Love Feigned and Unfeigned* while the doomed radicals of besieged Münster staged plays on the theme Lazarus and the Rich Man to boost morale.

As older, medieval forms declined, the Renaissance made its influence felt in the humanist drama aimed at the literate members of social elites. This genre began in the 1480s when Italian courts sponsored the revival of plays by Roman authors Plautus and Terence; original plays in Latin or the vernacular, modelled on strict classic artistic conventions soon followed. Ariosto at the Este court in Ferrara wrote comedies in this vein but the best was probably *Mandragola* in 1518 by Niccolò Machiavelli. Though these sorts of plays became most influential in France where they helped shape the theatre of the seventeenth century, they were popular among learned audiences all across Europe; at the Polish court, Jan Kochanowski's *The Dismissal of the Greek Envoys* (1578) drew on classical models as did Martin Držić's comedy *Dundo Maroje*, staged in Dubrovnik in 1551. Christian humanists adopted the form for use in schools; Melanchthon wrote prologues to classic dramas presented by his academy while Luther believed that such plays were an excellent way to teach Latin and to impart certain virtues to secondary school students. Later in the century the Jesuits made excellent use of school drama in aiding the Catholic cause.

Early sixteenth-century drama must not be confused with the sort of professional entertainments and public theatres associated with, for example, William Shakespeare and his contemporaries. Though much ingenuity and expense was lavished by courts, schools and civic groups on the staging and designing of the settings (both Leonardo da Vinci and Raphael were employed at various times for this purpose), there were, as yet, no permanent theatres. Productions were mounted in indoor halls, on moveable carts and stages or enclosed inn-yards – the first permanent Elizabethan house was built in 1576 while the great perspective theatre in Vicenza which seated 2,000 appeared only in 1584. Moreover, most plays depended on amateur or, at best, semi-professional actors. In Paris the comic 'soties' and farces were staged by the 'Enfans sans Souci', amateur dramatic guildsmen, while German Shrovetide plays also used citizens as actors. Georg Wickram's *Tobias*, for example, had speaking parts for eighty-eight burghers of Strassburg and took two days to complete. In London, law students at the Inns of Court performed tragedies based on Seneca while entertainments at royal courts were presented by servants who would return to more mundane duties after their performances were over.[13] It is not until mid-century that the first professional troupes of actors make their appearance in Italy in the productions of the 'commedia dell'arte'.

The commedia dell'arte grew out of the Italian farce tradition. The plays were improvised, based on a plot outline and a collection of a dozen or so stock characters, including the figures of Pulcinella (who in England evolved into Punch), Harlequin and Columbine. The company's 'zannis', or buffoons, were called upon to perform their individual talents, such as acrobatics, ventriloquism, or telling rude jests, after the main attraction. Companies were often related by family ties and toured extensively in foreign countries, relying on mime to overcome difficulties of language. The plot devices and characters of the commedia dell'arte particularly enriched the drama of England, Spain and eastern Europe.

The great flowering of sixteenth century European drama appeared in England and Spain, following the development of the professional acting companies and the public theatres which began to appear in the 1570s and which were widespread by the 1590s. Playwrights such as William Shakespeare (1564–1616) and Lope de Vega (1562–1635) created a new sort of literature, rejecting the limitations on language and style of native medieval drama and the restrictive conventions of the neo-classic. Playing freely with action in space and time (Lope de Vega boasted he locked up all the rules under ten keys when he set out to write a play), mixing the tragic and the comic and insisting on a high degree of psychological realism, these writers entertained audiences of all classes by exploring themes of enduring appeal with a strong measure of the didactic. To Lope de Vega, who wrote hundreds of comedies and tragedies in the late sixteenth and early seventeenth centuries, authority, loyalty and Catholic orthodox were powerful forces in the Spanish heart, forces that might clash with an equally powerful sense of individual honour, as can be seen in two of his best tragedies,

The Sheep Well and *The King, the Greatest Alcalde*. In his plays the dignity and moral worth of peasants is equal to that of lords. Shakespeare, too, probed the individual psyche and also found value in the strength of national and cosmic authority. Perhaps Shakespeare was more reluctant, though, than his contemporaries in asserting definite answers to moral problems and his ultimate greatness may lie in his willingness to raise hard questions about human existence.

It is interesting to consider why sixteenth century theatre reached its highest point in the England of Shakespeare, Jonson and Marlowe and the Spain of Lope de Vega and not, say, in Germany or Italy. The answer lies in the security and improved status provided for actors and playwrights by the professional companies established in their public theatres open to all classes and in the happy combination of a royal court and big-city audience found in London and Madrid. Writers could then adapt classical allusions and themes to more robust contemporary tastes and produce a drama appealing both to the educated elites and semi-literate urban crowds. In Italy and Germany, where court societies were not located in large urban centres, authors lacked this sort of audience and drama remained amateurish and sterile.

THE INTERNATIONAL DIMENSION

One of the most remarkable features of literature in the sixteenth century is the extent to which, in an age of increasing nationalism and the breakup of Christian unity, it displayed an international flavour. Literary themes, forms and artists jumped frontiers and found themselves influential far from their original home, leading some to suggest that Europe possessed a cultural unity much greater in the sixteenth century than today.[14]

To a certain extent this was true, in literature at least. Humanism provided a link between those educated in its precepts, wherever they lived (see p. 76). Its students, clerics, nobles, administrators and scholars were brought up reading the same classical literature, responding to the same allusions to Greek and Roman culture and trained in the same rhetorical techniques. Across Europe, these men of similar cultural training could communicate with each other in an international language. Renaissance humanists had made great

efforts to purge Latin of its medieval 'barbarisms', to return it to a
state of purity, and throughout the sixteenth century Latin
continued to be employed as a literary as well as an ecclesiastical,
diplomatic and scientific means of expression. Any author who
courted an international audience of the classically educated wrote
in Latin, of necessity. This enabled writers in areas on the fringe of
European culture, such as Scandinavia, Eastern Europe and Spanish
America to be connected to the main streams of literature. Thus the
first Swedish attempt at drama was in Latin, *Tobiae comedia* (1550) by
Olavus Petri (1493–1552), and the greatest Polish poet of the century,
Jan Kochanowski, also produced a large part of his work in Latin.

Much of what was written in Latin was imitative of Roman
models such as Plautus and Seneca in drama or Horace and Virgil
in poetry. The Scottish humanist George Buchanan, who might
serve as an example of how Latin helped fashion an international
literature, wrote classically-influenced plays and verse while
teaching in France. Though once regarded as one of the finest poets
of his age, Buchanan's *Jephthes* (1534) and *Baptistes* (1578) find few
admirers today; nor would the romances of the Scot John Barclay,
the orations of the Englishman Walter Haddon or the plays of the
Croatian Marko Marulić attract more than an antiquarian interest.
However, the language could be used with great originality and
some of the century's most striking literature was written in Latin.
The satiric *Praise of Folly* (1509) by Erasmus and *Utopia* (1516) by
Thomas More showed that Latin was still capable of expressing
considerable creative power. It must also be remembered that many
of the century's great vernacular works, such as Castiglione's
Courtier were translated into Latin for an international audience.

The sixteenth century was one of great activity for translators. A
large proportion of printed literature in many countries consisted of
translations from Latin or other vernaculars. French riddles became
popular reading in England; English plays were translated into
German; Italian drama was staged in Poland and French poetry was
re-cast into Scots. New literary life could often spring from
translations. For example, in *The Palace of Pleasure* (1566) by William
Painter (1525–95) short stories from many languages and traditions
were made available to the English reader. Shakespeare and John
Webster (1578–1632) then took plot ideas from this collection of
international literature and turned them into new creations such as
All's Well That Ends Well and *The Duchess of Malfi*. Translators
worked with more than just written literature; they were also called

upon to render dramatic performances intelligible to audiences who could not understand either the Latin of the school or Jesuit drama or the native tongue of the foreign players.[15] Ironically, one of the areas in which translation served to create an international literature was religious polemic. Out of the clamour and invective thrown up by the opposing forces in the struggles between Catholics and Protestants grew a literature of charge and counter-charge, attack and counter-attack. These books were frequently translated by religious authorities in order to show the people that their spiritual enemies were being properly rebutted or were smuggled across borders in order to win converts. The religious works of figures as diverse as Savonarola, Calvin, the Belgian monk Peter Frarin, the Jesuit St Peter Canisius and Luther were printed in English in the sixteenth century as part of this literary warfare in which translators played an indispensable part.

POPULAR LITERATURE

Much of the literature of the century did not appeal to the bulk of the people and, indeed, was deliberately not aimed at them by its authors. The French poet Joachim du Bellay proclaimed that a writer of poetry should be a learned man and avoid 'the ignorant people who are the enemies of all rare and ancient learning'. The Italian epic poet Torquato Tasso agreed, saying, 'I have never tried to please the stupid common people.' Works written in Latin for a scholarly or clerical readership also could have had little attraction for a vernacular readership, nor is it likely that courtly allegory or learned imitations of Seneca had popular appeal. What then did the ordinary literate European in the sixteenth century read?

As might be expected in a century dominated by the Protestant and Catholic Reformations, religious and devotional material was very popular. Prayer books, saints' lives, hymn books, paraphrases of psalms and collections of sermons could be found in many homes. Readers could also choose from books discussing the responsibilities of Christian parents, whether one might, in good conscience, lend money at interest or how to meet death with a strong faith. The primer was probably the most popular form of devotional material. It was a combination of a layman's prayer-book, a compendium of religious advice and a calender of canonical hours for Christian worship. The primer had evolved from the medieval Book of Hours which gave the proper time of day or night for the various offices of worship, telling when they should take place. But in the sixteenth century the primers included many more prayers, meditations and, at times, instructions on the 'ars moriendi'. As the century wore on the reformers used the great popularity of the primers, adapting them to their teaching, yet always allowing them to remain within their traditional forms. Martyrologies were common reading in both Catholic and Protestant countries; the most famous of these was the 1563 *Acts and Monuments of the Church* by John Foxe, better known as his *Book of Martyrs*. One of history's earliest books of trivia had religious content: a book originally written in German entitled *Spiritual Questions*, also known as 'The Pastor's Torment', was written to give young party-goers something else to do than drink. It asked, for example, 'Where is it written God watches over our hair?', hoping to elicit the answer Matthew 10: 30, 'the very hairs of your head are numbered'. *Spiritual Questions* was translated into other languages and went through numerous editions.[16]

At least as popular as religious material was the pseudo- scientific almanac. Cheap enough to be available to all but the poorest, almanacs gave their readers more than astronomical information such as phases of the moon. They provided astrological prognostications, agricultural and gardening tips, flood calendars and hints on how to read character from facial features. Almanacs also included recipes, medical advice, inspirational verses, information on markets and fairs, and aids to travellers such as distance tables and coastal landmarks. Though the vastly popular almanac *The Shepherd's Calendar* may not actually have been useful to shepherds and the rural poor, it and other prognostication books were big sellers throughout Europe for centuries.

Prose fiction was also popular with the common reader. Romances, with their tales of knighthood and love, had wide readership among women as did the sensational 'novellae' of Italy. Germans bought the novels of Georg Wickram (1520—60) with their affirmation of the values of the middle-class family while Spaniards loved the picaresque novel and its exploration of the seamy underside of life. Comic tales found readers everywhere. The pranks of the Saxon peasant trickster Till Eulenspiegel and the short story collection *Joyeux Devis* by Bonaventure des Periers amused Englishmen in translation as the deeds of 'Howleglas' and the

Mirour of Mirth. These humorous stories could be based around one character, as in Eulenspiegel or Old Hobson, or they could be random compilations full of the ribald doings of amorous monks, cuckolded millers and faithless wives. The 1555 *Rollwagenbüchlein* of Wickram was a widely imitated collection of anecdotes and light tales intended to be read by travellers on ships or stage-coaches.

In a great variety of 'how-to' books writers offered advice to their readers on a wide range of skills. Trade secrets and craft skills were now available to all with the price of a book and a curiosity about the workings of surgeons, carpenters or veterinarians. One might also learn how to swim, how to make cosmetics, how to fence, dance or do mental arithmetic. In by-passing the customary master/ student relationship and the demands of formal instruction, these books introduced a democratic and almost subversive element to sixteenth-century literature.

The most common form of popular literature was the ephemeral pamphlets and single-sheet broad-sides.[17] Used by all sides throughout the century to present religious and political propaganda, they could also entertain and inform. Broad-sides often consisted of printed ballads which conveyed either a light-hearted diversion like 'A New Merry Ballad of a Maid that would Marry with a Serving Man' or news in song of recent events such as 'A Brief Ballad Touching the Taking of Scarborough Castle'. Many of these were illustrated and some thoughtfully included the music for the song, though most just specified that the ballad was to be sung to a particular popular tune. This literature had a tendency to the bizarre and horrifying, showing a pronounced taste for news of comets, deformed births, assassinations and executions. Unlike book-sellers in their stalls and shops, ballad sellers, who would frequent taverns or barber-shops to sing a sample of their wares and peddle their merchandise, were often in trouble with the authorities and were classified with vagabonds as public nuisances. The very low price of these pamphlets and broad-sides guaranteed a wide readership among the urban working classes.

WOMEN IN LITERATURE

Since the time has come, Mademoiselle that the severe laws of men no longer prevent women from applying themselves to sciences and disciplines it seems to me that those who have that facility should employ that worthy freedom . . . and if one of us should reach such a level as to be able to put down her conceptions in writing, she should do it carefully and not disdain fame and make of it an adornment.[18]

So wrote the French poet Louise Labé in the dedication of her dialogue *The Debate of Love and Folly* (1555). The century did see increasing restrictions put on women in some professions (such as the drive by the male medical profession to regulate midwifery) but this was not the case in literature where female influence actually increased. Women such as Christine de Pisan and Juliana of Norwich had written books in the Middle Ages, but the customary function of women in literature had been as inspiration for male writers or as a topic of discussion, such as in the 'querrelle de femmes' where the proper attributes of their sex had been debated by numerous authors. Noble women might also serve as patrons, providing encouragement, protection or financial support to writers, who would, in turn dedicate their books to them. Women continued to play these roles in the sixteenth century but the number who actually produced literary works of their own multiplied greatly.

There are several reasons for this. Printing, as we have seen, greatly enhanced the chances for publication of all sorts of works and the religious upheavals of the age brought women to the fore in defending and propagating the faith. Probably most importantly, however, humanist education produced a number of very well-educated women who had been encouraged to become involved with literature − this would help account for the high proportion of women of rich or noble families among female writers. A popular exercise in humanist education was student translation of classic works and many women, particularly those of the nobility and even royalty, produced and published translations. Ann Bacon (1528–1610), for example, the wife of the Elizabethan Lord Keeper, translated into English the sermons of the Italian Protestant Bernard Ochino and Bishop Jewel's Latin *Apology of the Church of England*.

Though some women such as Louise Bourgeois (1563–1636), author of *Observations diverses* on the midwife's trade, might write non-fiction prose and an exceptionally influential woman such as Marguerite of Navarre might have a play produced, most women writers seem to have chosen poetry as their means of literary expression. In Italy, the aristocratic widow Vittoria Colonna (1492–1547), friend of Aretino and Michelangelo, wrote philosophical sonnets while the courtesan Tullia d'Aragona penned rather more uninhibited verses on love. In France, *Rimes* (1545) by Pernette du Guillet went through four editions; Louise Labé (1520–65), known as the 'French Sappho', produced love sonnets and elegies as well as her more famous dialogue quoted above and Nicole Estienne published verses on *The Miseries of the Married Woman*. Schoolmistress Anna Bijns (1493–1575) was one of the last great rhetorician-poets of Antwerp, attacking Lutheranism in her verse.

Religion figured largely in much of the writing by sixteenth-century women. The Spanish mystic St Teresa of Avila (1515–82) wrote of the contemplative soul's progress toward God in several works including the posthumously-published *The Way of Perfection* (1583). In England, Lady Elizabeth Fane's Biblical verse paraphrases in *Certaine Psalmes* appeared in 1550; later in the century Anne Dowriche's *French Historie* (1589) recounted in verse form the suffering of the persecuted Huguenots. The first poet in Europe to create a purely religious emblem book was the French Protestant Georgette de Montenay (1540–71) whose *Emblesmes ou Devises Chrestiennes* appeared in the year of her death. German women also took up the pen in defence of their religious views: in Strassburg, Katherine Zell defended the new Protestant practice of married clergy, while the Bavarian noblewoman Argula von Grumbach published a treatise attacking Catholics at the local university. Marguerite of Navarre, the most important female author of her time, wrote many works in different genres but her first publication was one with great appeal to her contemporaries, the 1531 *Miroir de l'âme pécheresse*, which was translated by the future Queen Elizabeth of England as *A Godly Meditation*. The religious element would also be a strong part of women's autobiography as can be seen in works as diverse as the *Memoires* of the French Catholic queen Marguerite de Valois (1553–1615) and the reminiscences of the English Puritan Rose Hickman (1526–1613).

Marguerite of Navarre's *The Heptameron* is best known to modern readers but other female authors of prose fiction include Jeanne Flore whose 1530 *Comptes amoureuses* dealt with the power of romantic love and Marguerite de Briet whose semi-autobiographical novel *Angoysses doloureuses* (1538) was the first in France to describe events from a woman's point of view.

De Briet's book was published under the pseudonym of Helisenne de Crenne. It was not uncommon for women writers to conceal their authorship, not just under assumed names but in a refusal to publish at all. Some women like Margaret Tyler were unashamed to state their sex and name, saying: 'my persuasion hath bene thus, that it is all one for a woman to pen a story as for a man to address his story to a woman',[19] but many of the century's best literary works by women, such as those of Pernette du Guillet, remained in manuscript until after their deaths. Indeed, Modesta Pozza's *Merit of Women* (1600) was published not only posthumously but also pseudonymously. The wide-spread reluctance of many female authors to be linked publicly with their art and the narrow range of topics considered suitable to be addressed by them (chiefly questions of love or religion) show that, despite the increased participation of women in literature, social restrictions were still keenly felt.

CENSORSHIP

One of the most important effects of the invention of printing was to take control of book production away from the Church and give it to lay entrepreneurs, a phenomenon which contributed greatly to the success of the Reformation (see pp. 160ff.). This did not mean, of course, that there was no censorship or that authors were completely free to write whatever they chose. In the first place, writers, who had no copyright protection, had to please both publisher and patron if they hoped to have their work printed and profit from it. There was also ecclesiastical and state censorship to reckon with. The 1515 Lateran Council demanded that all books be examined by Church authorities and the flood of Reformation literature shortly after that made both clergy and magistrates aware of the importance of controlling the press.

Some jurisdictions, more tolerant than others, sought only to preserve public harmony. A 1524 Strassburg law, for example, forbade the printing of anything that 'would provoke the ordinary Christian man to attack or ridicule his neighbour'.[20] Most legislation, however, was aimed at regulating orthodoxy, as in the northern French ordinance that prohibited folk from attempting to 'sing, or play or cause to be divulged, sung or played publicly, in company or private, any farces, ballads, songs, comedies, refrains, or other similar writings on any subject or in any language whatsoever, old or new, in which there be mixed any questions, propositions, or facts concerning our religion or ecclesiastical persons'.[21]

This latter regulation dated from 1560 and is typical of the mid-century attempt throughout Europe to tighten up censorship law and machinery; this was particularly so in Catholic Europe which heeded the Council of Trent's admonition that literature should be religiously and morally uplifting. The Italian city of Lucca published a list of prohibited books in 1547, an example followed by Milan and Venice in 1554 and the famous papal Index in 1559. The Index, of course, banned Protestant literature but also caught up others in its attack on 550 authors and 400 named books, including works by Machiavelli, Erasmus, Aretino, Boccaccio and Dante. (A 1564 version of the Index relaxed restrictions against fiction, especially by classical authors. This time Boccacio's *Decameron* was allowed to be published if stripped of its anti-clerical satire.) In England, the regime of Mary Tudor established the Stationers' Company in 1557 to regulate book production and banned the performance of plays as tending to incite the people to disorder. In Spain, the Inquisition condemned the poetry of Jorge Montemayor and imprisoned the poet Luis de León; in the Netherlands the popular rhetorical exhibitions were suppressed; in France mystery plays were banned.

How did the literary community react to these moves and what effect did censorship have on sixteenth-century literature? Printers and writers devised numerous ways of evading the authorities. Authors disguised their association with dangerous works by adopting pseudonyms, printers by using false colophons. A virulently anti-papal tract published by exiled English Protestants, for example, declared itself to have been published adjacent to the pope's palace. When regulation of printing establishments grew too rigorous, printers might resort to presses hidden in the countryside, as when English Puritans published their satirical attacks on the Church hierarchy in the Marprelate controversy. Books banned in one part of Europe might be printed abroad and distributed by smuggling or the author might simply move to a more tolerant country and work there. Writers of extreme unorthodoxy like Giordano Bruno might, however, flee to a number of foreign lands and still not find refuge.

There were other, more subtle, ways of avoiding censorship. By using a dialogue formāt a writer might publish suspect viewpoints with less risk of necessarily being identified as a proponent of them. Authors also used artful ambiguity to disguise their true beliefs; scholars still search Sir Philip Sidney's *Arcadia* and Edmund Spenser's *Faerie Queene* for clues as to the authors' views on contemporary personalities and politics. Finally, there was self-censorship where writers might refuse to publish at all or change their works in anticipation of official disapproval. The neurotic poet Tasso, desperate lest he have somehow offended the Church in his epic *Jerusalem Liberated*, made extensive changes to his work.

Censorship was often successful in encouraging authors to concentrate their creative energies in approved channels and in keeping banned works from the eyes of the people. Ironically, however, much of this censorship back-fired and only served to advertise works it meant to suppress. Indexes of prohibited literature were studied by book-sellers and printers looking for exciting material to stock or re-print. Those passages which Catholic censors cited for purgation only served to advertise where prominent authors had held anti-Roman opinion.[22] In the long run the future of European literature and the real power of the printing press would lie beyond the reach of censors of all kinds.

NOTES AND REFERENCES

1 See Elizabeth Eisenstein, *The Printing Press as an Agent of Change: Communications and cultural transformations in early-modern Europe*, 2 vols (Cambridge, 1979) and Miriam Usher Chrisman, *Lay Culture and Learned Culture: Books and Social Change in Strasbourg, 1480–1599* (New Haven, 1982).

2 Helena M. Shire, 'The Lyric and the Renaissance', in David Daiches and Anthony Thorlby, eds. *The Old World: Discovery and Rebirth* (London, 1974), p. 161.

3 Natalie Zemon Davis, 'Printing and the Peoples', in *Society and Culture in Early Modern France* (Stanford, 1975), p. 225.

4 In *English Essays from Sir Philip Sidney to Macaulay* (New York, 1910), p. 12.

5 A. Bartlett Giametti, *Exile and Change in Renaissance Literature* (New Haven, 1984), p. 4.

6   Jenny Wormald, *Court, Kirk, and Community: Scotland 1470–1625* (Toronto, 1981), pp. 185–86.

7   Konrad E. Eisenbuchler, 'The Religious Poetry of Michelangelo: the Mystical Sublimation', *Renaissance and Reformation*, 1987, p. 124.

8   Guillermo Diaz-Plaja, *A History of Spanish Literature* (New York, 1971), p. 76.

9   A. C. Hamilton, 'English Prose Fiction and Some Trends in Recent Criticism', *Renaissance Quarterly*, 1984, p. 28.

10 Deborah N. Losse, 'Authorial and Narrative Voice, in the *Heptameron*', *Renaissance and Reformation*, 1987, p. 237.

11 Mikhail Bakhtian, *Rabelais and His World*, tr., Helene Iswolsky (Bloomington, 1984), *passim*

12 I. D. Macfarlane, *A Literary History of France: Renaissance France, 1470–1589* (London, 1974), p. 189.

13 D. M. Loades, *The Tudor Court* (London, 1986), p. 111.

14 Victor E. Neuberg, *Popular Literature: A History and Guide* (Harmondsworth, 1977), p. 40.

15 Jerzy Limon, 'English Players "Beyond the Seas": Staging Problems', *The Elizabethan Theatre IX* (Port Credit, 1981), p. 191.

16 Harald Beyer, *A History of Norwegian Literature* (New York, 1956), p. 84.

17 See Marie-Hélène Davies, *Reflections of Renaissance England: Life, Thought and Religion Mirrored in Illustrated Pamphlets, 1535–1640* (Allison Park, 1986).

18 In Germaine Bree, *Women Writers in France* (New Brunswick, 1973), p. 25.

19 Margaret Tyler's introduction to her translation of Diego Ortunez de Calahorra, *The Mirror of Princely Deedes and Knighthood* (London, 1578), A5.

20 Chrisman, *Learned Culture, Lay Culture*, p. 27.

21 Cited in Robert Muchembled, *Popular Culture and Elite Culture in France, 1400–1750* (Baton Rouge, 1985), p. 162.

22 Eisenstein, *The Printing Press as an Agent of Change*, vol. 1, pp. 416–7.

15

FROM RENAISSANCE TO BAROQUE: ART, MUSIC AND SCIENCE

ART

The sixteenth century was the greatest single century in the history of European art. Between 1500 and 1600 more of the finest paintings and frescoes of Europe were painted, and in a greater and more contrasting variety of styles, than in any other similar period. If the same cannot be said with equal conviction of sculpture and architecture, yet these arts too achieved a most remarkable number and range of triumphs. Any attempt to give a comprehensive history of these achievements, in the space here available, and without illustrations, would soon deteriorate into a mere list of great artists and their masterpieces. We have therefore attempted to show the art, music and natural science of the sixteenth century not so much for their intrinsic values — these can easily be studied in the many excellent and illustrated books specifically devoted to them — than as functions and achievements of the creative energies of the men of the period and the societies they lived in.

THE ART OF THE HIGH RENAISSANCE IN ITALY

In 1500 the whole of Europe recognized the pre-eminence of Italian art. Its style, the style of the High Renaissance, was the culmination of two centuries of unparalleled creative endeavour by an astonishing succession of painters, sculptors and architects of genius.

Where the medieval artist had striven to represent an idea, a picture in his mind — the idea of the rose, for instance, or of the Holy Virgin — the Renaissance artist strove to imitate nature. By 1500 the Italians had solved the technical problems which this involved. Leonardo, Raphael and Michelangelo, to name only the greatest, had mastered the mathematics of perspective to such a degree that Michelangelo, for instance, could paint a seemingly outcurving figure on a concave surface.[1] They perfected the technique of perspective drawing not only because it made the image appear like the object but because they thought that this technique also described how objects appeared in men's vision. This belief enabled the Renaissance painters to claim that their art was also a science.[2] They studied and drew the shapes of plants and animals with hitherto unknown precision; they dissected the human body to learn the secrets of its bone structure and the mechanism of its muscles; they investigated the behaviour of light (optics) and the structure of the human eye, and they made all such studies a part of their quest for artistic naturalism. The realistic representation of nature was one aspect of classical Graeco-Roman art which the artists of the High Renaissance had managed to recapture. The other was the emulation of the classical concept of beauty which they sought, in Leonardo's words, in 'the harmonious proportion of the parts which compose the whole, which content the sense'.[3] This was achieved in various ways. In architecture, the different parts of a building might be related to each other in mathematical proportions which corresponded to the geometrical proportions of musical harmonies. In painting or drawing, the correct, and therefore beautiful, proportions of the human figure might be obtained by inscribing it with outstretched limbs into a circle, the perfect geometrical figure. Or again, the artist would simply rely on experience to confirm for him the idea of ideal beauty. Thus Raphael wrote to his friend, Count Baldassare Castiglione, a famous connoisseur: 'In order to paint a beautiful woman I would have to see more beautiful women and on condition that you help me to select them; but since there are so few beautiful women and so few good judges, I follow a certain idea I have in my mind.'[4]

If the results eventually depended more on the living tradition of the previous two hundred years of Italian art and a free assimilation of classical motifs, especially in architecture, than on a direct imitation of the ancients, this only serves to show the vitality of the Renaissance tradition and the originality of its achievements.

NEOPLATONISM AND ART

Thoughts of the ancient Greek philosopher Plato (427–347 B.C.) had been revived and modified many times in late antiquity and the Middles Ages (see p. 146). Plato's basic concept of the existence of external 'Ideas' above the everyday world, and of the imitation of these 'Ideas' in objects and beings in the world was combined with Christian teachings. Here the mind and the immortal soul became linked. Thus, the mind–soul of a person was thought to be capable of ascending through stages from the physical world of nature up to the eternal 'Ideas' and God. The soul was seen as having an innate desire for, and love of, beauty, truth and goodness. It sought them in their purest eternal form.

The Italian Renaissance placed a special emphasis on beauty in art and in the natural world. The association of this natural beauty with eternal beauty was revived and elaborated in the works of fifteenth century Florentine neo-platonists. With the help of Medici patronage, Marsilio Ficino and his brilliant younger associate, Count Giovanni Pico Della Mirandola, became pre-eminent in the Florentine academy. Their (highly eclectic) scholarship, translations and commentaries emphasized a spiritualized philosophy and theology, particularly, Ficino's *Theologia Platonica*.[5] The mind and soul of man was seen as having the capacity to transform itself in life. From merely mortal human nature man could either descend to sub-human and bestial nature, or ascend to angelic and divine nature. The route to ascent was through platonic love. The love of beauty, truth and goodness could inspire the seeker to direct human will and intellect towards higher realities. From the appropriate appreciation of external beauty, a beautiful landscape, a beautiful person, the soul could move to internal and immaterial levels of contemplation and to the higher stages of understanding, to universal reality and to God. (See Figure 1, p. 4)

The ideals and tremendous optimism of the academy continued to influence sixteenth-century artists and intellectuals, even though few imagined that they could reach the highest levels of apprehension. Terrestrial beauty, both in artistic cloak and/or in scientific detail, was seen as the reflection of superior and true beauty.

Michelangelo's artistic universality was animated and exalted by the dynamic image of intellectual and spiritual ascent through beauty: 'She (beauty) lifts to heaven hearts that truly know . . .'[6]

And the aristocratic intelligentsia, companions of Baldassar Castiglione at the court of Urbino, were intrigued with the, now fashionable, image of platonic love and the dynamic route through beauty to perfection. Thus they were entertained and excited by the poet, Pietro Bembo's climactic prayer: 'And since you (divine love) delight to inhabit the flower of beautiful bodies and beautiful souls, and there sometimes consent to reveal a little of yourself to those worthy to see you, I believe that you now dwell here among us.'[7] When Bembo was transported by the frenzy raised by his thoughts about these matters, another member of the circle, Emilia, urged him, with gentle irony, to watch out lest his soul leave his body on the spot.

The inspiration of the Florentine academy also extended to serious intellectuals in other countries, for example, the Oxford Reformers, John Colet and Thomas More in England, and French poets, musicians and universalists, the Pléiade poets, and Antoine de Baïf's academicians. Renaissance neo-platonism and pythagoreanism is also linked with the creative activity of the scientific revolution. These notions formed a significant part of the intellectual milieux and mentalities of Copernicus, Kepler, Galileo and Harvey. Related influences continued in the seventeenth century.[8]

BREAKDOWN OF THE SOCIAL AND PSYCHOLOGICAL BASIS OF RENAISSANCE ART

At the very moment when the artists of the High Renaissance achieved the classical balance of harmonious proportions and ideal beauty in their altarpieces, statues and churches, the social and psychological basis of their art was breaking down. This basis had been the Italian city state. The artists in their workshops shared the sense of citizenship of the Christian commune. They had helped to create it with the cathedrals they built, the bronze reliefs for baptistry doors which they cast, and the frescoes of biblical stories they painted inside the churches. As city after city fell under the rule of despots, many artists took commissions from the new courts. The portraits and paintings, or decorations, of classical themes which they now executed, in addition to the traditional altarpieces and biblical frescoes, show the sophisticated and complex iconographical content favoured in the highly educated new court society. From a skilled craftsman the artist was becoming a gentleman expected to possess a thorough humanist training. At the other end of the artistic social scale he was, perhaps inevitably, becoming an eccentric. The emperor Frederick III made Gentile Bellini a count palatine. Charles V bestowed similar titles on Titian and, by the end of the sixteenth century, artists frequently figured in 'honours lists'.[9] Princes and popes treated artists like Leonardo and Michelangelo with a deference and consideration for the vagaries of the artistic temperament — a psychological phenomenon that was discovered and exploited just then for the first time — which would have been unthinkable in earlier generations.[10] Artists themselves were convinced of their role as creators. Leonardo's self-portrait looks quite remarkably like the traditional representations of God the Father. Dürer's looks even more like those of Christ.[11] Michelangelo, with his broken nose, could not compete in this respect, although one could speculate about his *Moses*; but his own contemporaries referred to him as *il divino* — an epithet which stemmed from the classical Neoplatonic notion of divine frenzy. Never before, and rarely since, had the creative role of the artist been valued so highly.

For a time court and civic art could coexist, could stimulate each other, especially when the artists had gained their new freedom and status and while the courts were still informal. Such were the courts of Lorenzo de Medici in Florence, and those of the princes and princesses of the houses of Gonzaga, Este and Montrefeltre in Mantua, Ferrara and Urbino, who held court as if it were a kind of humanist salon. Raphael's friend, Castiglione, has given us the portrait of the ideal court of this kind — a society which could still draw on the living traditions of the city state and blend them with the individualism of the new rulers, the splendour of their patronage and the civilized tastes and liberal values of a humanistically educated aristocracy.[12] It was more than the background to the art of the High Renaissance; it was its condition.[13]

The development of artistic styles has a logic of its own, especially where there are strong and self-conscious artistic traditions, as there were during the Italian Renaissance. The very perfection of the classical style of the High Renaissance was likely to be a reason for its rejection by a younger generation of artists. In 1523 Parmigianino painted his self-portrait as seen in a convex mirror. Perhaps this was no more than a virtuoso performance of a young artist showing off his technical skill; yet, if one considers the giant hand in the foreground, the distorted yet expressive facial features in the centre and a background which appears to revolve around the sitter, one feels that here was a deliberate denial of the values of classical art, almost an artistic declaration of war on the High Renaissance. The startling fact is, however, that the great masters of the classical style, Michelangelo and even Raphael, had themselves already begun to break down their own canons during the second decade of the sixteenth century, some years before Parmigianino's *jeu d'esprit* with the convex mirror. The causes of this break in tradition are therefore likely to be more complex than the traditional conflict of generations. They are evident, nevertheless. The political and military disasters of the city states, the rise of religious mass movements, and the devastating attacks by Machiavelli, Erasmus, More and Luther on practically the whole range of established values – all these make the intellectual and emotional climate of the age unmistakable: the time was past for the painting of beautiful and serene madonnas enthroned in majestic repose over a rational and orderly world.

The crisis continued. The sack of Rome by the emperor's unpaid armies, in 1527, put an end to the first great period of papal patronage of the arts, the period when Bramante was designing St Peter's, when Michelangelo was sculpting the *Moses* for the tomb of Julius II and painting the ceiling of the Sistine Chapel, when Raphael not only painted his portraits, his madonnas and the frescoes in the Vatican Palace, but also supervised the excavations of the Forum Romanum. By 1527 Bramante and Raphael were already dead. The other artists were dispersed. The young Benvenuto Cellini had fired the shot which killed the leader of the besieging army, the Connétable de Bourbon – or so he later claimed in his famous autobiography. Milan became a Spanish appanage. The Medici, having finally overthrown the last Florentine republic, took the titles of dukes and married into the Spanish nobility. Their court, and the courts of the other Italian princes and despots, adopted Spanish etiquette and formality.

The artist and writer, like everyone else, had been changed from a free citizen into a subject.[14] One of the roots of the tradition of Renaissance art had been cut off: the artist's work as a free citizen for the whole community. He was now thrown back, almost entirely, on the patronage of princes, courts and private persons. Could Italian art survive this narrowing of its psychological basis, in contrast to its centuries-old tradition, without a loss in quality and a diminished appeal to the finest young creative talent?

ARTISTIC REBELLION AND QUEST FOR SECURITY – MANNERISM

The reaction of Italian artists to the crisis took several, often contradictory, forms. The first and most immediate reaction was that rejection of the traditional pattern of values which has already been described. It was the merit of a generation of young artists – Parmigianino, Pontormo, Rosso Fiorentino and others, as well as of the older Michelangelo – to have created a new style, later called Mannerism because it was supposedly based on the manner of the later works of Michelangelo. The style was deliberately anticlassical, often violent, sometimes downright ugly, but with subtly expressive pictorial rhythms and emotions that the present century has found easier to appreciate than some intervening ages.[15]

The second, opposite but equally natural, reaction was the quest for security. Many had welcomed the return of the Medici, even the domination of the Spaniards, for the peace and stability they promised after more than a generation of war and revolutions. The gentlemanliness of the artists was now stressed more than ever. Vasari, himself a gifted architect but second-rate painter, patronized by the Medici, had in his famous *Lives*[16] shown Raphael as the ideal personality of an artist in the then fashionable Neoplatonic view. In his works, it was thought, the artist's 'mind expresses itself not otherwise than a mirror reflects the face of a man who looks into it'.[17] A somewhat later theorist, Lomazzo, imagined that the notoriously difficult, withdrawn and ugly Michelangelo also fitted this ideal. But not all artists either could or even wanted to fit into Lomazzo's categories. Parmigianino's face in the convex mirror, as indeed the whole of his troubled life and his disastrous passion for necromancy were a striking rejection of the Platonic mirror metaphor. Characteristically for the artists of this period, however, Parmigianino's attitude was nevertheless ambiguous; for, from his last years, we have another self-portrait of his which, like Dürer's, shows an unmistakably Christlike face. In Bronzino's portraits of Florentine court society in the mid-sixteenth century one can glimpse the nervous tension behind the masks of formal dress and rigid court manners. The character of the sitter is no longer openly presented to the beholder, as it had been in the faces of Raphael's superman-portrait of Julius II, of the fat and astute aesthete Leo X, or the honest and sensitive Castiglione. Bronzino caught the pathos of inadequate personalities behind robes of courtly splendour in a way that no other portraitist did again until Velazquez's even more compassionate and moving portraits of the Spanish court, a hundred years later.

As the sixteenth century wore on, the small Italian courts were becoming more and more provincial and narrow. Inevitably, the same fate overtook the main academies which had been founded with much enthusiasm to defend the social status of the artist and the quality of artistic production. Worse was to come. From about 1550, the Roman Counter-Reformation, in the first flush of its reborn resolution, began to turn its newly found puritan convictions against the arts. Castiglione's *Courtier* was put on the Index, there to keep incongruous company with Machiavelli's *Prince*. The sculptor Ammanati publicly repented of having sculpted nudes — his small bronze nudes on the Neptune fountain in Florence are beautifully elegant; his attempt to create a monumental marble figure in the manner of Michelangelo was, characteristically, a disaster. Michelangelo's *Last Judgment*, in the Sistine Chapel, was declared obscene and its naked figures partly painted over on the orders of the papal court. As another sign of the times, Pietro Aretino, the satirist and former scourge of the pompous, high or low, was on this occasion baying with the hounds. Even Michelangelo's plans for St Peter's were changed for narrowly doctrinal reasons.

Art in Italy was being stifled. The first generation of Mannerists had created a revolution in style and much superbly sensitive and imaginative work. The second and third generations deteriorated into a new rigidity, a kind of mannerist academicism; and academicians, though frequently addicted to pontifical pronouncements, do not usually think it becoming to a gentleman to identify himself with the divine.

THE BEGINNINGS OF THE BAROQUE

Towards the end of the sixteenth century the climate changed again. Counter-Reformation puritanism, at least in the arts, was in retreat. Much was due to Sixtus V (1585–90) and his determination to make Rome a city intellectually and artistically worthy of being the centre of Christendom (see p. 121). Vignola, Fontana, Maderno and other architects developed a new architectural style, the Baroque, in which the severe mode of Renaissance classicism was transformed to produce dramatic and spectacular effects with richly decorated surfaces and interiors, where frescoes and sculptures were much more consistently treated as part of an overall design than had been usual in the Renaissance. It was both a counter-attack against the intellectual agonies of Mannerism and a deliberate attempt to combine different art forms in order to heighten the effect of the complete work of art. It also became immensely popular and spread from Rome through Italy to Catholic central Europe, as far as Poland, and through Spain and Portugual to Central and South America. It represented a great revival of popular religious art and this was, perhaps, one of the most effective weapons of the Catholic Reformation, for it touched, and continued to touch, the imagination of the Catholic population of Europe in a way that not even the sermons of the preachers of the new Orders could do. The new style, which was not, indeed, fully developed until the following century, seems to have successfully caught and expressed a new sensibility. While brilliantly suited to glorify the Church and its dignitaries, or for that matter a king and his court, it appealed at the same time both to a very personal piety and to religious mass emotion. In this way the contact between artist and a wider public was re-established, even if it remained rather precarious and subject to the patronage and tastes of the ecclesiastical and secular courts. Caravaggio, perhaps the greatest painter of the early Italian Baroque, was in constant trouble with both the ecclesiastical authorities and the academies for the realism he introduced into his religious paintings. His *Madonna of Loreto*, a madonna and child adored only by an old peasant couple, was said to be disliked by 'persons of taste' but popular with common people.[18]

Rome in 1600 was not provincial as Florence had become under the Medici dukes and grand-dukes. Concentrating within the city much of the wealth of the whole Catholic Church, the popes, papal nephews and cardinals could afford to recreate the splendours of the time of Julius II. But at that time Rome had been *primus inter pares*, the greatest of many great centres between which artists could wander, constantly enriching and fructifying the art of each with the traditions and skills of the others. Now, in 1600, Rome was alone, drawing to herself the finest creative talent from the whole peninsula – sometimes, it seemed, from the whole of Catholic Europe – and leaving the former centres of Renaissance art more desolate and provincial than ever. The last of these to maintain at least a semblance of the old tradition, Ferrara, was swallowed up by the Papal States after the death of the last Este duke, Alfonso II, in 1598, and the once brilliant court, the scene of Tasso's triumphs and miseries, became a memory.

ART IN VENICE

There was one city in Italy which does not fit into the general pattern of artistic development that we have tried to discern and which yet, by its very difference, confirms the prevalence of this pattern. This city was Venice. Venice, with its strong links with the east and its Byzantine tradition, had been late in adopting the principles and techniques of Renaissance art. When she did so, towards the end of the fifteenth century, she added her own special contribution: the incomparable rendering of colour, to which her painters were stimulated by the magical light which the lagoon reflects on the city – much as the seventeenth-century Dutch and the nineteenth-century English painters were to be enthralled by the water-reflected skies and trees of their countries. In the sixteenth century Venice was the one Italian state which successfully and self-consciously maintained the character of an independent city state. Here the artist remained a free citizen. When the Florentine sculptor, Jacopo Sansovino, fled to Venice after the sack of Rome in 1527, Titian and Aretino entreated him to remain in the Republic of St Mark, and not to be tempted by the false allurements of the court life of Rome or France. Sansovino took this advice and, with the Library of San Marco, the Loggietta and the Giant Staircase of the Ducal Palace, gave Venice its finest High Renaissance buildings and much of the character of the Square of St Mark and the Piazzetta as we know them now.

The crisis of Italian art barely touched Venice. Almost effortlessly the Venetian painters absorbed the Mannerist style and enriched and transformed it. The greatest exponents of Mannerism (always with the exception of the aging Michelangelo who, anyhow, is a case apart) were not its central Italian inventors but the

Venetians: the old Titian and the younger Tintoretto and Veronese and, later still, the Venetian-trained Greek master of Toledo, El Greco. From about the middle of the century, when Michelangelo had painted his last fresco, there was in the rest of Italy no painter of the stature of the great Venetians. Even Vasari who was not in sympathy with Tintoretto's passionate, swirling compositions was moved to describe him as 'the most awesome mind that ever was in painting'.

At the same time, in Venice, Palladio and his school created a new type of elegant and harmonious classical architecture that was destined to appeal just to those sections of aristocratic European society which were doctrinally or emotionally unwilling to accept the Roman Baroque style. The Venetian patricians, who formed the most exclusive of European aristocracies, still superbly sure of being able to manage their republic without the benefit of a Spanish-style court, a Rome-controlled Inquisition or a Jesuit-staffed university, were building their Palladian country houses for a new, cultured, aristocratic and non-courtly style of living that was still to bear fruit in eighteenth-century England. The contrast with the rest of Italy, clerical and court dominated as it had become, could hardly be more striking.

THE RENAISSANCE IN GERMANY

It was in southern Germany that the Italian High Renaissance made its earliest impact north of the Alps. Conditions were exceptionally favourable. German merchants traded in Venice and Milan and there acquired not only a knowledge of Italian bookkeeping but also a taste for Italian art. German pilgrims journeyed to Rome; German undergraduates studied at the universities of Bologna, Padua and Pavia and returned to professorships in the German universities. At the same time, German silver was flooding Europe and Nuremberg's arms, watches and instruments spread the fame of Germany's new technical skills. In 1500 the south German cities — city states, as free almost as their Italian counterparts — were richer and more self-confident than ever before. At least some of the German princes were giving their courts that curious mixture of an archaizing Burgundian-chivalresque and an advanced Italian-humanist tone which had been made fashionable by the emperor

Maximilian I, himself the author of a poem of chivalry and a patron of the new learning. These were the conditions in which the fine late-Gothic tradition of German art reached a climax which can be compared with the climax of the Italian High Renaissance. It turned out to be even more precarious, and this for very similar reasons.

None of the astonishingly large number of supremely gifted German painters, engravers, sculptors and wood carvers entirely escaped the impact of the Italian Renaissance. Riemenschneider's virtuoso transposition of Italian chiaroscuro into the light and shade effects of his seemingly Gothic wood carvings seems to show this no less than does Grünewald's use of colour and his modelling of the figures in that most shockingly powerful of all crucifixions, the Isenheim altar (1512–15). But it was only Dürer who made the deliberate attempt to marry the aesthetic philosophy and the technical achievements of the classical south to the very different traditions of the Gothic north. An unusually introspective and articulate artist who 'created' a scientific German prose, much as Luther 'created' the biblical-literary German language,[19] Dürer saw his problems both on the technical-artistic and on the sociological level. 'Here I am a gentleman,' he wrote from Venice in 1506, 'at home I am a parasite.'

The German artist, just emerging from the protective but restricting conditions of the old craft tradition, found himself in an immensely stimulating environment, but one in which accepted values were breaking down even more dramatically than in Italy. Riemenschneider, the wealthy and respectable burgomaster of Würzburg, supported the peasant revolt. He was imprisoned, tortured and broken. Grünewald, also involved in the revolt, ceased to paint. It is not clear whether this was for lack of commissions or whether he had become convinced by iconoclastic teaching of the idolatrous nature of religious art. The various forms of Protestantism in Germany, though not all equally hostile to art, provided at best a chilly climate for the artist; for in Germany, as everywhere else in Europe, most art had been religious art. Dürer was so famous and so sure of himself that he could attempt to create a Protestant iconography (notably his *Four Apostles*). But in the absence of Protestant ecclesiastical patronage for artists, even Dürer could not start a viable tradition. Holbein, the friend and portraitist of Erasmus, found the court of Henry VIII more congenial than the Protestant German and Swiss cities. Cranach, the successful court painter of the electors of Saxony, illustrated his friend Luther's Bible and books of sermons and also attempted a number of large-scale religious paintings. But, with very few exceptions, their artistic quality does not match that of his portraits and classical subjects. The Mannerist 'serpentine' line and rhythm of his Greek mythological figures in their northern setting is delightful and original; yet in some respects this art leaves us with a feeling of unease. Cranach's Venuses, clothed in their elaborate hats and diaphanous veils, seem to flaunt a wilful eroticism that goes far beyond the open sensuality of contemporary Italian Mannerist nudes.

THE DECLINE OF GERMAN ART

By the middle of the sixteenth century the conditions of the German 'Renaissance' had disappeared. Many of the cities had suffered political and military defeat. Economically they were hemmed in by the surrounding territorial states or tied by their bankers to the financial fortunes and inevitable bankruptcies of the Habsburg and Valois monarchies. As in Italy, the rigid court societies of the small principalities which were now beginning to ape the courts of Spain and France, imposed their blighting effects on art and literature. The philistinism and aridity of Lutheranism, after the first heroic generation of reformers had passed away, and the narrowness of the Jesuit-dominated Catholic courts only emphasized the pervasive provincialism of this society. There were more of these courts than there were in Italy; they were poorer and, having developed apart from the city state, they lacked the urbanity which the Florentine tradition could still impart to the court of the grand-dukes of Tuscany. The collapse of German art after the deaths of Holbein, Cranach and Dürer's gifted pupil, Baldung, was much more catastrophic than anything that happened in Italy.

During the last quarter of the sixteenth century the Emperor Rudolf II attracted to his court in Prague a brilliant and international company of scholars, artists, scientists and cranks. Germany provided one of the greatest scientists of the age, Kepler, but no painter or sculptor of note. The leading artistic figure in Prague was the Milanese, Giuseppe Arcimboldi, a Mannerist of Mannerists, whose portraits of the emperor made up of vegetables, or of a librarian made up of books, had then, and have had again in the twentieth century, a fashionable appeal of witty and not too abstruse symbolism. But even Rudolf's patent bestowing on Arcimboldi the dignity of a count palatine praised him as an ingenious, rather than a great, artist.[20] The court of Prague, cosmopolitan, fashionable, fantastical and civilized as it was, never became a genuinely creative centre for the arts. Its brilliance disappeared in the harsh realities of the political and religious strife of the early seventeenth century.

THE NETHERLANDS

The history of art in western Europe showed no such dramatic reversals as in Germany. In the Netherlands the splendid traditions of fifteenth-century painting — courtly and religious in an urban setting — continued into the sixteenth without a break. More easily than their German contemporaries, Gerard David, Quentin Matsys and Mabuse assimilated some of the vital principles of Italian Renaissance painting for their portraits and altarpieces. The court of Brussels, in the absence of its dukes, had undoubtedly lost something of the brilliance of the great days of Philip the Good and Charles the Bold, even though the highly civilized Habsburg lady-governors, Margaret of Austria and Mary of Hungary, tried to maintain the Burgundian tradition. But Breughel, the greatest Netherlands artist of the mid-sixteenth century, seems to have moved in bourgeois-Erasmian, rather than court circles. His style, derived from the demonological dream fantasies of Bosch, as well as from traditional Flemish realism, was able to absorb Italian Mannerist elements to create a wholly original, sometimes bitterly satirical, but always humanist and compassionate pictorial language.

It is not surprising that the iconoclastic movements and civil wars which broke out in 1566 should have cut off a vital artistic tradition. The surprise is that they did so only temporarily. In the middle of the civil wars Flemish designers and weavers produced a set of superbly beautiful tapestries which William of Orange sent to Catherine de Medici, partly as a diplomatic gift, but also as propaganda for his policy of peace and toleration; for they represent Catherine and her family presiding over splendid festivals celebrating the reconciliation of the parties and religions. Like Breughel's paintings, the *Valois Tapestries*, as they were to be known, are a visual embodiment of the Erasmian tradition of humanism in the Netherlands.[21] Around 1600, when the worst of the fighting was over, painting immediately revived and the two dominant elements of the Flemish style, the urban and the courtly, now tended to divide geographically, between the north and the south, in accordance with the prevalent social ethos of the two parts of the now divided Netherlands. But it was a sign, both of the international character of the Baroque style and of the growing provincialism of the southern Netherlands, that the two greatest Flemish exponents of Baroque, Rubens and Van Dyck, became cosmopolitan court painters, sought after from Rome to Madrid and from Genoa to London.

ENGLAND: COURT ART AND MINIATURES

England in the early sixteenth century had no surviving tradition in painting and sculpture comparable with that of Germany and the Netherlands. The Reformation, and especially the dissolution of the monasteries, sharply reduced ecclesiastical patronage and, in the general climate of hostility towards Rome, seems to have discouraged Italian influence on church building. The Perpendicular style, once boldly elegant and gay with its large bright glass surfaces, continued unchallenged, but now a little tired and mechanical. The doctrinal somersaults of the English Church, and the eventual Elizabethan compromise settlement with its concentration on verbal definitions, not unnaturally failed to stimulate a new visual sensibility in ecclesiastical architecture. It was in secular building that the Renaissance had a late but decisive influence. At first, Renaissance motifs were simply, and sometimes rather incongruously, added to traditional square country houses. But soon a new, much more integrated style developed which made the finest English country houses of 1600 imposing aristocratic structures, almost palaces, yet with a sense of privacy and a regard for physical comfort that resembled more the villas of Venetian patricians than the *châteaux* of the French high aristocracy.

A portrait gallery in the country houses was *de rigueur*; yet the wooden faces of the subjects, and the crude craftsmanship of the painting (unless the sitters had the imagination and the money to employ a foreign portraitist) show both the pervasive visual philistinism of the English upper classes and the inability of English painters to rise above the status of worthy but ultimately despised artisans.[22] Only in the painting of miniatures did English art, for one short generation, from about 1570 to about 1600, rise to the level of contemporary European painting. Its aim, as its most distinguished practitioner, Hilliard, expressed it, was 'to catch these lovely graces, witty smilings and these stolen glances which suddenly like lightning pass and another countenance taketh place'.[23] It was court art at its purest: a private, yet expensive art, for even the settings of the miniatures were rich and costly: an art for which, so Hilliard maintained, the 'limner' himself should be a gentleman; an art with no religious and few philosophical overtones; an art of a young, gay, fashionably dressed, self-confident and very exclusive society — in short, an art with the narrowest conceivable basis. After the turn of the century the very success of the miniatures gave them a snob appeal which rapidly led both to a wider diffusion and a coarsening of the art.

FRENCH ART AND THE INFLUENCE OF ITALY

In France, for simple geographical reasons and because there was no significant difference of religion before the middle of the century, the influence of Italian art was much greater than in England. From the time of the earliest French invasions, the kings of France had invited Italian artists to their courts, and some of the greatest, including Leonardo da Vinci and Andrea del Sarto, followed the call. Yet France had her own, lively, late-medieval traditions which were stylistically closer to those of the Netherlands than to the Italian Renaissance. It therefore took time for the full impact of Italian art to make itself felt. When it did, in the second quarter of the sixteenth century, it was the art of the Mannerists rather than that of the High Renaissance. It is not surprising that the mannered elegance of the work of Rosso Fiorentino, Primaticcio and Cellini should have appealed to the sophisticated court of Francis I, nor that it should have stimulated French artists to acclimatize and gallicize this style, as Clouet did for portraiture, and Goujon and Pilon for sculpture. But, just as happened in the Netherlands, the artistic life of France suffered a profound crisis during the civil and religious wars of the second half of the century. Where French Mannerist art had, up till then, been restrained and almost classical, it now looked to the most extreme of late Mannerist models.[24] A peripatetic court, torn by religious doubts and political factions, often fighting for the very survival of the monarchy against religious revolutionary movements, could still indulge in staging magnificent festivals with elaborate musical and aquatic displays. Exciting as they must have been, they were as ephemeral as they were fantastical, even when fate and human malice did not supply a final ironic twist, as they did when Catherine de Medici changed the most brilliant festival she ever planned into the massacre of St Bartholomew.[25] With Henry IV's restoration of the authority of the monarchy, the classical tradition re-emerged, and for the next hundred years it was to be the dominant characteristic of French art. But it took another half-century before the French court could effectively rival that of the popes of Rome as the greatest centre of European art.

SPANISH ART AND THE COUNTER-REFORMATION

Spain suffered no crisis of civil and religious war like France and the Netherlands. Its artistic traditions, however, were much more complex than those of other western European countries; for, together with the international Gothic style of the later Middle Ages, Spain had also inherited the Mudéjar style which was derived from the style of the Moorish caliphate of Córdova and the Moorish kingdom of Granada. Since the Muslims had no pictorial tradition. the assimilation of the Italian Renaissance style in Spanish painting proceeded smoothly enough. In architecture, however, the meeting of the different traditions produced one of the most original and charming inventions of the century, the Plateresque. In this style a rich variety of Gothic and Renaissance ornament was applied to relatively simple classical structures in the traditional manner of Moorish decorations, that is, as if a carpet were hung over the building. The style fell into disfavour in the severer climate of the Counter-Reformation, although one can detect some of its features, and certainly its spirit, in some later Baroque churches in Mexico (especially in Taxco). Philip II patronized by preference architects like Juan de Herrera who erected imposing and unornamental classical structures. At their best, as in Philip's monastic palace of El Escorial, they have a gloomy grandeur, in keeping both with the king's own spirit and the forbidding landscape of the Sierra da Guadarrama. More commonly, however, the style produced only ugly and pompous monumentality; in this it reflected the darker side of Philip II's monarchy with equal faithfulness.

Philip II was a passionate collector of paintings and a generous patron. He failed, however, to appreciate the genius of the greatest painter in his kingdom. The ecclesiastical authorities of Toledo and the Castilian grandees of that region fortunately did not make the same mistake about Domenikos Theotucopulos whom they called El Greco, the Cretan who, as a young man, had learnt his craft from Tintoretto in Venice. Toledo, the spiritual centre of Spanish catholicism, far removed from the mundane traditions of court life, proved the perfect setting for El Greco's genius and seems to have been completely congenial to him. El Greco's is the most anticlassical art of the sixteenth century, at any rate in a Mediterranean country. Realism was to him as unimportant as to the painters of Byzantine ikons which he had known in his youth. His landscape backgrounds are almost completely abstract. The expressive 'serpentine' line of the Mannerists and their elongated figures became on Greco's canvases so many flames rising towards heaven. No other artist has conveyed so powerfully the burning faith and the rapt devotion of the Counter-Reformation in its purest, most spiritual form.

MUSIC: THE PRE-EMINENCE OF THE NETHERLANDS SCHOOL OF MUSIC

If in 1500 the whole of Europe recognized the pre-eminence of Italian art, it equally recognized the pre-eminence of Flemish music. For a tune to be fashionable in good society, said Castiglione, it had to be ascribed to Josquin des Prés.[26] As late as 1567, an Italian writer compared Ockegem with Donatello as having 'rediscovered' music as Donatello had 'rediscovered' sculpture, and Josquin with Michelangelo, for both were, in their own arts, 'alone and without a peer; both one and the other have opened the eyes of all those who delight in these arts or are to delight in them in the future'.[27] In Italian collections of printed music of the early sixteenth century there was more Netherlands music than Italian.[28]

In the last quarter of the fifteenth and in the early sixteenth century Josquin and his contemporaries in the Netherlands and northern France perfected the polyphonic tradition of the later Middle Ages by conceiving of the different parts of a composition simultaneously, that is, in connection with every other part, instead of composing the voices successively and with little relation to each other, as medieval composers had done. In their masses and motets, their vespers and magnificats, they combined noble melodic lines with splendid choral sonorities, and their compositions have rightly been regarded as the musical counterpart to the classical harmonies of High Renaissance painting, while their virtuoso handling of the mathematical intricacies of counterpoint may be seen as analogous to the Renaissance painters' pride in mastering the geometry of perspective. Nowhere else did a young musician receive such a thorough and comprehensive musical training as in the church and cathedral schools of the Netherlands. Netherlands singers, choirmasters, organists and composers were in demand in courts and cathedrals all over Europe. The Emperor Charles V's Flemish *capilla* was the most famous choir in Europe. It accompanied him on his travels and did much to spread the fame of his Flemish subjects.

Even the civil wars of the second half of the sixteenth century did not break up the traditions of the Flemish choir schools. But the churches and cathedral chapters lost much of their former wealth. More than ever, the Netherlanders found musical careers abroad more attractive than staying at home. Charles V's *capilla* was dissolved after his abdication; but, from 1543 until 1612, the Austrian Habsburgs appointed seven Netherlanders successively as musical directors of their courts. The greatest Netherlands composer of the age, Orlando de Lassus, spent nearly all his working life at the court of the dukes of Bavaria, in Munich.[29]

The whole of European music was thus in the debt of the Netherlanders; but perhaps none more so than that of the Italians. In 1527 Adriaen Willaert was appointed organist and *maestro di capella* of St Mark's, Venice. In the following thirty-five years he and his compatriot and pupil, Cyprian de Rore, trained several generations of Italian musicians and founded the famous Venetian school of music. In 1581 Francesco Sansovino, writing one of the first guidebooks of Venice, could claim proudly that 'music has its very own home in this city'.[30] It could not have been said fifty years earlier. The same was true for Rome. Here, Palestrina, himself the pupil of a Flemish musician, had won for himself a reputation unequalled in Europe since Josquin, two generations before. When Sweelinck, the last of the line of great Netherlands composers, translated the Venetian Zarlino's *Institutioni harmoniche* into Dutch, it was a sign that the relative positions of Flemish and Italian music were becoming reversed. By 1600 the pre-eminence of Italian music was as firmly established as that of Flemish music had been in 1500.

MUSIC IN ITALY, DEVELOPMENT OF MUSICAL HARMONY

The Italian eulogists of Flemish music had perhaps done less than justice to the musical traditions of their own country. In 1501 the first musical press was set up in Italy and the rapid expansion of music publishing was a sign of the lively demand for music in Italian society. Leonardo had a great reputation as a lutanist, apart from all his other achievements. Benvenuto Cellini, although he affected to dislike music, characteristically claimed that, nevertheless, he was a superb flautist and that both his audience and he himself were always greatly moved by his playing. The Italian courts were centres for secular and private music making, enthusiastically described by Castiglione, in a way that hardly existed in the Netherlands. Most important of all, the Italians were discovering the magic of harmony and its power of expressing emotions. It was the combination of Italian harmonic thinking with the polyphonic-thematic composition of the Netherlands which opened the way for the uniquely rich and varied development of European music in the succeeding centuries.[31] One of its earliest fruits was the Italian madrigal, the setting for occasionally three but usually four or more voices of fairly short lyric poems, mostly about unrequited love, by the greatest Italian poets from Petrarch to Ariosto and Tasso. It was an art form which matched perfectly the highly developed personal sensibilities of a sophisticated lay society. Carlo Gesualdo, though neither the most famous nor the most prolific of the Italian madrigalists, may be taken as the embodiment of the personal and musical extremes to which those characteristics could lead. A member of the Neapolitan high nobility – he was prince of Venosa – Gesualdo surrounded himself with a circle of poets and musicians and, apparently, neglected his wife whom, in the true aristocratic fashion of the time, he had married for purely dynastic reasons. Finding her in *flagrante* with a lover, he murdered them both; but such was his social eminence that the murders evoked little more than a spate of elegiacal sonnets from Tasso and other friends of the unhappy couple. A contemporary genius, the lowly-born, bohemian and homosexual painter Caravaggio, did not get away so easily with a murder he committed, but had to spend the rest of his short life on the run. Gesualdo's own madrigals show a systematic use of discords, broken melodic lines and abrupt rhythmic changes, all employed most skilfully to heighten the expressiveness of the profoundly sad and disturbed texts he chose to set. His violent rejection of classical musical forms and traditional harmony has, rightly, been compared with the Mannerist rejection of classical forms in painting.[32]

THEORIES OF GOOD AND BAD MUSIC

It was not, however, always easy to combine the Flemish and the Italian traditions, and least of all at the very centre of sixteenth-century musical life, in church music. The very splendour of the Netherlands polyphonic style had raised enemies, at least against its use in church. There was the uneasy feeling, among the puritanically minded of all denominations, that music had a power all its own. This belief had respectable classical antecedents and it coincided, moreover, with another, related, classical tradition that went back to Plato's distinction between good and bad or, really, moral and immoral music. Luther, a passionate lover of music, was not worried. All music in the service of God was good, he claimed, and there was no reason why the devil should have all the best tunes. The musical tradition which he bequeathed to his church has been one of its greatest glories. Calvin's attitude was much more ambiguous. Music must not be condemned simply because it served our enjoyment, he wrote.[33] (Had someone in his circle, then, condemned music altogether?) The flute and the tambourine are bad only when abused; 'yet it is certain that the tambourine never sounds to rejoice men but there is some vanity in it . . .'[34] Music was like a funnel through which either good or evil could be instilled into men.

Calvin allowed the singing of psalms, and this practice became a most powerful, because highly popular, weapon in the spiritual and psychological armoury of the Huguenots. But he banned musical instruments from church service. Where this ban became effective it could lead, in the long run, to a terrible impoverishment of the musical tradition of the country concerned. Contemporaries were well aware of this danger, even before it became effective. In England, during the latter part of the sixteenth and the early seventeenth centuries, there appeared a remarkable number of verses in praise, and in defence, of music against the attacks of its enemies, those men whose souls were 'dark as Erebus' and who were 'fit for treasons, stratagems and spoils'.*

In spite of Calvin's strictures on popish music, the attitude of the Catholic Church was inspired by a puritanism similar to his own. Theologians and church councils consistently condemned over-elaborate church music which, they claimed, made the words of the liturgy unintelligible and seduced men's minds from attention to the word of God. While in the Netherlands the polyphonic tradition was strong enough to resist such attacks, Flemish composers who strove to assimilate the chromaticism of Italian secular music for the sake of heightening the emotional impact of their own religious music, were forced to do so secretly, by a method of musical notation which involved a double meaning: one, openly apparent, which accorded with the traditional rules of the church modes, and the other, secret or concealed, which was understood only by the initiated and which was frowned upon by the Church. It was a surprising development, even in an age as passionately devoted to allegories, anagrams and hidden meanings as the sixteenth century. Characteristically, it seems to have flourished among those Erasmian circles whose orthodoxy was suspect but who never chose openly to break with the Catholic Church.[35] The orthodox Catholic tradition was summed up by the Council of Trent with its decrees against the use of 'lascivious, impure and profane' music in church and its insistence on making music subservient to the word of God.[36] Palestrina fulfilled all these conditions in his noble, unaccompanied masses. Nevertheless it was fortunate for the future development of music that the decrees were silent on detail and left room for differing interpretations. While the more austere churchmen, such as St Carlo Borromeo, banned all instruments except the organ from divine service, this practice was not followed universally.

*Shakespeare, *Merchant of Venice*, Act V, Sc. 1. Cf. J. Hulton, 'Some English poems in praise of music', *English Mirsellamy*, vol. II, ed. M. Praz (Rome, 1951). For a contrary view of the relation between Calvinism and music, see P. Scholes, *The Puritans and Music* (London, 1934).

MUSIC AND PAINTING IN VENICE

By 1600, the phase of acute musical puritanism in the Catholic Church in Italy was already on the wane. It had never been strong in Venice, where the *capella* of St Mark's depended more on the secular than on the ecclesiastical authorities. Willaert had introduced the use of multiple choirs and these came soon to be accompanied, not only by the organ, but by trombones and strings. Towards the end of the century, Andrea and Giovanni Gabrieli, uncle and nephew, gave to Venetian music, both church and secular, a richness and variety of texture and tone colour that was the musical counterpart to contemporary Venetian painting. Certainly, the painters seem to have seen it in this way. In his *Marriage of Cana*, now in the Louvre, Veronese depicted a group of musicians in the very centre of his composition, and immediately below the figure of Christ; they were Titian playing a string bass, Tintoretto and Veronese himself playing viols, and Bassano playing the flute.

It was the Venetians who systematically developed the musical language and conventions for the expression of specific emotions. 'As poets are not supposed to compose a comedy in tragic verse,' wrote Zarlino, 'so musicians are not supposed to combine harmony and text in an unsuitable manner. Therefore, it would not be fitting to use a sad harmony and a slow rhythm with a gay text, or a gay harmony and light-footed rhythms to a tragic matter full of tears.'[37] To Zarlino's contemporaries this was not as obvious as it seems today, for in the earlier practice of composition these aspects of the art had by no means achieved the primacy which they did in the sixteenth century. But it was a French composer, Clément Jannequin, who invented the art of finding musical equivalents to the sounds of the world around him, in such compositions as *The Nightingale, The Cries of Paris* and *The Battle of Marignano*.[38]

THE INVENTION OF OPERA

Throughout the sixteenth century the musical humanists had sought to make music enhance the power of words. They believed it could do this because their predecessors thought that music represented directly the harmony and the mathematical structure of the universe. The Greeks — it was generally thought to have been

Pythagoras — had made the startling discovery that consonant intervals between notes in music, i.e. chords which were immediately pleasing to the ear, depended on simple numerical proportions. If you divide a string in half, i.e. in the ratio 2 : 1, and pluck it, you get an octave; if in the ratio of 3 : 2, a fifth; of 4 : 3, a fourth, and so on. This discovery became the basis of both a mathematical and a philosphical theory of music. It was easily Christianized; for did not the Bible assure us that God made all things in number, weight and measure? In the course of the sixteenth century the theoretical emphasis on harmony that was based on number theory became comparatively unimportant. Dissonance became acceptable, just as it was becoming acceptable in the Mannerist style of the visual arts, when it was used to emphasize an underlying harmony of the composition as a whole. A relation between music and nature was envisaged in terms of sympathy, as a kind of parallel between music and human emotions. This was the theoretical justification for the widening of music's emotional range.[39] What the musical humanists could discover about the music of the ancients only served to confirm this aim and, in consequence, their hostility to polyphony which tended to make the words incomprehensible. In the 1590s a group of Florentine musicians, of whom one of the most distinguished was Vincenzo Galilei, the father of the scientist, set themselves to recreate musical drama, and, in effect, invented opera. Naturally, they made use of existing traditions. Incidental music for festivals, processions and stage shows, particularly the so-called *intermezzi*, light musical entertainments between the acts of plays or other shows, which were all immensely popular with all classes of the public.

The rise of this new art form was meteoric. Only ten years separate the earliest opera, Peri's *Dafne* (1597, but now lost), from the oldest opera still in the twentieth-century repertoire, Monteverdi's *Orfeo* (1607). The previous generation of composers had developed the techniques of representing personal emotions in music, together with a subtlety of orchestration that could give a musical interpretation to the visual effects seen on the stage. Only at this point did opera become possible. It has been suggested that it was precisely this ability of music to satisfy the visual sense of the Italians (for whom the visual arts had been traditionally pre-eminent) which accounts for the rapid popularity of opera in Italy.[40]

ITALIAN MUSIC IN THE BAROQUE ERA

The astonishing rise of Italian music in the second half of the sixteenth century occurred at the very time when painting and sculpture, outside Venice, were suffering a relative decline (see p. 394 ff.) If the value judgements inherent in these propositions of rise and decline are accepted — and every history of any art form whatever is bound to make at least implicit value judgments by its selection of the works it discusses — it may be possible to see a connection between these two phenomena. Venice showed its enormous vitality by the role it played in the development of Italian music; but the contrast with other parts of Italy is not as striking as in the case of painting. The Counter-Reformation Church, even at its most rigid, was never actually hostile to church music in the way in which many Calvinist puritans seem to have been. Borromeo himself took a genuine, if austere, interest in church music. In the oratory of St Filippo Neri, in Rome, a new, non-liturgical form of religious music was cultivated which was soon to gain wide popularity as oratorio. The composers of church music never lost the vitalizing contact with a wide audience, their congregations, and the very personal religious sensibility of the Counter-Reformation found in religious music a new and satisfying emotional expression.

It is probably no accident that Caravaggio, the Italian painter who most powerfully expressed this sensibility, was fascinated by music and strongly attracted to Neri's circle. At the same time, the Italian courts of the period provided an ideal setting for the development of music. Rich courtiers and aristocratic amateurs collected groups of musicians in their houses to sing madrigals and play chamber music. It was court society which financed the new operas; and yet, this 'spectacle for princes' was soon to enjoy immense popularity among all classes of Italian society.

Music in Italy was both fashionable and popular; it was approved by lay and ecclesiastical authority; it had discovered hitherto unthought-of possibilities of emotional and dramatic expression. Here was an exciting challenge, and it came at a time of crisis in the visual arts. It seems at least possible to see the response to this challenge in a shift in creative activity, from painting and sculpture to music.[41] The Italian musician had few of the problems of the Italian painter, sculptor and poet who, if he did not exactly see his 'art made tongue-tied by authority',[42] at least found himself in a much less congenial environment.[43]

MUSIC IN FRANCE

Except for traditional popular music — mainly dances and songs — the music of the rest of Europe during the sixteenth century was all heavily dependent on Netherlands and Italian models. The two greatest Spanish composers of the century, Morales and Victoria, spent much of their lives in Italy, the latter as the most brilliant and original pupil of Palestrina. In France musical life tended to concentrate in the court and its imitators. Francis I and the later Valois kings invited Italian musicians to the royal choir, just as they invited Italian artists. But from about the middle of the century, French music came to be increasingly influenced by the humanists and poets of the circle of the *Pléiade* (see p. 368). More systematically even than their Italian counterparts they wanted to go back to classical models, and they saw music essentially as the servant of words, especially poetry. Charles IX's letters patent for Baïf's Academy, which was founded in 1570 to pursue precisely such aims, had this preamble:

> . . . it is most important for the morals of the citizens of a town that the music which is generally used in the country should be practised according to certain laws, since the minds of most men are formed, and their behaviour is influenced, by its character (i.e. of music); in such manner as where music is disordered, there morals become readily depraved, and where it is well-ordered, there good morals are instilled into men.[44]

The combination of poetry, music and dance which Baïf's Academy practised had a profound influence on the development of the *ballet de cour* and the magnificent court festivals organized by Catherine de Medici. These, in their turn, led to the development of French opera in the seventeenth century.

MUSIC IN ENGLAND

In England, after the splendid and very original outburst of musical activity in the early fifteenth century, the standard of musical life remained high. Like their Italian counterparts, English composers and musicians of the first half of the sixteenth century assimilated the polyphonic style of the Netherlands. The Reformation caused no break in this development; for the Anglican Church simply continued the musical tradition of the old religion, even though many musical instruments seem to have perished in the dissolution of the monasteries. Just as in France, musical life in England centred essentially on the capital and the court. In the reign of Edward VI the Chapel Royal employed some eighty professional musicians, and during the succeeding reigns the numbers remained substantially similar. There was, moreover, an enthusiastic public for music. In his dialogue, *A Plain and Easy Introduction to Practical Music*, first published in 1597, the composer Thomas Morley has a passage on the musical education of a gentleman of which Castiglione would undoubtedly have approved:

> . . . supper being ended, and Musicke bookes, according to the custome, being brought to the table: the mistresse of the home presented mee with a part, earnestly requesting me to sing. But when after many excuses, I protested unfainedly that I could not, every one began to wonder. Yea, some whispered to others, demaunding how I was brought up . . .[45]

One may wonder how much wishful thinking there was in Morley's famous anecdote and also how far his picture would have been true in the provinces. Nevertheless it was the combination of a long and vigorous tradition in ecclesiastical music with the italophile proclivities of a musically sophisticated London and court society that made possible the golden age of English music. It only lasted for the last one or two decades of the sixteenth century and the first two or three of the seventeenth.

Perhaps the most astonishing aspects of this greatest period of English music were its range and individuality, even though in sheer volume of output it never compared with that of Italy or the Netherlands. The English madrigal, although clearly derived from the Italian, was a more popular art form than its model, using light, popular verse, rather than the serious poetry of an Ariosto or a Tasso, and there were in England no madrigal academies nor professional madrigal singers, as there were in Italy. English keyboard music, while again influenced by Continental models, yet developed a wholly original style, and the same was true for Dowland's delightful songs with lute accompaniment. But church music was still the centre of musical activity, and Byrd's great masses are the last, and possibly the finest, fruit of the great Flemish–Italian polyphonic tradition. In its variety and range English music far surpassed contemporary English painting and rivalled Elizabethan and Jacobean drama and poetry. In its immediate impact on the rest of Europe, it was probably even more important.

MUSIC IN GERMANY

In Germany political fragmentation prevented the geographical concentration of musical life that was so characteristic of France and England. German church music was highly traditional and slow, even, to accept Flemish influences. Luther was a great admirer of Josquin; but it was only in the second half of the sixteenth century, when Lassus lived at the court of the dukes of Bavaria in Munich, and when his Flemish compatriots were the directors of music at the courts of Vienna, Prague and many of the smaller *Residenzstädte*, that Netherlands music made its greatest impact on Germany – at a time, that is, when it was itself already becoming Italianized. Especially conservative, and even hidebound in their narrow traditionalism, were the musical associations of the petty bourgeois master craftsmen, the master singers, immortalized by Wagner in his opera *Die Meistersinger von Nürnberg*. Yet the master singers maintained the tradition of an active participation in music among a much wider range of social classes than in any other European country, and this goes far to explain the extraordinary development of German music which began from about 1570.

It is tempting to see in the rise of German music a similar, perhaps even more decisive, shift in creative activity to that which we thought we could observe in Italy. The social and psychological traditions were in many respects similar. The decline of the imperial cities and the rise of the many small courts may have had a stifling effect on German painting and sculpture (see p. 335). But, as in Italy, courts and court society provided a congenial and stimulating life for composers and musicians. Fortunately, moreover, Calvinist puritanism had only limited footholds in Germany. Church music, both Catholic and Lutheran, therefore, continued to flourish, often with a pleasing lack of mutual discrimination. Thus Hans Leo Hassler, the first of the great German composers to be trained in the Venetian school, wrote both Protestant and Catholic motets and, at different times, enjoyed the patronage of both the Protestant elector of Saxony and the Catholic princely millionaire, Octavian II Fugger.[46]

Baroque music, like Baroque art, had the ability to please at all

414

levels, from the most sophisticated to the most popular. Moreover, in spite of the disapproval of the moralists, the distinction between church and secular music was by no means always observed. Luther himself used dance tunes for his chorales – *Vom Himmel hoch* is a famous example – and both Protestant and Catholic hymns were often musical parodies, that is tunes composed originally for secular texts.

In Germany the shift, if such it was, of creative activity from the visual arts into music was a permanent one. In Germany, as in Italy and very much in contrast to England, the highest musical tradition, once firmly established in the last decades of the sixteenth century, continued unbroken for the next three centuries.

SCIENCE

It is possible to argue that, if there was a shift in creative activity in Italy and Germany during the latter half of the sixteenth century, it included a shift into physical science. Such an argument must, to some extent, remain hypothetical; but it does seem at least very likely. At the same time, it is essential to discuss the development of science as part of the general social and intellectual history of Europe.

The history of science and scientific thought in the sixteenth century is a subject that is both intrinsically very difficult and also still very obscure. Its historiography has only quite recently emerged from a long-accepted teleological pattern which contrasted an obscurantist, or at least, irrelevant medieval view of science with the modern methods of experimental and inductive science as it was held to have developed in the 'scientific revolution' of the seventeenth century, very conveniently spelled out by Bacon. Such a contrast tended to produce the almost insoluble puzzle as to why men who had 'advanced' views on some topics should still have been 'bound by medieval traditionalism' in so many others.

THE WORLD PICTURE IN 1500

Niccolò Leoniceno, a distinguished professor of medicine in the University of Padua at the beginning of our period, may serve as a typical example of the problems facing the historian of sixteenth-century science. Attacking the then popular view that syphilis was a completely new disease (although nobody, at that time, attributed it to Columbus's sailors — this particular legend has a later origin), Leoniceno wrote in 1497:

> . . . When I reflect that men are endowed with the same nature, born under the same skies, brought up under the same stars, I am compelled to think that they have always been afflicted by the same diseases . . . For if the laws of nature are examined, they have existed unchanged on countless occasions since the beginning of the world. Wherefore I am prepared to show that a similar disease has arisen from similar causes also in past ages.[47]

At first sight this statement looks impeccably 'modern' and 'scientific'; yet Leoniceno went on to attribute the disease to a rise in the level of the Italian rivers, notably the Tiber, which, he argued, disturbed the humours. In traditional medical theory the humours were the chief bodily fluids: blood, phlegm, yellow bile and black bile, the balance of which determined both a man's health and his disposition, as sanguine, phlegmatic, melancholic or choleric. Leoniceno had, in fact, not advanced the argument beyond that of the ancients. From our point of view, however, the importance of Leoniceno's statement lies not so much in the fact that its apparently modern flavour did not prevent its author from uncritically accepting the authority of the classical writers on medicine, as in what it says about the contemporary views of the universe and of man's position in it. The key phrase here is 'that men are . . . born under the same skies, brought up under the same stars'. Man is subject to immutable laws because he is held to be part of the cosmos with its immutable laws. He is indeed a microcosm of the macrocosm of the universe.

Around 1500 this was the almost universally accepted world picture. The earth was a sphere at the centre of the universe,[48] the sublunar sphere of imperfect, material bodies. Beyond the earth, and revolving around it, were the perfect and incorruptible celestial spheres containing the moon, sun, planets and stars and ascending, in increasing purity, to the outermost sphere, the *primum mobile* and, beyond this again, to God himself. The contemplation and study of this orderly, hierarchical cosmos and of the laws of nature was as much a part of the contemplation and study of God as were theology and philosophy. At Wittenberg Melanchthon himself gave the lectures on physics and astronomy to the theology students of the university. Yet, even in 1500, half a century before Melanchthon's course of lectures, almost all aspects, and certainly many details, of this traditional view of the universe had come, or were shortly to come, under attack. These attacks proceeded from different directions; they were uncoordinated and, often, overlapping or contradictory; and the attacks which were eventually most effective were not always recognized as such at the time, nor were they always chronologically consecutive or logically dependent on each other.

THE CONTRIBUTION OF THE RENAISSANCE PAINTERS

It was in the first place the Renaissance painters, rather than the philosophers and scientists, who developed the habit of close and accurate observation of nature.[49] Landscapes might still be fantastical, as in Leonardo's two famous paintings of the *Madonna of the Rocks*; but the details of the plants and rock formations are as accurate as any modern naturalist would wish. Leonardo's anatomical drawings, in his notebooks, are in a class by themselves; but human anatomy was studied, and accurate drawings were made, in nearly all the workshops of the Renaissance masters. In textbooks of anatomy, however, they remained comparatively rare until Vesalius (1514–64) published his superbly illustrated *De Humani Corporis Fabrica* in 1543. From then on, no respectable book on anatomy could be without such illustrations – to the great profit of the teaching and understanding of the subject.

Equally important was the contribution of the painters of the Renaissance to the application of geometry in the theory of perspective. The practical problems of perspective representation forced on painters and aesthetic theoreticians the realization that space was not something rather indeterminate between objects but a geometrical concept which had to be constructed. In Aristotelian physics all objects, according to their inherent qualities, had a natural place to which they tended to move and where they would then be at rest. The 'discovery of space', that is the need to define the position of objects geometrically with relation to other objects, and not according to their own inherent qualities, helped to weaken the idea of place and was thus a precondition of the formulation of the laws of classical mechanics in the seventeenth century in which the concept of natural place was discarded altogether.

PHILOSOPHICAL AND PSYCHOLOGICAL ORIGINS OF THE SCIENTIFIC REVOLUTION

Even more significant than specific conceptual advances was the artists' and the scientists' view of the nature of the universe and of their role in discovering it. It is here that the Renaissance concept of universality played a crucial part. More than any other, Leonardo da Vinci has been regarded as an *uomo universale*, a universal man. This was not because he was a master of many subjects, although he certainly was that. He was a painter, sculptor and architect, a musician, a mathematician, a mechanical, civil and military engineer, a botanist, zoologist and geologist, an anatomist and a physiologist and, perhaps most famously, an inventor of forward-looking contrivances such as submarines. His universality lay rather in his view of a pervasive pattern or divine order of all existing things. Man could apprehend this divine order through experience and intellect and he could see it in all the myriad transformations which occurred in nature. The Latin poet Ovid's *Metamorphoses*, telling Greek legends of changes and transformations, such as that of the nymph Daphne who, to escape pursuit by the god Apollo, was changed into a bay tree, was one of the best-known and best-loved texts in the Renaissance. Understanding these transformations, the artist and the scientist could both imitate nature and beyond that, make new combinations and transformations. In this way, at least on a human level, he could emulate divine creativity. The understanding and control of nature, the 'second book of God', therefore became aims of human endeavour as divinely justified as the study of God's word in the traditional discipline of theology.[50]

Basic to the understanding of nature was an understanding of the laws which governed it. The concept of the laws of nature had appeared in a rudimentary form with the Greeks. It was fully developed only in the sixteenth and seventeenth centuries. The concept assumed a divine creator who had given laws to the cosmos. These laws were regarded as applying to all natural phenomena and all created beings.[51] A small but significant consequence of this view was the appearance at this time in Europe of the seemingly bizarre, but on the assumptions of the time quite rational, practice of the judicial trial of animals for behaving 'unnaturally'. That is, they were thought to have broken the laws of nature. Churchmen had traditionally pronounced anathemas against animal pests, such as locusts or mice. But this had really been only a kind of exorcism. Now we find formal trials, for instance of a cock in Switzerland which had laid eggs or of rats in France who were formally summoned to a law court and assigned a lawyer to defend them. In the event, he argued that their failure to answer the summons was justifiable because they had no safe-conduct and were therefore quite reasonably afraid of the local cats.[52]

More important for the development of natural science, the laws of nature were regarded as rational and comprehensible. Since they were divinely ordained, there was no inherent opposition between theology and science. Difficulties arose from the Churches' traditional claim that theology was the queen of the sciences and that all others were her handmaidens. To the scientists, however, it seemed more and more that, when the theologians pronounced on scientific matters, they did not know what they were talking about. Thus the famous anatomist Vesalius complained that at the university of Louvain, in the Netherlands, the lecturer who taught Aristotle was 'a theologian by profession and therefore . . . ready to mingle his pious views with those of the philosophers'. As a result he talked scientific nonsense, in this particular case about the structure of the human brain, and as a consequence misled his students not only about the true nature of the Creator's work but also in their religious beliefs.[53]

The scientists therefore attempted to fence off their work from interference by the theologians by drawing dividing lines between the realm of religion and that of science or, as they said, of natural philosophy. But was this possible? And even if it were, who was to draw the line, the scientist or the theologian? It was over this question that battle lines began to be drawn towards the end of the sixteenth century.

THE IMPORTANCE OF PRACTICAL PROBLEMS

In the meantime, the need to solve practical problems often proved to be a stimulus to the development of scientific ideas and practice. The inclusiveness of Renaissance humanistic and artistic education, and the common habit of arguing by means of analogy, favoured the transference of theories and skills from one field of study to another. Dürer wrote a book on the fortification of cities. Leonardo designed elaborate engines of war which, however, all remained on paper. But both he and Michelangelo served their native Florence as practical military engineers. Princes and governments employed mathematicians to make accurate maps, improve their artillery, invent ciphers for diplomatic correspondence or supervise their mints. The theories of surveying and mathematical projection, of ballistics, of cryptography, and of statistics and economics all benefited from such patronage.

A characteristic example is that of the German humanist Agricola (Georg Bauer, 1494–1555) who spent long years as a physician to the miners of Saxony and used this opportunity to study both mining techniques and geology. His best-known book, the *De re metallica*,[54] is a compendium of the sophisticated mining technology of his day. In this book and in his other works on geology Agricola showed his outstanding ability for critical observation combined with an unusual scepticism towards traditional views and miners' lore. His own theories on the effects of erosion on the shape of mountains and of the origin of ore deposits, while not always correct, foreshadowed much later developments in the science of geology. But perhaps even more important than Agricola's specific contributions to geology, chemistry and the spread of mining technology is the fact that he was an outstanding representative of an increasingly important trend in European thought: the fascination which mechanisms and machines of all types held for men in the later fifteenth and the sixteenth centuries — the projects recorded in Leonardo's notebooks and Charles V's passion for clocks are typical examples — and the slowly growing tendency to think of the universe in mechanistic terms.

Nevertheless, the impact of practical problems on the development of fundamental scientific ideas and of the world picture as it existed in 1500 can be exaggerated. Technology and theoretical science touched each other at some points, but as frequently ignored each other. Practical chemistry, as it developed, for instance, in the dyeing industry, had no influence on chemical theory. In medicine one of the most important practical advances of the sixteenth century, Ambroise Paré's treatment of bullet wounds with cool unguents instead of the conventional application of boiling oil (1537) was given neither a theoretical justification nor did it have any consequences for the theory of medicine. Even where practical and philosophical considerations are found together, it is not easy to determine their respective importance. At the very end of the century, the English physician William Gilbert (1540–1603) made his famous experimental investigations of magnetism which led him, among other theories, to the correct conclusion that the earth itself is a magnet. He hoped that his experiments would help practical navigation, for he thought that the inclination of the magnetic needle could indicate latitude. But it is a nice point whether it was this practical and, in the event, wrong conclusion that inspired Gilbert's investigations or whether it was an apparently useful by-product of his mystical philosophy which saw the earth as animated by magnetism and which, as Bacon said, 'made a philosophy out of the loadstone'.[55]

CLASSICAL GREEK TREATISES

At least as important as the stimulus of practical problems was the discussion and criticism of the theories of the classical writers. It was the humanist scholars who edited, and often translated into Latin, the original texts of the ancient Greek scientific treatises and who tried to disentangle them from the commentaries and interpretations of medieval Arabic translators and writers. In the course of the sixteenth century the great majority of those Greek texts which had survived at all were, in this way, made available. This work of recovery proved to be an essential precondition for future advance in scientific thinking. It became clear that the ancients were often not agreed among themselves about quite fundamental problems of science and that it would be necessary to rethink these problems from first principles. At the same time, it was not always immediately obvious that a great deal of the scientific literature of the ancients was of the most dubious value. Moreover, despite the advances made by the humanists in philology and textual criticism, the possibilities for misunderstanding and misinterpreting classical works were still immense.

One of the most fateful of such misinterpretations was the value which many of the humanists attached to the *Hermetica*. This was a collection of treatises on philosophy, astrology, magic and other occult arts, dating from the first to the fourth century A.D. and containing mostly ideas that were conventional in Hellenistic Alexandria during those centuries. The authorship of the *Hermetica* was ascribed to an Egyptian priest, Hermes Trismegistus, the 'Thrice Great'. The humanist Ficino (1433–99) who translated these treatises into Latin, and many humanists and scientists of the sixteenth century, followed the opinion of some of the early Christian fathers in dating this compendium as preceding Plato and the classical Greek philosophers. Popularized and conventionalized versions of their ideas were therefore held to be seminal and were invested with a wholly spurious aura of age and profundity. In particular, this misinterpretation did much to make magic and astrology respectable.[56]

It has been argued that this respectability assigned to magic involved a psychological change of the greatest importance. For, while the medieval philosopher had been willing to contemplate and investigate the world, he had thought that the wish to control or operate it could only be inspired by the devil. For the Renaissance philosopher, steeped in the occult learning of the *Hermetica* which had been approved by at least some of the great fathers of the Church, magic, and therefore operation (i.e. the actual use of man's knowledge and his power over nature) seemed both a dignified occupation and one approved by the will of God.[57] Whether or not we really have here one of the psychological origins or, rather, preconditions of the modern scientific attitude, there can be little doubt that the influence of the *Hermetica* explains some of the extraordinarily widespread belief in magic, astrology and the theories of alchemy among many of the greatest scientific minds of the sixteenth century.

COPERNICUS

Copernicus himself mentions Trismegistus in his revolutionary work[58] though this may not be more than a graceful literary flourish in his eulogium of the sun. The mystical importance which the sun had for Copernicus may well have played a part in the psychological motivation of his work, that is in his willingness to substitute the sun for the earth as the centre of the cosmos. The idea itself was not altogether new, and the theory of the rotation of the earth about its own axis had been specifically rejected by Ptolemy. Copernicus's great achievement was to work out the detailed mathematics of an astronomical model in which the earth and all the planets revolved around the stationary sun. The astronomical observations on which Copernicus based his calculations and many of the fundamental assumptions of the geometrical representation of the motions of celestial bodies were essentially those of Ptolemy. Moreover, while Copernicus's system was mathematically more elegant than that of Ptolemy, and while the astronomical tables based on it were somewhat more accurate, it was still highly complex and technically far from satisfactory. For instance, observational data did not permit Copernicus to place the sun actually at the centre of the earth's supposedly circular orbit and the mystical place assigned to the sun in Book I of his famous *De revolutionibus orbium coelestium* remains, at least in strict geometry, no more than a figure of speech.

The *De revolutionibus* was published in 1543, with a dedication to Pope Paul III and a preface by the Lutheran theologian Osiander, describing the work as merely a mathematical hypothesis. It was probably this interpretation of Copernicus's system which accounts for the substantial absence of theological opposition to his work in the first three or four decades after its publication. But, whatever Copernicus may have thought of Osiander's preface — and it is not even clear whether he had a chance to read it before his death — both he himself and his followers regarded his system not as a mathematical hypothesis but as a fully fledged new cosmology. As such it was to move into the centre of intellectual and religious controversy in Europe, but not until the last two decades of the sixteenth century. (See Figure 2, p. 5).

TYCHO BRAHE

By that time, other discoveries and theories had also come to undermine the traditional view of the universe. In 1572 a new star (a supernova) appeared in the constellation of Cassiopeia. It grew in brilliance but disappeared again after sixteen months. This phenomenon was followed, in 1577, by the appearance of a comet. The historical importance of both events lay in the observations and measurements to which they were subjected by the Danish astronomer Tycho Brahe (1546—1601) and in the conclusions which he drew from his observations. For the appearance and disappearance of a new star which, as Tycho's measurements proved, was situated far beyond the supposed lunar sphere of the traditional cosmos, demonstrated the fallacy of the view that all celestial bodies were incorruptible and not subject to growth and decay as were those of the sublunar sphere. More conclusive still, the comet of 1577 travelled across the supposedly impermeable crystalline celestial spheres. To Tycho and to many of his contemporaries all this proved clearly the non-existence of the traditional spheres. Copernicus seems to have still believed in these, even though his theory of the movement of the earth around the sun tended to break down the difference between the sublunar and the celestial spheres. Characteristically, Tycho rejected both the traditional, Ptolemaic, cosmos and Copernicus's heliocentric universe in favour of a compromise solution according to which the planets travelled around the sun, but the sun and all other heavenly bodies still circled around the stationary earth.

Tycho was a passionate alchemist and convinced astrologer. Indeed, it was the felt need for a more accurate science of astrology which provided the psychological impetus for much of the laborious work that was the basis of the great advances in astronomy and cosmology. Nor did this seem unreasonable or superstitious to intelligent men at the time. The English mathematician John Dee (1527—1608) remarked of those who disbelieved in astrology that:

they understand not (or will not understand) of the other workings and virtues of the heavenly sun, moon and stars: not so much as the mariner or husbandman . . . nor will allow these perfect and incorruptible mighty bodies so much radiation and force as they see in a little piece of a *Magnes stone* which, at great distance, showeth his operation.[59]

Tycho's greatest contribution to science lay in his method: accurate, systematic observation of natural phenomena over an extended period of time and a willingness to draw the logical conclusions from observed data and calculations, even if these contradicted time-hallowed theories. His conceptual failures were not due to his belief in astrology but to the psychological difficulties of following a chosen path with complete consistency.

KEPLER

Kepler, who made such good use of Tycho's data for his much more revolutionary and, in the end, correct theories of planetary motion (worked out between 1601 and 1609), was equally motivated by that curious mixture of Neoplatonic mysticism and a passion for astrology which was proving such an effective stimulus to scientific thinking. Kepler's religious veneration for the sun made both Copernicus's and Tycho's systems unacceptable to him, for he saw the sun as the actual motive force of the planets.[60]

Kepler's achievement, as that of Copernicus before him, was the result of a combination of conceptual insight with the sustained mathematical work necessary to make the available observational data fit into a coherent theory, and the intellectual honesty to reject his most cherished hypotheses when these did not fit. Kepler, the Neoplatonist, had thought that the radii of the supposedly circular orbits of the six planets revolving around the sun – Mercury, Venus, Earth, Mars, Jupiter, and Saturn – could be circumscribed to and inscribed in the five regular polyhedra and that in this fact lay an aspect of the fundamental harmony of the universe. His calculations, however, showed such an hypothesis would involve a deviation of eight minutes of arc from the data that Tycho had obtained by his observations. 'God's goodness', wrote Kepler in his *Astronomia Nova* (1609), 'has given [us] in Tycho Brahe a most careful observer. . . . It is fitting to recognize with a grateful heart this good gift of God and make use of it. . . . These eight minutes alone therefore have shown the way to the complete reform of astronomy.'[61] This reform was the discovery of the elliptical shape of the planetary orbits and of the fact that a line drawn from a given planet to the sun would describe equal areas in equal time – a fact which implied that celestial bodies did not move with uniform velocity, as had always been assumed.

PLATONISM AND THE IMPORTANCE OF MATHEMATICS

Underlying the work of Copernicus, Tycho Brahe and Kepler were two important Platonic-types of assumption: first, the progress of knowledge, as it applied to mundane affairs and the physical world, complemented, or harmonized with, providential wisdom. This was a belief in wisdom willed by God for both intellectual and spiritual progress. The second was the more specific assumption that the world could be explained in mathematical terms. But this assumption had been held to apply primarily to astronomy, that is to the eternal motions of the incorruptible, weightless celestial spheres and bodies. Aristotle, however, had not applied mathematics in any real sense to the heavens and his physics, the science of terrestrial nature, was sharply distinguished from mathematics. For Aristotle, mathematics could not adequately describe terrestrial motion because terrestrial objects did not move in abstract Euclidean space. It was a consequence of this view that Aristotelian physics was concerned with the quality of, and change in, objects and therefore tended to be partly chemistry. But, once it was assumed that the earth ceased to be the centre of the cosmos and moved around the sun in an orbit similar to that of the other planets, the old Aristotelian distinction between mathematical astronomy and mainly non-mathematical physics disappeared. It remained, however, to construct a new mathematical science of terrestrial physics and eventually to integrate this with Copernican and Keplerian astronomy in a new cosmology. This was fully achieved only by Newton late in the seventeenth century. Much of the groundwork on the basic terrestrial mechanics, however, was done by Galileo Galilei (1564–1642), a good deal of it before the end of the sixteenth century.

It seems to have been a fuller appreciation during the last quarter of the sixteenth century of the work of the Greek mathematician Archimedes (287–212 B.C.) which was the basis for the crucial advances in the science of mechanics. These advances were primarily theoretical and conceptual, even in the case of the Dutch engineer-mathematician Simon Stevin (1548–1620). They involved not only the disproving of specific Aristotelian theories of mechanics, such as that projectiles fly because they are propelled by the medium through which they travel (Galileo and others), or that heavy bodies fall more rapidly than light bodies (Stevin's experiments with lead balls, before 1586) but, more important still, they involved the rejection of the Aristotelian concept that the composition, quality and value of objects have any relevance to the problem of their motion in space. Only by a process of abstraction from the commonsense reality of the Aristotelian world was Galileo able to formulate his mathematical laws of terrestrial physics and thus (to many of his contemporaries paradoxically) to advance man's understanding of physical reality.[62]

This was not the only paradox. Unlike Tycho or Kepler, Galileo was comparatively free from belief in alchemy, astrology (though he did cast horoscopes), animism and the various forms of biblical, cabalistic or Pythagorean numerology which were fashionable in the sixteenth century. He hated mysticism and allegory even in poetry and therefore greatly preferred Ariosto to Tasso.[63] Yet it was precisely Galileo's rejection of an essential philosophical difference between the material world and geometrical figures – a distinction made by both Aristotelians and Platonists – which, so it has recently been argued, prevented him from accepting Kepler's theory of the elliptical shape of the orbits of the planets.[64] Galileo, just as Copernicus and Kepler, believed with Plato in the aesthetic perfection and beauty of the circle and the sphere. Since God had created the universe beautiful and harmonious it followed that the movements of the heavenly bodies had to be circular. Kepler, on the other hand, still held to the philosophical difference between geometry and reality and, in consequence, he was prepared to accept a deviation from the idea of circularity when observational evidence and his mathematical calculations demanded it.

COLLAPSE OF THE MEDIEVAL WORLD PICTURE

By the beginning of the seventeenth century the traditional world picture of the Middle Ages had collapsed. Ptolemy's complex mathematical model of a geocentric universe was being superseded by a simpler and better mathematical model of a heliocentric universe. Aristotle's physics had been shown in many respects to be wrong or inadequate and his conception of an elaborate hierarchical universe had been shattered. As yet there was no new, coherent cosmology to take the place of what had been lost. Not even the direction of future scientific advance was fully clear to contemporaries, as the controversies among even the most 'advanced' thinkers over the shape of the planetary orbits show. To the general public it was all very bewildering. The sophisticated discussions of magic, mysticism and theology, which formed such an integral part of the philosophical and scientific thinking of the age and without which there would probably have been no advance in science at all — all this was as incomprehensible to the ordinary man as was the advanced mathematics of these discussions. It was to be a long time before he would accept that the sun did not move around the earth and his everyday language, with such phrases as the rise and the setting of the sun, has not even yet managed to adapt itself to the Copernican revolution. At the same time, the scale, the conditions and, perhaps even the psychological atmosphere and motivation of scientific inquiry, were beginning to change.

INCREASING INTEREST IN SCIENCE

In the first place, it looks as if in 1600 there were far more men with a training and interest in one or more fields of science than there had been in 1500. New chairs of science, and particularly of medicine and its related disciplines, were being founded in the universities. It has been held that Vesalius's greatest achievement was the initiation of the sequence of master and pupil in the medical school of the University of Padua. It was Vesalius, too, who played a great role in the foundation of the famous medical school of Basle. This school from its reorganization as a Protestant university in 1532 until 1560 promoted only nine students as doctors of medicine. In the next twenty-five years the number rose to 114 and in the following quarter-century, from 1586 to 1610, to 454.[65] In 1560 Landgrave William IV of Hesse established the first permanent astronomical observatory in Europe with a full-time professional mathematician in charge. It was at the landgrave's suggestion that, in 1576, Frederick II of Denmark provided the young Tycho Brahe with his magnificent observatory of Uraniborg, on the island of Hven, where, for the first time, a team of trained observers could cooperate in systematic programmes of observation.

While discussion of scientific theories and discoveries was not unknown in the philosophical academies of the first half of the sixteenth century — it was the humanists, as we have seen, who were making available the bulk of Greek scientific writing — such discussions seem to have become much more common towards the end of the century. Baïf's Academy in Paris, which otherwise concentrated on poetry, music and dance, is a good example of this (see p. 412). Some academies even were founded specifically for and by scientists.[66] The most famous of these, although not the first, was the Accademia dei Lincei of Rome, founded in 1603 by a friend of Galileo, Prince Federico Cesi.

These were only the beginnings. The great age of the scientific societies was not the sixteenth but the seventeenth century. It may be that the greater number of scientists in 1600 simply reflected a general increase in the diffusion of learning and education. Yet one has the distinct impression that brilliant young men who, in 1500, would almost naturally have chosen the study of theology and the church as a career were, in 1600, beginning to turn to the study of science. It is true that there were probably more priests and theologians in 1600 than in 1500 — almost certainly so in Spain and Italy. Yet, the bitter religious quarrels of the sixteenth century and the disasters which had befallen western Europe in consequence of these quarrels, seem to have driven many of precisely the most gifted men away from theological controversies and towards activities which promised that peace and harmony which the conventional theology of both Catholic and Protestants was so signally failing to provide.

THE POLITIQUE SPIRIT AND THE QUEST FOR HARMONY

In a sense, this development was the intellectual counterpart to the growth of the Politique attitude in the religious politics of the last quarter of the sixteenth century. (See pp. 308 ff.) Its intellectual roots were, indeed, much older and can be traced, both to the Neoplatonism and Hermetism of Ficino and his followers for whom the disputes of the theologians seemed unimportant compared with the mystical religious knowledge to be derived from the Platonic philosophers and from Hermes Trismegistus, and to the beliefs of Erasmus and the Erasmians who sought to bridge the doctrinal differences between Catholics and Lutherans. But it was precisely in the last quarter of the sixteenth century, and even more in its last decade, that these varied traditions tended to come together. All had in common the quest for harmony, in politics and music, in poetry, art and cosmology. The interconnections were particularly clear in France, not only in Baïf's Academy which had both Catholic and Protestant members, but in the intellectual debates and splendid festivities at the court of Henry III and

429

Catherine de Medici (herself brought up in the Neoplatonic intellectual atmosphere of Florence).[67] Henry IV, the personal embodiment of the Politique idea, was hailed in intellectual circles all over Europe as the bringer of peace and harmony to a divided world. The expression of such hopes was one of the principal accusations against Giordano Bruno in his trial by the Inquisition, for it was interpreted as support for a heretic king.

Bruno (1548–1600) has no place in the history of scientific discoveries or of the development of scientific methods. His importance in the intellectual history of Europe lies rather in the fact that he embodied in his personality and career many of the aspects of the late sixteenth-century quest for harmony (see also p. 347). He was an ardent protagonist of the Copernican system which he enlarged into a belief in a limitless universe with an infinite number of worlds peopled by sentient beings; for nothing less, he argued, was fitting to the omnipotence of God. A prophet of the magic and the mystical religion of Hermetism, he travelled indifferently in Catholic Italy and France and in Protestant England, Switzerland and Germany, debating and preaching his doctrines and hoping in the end for a reform of the Catholic Church which should heal the schism of Christendom. In 1592 he was betrayed to the Venetian Inquisition and although he recanted all the heresies of which he was accused, he later withdrew his recantation before the Roman Inquisition and was burned alive, as a relapsed heretic, in Rome in 1600. Bruno's condemnation by the Inquisition was based primarily on his religious views. Yet his philosophical and cosmological theories were inseparable from these latter – as, indeed, they were for practically all of his contemporaries – and the Inquisition, of necessity, condemned the one with the others.[68] Thus arose the legend that Bruno was condemned by an obscurantist Church for his belief in the Copernican system. Yet Bruno's death, which created a sensation in intellectual Europe, did show that the Catholic Church was unwilling to accept tamely the destruction of a cosmology which, over the centuries, it had built into the very foundations of its dogma. It was Galileo's attempt to prevent the Church from making this, to his mind, fundamental mistake that led him into his own, even more famous, struggle with the Inquisition (1616–33).

In Italy the political aspects of the late sixteenth-century quest for harmony were not as prominent as in France; for Italy had escaped religious civil wars, and political harmony did not appear to have the same urgency as in western Europe. Characteristically, French Politique ideas were received with the greatest sympathy in Venice, the independent city republic manœuvring between the great powers and, at the turn of the century, drifting into an open quarrel with the papacy. In all non-political fields, however, the striving for harmony was as great in Italy as in France. In painting and architecture the new Baroque and classical styles of Caravaggio and the Carracci, of Vignola and of Maderna were a deliberate rejection of the tensions of the previous generation of Mannerism and a return to the classical harmony of the High Renaissance. Sculpture, painting and architecture were being treated as complementary arts, brought together to form a harmonic whole. Even more striking is the case of music. The quest for harmony − a harmony that, in some sense, mirrored the harmony of the universe and the music of the celestial spheres − had been the basis of musical composition throughout the sixteenth century. Throughout the century, too, music was composed to harmonize with words. But it was at Catherine de Medici's court that music came to be an integral part of the splendid spectacles which she loved to present and which were deliberately designed as propaganda for her policy of religious and political conciliation.[69] These spectacles were too expensive and too closely linked with specific political situations to become regular institutions and art forms. But opera, invented in Florence in the last decade of the sixteenth century, did not suffer from these drawbacks. With its combination of drama, poetry, music and the visual arts, opera embodied the contemporary quest for harmony more successfully than any single art form could do − and this may well account for its extraordinarily rapid rise in popularity in all levels of society.

GALILEO

It was in this atmosphere that Galileo Galilei grew up. His father, Vincenzo, was a prominent member of the circle of Florentine and Roman musicians and humanists who wished to recover the classical music of the ancients and who invented opera. Galileo himself had originally been inclined to study painting. He loved music and he was a poet and an accomplished Latinist. His artistic and literary tastes were distinctly classical.[70] For Galileo the study of

431

the universe and its laws was of a piece with the study and the practice of the arts; for, basic to both, was the harmony of the universe and of all its manifestations. Galileo's scientific inspiration was therefore not as different from that of his mystic friend, Kepler, as has sometimes been thought. What was new in the work of both, as it was also in the scientific work of their most distinguished contemporaries, was the consistent application of mathematical thinking to observed phenomena, the acceptance of the most revolutionary consequences of such thinking (although none of the scientists of this period managed to be completely consistent in this), and the actual scientific laws in physics and astronomy which they discovered and formulated. Galileo made his greatest contributions to science after 1600, when he was already middle-aged. It was then that he formulated his mathematical laws of motion which, if often not yet fully correct, cleared away most of the misconceptions of both Aristotelian physics and of its earlier critics, in whose attacks on Aristotle Galileo had eagerly joined in his earlier years, when he had been a professor of mathematics in the universities of Pisa and Padua. It was in 1609 that Galileo first turned a telescope towards the heavens and made those startling discoveries which revolutionized man's picture of the universe much more effectively than Copernicus's mathematical calculations had done. All this was given its fullest effect only by the impact of Galileo's personality on his contemporaries and on later generations. His passionate commitment to the Copernican world view, his fierce controversies with the Ptolemists and Aristotelians, his deliberate break with academic tradition in writing his scientific works not in Latin but in Italian, and in a most beautifully clear and readable Italian at that,[71] and finally his clashes with the Roman Inquisition – all this gave to the great debate about the nature of the universe a dramatic force which went even beyond John Donne's lament of 1611:

> 'Tis all in pieces, all coherence gone;
> All just supply, and all Relation.*

These lines were part of a lament for the death of a young girl, written for a patron. The point is that Donne should have thought it appropriate to include this reference to the contemporary perception of the world among his conventionally Christian expressions of lament. Perhaps the increasing attractiveness of scien-

*J. Donne, *An Anatomy of the World*. 'The First Anniversary', 213–14.

tific studies lay in just this combination of a quest for harmony, in a world that was becoming increasingly disillusioned with religious strife, with the exciting results which scientific studies seemed to promise.

This was not the whole story. The great advances which were made in the biological sciences during the sixteenth century do not easily fit into the pattern we have tried to discern, except that they shared with the physical sciences the growing importance of international collaboration and an acceptance that the republic of science, like the republic of letters, transcended national and denominational boundaries. Nor were all aspects of the political, intellectual and artistic life of Europe at the end of the sixteenth century a part of this quest for universal harmony. The contrary attitudes in politics, economics, religion and even art were still strong and, at the end of the second decade of the seventeenth century, they were to plunge Europe into new disasters. But for about a quarter of a century, from the early 1590s, the Politique spirit and the quest for universal harmony were triumphant. They gave Europe peace, after almost a century of dynastic, national, religious and civil wars, at least in part inspired and allowed it to enjoy the achievements of one of the great peaks of European civilization: for this was the age of Shakespeare and Cervantes, of Caravaggio and Rubens, of Gabrieli and Monteverdi, and, not least, of Kepler and Galileo.

NOTES AND REFERENCES

1 The prophet Jonah on the ceiling of the Sistine Chapel.

2 Dorothy Koenigsberger, *Renaissance Man and Creative Thinking: A History of Concepts of Harmony 1400–1700* (Hassocks, 1979), p. 268.

3 Quoted in K. Clark, *Leonardo da Vinci* (Harmondsworth, 1961), p. 75.

4 Quoted in E. Panofsky, *Idea*, 2nd edn (Berlin, 1960), p. 32.

5 Marsilio Ficino, *Theologia Platonica: de Immortalitate Animarum* (Platonic Theology: on the Immortality of the Souls. Written 1469–74; printed 1482).

6 'Per fido essempio' (G 164), trans. and quoted in Robert J. Clements, *The Poetry of Michelangelo* (New York, 1966), p. 208.

7   B. Castiglione, *The Book of the Courtier*, trans. C. S. Singleton (New York, 1954), p. 356.

8   For Neoplationism and its transmission and influence see D. Koenigsberger, *Renaissance Man and Creative Thinking*, pp. 71–73, 187–88, 226–34.

9   F. Haskell, *Patrons and Painters* (New York, 1963), p. 19, n. 4.

10 R. Wittkower, *Born under Saturn* (London, 1963), pp. 91 ff. and *passim*.

11 *Ibid*, p. 87.

12 B. Castiglione, *Il Cortegiano*, written between 1513 and 1518, and first published in 1528. First English translation, *The Book of the Courtier*, by Sir Thomas Hoby, published in 1561. There are several modern editions and translations.

13 We are not suggesting that every artist of the later fifteenth century was a court artist, nor that all those who were worked in the High Renaissance style as it was later defined by art historians. We are concerned with the dominant tendency in an immensely rich and varied artistic field.

14 For the effects of this change on historical and political writing see p. 103.

15 Cf. the enormous number of books on Mannerism published in the last several decades. For a typical example of the sometimes illuminating but often also fantastical attempts to establish parallelisms between Mannerism and twentieth-century art and literature, G. R. Hocke, *Die Welt als Labyrinth: Manier and Manie in der europäischen Kunst* (Hamburg, 1957).

16 G. Vasari, *Della Vite de' piu eccellenti pittori, scultori ed architettori* (Florence 1550; second enlarged ed, 1568). Historians of art differ about Vasari's reliability. His *Lives*, however, are the first systematic history of art, are very readable and give an excellent insight into sixteenth-century views on art.

17 From Marsilio Ficino, *Theologia Platonica*, quoted in Wittkower, *Born under Saturn*, p. 94.

18 R. Julian, *Caravage* (Lyons, Paris, 1961), pp. 112, 147.

19 E. Panofsky, *Albrecht Dürer*, vol. 1 (Princeton, 1945), pp. 244 ff. Panofsky's two-volume biography is by far the finest comprehensive work on Dürer.

20 G. R. Hocke, *Die Welt als Labyrinth*, pp. 144 ff.

21 F. Yates, *The Valois Tapestries* (Studies of the Warburg Institute, no. 23, London, 1959).

22 E. Mercer, *English Art 1553–1625* (Oxford, 1962), pp. 152 ff.

23 Quoted, E. Mercer, *English Art 1553–1625* (Oxford, 1962), pp. 199 ff.

24 A. Blunt, *Art and Architecture in France 1500 to 1700* (Harmondsworth, 1957) pp. 75 ff.

25 F. Yates, *The Valois Tapestries*, pp. 61 ff.

26 Castiglione, *The Book of the Courtier*, p. 133.

27 Cosimo Bartoli, *Ragionamenti accedemici*, quoted in G. Reese, *Music in the Renaissance* (New York, 1954), pp. 259 ff.

28 *Ibid.*, p. 185.

29 P. Nuten, 'Niederländische Musik. Die 2. Halfte des 16. Jahrhunderts', in F. Blume, *Die Musik in Geschichte und Gegenwart*, vol. IX (Kassel, 1961), pp. 1478 ff.

30 Quoted in G. M. Cooper, 'Instrumental Music', in *The Oxford History of Music*, 2nd edn, vol. 11, p. 422.

31 E. Lowinksy, 'Music in the Culture of the Renaissance', *Journal of the History of Ideas*, vol. XV (1954), p. 542.

32 D. B. Rowland, *Mannerism – Style and Mood* (New Haven and London, 1964), pp. 23–36.

33 J. Calvin, *The Institutes of the Christian Religion*, trans. F. C. Battles (Philadelphia, 1960), vol. 11, p. 721, n. 4.

34 Calvin, Sermon on the Book of Job, quoted in H. P. Clive, 'The Calvinist Attitude to Music', *Bibliothèque d'Humanisme et Renaissance*, vol. XX (1957), p. 93, n. 4.

35 E. Lowinsky, *Secret Chromatic Art in the Netherlands Motet* Columbia University Studies in Musicology, VI (New York, 1946).

36 *Canones et Decreta Sacrosancti oecumenici et generalis Concilii Tridentini* (Venice, 1564), p. 112.

37 Quoted from *Istituzioni harmoniche*, bk IV, ch. 32 (1558), by E. Lowinsky 'Music in the Culture of the Renaissance', p. 537.

38 *Ibid.*, p. 540.

39 D. Koenigsberger, *Renaissance Man and Creative Thinking*, pp. 185–93.

40 This point was made by Professor E. Lowinsky in a Renaissance Seminar in Chicago in January 1965.

41 H. G. Koenigsberger, 'Decadence or shift', *Trans. R. Hist. Soc.*, 5th ser., vol. X, 1960, pp. 1–18. The first, very rough draft of a theory which still needs considerable correction and elaboration. Cf. also L. Olschki, *The Genius of Italy* (London, 1950).

42 Shakespeare, *Sonnet No. 66.* Also quoted by Lowinsky in the context of the secret chromatic art of the Netherlands. See p. 408.

43 Cf. the methodologically similar analysis of the effect of this environment on Italian economic life in H. Trevor-Roper, 'Religion, the Reformation and Social Change', *Historical Studies*, vol. IV (London, 1963).

44 F. Yates, *The French Academies of the Sixteenth Century* (London, 1947), p. 319.

45 p. 1; also quoted in Lowinsky, 'Music in the Culture of the Renaissance', p. 520.

46 G. Reese, *Music in the Renaissance*, p. 685.

47 Quoted in W. P. D. Wightman, *Science and the Renaissance* (Edinburgh, 1962), vol. 1.

48 It is another later (and much more absurd) legend coupled with the name of Columbus that he had to prove to his unbelieving contemporaries that the world was round.

49 See the brilliant account of the history and psychology of naturalistic representation in E. H. Gombrich, *Art and Illusion* (London, 1962).

50 D. Koenigsberger, *Renaissance Man and Creative Thinking*, ch. 2. *Idem*, 'Decadence, shift, cultural changes and the universality of Leonardo da Vinci', in P. Mack and M. G. Jacob eds., *Politics and Culture in Early Modern Europe* (Cambridge, 1986), pp. 273–303.

51 J. Needham, 'Human Law and the Law of Nature', in *The Grand Titration: Science and Society in East and West* (London, 1969), pp. 299–331.

52 *Ibid.* and E. P. Evans, *The Criminal Prosecution and Capital Punishment of Animals* (London, 1987).

53 *Vesalius on the Brain*, ed. and trans. C. Singer (Oxford, 1952), pp. 4–6.

54 G. Agricola, *De re metallica*, Trans. Herbert C. Hoover and Lou H. Hoover (New York, 1950).

55 Quoted in M. Boass, *The Scientific Renaissance* (New York, 1962), p. 195.

56 F. A. Yates, *Giordano Bruno and the Hermitic Tradition* (London and Chicago, 1964), ch. 1 and 11. See also p. 347.

57 F. A. Yates, *Giordano Bruno and the Hermetic Tradition*, pp. 155 ff.

58 *Ibid.*, p. 254. E. J. Dijksterhuis, *The Mechanisation of the World Picture* trans. C. Dikshoorn (Oxford, 1962), p. 293.

59 *The Elements of Geometrie of . . . Euclid*, trans. H. Billingsley . . ., Preface made by M. I. Dee . . . (London, 1570), fo. b IIII.

60 Dijksterhuis, *The Mechanisation of the World Picture*, p. 305.

61 Quoted *ibid.*, p. 307.

62 A. Koyré, 'Galileo and Plato', *Journal of the History of Ideas*, vol. IV, no. 4 October 1943, pp. 403 ff, 417 ff.

63 E. Panofsky, *Gaileo as a Critic of the Arts* (The Hague, 1954), pp. 12 ff.

64 *Ibid.*, pp. 28 ff.

65 Wightman, *Science and the Renaissance*, vol. I, pp. 234 ff.

66 J. Ben-David, 'The scientific role: The conditions of its establishment in Europe', *Institute of International Studies*, University of California Reprint, pp. 204, Comparative International Series (Berkeley, 1966), pp. 33 ff.

67 F. A. Yates, *The French Academies of the Sixteenth Century* (London, 1947); ch. V, pp. 234 ff., 262 and *passim*.

68 Yates, *Bruno and the Hermetic Tradition*, ch. XIX

69 F. A. Yates, *The Valois Tapestries* (London, 1959), pt II, *passim*.

70 Panofsky, *Galileo as a Critic of the Arts*, pp. 4 ff.

71 There is a parallel here with Machiavelli's *Prince* whose beautiful Italian prose and consequent accessibility to a wide reading public made it seem much more obnoxious to the orthodox and conventional than it would have been in the form of a traditional Latin treatise.

APPENDIX: SIXTEENTH-CENTURY CHRONOLOGY

1490

POLITICS: Death of Matthias Corvinus of Hungary; succeeded as King by Vladislav II of the Polish line of Jagiello, already King of Bohemia; Maximilian of Habsburg acquires the Tyrol.

RELIGION: Birth of German Anabaptists Kaspar Schwenkfeld and Bernard Knipperdoling.

THE ARTS: Leonardo da Vinci, 'The Musician'.

EXPLORATIONS: The Talavera commission advises Spanish monarchy that a westward voyage to the Indies would be 'uncertain and impossible'.

SOCIETY: Strassburg authorities claim city contains fifty-seven secret 'nests of whores'.

1491

POLITICS: The future Henry VIII of England born.

RELIGION: Ignatius Loyola, founder of the Society of Jesus, born.

THE ARTS: Filippino Lippi, 'Sacrifice of Laocoön'. Giovanni Bazzi, 'Sodoma', apprentices as painter in Piedmont.

EXPLORATIONS: Death of William Caxton, first English printer. Columbus states his demands to Spanish court, including titles of admiral, governor and viceroy.

SOCIETY: English merchants granted trading rights in Danzig by Hanseatic League; Danzig merchants object.

1492

POLITICS: The Spanish conquer Granada, the last Moorish stronghold in Spain. Death of Lorenzo 'The Magnificent' de Medici; succeeded as ruler of Florence by son Piero. England invades France for backing the pretender Perkin Warbeck.

RELIGION: Spanish Jews are ordered to convert or leave the country. Pope Innocent VIII dies; Roderigo Borgia, Alexander VI, succeeds. Birth of Luis Vives, Spanish humanist.

THE ARTS: Birth of Pietro Aretino, Italian poet and Marguerite of

438

Navarre, author of the *Heptameron*. Boethius' treatise on music, *Opera*, published.

EXPLORATIONS: Christopher Columbus crosses Atlantic in search of the Indies and discovers the Caribbean islands.

SOCIETY: Peasant discontent widespread in Germany.

1493

POLITICS: Alexander VI publishes bull dividing the newly-discovered territories between Spain and Portugal. Peasant revolts, 'Bundschuh', break out in Germany.

RELIGION: Jacques Lefèvre d'Etaples, French humanist, publishes commentary on Aristotle.

THE ARTS: 'Nuremberg Chronicle' published.

EXPLORATIONS: Columbus's second voyage. Birth of Paracelsus, Swiss alchemist and physician.

SOCIETY: Introduction of maize to Europe from America. Spanish settlers populate Tenerife. 142,000 pilgrims flock to vial of sacred blood in Aix-la-Chapelle.

1494

POLITICS: Charles VIII of France invades Italy. The Medici are overthrown and the Florentine Republic re-established. By the treaty of Tordesillas, the Portuguese and Spanish agree on world partition. Ireland made dependency of England through 'Poynings' Law'.

RELIGION: Girolamo Savonarola establishes sway over Florence.

THE ARTS: Leonardo da Vinci begins 'Madonna of the Rocks'. Sebastian Brant, *The Ship of Fools*, social and anti-clerical satire. Birth of François Rabelais, French writer.

EXPLORATIONS: Columbus explores Cuba, convinced it is southern China, and Jamaica.

SOCIETY: Founding of King's College, Aberdeen.

1495

POLITICS: Charles VIII withdraws from Italy. John II of Portugal dies, succeeded by Manuel I.

RELIGION: Portuguese Jews expelled. John Bale, English reformer, dramatist and bishop of Ossory, born.

THE ARTS: Hieronymus Bosch, 'Temptation of St Anthony'. Leonardo da Vinci 'The Last Supper'.

EXPLORATIONS: Natives of Hispaniola rebel against Columbus and Spanish but are defeated by cavalry and firearms.

SOCIETY: Syphilis epidemic spreads through Europe.

1496

POLITICS: Scotland invades England in support of Perkin Warbeck.

RELIGION: Savonarola encourages Florentines to dispose of worldly objects in the 'burning of vanities'.

THE ARTS: Franchino Gafori, composer and theoretician, *Practica Musicae*.

EXPLORATIONS: Columbus returns from second voyage.

SOCIETY: First mention of tobacco by a European. Scottish landowners required by law to educate their sons.

1497

POLITICS: Cornishmen rise and march on London; Perkin Warbeck captured by Henry VII. Scandinavian union revived by Danes.
RELIGION: Savonarola excommunicated. Birth of Philip Melanchthon, German humanist and reformer.
THE ARTS: Birth of Hans Holbein the Younger.
EXPLORATIONS: John Cabot, in pay of England, mistakes coast of Canada for that of China. Vasco da Gama of Portugal rounds the Cape of Good Hope.
SOCIETY: Famine in Florence.

1498

POLITICS: Charles VIII dies, succeeded as King of France by Louis XII.
RELIGION: Savonarola executed in Florence. Erasmus of Rotterdam, Dutch humanist, lectures at Oxford.
THE ARTS: Aldus Manutius publishes comedies of Aristophanes. Ottaviano dei Petrucci first to print music with moveable type.
EXPLORATIONS: Da Gama reaches India by sea. Third voyage of Columbus.
SOCIETY: Cabot's discovery of Canadian fishing grounds frees England from reliance on Icelandic waters.

1499

POLITICS: Perkin Warbeck executed after escape attempt. Louis XII marries Anne of Brittany to add province to French crown.
RELIGION: Spanish Moors, ordered to convert, rebel in Granada.
THE ARTS: Birth of Sir Thomas Elyot, English author.
EXPLORATIONS: Second Cabot expedition reported lost at sea. Spanish discover Venezuelan pearl fishery.
SOCIETY: Plague in England (–1500).

1500

POLITICS: Future Emperor Charles V born. Moorish rebellion crushed.
RELIGION: Birth of Swiss theologian Johannes Stumpf.
THE ARTS: Benevenuto Cellini, Italian sculptor and goldsmith, born.
EXPLORATIONS: Pedro Alvares Cabral claims Brazil for Portugal. Amerigo Vespucci explores South American coast. Columbus sent back to Spain in irons. Death of Portuguese explorer Diaz.
SOCIETY: University of Valencia founded. 30,000 pilgrims reported dead of plague in Rome. Severe crop failures in Germany.

1501

POLITICS: Prince Arthur of England weds Catherine of Aragon. French army enters Rome; Louis XII declared King of Naples.
RELIGION: Erasmus's *Enchiridion*.

THE ARTS: Michelangelo begins 'David'. Albrecht Dürer, 'Life of the Virgin'. Masses by Josquin des Prés published.
EXPLORATIONS: Leonhard Fuchs, German botanist, born.
SOCIETY: First load of Indian spices arrives in Portugal.

1502
POLITICS: Spaniards conquer Naples. Peasant rebellions in Germany. English heir to throne Prince Arthur dies, leaving Prince Henry as heir.
RELIGION: Lady Margaret professorships of divinity established at Oxford and Cambridge.
THE ARTS: Lucas Cranach, 'Crucifixion'.
EXPLORATIONS: Columbus begins last voyage. da Gama establishes Portuguese colony in India at Cochin.
SOCIETY: Frederick of Saxony founds University of Wittenberg. Book censorship begins in Spain.

1503
POLITICS: James IV of Scotland marries Margaret Tudor, daughter of Henry VII.
RELIGION: Thomas à Kempis's *Imitation of Christ* published in English translation. William Warham appointed archbishop of Canterbury. Death of popes Alexander VI and successor Pius III. Guiliano della Rovere elected Pope Julius II.
THE ARTS: Da Vinci, 'Mona Lisa'. Thomas Wyatt, English poet, born.
EXPLORATIONS: Portuguese colony established on Zanzibar. Michel de Nostredame, 'Nostradamus', French astrologer, born.
SOCIETY: Paris surgeons treat syphilis with red-hot irons.

1504
POLITICS: Isabella of Spain dies; her mad daughter Juana proclaimed Queen of Castile.
RELIGION: Birth of Matthew Parker, first Elizabethan archbishop of Canterbury.
THE ARTS: Michelangelo, 'David'; Lucas Cranach, 'Rest on the Flight to Egypt'. Jacopo Sanazaro, *Arcadia*.
EXPLORATIONS: Columbus returns from his last voyage.
SOCIETY: Peter Henlein of Nuremberg invents first portable time-piece.

1505
POLITICS: Treaty of Salamanca establishes shared rule in Castile between Ferdinand of Aragon and Juana's husband, Philip of Burgundy.
RELIGION: Luther enters cloister in Erfurt. Birth of John Knox, Scottish Reformer.
THE ARTS: Giorgione, 'The Tempest'.
EXPLORATIONS: Portuguese Almeida reaches Ceylon. Sebastian Cabot enters Hudson Strait.
SOCIETY: College of Surgeons founded in Scotland.

441

1506

POLITICS: Council of Regency is established in Castile for Juana on death of her husband, Philip of Burgundy.

RELIGION: Birth of St Francis Xavier. Birth of George Buchanan, Scottish humanist.

THE ARTS: Rebuilding of St Peter's, Rome begins under Donato Bramante.

EXPLORATIONS: Death of Columbus.

SOCIETY: Florence forms militia, first national army in Italy.

1507

POLITICS: Margaret of Austria named regent of the Netherlands.

RELIGION: Martin Luther ordained priest.

THE ARTS: Petrucci publishes first printed lute tablature.

EXPLORATIONS: New World first called 'America' after Vespucci.

SOCIETY: Russians import Scottish gun makers.

1508

POLITICS: Maximilian I becomes Holy Roman Emperor.

RELIGION: Luther studies theology at Wittenberg University.

THE ARTS: Michelangelo begins painting the Sistine Chapel. Birth of Italian architect Andrea Palladio. First books printed in Scotland. Garcia de Montalvo, *Amadis of Gaul*.

EXPLORATIONS: Vespucci named pilot-major of Spain.

SOCIETY: French sermons attack extravagant women's hair-styles. First importation of African slaves to America.

1509

POLITICS: League of Cambrai formed against Venice. Henry VIII crowned King of England and marries Catherine of Aragon.

RELIGION: Birth of John Calvin, French Reformer. Johann Pfefferkorn leads attack on Jewish writings in Germany.

THE ARTS: Erasmus, *Praise of Folly*. Raphael, 'School of Athens'.

EXPLORATIONS: Spanish under Vasco Núñez de Balboa found Santa Maria de l'Antigua, first European settlement on the American continent.

SOCIETY: Earthquake rocks Constantinople. Jews attacked in Verona, Treviso and Asolo.

1510

POLITICS: Henry VIII executes his father's unpopular ministers Empson and Dudley.

RELIGION: Luther visits Rome.

THE ARTS: Death of Italian painter Botticelli. Death of Giorgione.

EXPLORATIONS: Portuguese take Goa.

SOCIETY: John Colet founds St Paul's School, London.

1511

POLITICS: Pope Julis II forms Holy League against France.

RELIGION: Birth of Michael Servetus, Spanish theologian and physician.

THE ARTS: Birth of Giorgio Vasari.
EXPLORATIONS: Portuguese take Malacca. Spanish discover gold in Cuba.
SOCIETY: Preachers blame earthquake in Venice on divine wrath against sodomy.

1512
POLITICS: France expelled from Italy. Florentine republic falls with the return of the Medici.
RELIGION: Fifth Lateran Council opens. Luther lectures on *Romans*.
THE ARTS: Michelangelo finishes the Sistine Chapel. Andrea del Sarto, 'The Annunciation'.
EXPLORATIONS: Nicholas Copernicus, Polish astronomer, concludes the planets circle the sun. Death of Vespucci. Ponce de Leon explores Florida. Birth of cartographer Gerardus Mercator.
SOCIETY: Dutch allowed by the Hanseatic League to trade in the Baltic.

1513
POLITICS: Scots defeated by England at Flodden; James IV of Scotland dies, succeeded by James V. Peasant revolt in Germany.
RELIGION: Lateran Council pronounces that the soul is immortal. Giovanni de Medici elected Pope Leo X, succeeding Julius II.
THE ARTS: Michelangelo, 'Moses'. Niccolò Machiavelli writes *The Prince*. Baldassare Castiglione begins writing *The Courtier* (–1518).
EXPLORATIONS: Portuguese reach the Spice Islands and China. Balboa discovers Pacific Ocean.
SOCIETY: 565 slaves from Guinea reach Portugal.

1514
POLITICS: Vasily III takes Smolensk. Peasant rebellion suppressed in Hungary.
RELIGION: Hunne case in London arouses strong anti-clericalism. Fuggers authorized to sell indulgences in Germany. Thomas Wolsey named archbishop of York.
THE ARTS: Hieronymous Bosch, 'The Garden of Earthly Delights'. Albrecht Dürer, 'Melancholia'.
EXPLORATIONS: Birth of Andreas Vesalius, Dutch anatomist.
SOCIETY: Hungarian peasants condemned to 'real and perpetual servitude'.

1515
POLITICS: French rout Swiss at Marignano. Francis I occupies Milan.
RELIGION: Lateran Council forbids publication of books unless examined by ecclesiastical authorities.
THE ARTS: *Letters of Obscure Men*, humanist satire. Antonio Allegri da Correggio, 'Madonna of St Francis'. Jacopo da Pontormo, 'Joseph of Egypt'.
EXPLORATIONS: Spanish reach Mexico.

SOCIETY: Louis XII gives vinegar-makers the right to distil brandy. Gypsies expelled from Burgundy. Hampton Court palace finished for Cardinal Wolsey.

1516

POLITICS: Charles V succeeds Ferdinand II as King of Spain. Birth of future Mary I of England.

RELIGION: Concordat of Bologna grants liberties to the Gallican Church. Erasmus publishes Greek and Latin New Testatment.

THE ARTS: Death of Bosch. Ludovico Ariosto writes *Orlando Furioso*; Thomas More, *Utopia*.

EXPLORATIONS: Peter Martyr's *Decades* discusses explorations in America.

SOCIETY: First Jewish ghetto in Venice. Bananas introduced to the West Indies from the Canary Islands.

1517

POLITICS: 'Evil May Day' riots in London; sixty hanged.

RELIGION: Luther publishes his '95 Theses'. End of Lateran Council.

THE ARTS: Ulrich von Hutten named 'King of Poets' by Emperor Maximilian I.

EXPLORATIONS: Ferdinand Magellan leaves Portuguese employ to work for Spain. Balboa executed on false charge of treason.

SOCIETY: Coffee introduced to Europe from East Africa. Wheel-lock musket invented in Nuremberg.

1518

POLITICS: Peace of London arranged by Wolsey between English, French, Empire, Pope and Spain.

RELIGION: Luther, under attack, refuses to recant.

THE ARTS: Raphael, 'Portrait of Leo X'. Machiavelli, *Mandragola*. Birth of Venetian painter, Tintoretto.

EXPLORATIONS: Spanish exploring east coast of Mexico.

SOCIETY: Royal College of Physicians founded. Charles V grants eight-year licence to import 4,000 African slaves into America.

1519

POLITICS: Charles V succeeds grandfather Maximilian I as Holy Roman Emperor.

RELIGION: Luther's Leipzig disputation with Johann Eck. Erasmus, *Colloquies*. Huldreych Zwingli begins to preach reform in Switzerland.

THE ARTS: Death of Leonardo.

EXPLORATIONS: Ferdinand Magellan leads Spanish expedition to circumnavigate the globe. Hernán Cortés begins conquest of Aztec kingdom in central Mexico.

SOCIETY: Augsburg establishes settlement for poor.

1520

POLITICS: Gustavus Vasa leads Swedish rebellion against Christian

II. Revolt of Comuneros in Spain. Suleiman the Magnificent becomes Ottoman Sultan.

RELIGION: Luther is excommunicated.

THE ARTS: Birth of Dutch painter Pieter Brueghel the Elder. Death of Raphael. Birth of French poet Louise Labé.

EXPLORATIONS: Portuguese traders established in China. Magellan rounds Cape Horn into the Pacific. Rifling on fire-arms devised by Gaspard Koller.

SOCIETY: Earthenware stoves appear in France. Chocolate appears in Europe from Mexico.

1521

POLITICS: Comunero revolt suppressed. Turks conquer Belgrade and move against Hungary.

RELIGION: Luther declared outlaw at Diet of Worms; he begins German translation of New Testament. Henry VIII named 'Defender of the Faith' for his book against Luther. Philip Melanchthon writes systematic treatment of Lutheran theology, *Loci Communes*.

THE ARTS: Machiavelli, *On the Art of War*. Death of Sebastian Brant and composer Josquin des Prés.

EXPLORATIONS: Magellan killed in the Philippines; expedition continues under del Cano.

SOCIETY: France begins to manufacture silk.

1522

POLITICS: Charles V allies with England against France.

RELIGION: Luther returns to Wittenberg and moves against sectaries. Election of Adrian VI, last non-Italian pope for over 450 years.

THE ARTS: Pontormo begins 'Passion Cycle'.

EXPLORATIONS: Cortés appointed governor of 'New Spain'. Spanish overland expedition reaches Peru.

SOCIETY: Hamburg physician executed for disguising himself as a woman in order to observe a birth.

1523

POLITICS: Danes depose Christian II and elect Frederick I. Knights' War in Germany ended.

RELIGION: Zwinglian reform wins Zürich. Adrian VI dies, succeeded by Clement VII, Giulio de Medici. Execution, in Brussels, of first Protestant martyr.

THE ARTS: Death of von Hutten. Tiziano Veccelli, Titian, 'Bacchus and Ariadne'. Parmigianino paints self-portrait in a convex mirror. Hans Sachs, 'Wittenberg Nightingale'.

EXPLORATIONS: Portuguese expelled from China.

SOCIETY: The plague attacks Paris.

1524

POLITICS: Peasant Revolt breaks out in Germany. French driven out of Italy. Sweden becomes independent of Denmark.

RELIGION: Thomas Münzer preaches imminent apocalypse.

THE ARTS: Cranach, 'Judgement of Paris'. Birth of Portuguese poet Luis Vaz de Camões. Johann Walther and Luther produce German hymn book.

EXPLORATIONS: Death of da Gama in India. Giovanni da Verrazano explores eastern American coast for France.

SOCIETY: Plague in Milan.

1525

POLITICS: French defeated by an imperial army at Pavia; Francis I taken prisoner. German peasant revolt crushed. Henry VIII forced by popular pressure to abandon Amicable Grant.

RELIGION: William Tyndale translates New Testament into English. Luther marries ex-nun Katharina von Bora. Anabaptists appear in Zürich. Thomas Münzer executed.

THE ARTS: Birth of French poet Pierre de Ronsard. Titian, 'Vanitas', 'Deposition'. Birth of Italian composer Giovanni Pierluigi da Palestrina.

EXPLORATIONS: German text *The Handywork of Surgery* translated into English.

SOCIETY: Zürich law decrees marriage for deflowered virgins.

1526

POLITICS: Turks defeat Hungarians at Mohacs, killing King Louis II. Peace of Madrid between Charles V and Francis I.

RELIGION: Luther writes 'German Mass'.

THE ARTS: Hans Holbein the Younger arrives in England. Dürer, 'The Four Apostles'.

EXPLORATIONS: Girolamo Cardano, Italian physician and mathematician, receives medical degree.

SOCIETY: Debasement of coinage in England. Piracy plagues Spanish shipping.

1527

POLITICS: Ferdinand of Habsburg, brother of Charles V, named King of Hungary. Imperial troops sack Rome; Clement VII imprisoned. Republic re-established in Venice. Birth of future Philip II, King of Spain.

RELIGION: Swedish Reformation begins.

THE ARTS: Holbein, portrait of Thomas More family. Death of Machiavelli.

EXPLORATIONS: Paracelsus publishes surgical manual *Die Kleine Chirurgia*.

SOCIETY: Foundation of Marburg University.

1528

POLITICS: England declares war on the emperor. Anti-Portuguese rising in East Africa.

RELIGION: Reformation under way in Scotland, Basel, Berne and Strassburg. Anabaptist leader Balthasar Hubmaier burnt in Vienna.

THE ARTS: Death of Dürer. Correggio, 'Reading Magdalene'.
Castiglione publishes *The Courtier*.
EXPLORATIONS: Paracelsus driven from medical lectureship at
Basel.
SOCIETY: Plague and peasant riots in England.

1529
POLITICS: Legatine court considers Henry VIII's divorce; Thomas
More replaces Wolsey as Chancellor. Turks lay siege to Vienna.
'Ladies' Peace' between France, emperor and England.
RELIGION: Lutheran and Swiss reformers meet at Colloquy of
Marburg. Diet of Speyer prompts Lutherans to be termed
'Protestants'.
THE ARTS: Birth of Italian composer Bartolommeo Spontone.
Albrecht Altdorfer 'Battle of Alexander'.
EXPLORATIONS: Spanish reach California.
SOCIETY: Francis I establishes College de France.

1530
POLITICS: Medici destroy Florentine Republic. Knights of St John
settle in Malta. Death of Wolsey after arrest for treason.
RELIGION: Lutheran Confession of Augsburg. Protestant princes
ally against emperor and Catholic forces.
THE ARTS: Birth of Andrea Amati, Italian violin-maker, and Polish
poet Jan Kochanowski.
EXPLORATIONS: Georgius Agricola, *Bermannus*, on mineralogy.
SOCIETY: Antwerp Exchange founded.

1531
POLITICS: Henry VIII named 'Protector and Supreme Head of the
church and clergy of England'. Ferdinand of Habsburg elected
King of the Romans.
RELIGION: Zwingli killed at Battle of Kappel between Protestant
and Catholic cantons. Servetus attacks Trinity.
THE ARTS: Erasmus publishes complete edition of Aristotle. Sir
Thomas Elyot, *The Book named the Governor*.
EXPLORATIONS: Francisco Pizzaro leads expedition against Peru.
SOCIETY: Halley's comet causes sensation in Europe. English law
decrees poisoners to be boiled to death.

1532
POLITICS: Turks invade Hungary.
RELIGION: Submission of the English Clergy.
THE ARTS: François Rabelais, *Pantagruel*. Birth of Dutch composer
Orlando de Lassus.
EXPLORATIONS: Pizarro kidnaps Inca Atahualpa to extort ransom.
SOCIETY: Augsburg Library opens. Plague in Edinburgh.

1533
POLITICS: Henry VIII marries Anne Boleyn; birth of future
Elizabeth I. Hungary partitioned; John Zapolya receives eastern

447

Hungary as Turkish vassal. Future Henry II of France weds Catherine de Medici.

RELIGION: Protestant movement in Lübeck. Thomas Cranmer named archbishop of Canterbury.

THE ARTS: Birth of Michel de Montaigne, French essayist. Holbein, 'The Ambassadors'. Titian, 'Charles V'.

EXPLORATIONS: Pizarro murders Atahualpa and consolidates conquest of Peru.

SOCIETY: Cooks accompanying Catherine de Medici to France introduce Italian cuisine.

1534

POLITICS: Anabaptist Kingdom established in Münster. English parliament enacts Act of Supremacy.

RELIGION: Ignatius Loyola founds Society of Jesus. Alessandro Farnese as Paul III succeeds Clement VII. Execution of Elizabeth Barton, 'Nun of Kent'.

THE ARTS: Rabelais, *Gargantua*. Michelangelo moves to Rome.

EXPLORATIONS: Jacques Cartier explores Canadian coast for France.

SOCIETY: English law forbids export of grain without royal licence.

1535

POLITICS: Execution of More, Cardinal Fisher and Carthusian monks for opposing Supremacy of Henry VIII. Münster Anabaptist regime suppressed. Charles V takes Tunis; takes Milan as fief after death of last Sforza.

RELIGION: Scottish act against heretical literature.

THE ARTS: Holbein, 'Henry VIII'; Angelo Bronzino, 'Portrait of a Young Man', in the Mannerist style.

EXPLORATIONS: Cartier's second voyage explores St Lawrence river.

SOCIETY: English pedlars criticized for bedazzling country folk with their sacks of 'artificial fantasies'.

1536

POLITICS: Pilgrimage of Grace, rebellion in northern England. Death of Catherine of Aragon; execution of Anne Boleyn. Henry VIII marries Jane Seymour.

RELIGION: First edition of Calvin's *Institutes*. Tyndale burnt at stake in Netherlands. Reginald Pole writes *Defence of the Unity of the Church* against Henry VIII; named cardinal. Suppression of English monasteries begins. Lutheran state church established in Denmark.

THE ARTS: Holbein becomes court painter to Henry VIII. First music publications of Gardano in Venice.

EXPLORATIONS: Spanish found Buenos Aires.

SOCIETY: Small books selling in France for the same price as a loaf of bread.

1537

POLITICS: Pilgrimage of Grace put down. Jane Seymour dies giving birth to future Edward VI.

RELIGION: First Roman Catholic hymnal. Paul III excommunicates all Catholics engaged in the slave trade.
THE ARTS: Michelangelo begins 'Last Judgment'. First music conservatories open in Italy.
EXPLORATIONS: Niccolò Tartaglia discusses science of ballistics in *La Nova Scientia*. Spanish found Asunción.
SOCIETY: First printing press in Mexico.

1538
POLITICS: Pause in French-Imperial war. James V of Scotland marries Marie de Guise.
RELIGION: Calvin and Guillaume Farel are expelled from Geneva; Calvin moves to Strassburg. Excommunication of Henry VIII.
THE ARTS: Michelangelo named architect of St Peter's.
EXPLORATIONS: Cartier proposes a voyage to discover the Kingdom of Saguenay in the Canadian interior.
SOCIETY: Johannes Sturm establishes public secondary school in Strassburg.

1539
POLITICS: England in fear of invasion from Scotland, France and emperor.
RELIGION: Six Articles Act in England affirms much traditional doctrine; Bishops Shaxton and Latimer resign sees in protest. Publication of Miles Coverdale's 'Great Bible'. Henry Niclaes establishes 'Family of Love' sect.
THE ARTS: Holbein's portrait of Anne of Cleves. Jacob Arcadelt, first book of five-part madrigals.
EXPLORATIONS: Luther calls Copernicus an 'upstart astrologer'.
SOCIETY: Printers go on strike in Lyon. Public lottery in France.

1540
POLITICS: Henry marries and subsequently annuls marriage to Anne of Cleves; marries Catherine Howard. Chancellor Thomas Cromwell executed.
RELIGION: French Edict of Fontainebleau against heresy. Last English monastery suppressed. Six new bishoprics in England.
THE ARTS: Sir David Lyndsay, *Ane Satyre of the Thrie Estates*, Scottish morality play.
EXPLORATIONS: Vannoccio Biringuccio, *Concerning Pyrotechnics*, first comprehensive work on metallurgy.
SOCIETY: London barber-surgeons given bodies of four dead criminals yearly for dissection.

1541
POLITICS: Henry VIII assumes title of King of Ireland.
RELIGION: Diet of Regensburg fails to achieve religious compromise in Empire. Calvin agrees to return to Geneva.
THE ARTS: Birth of El Greco. Gerardus Mercator's terrestrial globe.
EXPLORATIONS: Death of Paracelsus. Spanish explore Mississippi

River. Cartier's third expedition establishes colony at Cap Rouge. Murder of Pizarro.

SOCIETY: Jews expelled from Naples. All Englishmen aged 17–60 to have bows; boys from age 7 to be trained in their use.

1542

POLITICS: English crush Scots as Solway Moss; week-old Mary succeeds James V. Catherine Howard executed. War resumes between France and emperor.

RELIGION: Paul III establishes Roman Inquisition under Cardinal Carafa. Birth of Spanish mystic, St John of the Cross.

THE ARTS: Death of English poet Sir Thomas Wyatt.

EXPLORATIONS: Vesalius's *De humani corporis fabrica*, foundation of modern anatomy. Portuguese reach Japan and New Guinea. Fuchs's *Historia Stirpium* on natural history. Cartier abandons colony; Sieur de Roberval establishes another one in Canada.

SOCIETY: 'New Laws' in Spanish America for protection of natives.

1543

POLITICS: Henry VIII allies with Charles V; marries Catherine Parr. Charles V adds Duchy of Guelders to Netherlands.

RELIGION: Scottish act permits reading Scripture in the vernacular. Spain burns first Protestants.

THE ARTS: Holbein dies of the plague. Cellini's salt-cellar for Francis I and the 'Nymph of Fontainebleau'. Birth of English composer William Byrd.

EXPLORATIONS: Publication of Copernicus's *On the Revolution of the Celestial Spheres*; death of Copernicus. Roberval abandons colony.

SOCIETY: Population of Netherlands estimated at 3 million.

1544

POLITICS: French-Imperial peace of Crépy. Beginning of 'rough wooing' in Anglo-Scottish relations. England invades France.

RELIGION: Protestant Sir John Cheke named tutor to Prince Edward.

THE ARTS: Birth of Italian poet Torquato Tasso.

EXPLORATIONS: Mercator arrested for heresy. Sebastian Münster, *Cosmographia*

SOCIETY: French serfs in royal domains freed.

1545

POLITICS: English again invade Scotland. Birth of Don John of Austria.

RELIGION: Council of Trent meets. Palatinate becomes Lutheran. Massacre of Waldensians in France.

THE ARTS: Cellini returns to Florence.

EXPLORATIONS: Roger Ascham's treatise on archery, *Toxophilus*. Gerolamo Cardano *Ars magna*, solution of the cubic equation.

SOCIETY: Thirty-four executed for witchcraft in Geneva. The English warship 'Mary Rose' sinks.

1546
POLITICS: Scottish rebels murder Cardinal Beaton.
RELIGION: Death of Martin Luther. John Knox joins Scottish insurgents; later captured and sent to French galleys. Protestant Anne Askew burnt in England for heresy.
THE ARTS: Etienne de la Boétie, *Discourse on Voluntary Servitude.*
EXPLORATIONS: Mercator states earth has magnetic pole.
SOCIETY: First reference to bear-baiting in London. Henry VIII closes Bankside brothels.

1547
POLITICS: Death of Henry VIII; Edward VI succeeds as minor dominated by uncle Thomas Seymour. Francis I dies, succeeded by Henry II.
RELIGION: Six Articles repealed. France establishes the 'chambre ardente' against heresy. Council of Trent moves to Bologna.
THE ARTS: Birth of Spanish writer Miguel de Cervantes. Swiss musician Henricus Glareanus, *Dodecachordon.*
EXPLORATIONS: Bolivian silver-mining town Potosì founded. Death of Cortés.
SOCIETY: First poor-rate levied in England. English peers given benefit of clergy even if illiterate. Modena passes law against raucous 'mattinata' ceremonies.

1548
POLITICS: French peasants rebel against the salt tax. Mary Queen of Scots, betrothed to the Dauphin, sent to France.
RELIGION: Charles V promulgates the Augsburg Interim. Francis Xavier begins mission in Japan.
THE ARTS: Titian, 'Charles V at the Battle of Mühlberg'. John Bale, first English historical drama, *King John.*
EXPLORATIONS: Birth of Giordano Bruno, Italian cosmologist.
SOCIETY: Founding of Messina University.

1549
POLITICS: English rebellions in the south-west and Norfolk.
RELIGION: Introduction of new English Prayer Book. Zwinglianism and Calvinism reconciled in Consensus Tigurinus. Death of Paul III.
THE ARTS: Joachim du Bellay, *Défense de la langue Française.* Cellini, 'Perseus'. Death of Icelandic poet Jon Arason and Margaret of Navarre.
EXPLORATIONS: First anatomical theatre in Padua.
SOCIETY: Very bad harvests in England until 1552.

1550
POLITICS: Seymour overthrown by John Dudley, later duke of Northumberland.
RELIGION: Cardinal del Monte becomes Pope Julius III.
THE ARTS: Nicholas Udall, *Ralph Roister Doister*, first English comedy. Giorgio Vasari, *Lives of the Artists.*

EXPLORATIONS: Birth of mathematician John Napier.
SOCIETY: Decline in European meat consumption begins.

1551
POLITICS: Turks take Tripoli. Alliance between Henry II and
Maurice of Saxony.
RELIGION: Second session of Council of Trent (–1553). John Knox
named English court preacher.
THE ARTS: Claude Goudinel, *First Book of Psalms*. Palestrina director
of music at St Peter's.
EXPLORATIONS: Conrad von Gesner, first modern book on
zoology, *Historia animalium*. First English treatment of Copernican
system, Robert Recorde's *Castle of Knowledge*.
SOCIETY: First licensing of taverns and alehouses in England.
Influenza epidemic in England.

1552
POLITICS: France at war with Charles V. Ivan IV of Russia moves
against the Tartars. End of second Schmalkaldic War.
RELIGION: Second English Prayer Book.
THE ARTS: Pierre de Ronsard, *Amours*. Birth of English poet
Edmund Spenser.
EXPLORATIONS: Bartolommeo Eustachio, *Tabulae anatomicae*, on
Eustachian tube and valve.
SOCIETY: Edward VI establishes thirty-five grammar schools.

1553
POLITICS: Edward VI dies, succeeded (for nine-day coup) by Jane
Grey and by Mary I; Northumberland arrested.
RELIGION: Mary I moves against Protestant clergy. Servetus
executed for heresy in Geneva.
THE ARTS: Titian, 'Danae'. Death of Rabelais.
EXPLORATIONS: English merchants reach Archangel. Servetus
announces discovery of pulmonary circulation of the blood in
Christianismi Restitutio.
SOCIETY: 700 different legal codes in force in the Netherlands.

1554
POLITICS: Mary I puts down Wyatt's rebellion; weds Philip of
Spain. Jane Grey, husband and Northumberland executed. Princess
Elizabeth imprisoned in Tower.
RELIGION: Pole returns to England to accept country back into
Catholic Church; hundreds of Protestants flee to Continent.
THE ARTS: Palestrina's first book of masses. Philippe de Monte's
first book of madrigals. Birth of English poet Sir Philip Sidney.
Lazarillo de Tormes, anon., first picaresque novel.
EXPLORATIONS: Pure alcohol produced by Cardano. Birth of
English explorer, Sir Walter Raleigh.
SOCIETY: Muscovy Co. established for English trade with
Russia.

1555

POLITICS: Peace of Augsburg. Charles V turns over Netherlands to Philip. Elizabeth released from Tower.

RELIGION: English heresy laws revived; burning of Protestants starts. Calvin consolidates power in Geneva. Pope Julius III dies, succeeded by Marcello Cervino as Marcellus II; Marcellus II succeeded by Cardinal Carafa as Paul IV.

THE ARTS: Michelangelo, 'Pietà'. De Lassus's first book of madrigals. Georg Wickram, *Rollwagenbüchlein*.

EXPLORATIONS: Portuguese reach Macao. Death of Agricola.

SOCIETY: Tobacco reaches Europe from America. First coach in England. Bad harvests throughout western Europe.

1556

POLITICS: Charles V abdicates Spain to Philip II and Empire to Ferdinand I.

RELIGION: Cranmer executed, replaced as archbishop of Canterbury by Pole.

THE ARTS: Birth of Venetian composer Giovanni Gabrieli. De Lassus begins service at court of Duke of Bavaria. John Ponet, *Shorte Treatise of Politic Power*.

EXPLORATIONS: Agricola's work on mineralogy, *De re metallica*, published posthumously.

SOCIETY: French law sets age for marriage without parental consent at thirty for males and twenty-five for females. Worst harvest of century in England and Netherlands; price of grain three times normal.

1557

POLITICS: England joins Spain in war against France. John II of Portugal dies, succeeded by Sebastian I. Stafford invasion of England.

RELIGION: Scottish nobles form convenant for defence of Protestantism.

THE ARTS: Escorial Palace started. Birth of Italian composer Giovanni Gabrielli.

EXPLORATIONS: Recorde's *Whetstone of Wit* first to use '=' as equals sign. Deaths of Sebastian Cabot and Jacques Cartier.

SOCIETY: National bankruptcies in Spain and France. Algiers a centre for Mediterranean piracy.

1558

POLITICS: French take Calais from English. Mary Queen of Scots weds future Francis II. Charles V dies. Mary I dies, succeeded by Elizabeth I.

RELIGION: Knox's *First Blast of the Trumpet*. Death of Pole.

THE ARTS: Gioseffo Zarlino, *Institutioni harmoniche* on musical scales. Adrian Willaert, *Musica nova*. Marguerite of Navarre, *Heptameron* (posth.).

EXPLORATIONS: Thomas Gresham formulates 'Gresham's Law' on bad currency.

SOCIETY: Death penalty in Spain for importing or printing unauthorized books.

1559

POLITICS: Peace of Cateau-Cambrésis ends Anglo-French-Spanish war. Henry II killed in tournament; succeeded by Francis II under Guise regency.

RELIGION: New English prayer book; Act of Uniformity. 'Beggars' Summons', Scottish monks required to do charitable work. Paul IV dies, succeeded by Giovanni Angelo de Medici as Pius IV.

THE ARTS: Brueghel, 'Proverbs'. First papal Index of prohibited books.

EXPLORATIONS: Matteo Realdo Colombo, *De re anatomica*, accurate observations based on dissection.

SOCIETY: Glass window-panes common in England. Unauthorized printing punishable by death in France.

1560

POLITICS: Huguenot conspiracy of Amboise. Francis II dies, succeeded by Charles IX, with Catherine de Medici as regent. Spanish–Italian fleet routed by Turks off Tunisia. England intervenes in Scotland on behalf of Lords of the Covenant.

RELIGION: First edict of toleration in France. Church of Scotland founded. Death of Melanchthon. Felice Peretti, Inquisitor general in Venice (late Pope Sixtus V), recalled for severity.

THE ARTS: Uffizi palace in Florence built by Vasari as government offices. Birth of Italian composer Carlo Gesualdo.

EXPLORATIONS: 'Academia Secretorum Naturae', first scientific academy founded in Naples.

SOCIETY: Catherine de Medici uses snuff as a headache remedy. French nobles forbidden to engage in trade.

1561

POLITICS: Mary Queen of Scots returns to Scotland.

RELIGION: Thomas Norton's English translation of Calvin's *Institutes*.

THE ARTS: Sackville and Norton, *Gorboduc*, first English tragedy in blank verse. Palestrina, 'Improperia'. Birth of essayist, politician and scientist Francis Bacon.

EXPLORATIONS: Death of Roberval in Paris religious riot.

SOCIETY: Portuguese introduce printing in India. Spire of St Paul's, London destroyed by lightning.

1562

POLITICS: Elizabeth I almost dies from smallpox. First French War of Religion.

RELIGION: Last session of Council of Trent opens. Duc de Guise massacres Huguenots at Vassy.

THE ARTS: Cellini finishes autobiography. Death of Willaert. Birth

of English composer John Dowland and Spanish writer Lope de
Vega.
EXPLORATIONS: French establish settlement in Florida.
SOCIETY: John Hawkins begins English slave trade to America.
Dutch complain of increase in number of wolves.

1563

POLITICS: Peace of Amboise ends first French religious war.
RELIGION: Huguenots granted limited toleration. Council of Trent
closes. Church of England doctrine in the 39 Articles. Heidelberg
Catechism.
THE ARTS: Brueghel, 'Tower of Babel'. First English edition of
John Foxe's *Acts and Monuments*, 'Book of Martyrs'.
EXPLORATIONS: Mercator produces map of Lorraine.
SOCIETY: Plague in London. To aid fishing industry Wednesdays
added to Fridays as fish days in England.

1564

POLITICS: Emperor Ferdinand I dies, succeeded by son Maximilian
II. Ivan IV, 'the Terrible', forced to withdraw from Moscow.
RELIGION: Death of Jean Calvin. Revised papal Index of prohibited
books.
THE ARTS: Death of Michelangelo. Birth of English playwrights
William Shakespeare and Christopher Marlowe.
EXPLORATIONS: Death of Vesalius. Birth of Italian scientist
Galileo Galilei.
SOCIETY: Plague in Rennes causes Parlement to flee. Coldest winter
of the century in north-western Europe.

1565

POLITICS: Ivan IV sets up oprichnina. Knights of St John defeat
Turkish siege of Malta. Mary Queen of Scots marries Henry
Darnley.
RELIGION: Death of Pius IV. Beginning of vestiarian controversy in
English Church.
THE ARTS: De Lassus, 'Penetential Psalms'. Death of Louise
Labé.
EXPLORATIONS: Death of Conrad Gesner, Swiss naturalist. Start
of Filipino–Mexican convoys.
SOCIETY: Tobacco introduced in England. English begin
manufacture of pencils.

1566

POLITICS: Murder of Rizzio, secretary to Mary Queen of Scots;
birth of future James VI. Suleiman the Magnificent dies after
Hungarian campaign; succeeded by Selim II.
RELIGION: Iconoclastic riots in the Netherlands. Michaele Ghisileri
becomes Pius V.
THE ARTS: Brueghel, 'Wedding Dance'.
EXPLORATIONS: Death of Nostradamus.
SOCIETY: London Royal Exchange founded as the 'Bourse'.

1567

POLITICS: Darnley murdered; Lord Bothwell abducts and marries Mary Queen of Scots. Mary abdicates, with Earl of Moray as regent. Duke of Alva arrives in Netherlands and establishes Council of Troubles. Huguenots start second war of religion.

RELIGION: Birth of St Francis de Sales.

THE ARTS: Birth of Italian composer Claudio Monteverdi.

EXPLORATIONS: Francis Drake accompanies Hawkins expedition to West Africa and the Caribbean.

SOCIETY: Portuguese establish Rio De Janeiro.

1568

POLITICS: Mary Queen of Scots flees to England and never regains freedom. Revolt of Granada Moriscos. Second French religious war ends; third begins. Counts Egmont and Hoorne executed in Netherlands.

RELIGION: 'Bishops' Bible' published in England. English Catholic College established at Douai.

THE ARTS: Birth of actor-manager Richard Burbage.

EXPLORATIONS: Hawkins and Drake ambushed in Mexican port by the Spanish treasure fleet; all ships lost but two.

SOCIETY: Alexander Nowell, Dean of St Paul's, accidentally invents bottled beer.

1569

POLITICS: Grand Duchy of Tuscany established in Florence. Revolt of northern earls in England.

RELIGION: Northern Catholics support earls; Protestant prayer books burnt, Durham Cathedral sacked.

THE ARTS: Palestrina, first book of motets. Death of Brueghel.

EXPLORATIONS: Mercator uses cylindrical projection for maps.

SOCIETY: 50,000 die of fever in Lisbon. Public lottery in England to pay for harbour maintenance. Trained English bowmen forbidden to learn firearms.

1570

POLITICS: Peace of St Germain-en-Laye ends third French religious war. Turks take Nicosia, Cyprus. Ivan IV destroys Novgorod. Don John defeats Moriscos.

RELIGION: To support English Catholics Pius V excommunicates Elizabeth I. Consensus of Sendomir unites Polish Protestants.

THE ARTS: Birth of English playwright Thomas Dekker.

EXPLORATIONS: Japanese open Nagasaki to European trade.

SOCIETY: Spanish silver from the New World spreads through Europe. Serious flooding in the Netherlands.

1571

POLITICS: Ridolfi plot discovered in England. Turkish navy defeated by Spanish–Venetian–papal fleet led by Don John at Lepanto. Crimean Tartars burn Moscow.

RELIGION: Puritan pressure in Parliament to amend Prayer Book.

THE ARTS: Birth of German composer Michael Praetorius. Death of
Cellini.
EXPLORATIONS: Birth of German astronomer Johann Kepler.
SOCIETY: English population at 3.2 million. First permanent
gallows in London at Tyburn.

1572
POLITICS: St Bartolomew Massacre in Paris; fourth war of religion
begins. Duke of Norfolk executed for Ridolfi plot. Dutch revolt
against Spanish; Sea Beggars take Holland and Zeeland.
RELIGION: Puritan *Admonition to Parliament*. Death of John Knox.
Pius V dies, succeeded by Ugo Buoncampagni as Gregory XIII.
THE ARTS: Giovanni da Bologna, 'Mercury'. Birth of English poet
John Donne and English playwright Ben Jonson. Luis Camões,
The Lusiads.
EXPLORATIONS: Cardano arrested for heresy. Petrus Ramus,
French logician, killed in Paris massacre. Nova observed by Tycho
Brahe.
SOCIETY: Society of Antiquaries formed in London.

1573
POLITICS: Fourth religious war ends in France. Venice loses Cyprus
to Turks. Henry, Duc d'Anjou, elected Polish king; Pacta
Conventa limits rights of future Polish Kings. Alva leaves
Netherlands, replaced by Requesens.
RELIGION: Warsaw Compact affirms religious liberty in Poland.
THE ARTS: Birth of Italian painter Michelangelo Merisi,
'Caravaggio'. Francis Hotman, *Francogallia*.
EXPLORATIONS: Carolus Clusius, botanist, becomes head of
emperor's garden in Vienna.
SOCIETY: Famine and food riots in France. Establishment of
'trained bands', English militia.

1574
POLITICS: Death of Charles IX, succeeded by Henry III who
returns from Poland. Fifth war of religion erupts. Turks take
Tunis from Spain.
RELIGION: First Catholic missionary priests enter England.
THE ARTS: Tintoretto, 'Paradiso'.
EXPLORATIONS: Death of Eustachio. Tycho Brahe, Danish
astronomer, *De nova stella*, on astronomical nova.
SOCIETY: First Scottish Poor Law.

1575
POLITICS: Union of Protestants and Politiques in France. Duc
d'Alençon rebels.
RELIGION: Edmund Grindal becomes Archbishop of Canterbury.
Two Anabaptists burnt in London.
THE ARTS: William Byrd and Thomas Tallis, *Cantiones sacrae*.
EXPLORATIONS: Italians begin to imitate China porcelain. Birth of
William Oughtred, English inventor of the sliderule.

SOCIETY: Second national bankruptcy in Spain. Child labour abolished in Hungarian mines. Plague in Venice and much of Italy.

1576

POLITICS: Spanish authority collapses in the Netherlands; Pacification of Ghent; Don John of Austria named Governor. Henry of Navarre escapes from French court and declares for Protestant cause. Toleration granted; formation of Catholic Holy League. Rudolph II succeeds Maximilian II as Emperor.

RELIGION: Grindal refuses Elizabeth's order to suppress prophesying.

THE ARTS: Tintoretto, 'Ascencion of Christ'. Bodin's *Six Livres de la République*. Death of Hans Sachs.

EXPLORATIONS: Martin Frobisher embarks on search for Northwest Passage.

SOCIETY: 'The Theatre', London's first playhouse opens. Sir Christopher Hatton rents Ely Place for £10, ten loads of hay and a rose picked at midsummer.

1577

POLITICS: Sixth civil war in France begins and ends. William of Orange rejects Perpetual Edict, agreed by Don John and the States General. Don John restarts civil war.

RELIGION: Lutheran Formula of Concord. Grindal suspended as archbishop.

THE ARTS: Raphael Holinshed, *Chronicles*. Birth of Flemish painter Peter Paul Rubens.

EXPLORATIONS: Drake begins circumnavigation of globe. Frobisher's second voyage.

SOCIETY: Curtain Theatre opens in London.

1578

POLITICS: Death of Don John; replaced by duke of Parma. War in Netherlands continues. James VI assumes rule of Scotland. Elizabeth discusses marriage with Duc d'Anjou.

RELIGION: English Catholic College moved to Rheims.

THE ARTS: John Lyly, *Euphues, the Anatomy of Wit*.

EXPLORATIONS: Roman catacombs discovered. Frobisher's third voyage.

SOCIETY: Fireplaces still rare in Paris.

1579

POLITICS: Rebellion against English in Ireland. Netherlands divided by Unions of Utrecht and Arras.

RELIGION: English Jesuit College founded in Rome.

THE ARTS: Edmund Spenser, *Shephearde's Calendar*. *Vindiciae contra tyrannos* published.

EXPLORATIONS: Drake claims California for England.

SOCIETY: First Englishman, Father Thomas Stephens, settles in India.

1580

POLITICS: Spanish take Portugal; personal union until 1640. Ivan the Terrible kills his own son; loses territory to Swedes. Seventh French civil war.

RELIGION: Jesuit priests Campion and Persons enter England. Lutheran *Book of Concord.*

THE ARTS: Montaigne, *Essays.* Vincenzo Galileo, *Dialogo della musica antica e della moderna.* Sidney begins to write *Arcadia,* (published 1590 and 1593).

EXPLORATIONS: Drake completes circumnavigation. Pett and Jackman search for Northeast Passage to China.

SOCIETY: Earthquake shakes England, northern France and Netherlands; Arras decrees three weeks of sermons to admonish inhabitants for sins. Plague in Lisbon.

1581

POLITICS: Poland invades Russia. Act of Abjuration of seven northern Dutch provinces; Duc d'Anjou becomes official sovereign.

RELIGION: Campion executed for treason.

THE ARTS: Caravaggio, 'Martyrdom of St Maurice'. Richard Mulcaster's *Positions* urges education of girls.

EXPLORATIONS: Galileo enters University of Pisa to study medicine, observes pendulum effect.

SOCIETY: A single ballet at French court staged at cost of 3.6 million francs. First pumped water supply to London.

1582

POLITICS: James VI of Scotland kidnapped in Ruthven Raid. Russia loses Baltic territory to Poland. Parma wins military successes in Flanders and Brabant.

RELIGION: Grindal dies, replaced by John Whitgift. Jesuit missionaries reach China.

THE ARTS: Sir Thomas Smith, *De republica Anglorum.*

EXPLORATIONS: Gregory XIII reforms calender. Richard Hakluyt, *Discovery of America.*

SOCIETY: University of Edinburgh founded.

1583

POLITICS: Anjou retires from the Netherlands. Throckmorton plot against Elizabeth uncovered.

RELIGION: Whitgift demands subscription to anti-Puritan articles.

THE ARTS: Birth of Italian composer Girolamo Frescobaldi and English composer Orlando Gibbons.

EXPLORATIONS: Sir Humphrey Gilbert claims Newfoundland for England.

SOCIETY: Earliest life insurance policy in England.

1584

POLITICS: Death of Anjou makes Navarre heir to French throne. William of Orange assassinated. Death of Ivan the Terrible; succeeded as tsar by Feodor.

RELIGION: Bruno attacks Bible as source of astronomical knowledge.
THE ARTS: Birth of English playwright Francis Beaumont. Opening of Teatro Olimpico, Vicenza.
EXPLORATIONS: Hakluyt, *Western Discoveries*. Raleigh's expedition to Virginia.
SOCIETY: John Dee, English mathematician, tours Europe giving demonstrations of magic.

1585
POLITICS: Spain allies with French Catholic League. English expedition under earl of Leicester to aid Dutch rebels. Birth of future Cardinal Richelieu.
RELIGION: English act against Jesuits and seminary priests. Gregory XIII dies; succeeded by Felice Peretti as Sixtus V. Sixtus excommunicates Navarre.
THE ARTS: Birth of Heinrich Schütz, German composer.
EXPLORATIONS: Dutch mathematician Simon Stevin argues for use of decimal system.
SOCIETY: Barbary Company formed for English trade to North Africa.

1586
POLITICS: Babington plot to free Mary Queen of Scots and murder Elizabeth uncovered. Mary makes Philip II her heir to claim to English throne.
RELIGION: Sixtus V limits size of College of Cardinals.
THE ARTS: Death of Sidney of wounds in Netherlands. Death of Polish poet Jan Kochanowski.
EXPLORATIONS: Galileo describes hydrostatic balance. Stevin demonstrates two bodies of unequal weight fall at same speed.
SOCIETY: Frankfurt law decrees no foreigner can become a citizen unless he marries into a citizen's family. Lorraine prohibits duelling. Potatoes introduced in England.

1587
POLITICS: Mary Queen of Scots executed for treason. Navarre defeats royal army; League plots in Paris. Drake raids Cadiz. Boris Godunov becomes regent for imbecile Tsar Feodor.
RELIGION: Beginning of Catholic re-conquest of Poland. Portuguese missionaries banished from Japan.
THE ARTS: First book of Monteverdi madrigals.
EXPLORATIONS: Hakluyt, *Notable History*. Second attempt at colonizing Virginia.
SOCIETY: Start of witchcraft craze in Trier; 368 are executed in six years.

1588
POLITICS: Spanish Armada routed by English and bad weather. 'Day of Barricades' drives Henry III from Paris; Henry assassinates League leaders Duc de Guise and his brother.

RELIGION: Sixtus reorganizes Roman Curia. Beginning of Puritan 'Marprelate' tracts.
THE ARTS: Marlowe, *Doctor Faustus*. Birth of English philosopher Thomas Hobbes.
EXPLORATIONS: Thomas Hariot, *Brief and True Report on Virginia*, recommends medicinal use of tobacco.
SOCIETY: Influenza epidemic in Venice.

1589
POLITICS: Henry III assassinated; Henry of Navarre begins Bourbon dynasty. English attack Lisbon and send troops to aid Navarre.
RELIGION: Richard Bancroft argues for 'de iure divino' episcopacy.
THE ARTS: Byrd, *Cantiones sacrae, Songs of Sundrie Natures*.
EXPLORATIONS: Galileo lectures on mathematics at University of Pisa. Hakluyt, *Principal Navigations and Discoveries of the English Nation*.
SOCIETY: Grenoble Parlement flees plague.

1590
POLITICS: Henry IV lays siege to Paris but Parma relieves city. Duc de Mayenne sets up rival government.
RELIGION: Thomas Cartwright and other Puritan leaders arrested. Sixtus V dies, succeeded by Cardinal Castagna as Urban VII. After twelve days Urban dies, succeeded by Cardinal Sfondrato as Gregory XIV.
THE ARTS: Edmund Spenser, *Faerie Queene*.
EXPLORATIONS: Virginia colony found mysteriously abandoned.
SOCIETY: Carlo Gesualdo orders murder of unfaithful wife and her lover. Mamugna, alchemist, hanged for fraud on tinselled gallows in München.

1591
POLITICS: Dmitri, younger son of Ivan the Terrible, is murdered on orders of Godunov. Philip II crushes Aragonese rebellion. Emperor Rudolph attempts to bring peace between Spain and Netherlands.
RELIGION: Gregory XIV dies, succeeded by Antonio Faccinetti as Innocent IX.
THE ARTS: Shakespeare, *Henry VI part I*. Sidney, *Astrophel and Stella* (posth.).
EXPLORATIONS: James Lancaster leads three ships in first English expedition to the East Indies.
SOCIETY: William Hackett proclaims himself Jesus Christ and threatens to depose Elizabeth; executed with followers.

1592
POLITICS: John III of Sweden dies, succeeded by Sigismund III of Poland. English army supports Navarre in Normandy.
RELIGION: Innocent IX dies, succeeded by Cardinal Aldobrandini as Clement VIII.

THE ARTS: Death of Montaigne. Shakespeare, *Richard III, Comedy of Errors*. Thomas Nashe, *Pierce Pennilesse*.
EXPLORATIONS: Spanish explore British Columbia coast. François Viète, French mathematician, *Artem analyticum isagoge*, on symbolic algebra.
SOCIETY: Plague in London.

1593
POLITICS: Henry IV anounces his return to Catholicism. War between Turks and Empire.
RELIGION: Execution of John Penry, involved in the Marprelate controversy and two Separatists Henry Barrow and John Greenwood.
THE ARTS: El Greco, 'The Crucifixion'. Shakespeare, *Taming of the Shrew*. Death of Marlowe in tavern fight.
EXPLORATIONS: Inquisition extradites Bruno to Rome.
SOCIETY: Fear of worsening plague in London aroused when a heron perches on top of St Peter's, Cornhill.

1594
POLITICS: Henry IV enters Paris; grants toleration to Huguenots. Rebellion in Ireland.
RELIGION: Richard Hooker defends English Church in *Laws of Ecclesiastical Polity*.
THE ARTS: Gesualdo, first book of madrigals. Shakespeare, *Romeo and Juliet*. Death of Tintoretto.
EXPLORATIONS: Death of Mercator. Lancaster expedition returns with only one ship and twenty five men.
SOCIETY: Beginning of four consecutive bad harvests in England.

1595
POLITICS: Assassination attempt on Henry IV. France declares war on Spain.
RELIGION: Clement VII receives Henry IV back into Church and recognizes him as King of France. 'Wisbech Stirs' among English Catholic clergy begin.
THE ARTS: Sidney, *Defence of Poesie* (posth.)
EXPLORATIONS: Dutch begin colonization of East Indies.
SOCIETY: English army abandons bow as weapon.

1596
POLITICS: France allies with England and Netherlands against Spain. Second unsuccessful Spanish armada.
RELIGION: Union of Brześć between Polish Catholics and part of Lithuanian Greek Orthodox hierarchy.
THE ARTS: Caravaggio begins 'The Supper at Emmaus'. Death of Bodin.
EXPLORATIONS: Kepler, *Cosmographic Mystery*, on planetary motion. Death of Drake.
SOCIETY: Sir Thomas Harington invents first flush toilet. Plague in Spain and Mediterranean basin (−1600).

1597
POLITICS: Third unsuccessful Spanish Armada.
RELIGION: Death of Jesuit St Peter Canisius.
THE ARTS: Dowland, *First Book of Songs*. James VI, *Daemonologie*, on witchcraft. Jacopo Peri, 'Dafne', first opera.
EXPLORATIONS: Galileo tells Kepler he agrees with Copernican system.
SOCIETY: English Act for transportation of felons to the colonies.

1598
POLITICS: Death of Philip II, succeeded by Philip III. Irish rebels defeat English army. Peace between France and Spain. Feodor dies, ending Rurik dynasty; Boris Godunov elected Tsar.
RELIGION: Edict of Nantes grants toleration and liberties to Huguenots. 'Archpriest Controversy' over leadership of English Catholic clergy.
THE ARTS: Shakespeare, *Much Ado About Nothing*.
EXPLORATIONS: Brahe, *Astronomiae instauratae Mechanica*.
SOCIETY: 'The Theatre' is torn down and the timber used to build 'The Globe'.

1599
POLITICS: Earl of Essex concludes truce with Irish rebels and returns to England. Henry IV wins annulment of marriage to Marguerite de Valois.
RELIGION: Pope Clement refuses mercy to killers in Cenci murder scandal.
THE ARTS: Death of Spenser. Shakespeare, *Julius Caesar*. Birth of Spanish painter Diego Velasquez.
EXPLORATIONS: Ulisse Aldrovandi publishes on natural history.
SOCIETY: East India Company formed. Will Kemp morris-dances from London to Norwich.

1600
POLITICS: Henry IV marries Marie de Medici.
RELIGION: Persecution of Catholics in Sweden.
THE ARTS: Shakespeare, *Hamlet*. Giulio Caccini, 'Euridice'.
EXPLORATIONS: William Gilbert, *De magnete*, on magnetism. Execution of Bruno.
SOCIETY: Will Adams, first Englishman to land in Japan, stays on as shipbuilder to the shogun. Half of Frankfurt's elementary schools are operated by women.

1601
POLITICS: Essex, out of favour, attempts a coup against Elizabeth and is executed. Treaty of Lyon between France and Savoy. Birth of future Louis XIII. Elizabeth's 'Golden Speech' to parliament.
RELIGION: Francis Godwin, author of first science-fiction story in English, appointed bishop of Llandaff.
THE ARTS: Caccini, *Nuove musice*. Gesualdo madrigals.

EXPLORATIONS: Death of Brahe; Kepler succeeds him as Imperial Mathematician.
SOCIETY: English population at 4.1 million. Severe famine in Russia.

1602
POLITICS: Tax revolts in France. Savoy fails to capture Geneva. Robert Cecil negotiates English succession with James VI.
RELIGION: English government offers concessions to Catholic priests willing to acknowledge Elizabeth.
THE ARTS: Shakespeare, *All's Well That Ends Well.*
EXPLORATIONS: Galileo postulates law of falling bodies.
SOCIETY: Dutch East India Company formed. Plague in London. First copper coins in France.

1603
POLITICS: Elizabeth I dies; succeeded by James VI of Scotland as James I.
RELIGION: Millenary Petition. Jacobus Arminius lectures in theology at Leiden.
THE ARTS: Shakespeare's company, the Chamberlain's Co., tour English provinces for fear of London plague.
EXPLORATIONS: Death of botanist Andrea Cesalpino.
SOCIETY: Plague in London.

1604
POLITICS: Treaty of London, peace between England and Spain.
RELIGION: Death of Faustus Socinius, anti-trinitarian. Hampton Court Conference. Whitgift dies and is replaced as Archbishop of Canterbury by Richard Bancroft.
THE ARTS: Shakespeare, *Othello.*
EXPLORATIONS: Supernova appears, causing much astronomical speculation.
SOCIETY: The 'paulette' tax in France for venality of office. James I attacks tobacco. A House of Commons bill is rejected when a jackdaw – a sign of bad fortune – flies through chamber.

1605
POLITICS: English Catholics form Gunpowder Plot. Death of Boris Godunov; succeeded first by Feodor II, who is assassinated, and then by the 'False Dmitri'.
RELIGION: Death of Clement VIII, succeeded by Alessandro de Medici as Pope Leo XI; he dies and is succeeded by Camillo Borghese as Paul V.
THE ARTS: Miguel de Cervantes, *Don Quixote.* Michael Drayton, *Poems.* Shakespeare, *King Lear.*
EXPLORATIONS: Francis Bacon, *On the Advancement of Learning.* French establish colony at Port Royal.
SOCIETY: First public library opens in Rome.

1606
POLITICS: 'False Dmitri' is assassinated by Vasili Shuisky who becomes tsar.

RELIGION: New oath of allegiance tor Catholics in England; Paul V commands them not to take it.
THE ARTS: Shakespeare, *Macbeth*. Jonson, *Volpone*.
EXPLORATIONS: Death of Aldrovandi.
SOCIETY: Scottish attempt to colonize Lewis with lowlanders.

1607
POLITICS: Flight of Irish earls; leads to plantation of English and Scots in Ulster.
RELIGION: Persecution of Protestants in Bavaria.
THE ARTS: Monteverdi, 'Orfeo'. Honoré d'Urfé, *Astrée*.
EXPLORATIONS: English establish Jamestown colony in Virginia.
SOCIETY: Anti-enclosure riots in English Midlands.

1608
POLITICS: Second 'False Dmitri' rebels. Protestant Union formed in the Rhineland. Jesuits establish own state in Paraguay.
RELIGION: St Francis de Sales, *Introduction to the Devout Life*. William Perkins, Puritan divine, writes *Discourse of the Damned Art of Witchcraft*.
THE ARTS: Frescobaldi organist at St Peter's. Birth of English poet John Milton.
EXPLORATIONS: Dutch spectacle-maker Hans Lippershey invents telescope. Samuel de Champlain establishes French colony at Quebec.
SOCIETY: Post horses rent in England for three pence a mile.

1609
POLITICS: Twelve-year truce between Spain and Netherlands.
RELIGION: Freedom of religion in Bohemia.
THE ARTS: Heinrich Schütz in Venice.
EXPLORATIONS: Kepler, *Astronomia nova*. Henry Hudson explores Hudson River.
SOCIETY: Tea introduced to Europe. Animal fights in Tower of London end when bear kills child.

1610
POLITICS: Assassination of Henry IV, succeeded by Louis XIII, with Marie de Medici as regent.
RELIGION: Death of English Jesuit controversialist, Robert Persons. Death of Bancroft.
THE ARTS: Death of Caravaggio.
EXPLORATIONS: Galileo, *Starry Messenger*.
SOCIETY: Italy the most popular travel destination for European nobility.

BIBLIOGRAPHY

This bibliography is necessarily selective. We have tried to give titles for all the topics discussed in this volume and, wherever possible, in English. But not all the best foreign works have been translated, nor have all topics been adequately covered in English. We have therefore also included important books and occasional articles in French, German, Italian and Spanish, in this order of frequency.

INTRODUCTION

For the medieval antecedents of the sixteenth century: H. G. Koenigsberger, *Medieval Europe 400–1500* (London, 1987). For the place of the century in general history: H. G. Koenigsberger, *Early Modern History 1500–1789*, (London, 1987). For the concept of universal hierarchy see the classic by A. O. Lovejoy, *The Great Chain of Being: A Study in the History of an Idea* (1936. Harper Torch Books, New York, 1960). The importance of the idea of harmony is discussed in Dorothy Koenigsberger, *Renaissance Man and Creative Thinking: A History of Concepts of Harmony 1400–1700* (Hassocks, 1979). The 'Discovery of the World and of Man' is the title of the famous Part IV of Jacob Burckhardt's *The Civilization of the Renaissance in Italy* (First published in German in 1860. Many new editions and translations). A modern study of such attitudes in Keith Thomas, *Man and the Natural World: Changing Attitudes in England 1500–1800* (Penguin Books, Harmondsworth,

1983). See also D. J. Boorstin, *The Discoverers: A History of Man's Search to know the World and Himself* (New York, 1983. Penguin Books, Harmondsworth, 1986). E. Panofsky, *Renaissance and Renascences in Western Art* (Stockholm, 1960) investigates aspects of the differences between the Renaissance and earlier renaissances. On Montaigne it is best and most pleasurable to read his *Essays* (five editions in his lifetime, 1580–88. First English translation by John Florio, 1603. Many modern editions and translations). See also M. A. Screech, *Montaigne and Melancholy: the wisdom of the Essays* (London, 1983), and R. H. Popkin, *The History of Scepticism from Erasmus to Spinoza*, (rev. edn, Berkeley, 1979).

ECONOMIC LIFE

The literature on this subject has greatly expanded in the last twenty-five years and much of it is to be found in the articles of specialized journals: *The Economic History Review, Past and Present, The Journal of Economic History, Annales: Economies, Sociétés, Civilisations,* the *Vierteljahrschrift für Sozial- und Wirtschaftsgeschichte,* etc. The most useful single volumes for the century are H. A. Miskimin, *The Economy of Later Renaissance Europe 1460–1600* (Cambridge, 1977) and R. Davis, *The Rise of the Atlantic Economies* (Ithaca, 1973). H. Kellenbenz, *The Rise of the European Economy: an economic history of Continental Europe from the fifteenth to the eighteenth century* (London, 1976) is useful for a longer view. On a much larger scale are the magisterial volumes by F. Braudel, *The Mediterranean and the Mediterranean World in the Age of Philip II* (covering in fact a rather longer period), 2 vols., trans. S. Reynolds (London, 1972), and *Civilization and Capitalism,* 3 vols., trans. S. Reynolds (London, 1981–84). There are chapters of varying quality on different topics in C. M. Cipolla, ed., *The Fontana Economic History of Europe, Vol. II; The Sixteenth and Seventeenth Centuries* (London, 1974) and in *The Cambridge Economic History,* IV, Particularly useful for the history of money and prices is the chapter by F. Braudel and F. C. Spooner, 'Prices in Europe from 1450 to 1750'. For the English side of this topic see R. B. Outhwaite, *Inflation in Tudor and early Stuart England,* 2nd edn (London, 1977). The rise and decline of monetarist economic theories in the

1980s has had little influence on the historiographical debates about the price revolution of the sixteenth century. The connections between agrarian history and the development of capitalism are controversially explored in I. Wallerstein, *The Modern World-System: capitalist agriculture and the origins of the European world-economy in the Sixteenth Century* (New York and London, 1974). For a contrary view see for instance, P. O'Brien, 'European economic development: the contribution of the periphery,' *Economic History Review*, Second Ser. XXXV, 1, 1982. Opposing views are also presented in T. H. Aston and C. H. E. Pilpin, eds., *The Brenner Debate: agrarian class structure and economic development in pre-industrial Europe* (Cambridge 1986). This book, however, covers a much longer period. For the economic history of a single country, D. C. Coleman, *The Economy of England 1450–1750* (Oxford, 1977) is a good example. For English agrarian history the standard work is J. Thirsk, ed., *The Agrarian History of England and Wales*, vol. 4, *1500–1640* (Cambridge 1967). For France the outstanding of many excellent regional studies is E. Leroy Ladurie, *The Peasants of Languedoc*, trans. J. Day (Urbana, 1974) and, more generally, his *French Peasantry 1450–1660*, trans. A. Sheridan (Aldershot, 1987).

A model of the judicious use of theory in economic history is J. de Vries, *The Dutch Rural Economy in the Golden Age, 1500–1700* (Newhaven, 1974). For the nobility, L. Stone, *The Crisis of the Aristocracy 1558–1641* (Oxford 1965) goes far beyond any comparable work on the nobility of any continental country. The best concise account of the rise of the Junkers in East–Central Europe is still Part II of F. L. Carsten, *The Origins of Prussia* (Oxford, 1954) and, at greater length, Carsten, *The Junkers* (Aldershot, 1989). For international trade and finance there is a useful short introduction by J. N. Ball, *Merchants and Merchandise* (London, 1977). Apart from the relevant chapters in Braudel's volumes we have P. Chaunu's exhaustive study, *Seville et l'Atlantique (1504–1650)*, 8 vols. in 11 parts (Paris 1959). For Antwerp R. Ehrenberg, *Das Zeitalter der Fugger*, 2 vols. (Jena, 1896) with a much abbreviated translation by H. M. Lucas, *Capital and Finance in the Age of the Renaissance* (London, 1928) is still useful but should be supplemented by H. van der Wee, *The Growth of the Antwerp Market and the European Economy*, 3 vols. (The Hague, 1963). C. D. Ramsay, *English Overseas Trade during the Centuries of Emergence* (London, 1957) is a valuable general survey. The same author's *The City of London in International Politics at the Accession of Elizabeth Tudor* (Manchester, 1975) and *The Queen's Merchants and the Revolt of the Netherlands* (Manchester, 1986) are especially illuminating on the interaction of trade and politics. Of the many monographs on English trade, T. S. Willan, *The Early History of the Russia Company* (Manchester, 1956) is a good example. A. E. Christensen, *Dutch Trade in the Baltic about 1600* (Copenhagen, 1941) is basic for the history of international trade in the Baltic. Of the many excellent French monographs, H. Lapeyre, *Simon Ruiz et les asientos de Philippe II* (Paris, 1953) may serve as an example. The economic life of an Italian village under the typical sharecropping system (*métayage, mezzadria*) of Mediterranean agriculture is studied in F. McArdle, *Altopascio* (Cambridge, 1974).

SOCIAL HISTORY

M. W. Flinn, *The European Demographic System 1500–1820* (Brighton, 1981) is an excellent introduction to the new demographic history. See also E. A. Wrigley and R. S. Schofield, *The Population History of England, 1541–1871* (Cambridge, 1981) and T. H. Hollingsworth, *Historical Demography* (Ithaca, 1969). The new demography is applied to English social history in Peter Laslett, *The World We Have Lost*, 3rd edn (Cambridge, 1983). The history of the family is still highly controversial. P. Ariès, *Centuries of Childhood* (Harmondsworth, 1973) is readable but impressionistic. Steven Ozment's *When Fathers Ruled* (Cambridge, Mass. 1983) examines the Reformation's impact on the family while François Lebrun, *La Vie Conjugale sous l'Ancien Régime* (Paris 1975) and R. Pillorget, *La tige et le rameau: familles anglaises et françaises 16e–18e siècle* (Paris, 1979) look at the French family. Michael Mitterauer and Reinhard Sieder's *The European Family: Patriarchy to Partnership from the Middle Ages to the Present* (Chicago 1982) concentrates on Central Europe. Lawrence Stone, *The Family, Sex and Marriage in England, 1500–1800* (London, 1977) and Ralph Houlbrooke, *The English Family 1450–1700* (London, 1984) have much to say about England. An excellent summary of recent research is contained in Joyce Youings' volume in the Pelican Social History of Britain series, *Sixteenth Century England*

(Harmondsworth, 1984). Women's history is a rapidly growing field. Five of the best recent works are Natalie Zemon Davis, 'Women on top', in *Society and Culture in Early Modern France* (Stanford, 1975); Mary Beth Rose, *Women in the Middle Ages and the Renaissance: literary and historical perspectives* (Syracuse, 1986); Ian Maclean, *The Renaissance Notion of Women* (Cambridge, 1980); Christiane Klapisch-Zuber, *Women, Family and Ritual in Renaissance Italy* (Chicago, 1985) and Merry E. Wiesner, *Working Women in Renaissance Germany* (New Brunswick, NJ, 1986). Education in England is the topic of Rosemary O'Day, *Education and Society, 1500–1800,* (London, 1982); James McConica, *The History of the University of Oxford*, vol. 3 (Oxford, 1985) covers the life of the sixteenth-century university. The problems of determining literacy are taken up by François Furet and Jacques Ozouf, *Reading and writing: literacy in France from Calvin to Jules Ferry* (Cambridge, 1982) and David Cressy, *Literacy and the Social Order: Reading and Writing in Tudor and Stuart England* (Cambridge, 1980). A valuable look at the practice of humanist education can be found in Anthony Grafton and Lisa Jardine, *From Humanism to the Humanists: Education and the Liberal Arts in Fifteenth and Sixteenth-Century Europe* (Cambridge, MA, 1986).

For disease, hospitals and charity there is no single work for all of Europe, but there are very good studies of different countries and cities: e.g. W. K. Jordan, *Philanthropy in England, 1480–1660,* (London, 1959), B. Pullan, *Rich and Poor in Renaissance Venice,* (Oxford, 1971), L. Martz, *Poverty and Welfare in Habsburg Spain,* (Cambridge, 1983), R. Jütte, *Obrigkeitliche Armenfursorge in deutschen Reichsstädten der frühen Neuzeit* (Cologne, 1984) and R. Porter, *Disease, Medicine and Society in England 1550–1860* (London, 1987). Attitudes to death are discussed by P. Ariès, *The Hour of Our Death*, trans. H. Weaver (Harmondsworth, 1981) and, more philosophically, N. Elias, *The Loneliness of Dying* (Oxford, 1985).

Witchcraft historiography has undergone great changes in the last twenty years. A good introduction is G. Scarre, *Witchcraft and Magic in the Sixteenth and Seventeenth Century* (Basingstoke, 1987). The British experience is covered by Keith Thomas, *Religion and the Decline of Magic* (London, 1971), Alan Macfarlane, *Witchcraft in Tudor and Stuart England* (London, 1970) and Christina Larner, *Enemies of God: the witch-hunt in Scotland* (Baltimore, 1981). Larner makes provocative observations on the whole phenomenon in

Witchcraft and Religion: the politics of popular belief (New York, 1984). For the Continent: H. C. Erik Midelfort, *Witch Hunting in Southwestern Germany 1562–1684* (Stanford, 1972); Robert Muchembled, Willem Frijhoff and Marie-Sylvie Dupont-Bouchat, *Prophètes et Sorciers dans le Pays-Bas, XVI–XVIII siècle* (Paris, 1978); Norman Cohn, *Europe's Inner Demons* (New York, 1975); Carlo Ginzburg, *The Night Battles: witchcraft and agrarian cults in the sixteenth and seventeenth century* (London, 1983); A. Charpentier, *La sorcellerie en pays basque* (Paris, 1977); J. Fauret-Saadra, *Deadly Words: witchcraft in the Bocage* (Cambridge, 1980).

The impact of war on society has recently been brilliantly summarized by J. R. Hale, *War and Society in Renaissance Europe 1450–1620* (Leicester, 1985). On recruitment and military organization: F. Redlich, *The German Military Enterpriser and His Work Force*, 2 vols., *Vierteljahrschrift für Sozial- und Wirtschaftsgeschichte*, Beiheft 47 and 48 (Wiesbaden, 1964–65); I. A. A. Thompson, *War and Government in Habsburg Spain 1520–1620* (London, 1976); and J. R. Hale's part of M. E. Mallett and J. R. Hale, *The Military Organization of a Renaissance State: Venice c. 1400–1617* (Cambridge, 1984).

On court society, N. Elias, *The Court Society*, tr. E. Jephcott, (New York, 1984), an older book only recently translated, opened up this subject. More recent studies may be found in A. G. Dickens, *The Courts of Europe* (London, 1977), and J. H. Elliott, 'The Court of the Spanish Habsburgs: a peculiar institution?', in P. Mack and M. C. Jacob, *Politics and Culture in Early Modern Europe* (London, 1987). On court festivals, J. G. Russell, *The Field of the Cloth of Gold* (London, 1969) is exhaustive on details. More perceptive are Roy Strong, *Splendour at Court: Renaissance spectacle and illusion* (London, 1973) and especially F. A. Yates, *The Valois Tapestries* (London, 1959), a classic of its kind. The results of an especially interesting international conference are published in R. G. Asch *et al.*, eds., *Politics, Patronage and the Nobility: the court at the beginning of the modern age* (Oxford, 1989).

For the other end of the social scale see M. Mullett, *Popular Culture and Popular Protest in Late Medieval and Early Modern Europe* (London, 1987). Peter Burke, *Popular Culture in Early Modern Europe*, (New York, 1975) and *The Historical Anthropology of Early Modern Italy* (Cambridge, 1987) are stimulating looks at popular culture. David Warren Sabean, *Power in the Blood: popular culture and village discourse in early modern Germany* (Cambridge, 1984) presents an important re-assessment of the functioning of peasant society.

TOWNS

Unlike the medieval town, on the one hand, and the modern industrial town, on the other, the Renaissance and Baroque town has rarely been studied as a historical phenomenon. From an economic and demographic point of view there is now J. de Vries, *European Urbanization 1500–1800* (London, 1984). For the Holy Roman Empire H. Mauersberg, *Wirtschafts- und Sozialgeschichte zentraleuropäischer Städte in neuerer Zeit* (Göttingen 1960) is still useful, as is the classic article by O. Brunner, 'Soveränitätsproblem und Sozialstruktur in den deutschen Reichsstädten der früheren Neuzeit', in *Vierteljahrschrift für Sozial- und Wirtschaftsgeschichte*, vol. L, 1963). For South Germany, T. A. Brady Jr., *Turning Swiss: cities and empire, 1450–1550* (Cambridge, 1985) is a model of an up-to-date approach to urban history. Many of the recent studies of German cities centre on the introduction of the Reformation, but also contain much information on the structure and history of the cities. Good examples are B. Moeller, *Imperial Cities and the Reformation*, transl. H. C. E. Midelfort and M. U. Edwards, Jr. (Philadelphia, 1975) and A. G. Dickens, *The German Nation and Martin Luther* (New York 1974). For single German cities a good example is G. Strauss, *Nuremberg in the Sixteenth Century* (New York and London, 1966) published in a useful series *Historical Cities*, ed. N. F. Cantor, which also includes E. W. Monter, *Calvin's Geneva* (New York, 1967). An excellent study of Lübeck in this period is A. von Brandt, *Geist und Politik in der lübeckischen Geschichte* (Lübeck, 1954). See also P. Dollinger, *The German Hansa*, trans. D. S. Ault and S. H. Steinberg (London, 1970).

For England, W. G. Hoskins, *Provincial England* (London 1963) should be supplemented by P. Clark and P. Slack, eds., *English Towns in transition 1500–1700* (Oxford, 1976). For the rest, we have studies of some individual English cities of varying quality. There is no modern history of London in the sixteenth century; but A. L. Beier and R. Finley, eds., *London 1500–1700: the making of the metropolis*, (London, 1986) contains interesting articles.

For the major Italian cities J. Delumeau, *Vie économique et sociale de Rome dans la seconde moitié du XVIe siècle*, 2 vols. (Paris, 1957–59) is a model of its kind. Histories of Venice tend to cover a longer period or even the republic's whole history, such as the recent A. Zorzi, *Venice 697–1797, City and Republic* (1983). F. C. Lane, *Venice, a maritime Republic* (Baltimore, 1973) and W. H. McNeill, *Venice, the Hinge of Europe* set Venetian history in a wider historical perspective. J. J. Norwich, *A History of Venice*, (London, 1982) provides a readable political history. A Tenenti, *Piracy and the Decline of Venice*, trans. J. and B. Pullan (London, 1967) and J. C. Davis, *The Decline of the Venetian Nobility as a Ruling Class* (Baltimore 1962), deal with important aspects of the decline of Venice. D. S. Chambers, *The Imperial Age of Venice 1380–1580* (London, 1970) and O. Logan, *Culture and Society in Venice 1470–1790* (London, 1972) provide useful summaries of Venetian cultural history. The position of Venetian Jews can be seen in B. Ravid, 'The Venetian Ghetto in historical perspective', in *The Autobiography of a Seventeeth Century Rabbi: Leon Modena's Life of Judah* ed. M. R. Cohen (Princeton, 1988).

For Florence we have a wealth of excellent studies of the fifteenth and early sixteenth centuries but little for the period after 1530. G. Brucker, *Renaissance Florence* (Berkeley, 1969, bibliog. suppl. 1983) is a good introduction to the structure and politics of the Florentine republic. J. R. Hale, *Machiavelli and Renaissance Italy* (London, 1961) is excellent on the political and intellectual background of Machiavelli's career. M. Bullard, *Filippo Strozzi and the Medici* (Cambridge, 1980), illuminates Florentine family politics and the republic's financial exploitation by the Medici popes, Leo X and Clement VII. H. C. Butters, *Governors and Government in Early Sixteenth-Century Florence, 1502–1519* (Oxford, 1985) sums up much recent work. S. Berner, 'Florentine society in the late sixteenth and early seventeenth centuries', *Studies in the Renaissance* XVIII, 1971, is a useful article in a largely neglected field.

Ch. Petit-Dutaillis, *Les communes françaises* (Paris, 1947) is still worth consulting. R. Mousnier, Paris, *Fonction d'une capitale, Colloques Cahiers de Civilisation* (Paris, n.d.) is a brilliant short analysis of the functional role of Paris as a capital in French history. For a fine modern study of a provincial town see P. Benedict, *Rouen during the Wars of Religion*, (Cambridge 1981). See also G. Duby, ed., *Histoire de la France urbaine*, vol. 3, *La ville classique*, ed. E. Le Roy Ladurie (Paris 1981).

For Spain, J. Pérez, *La révolution des 'Comunidades' de Castille* (*1520–1521*) (Bordeaux, 1970) should be used in conjunction with S. Haliczer, *The Comuneros of Castile: The Forging of a Revolution 1475–1521* (Madison, 1981). For a city in the later sixteenth century see B. Bennassar, *Valladolid au siècle d'or: une ville de Castille et sa campagne au XVIe siècle* (Paris, The Hague, 1967). The political structure and history of Antwerp (as against that city's economic history, for which see the bibliography for chapter 3) is brilliantly treated in a forthcoming book by G. E. Wells, *Antwerp and the Government of Philip II, 1555–67*.

Italian republicanism has an extensive literature, from Machiavelli, *The Discourses*, trans. L. J. Walker (Penguin Classics, Harmondsworth, 1970) to excellent modern studies, such as W. J. Bouwsma, *Venice and the Defence of Republican Liberty* (Berkeley, 1968) and Q. Skinner, *The Foundations of Modern Political Thought*, vol. I: *The Renaissance*, (Cambridge, 1978). For the rest of Europe see the short sketch by Y. Durand, *Les républiques au temps des monarchies* (Paris, 1973), J. A. Maravall, *Las Comunidades de Castilla* (Madrid, 1963), and H. G. Koenigsberger and E. Müller-Luckner, eds., *Republiken und Republikanismus im Europa der frühen Neuzeit* (Munich, 1988), with contributions in English, German and French.

The architecture and town planning of this period is treated systematically in P. Lavedan, *Histoire de l'urbanisme. Renaissance et temps modernes*, (Paris, 1941). Cf. also Lavedan, *Les villes françaises* (Paris, 1960). G. Braun and F. Hogenberg, *Civitates Orbis Terrarum* (Cologne 1572–1618), a kind of sixteenth–seventeenth century super-guidebook with magnificent engravings of townscapes has been republished in facsimile (Cologne, 1965).

THE REFORMATION

Richard L. De Molen, *Essays on the Works of Erasmus* (New Haven, 1976), James D. Tracy, *The Politics of Erasmus: a pacifist intellectual and his political milieu* (Toronto, 1978) and Roland Bainton, *Erasmus of Christendom* (New York, 1969) deal with the prince of humanists. Steven Ozment, *The Age of Reform, 1250–1550* (New Haven, 1980), Gerald Strauss, *Manifestations of Discontent in Germany on the Eve of the Reformation* (Bloomington,

1971). A. E. McGrath, *Origins of the European Reformation* (Oxford, 1987) and H. G. Koenigsberger, 'The unity of the Church and the Reformation', in *Politicians and Virtuosi* (London, 1986) are valuable for the background to the Reformation. Carlos M. N. Eire, *War Against the Idols: the reformation of worship from Erasmus to Calvin* (Cambridge, 1986) makes the question of 'idolatry' central to the course of the Reformation. Roland Bainton, *Here I Stand: a life of Martin Luther* (Nashville, 1950) is the standard popular biography of the reformer while A. G. Dickens places Luther's work in its context in *The German Nation and Martin Luther* (London, 1974). Steven Ozment, *The Reformation in the Cities* (New Haven, 1975) and Kaspar von Greyerz, *The Late City Reformation in Germany: the case of Colmar 1522–1628* (Wiesbaden, 1980) chart the progress of the urban Reformation in Germany. Two recent biographies of note are Mark U. Edwards, *Luther's Last Battles: politics and polemics 1531–46* (Ithaca, 1983) and Eric W. Gritsch, *Martin – God's Court Jester: Luther in retrospect* (Philadelphia, 1983). Gerald Strauss's *Luther's House of Learning: indoctrination of the young in the German Reformation* (London, 1978) examines the reception of Lutheran thought. A. E. McGrath, *Reformation Thought: An Introduction* (Oxford, 1988) is valuable. George Williams, *The Radical Reformation* (Philadelphia, 1962) comprehensively covers Anabaptism and related movements. A good introduction to leading figures can be found in H.-J. Goertz, *Profiles of Radical Reformers: biographical sketches from Thomas Müntzer to Paracelsus* (Scottdale, 1982). An important work pointing out the small scale of the radical reformation is Claus-Peter Clasen's *Anabaptism: a social history, 1525–1618* (Ithaca, 1972). Steven Ozment, *Mysticism and Dissent: religious ideology and social protest in the sixteenth century* (New Haven, 1983) deals with a number of Anabaptist thinkers. Eric W. Gritsch, *Reformer Without a Church* (Philadelphia, 1967) is still the best biography in English of Thomas Münzer, while Frank E. Manuel and Fritzie P. Manuel concentrate on his millenarianism in *Utopian Thought in the Western World* (Cambridge, Mass., 1979). Irwin Horst, *The Radical Brethren: Anabaptism and the English Reformation to 1558* (Nieuwkoop, 1972) deals with English Anabaptism and James Stayer's *Anabaptists and the Sword* (Lawrence, 1972) discusses Anabaptist political thought. Good introductions to the historiography of the Peasants' War are R. W. Scribner, *The German Peasants' War 1525: new viewpoints* (London, 1979) and

Tom Scott, 'The Peasants' War: a historiographical review', *Historical Journal* 1979, pp. 693–720 and 953–74. Peter Blickle, *The Revolution of 1525*, trans. T. A. Brady and H. C. E. Midelfort (Baltimore, 1981) is an excellent account of the struggle.

Zwingli (Cambridge, 1976) by G. R. Potter is the best biography of the Swiss theologian; Robert C. Walton, *Zwingli's Theocracy* (Toronto, 1967) and Gottfried W. Locher, *Zwingli's Thought: new perspectives* (Leiden, 1981) are also useful. Philip Edgcumbe Hughes in his *Lefèvre: Pioneer of Ecclesiastical Renewal in France* (Grand Rapids, 1984) argues for the importance of Lefèvre d'Etaples in the history of the French Reformation. A neglected reformer is given his due in J. W. Baker, *Heinrich Bullinger and the Covenant* (Athens, Ohio, 1980). T. H. Parker, *John Calvin: a biography* (Philadelphia, 1975) is the standard biography while Eric Fuchs, *La Morale selon Calvin* (Paris, 1986), Harro Hopfl, *The Christian Polity of John Calvin* (Cambridge, 1982) and Andre Bieler, *La Pensée économique et sociale de Calvin* (Geneva, 1959) deal with aspects of Calvin's thought. Roland Bainton's *Hunted Heretic: the life and death of Michael Servetus* (Boston, 1960) and Jerome Friedman, *Michael Servetus: a case study in total heresy* examine Calvin's most famous opponent. Calvin's successor is the subject of T. Maruyama, *The Ecclesiology of Theodore Beza: the reform of the true church* (Geneva, 1978).

John Bossy, 'The Counter-Reformation and the people of Catholic Europe', *Past and Present* 1970, pp. 51–70, Jean Delumeau *Catholicism between Luther and Voltaire* (Paris, 1971, English trans., London, 1977) and A. D. Wright's *The Counter-Reformation: Catholic Europe and the non-Christian world* (New York, 1982) are provocative discussions of the importance of the Catholic Reformation. A. G. Dickens, *The Counter-Reformation* (New York, 1969) and Marvin R. O'Connell, *The Counter Reformation, 1554–1610* (New York, 1974) are less controversial renderings. Hubert Jedin, *A History of the Council of Trent* (St Louis, 1957) is the best account in English of the Catholic Reformation's central act. J. C. Olin, ed., *The Autobiography of St Ignatius Loyola* (New York, 1974) is good for the founder of the Society of Jesus. Robert Muchembled, *Popular Culture and Elite Culture in France, 1400–1750*, trans. Lydia Cochrane (Baton Rouge, 1985) discusses popular religion. R. P. Hsia's *Society and Religion in Muenster, 1535–1618* (New Haven, 1984), William A. Christian *Local Religion in Sixteenth-Century Spain* (Princeton, 1981), A. N. Galpern,

The Religions of the People in Sixteenth Century Champagne (Cambridge, Mass., 1976) and Philip Hoffman's *Church and Community in the Diocese of Lyon, 1500–1789* (New Haven, 1984) are excellent local studies. David Loades, *The Reign of Mary Tudor* (London, 1979) shows how her Catholic restoration was attempted; Mary's archbishop of Canterbury is the subject of Dermot Fenlon's *Heresy and Obedience in Tridentine Italy: Cardinal Pole and the Counter Reformation* (Cambridge, 1972). John Bossy, *The English Catholic Community, 1570–1850* (New York, 1976) puts his subject in the context of English non-conformism. A good idea of the large amount of work done in recent years on the Inquisition and its social, as well as religious, functions can be gained from S. Haliczer, ed., *Inquisition and Society in Early Modern Europe* (London, 1986), and from G. Hennigsen and J. Tedeschi, eds., *The Inquisition in Early Modern Europe: studies on sources and methods* (Dekalb, Ill. 1986).

EMPIRES

G. R. Elton, *Reformation Europe 1517–1559* (Fontana History of Europe, London, 1963) is an excellent introduction to the political history of western Europe in the first half of the sixteenth century. M. Fernández Alvarez, *Charles V: Elected emperor and hereditary ruler,* (London, 1975) is a short scholarly biography, concentrating on the political side. It does not supersede the old standard biography by K. Brandi, *The Emperor Charles V,* trans. C. V. Wedgwood (London, 1939). These biographies should be supplemented by P. Rassow, *Die Kaiser-Idee Karls V* (Berlin, 1932) and by the somewhat controversial contributions to two quatercentenary publications, *Charles Quint et son temps,* (Centre nationale de la recherche scientifique, Paris, 1959) and P. Rassow and F. Schalk, eds., *Karl V: Der Kaiser und seine Zeit* (Cologne, 1960. Contributions in different languages). Cf. also H. G. Koenigsberger, 'The Empire of Charles V in Europe,' *New Cambridge Modern History,* vol II, 2nd edn. For Gattinara see J. M. Headley *The Emperor and his Chancellor* (Cambridge, 1983). For the end of the reign see J. M. Rodríguez-Salgado, *The Changing Face of Empire: Charles V, Philip II and Habsburg Authority, 1551–1559* (Cambridge, 1988). H. Lutz, ed., *Das römisch-deutsche*

Reich im politischen System Karls V (Munich, 1982) has the most up-to-date discussions of Charles V and the Holy Roman Empire. A verbal discussion is by H. G. Koenigsberger and G. Parker, *Charles V* (Sussex Tapes HE 26, 1983).

On the Ottoman Empire, P. Wittek, *The Rise of the Ottoman Empire* Royal Asiatic Society Monographs XXIII (London, 1938) is still basic. P. Coles, *The Ottoman Impact on Europe* (London, 1968) is a useful introduction to the subject. Specifically on the Holy Roman Empire this impact is studied in W. Schulze, *Reich und Türkengefahr im späten sechzehnten Jahrhundert* (Munich, 1978). R. B. Merriman, *Suleiman the Magnificent* (Cambridge, Mass, 1944) is factual but superficial. Cf. also H. Inalcik, 'Ottoman methods of conquest', *Studia Islamica*, II (Paris 1954) and B. Lewis, 'The decline of the Ottoman Empire', *ibid.*, IX (1958). F. Braudel, *The Mediterranean* (*cit.* ch. III) has some suggestive passages on the Ottoman Empire. C. H. Fleischer, *Bureaucrat and Intellectual in the Ottoman Empire: The historian Mustafa Âli (1541–1600)* (Guildford, 1987) is one of the very few accessible modern monographs on a non-military figure of the period.

On Russia, H. Willetts, 'Poland and the evolution of Russia', in H. Trevor-Roper, ed., *The Golden Age of Europe* (London, 1968 and 1987) is a good short introduction, as is J. L. I. Fennell, 'Russia, 1462–1583', *New Cambridge Modern history*, vol. II. See also I. Grey, *Ivan the Terrible* (London, 1964) and J. H. Billington, *The Icon and the Axe* (London, 1966). The problem of Russian imperialism is discussed in M. Cherniavsky, *Tsar and People: studies in Russian myths* (New Haven and London 1961), in W. K. Medlin, *Moscow and East Rome* (Geneva, 1952), and in H. Schaeder, *Moskau das dritte Rom*, 2nd edn. (Darmstadt, 1957). The most recent textbook is R. O. Crummey, *The Formation of Muscovy 1304–1643* (London, 1987).

A good introduction to the Portuguese overseas empire is C. R. Boxer, *Four Centuries of Portuguese Expansion, 1425–1825* (Johannesburg, 1961) and *Race Relations in the Portuguese Colonial Empire* (Oxford, 1963). Very useful for both the Portuguese and the Spanish overseas empires is R. Konetzke, *Süd- und Mittelamerika*, I, Fischer Weltgeschichte, vol. XXII (Frankfurt, 1965). For the latter empire there are the authoritative studies by J. H. Parry, *The Spanish Theory of Empire in the Sixteenth Century* (Cambridge, 1940), *The Age of Reconnaissance* (London and Cleveland, 1963) and *The Spanish Seaborne Empire* (London, 1965), and L. Hanke, *The Spanish Struggle for Justice in the Conquest of America* (Philadelphia, 1949) and *Bartolomé de las Casas* (The Hague, 1951). The theories of Vitoria and other Spanish theologians are analysed by Bernice Hamilton, *Political Thought in Sixteenth-Century Spain* (Oxford, 1963), and by J. A. Fernández-Santamaria, *The State, War and Peace: Spanish Political Thought in the Renaissance 1516–1559* (Cambridge, 1977).

For the general concept of empire in the sixteenth century see the subtle analysis by F. Yates, *Astraea: the imperial theme in the sixteenth century* (Penguin Books, Harmondsworth, 1977).

The historical role of the 'New Monarchies' is discussed, with extensive bibliographical references, by F. Hartung and R. Mousnier, 'Quelques Problèmes concernant la Monarchie absolue', in *X International Congress of Historical Science*, Rome, 1955, *Relazioni*, IV. This discussion is continued by J. Vicens Vives, 'Estructura administrativa estatal en los siglos XVI y XVII', in *XI International Congress of Historical Sciences*, Stockholm, 1960, *Rapports*, IV. Excellent comparative studies are the relevant chapters in the *New Cambridge Modern History*, vol. II, 2nd edn. and vol. III. Both V. G. Kiernan, *State and Society in Europe 1550–1650* (Oxford, 1980), and for a longer period P. Anderson, *Lineages of the Absolutist State* (London, 1974), are Neo-Marxist interpretations. For a different view of the early modern period see H. G. Koenigsberger, *Early Modern Europe*, (*cit*. ch. I).

For the separate countries the following are especially useful.

ENGLAND

Useful for overviews of political and administrative history are G. R. Elton, *England Under the Tudors* (Cambridge, 1955) and Penry Williams, *The Tudor Regime* (Oxford, 1980). Differing views of Parliament are expressed in J. E. Neale, *Elizabeth I and her Parliaments*, 2 vols. (London, 1953–57) and G. R. Elton, *Parliament in England, 1559–81* (Cambridge, 1986). Parliamentary debates themselves are available in *Proceedings in the Parliaments of Elizabeth I, 1558–81* (Leicester, 1981), ed. T. E. Hartley. The history of Henrician England is undergoing some revision. For new approaches to Henry's reign see: David Starkey, *The Reign of Henry VIII* (London, 1985), David Starkey and Christopher Coleman, eds., *Revolution Reassessed: revisions in the history of Tudor government and administration* (Oxford, 1986), Maria Dowling, *Humanism in the Age of Henry VIII* (London, 1986), E. W. Ives, *Anne Boleyn* (New York, 1986) and Alistair Fox and John Guy, *Reassessing the Henrician Age* (Oxford, 1986). The English Reformation is best approached through A. G. Dickens, *The English Reformation* (London, 1964), Norman Jones, *Faith By Statute: parliament and the settlement of religion* (London, 1982), Claire Cross, *Church and People, 1450–1660: the triumph of the laity in the English Church* (Hassocks, 1976), Rosemary O'Day, *The English Clergy* (Leicester, 1979) and Patrick Collinson, *The Elizabethan Puritan Movement* (London, 1967) and *The Religion of Protestants* (London, 1982). Peter Lake and Maria Dowling, eds., *Protestantism and the National Church in Sixteenth Century England* (London, 1987) offers a number of important revisionist essays. Peter Lake, *Moderate Puritans and the Elizabeth Church* (Cambridge, 1982) looks at the careers and ideology of Puritan clerics. William Hunt, *The Puritan Moment* (Cambridge, Mass., 1983), Margaret Bowker, *The Henrician Reformation: the diocese of Lincoln under John Langland* (Cambridge, 1981) and Christopher Haigh, *Reformation and Resistance in Tudor Lancashire* (Cambridge, 1975) are good local studies. For casuistry see G. M. Mosse, *The Holy Pretence* (Oxford, 1957)

FRANCE

R. Doucet, *Les institutions de la France au XVIe siècle*, 2 vols. (Paris, 1948) is encyclopaedic and still worth consulting. Very useful are J. R. Major, *Representative Institutions in Renaissance France* (Madison, 1960) and the same author's *Representative Government in Early Modern France* (New Haven and London 1980). The development of the modern concept of the state is discussed by H. A. Lloyd, *The State, France and the Sixteenth Century* (London, 1983), and an important institution of the French monarchy by S. Hanley, *The Lit de Justice of the Kings of France: constitutional ideology in legend, ritual and discourse* (Princeton, 1983). R. J. Knecht, *Francis I* (Cambridge, 1982) is a good biography.

SPAIN

J. H. Elliott, *Imperial Spain 1469–1716* (London, 1963) and J. Lynch, *Spain under the Habsburgs*, vol. 1, 2nd edn. (Oxford, 1981) supersede all earlier textbooks. I. A. A. Thompson, *War and Government in Habsburg Spain 1560–1620* (London, 1976) and A. W. Lovett, Philip II *and Mateo Vázquez de Leca: the Government of Spain (1572–1592)* (Geneva, 1977) show the actual funtioning of the Spanish government. This is also shown for Spanish government of its Italian dominions in H. G. Koenigsberger, *The Practice of Empire: the government of Sicily under Philip II of Spain* (London and Ithaca, 1951, 1969) and by V. Sciuti Russi, *Astrea in Sicilia: II Ministero togato nella Società Siciliana dei Secoli XVI e XVII* (Naples, 1983). For Naples see A. Cernigliaro, *Sovranità e Feudo nel Regno di Napoli 1505–1557*, 2 vols (Naples, 1983).

GERMANY

F. L. Carsten, *The Origins of Prussia* (Oxford 1954) and *Princes and Parliaments in Germany* (Oxford, 1959) were almost the first real break with traditional conservative historiography in this field; but they have now been followed by a rich and varied historiography. See for instance G. Oestreich, *Neostoicism and the early modern state*, ed. H. G. Koenigsberger and B. Oestreich, trans. D. McLintock (Cambridge, 1982), or the collection of papers in P. Baumgart, ed., *Ständetum und Staatsbildung in Brandenburg-Preussen* (Berlin, 1983).

SWEDEN

I. Andersson, *A History of Sweden*, trans. C. Hannay (London, 1956) and especially M. Roberts, *The Early Vasas: A History of Sweden, 1523–1611* (Cambridge, 1968). Cf. also M. F. Metcalf, ed., *The Riksdag: A History of the Swedish Parliament* (Stockholm, 1987) and S. Lundkvist, 'The European powers and Sweden in the reign of Gustav Vasa', in E. I. Kouri and T. Scott, eds., *Politics and society in Reformation Europe* (London, 1987).

POLAND

There is now a good modern textbook in Norman Davies, *God's Playground; a history of Poland*, vol. I (Oxford, 1981).

There is no full study of nationalism in this period. H. Kohn, *The Idea of Nationalism* (New York, 1945) is a useful introduction. O. Ranum, ed., *National Consciousness, History and political Culture in Early Modern Europe* (Baltimore, Md., 1975) has chapters on six major European countries. R. Mousnier, *La vénalité des offices sous Henri IV et Louis XIII* (Rouen, 1946) is exhaustive about this characteristic sixteenth-century phenomenon in France. K. W. Swart, *Sale of Offices in the Seventeenth Century* (The Hague, 1949) has some useful pages on other countries. Patronage is treated in a composite volume by A. Mączak, ed., *Patronage and Clientage in Early Modern Europe* (Munich, 1988). Representative assemblies and other topics within the general topic of monarchies are treated in H. G. Koenigsberger, *Estates and Revolutions: essays in early Modern European history* (Ithaca, 1971) and *Politicians and Virtuosi: essays in early modern history* (London, 1986).

THE AGE OF PHILIP II

A general introduction is provided by H. G. Koenigsberger, 'Western Europe and the power of Spain', *New Cambridge Modern History* vol. III, reprinted in H. G. Koenigsberger, *The Habsburgs and Europe* 1516–1660 (Ithaca, 1971). An excellent longer introduction is J. H. Elliott, *Europe Divided 1559–1598* (Fontana History of Europe, London, 1968). Braudel, *The Mediterranean* (*cit*. Ch. 3) is indispensable on Spanish-Mediterranean history and has some interesting things to say on Spanish foreign policy in general. Very good recent biographies of Philip II are P. Pierson, *Philip II of Spain*, (London, 1975) and, on a more personal level, G. Parker, *Philip II*, (Boston, 1978). For the early years of the reign see J. M. Rodriguez-Salgado, *The Changing Face of Empire*. J. F. Guilmartin Jr., *Gunpowder and Galleys: changing technology and Mediterranean warfare at sea in the sixteenth century* (Cambridge, 1974) is an excellent, if at some points controversial, study. A. C. Hess, *The Forgotten Frontier: a history of the sixteenth-century Ibero-African Frontier*, (Chicago, 1978) is one of the rare studies in

English based also on Islamic sources and it offers a very different interpretation from Braudel's.

On the Netherlands, P. Geyl's classic account, *The Revolt of the Netherlands*, 2nd edn (London, 1958) is now dated in many respects, but still worth reading. A modern account is G. Parker, *The Dutch Revolt* (Penguin Books, London, 1977). Parker's *Spain and the Netherlands 1559–1659* (Fontana Books, Glasgow, 1979) investigates the Spanish side of the revolt; his *The Army of Flanders and the Spanish Road 1569–1659* (Cambridge, 1976) is indispensable for the military aspect. W. S. Maltby, *Alba* (Berkeley, 1983) is an adequate biography of one of the principal actors on the Spanish side. J. den Tex, *Oldenbarnevelt*, vol. I, trans. R. B. Powell (Cambridge, 1973) covers the first, and here relevant, half of the life of the Dutch statesman. One of the smaller Dutch cities is studied in C. C. Hibben, *Gouda in Revolt*. C. V. Wedgwood, *William the Silent* (London, 1944), while very readable, is now rather dated. An authoritative biography of William by K. W. Swart is forthcoming. For topics in both Spanish and Netherlands history in this period see also H. G. Koenigsberger, *Politicians and Virtuosi* (cit. Ch. 7).

FRANCE

There has been a great deal of first class work done in the last twenty-five years. J. H. M. Salmon, *Society in Crisis: France in the sixteenth century* (London, 1975) paints his picture on a wide canvas and even wider in his recent *Renaissance and Revolt: essays in intellectual and social history of early modern France* (Cambridge, 1987). The rulers of provincial France are studied in R. R. Harding, *Anatomy of a Power Elite: the provincial governors of early modern France* (New Haven, 1978). For a provincial city see P. Benedict, *Rouen during the Wars of Religion*. L. Romier, *Le royaume de Cathérine de Médicis*, 2 vols. (Paris, 1913–14) is still indispensable for the beginnings of the civil wars, together with R. M. Kingdon, *Geneva and the Coming of the Wars of Religion* (Geneva, 1954) and his *Geneva and the Consolidation of the French Protestant Movement* (Geneva, 1967). These works should be used in conjunction with D. R. Kelley, *The Beginning of Ideology: consciousness and society in the French Reformation* (Cambridge, 1981) and Henry Heller, *The Conquest of Poverty: the Calvinist revolt in sixteenth-century France* (Leiden, 1986). Religious passions, fears and hostilities, with special emphasis also on the role of women, are brilliantly analysed in essays which have already become classics: N. Z. Davis, *Society and Culture in Early Modern France* (Standford, 1975), the massacre of St Bartholomew (in the late twentieth century, unsurprisingly, still a live and controversial subject) is analysed in its wider historical context by N. M. Sutherland, *The Massacre of St Bartholomew and the European Conflict 1559–1572* (New York, 1973), in A. Soman, ed., *The Massacre of St Bartholomew: reappraisals and documents* (The Hague, 1974), and in R. M. Kingdon, *Myths about the St Bartholomew's Massacre 1572–1576,* (Cambridge, Mass., 1988). For the latter part of the civil war period see D. L. Jensen, *Diplomacy and Dogmatism* (Cambridge, Mass., 1964); E. Barnavi, *Le Parti de Dieu: Etude sociale et politique des chefs de la Lique parisienne 1585–1594* (Louvain, 1980); and for the Politique party M. P. Holt, *The Duke of Anjou and the Politique Struggle during the Wars of Religion* (Cambridge, 1986). There are very useful articles on Catherine de Medici, Coligny and other topics in N. M. Sutherland, *Princes, Politics and Religion 1547–1589* (London, 1984). A new form of history writing in the full-length reconstruction of specific incidents is exemplified in the highly readable N. Z. Davis, *The Return of Martin Guerre* (Penguin Books, Harmondsworth, 1983. It is also the basis of a visually very evocative French film of 1985) and E. Leroy Ladurie, *Carnival in Romans: a people's uprising at Romans 1579–1580,* trans. M. Feeney (Harmondsworth, 1981).

The recent literature on Henry IV's reign is not as extensive as that on the wars of religion. See R. Mousnier, *L'assassinat de Henri IV,* (Paris, 1964); D. J. Buisseret, *Sully and the Growth of Centralized Government in France 1598–1610* (London, 1968), and his *Henry IV,* (London, 1984); see also M. Greengrass, *France in the age of Henry IV* (London, 1984).

For nothern and central Europe the relevant chapters in *The New Cambridge Modern History,* vol. III should be supplemented by M. Roberts, *The Early Vasas*; R. J. W. Evans, *Rudolf II and his World* (Oxford, 1973); and A. Maçzak, 'The conclusive years: the end of the sixteenth century as the turning point of Polish history', in Kouri and Scott, *Politics and Society in Reformation Europe.* P. Clark, ed., *The European Crisis of the 1590's* (London, 1985) contains informative articles on different countries but fails to establish a specific crisis for that decade. P. Zagorin, *Rebels and Rulers 1500–1660*, 2 vols. (Cambridge, 1982) contains a useful compendium of revolts and revolutions in this period.

The 400th anniversary of the sailing of the Spanish Armada has led to the republication of Garrett Mattingly's classic *The Defeat of the Spanish Armada* (Harmondsworth, Penguin, 1988) and several beautifully illustrated new studies. See especially *Armada 1588–1988*, the catalogue of an exhibition at the National Maritime Museum, Greenwich, England, with a very scholarly introduction by M. J. Rodríguez-Salgado (London, Penguin, 1988); C. Martin and G. Parker, *The Spanish Armada* (London, 1988) which makes use of recent underwater archaeology; and Peter Kemp, *The Armada* (London, 1988), written by an expert on naval warfare.

POLITICAL THOUGHT

A good introduction to sixteenth–century political thought is Quentin Skinner, *Foundations of Modern Political Thought*, 2 vols. (Cambridge, 1978). A Pagden, ed., *The Languages of Political Theory in Early-Modern Europe* (Cambridge, 1987) contains a number of essays on one of the new ways of approaching this subject. R. Linder, *The Political Thought of Pierre Viret* (Geneva, 1964), W. D. J. Cargill-Thompson, *The Political Thought of Martin Luther*, James Stayer, *Anabaptists and the Sword* (Lawrence, 1972), and Lowell H. Zuck, *Christianity and Revolution* (Philadelphia, 1975) cover a wide variety of Protestant thinking. Donald R. Kelley's *The Beginning of Ideology* (Cambridge, 1981) and Frederic Baumgartner, *Radical Reactionaries: the political thought of the French Catholic League* (Geneva, 1976) examine French thought in the second half of the century. Peter Holmes, *Resistance and Compromise* (Cambridge, 1982) deals with English Catholic political thought. Bernice Hamilton, *Political Thought in Sixteenth-Century Spain* (Oxford, 1963) covers important Spanish writers. English translations of sixteenth–century resistance writings are many: Robert M. Kingdon, *The Political Thought of Peter Martyr Vermigli: selected texts and commentary* (Geneva, 1980); *Francogallia*, eds. J. H. Salmon and Ralph Giesey (Cambridge, 1972); *Vindiciae contra tyrannos* as *A Defence of Liberty against Tyrants,* ed. Harold J. Laski (Gloucester, 1963); Etienne de la Boétie's *Discours de la Servitude Volontaire* as *The Politics of Obedience: the discourse of voluntary servitude,* ed. Murray Robthard (New York, 1975).

LITERATURE

The history of sixteenth-century literature has tended to be written as national surveys or examinations of separate genres but A. J. Krailsheimer, ed., *The Continental Renaissance, 1500–1600* (Harmondsworth, 1971) is a helpful exception. David Daiches and Anthony Thorlby, eds., *The Old World: discovery and rebirth* (London, 1974) contains a wide range of valuable articles. Elizabeth Eisenstein, *The Printing Press as an Agent of Cultural Change,* 2 vols. (Cambridge, 1979) and Miriam Usher Chrisman, *Lay Culture amd Learned Culture: books and social change in Strasbourg, 1480–1599* (New Haven, 1982) are essential for an understanding of the impact of the printing press. For England, C. S. Lewis, *English Literature in the Sixteenth Century, Excluding Drama* (Oxford, 1954) is still readable but John N. King, *English Reformation Literature* (Princeton, 1982) challenges Lewis on the drabness of early Tudor writing. Robert Potter, *The English Morality Play* (London, 1975) and Rosemary Woolf, *The English Mystery Plays* (Berkeley, 1972) treat those two theatrical forms. *Society and History in English Renaissance Verse* (London, 1985) examines the ralationship between literature and society in sixteenth-century England. Michael Hathaway, *Elizabethan Popular Theatre: plays in performance* (London, 1982) examines production techniques and conventions of the theatre. The new series of *Renaissance Drama* issued yearly by Northwestern University contains valuable articles concentrating on the English theatre but occasionally deals with the Continental experience. The study of William Shakespeare is a veritable cultural industry and books about him are legion. L. S. Champion, *The Essential Shakespeare: an annotated bibliography of major studies* (Boston, 1982) is the best guide to the immense body of literature on Shakespeare. The *Shakespeare Quarterly* and *Shakespeare Studies* produce a regular supply of articles on the playwright and his age. A readable English biography of Spain's great dramatist is F. C. Hayes, *Lope de Vega* (New York, 1967). I. D. McFarlane, *Renaissance France,*

1470–1589 (London, 1974) is a comprehensive treatment of the French literary experience while Dorothy Gabe Coleman, *The Gallo-Roman Muse* (Cambridge, 1979) handles the question of classical Roman influences on French literature. Germaine Bree, *Women Writers in France* (New Brunswick, NJ, 1973) deals with some sixteenth-century examples. Marc Fumaroli, *L'Age de l'Eloquence* (Geneva, 1980) concentrates on the importance of rhetoric in French literature. French theatre is the subject of two works by Madeleine Lazard: *La Comédie humaniste au XVIe siècle et ses personnages* (Paris, 1978) and *Le Théatre en France au XVIe siècle* (Paris, 1980). Michael Bakhtin, *Rabelais and His World* (Bloomington, 1984) ties Rabelais to European folk culture. Also useful for Rabelais are M. A. Screech, *Rabelais* (Ithaca, 1979) and Donald M. Frame, *François Rabelais: A Study* (New York, 1977). Henry F. Salerno, *Scenarios of the Commedia dell'Arte: Flaminio Scala's Il Teatro della favole rappresentative* (New York, 1967) reprints fifty scenarios from this genre. Peter M. Daly, *Literature in the Light of the Emblem* (Toronto, 1979) is a look at the emblem book phenomenon. Victor E. Neuberg, *Popular Literature: a history and guide* (Harmondsworth, 1977) and Natalie Zenon Davis, 'Printing and the people' in *Society and Culture in Early Modern France* (Stanford, 1975) are good introductions to popular literature. P. M. Zell, *A Hundred Merry Tales and other English Jestbooks of the Fifteenth and Sixteenth centuries* (Lincoln, 1963) reprints a selection of popular literature. Carlo Ginzburg, *The Cheese and the Worms: the cosmos of a sixteenth century miller* (Baltimore, 1980) provides food for thought on what might have constituted popular reading material. Guillermo Diaz-Plaja, *A History of Spanish Literature* (New York, 1971) and J. R. Stamm, *A Short History of Spanish Literature*, rev. edn (New York, 1979) have good sections on the sixteenth century. There are numerous modern English translations available of some of the century's most influential works including Cervantes's *Don Quixote*, Sannazaro's *Arcadia*, Tasso's *Jerusalem Delivered*, Ariosto's *Orlando Furioso* and Marguerite of Navarre's *Heptameron*.

FROM RENAISSANCE TO BAROQUE

The literature of sixteenth-century art is enormous, and fine new illustrated books on aspects of the subject, or on the work of individual artists, are constantly being published. R. Wittkower, *et al.*, 'The arts in western Europe', ch. VI in *New Cambridge Modern History*, vol. II, is a good introduction. H. Wölfflin, *Classic Art*, 2nd edn (London, 1953) is still a good stylistic analysis of the High Renaissance. For Mannerism (a style which Wölfflin did not recognize), cf. W. F. Friedländer, *Mannerism and Anti-Mannerism in Italian Painting* (New York, 1957), J. Shearman, *Mannerism*, (Harmondsworth, 1967), and L. Murray, *The High Renaissance and Mannerism: Italy, the North and Spain 1500–1600*, (London, 1967). G. Vasari, *The Lives of the Painters* (1550. 4 vols. trans. A. B. Hind, New York, 1927. A large selection, trans. G. Bull, 2 vols. Penguin Classics, Harmondsworth 1965–87), although not reliable in all details is still a basic source and gives a splendid picture of Italian art and artists during the period. Vasari should be supplemented by such modern works as R. and M. Wittkower, *Born under Saturn* (London, 1963) which studies Renaissance perceptions of the artist, and by biographies such as the popular K. Clark, *Leonardo da Vinci* (Harmondsworth, 1961) and the recent very scholarly M. Kemp, *Leonardo da Vinci: the marvellous works of nature* (London, 1981); C. de Tolnay, *Michelangelo*, 5 vols. (Princeton, 1943–60); H. Tietze, *Tizian* (Vienna, 1936, abridged translation, *Titian*, London, 1950); W. F. Friedländer, *Caravaggio Studies* (Princeton, 1955). The social and political world of the artist is discussed in D. S. Chambers, *Patrons and Artists in the Italian Renaissance* (London, 1970), in P. Burke, *Tradition and Innovation in Renaissance Italy: a sociological approach* (London, 1974), and in H. Trevor-Roper, *Princes and Artists: patronage and ideology at four Habsburg courts 1517–1633* (London, 1976). For Spain and the art of the Counter-Reformation cf. David Davies, *El Greco*, (Oxford, 1976). The highly sophisticated study of the religious, philosophical and literary ideas underlying sixteenth-century art is best exemplified in the magisterial writings of E. Panofsky, e.g. *Idea*, 2nd edn (Berlin, 1960) and *Studies in Iconology*, 2nd edn (New York, 1962). For architecture cf. R. Wittkower, *Architectural Principles in the Age of Humanism* (London, 1962). For transalpine Europe, O. Benesch, *The Art of the Renaissance in Northern Europe* (Cambridge, Mass., 1945) is a good survey. E. Panofsky, *Albrecht Dürer*, 3rd edn (Princeton, 1948) is definitive. A. Blunt, *Art and Architecture in France, 1500–1700*, Pelican History of Art (Harmondsworth, 1953) is indispensable. E. Mercer, *English Art 1553–1625* is useful

For music, the German encyclopaedia, *Die Musik in Geschichte und Gegenwart*, ed. F. Blume, 17 vols. (Kassel, 1949–86), and *The New Grove Dictionary of Music*, ed. S. Sadie (London, 1980) are superb reference works. The long articles, in *Grove*, on Josquin, Palestrina, Lassus, Byrd and Victoria have been separately published under the title *High Renaissance Masters* (London, 1984). For patronage of music and its social background see, for instance, D. C. Price, *Patrons and Musicians of the English Renaissance* (Cambridge, 1981). Music for the stage is discussed by N. Pirotta, *Music and Theatre from Poliziano to Monteverdi* (Cambridge, 1982). For the relations between humanism and music see D. P. Walker, *Music, Spirit and Language in the Renaissance*, ed. P. Gouk (London, 1985) and *idem*, *Studies in Musical Science in the Late Renaissance* (Leiden), 1978). Cf. also C. V. Palisca, *Humanism in Italian Renaissance Musical Thought* (New Haven, 1986). For the reformers' views on music see F. Blume, 'Luther the musician', in H. G. Koenigsberger, ed., *Luther: a profile* (New York and London, 1973); C. Garside, *Zwingli and the Arts* (New Haven, 1966), and H. P. Clive, 'The Calvinist attitude to music', *Bibliothèque d'Humanisme et Renaissance*, XIX (1957). G. Reese, *Music in the Renaissance* (New York, 1954) is still a useful general textbook. An outstanding example of a monumental work on a specific genre is A. Einstein, *The Italian Madrigal*, 3 vols., trans. A. Krappe *et al.* (Princeton, 1959). For theories of the science of music, a very important topic in this period, see H. F. Cohen, *Quantifying Music* (Dordrecht, Boston, Lancaster, 1984).

In the history of science, many of the textbooks for this period are now dated. P. M. Harman, *The Scientific Revolution* (London, 1983) is a useful first introduction. See also A. G. Debus, *Man and Nature in the Renaissance* (Cambridge, 1978). E. J. Dijksterhuis, *The Mechanization of the World Picture*, trans. C. Dijkshoorn (Oxford, 1961) is still indispensable for the physical sciences. Thomas S. Kuhn, *The Copernican Revolution: planetary astronomy in the development of western thought* (Cambridge, Mass., 1957) and *The Structure of Scientific Revolutions* (Chicago, 1962), proposes a now well-known, but also very controversial, theory of major advances in scientific thought. The *Past Masters* series has an excellent short biography by Stillman Drake, *Galileo* (Oxford, 1980), and the same author's *Discoveries and Opinions of Galileo* (Garden City, N.Y., 1957) has a useful introduction to some of Galileo's most important writings. The complex and varied intellectual sources of Renaissance scientific thought are exemplified, for example, in W. Pagel, *Paracelsus* (Basel and New York, 1958), in F. Yates, *Giordano Bruno and the Hermetic Tradition* (London, 1964), and in B. Vickers, ed., *Occult and Scientific Mentalities in the Renaissance* (Cambridge, 1984). See also the very scholarly study by D. P. Walker, *Spiritual and Demonic Magic from Ficino to Campanella* (London, 1958). There are several relevant essays in P. Curry, ed., *Astrology, Science and Society* (Woodbridge, Suffolk, 1987).

For the importance of printing in the development of science see E. L. Eisenstein, *The Printing Press as an Agent Of Change*, 2 vols. (Cambridge, 1979), and G. P. Tyson and S. S. Wagonheim, eds., *Print and Culture in the Renaissance* (London and Toronto, 1986).

The intellectual relations between different disciplines and the important Renaissance concept of harmony are discussed in Dorothy Koenigsberger, *Renaissance Man and Creative Thinking* (Hassocks, Sussex, 1979). For the social and political conditions of creativity in literature, art, music and science see H. G. Koenigsberger, *Politicians and Virtuosi* (London, 1986), chapters 9–11.

GENEALOGICAL CHARTS

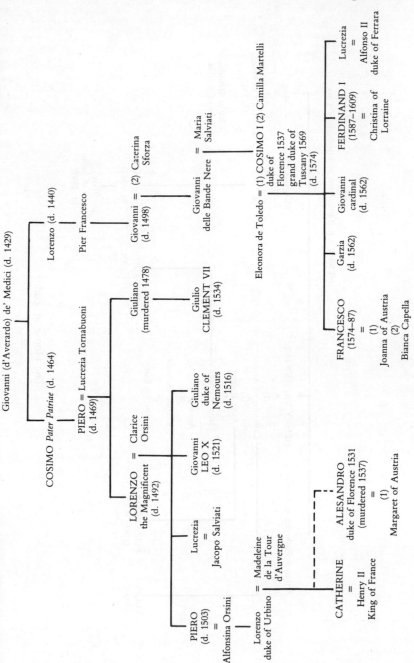

1. The House of Medici

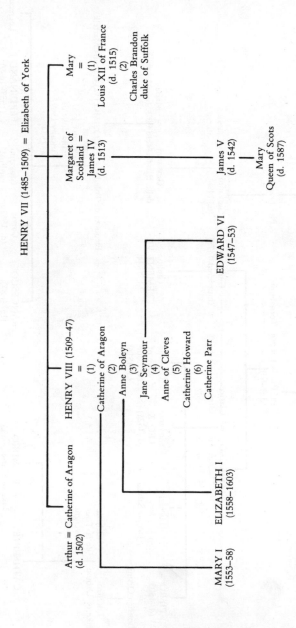

2. The House of Tudor

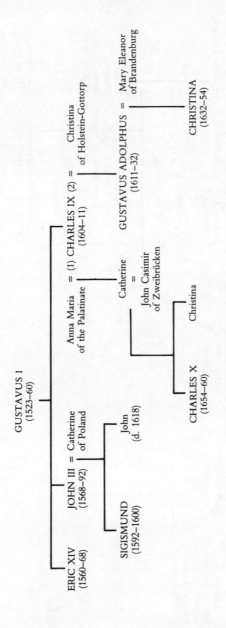

3. The House of Vasa

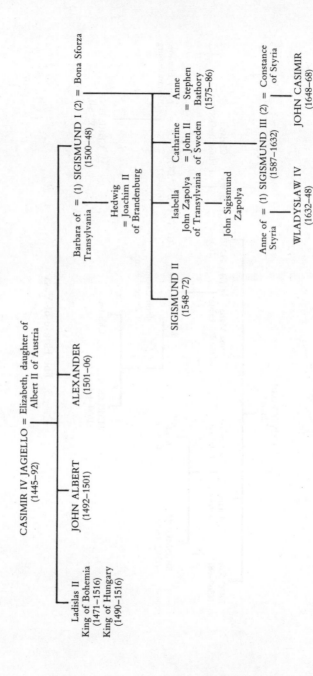

4. Kings of Poland

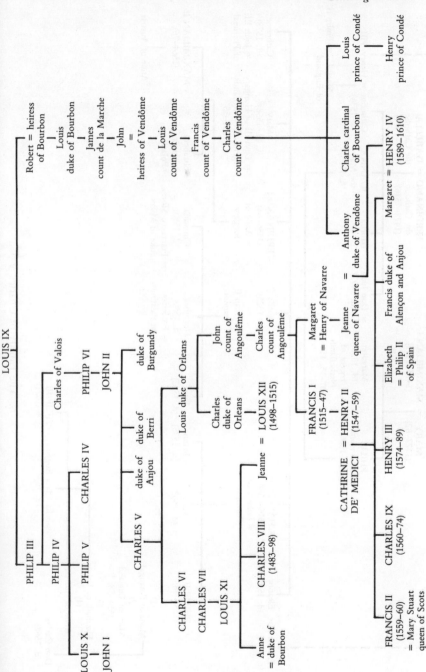

5. The Houses of Valois and Bourbon (to 1610)

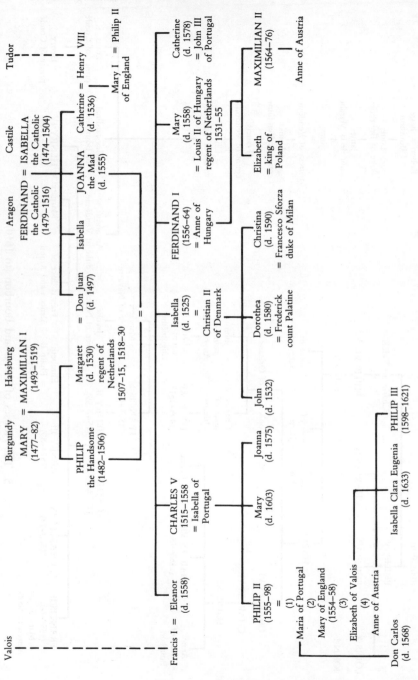

6. The Family of Charles V

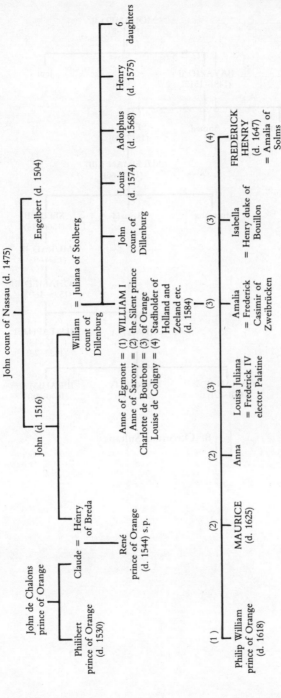

7. The House of Orange–Nassau

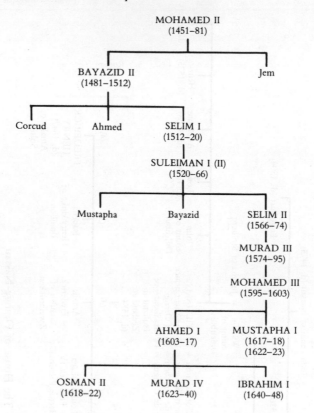

8. Ottoman Sultans

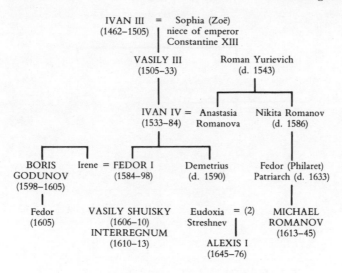

IVAN III = Sophia (Zoë)
(1462–1505) │ niece of emperor
Constantine XIII

VASILY III   Roman Yurievich
(1505–33)   (d. 1543)

IVAN IV = Anastasia   Nikita Romanov
(1533–84)   Romanova   (d. 1586)

BORIS   Irene = FEDOR I   Demetrius   Fedor (Philaret)
GODUNOV   (1584–98)   (d. 1590)   Patriarch (d. 1633)
(1598–1605)

Fedor   VASILY SHUISKY   Eudoxia = (2)   MICHAEL
(1605)   (1606–10)   Streshnev   ROMANOV
            INTERREGNUM   (1613–45)
             (1610–13)   ALEXIS I
                               (1645–76)

9. The Houses of Rurik and Romanov

Alexander VI (Borgia), 1492–1503
Pius III, 1503
Julius II (della Rovere), 1503–1513
Leo X (Medici), 1513–1521
Hadrian VI (Dedel), 1522–1523
Clement VII (Medici), 1523–1534
Paul III (Farnese), 1534–1549
Julius III (del Monte), 1550–1555
Marcellus II (Cervini), 1555
Paul IV (Caraffa), 1555–1559
Pius IV (Medici)★, 1559–1564
Pius V (Ghislieri), 1566–1572
Gregor XIII (Boncompagni), 1572–1585
Sixtus V (Peretti), 1585–1590
Urban VII (Castagna), 1590
Gregory XIV (Spondrato), 1590–1591
Innocent IX (Fachinetti), 1591
Clement VIII (Aldobrandini), 1592–1605

★ Not related to the Florentine Medici popes, Leo X and Clement VII.

10. Popes

MAPS

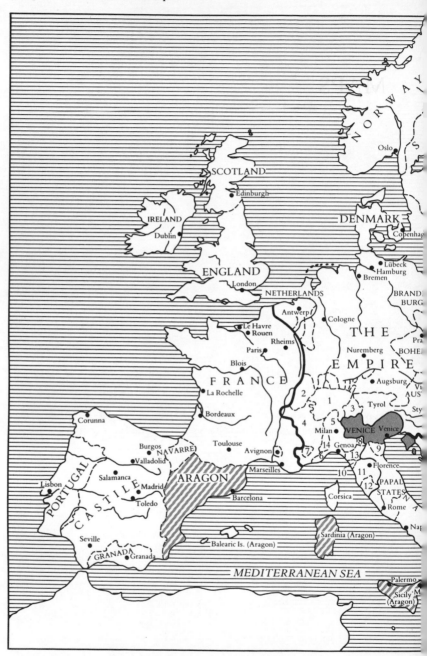

Map 1 Europe: frontiers about 1500.

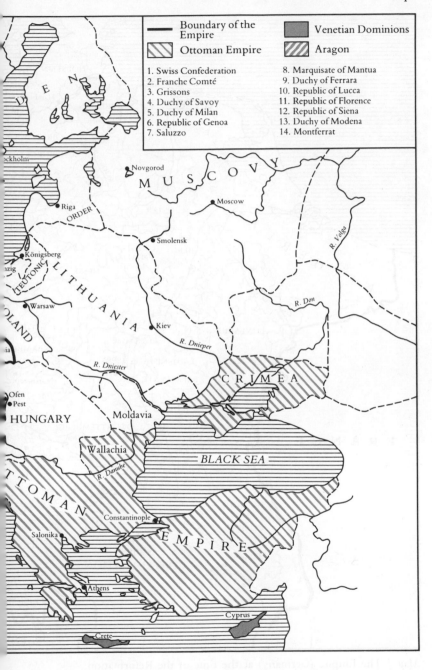

Map 2 The Empire (Germany) at the time of the Reformation.

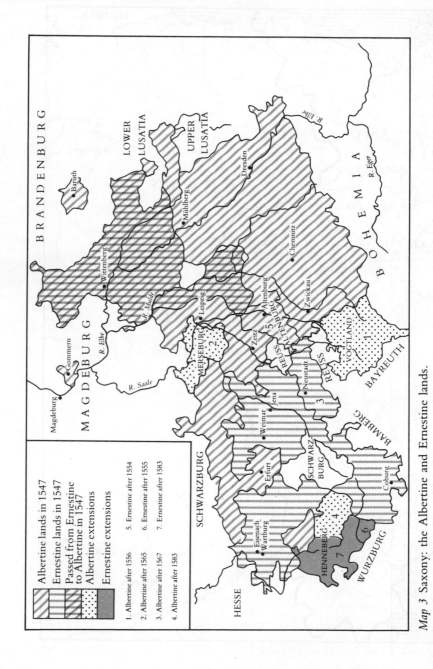

Map 3 Saxony: the Albertine and Ernestine lands.

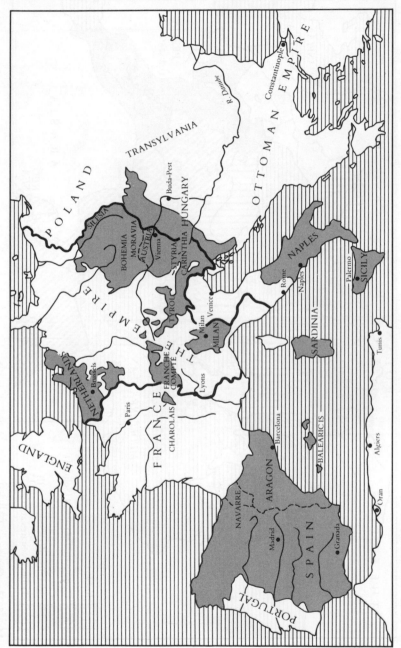

Map 4 The Empire of Charles V.

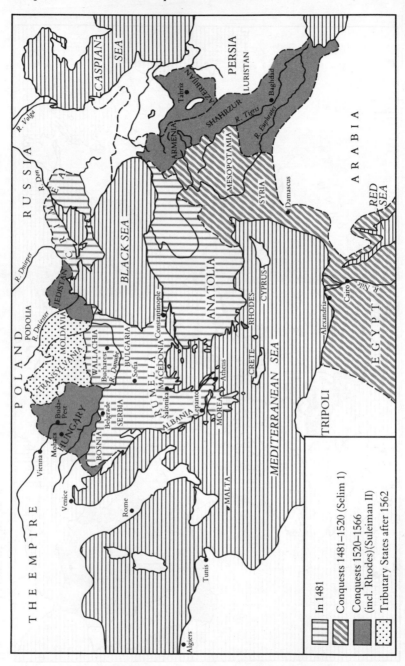

Map 5 The Ottoman Empire.

In 1481

Conquests 1481–1520 (Selim 1)

Conquests 1520–1566
(incl. Rhodes)(Suleiman II)

Tributary States after 1562

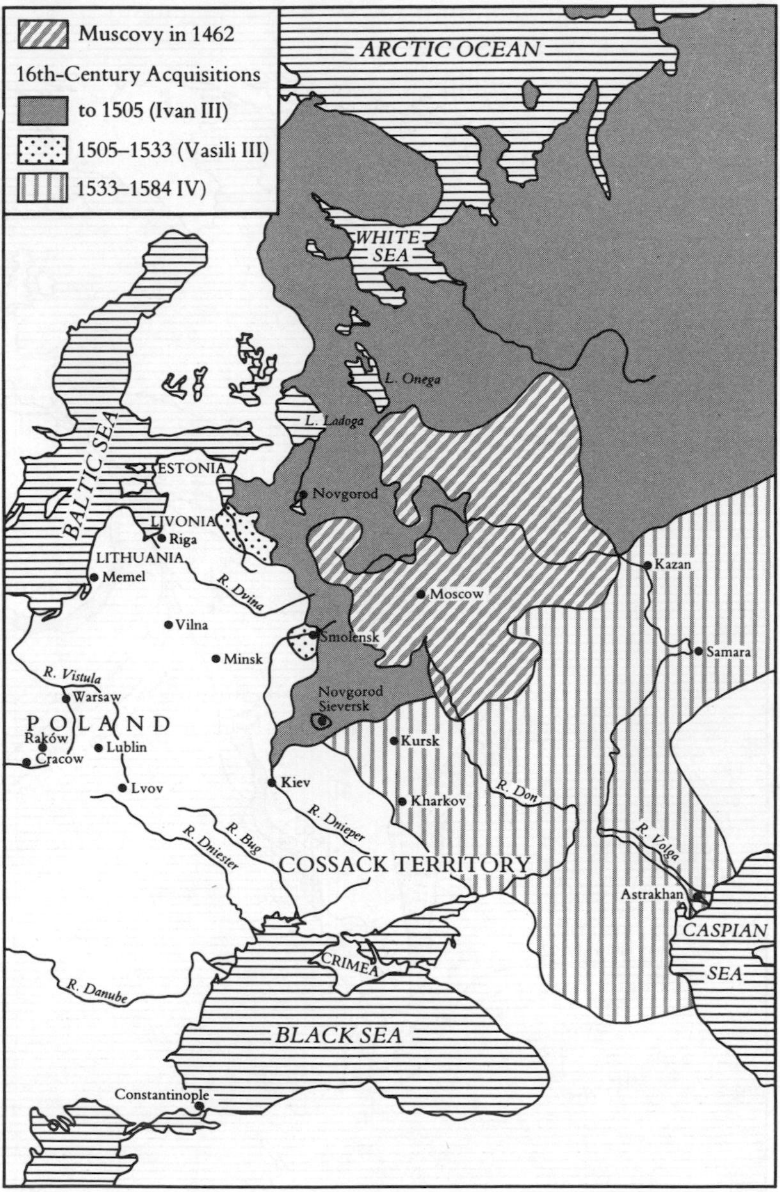
Muscovy in 1462
16th-Century Acquisitions
to 1505 (Ivan III)
1505–1533 (Vasili III)
1533–1584 IV)
ARCTIC OCEAN
WHITE SEA
L. Onega
L. Ladoga
BALTIC SEA
ESTONIA
Novgorod
LIVONIA
Riga
LITHUANIA
Memel
R. Dvina
Moscow
Kazan
Vilna
Smolensk
Samara
Minsk
R. Vistula
Warsaw
Novgorod Sieversk
POLAND
Raków
Lublin
Cracow
Kursk
Lvov
Kiev
Kharkov
R. Don
R. Dnieper
R. Bug
R. Dniester
R. Volga
COSSACK TERRITORY
Astrakhan
CASPIAN SEA
CRIMEA
R. Danube
BLACK SEA
Constantinople

Map 6 Muscovy and Eastern Europe.

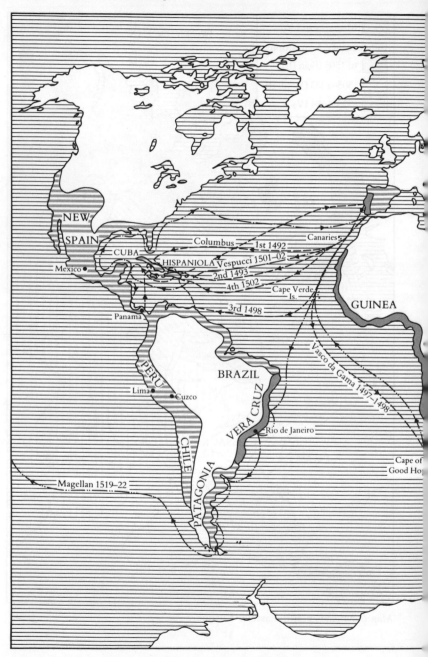

Map 7 The Portuguese and Spanish Overseas Empires.

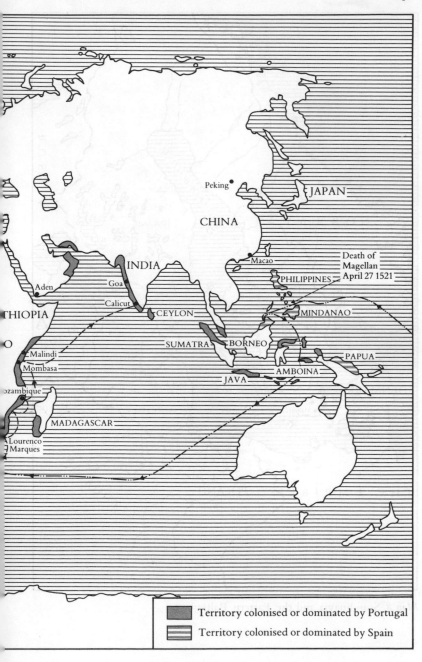

Aden

Goa

INDIA

THIOPIA

O

Calicut

CEYLON

Malindi

Mombasa

SUMATRA

BORNEO

JAVA

ozambique

MADAGASCAR

Lourenco
Marques

Peking

CHINA

JAPAN

Macao

PHILIPPINES

MINDANAO

AMBOINA

PAPUA

Death of
Magellan
April 27 1521

Territory colonised or dominated by Portugal

Territory colonised or dominated by Spain

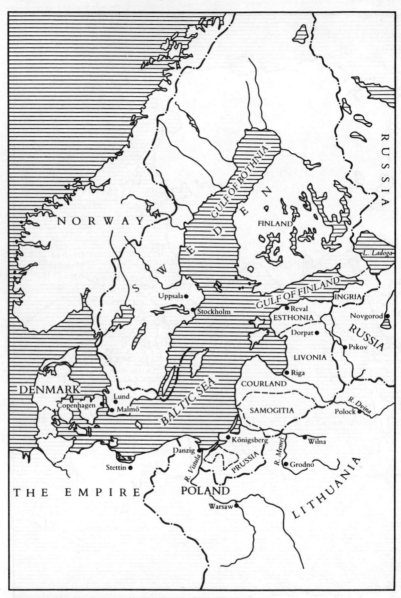

Map 8 Scandinavia and the Eastern Baltic.

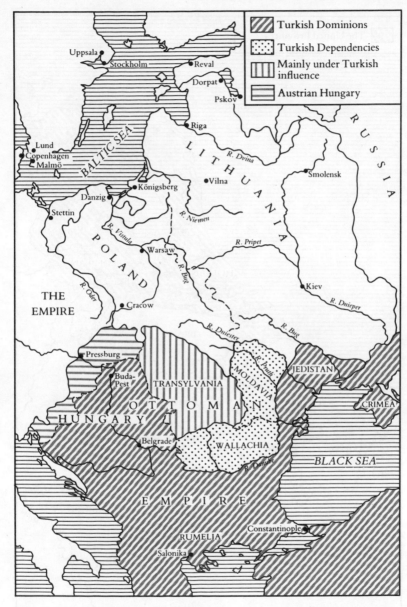

Map 9 Poland-Lithuania and Hungary.

Map 10 The Netherlands.

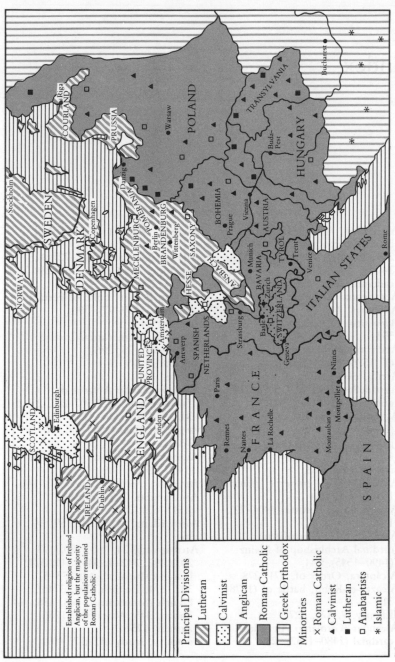

Map 11 Europe: religious divisions about 1600.

Index

Abjuration, Act of (1581), 98, 318
absolutism, political, 29, 50, 189,
  245, 252–3, 276, 282, 288, 327,
  340
academies, 428–9
Accademia dei Lincei, 429
Adamites, 140
Admonition to Parliament (1572),
  353
Aerschot, Philippe de Croy, duke
  of (1526–95), 312, 316
Africa, exploration of, 52
Agnadello, battle of (1509), 105
agnostics, Christian, 348
Agricola (Georg Bauer)
  (1494–1555), 420
agricultural specialization, 35–6,
  45
aides, clerical, 283
Akbar, Moghul emperor (*regnabat*
  1556–1605), 244
Alberti, Leon Battista (1404–72),
  119
Albrecht of Hohenzollern,
  cardinal Archbishop of Mainz
  (1490–1545), 144
Alcántara, Order of, 271, 278
Alcazar-el-Kebir, battle of (1578),
  319
alchemy, 7, 424, 427
Aleander (Girolamo Aleandro),
  cardinal (1480–1532), 232

Alemán, Mateo (1547–*c.* 1614),
  371
Alessi, Galeazzo, (1512–72), 115
Alexander the Great (356–323
  B.C.), 244
Alfonso II Este, duke of Ferrara
  (*regnabat* 1559–97), 396
Algiers, 244
Allen, William, cardinal,
  (1532–94), 25, 296
almanacs, 379
Alsace, 128
Alva, Fernando Álvarez de
  Toledo, duke of (1507–82), 239,
  307, 314–15, 316, 319
Amadis of Gaul (1540–48), 369,
  370
Amboise, George d', cardinal
  (1460–1510), 286
America, discovery of, 52–3, 141
Ammananti, Bartolommeo
  (1511–92), 394
Amsterdam, 34, 39, 42, 59, 94,
  96
Anabaptists, 24, 169, 180, 197,
  203, 292, 342–4, 345, 346, 374;
  Dutch (Munster), 42, 173–5,
  302, 374; English, 296, 374;
  French (Strassburg), 186, 188;
  Italian, 345; Moravian, 175;
  Zurich, 175
anatomy, study of, 417, 419